PART 7 READING

解きまくれ！
リーディングドリル
TOEIC® L&R TEST PART 7

TOEIC is a registered trademark of ETS.
This publication is not endorsed or approved by ETS.
*L&R means LISTENING AND READING.

著：大里秀介

スリーエー
ネットワーク

Published by 3A Corporation
Trusty Kojimachi Bldg., 2F, 4, Kojimachi 3-Chome, Chiyoda-ku, Tokyo 102-0083, Japan

ISBN 978-4-88319-892-4 C0082

First published 2021
Printed in Japan

はじめに

　2016年5月のTOEIC公開テストから、一部問題形式が変更になり5年以上経過しました。以来、Part 7の長文読解問題は、そのウエイトが以前にも増して高くなり、文脈や複数箇所を関連付けて解く文挿入位置問題、意図問題、3文書参照型問題、オンラインチャット問題が追加されたことで、より深く内容を理解して解く必要が出てきました。長文が苦手な人は、より苦手意識が高まり、『正解や正解の根拠を時間内に見つけることができない』『時間内に解き終わらない』、そんな声を今でも聞くことがあります。

　最近はいろいろな対策本が出現してきましたので、『こうすれば解けるのか！』といった気づきにつながる一方で、それが本当に実際のテストで役立つのか？　と感じる人がいることも事実です。

　本書は、タイトルの通り、自分の実力がどの程度なのか、『解きまくる』ことで確認するためのドリル的な本です。攻略的な要素というより、解いて、解いて、解説を読んで、また解いて、と問題を解くことで感じる、タイムマネジメントやどうやって正解にたどり着くか、というアプローチを全面に押し出した本です。

　私も、旧型式のTOEICテストで990点満点を取る際には、この解きまくれシリーズをやりこみ、読解力を高めていきました。『どうしてこれが正解なんだ？』『どうすれば正解にたどり着けるんだ？』そんなことを毎日思い悩んで、スコアアップさせた日々が改めてよみがえってきます。そんな私の体験を皆さんにも味わってもらいたく、良質な問題を432問用意させていただきました。そして、全ての問題に難易度レベルを5段階でつけておりますので、参考にしていただければと思います。

　ただ解いて、実力を確かめるだけでもかまいません。毎日少しずつ解きながら、時間管理や読解問題の形式に慣れる、問題を解かずにただ文書を読んで、TOEIC形式の文書スタイルを理解しながら読解力を高める、設問だけを読んで問題自体の分類や性質に慣れる等、いろいろな使い方があります。是非、自分の解き方スタイルを、『解きまくり』ながら、確立していただければと思います。

　2020年、2021年は、新型コロナウィルス感染拡大防止のため、長期間にわたる自粛期間やイベントの中止・延期等、さまざまなことがありました。そして、それは今後の学び方、働き方、生き方にも影響を与えようとしています。このような状況下で、進学、留学、転職、昇進に関わらず、リモートかつグローバルな仕事の機会が増えることが予想され、メールや文書を英語で読むことは、増えてくると思います。そういう意味では、TOEIC L&Rテスト、とりわけPart 7の長文読解問題は、私自身の過去の海外留学・駐在の経験からみても、日常で使う表現、ビジネスで使える表現がかなり増え、大変役に立ちます。つまり、単にスコアを取るだけのテストではなく、実践力の素地を養い、アウトプット力を身に着けられる、良いテストになったと感じています。

　TOEIC L&Rテストも日々進化をしています。是非この本を使い倒していただき、皆さん自身のスコアアップ、ひいては夢や目標を達成し、人生を更に充実させたものにし、将来を切り拓いていくことを切に願っております。

2021年12月　大里 秀介

目次

※ マークシート（解答用紙）は、一番最後のページに付いています。

PART 7 設問タイプについて

本書では、以下のタイプの設問には、解説箇所に表示をしています。解説を読む際に、どのタイプの問題なのかを参考にしてみてください。

▶ NOT 問題

NOT 問題は「文書に書かれていないもの」が正解になるタイプの設問です。4 つの選択肢のうち 3 つが文書の内容と合致しており、残った 1 つが正解となります。そのため、すべての選択肢を照合する必要があり、解答に時間を要します。

▶ 文挿入位置問題

文挿入位置問題は、設問に示された文（挿入文）が入る適切な箇所を、文書内にある空所 [1] ～ [4] から選ぶタイプの設問です。文書の全体像、挿入箇所の前後の文脈などをきちんと理解し、自然な文脈になる適切な箇所を選びます。

▶ 同義語問題

同義語問題は、文書にある語（句）と同じ意味の語（句）を選択肢から選ぶタイプの設問です。問われている語が多義語の場合も多く、文脈を確認して解く必要がありますので、注意が必要です。

▶ 意図問題

意図問題は、テキストメッセージ・オンラインチャットなどの文書で出題されます。発言の意図を問うタイプの設問で、なぜその発言をしたのか、その理由を選択肢から選びます。口語表現の知識がなくとも、会話の流れ（文脈）の理解で解くことができます。

▶ クロスリファレンス問題

ダブルパッセージ（2 文書）、トリプルパッセージ（3 文書）の大問で、解答の根拠が複数の文書にまたがっているタイプの設問です。両文書参照型問題、複数文書参照型問題とも呼ばれています。複数の文書の内容を把握し、各文書にある解答の根拠を関連付けて、正解を選びます。このタイプの設問は解答に時間がかかるため、難問の部類に入ります。

※このほか、解説中に「選択肢照合型問題」という説明がある設問があります。この「選択肢照合型問題」は、ピンポイントで 1 つの選択肢を選べず、4 つの選択肢すべてを文書と照合して解かなくてはいけないタイプの問題です。誤答となる選択肢は「文書に記載がない」「文書の内容と異なる」という根拠が挙げられます。

本書の構成と使い方

本書は、問題ページ → 解説ページを繰り返す、ドリル形式の問題集で、TEST 8 回分（432 問）を収録しています。また、試験と同じ流れで解きたい方、設問タイプ（single、double、triple）で解きたい方のどちらにでも対応できるような構成になっています。

【特長】

● 問題ページのみ、右にインデックスがあり、single 2Q（2 つの設問）、single 3Q、single 4Q、double、triple の 5 つのタイプになっています。それぞれの問題タイプのみを解きたい方は、このインデックスを使えば、検索できます。

● 問題ページ左端には 3 回分のチェックボックスを設けています。間違えた問題にチェックを入れることで、復習の際に容易に探せるようになっています。

● 巻末には 3 回分のマークシートが収録されています。

（問題ページ）

single 2Q のみ、大問 2 つが見開きに並んで収録されていますが、その他は見開きに大問 1 つです。

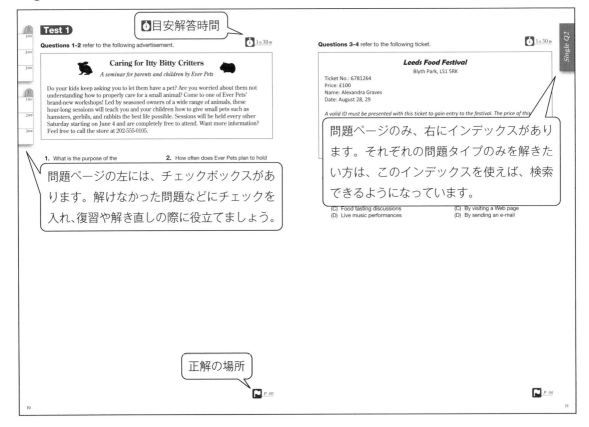

（解答ページ）

解答ページは、問題ページのすぐ後にあります（single 2Q の Questions 3-4、Questions 5-6 のみ例外です）。

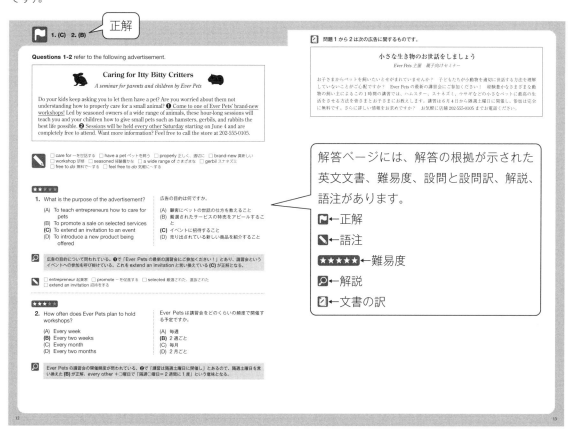

アプリのご利用

■ AI英語教材 abceed

株式会社Globeeが提供する、マークシート連動型アプリで解答ができます。

abceed

https://www.abceed.com/

（アプリのダウンロード、その他アプリに関する不具合やご質問に関しましては、上記の配信先へお問い合わせください。弊社ではお答えいたしかねますので、ご了承ください）

Test

1

Test 1

Questions 1-2 refer to the following advertisement.

 1分30秒

 Caring for Itty Bitty Critters

A seminar for parents and children by Ever Pets

Do your kids keep asking you to let them have a pet? Are you worried about them not understanding how to properly care for a small animal? Come to one of Ever Pets' brand-new workshops! Led by seasoned owners of a wide range of animals, these hour-long sessions will teach you and your children how to give small pets such as hamsters, gerbils, and rabbits the best life possible. Sessions will be held every other Saturday starting on June 4 and are completely free to attend. Want more information? Feel free to call the store at 202-555-0105.

1. What is the purpose of the advertisement?

   (A) To teach entrepreneurs how to care for pets
   (B) To promote a sale on selected services
   (C) To extend an invitation to an event
   (D) To introduce a new product being offered

2. How often does Ever Pets plan to hold workshops?

   (A) Every week
   (B) Every two weeks
   (C) Every month
   (D) Every two months

 P. 12

Questions 3-4 refer to the following ticket.

 1分30秒

Leeds Food Festival
Blyth Park, LS1 5RK

Ticket No.: 6781264
Price: £100
Name: Alexandra Graves
Date: August 28, 29

A valid ID must be presented with this ticket to gain entry to the festival. The price of this ticket covers all food and drink, including access to taster sessions and mini concerts. All chef-led training seminars require a nominal booking fee not included in the ticket price. For more information about the event, or to volunteer as staff, please call 0113 189 2458 or go to www.leedsfoodfest.co.uk. Contact support@leedsfoodfest.co.uk to request a refund or any other changes.

3. According to the ticket, for what would an extra fee be charged?

(A) Cooking lessons
(B) Improper identification
(C) Food tasting discussions
(D) Live music performances

4. How can Ms. Graves get her money back?

(A) By asking staff at the event
(B) By calling a staff member
(C) By visiting a Web page
(D) By sending an e-mail

Questions 1-2 refer to the following advertisement.

 ## Caring for Itty Bitty Critters

A seminar for parents and children by Ever Pets

Do your kids keep asking you to let them have a pet? Are you worried about them not understanding how to properly care for a small animal? ❶ Come to one of Ever Pets' brand-new workshops! Led by seasoned owners of a wide range of animals, these hour-long sessions will teach you and your children how to give small pets such as hamsters, gerbils, and rabbits the best life possible. ❷ Sessions will be held every other Saturday starting on June 4 and are completely free to attend. Want more information? Feel free to call the store at 202-555-0105.

□ care for 〜を世話する   □ have a pet ペットを飼う   □ properly 正しく、適切に   □ brand-new 真新しい
□ workshop 研修   □ seasoned 経験豊かな   □ a wide range of さまざまな   □ gerbil スナネズミ
□ free to *do* 〜するのは無料である   □ feel free to *do* 気軽に〜する

★★☆☆☆

1. What is the purpose of the advertisement?

(A) To teach entrepreneurs how to care for pets
(B) To promote a sale on selected services
(C) To extend an invitation to an event
(D) To introduce a new product being offered

広告の目的は何ですか。

(A) 顧客にペットの世話の仕方を教えること
(B) 厳選されたサービスの特売をアピールすること
(C) イベントに招待すること
(D) 売り出されている新しい商品を紹介すること

広告の目的について問われている。❶で「Ever Pets の最新の講習会にご参加ください！」とあり、講習会というイベントへの参加を呼び掛けている。これを extend an invitation と言い換えている **(C)** が正解となる。

□ entrepreneur 起業家   □ promote 〜を促進する   □ selected 厳選された、選抜された
□ extend an invitation 招待をする

★★★☆☆

2. How often does Ever Pets plan to hold workshops?

(A) Every week
(B) Every two weeks
(C) Every month
(D) Every two months

Ever Pets は講習会をどのくらいの頻度で開催する予定ですか。

(A) 毎週
(B) 2週ごと
(C) 毎月
(D) 2月ごと

Ever Pets の講習会の開催頻度が問われている。❷で「講習は隔週土曜日に開催し」とあるので、隔週土曜日を言い換えた **(B)** が正解。every other ＋○曜日で「隔週○曜日＝2週間に1度」という意味となる。

小さな生き物のお世話をしましょう

Ever Pets 主催　親子向けセミナー

お子さまからペットを飼いたいとせがまれていませんか？　子どもたちが小動物を適切に世話する方法を理解していないことがご心配ですか？　Ever Pets の最新の講習会にご参加ください！　経験豊かなさまざまな動物の飼い主によるこの1時間の講習では、ハムスター、スナネズミ、ウサギなどの小さなペットに最高の生活をさせる方法を皆さまとお子さまにお教えします。講習は6月4日から隔週土曜日に開催し、参加は完全に無料です。さらに詳しい情報をお求めですか？　お気軽に店舗202-555-0105までお電話ください。

Questions 3-4 refer to the following ticket.

Leeds Food Festival

Blyth Park, LS1 5RK

Ticket No.: 6781264
Price: £100
❶ Name: Alexandra Graves
Date: August 28, 29

A valid ID must be presented with this ticket to gain entry to the festival. The price of this ticket covers all food and drink, including access to taster sessions and mini concerts. ❷ All chef-led training seminars require a nominal booking fee not included in the ticket price. For more information about the event, or to volunteer as staff, please call 0113 189 2458 or go to www.leedsfoodfest.co.uk. ❸ Contact support@leedsfoodfest.co.uk to request a refund or any other changes.

□ valid 有効な □ present ～を提示する □ gain entry 入場する、入る □ cover ～を含む（≒ include）
□ access 利用（参加）の権利 □ taster session 試食会 □ chef-led シェフ主導の（○○ -led: ○○主導の）
□ nominal 少額の、わずかな □ booking fee 予約金 □ refund 払い戻し

★★★★★

3. According to the ticket, for what would an extra fee be charged?

(A) Cooking lessons
(B) Improper identification
(C) Food tasting discussions
(D) Live music performances

チケットによると、何について追加料金が課金されますか。

(A) 料理のクラス
(B) 不適切な身分証明書
(C) 試食の議論
(D) 生演奏

追加料金が課せられるものについて問われている。❷で「シェフによるすべての研修会には少額の予約金が必要で、チケット代には含まれていない」とあるため、「シェフによる研修会＝追加料金が必要」だとわかる。よって、正解は **(A)** となる。(C) は❷の前で「試食会はチケットに含まれている」とあるため不正解。

□ improper 適切ではない □ identification 身分証明書 □ food tasting 試食

★★★★★

4. How can Ms. Graves get her money back?

(A) By asking staff at the event
(B) By calling a staff member
(C) By visiting a Web page
(D) By sending an e-mail

Graves さんはどうすれば返金を受けられますか。

(A) イベント会場でスタッフに尋ねる
(B) スタッフに電話をする
(C) ウェブページにアクセスする
(D) Eメールを送る

Graves さんがどうすれば返金を受けられるかが問われている。Graves さんは、❶から、チケットの持ち主であることがわかる。❸で、「払い戻しやその他の変更をご希望の場合は、指定メールアドレスまでお問い合わせを」と書かれているので、ここから **(D)** が正解とわかる。(B) と (C) は、イベントの詳細やスタッフの志願に関する問い合わせ先のため、不正解。

問題 3 から 4 は次のチケットに関するものです。

Leeds フードフェスティバル
Blyth Park, LS1 5RK

チケット番号：6781264
価格：100 ポンド
お名前：Alexandra Graves
日程：8 月 28 日、29 日

フェスティバルへの入場には、このチケットと一緒に有効な身分証明書をご提示いただく必要がございます。このチケット代には、試食会やミニコンサートの入場を含め、すべての飲食が含まれています。すべてのシェフによる研修会には少額の予約金が必要で、チケット代には含まれていません。イベントの詳細やスタッフの志願については、0113 189 2458 までお電話いただくか、www.leedsfoodfest.co.uk をご覧ください。払い戻しやその他の変更をご希望の場合は、support@leedsfoodfest.co.uk までお問い合わせください。

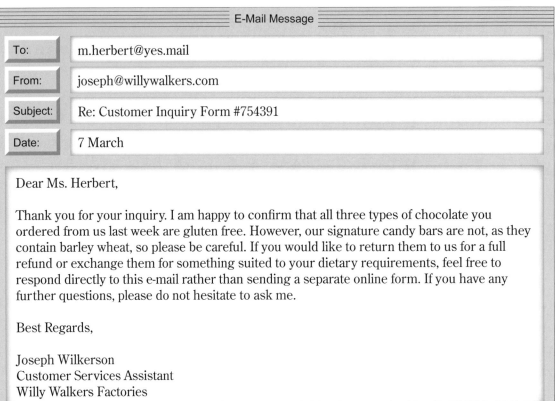

E-Mail Message

To: m.herbert@yes.mail

From: joseph@willywalkers.com

Subject: Re: Customer Inquiry Form #754391

Date: 7 March

Dear Ms. Herbert,

Thank you for your inquiry. I am happy to confirm that all three types of chocolate you ordered from us last week are gluten free. However, our signature candy bars are not, as they contain barley wheat, so please be careful. If you would like to return them to us for a full refund or exchange them for something suited to your dietary requirements, feel free to respond directly to this e-mail rather than sending a separate online form. If you have any further questions, please do not hesitate to ask me.

Best Regards,

Joseph Wilkerson
Customer Services Assistant
Willy Walkers Factories

5. What is the purpose of the e-mail?

(A) To revise an online order
(B) To answer a question
(C) To inquire about a refund
(D) To request edits to a form

6. Where does Mr. Wilkerson most likely work?

(A) A grocery store
(B) A health clinic
(C) A food manufacturer
(D) A wheat factory

P. 18

Questions 7-8 refer to the following text-message chain.

1分30秒

Oliver Thorne (11:14 A.M.)

Hi, May, do you have any slots available this Thursday afternoon? Suzanne Joyce, one of my regulars, wants to come in, but I'm fully booked.

May Lin (11:16 A.M.)

I only have one hour free. What does she need done?

Oliver Thorne (11:17 A.M.)

I think just coloring. She said she needed it done by Friday evening because she's going to a wedding, and she wants to look her best.

May Lin (11:20 A.M.)

Well, I could see her Friday morning. Would she be okay with that?

Oliver Thorne (11:22 A.M.)

Maybe, but I can't call her right now. Could you give her a call? Her number is (408) 873-9131.

May Lin (11:29 A.M.)

Okay, all sorted.

Oliver Thorne (11:30 A.M.)

Thanks! Take good care of her for me.

---

7. Who most likely are Mr. Thorne and Ms. Lin?

(A) Tailors
(B) Hairstylists
(C) Florists
(D) Wedding planners

8. At 11:29 A.M., what does Ms. Lin most likely mean when she writes, "all sorted"?

(A) She will come into work early.
(B) She plans to contact Ms. Joyce.
(C) She accepted an appointment.
(D) She has asked someone else to do a job.

P. 20

Questions 5-6 refer to the following e-mail.

E-Mail Message

To:	m.herbert@yes.mail
From:	joseph@willywalkers.com
Subject:	❶ Re: Customer Inquiry Form #754391
Date:	7 March

Dear Ms. Herbert,

❷ Thank you for your inquiry. I am happy to confirm that ❸ all three types of chocolate you ordered from us last week are gluten free. However, ❹ our signature candy bars are not, as they contain barley wheat, so please be careful. If you would like to return them to us for a full refund or exchange them for something suited to your dietary requirements, feel free to respond directly to this e-mail rather than sending a separate online form. If you have any further questions, please do not hesitate to ask me.

Best Regards,

Joseph Wilkerson
Customer Services Assistant
Willy Walkers Factories

□ inquiry 問い合わせ □ confirm ～を確認する □ gluten free グルテンを含まない □ signature 代表的な
□ contain ～を含む □ barley 大麦 □ full refund 全額払い戻し □ exchange A for B A と B を交換する
□ suited to ～に合致した □ dietary requirement 食事要件 □ feel free to *do* 気軽に～する □ directly 直接
□ rather than ～より □ separate 別々の

★☆☆☆☆

5. What is the purpose of the e-mail?

(A) To revise an online order
(B) To answer a question
(C) To inquire about a refund
(D) To request edits to a form

このEメールの目的は何ですか。

(A) オンラインでの注文の変更をすること
(B) 質問に答えること
(C) 払い戻しについて問い合わせること
(D) フォームの編集を頼むこと

Eメールを送った目的が問われている。❶で「問い合わせフォームへの返答」、❷で「お問い合わせのお礼」が書かれていることから、お客からの問い合わせに対する返答だとわかる。よって、正解は **(B)**。Eメールの件名、冒頭には、その目的を表すヒントが置かれている場合が多いので、注意して読もう。

□ revise ～を変更する □ inquire 尋ねる □ edit 編集（作業）

★★☆☆☆

6. Where does Mr. Wilkerson most likely work?

(A) A grocery store
(B) A health clinic
(C) A food manufacturer
(D) A wheat factory

Wilkerson さんはどこで働いていると考えられますか。

(A) 食料品店
(B) 診療所
(C) 食品メーカー
(D) 小麦の工場

 メールの送信者である Wilkerson さんがどこで働いているかが問われている。❸の「当社から注文していただいたチョコレート」、❹の「当社の代表的なキャンディーバー」から、お菓子を取り扱っている会社であることが考えられる。よって、正解は **(C)**。文書に出てくる "wheat" という単語で (D) を選ばないように気を付けよう。

 □ wheat 小麦

問題 5 から 6 は次の E メールに関するものです。

受信者:	m.herbert@yes.mail
送信者:	joseph@willywalkers.com
件名:	Re: 顧客問い合わせフォーム #754391
日付:	3 月 7 日

Herbert 様

お問い合わせいただき、ありがとうございます。先週当社にご注文いただいた 3 種類のチョコレートはすべてグルテンを含まないことを確認いたしました。ただし、当社の代表的なキャンディーバーはそうではなく、大麦が含まれておりますので、ご注意ください。返品による全額返金、またはお客様の食事の要件に合うものとの交換をご希望でしたら、新たにオンラインフォームをお送りいただかず、お気軽にこちらの E メールに直接返信してください。この他にご質問がある場合は、ご遠慮なくお尋ねください。

よろしくお願いいたします。

Joseph Wilkerson
顧客サービス係
Willy Walkers Factories

Questions 7-8 refer to the following text-message chain.

Oliver Thorne (11:14 A.M.)

Hi, May, do you have any slots available this Thursday afternoon? Suzanne Joyce, one of my regulars, wants to come in, but I'm fully booked.

May Lin (11:16 A.M.)

I only have one hour free. What does she need done?

Oliver Thorne (11:17 A.M.)

❶ I think just coloring. ❷ She said she needed it done by Friday evening because she's going to a wedding, and she wants to look her best.

May Lin (11:20 A.M.)

❸ Well, I could see her Friday morning. Would she be okay with that?

Oliver Thorne (11:22 A.M.)

Maybe, but I can't call her right now. ❹ Could you give her a call? Her number is (408) 873-9131.

May Lin (11:29 A.M.)

Okay, ❺ all sorted.

Oliver Thorne (11:30 A.M.)

❻ Thanks! Take good care of her for me.

□ slot 時間帯　□ available 空いている　□ fully booked 予約ですっかり埋まっている　□ coloring (髪の) 染色
□ look one's best 自分を一番よく見せる　□ okay with ～で構わない　□ right now 今すぐ
□ take care of ～ for A A の代わりに～の面倒をみる

`★★☆☆☆`

7. Who most likely are Mr. Thorne and Ms. Lin?

(A) Tailors
(B) Hairstylists
(C) Florists
(D) Wedding planners

Thorne さんと Lin さんはおそらく誰ですか。

(A) 仕立て屋
(B) 美容師
(C) 花屋
(D) ウェディングプランナー

Thorne さんと Lin さんが誰なのかが問われている。選択肢を見ると、それぞれ職業が並んでいる。Thorne さんは❶で「カラーリングだけだと思う」、❷で「(お客さんは) 結婚式に行くために、金曜日の夜までに行わなければならない」と述べているので、ヘアカラーをする仕事をしていると考えられる。よって、**(B)** が正解。

□ tailor (服の) 仕立て屋　□ florist 花屋

8. At 11:29 A.M., what does Ms. Lin most likely mean when she writes, "all sorted"?

(A) She will come into work early.
(B) She plans to contact Ms. Joyce.
(C) She accepted an appointment.
(D) She has asked someone else to do a job.

午前 11 時 29 分に、Lin さんは "all sorted" という発言で、何を意味していると考えられますか。

(A) 早めに職場に来る。
(B) Joyce さんに連絡をする予定である。
(C) 予約を受け付けた。
(D) 他の誰かに仕事を頼んだ。

意図問題。問われている表現の❺は、「all sorted（すべて解決した）」という意味となる。この前後の流れを見ていくと、❸「金曜の朝なら対応可能」→❹「電話して確認してもらえるか」→❺「解決した」→❻「ありがとう」という流れになっており、Lin さんがお客の Joyce さんへ電話をし、予約を受け付けたことがわかる。よって、正解は **(C)**

□ come into work 職場に来る、出社する

問題 7 から 8 は次のテキストメッセージのやりとりに関するものです。

Oliver Thorne（午前 11 時 14 分）
こんにちは May さん、今週木曜日の午後に担当可能な時間はありますか？ Suzanne Joyce さんという私の常連の一人が来店されたいそうなのですが、私は終日空いていないんです。

May Lin（午前 11 時 16 分）
1 時間だけなら大丈夫です。彼女の希望内容は何ですか？

Oliver Thorne（午前 11 時 17 分）
カラーリングだけだと思います。結婚式に行くために金曜日の夜までに行わなければならないとのことで、最高にきれいにしたいそうです。

May Lin（午前 11 時 20 分）
ええと、金曜日の朝なら担当可能です。それでも大丈夫そうですか？

Oliver Thorne（午前 11 時 22 分）
おそらくは。でも、私は今すぐに電話ができません。彼女に電話をしてもらってもいいですか？ 彼女の電話番号は (408) 873-9131 です。

May Lin（午前 11 時 29 分）
はい、すべて解決しました。

Oliver Thorne（午前 11 時 30 分）
ありがとうございます！ 私の代わりにどうかよろしくお願いします。

---

http://www.lingojob.co.uk/vacancies/56025

Position: Japanese to English PR Translator   **Reference Number:** 56025
Company: Rising Sun Translations   **Application Deadline:** September 8

Headquartered in London, and with branches in both South Korea and Japan, Rising Sun Translations is one of the world's leading translation firms specializing in East Asian languages. We are currently looking for a skilled translator to join the team at our head office. — [1] —. Only local candidates may apply.

The successful candidate will translate a variety of Japanese texts into English for the U.K. market, including press releases, ad copy, and so on. — [2] —. Furthermore, to be considered for this position, applicants must have relevant college-level education, a passion for languages and creative writing, and three professional or academic references. — [3] —. Experience in a similar role is not necessary in order to apply, as we offer a comprehensive, six-month training program, which includes brief visits to our branches overseas. — [4] —.

Applications can be downloaded or printed by entering the reference number at www.risingsuntr.co.uk/apply/

9. Where will the successful candidate live?

(A) In the United Kingdom
(B) In the United States
(C) In South Korea
(D) In Japan

10. What is stated about the job being advertised?

(A) It is a managerial position.
(B) It involves international travel.
(C) Students are welcome to apply.
(D) Translation experience is required.

11. In which of the positions marked [1], [2], [3], and [4] does the following sentence best belong?

"Thus, fluency in Japanese and native-level British English are essential."

(A) [1]
(B) [2]
(C) [3]
(D) [4]

P. 24

Questions 9-11 refer to the following Web page.

◀ ▶   http://www.lingojob.co.uk/vacancies/56025   ▶

Position: Japanese to English PR Translator   **Reference Number:** 56025
Company: Rising Sun Translations   **Application Deadline:** September 8

❶ Headquartered in London, and with branches in both South Korea and Japan, Rising Sun Translations is one of the world's leading translation firms specializing in East Asian languages. ❷ We are currently looking for a skilled translator to join the team at our head office. — [1] —. Only local candidates may apply.

❸ The successful candidate will translate a variety of Japanese texts into English for the U.K. market, including press releases, ad copy, and so on. — [2] —. ❹ Furthermore, to be considered for this position, applicants must have relevant college-level education, a passion for languages and creative writing, and three professional or academic references. — [3] —. ❺ Experience in a similar role is not necessary in order to apply, as we offer a comprehensive, six-month training program, which includes brief visits to our branches overseas. — [4] —.

Applications can be downloaded or printed by entering the reference number at www.risingsuntr.co.uk/apply/

☐ translator 翻訳者 ☐ reference number （対象の）参照番号 ☐ headquartered in ～に本社を置いている
☐ branch 支社 ☐ leading 主要な ☐ firm 会社 ☐ specialize in ～を専門とする ☐ skilled 熟練の
☐ head office 本社 ☐ successful candidate 採用された候補者、合格者 ☐ a variety of さまざまな
☐ text 文書、テキスト ☐ press release 報道発表、プレスリリース ☐ ad copy 広告のコピー
☐ and so on ～など ☐ furthermore さらに ☐ considered for ～として考慮される ☐ position 職
☐ relevant 関連した ☐ college-level education 大学レベルの教育 ☐ passion 情熱
☐ creative writing 創作作品 ☐ professional 職務経験 ☐ academic 教育に関する ☐ reference 推薦状
☐ comprehensive 総合的な、包括的な ☐ brief visit 短期訪問 ☐ overseas 海外の
☐ download ～をダウンロードする

★★☆☆☆

9. Where will the successful candidate live?

   (A) In the United Kingdom
   (B) In the United States
   (C) In South Korea
   (D) In Japan

採用者はどこに住むことになりますか。

   (A) イギリス
   (B) アメリカ合衆国
   (C) 韓国
   (D) 日本

採用者がどこに住むことになるかが問われている。❶で「本社がロンドンにあること」、❷で「本社の求人であること」がわかるため、採用された方はロンドン、つまりイギリス国内に住むことがわかる。以上より、正解は **(A)**。本社の場所がどこかに加え、本社採用であることを見抜くことがカギ。"headquartered" と "at our head office" が言い換えになっていることを押さえておこう。

10. What is stated about the job being advertised?

(A) It is a managerial position.
(B) It involves international travel.
(C) Students are welcome to apply.
(D) Translation experience is required.

広告の求人情報について何が述べられていますか。

(A) 管理職である。
(B) 海外への出張を伴う。
(C) 学生からの応募を歓迎している。
(D) 翻訳の経験が必要である。

求人広告で何が述べられているかを問う選択肢照合型問題。❺の後半で「弊社では海外支店への短期訪問を含む6カ月間の総合研修プログラムを実施する」と述べているため、海外研修を行うことがわかる。よって、これを言い換えた **(B)** が正解。❺の "brief visits to our branches overseas" が選択肢では international travel となっていることを押さえておこう。(A) と (C) については記載がなく、(D) は❺の前半で「同様の職務経験は必要条件ではない」と述べているので、いずれも不正解。

☐ managerial position 管理職　☐ translation experience 翻訳の経験

★★★☆☆ 文挿入位置問題

11. In which of the positions marked [1], [2], [3], and [4] does the following sentence best belong?

"Thus, fluency in Japanese and native-level British English are essential."

(A) [1]
(B) [2]
(C) [3]
(D) [4]

次の文は [1]、[2]、[3]、[4] のどの位置に最もよく当てはまりますか。

「そのため、流ちょうな日本語と母国語相当のイギリス英語の力が必須です」

(A) [1]
(B) [2]
(C) [3]
(D) [4]

問われた文の位置を問う問題。問われた文は「そのため、流ちょうな日本語と母国語相当のイギリス英語の力が必須」となっている。❸で「採用された方には、さまざまな日本語のテキストを英語に翻訳してもらう」と、日本語と英語を使う業務について述べられ、❹では追加された要件が挙げられている。この間に問われた文を挿入すると、業務に必要な日英の流暢さのレベルを明確にし、さらに追加の要件を挙げる、という流れができる。よって、正解は **(B)**。

問題 **9** から **11** は次のウェブページに関するものです。

◀ ▶ http://www.lingojob.co.uk/vacancies/56025 ▶

仕事：プレスリリースの日英翻訳　　　照会番号：56025
会社名：Rising Sun Translations　　　応募締切：9月8日

ロンドンに本社を置き、韓国と日本に支社を持つ Rising Sun Translations は、東アジア言語を専門とする世界有数の翻訳会社です。現在、私たちは本社のチームに参加していただける技術力のある翻訳者を探しています。—[1]—国内からのみ受け付けております。

採用された方には、プレスリリースや広告コピーなどのさまざまな日本語のテキストを英国市場向けに英語に翻訳していただきます。—[2]—そのため、流ちょうな日本語と母国語相当のイギリス英語の力が必須です。さらに、この職への応募をご希望の方には、関連分野の大学レベルの教育を受けていること、言語と創作作品に対する情熱があること、職務上または学業上の推薦状が3通必要です。—[3]—弊社では海外の支店への短期訪問を含む6カ月間の総合研修プログラムを実施するため、同様の職務経験は応募の必要条件ではありません。—[4]—

応募用紙は照会番号を入力することにより www.risingsuntr.co.uk/apply/ からダウンロードまたは印刷できます。

Questions 12-14 refer to the following e-mail.

To: Maria Cruz <maricru@springblog.com>
From: Lola Hawkins <lhawkins@neodes.com>
Subject: Site Redesign
Date: 19 January

Dear Maria,

Thank you for your patience during this busy time. I'm happy to announce that we have completed the redesign of your Web site. When you get a chance, please go to www.springblog.com to see how the new site looks. We changed the layout to match your latest specifications, but please do not hesitate to ask if it requires any further adjustments.

You can access the site's administrator dashboard using the login details listed below:

URL: www.springblog.com/admin
Username: mariacruz
Password: feSr27nJs5

From the dashboard, you can draft new blog posts, edit pages, and view your site's traffic. Please make sure that the dashboard is working properly for you. Although all major bugs have been dealt with, there may be some smaller issues that we did not notice during our initial testing. We'll be happy to fix any problems you find.

By the way, while working on this job, I noticed that you have a few other sites that you run in addition to Spring Blog. While I didn't notice any technical problems, the designs of these sites are quite outdated. If you're interested in updating them, we have special rates for repeat customers.

Sincerely,

Lola Hawkins
Project Manager, Neodes

12. Why did Ms. Hawkins send the e-mail?

    (A) To thank a client
    (B) To advertise a new blog
    (C) To request changes to a site
    (D) To report a job's status

13. What does Ms. Hawkins ask Ms. Cruz to do?

    (A) Make a list of problems
    (B) Write a blog post
    (C) Log in to a Web site
    (D) Send design specifications

14. What does Ms. Hawkins offer to do?

    (A) Build an additional Web site
    (B) Provide a discount
    (C) Fix some technical errors
    (D) Review some designs

P. 28

Questions 12-14 refer to the following e-mail.

To: ❶ Maria Cruz <maricru@springblog.com>
From: ❷ Lola Hawkins <lhawkins@neodes.com>
Subject: Site Redesign
Date: 19 January

Dear Maria,

Thank you for your patience during this busy time. ❸ I'm happy to announce that we have completed the redesign of your Web site. ❹ When you get a chance, please go to www.springblog.com to see how the new site looks. We changed the layout to match your latest specifications, but please do not hesitate to ask if it requires any further adjustments.

You can access the site's administrator dashboard using the login details listed below:

URL: www.springblog.com/admin
Username: mariacruz
Password: feSr27nJs5

From the dashboard, you can draft new blog posts, edit pages, and view your site's traffic. Please make sure that the dashboard is working properly for you. Although all major bugs have been dealt with, there may be some smaller issues that we did not notice during our initial testing. We'll be happy to fix any problems you find.

By the way, while working on this job, I noticed that you have a few other sites that you run in addition to Spring Blog. While I didn't notice any technical problems, the designs of these sites are quite outdated. ❺ If you're interested in updating them, we have special rates for repeat customers.

Sincerely,

Lola Hawkins
Project Manager, Neodes

✏️ ☐ redesign 再設計　☐ patience 辛抱、我慢　☐ layout レイアウト　☐ match 〜に合う　☐ latest 最新の
☐ specification 仕様　☐ further さらなる　☐ adjustment 調整　☐ administrator 管理者
☐ dashboard ダッシュボード（ウェブサイトに関するさまざまな情報の管理などを行うページのこと）
☐ login detail ログインの詳細情報　☐ draft 〜を下書きする　☐ post 投稿　☐ edit 〜を編集する
☐ traffic （ウェブサイトの）アクセス状況　☐ work properly 正しく動作する　☐ major 主要な
☐ bug 欠陥、不具合　☐ deal with 〜に対応する　☐ initial testing 初期テスト　☐ fix 〜を修復する
☐ by the way ところで　☐ run 〜を運営する　☐ in addition to 〜に加えて　☐ update 〜を更新する
☐ special rate 特別価格

★★☆☆☆

12. Why did Ms. Hawkins send the e-mail?

    (A) To thank a client
    (B) To advertise a new blog
    (C) To request changes to a site
    (D) To report a job's status

Hawkins さんが E メールを送ったのはなぜですか。

    (A) 顧客に感謝するため
    (B) 新しいブログを宣伝するため
    (C) ウェブサイトの変更を要求するため
    (D) 仕事の状況を報告するため

🔍 Hawkins さんが E メールを送付した目的が問われている。Hawkins さんは❸で「お客様のウェブサイト再設計が完了したことを知らせる」と述べており、依頼された仕事の状況を知らせるために連絡したことがわかる。以上から、❸の "we have completed the redesign of your Web site" を a job's status と表現した **(D)** が正解となる。job status は仕事の進行状況を伝える際に使うことができる表現として押さえておこう。

✏️ ☐ thank 〜に感謝する　☐ advertise 〜を広告する　☐ status 進行状況

13. What does Ms. Hawkins ask Ms. Cruz to do?

(A) Make a list of problems
(B) Write a blog post
(C) Log in to a Web site
(D) Send design specifications

Hawkins さんは Cruz さんに対して何をするように頼んでいますか。

(A) 問題のリストを作成する
(B) ブログの投稿を書く
(C) ウェブサイトにログインする
(D) 設計仕様書を送る

Hawkins さんが Cruz さんに依頼していることが問われている。まず、❶・❷からこの E メールは Hawkins さんが Cruz さんに送っていることがわかる。次に、❹で Hawkins さんは「時間のある際に、指定アドレスにアクセスしウェブサイトを確認してほしい」と述べている。以上から、正解は (C) となる。"go to www.springblog. com" が、Log in to a Web site と言い換えられていることもチェックしておこう。また、Hawkins さんが❸で "your Web site" と述べているため、この Web site は Cruz さんのウェブサイトであることもしっかり理解しておこう。

14. What does Ms. Hawkins offer to do?

(A) Build an additional Web site
(B) Provide a discount
(C) Fix some technical errors
(D) Review some designs

Hawkins さんは何をすることを申し出ていますか。

(A) 他にもウェブサイトを作成する
(B) 割引をする
(C) 技術的な問題点を修正する
(D) デザインを確認する

Hawkins さんが申し出ていることが問われている。Hawkins さんは最終段落で、Cruz さんの他のウェブサイトも閲覧したことを述べ、❺で「新しくすることを検討しているのであれば、特別料金がある」と割安で対応することを申し出ている。以上から、**(B)** が正解。❺の "special rate for ~ " が provide a discount の言い換えになっている。新しくすること（update）と言っているが、一から作成するとは述べていないので、(A) は不正解。

☐ build ～を作成、構築する　☐ provide ～を提供する　☐ fix ～を修復する　☐ review ～を確認する

📝 問題 12 から 14 は次の E メールに関するものです。

受信者：　Maria Cruz <maricru@springblog.com>
送信者：　Lola Hawkins <lhawkins@neodes.com>
件名：　　ウェブサイトの再設計
日付：　　1 月 19 日

Maria 様

お忙しいところ、お待ちいただきありがとうございます。お客様のウェブサイトの再設計が完了したことを喜んでお知らせいたします。お時間のある時に、www.springblog.com にアクセスいただき、新しいサイトの見栄えをご確認ください。お客様の最新の仕様に合うようにレイアウトを変更しましたが、さらなる調整が必要な場合は、お気兼ねなくご連絡ください。

以下のログイン情報を使ってサイトの管理者用ダッシュボードにアクセスできます。

URL: www.springblog.com/admin
ユーザー名：mariacruz
パスワード：feSr27nJs5

ダッシュボードからは新しいブログの投稿の下書き、ページの編集、ウェブサイトのアクセス状況を見ることができます。ダッシュボードが正しく機能していることをご確認ください。主要な欠陥は解決されましたが、初期のテストで見落とされた小さな問題がある可能性があります。問題が見つかった場合は喜んで修正いたします。

話は変わりますが、このお仕事をさせていただいている間に、お客様が Spring Blog の他にもいくつかのサイトを運営されていることを拝見しました。技術的な問題はございませんでしたが、サイトのデザインはかなり時代遅れです。新しくすることをお考えでしたら、リピーターのお客様向けには特別料金をご用意しています。

よろしくお願いいたします。

Lola Hawkins
Neodes プロジェクトマネージャー

Luke Ray <l-ray@vizion.com>
Evie Thornton <e-thornton@vizion.com>
RE: Application
June 25

Dear Ms. Thornton,

Thank you for your application for the position of Senior Creative Consultant. As you may know, we screen all internal referrals before advertising any position outside of the company. I have spoken to your current manager, and he has spoken highly of your creative abilities and determination to succeed. With this in mind, I am pleased to inform you that you have made it to the next stage in the application process.

I would like to schedule a meeting to discuss what the position entails and determine whether it would be a good fit for you. I should mention that this position involves very little graphic design work, so it is quite different from what you are currently doing. If you are still interested in the possibility of being promoted to this position, please let me know which date and time is best for you from the list below.

06/28 9:30 A.M.
06/28 1:45 P.M.
06/29 5:30 P.M.

Best regards,

Luke Ray
Hiring Manager
Vizion Arts

15. What is the purpose of the e-mail?

    (A) To apply for a position
    (B) To set up an interview
    (C) To praise an employee
    (D) To describe an assignment

16. What is NOT suggested about Ms. Thornton?

    (A) She is a dedicated employee.
    (B) She is a graphic designer.
    (C) She has applied for a promotion.
    (D) She has experience as a manager.

17. The word "screen" in paragraph 1, line 2, is closest in meaning to

    (A) examine
    (B) accept
    (C) prefer
    (D) cover

P. 32

Questions 15-17 refer to the following e-mail.

From: Luke Ray <l-ray@vizion.com>
To: Evie Thornton <e-thornton@vizion.com>
Subject: RE: Application
Date: June 25

Dear Ms. Thornton,

❶ Thank you for your application for the position of Senior Creative Consultant. As you may know, we ❷ screen all internal referrals before advertising any position outside of the company. I have spoken to your current manager, and ❸ he has spoken highly of your creative abilities and determination to succeed. With this in mind, I am pleased to inform you that you have made it to the next stage in the application process.

❹ I would like to schedule a meeting to discuss what the position entails and determine whether it would be a good fit for you. ❺ I should mention that this position involves very little graphic design work, so it is quite different from what you are currently doing. ❻ If you are still interested in the possibility of being promoted to this position, please let me know which date and time is best for you from the list below.

06/28 9:30 A.M.
06/28 1:45 P.M.
06/29 5:30 P.M.

Best regards,

Luke Ray
Hiring Manager
Vizion Arts

□ screen ～を選別する □ internal 内部の □ referral 推薦された人 □ speak highly of ～のことをほめる
□ determination 決意 □ with this in mind この点を考慮して □ next stage 次の段階
□ application process 応募の過程 □ entail ～を必要とする □ a good fit ぴったりなもの □ involve ～を含む
□ be promoted to ～に昇進する

★★☆☆☆

15. What is the purpose of the e-mail?

(A) To apply for a position
(B) To set up an interview
(C) To praise an employee
(D) To describe an assignment

Ｅメールの目的は何ですか。

(A) 仕事に応募すること
(B) 面接を設定すること
(C) 従業員を称賛すること
(D) 課題について説明すること

Ｅメールの目的が問われている。メールの送信者は、❶で求人への応募のお礼を伝え、❹で「仕事内容と適性の有無について話し合う面談をしたい」と述べているため、ここから求人募集に関する面談を設定したい趣旨でメールを送付していることがわかる。以上から、面談を interview と言い換えた **(B)** が正解となる。(D) を「職務内容の説明」と解釈すれば正解のように見えるが、❹ "what the position entails（その職が必要としている要件)" であって、「職務内容」とは異なるので不正解。entail（～を必要とする、伴う）は難しい語だが、require, involve の同義語としてインプットしておこう。

□ apply for ～に申し込む・応募する □ set up ～を設定する □ praise ～を褒める □ describe ～を説明する
□ assignment 業務、課題

★★★★☆ NOT 問題

16. What is NOT suggested about Ms. Thornton?

(A) She is a dedicated employee.
(B) She is a graphic designer.
(C) She has applied for a promotion.
(D) She has experience as a manager.

Thornton さんについて示唆されていないことは何ですか。

(A) 献身的な従業員である。
(B) グラフィックデザイナーである。
(C) 昇進を申し込んだ。
(D) 管理職としての経験がある。

 NOT 問題。Thornton さんについて示されていないことが問われている。Thornton さんはこのEメールの受信者である。❸の「創造的な能力と成功への決意を高く評価されている」が (A) に、❺の「現在行っているグラフィックデザイン業務とは違う」が (B) に、❻の「昇進の可能性についてまだ興味があるなら」が (C) に、それぞれ該当する。残った **(D)** が本文に示されていないため、これが正解となる。(A)dedicated（献身的）の本文の言い換えが少し難しいので、抜き出して再度参照し、言い換えとして反応できるようにしておこう。

□ dedicated 献身的な

 ★★★★☆ 同義語問題

17. The word "screen" in paragraph 1, line 2, is closest in meaning to

(A) examine
(B) accept
(C) prefer
(D) cover

第 1 段落・2 行目にある "screen" に最も意味が近いのは

(A) ～を精査する
(B) ～を受け容れる
(C) ～を好む
(D) ～を覆う、報道する

 同義語問題。問われている❷ "screen" は「（社内人員）を検査・選抜する」という意味。これと同義語になるのは **(A)**。screen は「フィルターにかけて検査、選抜する」という意味もあるので押さえておこう。パッと見るだけだと、つい (D) を選びそうだが、ここでは文脈で意味を考えないといけない。

問題 15 から 17 は次のEメールに関するものです。

送信者： Luke Ray <l-ray@vizion.com>
受信者： Evie Thornton <e-thornton@vizion.com>
件名： RE: 応募
日付： 6 月 25 日

Thornton 様

シニアクリエイティブコンサルタントの職にご応募いただきありがとうございます。ご存じとは思いますが、当社では、社外に求人を出す前に社内の候補者を審査しています。あなたの現在の上司と話したところ、あなたの創造的な能力と成功への決意を高く評価されていました。この点を考慮して、応募プロセスの次の段階に進まれたことをお知らせします。

仕事内容とあなたに適しているかどうかについて話し合う面談を予定したいと思います。お伝えしておくべきことは、この職ではグラフィックデザインの仕事はほとんどないということです。つまり、現在あなたが行っていることとはかなり違います。それでもなお、この職へ昇進することに興味がおありでしたら、下記の日程の中から最も都合がいいものを教えてください。

6 月 28 日午前 9 時 30 分
6 月 28 日午後 1 時 45 分
6 月 29 日午後 5 時 30 分

よろしくお願いいたします。

Luke Ray
Vizion Arts 人事部長

4分00秒

FOR IMMEDIATE RELEASE	**Contact:** Lois Pennington **E-mail:** lpen@westmidlib.co.uk

Adorable New Additions at West Midlands Library

Grown-ups aren't the only ones who can teach children—pets can too! That's the lesson being taught by the unique Susanna Fisher, a rising star in the world of children's literature. Her *My Little Friend* series combines moral lessons with adorable illustrations from a range of handpicked local artists.

Fisher's most celebrated works include *Fish are Friends*, *Bye-bye Bertie*, and *Guinea Gangsters*, all of which are filled with characterful animals kids can't help but fall in love with. The same is true of her latest work, *Penny and Prue*, which was released last month. It is our great pleasure to announce that these iconic books will be joining our expansive collection at West Midlands Library. Please be aware that since we have been getting calls from so many people eager to borrow these books, we will only be offering short loans, and stock will likely run out quickly.

To celebrate her newest title, Fisher will also be doing a regional library tour across the West Midlands, starting here in Birmingham on 6 August, before moving on to Wolverhampton (10 August), Coventry (14 August), and Dudley (18 August). During each one-day visit, fans are invited to meet the author, have their books signed, and even have their picture taken with her. Don't miss this amazing opportunity!

18. Who most likely is Susanna Fisher?

    (A) A schoolteacher
    (B) An author of children's stories
    (C) A book illustrator
    (D) A TV show host

19. What is indicated about *Penny and Prue*?

    (A) It is about children.
    (B) It will be released soon.
    (C) It features animals.
    (D) It is the final title in a series.

20. What is suggested about the new collection?

    (A) It is on sale for a limited time.
    (B) It is written by multiple authors.
    (C) It will move to different libraries.
    (D) It is expected to be popular.

21. What can participants do at the library tour events?

    (A) Buy publications at a lower price
    (B) Purchase signed merchandise
    (C) Eat lunch with an author
    (D) Take a commemorative photograph

Single Q4

P. 36

Questions 18-21 refer to the following press release.

FOR IMMEDIATE RELEASE	**Contact:** Lois Pennington **E-mail:** lpen@westmidlib.co.uk

Adorable New Additions at West Midlands Library

Grown-ups aren't the only ones who can teach children—pets can too! That's the lesson being taught by the unique Susanna Fisher, ❶ a rising star in the world of children's literature. Her *My Little Friend* series combines moral lessons with adorable illustrations from a range of handpicked local artists.

❷ Fisher's most celebrated works include *Fish are Friends*, *Bye-bye Bertie*, and *Guinea Gangsters*, all of which are filled with characterful animals kids can't help but fall in love with. The same is true of her latest work, *Penny and Prue*, which was released last month. It is our great pleasure to announce that these iconic books will be joining our expansive collection at West Midlands Library. ❸ Please be aware that since we have been getting calls from so many people eager to borrow these books, we will only be offering short loans, and stock will likely run out quickly.

❹ To celebrate her newest title, Fisher will also be doing a regional library tour across the West Midlands, starting here in Birmingham on 6 August, before moving on to Wolverhampton (10 August), Coventry (14 August), and Dudley (18 August). ❺ During each one-day visit, fans are invited to meet the author, have their books signed, and even have their picture taken with her. Don't miss this amazing opportunity!

□ immediate release 速報　□ adorable 魅力的な　□ addition 付け加えたもの　□ grown-up 大人
□ rising star 期待の星　□ literature 文学　□ combine A with B A と B を組み合わせる
□ moral lesson 道徳教育　□ illustration イラスト　□ a range of 多様な　□ handpicked 厳選された
□ celebrated 有名な　□ filled with ～であふれている　□ characterful 個性的な
□ can't help but ～せずにいられない　□ fall in love with ～を愛する　□ latest 最新の　□ work 作品
□ iconic 象徴的な　□ expansive 広大な　□ be aware that ～に留意する　□ eager to ～することを熱望する
□ short loan 短期の貸し出し　□ stock 在庫　□ likely おそらく　□ run out 品切れとなる　□ regional 地域の
□ Don't miss ～を見逃すな　□ amazing 驚くべき　□ opportunity 機会

★★★★☆

18. Who most likely is Susanna Fisher?

  (A) A schoolteacher
  (B) An author of children's stories
  (C) A book illustrator
  (D) A TV show host

Susanna Fisher さんは誰であると考えられますか。

  (A) 教師
  (B) 子ども向けの物語を書く作家
  (C) 本のイラストレーター
  (D) テレビ番組の司会者

Susanna Fisher さんが誰かが問われている。❶で、Susanna Fisher さんは「児童文学界の新星」と表現されていることから、これを言い換えた **(B)** が正解。イラストが本に載っていることがうかがえるため、(C) を選んでしまったかもしれないが、イラストは地元のイラストレーターが書いている。

 □ illustrator イラストレーター（絵や図を描くことを職業とする人）　□ TV show テレビ番組　□ host 司会者

19. What is indicated about *Penny and Prue*?

   (A) It is about children.
   (B) It will be released soon.
  (C) It features animals.
   (D) It is the final title in a series.

Penny and Prue について何が示されています
か。

   (A) 子どもたちについてのものである。
   (B) 間もなく発売される。
  (C) 動物が登場する。
   (D) シリーズ最後の作品である。

Penny and Prue について何が示されているかを問う選択肢照合型問題。❷で Susanna Fisher さんの代表作について触れ、「代表作はすべて、個性的な動物たちであふれ、Penny and Prue も同様である」と述べている。これを言い換えた **(C)** が正解となる。(A) は児童文学だが、この作品が子どもについて書かれたとは述べられていない、(B) は先月発売されたものである、(D) はこの作品はシリーズ最新作だが、シリーズ最後とは言及されていないので、それぞれ不正解。

□ release 〜を発売、発表する　□ feature 〜を呼び物にする

20. What is suggested about the new collection?

   (A) It is on sale for a limited time.
   (B) It is written by multiple authors.
   (C) It will move to different libraries.
  (D) It is expected to be popular.

新しい蔵書について何が示唆されていますか。

   (A) 期間限定で販売される。
   (B) 複数の著者によって書かれている。
   (C) 他の図書館へ移管される。
  (D) 人気が出ると予想される。

新しい蔵書について何が示唆されているかを問う選択肢照合型問題。❸で「これらの本を借りることを希望する多くの方から電話をいただいているため、短期間での貸出しになり、在庫はすぐになくなる見込みだ」と述べているので、この蔵書が人気になることが予測できる。以上から、**(D)** が正解となる。(A)(B)(C) については言及がないため、いずれも不正解。

□ collection コレクション、蔵書　□ on sale 販売中である　□ for a limited time 期間限定で　□ multiple 多数の
□ be expected to 〜することが予想される

21. What can participants do at the library tour events?

   (A) Buy publications at a lower price
   (B) Purchase signed merchandise
   (C) Eat lunch with an author
  (D) Take a commemorative photograph

図書館のツアーイベントで参加者は何ができますか。

   (A) 低価格で出版物の購入ができる
   (B) サイン入りの商品を購入できる
   (C) 著者と昼食を食べられる
  (D) 記念写真の撮影ができる

図書館のツアーイベントで参加者は何ができるかが問われている。❹でツアーイベントが最新作の記念イベントであることがわかり、❺では「(イベントでは) 著者との交流、本にサインをもらうこと、一緒に写真撮影ができる」と述べられている。よって、この「写真撮影」を言い換えた **(D)** が正解となる。(B) はサイン入りの商品を購入ではなく、「本にサインをしてもらえる」なので不正解。(A) と (C) については文書に言及がなく、いずれも不正解。

□ participant 参加者　□ publication 出版物　□ at a lower price 低価格で　□ signed サイン入りの
□ merchandise 商品　□ commemorative 記念の

問題 18 から 21 は次のプレスリリースに関するものです。

速報	連絡先：Lois Pennington E メール：lpen@westmidlib.co.uk

West Midlands 図書館のかわいらしい新刊図書

子どもたちに何かを教えることができるのは大人たちだけではありません。ペットにも可能です！　この教訓は児童文学界の新星、唯一無二の Susanna Fisher さんによるものです。彼女の *My Little Friend* シリーズは、道徳的な教訓と、厳選された地元のアーティストによるかわいらしいイラストを組み合わせています。

Fisher さんの最も有名な作品には、*Fish are Friends*、*Bye-bye Bertie, Guinea*、*Gangsters*、などがあり、これらはすべて、子どもたちが愛さずにはいられない個性的な動物たちでいっぱいです。先月発売された最新作 *Penny and Prue* についても同様です。これらの象徴的な本が West Midlands 図書館の膨大な蔵書に加わることを発表でき、大変うれしく思います。これらの本を借りることをご希望する多くの方からお電話をいただいていますので、短期間での貸し出しのみとなること、在庫がすぐになくなる可能性があることにご注意ください。

最新作を記念して、Fisher さんは West Midlands 地方で図書館ツアーを行う予定で、8 月 6 日にここ Birmingham から開始し、Wolverhampton（8 月 10 日）、Coventry（8 月 14 日）、Dudley（8 月 18 日）と移動します。各地での 1 日滞在で、ファンの皆さまは、著者との交流、書籍へのサイン、そして一緒に写真撮影をすることもできます。この素晴らしい機会をお見逃しなく！

Questions 22-25 refer to the following online chat discussion.

 4分00秒

Group Chat

Lloyd Carr (5:46 P.M.)

My meeting with Mr. Bowden lasted much longer than I expected. Sorry, but I won't be able to get to the dinner until around 7:00 at the earliest.

Elaine Metcalfe (5:51 P.M.)

I see. Our reservation is at 6:15, but I haven't heard from Tina and Ms. Newman. If they're running late too, maybe I should change our reservation to a later time.

Tina Powell (5:54 P.M.)

Actually, we'll be there in about five minutes. Ms. Newman and I are sharing a taxi from the conference hall.

Lloyd Carr (5:55 P.M.)

OK. Feel free to eat before I get there. And please tell Ms. Newman I'm sorry for being so late.

Elaine Metcalfe (5:56 P.M.)

You got it. By the way, what did Mr. Bowden think of our designs for the art center?

Lloyd Carr (5:57 P.M.)

He loved them. He said that he'd like to receive the entire set of blueprints by the end of the month so that he can show them to the builders.

Elaine Metcalfe (5:57 P.M.)

That's really soon. I'll call Jennifer Grey tomorrow morning to check if she can finish them before then.

Tina Powell (5:58 P.M.)

I wouldn't worry about it. Jennifer told me yesterday that she's almost done with them. But let's worry about that tomorrow. Tonight we need to celebrate successfully completing another job for AWT Construction!

22. Where do the writers most likely work?

    (A) At a restaurant
    (B) At an art center
    (C) At an architectural firm
    (D) At a conference hall

23. What is suggested about Ms. Newman?

    (A) She will arrive at the restaurant on time.
    (B) She has requested some new designs.
    (C) She gave a presentation at a conference.
    (D) She owns a construction company.

24. At 5:56 P.M., what does Ms. Metcalfe most likely mean when she writes, "You got it"?

    (A) She understands the meaning of Mr. Carr's request.
    (B) She will apologize on behalf of Mr. Carr.
    (C) She wants Mr. Carr to clarify a request.
    (D) She wants to talk about something else.

25. What is suggested about Ms. Grey?

    (A) She is a colleague of Ms. Newman.
    (B) She is creating blueprints for a building.
    (C) She will attend the dinner.
    (D) She met with Mr. Bowden earlier.

Single Q4

 P. 42

Questions 22-25 refer to the following online chat discussion.

Group Chat
Lloyd Carr (5:46 P.M.) My meeting with Mr. Bowden lasted much longer than I expected. Sorry, but ❶ I won't be able to get to the dinner until around 7:00 at the earliest.
Elaine Metcalfe (5:51 P.M.) I see. ❷ Our reservation is at 6:15, but I haven't heard from Tina and Ms. Newman. If they're running late too, maybe I should change our reservation to a later time.
Tina Powell (5:54 P.M.) Actually, ❸ we'll be there in about five minutes. Ms. Newman and I are sharing a taxi from the conference hall.
Lloyd Carr (5:55 P.M.) OK. Feel free to eat before I get there. And ❹ please tell Ms. Newman I'm sorry for being so late.
Elaine Metcalfe (5:56 P.M.) ❺ You got it. By the way, what did Mr. Bowden think of ❻ our designs for the art center?
Lloyd Carr (5:57 P.M.) He loved them. He said that he'd like to receive ❼ the entire set of blueprints by the end of the month so that he can ❽ show them to the builders.
Elaine Metcalfe (5:57 P.M.) That's really soon. ❾ I'll call Jennifer Grey tomorrow morning to check if she can finish them before then.
Tina Powell (5:58 P.M.) I wouldn't worry about it. Jennifer told me yesterday that she's almost done with them. But let's worry about that tomorrow. Tonight we need to celebrate successfully completing another job for AWT Construction!

□ last 続く □ run late 遅れる □ share ～を共有する □ feel free to *do* 気軽に～する
□ entire set of 一式の □ blueprint 設計図 □ builder 建築業者 □ worry about ～を心配する
□ successfully 無事に成功して

★★★☆☆

22. Where do the writers most likely work?

 (A) At a restaurant
 (B) At an art center
 (C) At an architectural firm
 (D) At a conference hall

メッセージを書いている人たちはどこで働いている
と考えられますか。

 (A) レストランで
 (B) 芸術センターで
 (C) 建築会社で
 (D) 会議場で

> メッセージのやりとりしている人たちがどこで働いているかが問われている。❻で「当社のデザイン」、❼・❽で「すべての設計図」「建設業者に見せる」という言及があり、ここからこの人達が設計図面を書く仕事をしていると考えることができる。以上から、正解はこれを言い換えた **(C)** となる。

□ architectural firm 建築会社

23. What is suggested about Ms. Newman?

(A) She will arrive at the restaurant on time.
(B) She has requested some new designs.
(C) She gave a presentation at a conference.
(D) She owns a construction company.

Newman さんについて何が示唆されていますか。

(A) レストランには時間どおりに到着する。
(B) 新しいデザインを要求した。
(C) 協議会で発表を行った。
(D) 建設会社を所有している。

Newman さんについて何が示唆されているかを問う選択肢照合型問題。まず、❶で「夕食会」の話題であることがわかる。次に❷・❸で「予約は 6 時 15 分」「Newman さんは同乗のタクシーで 6 時には着く」と言及されているので、ここから Newman さんは予約しているレストランには時間どおり着くことになるとわかる。よって、これを言い換えた **(A)** が正解となる。

□ own ～を所有する

★★★☆☆ 意図問題

24. At 5:56 P.M., what does Ms. Metcalfe most likely mean when she writes, "You got it"?

(A) She understands the meaning of Mr. Carr's request.
(B) She will apologize on behalf of Mr. Carr.
(C) She wants Mr. Carr to clarify a request.
(D) She wants to talk about something else.

午後 5 時 56 分に、Metcalfe さんは "You got it" という発言で、何を意味していると考えられますか。

(A) Carr さんの要求が意味することを理解している。
(B) Carr さんに代わって謝罪する。
(C) Carr さんに要求について詳しく説明してほしい。
(D) 何か他のことについて話したい。

意図問題。問われている❺は「あなたはそれ（直前に触れた内容）を得た」、つまり「了解」という意味となる。そのため直前の❹を見ると、「(Carr さんが) Newman さんに謝っておいてほしい」とお願いしているので、Metcalfe さんは、Carr さんの代わりに謝ることを意図していることがわかる。よって、正解は **(B)**。"You got it." の意図問題は必ず直前を確認しよう。

□ on behalf of ～の代わりに   □ clarify ～を詳しく説明する

★★★★☆

25. What is suggested about Ms. Grey?

(A) She is a colleague of Ms. Newman.
(B) She is creating blueprints for a building.
(C) She will attend the dinner.
(D) She met with Mr. Bowden earlier.

Grey さんについて何が示唆されていますか。

(A) Newman さんの同僚である。
(B) 建物の設計図を作成している。
(C) 夕食に参加する。
(D) Bowden さんに先ほど会った。

Grey さんについて述べられていることを問う選択肢照合型問題。Carr さんが❼・❽を含む文で「(Bowden さんが) 月末までにすべての設計図を受け取りたいとのことだ」と話し、それに対し Metcalfe さんが❾で「Grey さんにそれまでに完了するか確認する」と述べている。ここから、Grey さんが設計図を作成していることがわかるので、これを言い換えた **(B)** が正解。Grey さんが夕食会に参加する記載はないため、(C) は不正解。

□ earlier 少し前に

グループチャット
Lloyd Carr（午後 5 時 46 分） Bowden さんとの会議が予想していたよりずっと長くなってしまいました。すみませんが、夕食会には早くても、7 時くらいまで到着できそうにありません。
Elaine Metcalfe（午後 5 時 51 分） わかりました。予約は 6 時 15 分ですが、Tina さんと Newman さんからはまだ連絡がありません。もし彼女たちも遅くなるようなら、予約を遅い時間に変更したほうがよさそうですね。
Tina Powell（午後 5 時 54 分） 実は、私たちは 5 分後にそこに着きます。Newman さんと私は会議場からタクシーに一緒に乗っています。
Lloyd Carr（午後 5 時 55 分） わかりました。私が到着する前にどうぞ食べていてください。Newman さんに遅くなることについて謝っておいてもらえますか。
Elaine Metcalfe（午後 5 時 56 分） 了解しました。ところで、Bowden さんは当社の芸術センターのデザインについてどう思っていましたか？
Lloyd Carr（午後 5 時 57 分） とても気に入ってくれました。建設業者に見せられるように、今月末までにすべての設計図を受け取りたいとのことでした。
Elaine Metcalfe（午後 5 時 57 分） それは、急ぎですね。明日の朝、Jennifer Grey さんに電話して、それまでに終わらせられるか確認します。
Tina Powell（午後 5 時 58 分） 心配しなくても大丈夫だと思います。Jennifer さんは、昨日、完成間近だと言っていましたから。その心配をするのは明日になってからにしましょう。今夜は AWT Construction 社との別の仕事が無事に終わったことのお祝いをしなければ！

GO ON TO THE NEXT PAGE!

Tennant Sports
28 Learmouth Street
LYONS VIC 3304

20 December

Dear Ms. Lakes,

As one of our long-term customers, we would like to thank you for choosing Mail My Style to assist in the design of your personal wardrobe. — [1] —.

We are excited to announce that next month we will begin offering a premium version of our service that features products from companies like Vera One, Chocolate Stitches, and Mark Wesley. — [2] —. The premium membership is recommended for customers that are able to spend a little bit more money in exchange for access to the latest in luxury fashion. — [3] —. If you would like to upgrade to a premium membership, please fill out and mail the form on the back of this letter.

Regardless of whether you choose to upgrade, the personal stylist assigned to your account will not be changed, so you do not need to worry about having clothing sent to your home that does not match your preferences. — [4] —. As always, if you have any comments for your stylist, you can reach them by logging in to your account and using the link at the top right of the page to access our secure message center. If you have any further questions about premium membership, please call our membership specialist, Henry Pinto, at 858-555-3272.

Best regards,

Delilah Weber

Delilah Weber, CEO, Mail My Style, Inc.

26. What type of business most likely is Mail My Style, Inc.?

    (A) A clothing manufacturer
    (B) An apparel delivery service
    (C) A fashion magazine
    (D) A department store

27. How does the premium membership differ from the regular membership?

    (A) It is more affordable.
    (B) It features brand-name goods.
    (C) It comes with a personal stylist.
    (D) It can be purchased annually.

28. According to the letter, how can Ms. Lakes contact a stylist?

    (A) By sending an e-mail
    (B) By calling a phone number
    (C) By opening an account
    (D) By visiting a Web site

29. In which of the positions marked [1], [2], [3], and [4] does the following sentence best belong?

"Best of all, we are able to acquire these at exclusive discount prices."

    (A) [1]
    (B) [2]
    (C) [3]
    (D) [4]

Single Q4

P. 48

Questions 26-29 refer to the following letter.

Tennant Sports
28 Learmouth Street
LYONS VIC 3304

20 December

Dear Ms. Lakes,

❶ As one of our long-term customers, we would like to thank you for choosing Mail My Style to assist in the design of your personal wardrobe. — [1] —.

❷ We are excited to announce that next month we will begin offering a premium version of our service that features products from companies like Vera One, Chocolate Stitches, and Mark Wesley. — [2] —. ❸ The premium membership is recommended for customers that are able to spend a little bit more money in exchange for access to the latest in luxury fashion. — [3] —. If you would like to upgrade to a premium membership, please fill out and mail the form on the back of this letter.

Regardless of whether you choose to upgrade, the personal stylist assigned to your account will not be changed, so ❹ you do not need to worry about having clothing sent to your home that does not match your preferences. — [4] —. ❺ As always, if you have any comments for your stylist, you can reach them by logging in to your account and using the link at the top right of the page to access our secure message center. If you have any further questions about premium membership, please call our membership specialist, Henry Pinto, at 858-555-3272.

Best regards,

Delilah Weber
Delilah Weber, CEO, Mail My Style, Inc.

☐ long-term 長期間の ☐ wardrobe 持ち衣裳 ☐ premium 高級な ☐ feature ～を取り扱う
☐ premium membership プレミアム会員 ☐ in exchange for ～を見返りとして ☐ access to ～への案内
☐ latest 最新のもの ☐ on the back of ～の裏に ☐ regardless of ～に関わらず
☐ personal stylist 専任スタイリスト ☐ assigned to ～に割り当てられる
☐ match one's preference ～の好みに合う ☐ as always いつもどおり ☐ log in to ～にログインする
☐ secure 安全な ☐ specialist 専門家

★★★☆☆

26. What type of business most likely is Mail My Style, Inc.?

(A) A clothing manufacturer
(B) An apparel delivery service
(C) A fashion magazine
(D) A department store

Mail My Style 社はどのような業種だと考えられますか。

(A) 衣料品メーカー
(B) アパレル配送サービス
(C) ファッション雑誌
(D) デパート

🔍 Mail My Style 社がどのような業種かが問われている。❶・❹で「お客様の衣裳部屋のデザインのお手伝い」、「お好みでない洋服が自宅に送られる心配は不要」と述べられており、顧客に対して衣料品を送付するサービス会社だとわかる。ここから、正解は **(B)**。自前で衣料品を製造している記載はないため、(A) は不正解。

✎ ☐ clothing manufacturer 衣料品メーカー ☐ apparel 衣料品、アパレル

27. How does the premium membership differ from the regular membership?

    (A) It is more affordable.
    (B) It features brand-name goods.
    (C) It comes with a personal stylist.
    (D) It can be purchased annually.

プレミアム会員は通常会員とどのように異なりますか。

    (A) より安価である。
    (B) ブランド品を取り扱っている。
    (C) 専任スタイリストが付く。
    (D) 毎年購入できる。

プレミアム会員と通常会員の違いが問われている。❷・❸でプレミアムサービスについての言及があり、「ブランド製品を含む、当社サービスのプレミアム版の提供」「高級ファッションの新作を利用できる」と述べられている。よって、**(B)** が正解となる。

☐ affordable 手ごろな価格で　☐ feature ～を取り扱う　☐ come with ～が付く　☐ annually 毎年

---

28. According to the letter, how can Ms. Lakes contact a stylist?

    (A) By sending an e-mail
    (B) By calling a phone number
    (C) By opening an account
    (D) By visiting a Web site

手紙によると、Lakes さんはどうやってスタイリストに連絡できますか。

    (A) Eメールを送ることにより
    (B) 電話番号に連絡することにより
    (C) 口座を開設することにより
    (D) ウェブサイトを訪れることにより

手紙の受取人である Lakes さんがスタイリストに連絡する方法が問われている。❺で「スタイリストにご意見がある場合は、お客様のアカウントにログインし、ページ右上のリンクからメッセージセンターにアクセスを」と述べられているので、あるウェブサイトにアクセスすることが連絡手段だとわかる。以上から、これを言い換えた **(D)** が正解。(B) は❺の直後に「プレミアム会員に関する質問は電話を」とあるので不正解。

☐ open an account 口座を開設する

---

29. In which of the positions marked [1], [2], [3], and [4] does the following sentence best belong?

"Best of all, we are able to acquire these at exclusive discount prices."

    (A) [1]
    (B) [2]
    (C) [3]
    (D) [4]

次の文は、[1]、[2]、[3]、[4] のどの位置に最もよく当てはまりますか。

「何よりも、当社はこれらを特別に安価で仕入れることができます」

    (A) [1]
    (B) [2]
    (C) [3]
    (D) [4]

文の位置を問う問題。問われている文は「何よりも、これらを特別に安価で仕入れることができる」とあるため、「これら (these)」が指す箇所を探す必要がある。❷に「Vera One、Chocolate Stitches、Mark Wesley などのブランドの製品」という複数のブランド製品が書かれており、❷の直後に当てはめると、「来月には複数のブランドの製品を含む当社のサービスのプレミアム版の提供開始」→「これらを特別に安価で入手できる」→「少額の追加費用で利用できるプレミアム版の案内」と、複数のブランドを安く調達できるからこのサービスが実現したとなり、文意も合致する。よって正解は **(B)**。

☐ acquire ～を獲得する　☐ exclusive 特別の

Tennant Sports
28 Learmouth Street
LYONS ビクトリア州 3304

12月20日

Lakes 様

長きにわたり、お客様の衣類のデザインのお手伝いをするのに Mail My Style 社をお選びいただき、感謝申し上げます。
— [1] —

来月には Vera One、Chocolate Stitches、Mark Wesley などのブランドの製品を含む、当社サービスのプレミアム版の提供を開始することをお知らせします。— [2] — 何よりも、当社はこれらを特別に安価で仕入れることができます。プレミアム会員権は、高級ファッションの新作をご利用できるのと引き換えに、少額の追加費用を支払うことができるお客様にお勧めしております。— [3] — プレミアム会員へのアップグレードをご希望でしたら、このお手紙の裏面の書式にご記入いただき、ご郵送ください。

アップグレードの有無にかかわらず、お客様のアカウントに割り振られた専任スタイリストは変更されませんので、お好みでない洋服がご自宅に送られてしまわないかというご心配は不要です。— [4] — いつものとおり、スタイリストにご意見がある場合は、お客様のアカウントにログインしていただき、ページの右上にあるリンクから安全なメッセージセンターにアクセスしてください。プレミアム会員についてその他ご質問がございましたら、当社の会員担当、Henry Pinto 858-555-3272 までお電話ください。

よろしくお願いいたします。

Delilah Weber

Mail My Style 社 最高経営責任者 Delilah Weber,

Live Music at The Lion Bar

Friday, April 12	**Saturday, April 13**
Mono Tony's	Believing Girls
Hip-hop	Electric pop
Friday, April 19	**Saturday, April 20**
Panorama Paranoia	See Foam
Indie rock	Ethereal folk
Friday, April 26	**Saturday, April 27**
Jet Shot	Anarchysta
Acoustic pop	Classic punk

· All performances are from 9:00 P.M.—closing
· Advanced tickets $5 (online booking only)
· $10 fee required for tickets purchased at the door

Be sure to arrive early, especially if you're buying tickets at the door. And don't forget to sign up for our newsletter to stay up to date on the latest shows being performed.

www.lionbar.com/livemusic
(637) 502-5024
21 Third Street, Springfield, OR

Opening Hours:
Monday to Thursday 11:00 A.M.—11:00 P.M.
Friday to Saturday 12:00 P.M.—12:00 A.M.

From: mattydee@onemail.com
To: live@lionbar.com
Date: April 22
Subject: Performance Inquiry
Attachment: 📎 LL_demo

To Whom It May Concern,

I would like to inquire as to whether I could book a spot to perform for one of your upcoming live music nights. My friends' rock band played at your venue this month, and they were very happy with the professionalism of your staff, the quality of your equipment, and the enthusiasm of your patrons.

I'm the lead singer of electronic punk band Last Light. You may have heard of us, as we were recently interviewed on several local radio stations. We have been the opening act for hugely popular bands such as The Blue Spots and Calendar Error. For our solo shows, we typically perform at bars and other small venues.

We have quite a substantial following, both locally and nationwide, so I'm sure we could bring The Lion Bar plenty of customers. We played at Limelight Tavern, which is right next door to The Lion Bar, a few months ago to a sold-out crowd.

I have attached our demo should you be interested.

Best Regards,

Matthew Dee

30. How long do performances at The Lion Bar last?

(A) One hour
(B) Two hours
(C) Three hours
(D) Four hours

31. According to the schedule, how can concertgoers save money?

(A) By purchasing tickets from a Web site
(B) By arriving at the venue early
(C) By signing up for a newsletter
(D) By buying tickets in bulk

32. Which performers did Mr. Dee most likely speak with?

(A) Mono Tony's
(B) Believing Girls
(C) Panorama Paranoia
(D) See Foam

33. What is most likely true about Last Light?

(A) They primarily use acoustic instruments.
(B) They recently changed their band's name.
(C) They only play at small venues.
(D) They have a large fan club.

34. What is indicated about Limelight Tavern?

(A) It is smaller than The Lion Bar.
(B) It is located on Third Street.
(C) It is a nationwide chain.
(D) It is popular among pop music fans.

Double

 P. 54

Questions 30-34 refer to the following schedule and e-mail.

Live Music at The Lion Bar

❶ Friday, April 12	❷ Saturday, April 13
Mono Tony's Hip-hop	Believing Girls Electric pop
❸ Friday, April 19 ❹ Panorama Paranoia Indie rock	❺ Saturday, April 20 See Foam Ethereal folk
❻ Friday, April 26 Jet Shot Acoustic pop	❼ Saturday, April 27 Anarchysta Classic punk

· ❽ All performances are from 9:00 P.M.—closing
· ❾ Advanced tickets $5 (online booking only)
· ❿ $10 fee required for tickets purchased at the door

Be sure to arrive early, especially if you're buying tickets at the door. And don't forget to sign up for our newsletter to stay up to date on the latest shows being performed.

www.lionbar.com/livemusic
(637) 502-5024
⓫ 21 Third Street, Springfield, OR

Opening Hours:
Monday to Thursday 11:00 A.M.—11:00 P.M.
⓬ Friday to Saturday 12:00 P.M.—12:00 A.M.

From: mattydee@onemail.com
To: live@lionbar.com
Date: April 22
Subject: Performance Inquiry
Attachment: 📎 LL_demo

To Whom It May Concern,

I would like to inquire as to whether I could book a spot to perform for one of your upcoming live music nights. ⓭ My friends' rock band played at your venue this month, and they were very happy with the professionalism of your staff, the quality of your equipment, and the enthusiasm of your patrons.

⓮ I'm the lead singer of electronic punk band Last Light. You may have heard of us, as we were recently interviewed on several local radio stations. We have been the opening act for hugely popular bands such as The Blue Spots and Calendar Error. For our solo shows, we typically perform at bars and other small venues.

⓯ We have quite a substantial following, both locally and nationwide, so I'm sure we could bring The Lion Bar plenty of customers. ⓰ We played at Limelight Tavern, which is right next door to The Lion Bar, a few months ago to a sold-out crowd.

I have attached our demo should you be interested.

Best Regards,

⓱ Matthew Dee

★★★☆☆

30. How long do performances at The Lion Bar last?

(A) One hour
(B) Two hours
(C) Three hours
(D) Four hours

The Lion Bar での演奏はどのくらいの時間行われますか。

(A) 1 時間
(B) 2 時間
(C) 3 時間
(D) 4 時間

🔍 The Lion Bar での演奏時間が問われている。1 文書目の予定表を読むと、❶～❸、❺～❼で、ライブ演奏を開催する曜日が書かれており、金曜日と土曜日に開催ということがわかる。次に❽から「演奏は全日程、午後 9 時から閉店まで」ということがわかる。そして、⓬から、金曜日と土曜日の営業が午前 0 時までだとわかる。これらの情報から、演奏時間は金曜日と土曜日の午後 9 時から閉店の午前 0 時までの 3 時間ということになるため、正解は **(C)** となる。分散している情報を組み合わせて考える必要があるので注意しよう。

★★☆☆☆

31. According to the schedule, how can concertgoers save money?

(A) By purchasing tickets from a Web site
(B) By arriving at the venue early
(C) By signing up for a newsletter
(D) By buying tickets in bulk

予定表によると、コンサートの客がお金を節約するにはどうしたらいいですか。

(A) ウェブサイトでチケットを購入する
(B) 早めに会場に到着する
(C) ニュースレターに登録する
(D) チケットをまとめて購入する

🔍 予定表から、コンサートの客がお金を節約する方法を探す問題。予定表の❾から「前売りチケットの価格が 5 ドルで、オンライン予約のみ」という記載があるため、これを言い換えた **(A)** が正解。"advanced（事前の）""booking（予約）" は頻出表現なので押さえておこう。なお、❿の "at the door" は「開催する建物で」＝「当日窓口で」という意味で、❾との対比となっていることも注意しよう。また、設問の concertgoer は live music に行く人を指しており、TOEIC には頻出の表現なので慣れておこう。

✏️ ☐ concertgoer 演奏会に行く人　☐ venue 場所　☐ sign up for ～に登録する・申し込む　☐ in bulk 一括で、大量に

32. Which performers did Mr. Dee most likely speak with?

(A) Mono Tony's
(B) Believing Girls
(C) Panorama Paranoia
(D) See Foam

Dee さんが話をした演奏者は誰であると考えられますか。

(A) Mono Tony's
(B) Believing Girls
(C) Panorama Paranoia
(D) See Foam

 Dee さんが話をした演奏者はおそらく誰かが問われている。Dee さんは❶からEメールの送信者だとわかる。❸で「友人のロックバンドが Lion Bar で演奏し、満足していると言っていた」と述べている。ここから Dee さんには、The Lion Bar で演奏したロックバンドの友人がいることがわかる。1 文書目の予定表を参照すると、❹のバンドがロックを演奏していることがわかる。以上から **(C)** が正解。予定表に複数の比較できる情報がある時、別の文書に手掛かりがあるというのはよくあるパターンなので押さえておこう。

---

33. What is most likely true about Last Light?

(A) They primarily use acoustic instruments.
(B) They recently changed their band's name.
(C) They only play at small venues.
(D) They have a large fan club.

Last Light についておそらく当てはまるものはどれですか。

(A) 主にアコースティック楽器を使用している。
(B) 最近、バンドの名称を変更した。
(C) 小さな会場でのみ演奏する。
(D) 大きなファンクラブを持っている。

 Last Light についておそらく当てはまるものが何かを選ぶ問題。E メールの差出人である Dee さんは❶で、自分がバンド Last Light の一員であることを明かし、❶で「地元にも全国的にもかなりのファンがいる」と述べている。ここから、Last Light は全国に多数のファンがおり、ファンクラブのような団体がいることが推測できるので、正解は **(D)** となる。(A) 使用する楽器、(B) 名称変更、については触れられておらず、(C) 演奏会場の規模については、小さな会場でのみとは述べていないため、それぞれ不正解。

 □ primarily 主に　□ acoustic instrument アコースティック楽器

---

34. What is indicated about Limelight Tavern?

(A) It is smaller than The Lion Bar.
(B) It is located on Third Street.
(C) It is a nationwide chain.
(D) It is popular among pop music fans.

Limelight Tavern について何が示されていますか。

(A) The Lion Bar よりも小さい。
(B) Third Street にある。
(C) 全国チェーンである。
(D) ポップスファンに人気がある。

 Limelight Tavern について述べられていることが問われている選択肢照合型問題。2 文書目のEメールの❶で Dee さんは「The Lion Bar のすぐ隣にある Limelight Tavern で演奏した」と述べているため、Limelight Tavern は演奏会場だということがわかる。次に、1 文書目の予定表の⓫で Limelight Tavern の隣にある The Lion Bar が Third Street にあるということがわかる。よって、**(B)** が正解となる。Limelight Tavern の情報がどこにあるかを探し、それを The Lion Bar と関連付けて、予定表に戻って解く、という参照順がカギ。(A) 会場規模、(C) チェーン展開、(D) 人気層、については述べられていないため、それぞれ不正解。

 □ nationwide 全国の

The Lion Bar ライブ演奏

4月12日金曜日 Mono Tony's ヒップホップ	4月13日土曜日 Believing Girls エレクトロ・ポップ
4月19日金曜日 Panorama Paranoia インディー・ロック	4月20日土曜日 See Foam エーテル・フォーク
4月26日金曜日 Jet Shot アコースティック・ポップ	4月27日土曜日 Anarchysta クラシック・パンク

・演奏は全日程午後9時から閉店までです。
・前売りチケット5ドル（オンラインでの予約のみ）
・当日のチケットは10ドルです。

特に当日のチケットをお求めの場合は、お早めにお越しください。ニュースレターに登録して、公演イベントに関する最新情報を入手することもお忘れなく。

www.lionbar.com/livemusic
(637) 502-5024
21 Third Street, Springfield, オレゴン州

営業時間：
月曜日から木曜日 午前11時から午後11時
金曜日から土曜日 正午から午前0時

送信者：	mattydee@onemail.com
受信者：	live@lionbar.com
日付：	4月22日
件名：	演奏についての問い合わせ
添付：	🔗 LL_demo

ご担当者様

今度の夜のライブ演奏のどこかで出演させていただけないかと思い、ご連絡いたしました。友人のロックバンドが今月そちらの会場で演奏をさせていただき、従業員の方のプロ意識や機器の品質、常連客たちの熱意にとても満足していました。

私は、エレクトロニック・パンクバンド Last Light のメインボーカルです。最近、地元のいくつかのラジオ局でインタビューを受けたので、私たちのことをお聞きになったことがあるかもしれません。The Blue Spots や Calendar Error などの非常に人気のあるバンドの前座を務めたこともあります。バンド単体のショーでは、主にバーや他の小さな会場で演奏をしています。

私たちは地元にも全国的にもかなりのファンがいるので、The Lion Bar に多くの集客をもたらすことができるでしょう。数カ月前、The Lion Bar のすぐ隣にある Limelight Tavern で演奏をし、チケットは完売しました。

私たちのデモを添付しましたので、ご興味があればお聞きください。

よろしくお願いいたします。

Matthew Dee

Questions 35-39 refer to the following Web page and letter.

⏱ 5分00秒

| ◀ ▶ | https://shieldsmarket.com/announcements | ▶ |

Shields Supermarket

| Home | Shop | About | Announcements |

We are currently hiring for multiple positions over the holiday season, which is our busiest time of year.

FULL-TIME POSITIONS

Checkout Clerk—Applicants for this customer-facing role must be sociable and proactive. Experience desired but not necessary.

Shelf Stocker—This job involves moving stock around the warehouse, taking stock counts, and stacking shelves where necessary. Must be able to work and communicate in a large team.

PART-TIME POSITIONS

Customer Service Assistant—A role for more mature applicants that have experience in retail and dealing with complaints.

Delivery Driver—Looking for applicants in possession of a Commercial Driver's License to make deliveries to customers' homes. Heavy lifting is a major part of this role. Must be able to work night and weekend shifts.

If you are interested in any of the above roles, please e-mail us at recruitment@shieldsmarket.com by 20 November. Please note only successful candidates will be contacted. Interviews will start within one week of the closing date.

Heather Boyer
300 Victoria Ave
Whanganui, 4500

15 November

Dear Ms. Boyer,

It is my great pleasure to welcome you to our team here at Shields. In this welcome packet, you'll find your new ID card and employee handbook. I've also included a copy of the work contract you signed when we met last week. Please be sure to memorize the code on the back of your ID card before your first day of work, as you will need it in order to work the cash register. The employee handbook lays out the various rules and regulations for staff members, including details regarding our dress code.

During your interview, you mentioned that your brother was looking for a job that he could do for a few hours a day while he is home from university. Based on what you told me about him, we have some openings that seem like a good fit, so please have him call me if he is interested. It is OK if he does not have prior experience.

Best regards,

Collin Brady

Collin Brady, General Manager, Shields Supermarket

35. What is true about all the job openings?

(A) They require flexible schedules.
(B) They can lead to full-time positions.
(C) They involve talking to customers.
(D) They are temporary positions.

36. What is indicated about the application process?

(A) A curriculum vitae must be submitted.
(B) Candidates will be told if they are rejected.
(C) Applications must be sent by e-mail.
(D) Interviews will take one week.

37. What position did Ms. Boyer most likely apply for?

(A) Checkout Clerk
(B) Shelf Stocker
(C) Customer Service Assistant
(D) Delivery Driver

38. What is suggested about Ms. Boyer's brother?

(A) He lives with his sister.
(B) He met with Mr. Brady.
(C) He has a driver's license.
(D) He attends a school in Whanganui.

39. In the letter, the phrase "lays out" in paragraph 1, line 5, is closest in meaning to

(A) assembles
(B) defines
(C) directs
(D) determines

Double

P. 60

Questions 35-39 refer to the following Web page and letter.

| ◀ ▶ | https://shieldsmarket.com/announcements | ▶ |

Shields Supermarket

| Home | Shop | About | Announcements |

❶ We are currently hiring for multiple positions over the holiday season, which is our busiest time of year.

FULL-TIME POSITIONS

❷ **Checkout Clerk**—Applicants for this customer-facing role must be sociable and proactive. Experience desired but not necessary.

Shelf Stocker—This job involves moving stock around the warehouse, taking stock counts, and stacking shelves where necessary. Must be able to work and communicate in a large team.

PART-TIME POSITIONS

Customer Service Assistant—A role for more mature applicants that have experience in retail and dealing with complaints.

❸ **Delivery Driver**—Looking for applicants in possession of a Commercial Driver's License to make deliveries to customers' homes. Heavy lifting is a major part of this role. Must be able to work night and weekend shifts.

❹ If you are interested in any of the above roles, please e-mail us at recruitment@shieldsmarket.com by 20 November. Please note only successful candidates will be contacted. Interviews will start within one week of the closing date.

Heather Boyer
300 Victoria Ave
Whanganui, 4500

15 November

Dear Ms. Boyer,

It is my great pleasure to welcome you to our team here at Shields. In this welcome packet, you'll find your new ID card and employee handbook. I've also included a copy of the work contract you signed when we met last week. Please be sure to memorize the code on the back of your ID card before your first day of work, as ❺ you will need it in order to work the cash register. The employee handbook ❻ lays out the various rules and regulations for staff members, including details regarding our dress code.

During your interview, ❼ you mentioned that your brother was looking for a job that he could do for a few hours a day while he is home from university. ❽ Based on what you told me about him, we have some openings that seem like a good fit, so please have him call me if he is interested. It is OK if he does not have prior experience.

Best regards,

Collin Brady
Collin Brady, General Manager, Shields Supermarket

ウェブページ

☐ currently 現在　☐ multiple 多数の　☐ busiest time 最も繁忙な時期　☐ checkout clerk レジ係
☐ applicant 申込者　☐ customer-facing role 顧客と対面する仕事　☐ sociable 社交的な　☐ proactive 積極的な
☐ experience desired 経験があることが望ましい　☐ stock 在庫
☐ stack shelf (商品等の) 品出しをする、棚に積み込む　☐ where necessary 必要な場所に　☐ mature 熟練の
☐ in retail 小売業で　☐ deal with complaint 苦情に対応する　☐ in possession of ～を所有して
☐ heavy lifting 重いものを持ち上げること　☐ closing 締切

手紙

☐ packet (品物が入っている) 包み、袋　☐ work contract 労働契約書　☐ memorize ～を記憶する・覚える
☐ code 番号、コード　☐ lay out ～を記載している　☐ various さまざまな　☐ detail 詳細
☐ regarding ～に関する　☐ dress code 服装規定　☐ based on ～にもとづいて　☐ opening 職、仕事
☐ a good fit ぴったり合っているもの

★★☆☆☆

35. What is true about all the job openings?

(A) They require flexible schedules.
(B) They can lead to full-time positions.
(C) They involve talking to customers.
(D) They are temporary positions.

すべての求人について当てはまることは何ですか。

(A) 予定に柔軟に対応できることを求められる。
(B) 常勤の職につながる可能性がある。
(C) 顧客と話すことがある。
(D) 一時的な仕事である。

すべての求人について当てはまることが問われている。ウェブページの❶で「当店では現在、年間で最も忙しい時期の求人を募集」とあり、ここから期間限定の一時的な求人を募集していることがわかる。よって、「一時的な」をtemporary に言い換えた **(D)** が正解となる。(A) に関しては、❶以降に "FULL-TIME POSITIONS (常勤)" とあるので、必ずしも予定に柔軟とはいえない。(B) は "PART-TIME POSITIONS (非常勤)" に、常勤の職につながる可能性が記載されておらず、(C) はすべての職が顧客対応すると述べられていないので、いずれも不正解。

☐ flexible 柔軟な　☐ involve ～を含む　☐ temporary 一時的な

★★★☆☆

36. What is indicated about the application process?

(A) A curriculum vitae must be submitted.
(B) Candidates will be told if they are rejected.
(C) Applications must be sent by e-mail.
(D) Interviews will take one week.

応募の手順について何が示されていますか。

(A) 履歴書を送る必要がある。
(B) 候補者が不採用となった場合は通知される。
(C) 申し込みはEメールで送る必要がある。
(D) 面接には1週間かかる。

応募の手順について何が示されているかを問う選択肢照合型問題。ウェブページの❹に「以上の仕事のいずれかに興味があれば、期日までにメールで連絡を」とあり、❹以降で期日後に面接が行われると記載されている。つまり、"メール連絡＝申し込み" ということがわかる。このメールで申し込んだ一連の対応を、application、by e-mail を使って言い換えた **(C)** が正解。(A) は履歴書の送付に関する記載はなく、(B) は❹以降に「審査を通った方のみに連絡をする」とある。(D) は、面接開始時期については書かれているが、面接にかかる期間は書かれていないので、いずれも不正解。

☐ curriculum vitae 履歴書　☐ candidate 候補者　☐ application 申し込み　☐ deadline 期日

37. What position did Ms. Boyer most likely apply for?

(A) Checkout Clerk
(B) Shelf Stocker
(C) Customer Service Assistant
(D) Delivery Driver

Boyer さんは、どの仕事に応募したと考えられますか。

(A) レジ係
(B) 品出し係
(C) 顧客対応係
(D) 配達ドライバー

Boyer さんが応募した仕事について問われている。2文書目の手紙の❺で「レジで作業をする際に（ID カードの裏の番号が）必要」と述べているので、Boyer さんはレジで作業することがわかる。1文書目のウェブページを参照すると、❷にレジ係の募集があるため、おそらくこれに応募したものと推察ができる。よって、正解は **(A)**。checkout clerk ＝レジ係、と見抜けるかがポイント。checkout clerk の意味がわからない場合、❷の「客と対面する仕事」というところをヒントにして解答を導こう。

□ checkout（店舗の）レジ

....

38. What is suggested about Ms. Boyer's brother?

(A) He lives with his sister.
(B) He met with Mr. Brady.
(C) He has a driver's license.
(D) He attends a school in Whanganui.

Boyer さんの兄弟について何が示唆されていますか。

(A) 姉妹と一緒に住んでいる。
(B) Brady さんと会った。
(C) 運転免許を持っている。
(D) Whanganui の学校に在籍している。

Boyer さんの兄弟について示唆されていることを問う選択肢照合型問題。2文書目の手紙の❼・❽で、兄弟についての言及があり、「兄弟が大学から帰省している間、1日に数時間の勤務が可能な仕事を探していると聞いたが、現在の求人にちょうどよい仕事がある」と述べている。ここから、1文書目のウェブページを参照すると、❸の配達ドライバーに「夜間と週末のシフトで働ける必要がある」と書かれている。つまり、Boyer さんの兄弟にちょうどよいのは配達ドライバーの仕事であるため、何らかの商用に関わる運転免許証を持っていることが考えられる。よって、正解は **(C)** となる。(A)(B)(D) はそれぞれ文書に相当する記載がなく、いずれも不正解。

....

39. In the letter, the phrase "lays out" in paragraph 1, line 5, is closest in meaning to

(A) assembles
(B) defines
(C) directs
(D) determines

手紙の、第1段落目・5行目にある "lays out" に最も意味が近いのは

(A) ～を組み立てる
(B) ～を明確にする
(C) ～を指揮する
(D) ～を決定する

同義語問題。❻の "lays out" が含まれた文は、「従業員ハンドブックには職員向けのさまざまな規則や規定を記載している」という内容。ここでは「～をはっきりと説明する、提示する」という意味で使用している。よって、「明確にする、規定する」という意味を持つ **(B)** が正解。define は「定義する」の他に、今回のような意味も持っていることを覚えておこう。

---

https://shieldsmarket.com/announcements

Shields Supermarket

トップ	店舗	当店について	お知らせ

当店では現在、年間で最も忙しい年末に向けて複数の職種で求人を行っています。

常勤

レジ係—顧客と対面で対応するお仕事ですので、応募者は社交的かつ積極的である必要があります。経験者であることが望ましいですが、必須ではありません。

品出し係—この仕事は倉庫内での在庫の移動、在庫数の確認、必要に応じて品出しを行います。大きなチームの中で作業をし、意思疎通ができる必要があります。

非常勤

顧客対応係—小売業で苦情対応をしたことのある、経験値の高い応募者向けのお仕事です。

配達ドライバー—顧客の家まで配達するので、商用運転免許証を所持している応募者を必要としています。重い荷物を運ぶことが主な仕事です。夜間と週末のシフトで働ける必要があります。

以上の仕事のいずれかに興味がありましたら、11 月 20 日までに recruitment@shieldsmarket.com まで E メールにてご連絡ください。審査に通った方にのみご連絡いたしますのでご注意ください。面接は締め切り日から 1 週間以内に始まります。

Heather Boyer
300 Victoria Ave
Whanganui, 4500

11 月 15 日

Boyer 様

ここ Shields のメンバーとしてお迎えできることを大変喜ばしく思います。この歓迎パケットには新しい ID カードと従業員ハンドブックが入っています。先週お会いした時にご署名いただいた労働契約の写しも同封しました。ID カードの裏にある番号は、レジで作業をする際に必要となりますので、出勤初日までに必ず覚えてください。従業員ハンドブックには服装規定の詳細を含め、職員向けのさまざまな規則や規定を記載しています。

面接の際に、ご兄弟が大学から帰省している間、1 日に数時間でできる仕事を探していると話していましたね。お聞きした内容から、当店にちょうどよさそうな仕事があります。もし興味がおありでしたら、電話をくださるようにお伝えください。経験がなくても大丈夫です。

よろしくお願いいたします。

Collin Brady
Shields Supermarket 業務部長 Collin Brady

Questions 40-44 refer to the following instructions, e-mail, and review. 5分30秒

How to Use the Kitchart XR-100 Yogurt Maker

Using the Kitchart XR-100 electric yogurt maker is not only easy but also hassle-free. Follow these instructions to make a perfect batch of fresh yogurt.

Step One: Put all of your chosen ingredients into the plastic yogurt container (for recipe ideas, please visit our Web site). Cover the container with its lid. Make sure to wipe any drips off the outside of the container so the yogurt maker remains clean.

Step Two: Place the filled container into the yogurt maker and close the top of the device.

Step Three: Plug in the yogurt maker and set the preparation time (10 hours for a regular full batch). After setting the time, press the "Start" button on the LED display.

Step Four: After the set number of hours have passed, the device will automatically turn off. The container can now be removed from the device and placed in the refrigerator to cool.

To: Lindsey Barrett
From: Kitchart Customer Support
Date: February 7
Subject: Kitchart XR-100

Dear Ms. Barrett,

We received your e-mail regarding the Kitchart XR-100 yogurt maker you recently purchased from our online store. Since we inspect each and every item before they leave our warehouse, we were surprised to read your description of the product delivered to you. We suspect that some accident occurred during shipping, and we will continue looking into the matter with the aim of ensuring this problem does not reoccur.

Kitchart will replace the yogurt maker and pay the shipping cost to return it. By February 10, you will receive by mail some packing materials, a product return form, and a pre-paid label with our address. Please fill out the form and send it to us together with the appliance. About one week after we receive those, we will send you a brand-new Kitchart XR-100 yogurt maker.

We hope you will accept our apologies for the inconvenience and do business with us again.

Sincerely,

Michael Alvarado
Customer Support
Kitchart Corporation

Kitchart XR-100 (63 comments)

The XR-100 meets my needs perfectly. I can use it to make flavored yogurt with berries, which is lighter and fluffier than what I can buy at stores. When I first used the XR-100, I filled the separate plastic container with the ingredients and put it in the yogurt maker, but I couldn't get the device to close. That's when I realized the top was dented. It looked as if something heavy might have fallen on it. I sent a complaint to Kitchart Corporation, and one of their customer support representatives got back to me within an hour. I was impressed by how quick they were. He explained the process for returning and replacing the yogurt maker, and about a week later I had a new one on my kitchen counter. Like I said, it's perfect for me and makes great yogurt.

Name:

Lindsey Barrett

Date:

February 28

40. What is NOT explained in the instructions?

(A) What ingredients to include
(B) How long yogurt preparation takes
(C) How to activate the device
(D) When the device will shut down

41. Why was Mr. Alvarado surprised?

(A) A product was shipped without a component.
(B) A customer was sent the wrong package.
(C) A delivery arrived much later than expected.
(D) A customer received a damaged product.

42. According to Mr. Alvarado, what should Ms. Barrett do?

(A) Replace a part
(B) Unplug a faulty device
(C) Pay a shipping fee
(D) Complete a document

43. What step in the instructions does Ms. Barrett indicate she had difficulty with?

(A) Step One
(B) Step Two
(C) Step Three
(D) Step Four

44. Why was Ms. Barrett impressed with Mr. Alvarado?

(A) He sent her a new product immediately.
(B) He explained a procedure slowly.
(C) He addressed her complaint promptly.
(D) He provided a yogurt recipe clearly.

Triple

P. 66

Questions 40-44 refer to the following instructions, e-mail, and review.

How to Use the Kitchart XR-100 Yogurt Maker

Using the Kitchart XR-100 electric yogurt maker is not only easy but also hassle-free. Follow these instructions to make a perfect batch of fresh yogurt.

Step One: ❶ Put all of your chosen ingredients into the plastic yogurt container (for recipe ideas, please visit our Web site). Cover the container with its lid. Make sure to wipe any drips off the outside of the container so the yogurt maker remains clean.

Step Two: ❷ Place the filled container into the yogurt maker and close the top of the device.

Step Three: ❸ Plug in the yogurt maker and set the preparation time (❹ 10 hours for a regular full batch). ❺ After setting the time, press the "Start" button on the LED display.

Step Four: ❻ After the set number of hours have passed, the device will automatically turn off. The container can now be removed from the device and placed in the refrigerator to cool.

To: Lindsey Barrett
From: Kitchart Customer Support
Date: February 7
Subject: Kitchart XR-100

Dear Ms. Barrett,

We received your e-mail regarding the Kitchart XR-100 yogurt maker you recently purchased from our online store. Since we inspect each and every item before they leave our warehouse, ❼ we were surprised to read your description of the product delivered to you. We suspect that some accident occurred during shipping, and we will continue looking into the matter with the aim of ensuring this problem does not reoccur.

Kitchart will replace the yogurt maker and pay the shipping cost to return it. ❽ By February 10, you will receive by mail some packing materials, a product return form, and a pre-paid label with our address. ❾ Please fill out the form and send it to us together with the appliance. About one week after we receive those, we will send you a brand-new Kitchart XR-100 yogurt maker.

We hope you will accept our apologies for the inconvenience and do business with us again.

Sincerely,

❿ Michael Alvarado
Customer Support
Kitchart Corporation

Kitchart XR-100 (63 comments)

The XR-100 meets my needs perfectly. I can use it to make flavored yogurt with berries, which is lighter and fluffier than what I can buy at stores. ⓫ When I first used the XR-100, I filled the separate plastic container with the ingredients and put it in the yogurt maker, but I couldn't get the device to close. ⓬ That's when I realized the top was dented. It looked as if something heavy might have fallen on it. ⓭ I sent a complaint to Kitchart Corporation, and one of their customer support representatives got back to me within an hour. I was impressed by how quick they were. He explained the process for returning and replacing the yogurt maker, and about a week later I had a new one on my kitchen counter. Like I said, it's perfect for me and makes great yogurt.

Name:	Date:
Lindsey Barrett	February 28

取扱説明書
- ☐ hassle-free 手間のかからない ☐ instruction 手順 ☐ batch of 1 回分の ☐ ingredient 材料、原料
- ☐ wipe off ～を拭きとる ☐ drip 漏れ ☐ remain ～のままである ☐ device 装置
- ☐ plug in ～をコンセントにつなぐ ☐ preparation time 調理時間 ☐ automatically 自動的に
- ☐ turn off 消える ☐ refrigerator 冷蔵庫 ☐ cool ～を冷却する

E メール
- ☐ regarding ～に関する ☐ inspect ～を点検する ☐ description 記載、説明 ☐ occur 発生する
- ☐ shipping 配送 ☐ look into ～を調査する ☐ with the aim of ～を目的として ☐ reoccur 再発する
- ☐ replace ～を交換する ☐ packing material 包装資材 ☐ product return form 返品用紙
- ☐ pre-paid label 料金前払い済のラベル ☐ appliance 機器 ☐ brand-new 新品の

レビュー
- ☐ need 要求 ☐ flavored 風味を付けた ☐ berry ベリー ☐ fluffy なめらかな ☐ top 上部
- ☐ dented へこんでいる ☐ fall on ～の上に落ちる ☐ complaint 苦情
- ☐ customer support representative お客様対応係 ☐ get back to ～に折り返し連絡する
- ☐ be impressed 感激する

★★★☆☆ NOT 問題

40. What is NOT explained in the instructions?

(A) What ingredients to include
(B) How long yogurt preparation takes
(C) How to activate the device
(D) When the device will shut down

取扱説明書で説明されていないことは何ですか。

(A) どんな材料を入れるか
(B) ヨーグルト作りにどのくらいの時間がかかるか
(C) どのように機器を作動するか
(D) いつ機器が停止するか

NOT 問題。取扱説明書で説明されていないことが問われている。取扱説明書を読むと、❹の通常の（ヨーグルト）仕上がり時間」が (B) に、❸・❹・❺の「ヨーグルトメーカーをコンセントにつなぎ、調理時間を設定」「時間を設定したら "Start" ボタンを押す」が (C) に、❻の「設定した時間が経過すると、機器の電源が自動的に停止する」が (D) に、それぞれ合致する。よって、残った **(A)** が正解。材料を入れることについて❶に記載はあるが、ユーザーが好きなものを入れることとなっており、どんな材料を入れるかの説明はされていない。

- ☐ activate（機械など）を作動させる ☐ shut down 停止する

41. Why was Mr. Alvarado surprised?

    (A) A product was shipped without a component.

    (B) A customer was sent the wrong package.

    (C) A delivery arrived much later than expected.

    (D) A customer received a damaged product.

Alvarado さんはなぜ驚きましたか。

    (A) 製品が付属部品を付けずに出荷されたため。

    (B) 顧客に間違った荷物が送られたため。

    (C) 配達物が予想よりもはるかに遅れて到着したため。

    (D) 顧客が破損した製品を受け取ったため。

Alvarado さんがなぜ驚いたのかが問われている。2 文書目の E メールの❿から Alvarado さんはヨーグルトメーカーの社員だとわかり、❼で「お客様に配送された製品のご説明に驚いた」とある。次に 3 文書目のレビューを見ると、Barrett さんは⓫・⓬で「XR-100 をはじめて使った際に、機器を閉じることができず、その際に部品のへこみを発見した」と述べており、ここから Barrett さんが破損した製品を受け取ったことが推察される。よって、**(D)** が正解となる。

□ component 付属品　□ wrong 間違った　□ a damaged product 破損した製品

42. According to Mr. Alvarado, what should Ms. Barrett do?

    (A) Replace a part

    (B) Unplug a faulty device

    (C) Pay a shipping fee

    (D) Complete a document

Alvarado さんによると、Barrett さんは何をすべきですか。

    (A) 部品を交換する

    (B) 欠陥品のコンセントを抜く

    (C) 送料を支払う

    (D) 文書を完成させる

Alvarado さんが Barrett さんに対して何をすべきだと言っているかが問われている。Alvarado さんは 2 文書目の E メールの❽・❾で、「2 月 10 日までに返送に必要なものを郵送するので、用紙に記入し、製品と一緒に送ってください」とお伝えしている。ここから、"Please fill out the form" を Complete a document と言い換えた **(D)** が正解となる。(A) や (B) のような部品の修理等に関わる記載はなく、(C) は❽の前に、返送の必要経費はメーカー負担と述べているため、いずれも不正解。

□ replace 〜を交換する　□ unplug 〜をコンセントから抜く　□ a faulty device 欠陥がある装置

43. What step in the instructions does Ms. Barrett indicate she had difficulty with?

    (A) Step One

    (B) Step Two

    (C) Step Three

    (D) Step Four

Barrett さんは取扱説明書のどの手順で問題が生じたと述べていますか。

    (A) 手順 1

    (B) 手順 2

    (C) 手順 3

    (D) 手順 4

Barrett さんは取扱説明書のどの手順で問題が生じたと述べているかが問われている。Barrett さんは 3 文書目のレビューの⓫で「ヨーグルトメーカーに容器をセットしたが、機器を閉じることができなかった」と述べている。1 文書目の取扱説明書を読むと、STEP 2 の❷で「中身の入った容器をヨーグルトメーカーに入れ、デバイスの上部を閉じるように」と書いてある。ここから正解は **(B)** だとわかる。問題の記載を読んで、どの手順・順番に当たるかを探させる問題は、典型的なクロスリファレンス問題なので、しっかりとマスターしよう。

44. Why was Ms. Barrett impressed with Mr. Alvarado?

   (A) He sent her a new product immediately.
   (B) He explained a procedure slowly.
   (C) He addressed her complaint promptly.
   (D) He provided a yogurt recipe clearly.

Barrett さんはなぜ Alvarado さんに感銘を受けましたか。

   (A) すぐに新しい製品を送ってくれたため。
   (B) ゆっくりと手順を説明してくれたため。
   (C) 苦情に迅速に対応してくれたため。
   (D) ヨーグルトのレシピをわかりやすく教えてくれたため。

Barrett さんがなぜ Alvarado さんに感銘を受けたのかが問われている。3 文書目のレビューの❸で、Barrett さんが「Kitchart Corporation に苦情を申し立てたところ、1 時間以内に顧客サポートの担当者が返信をくれ、その早い対応に感動した」と書いてある。次に 2 文書目の E メールを見ると、実際に顧客サポートしているのは Alvarado さんであるため、この担当者は Alvarado さんのことを指しているとわかる。以上から、**(C)** が正解。❸と **(C)** の言い換えである "get back to me" = address her complaint と "within an hour" = promptly を、それぞれキャッチできるようにしておこう。promptly は immediately の同義語で Part 5 にも語彙問題として出題される。

□ immediately 早急に　□ procedure 手順　□ address (問題など) に対応する　□ promptly 迅速に
□ recipe レシピ　□ clearly 明確に、はっきりと

問題 40 から 44 は次の取扱説明書、E メール、レビューに関するものです。

Kitchart XR-100 ヨーグルトメーカーの使い方

Kitchart XR-100 電動ヨーグルトメーカーの使い方は、簡単なだけでなく、手間いらずです。完璧で新鮮なヨーグルトを作るにはこの手順に従ってください。

手順 1：選んだすべての材料をプラスチックのヨーグルト容器に入れてください（レシピのアイデアについては当社のウェブサイトをご覧ください）。容器に専用のふたをしてください。ヨーグルトメーカーを清潔に保つため、容器の外に漏れたものは必ず拭き取ってください。

手順 2：中身の入った容器をヨーグルトメーカーに入れ、機器の上部を閉じてください。

手順 3：ヨーグルトメーカーをコンセントにつなぎ、調理時間を設定してください（通常の仕上がりは 10 時間）。時間を設定したら、LED ディスプレイにある "Start" ボタンを押してください。

手順 4：設定した時間が経過すると、機器の電源が自動的に停止します。容器は機器から取り外して、冷蔵庫で冷やすことができます。

受信者： Lindsey Barrett
送信者： Kitchart 顧客サポート
日付：　 2 月 7 日
件名：　 Kitchart XR-100

Barrett 様

当社のオンラインショップで先日ご購入になった Kitchart XR-100 ヨーグルトメーカーについて、メールをいただきました。当社ではすべての製品を倉庫から出荷する前に点検しておりますので、お客様に配送された製品のご説明に驚きました。おそらく配送中に問題が起きたのではないかと思われます。このような問題が再び起きないように、引き続き原因を調査いたします。

Kitchart はヨーグルトメーカーの交換を行い、返送に掛かる送料を負担いたします。2 月 10 日までに、梱包材、製品の返品用紙、当社の住所入りの料金前払い済のラベルを郵送でお届けします。用紙にご記入いただき、機器と一緒に当社まで送ってください。当社に届いてから 1 週間程度で新品の Kitchart XR-100 ヨーグルトメーカーをお送りいたします。

ご不便をおかけし、申し訳ございません。今後もどうぞよろしくお願いいたします。

敬具

Kitchart Corporation
顧客サポート
Michael Alvarado

Kitchart XR-100 （63 の口コミ）

XR-100 はまさに欲しかった商品です。ベリーを使ったフレーバーヨーグルトが作れて、お店で売っているものよりも低カロリーでなめらかです。XR-100 をはじめて使った際に、取り外しのできるプラスチック容器に材料を入れた後、ヨーグルトメーカーにセットしましたが、機器を閉じることができませんでした。その時に上部がへこんでいることに気がつきました。何か重いものがその上に落ちたかのようでした。Kitchart Corporation に苦情を申し立てたところ、1 時間以内に顧客サポートの担当者が返信をくれました。早い対応に感動しました。彼はヨーグルトメーカーの返送と交換の手順を説明してくれて、およそ 1 週間後、わが家のキッチンカウンターには新品がありました。先に書いたように、これはまさに欲しかったもので、完璧なヨーグルトが作れます。

名前：

Lindsey Barrett

日付：

2 月 28 日

GO ON TO THE NEXT PAGE!

Questions 45-49 refer to the following e-mail, coupon, and schedule.

5分30秒

1回目

2回目

3回目

	E-Mail Message
To:	Ken Edwards
From:	Elena Rivera
Date:	August 21
Subject:	Marino Charters

Hi Ken,

Al Rossetti and Diane Smith from Marino Charters will be visiting our showroom tomorrow. They want to add a fishing boat to their fleet, and they are also considering purchasing a larger vessel for tours. You and I will show them the models we have in stock as well as those in the latest catalogs we have.

Marino Charters has been a valuable customer to us over the years. To show our appreciation, I will take Al and Diane out to dinner after their visit. I would like you to join us since you know them so well after all the sales support you've provided for them.

I made a reservation today for four people on the Casbay Yacht Dinner Cruise. I heard the food is quite good and a pop music band will be playing on the boat tomorrow night. According to the brochure, the cruise lasts three hours. There is also a coupon in there for twelve dollars off, so I picked up enough copies from the Tourist Information Center for all of us. Assuming that you can join us, let's leave the showroom at five o'clock.

Best regards,

Elena

CASBAY YACHT DINNER CRUISE

Issue Date: August 7

The Casbay Yacht departs from the Sunbridge Dock at 43 Queens Road every Thursday, Friday, Saturday, and Sunday at 6 P.M.

Cut this out and get

12.00 DOLLARS OFF!

Present this coupon when you come on board the Casbay.
This coupon is good for one person and one cruise only.
It is not valid with any other discounts or promotions.

(For reservations, call 555-0158. Reservation deadline: Noon of the previous day.)
This offer expires on August 31.

Casbay Yacht Dinner Cruise Schedule

Every Thursday: Choose from a wide range of delicious dishes in our extensive buffet while listening to jazz band The Boogie Shakers. The Casbay cruises around Mugg's Island on Thursdays for incredible views of the cityscape at night.	**Every Friday:** Fridays are for seafood on the Casbay, as we offer everything from crab and mussels to lobster and swordfish. The boat sails to Hutton Lighthouse and back with pop music band The Brave Begonias on stage to entertain you.
Every Saturday: Enjoy spectacular views of the city's skyline while cruising to Thompson Bridge and listening to country music band The Dusky Dolphins. Also, Saturdays are for barbecue lovers, with a big variety of grilled dishes on the buffet.	**Every Sunday:** As The Wobbly Wheels play classic rock and roll hits, sail around the lake and pick from over 130 tasty choices in our wide-ranging buffet. Make sure to bring a camera to catch the beautiful views and sunset.

45. Where most likely does Mr. Edwards work?

(A) On a cruise ship
(B) At an information center
(C) At a boat store
(D) At a tour company

46. What is probably true about Ms. Rivera?

(A) She made a cruise reservation in the morning.
(B) She will order some new boat catalogs.
(C) She will get off from a boat after 10 P.M. tomorrow.
(D) She met her coworkers at the Sunbridge Dock today.

47. What can be inferred about the coupon?

(A) It can be combined with other coupons.
(B) It should be presented when making a reservation.
(C) It is for a dinner cruise on a lake.
(D) It is valid for the entire month of August.

48. What band will the Marino Charters employees probably see perform?

(A) The Boogie Shakers
(B) The Brave Begonias
(C) The Dusky Dolphins
(D) The Wobbly Wheels

49. What is one common feature of all the cruise nights?

(A) A band that plays country music
(B) A buffet with a large selection
(C) A view from underneath a bridge
(D) An opportunity to catch some fish

P. 74

Triple

73

Questions 45-49 refer to the following e-mail, coupon, and schedule.

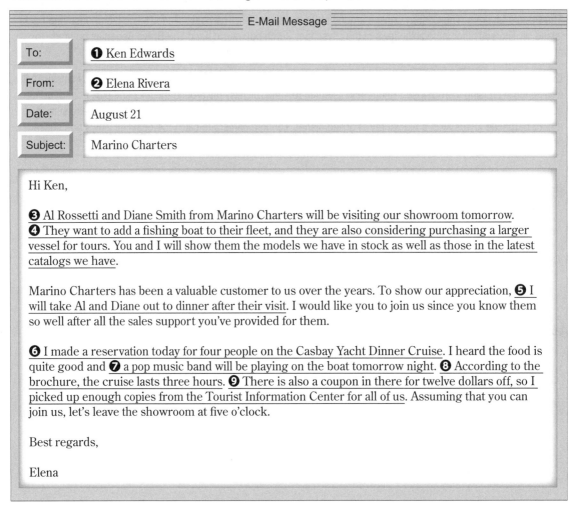

================= E-Mail Message =================

To:	❶ Ken Edwards
From:	❷ Elena Rivera
Date:	August 21
Subject:	Marino Charters

Hi Ken,

❸ Al Rossetti and Diane Smith from Marino Charters will be visiting our showroom tomorrow. ❹ They want to add a fishing boat to their fleet, and they are also considering purchasing a larger vessel for tours. You and I will show them the models we have in stock as well as those in the latest catalogs we have.

Marino Charters has been a valuable customer to us over the years. To show our appreciation, ❺ I will take Al and Diane out to dinner after their visit. I would like you to join us since you know them so well after all the sales support you've provided for them.

❻ I made a reservation today for four people on the Casbay Yacht Dinner Cruise. I heard the food is quite good and ❼ a pop music band will be playing on the boat tomorrow night. ❽ According to the brochure, the cruise lasts three hours. ❾ There is also a coupon in there for twelve dollars off, so I picked up enough copies from the Tourist Information Center for all of us. Assuming that you can join us, let's leave the showroom at five o'clock.

Best regards,

Elena

CASBAY YACHT DINNER CRUISE

❿ *Issue Date: August 7*

⓫ The Casbay Yacht departs from the Sunbridge Dock at 43 Queens Road
every Thursday, Friday, Saturday, and Sunday at 6 P.M.
Cut this out and get

12.00 DOLLARS OFF!

⓬ Present this coupon when you come on board the Casbay.
This coupon is good for one person and one cruise only.
⓭ It is not valid with any other discounts or promotions.

(For reservations, call 555-0158. ⓮ Reservation deadline: Noon of the previous day.)
This offer expires on August 31.

Casbay Yacht Dinner Cruise Schedule

Every Thursday: Choose from ⓯ a wide range of delicious dishes in our extensive buffet while listening to jazz band The Boogie Shakers. The Casbay cruises around Mugg's Island on Thursdays for incredible views of the cityscape at night.	**Every Friday:** Fridays are for seafood on the Casbay, as ⓰ we offer everything from crab and mussels to lobster and swordfish. The boat sails to Hutton Lighthouse and back ⓱ with pop music band The Brave Begonias on stage to entertain you.
Every Saturday: Enjoy spectacular views of the city's skyline while cruising to Thompson Bridge and listening to country music band The Dusky Dolphins. Also, Saturdays are for barbecue lovers, ⓲ with a big variety of grilled dishes on the buffet.	**Every Sunday:** As The Wobbly Wheels play classic rock and roll hits, ⓳ sail around the lake and pick from over ⓴ 130 tasty choices in our wide-ranging buffet. Make sure to bring a camera to catch the beautiful views and sunset.

E メール
☐ showroom 展示室　☐ vessel 船　☐ have in stock 在庫がある　☐ latest 最新の　☐ valuable 貴重な
☐ pop music ポップ（ポピュラー）音楽　☐ brochure パンフレット　☐ last 続く
☐ assuming that 〜と仮定すると

クーポン券
☐ depart from 〜を出発する　☐ present 〜を提示する　☐ come on board 〜に搭乗する
☐ good for 〜に有効な　☐ valid 有効な　☐ promotion キャンペーン　☐ the previous day 前日

予定表
☐ a wide range of 多様な　☐ extensive 大型の　☐ incredible 素晴らしい　☐ cityscape 都市景観　☐ crab カニ
☐ mussel ムール貝　☐ swordfish メカジキ　☐ sail to （船が）〜へ運航する　☐ entertain 〜をもてなす
☐ spectacular 素晴らしい　☐ skyline スカイライン（空を背景とした景色）　☐ a big variety of たくさんの種類の
☐ wide-ranging 多種の　☐ sunset 夕焼け

★★★☆☆

45. Where most likely does Mr. Edwards work?

(A) On a cruise ship
(B) At an information center
(C) At a boat store
(D) At a tour company

Edwards さんはどこで働いていると考えられますか。

(A) クルーズ船で
(B) 案内所で
(C) 船舶販売店で
(D) ツアー会社で

Edwards さんがおそらくどこで働いているかが問われている。1 文書目の E メールの❶・❷から、Edwards さんに Rivera さんが E メールを送っていることがわかる。次に❸・❹から、この 2 人が新たな船の購入を検討している顧客の応対をすることがわかる。ここから Edwards さんと Rivera さんは、船舶を販売する職業に関与していることが推察される。以上より、正解は **(C)**。(D) は、顧客の Rossetti さんと Smith さんのこと。どの人物が何をやっているのか整理して読もう。

46. What is probably true about Ms. Rivera?

  (A) She made a cruise reservation in the morning.
  (B) She will order some new boat catalogs.
  (C) She will get off from a boat after 10 P.M. tomorrow.
  (D) She met her coworkers at the Sunbridge Dock today.

Rivera さんについておそらく当てはまることは何ですか。

  (A) 朝、クルーズの予約をした。
  (B) 新しい船舶のカタログを注文する。
  (C) 明日の午後 10 時以降に船を降りる。
  (D) 今日、Sunbridge Dock で同僚と会った。

Rivera さんについておそらく当てはまることを選ぶ選択肢照合型問題。1 文書目の E メールの❺・❻で、Rivera さんは顧客 2 人を明日クルーズディナーに連れていく予定で、本日予約をしたということがわかり、さらに❾でクーポンを利用することがわかる。次に 2 文書目のクーポン券を見ると、⓮で「予約の締め切りは前日の正午まで」と記載されている。ここから Rivera さんは、明日のクルーズを前日の昼までに予約したことがわかる。以上より、正解は **(A)** となる。(C) は❽・⓫から 6 時から 9 時の 3 時間だとわかるため、不正解となる。他の選択肢は本文に根拠がなく不正解。

□ get off from 〜から降りる　□ coworker 同僚

47. What can be inferred about the coupon?

  (A) It can be combined with other coupons.
  (B) It should be presented when making a reservation.
  (C) It is for a dinner cruise on a lake.
  (D) It is valid for the entire month of August.

クーポンについて何が推測できますか。

  (A) 他のクーポンと併用することができる。
  (B) 予約時に提示されなければならない。
  (C) 湖でのディナークルーズ用である。
  (D) 8 月中いつでも有効である。

クーポンについて何が推測できるかを問う選択肢照合型問題。2 文書目のクーポン券の表題から、ディナークルーズのクーポン券であることがわかり、かつ⓫でこのディナークルーズのヨットは毎週木曜日、金曜日、土曜日、日曜日に出発していることがわかる。次に 3 文書目の予定表を見ると、⓳の日曜日の欄には「湖の周りを航行する」とある。ここから、その 2 つの条件を満たした選択肢 **(C)** が正解となる。これはクーポン券と予定表の 2 つの文書を読んで解くクロスリファレンス問題。(A) は⓭に他のクーポンとの併用不可、(B) は⓬に乗船時の提示、(D) は⓾に 8 月 7 日発行、とあるので、いずれも記載内容とは異なり、不正解。

□ be combined with 〜と組み合わせられる・併用される　□ vaild 有効な　□ entire 全体の

48. What band will the Marino Charters employees probably see perform?

  (A) The Boogie Shakers
  (B) The Brave Begonias
  (C) The Dusky Dolphins
  (D) The Wobbly Wheels

Marino Charters 社の従業員たちがおそらく見ることになる演奏はどのバンドのものですか。

  (A) The Boogie Shakers
  (B) The Brave Begonias
  (C) The Dusky Dolphins
  (D) The Wobbly Wheels

Marino Charters 社の従業員が演奏を見るバンドが問われている。1 文書目の E メールで Marino Charters 社の Rossetti さんと Smith さんをクルーズディナーに連れていく計画を立てていることがわかる。次に、2 文書目の E メールの❼で、「明日の夜はポップバンドが演奏をする」と述べている。そして、予定表の⓱を見ると、「ポップバンド The Brave Begonias のステージを」と書かれているので、ここから **(B)** が正解だとわかる。E メールの「ポップバンドの演奏」という情報から、予定表を見て、正解にたどり着くという問題。他の選択肢は、予定表から、いずれもポップバンドではないとわかるため不正解。

49. What is one common feature of all the cruise nights?

(A) A band that plays country music
(B) A buffet with a large selection
(C) A view from underneath a bridge
(D) An opportunity to catch some fish

すべての夜のクルーズに共通している特徴は何ですか。

(A) カントリー音楽を演奏するバンド
(B) 品揃え豊富なビュッフェ
(C) 橋の下からの眺め
(D) 魚を釣る機会

すべての夜のクルーズに共通している特徴が問われている。3 文書目の予定表をくまなく見ていくと、木曜日は❶大型ビュッフェ、金曜日は❶あらゆる海鮮料理を提供、土曜日は❶ビュッフェにはさまざまなグリル料理、日曜日は❷種類が豊富なビュッフェ、と記載があり、それぞれ豊富なメニューの食べ放題となっていることがわかる。よって、豊富さを a large selection と言い換えた **(B)** が正解。金曜日の "offer everything from crab and mussels to lobster and swordfish" が buffet の言い換えになっていることにも注目。(A) と (C) は土曜日のみで、(D) は記載がないため、いずれも不正解。

✎ □ underneath 〜の下に

 問題 45 から 49 は次の E メール、クーポン券、予定表に関するものです。

受信者：	Ken Edwards
送信者：	Elena Rivera
日付：	8 月 21 日
件名：	Marino Charters 社

こんにちは、Ken さん

Marino Charters 社の Al Rossetti 様と Diane Smith 様が、明日当社の展示室を訪問されます。あちらの船団に漁船を加えたいそうで、ツアー用のより大きな船の購入も考えているそうです。Ken さんと私で、ここに在庫してあるモデルと最新カタログに載っているモデルをお見せしようと思います。

Marino Charters 社は長年にわたる当社の貴重な顧客です。感謝の気持ちを表すためにも、訪問の後に Al さんと Diane さんを夕食にお連れしようと思います。Ken さんは販売時によくあちらの購入サポートをしてくださったこともあり、お二人をよく知っているでしょうから、ぜひ参加してほしいです。

今日、Casbay Yacht Dinner Cruise に 4 人分の予約を入れました。お料理はとてもおいしいと聞いていますし、明日の夜はポップバンドが船で演奏をするそうです。パンフレットによると、クルーズは 3 時間です。12 ドル引きのクーポンも付いていたので、観光案内所で全員分を取ってきました。Ken さんが参加できるなら、5 時に展示室を出発しましょう。

よろしくお願いいたします。

Elena

Casbay Yacht Dinner Cruise 予定表	
毎週木曜日：ジャズバンド The Boogie Shakers を聴きながら、大型ビュッフェでたくさんの種類のおいしいお食事からお選びください。Casbay 号は木曜日に Mugg's Island を周遊し、夜の素晴らしい景色をご覧いただけます。	**毎週金曜日**：金曜日は Casbay 号の海鮮料理の日で、カニやムール貝からロブスターやメカジキまで、あらゆる魚介類を提供いたします。ポップバンド The Brave Begonias のステージをお楽しみいただきつつ、船は Hutton Lighthouse まで往復します。
毎週土曜日：カントリー音楽バンドの The Dusky Dolphins を聴きながら、Thompson Bridge をクルーズします。素晴らしい街のスカイラインをお楽しみください。また、土曜日はバーベキュー好きのための日で、ビュッフェにはさまざまな種類のグリル料理があります。	**毎週日曜日**：The Wobbly Wheels がクラッシックロックンロールのヒット曲を演奏する中、湖の周りを航行します。種類の豊富なビュッフェで130種類以上のおいしいお料理の中からお選びいただけます。美しい景色と夕焼けを写真に収めるために、カメラをお忘れなく。

GO ON TO THE NEXT PAGE!

Abbott Photo Contest Submissions

The Abbott Gallery will be accepting entries from October 1 to 31 for its eighth annual photography competition. The theme of the contest this year is "Metropolitan Nature," and accordingly all submitted photos must show wildlife in an urban setting. They can be either in color or in black and white. Contestants are permitted to submit one entry only. Photographs will be accepted as attachments sent by e-mail to contest@abbottgallery.org.

A panel of judges will select the best photographs on November 5, and their decision will be posted on our Web site that same day. Prizes will be awarded to the first-, second-, and third-place winners. The top prize will be a Flentak QX650 camera. The second- and third-place winners will receive an Andian DSLR 500 camera and an Alpix Snapshot compact camera, respectively. In addition, the winning photographs will be exhibited in the lobby of our gallery for all to see until March 5.

E-Mail Message

To:	Evelyn Glover
From:	Dwight Garcia
Date:	November 6
Re:	Abbott Photo Contest

Dear Ms. Glover:

It is my pleasure to inform you that your entry has tied for third place in the Abbott Gallery's "Metropolitan Nature" photography contest. Congratulations! We are excited to present you with your prize and exhibit your striking black and white photo.

On Saturday, November 21, we will hold a small gathering at our gallery to present the winners with their awards, which will begin at 4:00 P.M. Your photo, along with those of the other winners, will be unveiled to the public at that time as well. Please RSVP at your earliest convenience by either return e-mail or phone (555-0135).

We look forward to meeting you, and congratulations again on taking such a remarkable picture!

Yours sincerely,

Dwight Garcia, Director
Abbott Gallery

Abbott Photo Contest Winners Acknowledged

Wainston City (Nov. 22)—One morning, while Nella Cohen was walking her dog along the Agawan River in Wainston, she spotted a beaver standing by the riverbank. Luckily, she had her camera with her, and she captured a shot of the animal, which appears to be looking at the city's tall skyscrapers not so far from its small natural habitat. This delightful photo won first prize in the Abbott Photo Contest this year.

More than 150 Wainston residents submitted photographs for consideration in the contest, and the judges were so impressed by so many of them, it was hard for them to pick the winners. In fact, two people tied for third place: Evelyn Glover and Wei Zhang. One had entered a black and white photo of an owl on a chimney, and the other had submitted a picture of a hummingbird drinking from a red flower in the garden of the city's courthouse. Amber Doyle, who came in third place in last year's contest, won the second-place prize this year for her photo of a fox in a shadowy alleyway. All of the winners received their prizes at the gallery yesterday.

For the past eight years, the competition has focused on various aspects of everyday life in Wainston. The winning photographs from all eight contests can be viewed on the Abbott Gallery's Web site.

50. What is NOT mentioned in the notice?

(A) The photography contest is held every year.
(B) Photos of natural landscapes are acceptable.
(C) Contestants' photos should be submitted by e-mail.
(D) Contest results will be posted on November 5.

51. What is one purpose of the e-mail?

(A) To provide a list of contest winners
(B) To request a title for a photograph
(C) To thank a contestant for participating
(D) To invite a contestant to an awards ceremony

52. What is probably true about Ms. Glover?

(A) She entered a photograph in the contest in previous years.
(B) She was awarded an Alpix Snapshot compact camera.
(C) She lives near the Agawan River in Wainston City.
(D) She was unable to attend the Abbott Gallery ceremony.

53. Who entered a photograph of a hummingbird in the contest?

(A) Nella Cohen
(B) Evelyn Glover
(C) Wei Zhang
(D) Amber Doyle

54. What is suggested about Ms. Doyle?

(A) A number of her photographs are featured on a Web site.
(B) Her camera only takes black and white pictures.
(C) She was with her pet when she took a photograph.
(D) She received a better prize last year.

P. 82

Questions 50-54 refer to the following notice, e-mail, and article.

Abbott Photo Contest Submissions

The Abbott Gallery will be accepting entries from October 1 to 31 for ❶ its eighth annual photography competition. ❷ The theme of the contest this year is "Metropolitan Nature," and accordingly all submitted photos must show wildlife in an urban setting. They can be either in color or in black and white. Contestants are permitted to submit one entry only. ❸ Photographs will be accepted as attachments sent by e-mail to contest@abbottgallery.org.

❹ A panel of judges will select the best photographs on November 5, and their decision will be posted on our Web site that same day. Prizes will be awarded to the first-, second-, and third-place winners. The top prize will be a Flentak QX650 camera. ❺ The second- and third-place winners will receive an Andian DSLR 500 camera and an Alpix Snapshot compact camera, respectively. In addition, the winning photographs will be exhibited in the lobby of our gallery for all to see until March 5.

E-Mail Message

To:	Evelyn Glover
From:	Dwight Garcia
Date:	November 6
Re:	Abbott Photo Contest

Dear Ms. Glover:

❻ It is my pleasure to inform you that your entry has tied for third place in the Abbott Gallery's "Metropolitan Nature" photography contest. Congratulations! ❼ We are excited to present you with your prize and exhibit your striking black and white photo.

❽ On Saturday, November 21, we will hold a small gathering at our gallery to present the winners with their awards, which will begin at 4:00 P.M. Your photo, along with those of the other winners, will be unveiled to the public at that time as well. ❾ Please RSVP at your earliest convenience by either return e-mail or phone (555-0135).

We look forward to meeting you, and congratulations again on taking such a remarkable picture!

Yours sincerely,

Dwight Garcia, Director
Abbott Gallery

Abbott Photo Contest Winners Acknowledged

Wainston City (Nov. 22) — One morning, while Nella Cohen was walking her dog along the Agawan River in Wainston, she spotted a beaver standing by the riverbank. Luckily, she had her camera with her, and she captured a shot of the animal, which appears to be looking at the city's tall skyscrapers not so far from its small natural habitat. This delightful photo won first prize in the Abbott Photo Contest this year.

More than 150 Wainston residents submitted photographs for consideration in the contest, and the judges were so impressed by so many of them, it was hard for them to pick the winners. In fact, ❿ two people tied for third place: Evelyn Glover and Wei Zhang. ⓫ One had entered a black and white photo of an owl on a chimney, and the other had submitted a picture of a hummingbird drinking from a red flower in the garden of the city's courthouse. ⓬ Amber Doyle, who came in third place in last year's contest, won the second-place prize this year for her photo of a fox in a shadowy alleyway. All of the winners received their prizes at the gallery yesterday.

For the past eight years, the competition has focused on various aspects of everyday life in Wainston. ⓭ The winning photographs from all eight contests can be viewed on the Abbott Gallery's Web site.

お知らせ
☐ submission 提出、投稿　☐ accept entry 応募を受け付ける　☐ competition 競技会、コンテスト
☐ metropolitan 大都会の　☐ accordingly 従って　☐ wildlife 野生動物　☐ urban setting 都市環境
☐ either in color or in black and white カラー、白黒のいずれか　☐ contestant 応募者
☐ a panel of ～の（審査）委員会　☐ judge 審査員　☐ post ～を掲載する　☐ award ～を贈呈する
☐ top prize 優勝賞品　☐ exhibit ～を展示する

E メール
☐ inform ～に知らせる　☐ tie for ... place …位タイとなる　☐ striking 素晴らしい
☐ small gathering 小規模な集まり　☐ along with ～とともに　☐ unveil ～ to the public ～を一般公開する
☐ as well 同様に　☐ RSVP お返事をお願いします（仏語の répondez s'il vous plaît の省略形から）
☐ at one's earliest convenience 一番早い都合の良い時期に　☐ remarkable 素晴らしい

記事
☐ acknowledged 承認された　☐ walk ～を散歩させる　☐ spot ～を発見する　☐ beaver ビーバー
☐ riverbank 川岸　☐ capture a shot of ～の撮影をする　☐ appear to be ～のように見える
☐ skyscraper 高層ビル　☐ habitat 生息域　☐ delightful 愉快な　☐ for consideration 審査してもらうために
☐ be impressed 感銘を受ける　☐ pick ～を選ぶ　☐ owl フクロウ　☐ chimney 煙突　☐ hummingbird ハチドリ
☐ courthouse 裁判所　☐ fox キツネ　☐ shadowy 暗い　☐ alleyway 路地　☐ focus on ～に焦点を当てる
☐ various さまざまな　☐ aspect 側面

50. What is NOT mentioned in the notice?

(A) The photography contest is held every year.
(B) Photos of natural landscapes are acceptable.
(C) Contestants' photos should be submitted by e-mail.
(D) Contest results will be posted on November 5.

お知らせで言及されていないことは何ですか。

(A) 写真コンテストは毎年行われている。
(B) 自然の風景の写真は受け付けられている。
(C) 参加者の写真はＥメールで提出される必要がある。
(D) コンテストの結果は 11 月 5 日に掲載される。

NOT 問題。1 文書目のお知らせで言及されていないことが問われている。お知らせの❶「年次写真コンテスト」が (A) に、❸の「（コンテスト用の）写真はメール添付で」が (C) に、❹の「11 月 5 日に入賞者の写真を選出し、同日に結果をウェブサイトに掲載」が (D) に、それぞれ該当するため、残った **(B)** が正解。❷に写真のテーマは「大都会の自然」とあるが、自然の風景ではなく、「都市環境における野生生物」を入れた写真でなければならない。

☐ natural landscape 自然の風景　☐ acceptable 受け付けられる　☐ contest results コンテストの結果
☐ post 〜を掲示する

---

51. What is one purpose of the e-mail?

(A) To provide a list of contest winners
(B) To request a title for a photograph
(C) To thank a contestant for participating
(D) To invite a contestant to an awards ceremony

Ｅメールの 1 つの目的は何ですか。

(A) コンテスト入賞者のリストを提供すること
(B) 写真の題名を依頼すること
(C) 参加者に参加のお礼をすること
(D) 参加者を授賞式に招待すること

2 文書目のＥメールの目的が問われている。Ｅメールの最初の段落❻・❼で、受賞の旨と賞品贈呈と展示に触れ、第 2 段落の❽・❾で「授賞式開催と出欠可否の問い合わせ」について触れている。ここから、参加者を授賞式に招待していることがわかる。よって、コンテスト参加者を contestant と表現した **(D)** が正解となる。

☐ contestant コンテストの参加者

---

52. What is probably true about Ms. Glover?

(A) She entered a photograph in the contest in previous years.
(B) She was awarded an Alpix Snapshot compact camera.
(C) She lives near the Agawan River in Wainston City.
(D) She was unable to attend the Abbott Gallery ceremony.

Glover さんについておそらく当てはまることは何ですか。

(A) 過去のコンテストで写真を応募した。
(B) Alpix Snapshot コンパクトカメラを授与された。
(C) Wainston 市にある Agawan River の近くに住んでいる。
(D) Abbott Gallery での式典に出席することはできなかった。

Glover さんについておそらく当てはまることは何かが問われている、選択肢照合型問題。Glover さんは 2 文書目のＥメールの受信者で、❻から、コンテストで 3 位になったことがわかる。次に 1 文書目のお知らせを読んでいくと、❺で、3 位の入賞者には Alpix Snapshot コンパクトカメラが贈呈されることがわかる。以上から、正解は **(B)**。❺の respectively（それぞれ）は、A and B will receive C and D, respectively で「A（2 位）は C（DSLR カメラ）、B（3 位）は D（コンパクトカメラ）を受け取る」という意味。他の選択肢は本文に記載がなく、不正解。

☐ award 〜を授与する

53. Who entered a photograph of a hummingbird in the contest?

(A) Nella Cohen
(B) Evelyn Glover
(C) Wei Zhang
(D) Amber Doyle

コンテストにハチドリの写真を応募したのは誰ですか。

(A) Nella Cohen
(B) Evelyn Glover
(C) Wei Zhang
(D) Amber Doyle

コンテストで「ハチドリの写真」を応募した人物が問われている。3文書目の記事の❿・⓫を読むと、3位はEvelyn Glover さんと Wei Zhang さんの2人で、一人は煙突にいるフクロウの白黒写真を応募し、もう一人は市の裁判所の庭に咲く赤い花から何かを飲むハチドリの写真を投稿したとある。よって、正解は **(C)** だとわかる。この英文は、Ⓐ and Ⓑ , one (Ⓐ) is XX and the other (Ⓑ) is YY. のように、ⒶとⒷを one と the other という代名詞を使って、それぞれ説明している関係を見抜く必要がある。(B) を選ばないように注意しよう。

- -

54. What is suggested about Ms. Doyle?

(A) A number of her photographs are featured on a Web site.
(B) Her camera only takes black and white pictures.
(C) She was with her pet when she took a photograph.
(D) She received a better prize last year.

Doyle さんについて何が示唆されていますか。

(A) 彼女が撮った数枚の写真がウェブサイトで取り上げられている。
(B) 彼女のカメラは白黒写真しか撮れない。
(C) 彼女が写真を撮った時、ペットと一緒にいた。
(D) 昨年はより良い賞を受賞した。

Doyle さんについて何が示唆されているかを問う選択肢照合型問題。まず3文書目の記事を読むと、⓬から Doyle さんは昨年と今年のコンテストの入賞者だとわかる。次に⓭で「全8回のコンテストのすべての入賞写真はウェブサイトで閲覧できる」とある。Doyle さんは昨年のコンテストでも3位に入賞したことから、今年と昨年の写真が掲載されていることがわかる。以上から、正解は **(A)**。(B) は記載がなく、(C) は1位の Cohen さんのこと、(D) は昨年より今年の方がより良い順位だったため、それぞれ不正解。

□ feature 〜を掲載する・取り上げる　□ prize 賞

問題 **50** から **54** は次のお知らせ、Eメール、記事に関するものです。

Abbott 写真コンテストへの投稿

The Abbott Gallery は第8回年次写真コンテストへのご応募を10月1日から31日まで受け付けております。今年のテーマは「大都会の自然」で、テーマにあるとおり、投稿写真には必ず都市環境で生きる野生生物が写っている必要があります。カラーでも白黒でも構いません。参加者は1つの作品のみ応募が可能です。写真は contest@abbottgallery.org まで、メール添付で受け付けています。

審査員は11月5日に入賞者の写真を選出し、結果は同日に当ウェブサイトに掲載されます。賞品は1位、2位、3位の入賞者に授与されます。優勝賞品は Flentak QX650 カメラです。2位と3位の入賞者にはそれぞれ、Andian DSLR 500 カメラ、Alpix Snapshot コンパクトカメラが贈られます。また、入賞写真はみなさんにご覧いただけるように、3月5日まで当ギャラリーのロビーに展示されます。

受信者：	Evelyn Glover
送信者：	Dwight Garcia
日付：	11 月 6 日
返信：	Abbott 写真コンテスト

Glover 様

Abbott Gallery の「大都会の自然」写真コンテストで、投稿写真が 3 位となったことをお知らせいたします。おめでとうございます！ Glover 様に賞品をお渡しするとともに、素晴らしい白黒写真を展示できることをうれしく思います。

11 月 21 日土曜日に当ギャラリーにて小規模な集会を開催し、入賞者に表彰を行います。集会は午後 4 時開始です。Glover 様のお写真も他の入賞者の写真とともに一般公開されます。できるだけ早く E メールかお電話 (555-0135) で出欠のお返事をお願いします。

お会いできるのを楽しみにしております。また、素晴らしい写真をお撮りになったことを重ねてお祝いいたします。

よろしくお願いいたします。

Abbott Gallery 取締役
Dwight Garcia

Abbott 写真コンテストの入賞者決まる

Wainston City (11 月 22 日) —ある朝、Nella Cohen が Wainston の Agawan River 沿いで犬を散歩させていたとき、川岸に立っているビーバーを発見した。運よくカメラを持って来ていたので、その小さな自然環境からさほど離れていない街の高層ビルを眺めているような、その動物の写真を撮影した。この愉快な写真は今年の Abbot 写真コンテストで 1 位を獲得した。

150 人以上の Wainston の住民が、このコンテストのために写真を投稿し、審査員たちはその多くに感銘を受け、入賞者を選ぶのは困難なことであった。事実、2 人が 3 位で同位だった。Evelyn Glover 氏と Wei Zhang 氏である。一人は煙突にいるフクロウの白黒写真を応募し、もう一人は市の裁判所の庭に咲く赤い花から何かを飲むハチドリの写真を投稿した。昨年のコンテストで 3 位だった Amber Doyle 氏は今年、暗い路地にいるキツネの写真で 2 位に入賞した。すべての入賞者は昨日ギャラリーで賞品を受け取った。

過去 8 年間、コンテストでは Wainston の日常生活のさまざまな面に焦点が当てられてきた。8 回のコンテストのすべての入賞写真は Abbott Gallery のウェブサイトで閲覧できる。

Test

2

TOKIMAKURE!

Questions 1-2 refer to the following e-mail.

1分30秒

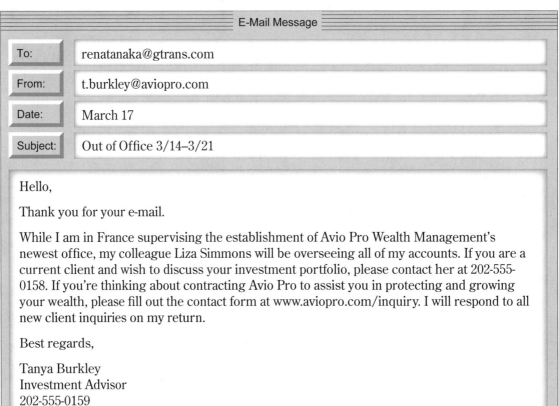

E-Mail Message

To:	renatanaka@gtrans.com
From:	t.burkley@aviopro.com
Date:	March 17
Subject:	Out of Office 3/14–3/21

Hello,

Thank you for your e-mail.

While I am in France supervising the establishment of Avio Pro Wealth Management's newest office, my colleague Liza Simmons will be overseeing all of my accounts. If you are a current client and wish to discuss your investment portfolio, please contact her at 202-555-0158. If you're thinking about contracting Avio Pro to assist you in protecting and growing your wealth, please fill out the contact form at www.aviopro.com/inquiry. I will respond to all new client inquiries on my return.

Best regards,

Tanya Burkley
Investment Advisor
202-555-0159

1. Why is Ms. Burkley not available at the moment?

(A) She is on vacation.
(B) Her schedule is full.
(C) She is on a business trip.
(D) She has to meet a client.

2. What are potential clients advised to do?

(A) Visit a Web site
(B) Call Ms. Simmons
(C) Wait for Ms. Burkley to return
(D) Mail a form

P. 90

ATTENTION

We are excited to announce that Catz Coffee Shop will be getting a new look! Aside from all new tables, chairs, and other furnishings, we are also going to be updating our menu, which will now feature a variety of locally roasted coffees. This store will be closed from Friday, July 5th, until Sunday the 7th while we implement these changes. During this time, you can still enjoy delicious food and drinks at our store on Lincoln Avenue. Upon reopening, we'll be holding an exclusive lunch party to celebrate the changes mentioned above. To book your place, please call 555-0908. Hope to see you there!

Ruby McDonald, Manager, Catz Coffee Shop

3. For whom is the notice intended?

(A) Employees
(B) Customers
(C) Caterers
(D) Suppliers

4. Why will the coffee shop be closed?

(A) A private party will be held.
(B) It is changing ownership.
(C) It is moving to a new location.
(D) It will be redecorated.

P. 92

Questions 1-2 refer to the following e-mail.

E-Mail Message

To:	renatanaka@gtrans.com
From:	t.burkley@aviopro.com
Date:	❶ March 17
Subject:	Out of Office 3/14–3/21

Hello,

Thank you for your e-mail.

❷ While I am in France supervising the establishment of Avio Pro Wealth Management's newest office, my colleague Liza Simmons will be overseeing all of my accounts. If you are a current client and wish to discuss your investment portfolio, please contact her at 202-555-0158. ❸ If you're thinking about contracting Avio Pro to assist you in protecting and growing your wealth, please fill out the contact form at www.aviopro.com/inquiry. I will respond to all new client inquiries on my return.

Best regards,

Tanya Burkley
Investment Advisor
202-555-0159

□ supervise ～を管理、監督する　□ establishment 設立　□ oversee ～を監督する　□ account 顧客
□ investment portfolio 保有証券　□ contact ～に連絡を取る　□ contract ～と契約する　□ protect ～を保護する
□ grow ～を増やす　□ wealth 資産　□ inquiry 問い合わせ　□ on one's return ～が戻り次第

★★☆☆☆

1. Why is Ms. Burkley not available at the moment?

(A) She is on vacation.
(B) Her schedule is full.
(C) She is on a business trip.
(D) She has to meet a client.

Burkley さんは現在なぜ対応ができないのですか。

(A) 休暇中である。
(B) 予定表がいっぱいである。
(C) 出張中である。
(D) 顧客に会わなければならない。

メールの送信者である Burkley さんが現在対応できない理由が問われている。❶で「現在（3 月 17 日）は事務所不在であること」がわかり、❷で「フランスで新事務所設立を監督している間は、同僚が私のすべての案件を取り仕切る」と伝えていることから、現在 Burkley さんは仕事でフランスに行っていることがわかる。これを on a business trip と言い換えた **(C)** が正解となる。"Out of Office" は、出張以外に、外出、休暇等にも使われる。用途を決め付けず、文書の手掛かりで正解にたどり着けるようにしよう。

 □ on vacation 休暇中の　□ on a business trip 出張中の

2. What are potential clients advised to do?

 (A) Visit a Web site
 (B) Call Ms. Simmons
 (C) Wait for Ms. Burkley to return
 (D) Mail a form

潜在的な顧客は何をするように勧められていますか。

 (A) ウェブサイトを訪れる
 (B) Simmons さんに電話をする
 (C) Burkley さんが戻るのを待つ
 (D) 書式を郵送する

潜在的な顧客がするように勧められていることが問われている。❸で、「資産の保護と増資に関する契約を検討されている場合は、指定アドレスのお問い合わせフォームに記入を」とお願いしているので、ここから「潜在的な顧客＝金融に関する契約検討者」と読み替えることができる。よって、勧められているのは、お問い合わせフォームに記入するためにアドレス先（ウェブサイト）を訪れることだとわかるため、正解は **(A)** となる。

□ mail ～を郵送する

問題 1 から 2 は次の E メールに関するものです。

受信者：	renatanaka@gtrans.com
送信者：	t.burkley@aviopro.com
日付：	3 月 17 日
件名：	3 月 14 日から 3 月 21 日まで事務所不在

こんにちは。

E メールをありがとうございます。

私がフランスで Avio Pro Wealth Management の新しい事務所の設立を監督している間、同僚の Liza Simmons さんが私のすべての案件を取り仕切ります。保有証券についてご相談をご希望の既契約者様は、彼女（202-555-0158）までご連絡をお願いいたします。資産の保護と増資のお手伝いについて Avio Pro との契約を検討されている方は、www.aviopro.com/inquiry のお問い合わせフォームにご記入ください。新規のお客様には、帰国後に私からご返信いたします。

よろしくお願いいたします。

Tanya Burkley
投資顧問
202-555-0159

Questions 3-4 refer to the following notice.

ATTENTION

❶ We are excited to announce that Catz Coffee Shop will be getting a new look! ❷ Aside from all new tables, chairs, and other furnishings, we are also going to be updating our menu, which will now feature a variety of locally roasted coffees. ❸ This store will be closed from Friday, July 5th, until Sunday the 7th while we implement these changes. During this time, you can still enjoy delicious food and drinks at our store on Lincoln Avenue. Upon reopening, we'll be holding an exclusive lunch party to celebrate the changes mentioned above. ❹ To book your place, please call 555-0908. Hope to see you there!

Ruby McDonald, Manager, Catz Coffee Shop

□ attention 注意、注目　□ new look 新たな外観、改装後の有り様　□ aside from ～に加えて
□ furnishings 家具　□ update ～を新しくする　□ feature ～を取り扱う　□ a variety of さまざまな種類の
□ roasted coffee 焙煎コーヒー　□ implement ～を実行する　□ upon reopening 再オープン時に
□ exclusive 特別な　□ lunch party 昼食会　□ mentioned above 上述の　□ book ～を予約する

★★☆☆☆

3. For whom is the notice intended?

(A) Employees
(B) Customers
(C) Caterers
(D) Suppliers

お知らせは誰を対象としていますか。

(A) 従業員
(B) 顧客
(C) ケータリング業者
(D) 仕入れ先

このお知らせが誰を対象にしているかが問われている。❶で「改装のお知らせ」をし、❹で「予約時の連絡先」を伝えているので、このお知らせはお客様宛のものだとわかる。よって、正解は **(B)** となる。❶のみだと顧客、従業員、関係業者すべて当てはまってしまうので、読み進めて決定的な手掛かりを見つけるようにしよう。

□ caterer ケータリング（出前）業者

★★☆☆☆

4. Why will the coffee shop be closed?

(A) A private party will be held.
(B) It is changing ownership.
(C) It is moving to a new location.
(D) It will be redecorated.

喫茶店はなぜ閉店しますか。

(A) 貸切パーティーが開かれる。
(B) 所有権が変わる。
(C) 移転する。
(D) 改装される。

喫茶店がなぜ閉店するかが問われている。❸で「当店はこれらの変更を行うために閉店する」と述べている。「これらの変更」は、直前の❷に書いてある「すべての、新しいテーブル、イス、その他のインテリアのほかに、メニューも新しくなる」を指している。ここから、正解は「改装する」という意味の redecorate を受け身で言い換えた **(D)** となる。

□ private party 貸切パーティー　□ ownership 所有権　□ redecorate ～を改装する、～の模様替えをする

問題 3 から 4 は次のお知らせに関するものです。

ご注意ください

Catz Coffee Shop が改装されることを喜んでお知らせいたします！ すべての、新しいテーブル、イス、その他のインテリアのほかに、メニューも一新し、地元で焙煎されたさまざまなコーヒーを取り扱います。当店は 7 月 5 日金曜日から 7 日日曜日まで、これらの変更を行うため、閉店となります。この期間は、Lincoln Avenue にある店舗でおいしい食べ物や飲み物をお楽しみいただけます。新装開店の際は、前述の変更を祝うための特別昼食会を開催します。ご予約は 555-0908 までご連絡ください。皆さまにお会いできるのを楽しみにしております！

Catz Coffee Shop マネージャー、Ruby McDonald

Sorry we missed you...

We tried to deliver a: ☐ Letter ☐ Large envelope ☒ Parcel
☐ Perishable item ☒ Fragile item ☒ Large item

Date: *December 18*
Tracking number: *994238532754*
Recipient: *Geoffrey Blair*
Sender: *Taylor Mobile Technology*

We will try again on *December 19*.
Your action is required:
    ☒ Someone must be present to sign for your delivery
    ☐ Must be 21 years of age or older
    ☒ We can leave your package if you fill out and sign the back of this form
    ☐ Your package has a collection-on-delivery payment due of $ _____
    ☒ Your delivery is also available for collection after 3:00 P.M. at:

OCPS Delivery Center
4 Genor Court, Owai City, HI, 96701

Items are kept available for collection for one week before being returned to the sender.

---

5. What most likely is being delivered to Mr. Blair?

  (A) A smartphone
  (B) A television
  (C) T-shirts
  (D) Food

6. What is NOT one way that Mr. Blair can obtain his package?

  (A) By being at home the following day
  (B) By scheduling a new delivery time
  (C) By visiting a delivery center
  (D) By providing his signature on the form

 P. 96

Questions 7-8 refer to the following online chat discussion.

Norman McCafferty 9:12 A.M.

Varun, will you be here later today? Mr. Park from the corporate office is coming to do an inspection.

Varun Sharma 9:25 A.M.

I have a meeting with Ms. Potter across town this afternoon.

Norman McCafferty 9:26 A.M.

What about Karlee Digby?

Varun Sharma 9:27 A.M.

She's coming with me this afternoon. Why don't you ask Rebecca Watts?

Norman McCafferty 9:30 A.M.

Well, Mr. Park also wanted to review our latest financial statements, so I thought someone from your department should meet with him.

Varun Sharma 9:31 A.M.

I think she can handle it. The statements are pretty simple to read.

Norman McCafferty 9:32 A.M.

You have a point. OK, I'll put together some materials for her.

7. Who most likely will meet with Mr. Park today?

(A) Mr. McCafferty
(B) Mr. Sharma
(C) Ms. Digby
(D) Ms. Watts

8. At 9:32 A.M., what does Mr. McCafferty most likely mean when he writes, "You have a point"?

(A) He needs to prepare some financial documents.
(B) An assignment is not very difficult.
(C) Mr. Park will not require assistance.
(D) Mr. Sharma is the best person for the job.

 P. 98

Questions 5-6 refer to the following form.

Sorry we missed you...

We tried to deliver a: ☐ Letter ☐ Large envelope **❶** ☒ Parcel
☐ Perishable item **❷** ☒ Fragile item **❸** ☒ Large item

Date: *December 18*
Tracking number: *994238532754*
Recipient: *Geoffrey Blair*
Sender: **❹** *Taylor Mobile Technology*

We will try again on *December 19*.
Your action is required:
❺ ☒ Someone must be present to sign for your delivery
☐ Must be 21 years of age or older
❻ ☒ We can leave your package if you fill out and sign the back of this form
☐ Your package has a collection-on-delivery payment due of $ _____
❼ ☒ Your delivery is also available for collection after 3:00 P.M. at:

OCPS Delivery Center
4 Genor Court, Owai City, HI, 96701

Items are kept available for collection for one week before being returned to the sender.

☐ deliver ～を届ける ☐ parcel 小包 ☐ perishable 生鮮な ☐ fragile 壊れやすい
☐ tracking number 追跡番号 ☐ recipient 受取人 ☐ sender 送り主 ☐ try again 再度行う
☐ present 居合わせる ☐ leave ～を置いておく ☐ package 荷物 ☐ the back of ～の裏面
☐ collection-on-delivery payment 代金引換払い ☐ due of ～の支払い義務 ☐ collection 引き取り、収集

★★★★★

5. What most likely is being delivered to Mr. Blair?

(A) A smartphone
(B) A television
(C) T-shirts
(D) Food

Blair さんに届けられたものはおそらく何ですか。

(A) スマートフォン
(B) テレビ
(C) T シャツ
(D) 食べ物

🔍 不在通知の受取人である Blair さんに届けられたものは何かが問われている。チェックボックスの❶「小包」、❷「ワレモノ」、❸「大型の品物」という情報と、❹の「依頼主名が技術関係に関連する会社から送られている」という情報から、大型の家電製品だと推測できる。よって、**(B)** が正解となる。❹の "Mobile" から、携帯電話会社＝スマートフォン、と安易に判断しないように注意しよう。

6. What is NOT one way that Mr. Blair can obtain his package?

(A) By being at home the following day
(B) By scheduling a new delivery time
(C) By visiting a delivery center
(D) By providing his signature on the form

Blair さんが配達品を引き取ることのできる方法ではないものは何ですか。

(A) 翌日家に居ること
(B) 新たに配達時間を設定すること
(C) 配送センターを訪れること
(D) 書式に署名をすること

NOT 問題。Blair さんが配達物を引き取ることのできる方法ではないものは何かが問われている。❺の「配達に際し、誰かの署名が必要」が「誰か在宅していること」と同じ意味で (A) に、❻の「この書式の裏面に記入及び署名」が (D) に、❼の「指定時間に配送センターで引き取り」が (C) に、それぞれ対応している。残った **(B)** のみが記載されていないため、これが正解となる。**(B)** は日本の配送サービスがやってくれそうなサービスだが、本文に記載されていない。思い込みで解かないように注意しよう。

□ the following day 翌日　□ delivery time 配達時間　□ provide one's signature 署名をする

問題 5 から 6 は次の書式に関するものです。

ご不在時にお伺いしました…

配達品：□ 手紙　□ 大型の封筒　☒ 小包
　　　　□ 生鮮食品　☒ ワレモノ　☒ 大型の品物
日付：12 月 18 日
追跡番号：994238532754
受取人：Geoffrey Blair
ご依頼主：Taylor Mobile Technology

再配達日　12 月 19 日
お手数をおかけしますが：
　☒ 配達に際し、どなたかにご署名をいただく必要があります
　□ 21 歳以上である必要があります
　☒ こちらの書式の裏面にご記入およびご署名いただければ、配達品を置いて行きます
　□ お客様の荷物は代金引換払いで、＿＿＿＿＿＿＿ドルのお支払いが必要です
　☒ 午後 3 時以降に次の場所へお引き取りに来ていただくことも可能です：

OCPS 配送センター
4 Genor Court, Owai City, ハワイ州 , 96701

配達品は送り主に返送するまで 1 週間お預かりいたしますので、その間にお引き取りいただけます。

Questions 7-8 refer to the following online chat discussion.

Norman McCafferty 9:12 A.M.

Varun, will you be here later today? ❶ Mr. Park from the corporate office is coming to do an inspection.

Varun Sharma 9:25 A.M.

I have a meeting with Ms. Potter across town this afternoon.

Norman McCafferty 9:26 A.M.

What about Karlee Digby?

Varun Sharma 9:27 A.M.

She's coming with me this afternoon. ❷ Why don't you ask Rebecca Watts?

Norman McCafferty 9:30 A.M.

Well, ❸ Mr. Park also wanted to review our latest financial statements, so I thought someone from your department should meet with him.

Varun Sharma 9:31 A.M.

❹ I think she can handle it. ❺ The statements are pretty simple to read.

Norman McCafferty 9:32 A.M.

❻ You have a point. ❼ OK, I'll put together some materials for her.

□ corporate office 本社　□ inspection 検査、点検　□ review 〜を確認する　□ latest 最新の
□ financial statement 財務諸表、財務明細表　□ handle 〜を処理する　□ simple to read 読みやすい
□ You have a point もっともである　□ put together 〜をまとめる　□ material 資料

7. Who most likely will meet with Mr. Park today?

(A) Mr. McCafferty
(B) Mr. Sharma
(C) Ms. Digby
(D) Ms. Watts

今日 Park さんと会うのはおそらく誰ですか。

(A) McCafferty さん
(B) Sharma さん
(C) Digby さん
(D) Watts さん

🔍 今日 Park さんと誰がおそらく会うかが問われている。まず冒頭の❶で McCafferty さんが「本社の Park さんが検査に来る」切り出し、その対応者を人選していると、❷で Sharma さんが「Watts さんはどうか？」と提案している。❸で McCafferty さんが「最新の財務情報に対応できる人」と条件を付けたところ、Sharma さんは❹で「それは彼女（Watts さん）が対応できると思う」と述べている。その後、❼で「彼女（Watts さん）のために資料をまとめておく」と述べていることから、Watts さんが Park さんに会うことが推測される。よって、正解は **(D)** となる。

8. At 9:32 A.M., what does Mr. McCafferty most likely mean when he writes, "You have a point"?

(A) He needs to prepare some financial documents.
(B) An assignment is not very difficult.
(C) Mr. Park will not require assistance.
(D) Mr. Sharma is the best person for the job.

午前 9 時 32 分に、McCafferty さんは "You have a point" という発言で、何を意味していると考えられますか。

(A) 財務書類を準備する必要がある。
(B) 仕事はそれほど難しくはない。
(C) Park さんに手助けは必要ない。
(D) Sharma さんがその仕事に適任である。

意図問題。問われている❻は「あなたはポイントを持っている＝あなたの言うことはもっともだ」という意味となる。前後の流れを見ていくと、❹「それは彼女（Watts さん）が対応できると思う」→❺「財務明細書はとてもわかりやすい」→❻「あなたの言うことはもっともだ」という流れになっている。つまり、財務明細書はとてもわかりやすいので、Watt さんでも容易に対応ができるということがわかる。よって、これを言い換えた **(B)** が正解。

☐ financial document　財務書類　☐ assignment 任務、タスク
☐ the best person for the job その仕事に適任の人物

問題 7 から 8 は次のオンラインチャットの話し合いに関するものです。

Norman McCafferty 午前 9 時 12 分
Varun さん、今日こちらに来られますか？　本社の Park さんが検査に来ます。

Varun Sharma 午前 9 時 25 分
今日の午後に Potter さんと町の反対側で会議があります。

Norman McCafferty 午前 9 時 26 分
Karlee Digby さんはどうですか？

Varun Sharma 午前 9 時 27 分
彼女は今日の午後私に同行します。Rebecca Watts さんに聞いてみるのはどうですか？

Norman McCafferty 午前 9 時 30 分
Park さんは最新の財務諸表を確認したいとも言っていたので、そちらの部署の誰かに会っていただけたらと思ったのですが。

Varun Sharma 午前 9 時 31 分
彼女ならできると思います。その財務諸表はとてもわかりやすいですから。

Norman McCafferty 午前 9 時 32 分
そうですね。では、Rebecca Watts さんのために資料をまとめておきます。

How the Pros Fly
Professional Helicopter Piloting at Whirlybirds Flight School
555-875-9090 ◆ www.whirlybirds.com ◆ info@whirlybirds.com

Whirlybirds is excited to announce that respected helicopter pilot Reginald Baltimore will be giving a presentation titled "How the Pros Fly" at our newly opened pilot school in Chesterfield on Saturday, April 14. Mr. Baltimore, who has been flying helicopters professionally for over 30 years, only comes to Whirlybirds to give these seminars once every few years, so this is a rare opportunity.

During his presentation, he will explain in detail the exact steps that you need to take to start working as a professional helicopter pilot. If you're hoping to turn your hobby into a career in the near future, then this is an event that you won't want to miss. Although there is no charge for attendance, space is limited. You can secure a place by submitting the registration form located on our Web site.

Whether you're an intermediate or an advanced pilot, the event is sure to be both fun and educational, just like the courses we teach at Whirlybirds. If you're interested in what we have to offer, along with the various prices we charge for courses, please call or e-mail us at your earliest convenience.

9. What is being advertised?

    (A) An introductory course
    (B) A job fair for helicopter pilots
    (C) A store's grand opening celebration
    (D) A complimentary seminar

10. What should people do if they want to attend the event?

    (A) Make a telephone call
    (B) Send an e-mail
    (C) Visit an office
    (D) Fill out a form online

11. For whom is the advertisement most likely intended?

    (A) People who want to change professions
    (B) People who fly helicopters professionally
    (C) People who travel frequently
    (D) People who attended a course last year

Single Q3

P. 102

Questions 9-11 refer to the following advertisement.

How the Pros Fly
Professional Helicopter Piloting at Whirlybirds Flight School
555-875-9090 ◆ www.whirlybirds.com ◆ info@whirlybirds.com

Whirlybirds is excited to announce that ❶ respected helicopter pilot Reginald Baltimore will be giving a presentation titled "How the Pros Fly" at our newly opened pilot school in Chesterfield on Saturday, April 14. Mr. Baltimore, who has been flying helicopters professionally for over 30 years, only comes to Whirlybirds to give these seminars once every few years, so this is a rare opportunity.

During his presentation, he will explain in detail the exact steps that you need to take to start working as a professional helicopter pilot. ❷ If you're hoping to turn your hobby into a career in the near future, then this is an event that you won't want to miss. Although ❸ there is no charge for attendance, space is limited. ❹ You can secure a place by submitting the registration form located on our Web site.

Whether you're an intermediate or an advanced pilot, the event is sure to be both fun and educational, just like the courses we teach at Whirlybirds. If you're interested in what we have to offer, along with the various prices we charge for courses, please call or e-mail us at your earliest convenience.

□ respected 尊敬されている、敬愛されている　□ titled ○○　○○というタイトルの
□ newly opened 新規にオープンした　□ rare めったにない　□ opportunity 機会　□ in detail 詳細に
□ turn A into B A を B にする　□ in the near future 近い将来　□ miss ～を見逃す
□ no charge for ～に費用が掛からない　□ attendance 出席　□ secure ～を確保する
□ registration form 申込フォーム　□ located on ～にある　□ intermediate 中級の　□ advanced 上級の
□ educational 教育的な　□ along with ～と共に　□ at one's earliest convenience ～のできる限り早めに

★★★☆☆

9. What is being advertised?

(A) An introductory course
(B) A job fair for helicopter pilots
(C) A store's grand opening celebration
(D) A complimentary seminar

何が宣伝されていますか。

(A) 入門コース
(B) ヘリコプター操縦士向けの就職説明会
(C) 店の新装開店祝い
(D) 無料講習会

文書で宣伝されているものは何かが問われている。❶で「ヘリコプター操縦士による講習会」と触れ、❸で「参加に費用は掛かりません」とある。よって、❶の "presentation" を seminar、❸の "no charge" を complimentary と言い換えた (D) が正解。最終段落に "the various prices we charge for course" などの有料を意味する箇所があるが、これは講習会ではなく、Whirlybirds の別のサービスに関する内容。

□ introductory course 入門者、初級者向けのコース　□ job fair 就職説明会
□ grand opening (店舗等の) グランドオープン　□ complimentary 無料の

10. What should people do if they want to attend the event?

(A) Make a telephone call
(B) Send an e-mail
(C) Visit an office
(D) Fill out a form online

イベントに参加したい場合はどうしたらいいですか。

(A) 電話をかける
(B) メールを送信する
(C) 事務所を訪れる
(D) オンラインでフォームに入力する

イベントに参加するためにはどうするかが問われている。❹で「席の確保はウェブサイトにある申込フォームを送信するように」と述べている。これを「オンラインでフォームに入力する」と言い換えた **(D)** が正解。❹の "secure a place" と設問の attend が言い換えとなっているので押さえておこう。

□ fill out（書式等）に記入する・入力する

---

11. For whom is the advertisement most likely intended?

(A) People who want to change professions
(B) People who fly helicopters professionally
(C) People who travel frequently
(D) People who attended a course last year

広告は誰を対象にしていると考えられますか。

(A) 職業を変えたい人たち
(B) プロとしてヘリコプターを操縦している人たち
(C) 頻繁に旅行をする人たち
(D) 昨年コースに参加した人たち

広告の対象者は誰かが問われている。第2段落の❷で「将来趣味を仕事に変えたいのなら、これは見逃せないイベントだ」と述べている。つまり、「いずれ趣味を仕事にすることを考えている＝職業を変更しようと考えている人」を対象にしたイベントと考えることができる。よって、これを言い換えた **(A)** が正解となる。❷の "hoping to turn your hobby into a career" が、(A) の want to change professions に対応していると考えよう。

□ profession 職業　□ frequently 頻繁に

問題 9 から 11 は次の広告に関するものです。

プロの飛び方

Whirlybirds Flight School でプロのヘリコプター操縦士の飛び方体験

555-875-9090 ◆ www.whirlybirds.com ◆ info@whirlybirds.com

Whirlybirds は、4 月 14 日土曜日、Chesterfield に新しく開校した操縦士学校にて、尊敬されるヘリコプター操縦士の Reginald Baltimore さんによる「プロの飛び方」と題した講習会を行うことをお知らせします。30 年以上、プロのヘリコプター操縦士として飛び続けている Baltimore さんが、このような講習会を行うために Whirlybirds へ来るのは、何年かに 1 度だけですので、これはめったにない機会です。

講習会では、プロのヘリコプター操縦士として働き始めるために踏まなければならない段階を、詳しくご説明いたします。近い将来趣味を仕事にしたいとお考えの方には、見逃せないイベントです。参加費は無料ですが、お席には限りがございます。当校のウェブサイトにある申込フォームを送信することで、お席をお取りいただけます。

中級者、上級者どちらにとっても、このイベントは Whirlybirds で教えられているコースと同様に、楽しく、学ぶことの多いものとなるはずです。当校が提供するものや、さまざまな金額の受講料に関心をお持ちでしたら、お電話か E メールで、できる限り早めにお問い合わせください。

Questions 12-14 refer to the following e-mail.

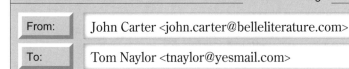 2分45秒

E-Mail Message	
From:	John Carter <john.carter@belleliterature.com>
To:	Tom Naylor <tnaylor@yesmail.com>
Subject:	Short Story Competition Results
Date:	January 3
Attachment:	📎 Statement_of_permission.pdf

Dear Mr. Naylor,

It is my great pleasure to inform you that your short story entitled "The Withered Beam" was selected to receive Belle Literature's third annual Emerging Authors Award. In addition to having your submitted story appear in next month's issue of our magazine, one of our editors will be assigned to you for one year to help you get your very first novel published. — [1] —.

You must confirm your acceptance of this award no later than January 10. — [2] —. Just sign and e-mail the statement of permission attached to this message, which grants us permission to publish your work. — [3] —. You are also welcome to request a specific editor to have assigned to you. Editor profiles can be found at www.belleliterature.com/editors. We will do our best to match you with someone who can bring out your best work. — [4] —.

John Carter
Social Media Manager
Belle Literature

12. Why was the e-mail sent?

    (A) To confirm a competition entry
    (B) To congratulate a published author
    (C) To inform a winner of their prize
    (D) To advertise an editing service

13. How can Mr. Naylor get his short story published?

    (A) By requesting an editor
    (B) By responding to the e-mail
    (C) By visiting a printing company
    (D) By mailing a signed document

14. In which of the positions marked [1], [2], [3], and [4] does the following sentence best belong?

"Failure to do so by then will result in the prize being given to the second-place contestant."

    (A) [1]
    (B) [2]
    (C) [3]
    (D) [4]

P. 106

Questions 12-14 refer to the following e-mail.

E-Mail Message

From:	John Carter <john.carter@belleliterature.com>
To:	Tom Naylor <tnaylor@yesmail.com>
Subject:	Short Story Competition Results
Date:	January 3
Attachment:	📎 Statement_of_permission.pdf

Dear Mr. Naylor,

It is my great pleasure to inform you that ❶ your short story entitled "The Withered Beam" was selected to receive Belle Literature's third annual Emerging Authors Award. In addition to having your submitted story appear in next month's issue of our magazine, one of our editors will be assigned to you for one year to help you get your very first novel published. — [1] —.

❷ You must confirm your acceptance of this award no later than January 10. — [2] —. ❸ Just sign and e-mail the statement of permission attached to this message, which grants us permission to publish your work. — [3] —. You are also welcome to request a specific editor to have assigned to you. Editor profiles can be found at www.belleliterature.com/editors. We will do our best to match you with someone who can bring out your best work. — [4] —.

John Carter
Social Media Manager
Belle Literature

□ entitled ～というタイトルの □ in addition to ～に加えて □ have ○○ appear in ○○ を～に掲載する
□ issue (雑誌の) ～号 □ assign ～に担当させる □ confirm ～を確認する □ acceptance 承諾
□ statement of permission 許可書 □ attached to ～に添付した □ grant (～に) ～を与える
□ profile 人物紹介 □ match A with B AをBと組み合わせる □ bring out ～をもたらす・引き出す

★★☆☆☆

12. Why was the e-mail sent?

(A) To confirm a competition entry
(B) To congratulate a published author
(C) To inform a winner of their prize
(D) To advertise an editing service

Eメールが送られたのはなぜですか。

(A) コンテストへの参加を確認するため
(B) 著書を出版した著者を祝うため
(C) 受賞者に知らせるため
(D) 編集サービスを宣伝するため

🔍 Eメールが送られた理由が問われている。❶で「貴殿の短編小説が賞に選ばれた」という内容が述べられているので、受賞者への通知をしていることがわかる。以上から、正解は **(C)**。

□ confirm ～を確認する □ competition entry 競技会への参加登録 □ inform A of B AにBを知らせる
□ editing service 編集サービス

13. How can Mr. Naylor get his short story published?

(A) By requesting an editor
(B) By responding to the e-mail
(C) By visiting a printing company
(D) By mailing a signed document

Naylor さんはどのように短編小説を出版できますか。

(A) 編集者を要望する
(B) Eメールに返信する
(C) 印刷会社を訪れる
(D) 署名入りの書類を郵送する

🔍 Naylor さんがどうやって短編小説を出版できるかが問われている。❸で Naylor さんは「メール添付されている、当社に貴殿の作品を出版することについての許諾書に署名していただき、Eメールで返送すれば結構です」と述べている。よって、これを言い換えた **(B)** が正解となる。(D) が正解と思ったかもしれないが、この mail は「〜を郵送する」という意味。

✏️ □ signed document 署名入りの文書

★★★☆☆ 文挿入位置問題

14. In which of the positions marked [1], [2], [3], and [4] does the following sentence best belong?

"Failure to do so by then will result in the prize being given to the second-place contestant."

(A) [1]   (C) [3]
(B) [2]   (D) [4]

次の文は、[1]、[2]、[3]、[4] のどの位置に最もよく当てはまりますか。

「それまでにそうしなければ、結果的に受賞は次席の方にお譲りすることとなります」

(A) [1]   (C) [3]
(B) [2]   (D) [4]

🔍 位置問題。問われている文は「それまでに対応しなければ、次席の方に譲る」という意味になっている。ここから、「次席の方に賞を譲られないようにすること＝受賞条件に関わる内容」が書かれているところがヒントだとわかる。よって、❷「1月10日までに、受賞を承諾する必要あり」と述べている直後の **(B)** が正解。❷の "no later than January 10（遅くても1月10日までに）" が、挿入文の "by then（それまでに）" と、直前を受けた表現になっていることに気づくと、正解にたどり着きやすくなる。

✏️ □ failure to *do* 〜しないこと   □ result in 結果として〜となる   □ contestant 出場者

📝 **問題 12 から 14 は次のEメールに関するものです。**

送信者：	John Carter <john.carter@belleliterature.com>
受信者：	Tom Naylor <tnaylor@yesmail.com>
件名：	短編小説コンテスト結果
日付：	1月3日
添付：	📎 許諾書 .pdf

Naylor 様

貴殿の短編小説 "The Withered Beam" が Belle Literature の第3回年次新人作家賞に選ばれたことをお知らせできることを大変喜ばしく思います。投稿された小説が来月発行の当社の雑誌に掲載されることに加え、処女小説の出版のために当社から1年間、編集者を1人担当におつけします。— [1] —

1月10日までにこの賞を受賞することをご承諾いただく必要があります。— [2] — 確認がとれなかった場合、賞は次席の方に授与されることとなります。このメッセージに添付されている、当社に貴殿の作品を出版することについての許諾書にご署名のうえ、Eメールでお送りいただくだけで結構です。— [3] —また、特定の編集者を担当にご指名いただくことができます。編集者のプロフィールは、www.belleliterature.com/editors でご覧いただけます。最高の作品を引き出せる人材をご紹介できるよう最善をつくします。— [4] —

John Carter
Belle Literature ソーシャルメディアマネージャー

MEMO

To: All
From: Events Management
Date: 4 May
Subject: Charity Fun Run

Hi everyone,

As you may know, it's almost time for our annual charity event. This year, we have decided to throw a fun run. The proceeds from the event will go to Greener Than Yesterday, a local organization that works to clean up and improve the city's local parks.

The run will span 24 kilometers, from the nearby Spring Park, then along the river, before setting up for the night at Starling campsite. The following day, we will be running through Westbury forest, eventually finishing at the central square near Castleton Station. The event will probably be held in late July, but please bear in mind this may be subject to change.

If you would like to train for the event, our very own Vicky Lemont will be holding a free seven-day boot camp. All attendees will be given five days' extra paid holiday to attend. However, spaces are limited and will be assigned on a first-come-first-served basis. To request a place, please contact Jessica Sharpe in the HR Department.

We will be holding a one-hour meeting about the fun run on Wednesday, 7 May. Even if you will be unable to participate in the event, attendance is required. We will be covering details such as how sponsorship works and safety during long-distance runs. We will also have a sign-up sheet for those wishing to volunteer as helpers.

15. According to the memo, how long will the event last?

(A) One day
(B) Two days
(C) One week
(D) Two weeks

16. Who is asked to contact Ms. Sharpe?

(A) People who cannot attend the event
(B) People who want to volunteer
(C) People with professional running experience
(D) People who wish to attend the training

17. What is indicated about the meeting on Wednesday?

(A) It will be hosted by event sponsors.
(B) It will be held during lunch.
(C) All staff members must go to it.
(D) Space for attendees is limited.

P. 110

Questions 15-17 refer to the following memo.

MEMO

To: All
From: Events Management
Date: 4 May
Subject: Charity Fun Run

Hi everyone,

As you may know, it's almost time for our annual charity event. This year, we have decided to throw a fun run. The proceeds from the event will go to Greener Than Yesterday, a local organization that works to clean up and improve the city's local parks.

❶ The run will span 24 kilometers, from the nearby Spring Park, then along the river, before setting up for the night at Starling campsite. The following day, we will be running through Westbury forest, eventually finishing at the central square near Castleton Station. The event will probably be held in late July, but please bear in mind this may be subject to change.

❷ If you would like to train for the event, our very own Vicky Lemont will be holding a free seven-day boot camp. All attendees will be given five days' extra paid holiday to attend. However, spaces are limited and will be assigned on a first-come-first-served basis. ❸ To request a place, please contact Jessica Sharpe in the HR Department.

❹ We will be holding a one-hour meeting about the fun run on Wednesday, 7 May. ❺ Even if you will be unable to participate in the event, attendance is required. We will be covering details such as how sponsorship works and safety during long-distance runs. We will also have a sign-up sheet for those wishing to volunteer as helpers.

□ As you may know ご存知のとおり □ annual 年次、例年の □ proceeds 収入、収益
□ span ～に広がる、及ぶ □ the following day 翌日 □ eventually 結局、最終的に
□ bear in mind ～を心に留める □ subject to change 変更する場合がある □ attendee 出席者
□ paid holiday 有給休暇 □ assign ～を割り当てる □ on a first-come-first-served basis 先着順に
□ HR Department 人事部 ※ HR Human Resources □ fun run 市民マラソン
□ even if ... たとえ…だとしても □ long distance 長距離 □ sign-up sheet 登録用紙

★★☆☆☆

15. According to the memo, how long will the event last?

(A) One day
(B) Two days
(C) One week
(D) Two weeks

連絡メモによると、イベントの期間はどのくらいですか。

(A) 1日
(B) 2日
(C) 1週間
(D) 2週間

イベントはどれくらい続くかが問われている。❶でコースの距離と場所について触れ、「キャンプ場で一晩過ごし、翌日ゴールとなる」と述べているので、ここから2日間のイベントであることがわかる。以上より、**(B)** が正解。❶の "the following day" が正解を見分けるポイントとなる。

16. Who is asked to contact Ms. Sharpe?

- (A) People who cannot attend the event
- (B) People who want to volunteer
- (C) People with professional running experience
- **(D)** People who wish to attend the training

Sharpe さんに連絡をするようにお願いされているのは誰ですか。

- (A) イベントに参加できない人たち
- (B) ボランティアをしたい人たち
- (C) プロとしてのランニングの経験がある人たち
- **(D)** トレーニングに参加したい人たち

 誰が Sharpe さんに連絡するようにお願いされているかが問われている。❷で「イベントのためのトレーニング」があることに触れ、❸で「参加希望の方は、人事部の Sharpe さんに連絡を」と述べている。ここから、トレーニング参加希望者が Sharpe さんに連絡をするように依頼されていることがわかるので、正解は **(D)** となる。❸だけでは、何に参加したいかがわからないので、第3段落をしっかり読み込んで解答しよう。

✎ □ volunteer ボランティアとして働く

---

17. What is indicated about the meeting on Wednesday?

- (A) It will be hosted by event sponsors.
- (B) It will be held during lunch.
- **(C)** All staff members must go to it.
- (D) Space for attendees is limited.

水曜日の会議について何が示されていますか。

- (A) イベントのスポンサーが主催する。
- (B) 昼食時に開催される。
- **(C)** スタッフ全員が行かなければならない。
- (D) 出席できる人数に制限がある。

 水曜日の会議について何が示されているかが問われている選択肢照合型問題。❹・❺で「5月7日の水曜日に市民マラソンの会議を開催する」「イベント不参加でも出席が必要」と述べているため、水曜日にスタッフ全員が会議に参加する必要があることがわかる。以上より、これを言い換えた **(C)** が正解。

✎ □ host ～を開催する

📝 問題 15 から 17 は次の連絡メモに関するものです。

連絡メモ

宛先： すべての方
差出人：イベント管理者
日付： 5月4日
件名： チャリティー市民マラソン

みなさん、こんにちは。

ご存じのように、例年のチャリティーイベントの時期が近づいてきました。今年は市民マラソンを開催します。イベントの収益は、市内の公園の清掃と改善に取り組んでいる地元団体の Greener Than Yesterday に寄付されます。

コースは 24 キロメートルに及び、近くの Spring Park から川に沿って走り、その後 Starling キャンプ場で一晩を過ごします。翌日、Westbury forest を走り抜け、最終的には Castleton 駅近くの中央広場でゴールとなります。イベントは 7 月末に開催される予定ですが、変更となる可能性もあるのでご注意ください。

イベントのためのトレーニングをご希望する方のために、当社の Vicky Lemont が無料 7 日間ブートキャンプを開催します。参加者全員には 5 日間の追加有給休暇が与えられます。ただし、参加できる人数には限りがあり、先着順となります。参加をご希望の方は人事部の Jessica Sharpe までご連絡ください。

5月7日水曜日に市民マラソンについての1時間の会議を開催します。イベントに参加ができない場合でも、出席が必要です。スポンサー契約の仕組みや長距離走での安全性などの詳細についてお話しします。手伝い人としてボランティアをご希望される方たちの参加用紙もご用意しております。

Questions 18-21 refer to the following memo.

MEMO

To: All staff
From: HR Department (Corporate)
Date: 18 July
Subject: BGC Conference

This is a reminder that any employee wishing to attend the BGC Conference in Hong Kong at the end of this year must apply no later than 1 August. As you know, the BGC Conference is important for creating and maintaining good relationships with our various partners in Asia. — [1] —. In addition to a core team that is sent from our corporate office on an annual basis, up to 20 employees from regional branches across the US are also eligible to attend. — [2] —.

By attending the conference, regional branch employees can gain a better understanding of Delphin Products' business model, discuss sales strategies with staff from other regions of the country and find out what has been successful for them, and strengthen our relationships with representatives of other businesses attending the conference. — [3] —. For these reasons, we give priority to members of the company who are sociable, hard-working, and interested in building a lengthy career with Delphin Products. — [4] —.

Applications can be submitted to your local HR department manager.

HR Department, Corporate Office
Delphin Products

18. What is the purpose of the memo?

    (A) To announce changes to an application process
    (B) To warn employees that a deadline is approaching
    (C) To describe the benefits of the BGC Conference
    (D) To clarify the requirements for applicants

19. According to the memo, what is true about Delphin Products?

    (A) It is seeking employees to move to its corporate office.
    (B) It has branches both in the US and Asia.
    (C) It participates in the BGC Conference each year.
    (D) It pays for all employee travel expenses.

20. Why are employees from regional branches sent to the conference?

    (A) To discover business strategies used at other branches
    (B) To motivate them to stay at the company for longer
    (C) To examine the business models of competitors
    (D) To secure new clients for Delphin Products

21. In which of the positions marked [1], [2], [3], and [4] does the following sentence best belong?

"If this sounds like you, please don't hesitate to apply."

    (A) [1]
    (B) [2]
    (C) [3]
    (D) [4]

Single Q4

P. 114

Questions 18-21 refer to the following memo.

MEMO

To: All staff
From: HR Department (Corporate)
Date: 18 July
Subject: BGC Conference

❶ This is a reminder that any employee wishing to attend the BGC Conference in Hong Kong at the end of this year must apply no later than 1 August. As you know, the BGC Conference is important for creating and maintaining good relationships with our various partners in Asia. —— [1] ——. ❷ In addition to a core team that is sent from our corporate office on an annual basis, up to 20 employees from regional branches across the US are also eligible to attend. —— [2] ——.

❸ By attending the conference, regional branch employees can gain a better understanding of Delphin Products' business model, discuss sales strategies with staff from other regions of the country and find out what has been successful for them, and strengthen our relationships with representatives of other businesses attending the conference. —— [3] ——. ❹ For these reasons, we give priority to members of the company who are sociable, hard-working, and interested in building a lengthy career with Delphin Products. —— [4] ——.

Applications can be submitted to your local HR department manager.

HR Department, Corporate Office
Delphin Products

□ reminder 思い出させるもの □ no later than 遅くとも〜までに □ maintain 〜を維持する
□ relationships with 〜との関係 □ various さまざまな □ in addition to 〜に加えて □ core 中核となる
□ corporate office 本社 □ regional branch 地方の支社 □ eligible to do 〜する資格がある
□ gain an understanding of 〜を理解する □ sales strategy 営業戦略 □ region 地域
□ strengthen 〜を強化する □ representative 代表者 □ priority 優先 □ sociable 社交的な
□ hard-working 勤勉な □ lengthy 長期的な

★★☆☆☆

18. What is the purpose of the memo?

(A) To announce changes to an application process
(B) To warn employees that a deadline is approaching
(C) To describe the benefits of the BGC Conference
(D) To clarify the requirements for applicants

連絡メモの目的は何ですか。

(A) 申請方法の変更を知らせること
(B) 従業員たちに対し期限が近づいていることを警告すること
(C) BGC 協議会の利点について説明すること
(D) 申請者の要件を明確にすること

連絡メモの目的は何かが問われている。冒頭の❶で、このメモが「BGC 協議会に参加を希望している従業員に、8月1日までに申し込みが必要なことを再度知らせるためのものだ」と述べていることから、従業員にある期限を繰り返し知らせていることがわかる。以上から、これを "warn" という少し厳しい表現を使用して言い換えた **(B)** が正解となる。

□ application process 申請方法 □ warn 人 that 人に〜と警告する □ approach 近づく
□ describe 〜を説明する □ clarify 〜を明確にする □ requirement 要件 □ applicant 申請者

19. According to the memo, what is true about Delphin Products?

(A) It is seeking employees to move to its corporate office.
(B) It has branches both in the US and Asia.
(C) It participates in the BGC Conference each year.
(D) It pays for all employee travel expenses.

連絡メモによると、Delphin Products 社について当てはまることは何ですか。

(A) 本社に異動する従業員を探している。
(B) 米国とアジア両方に支社がある。
(C) BGC 協議会に毎年参加している。
(D) すべての従業員の旅費を支払う。

Delphin Products 社について当てはまることを問う選択肢照合型問題。❷で、BGC 協議会について触れ、「毎年中核となるチームを本社から派遣するほかに、～」と述べていることから、この協議会には毎年参加していることがわかる。以上から、正解は **(C)**。❷で "a core team that is sent from our corporate office on an annual basis" とさらっと触れているので、しっかり読み取って解くようにしよう。

□ seek ～を探す　□ branch 支社　□ participate in ～に参加する
□ pay for ～の費用を支払う　□ travel expense 旅費

20. Why are employees from regional branches sent to the conference?

(A) To discover business strategies used at other branches
(B) To motivate them to stay at the company for longer
(C) To examine the business models of competitors
(D) To secure new clients for Delphin Products

協議会に地域支社の従業員が派遣されるのはなぜですか。

(A) 他の支社の事業戦略を見つけるため
(B) 会社に長期間残るよう促すため
(C) 競合他社のビジネスモデルを検証するため
(D) Delphin Products 社の新しい顧客を確保するため

協議会に地域支社の従業員が送られるのはなぜかが問われている。❸で「協議会に参加することで、地域支社の従業員は Delphin Products 社のビジネスモデルを理解し、他の地域の職員と販売戦略について話し合い、成功した事例を見つけ、協議会に参加している他の企業の代表者たちとの関係強化が可能」と述べている。ここから、他支社の事業戦略や成功事例を共有・発見できることがわかるので、これを言い換えた **(A)** が正解。

□ business strategy 事業戦略　□ motivate ～を促す、奮起させる　□ for longer 長期間　□ competitor 競合他社
□ secure ～を確保する

21. In which of the positions marked [1], [2], [3], and [4] does the following sentence best belong?

"If this sounds like you, please don't hesitate to apply."

(A) [1]
(B) [2]
(C) [3]
(D) [4]

次の文は、[1]、[2]、[3]、[4] のどの位置に最もよく当てはまりますか。

「もし自分がそれに当てはまるとお考えでしたら、ためらわずにお申し込みください」

(A) [1]
(B) [2]
(C) [3]
(D) [4]

適切な文の位置を探す問題。問われている文は「当てはまれば、お申し込みください」という勧誘表現になっている。つまり、この文の前には、当てはまるための条件が来ることが考えられる。❹を見ると、「社交的、勤勉、そして Delphin Products 社での長期的なキャリア構築をすることに関心がある社員を優先する」と、選考条件を述べているため、この直後が最も適切だと考えられる。以上より、正解は **(D)** となる。

問題 **18** から **21** は次の連絡メモに関するものです。

連絡メモ

宛先: 全従業員
差出人: 人事部 (本社)
日付: 7 月 18 日
件名: BGC 協議会

これは、今年の年末の香港での BGC 協議会に参加を希望している従業員に向け、8 月 1 日までに申し込みが必要であることを再度お知らせするためのものです。ご存じのとおり、BGC 協議会はアジアにおける当社のパートナー企業との良好な関係を構築、維持するのに重要です。— [1] —毎年中核となるチームを本社から派遣するほかに、米国各地の支社から最大 20 名の従業員にも参加する資格が与えられます。— [2] —

協議会に参加することにより、地域支社の従業員は Delphin Products のビジネスモデルについて理解を深め、国内の他の地域の職員たちと販売戦略について話し合い、成功した事例を見つけ、協議会に参加している他の企業の代表者たちとの関係を強化することができます。— [3] —これらの理由から、社交的、勤勉、そして Delphin Products での長期的なキャリア構築をすることに関心がある社員を優先します。— [4] — もし自分がそれに当てはまるとお考えでしたら、ためらわずにお申し込みください。

申請書は勤務地の人事部長に提出してください。

Delphin Products 本社人事部

GO ON TO THE NEXT PAGE!

◀ ▶   http://www.folksyfarm.com/whatson   ▶

Folksy Farm

| Home | Petting Zoo | Farm Activities | Buy Tickets |

Are you or your children interested in agriculture? Do you love animals? Then come to Folksy Farm, where you can learn about both in a safe and exciting environment! Here is our schedule of activities available for the current season:

Dairy Farmers—Tuesdays and Saturdays, 10:00 A.M.–2:00 P.M.
Milk some cows before taking a tractor ride to see all our different kinds of cattle.

Shepherds—Wednesdays and Fridays, 10:00 A.M.–2:00 P.M.
Bottle-feed our adorable spring lambs and learn how to give sheep a proper haircut.

Stable Hands—Saturdays and Sundays, 1:00 P.M.–5:00 P.M.
Master the basics of horse riding and feed our ponies some of their favorite snacks.

Poultry Farmers—Mondays and Thursdays, 1:00 P.M.–5:00 P.M.
Join an egg-hunting contest before visiting our incubation room, where you can pet baby chicks.

Order tickets in advance from our Web site for a 10% discount. *Or just come straight to the farm.

Folksy Farm is located about an hour south of the city, in the small town of Chester Flats, which has a population of only 200 people! It can be reached by via Highway 47. Take Exit 14 and turn left. We hope to see you soon!

Please e-mail us at info@folksyfarm.com before visiting if you plan to arrive with a large group.

22. According to the Web page, what is true about Folksy Farm?

    (A) It is exclusively for adults.
    (B) It sells food to customers.
    (C) It is open every day of the week.
    (D) It does not require an entry fee.

23. What do all the activities have in common?

    (A) They start in the morning.
    (B) They involve touching animals.
    (C) They include harvesting crops.
    (D) They deal with baby animals.

24. How can visitors pay a lower price?

    (A) By sending an e-mail
    (B) By going to the farm in person
    (C) By visiting with a large group
    (D) By purchasing tickets online

25. What is suggested about Folksy Farm?

    (A) It is most popular on the weekends.
    (B) It is located in a rural area.
    (C) It posts advertisements in multiple cities.
    (D) It opened last year.

Single Q4

P. 120

Questions 22-25 refer to the following Web page.

http://www.folksyfarm.com/whatson

Folksy Farm

| Home | Petting Zoo | Farm Activities | Buy Tickets |

Are you or your children interested in agriculture? Do you love animals? Then come to Folksy Farm, where you can learn about both in a safe and exciting environment! Here is our schedule of activities available for the current season:

Dairy Farmers— ❶ **Tuesdays and Saturdays,** 10:00 A.M.–2:00 P.M.
❷ Milk some cows before taking a tractor ride to see all our different kinds of cattle.

Shepherds— ❸ **Wednesdays and Fridays,** 10:00 A.M.–2:00 P.M.
❹ Bottle-feed our adorable spring lambs and learn how to give sheep a proper haircut.

Stable Hands— ❺ **Saturdays and Sundays,** 1:00 P.M.–5:00 P.M.
❻ Master the basics of horse riding and feed our ponies some of their favorite snacks.

Poultry Farmers— ❼ **Mondays and Thursdays,** 1:00 P.M.–5:00 P.M.
❽ Join an egg-hunting contest before visiting our incubation room, where you can pet baby chicks.

❾ Order tickets in advance from our Web site for a 10% discount. *Or just come straight to the farm.

❿ Folksy Farm is located about an hour south of the city, in the small town of Chester Flats, which has a population of only 200 people! It can be reached by via Highway 47. Take Exit 14 and turn left. We hope to see you soon!

Please e-mail us at info@folksyfarm.com before visiting if you plan to arrive with a large group.

□ pet（動物・子ども）をなでる、触れる　□ agriculture 農業　□ environment 環境　□ cow 乳牛
□ tractor トラクター　□ cattle 家畜の牛　□ bottle-feed ～に哺乳びんでミルクを与える　□ adorable かわいい
□ lamb 子羊　□ sheep ひつじ　□ proper 正しい　□ stable hands 馬の飼育係　□ master ～を習得する
□ pony 仔馬　□ snack おやつ　□ poultry 家禽　□ egg-hunting 卵狩り　□ incubation room ふ化室
□ baby chick ひよこ　□ in advance 事前に　□ come straight to 直接～に来る　□ population 人口
□ via ～経由で

★★★★★

22. According to the Web page, what is true about Folksy Farm?

(A) It is exclusively for adults.
(B) It sells food to customers.
(C) It is open every day of the week.
(D) It does not require an entry fee.

ウェブページによると、Folksy Farm について正しいことは何ですか。

(A) 大人専用である。
(B) 食品を顧客に販売している。
(C) 毎日営業している。
(D) 入場料は不要である。

Folksy Farm について正しいことは何かを問う選択肢照合型問題。❶・❸・❺・❼に、それぞれの体験活動営業日が記載されており、すべての曜日があることから、毎日営業していることがわかる。以上より、それを言い換えた **(C)** が正解となる。入場料が不要という記載はないので (D) は不正解。

☐ exclusively for ～専用 ☐ entry fee 入場料

★★★★★

23. What do all the activities have in common?

(A) They start in the morning.
(B) They involve touching animals.
(C) They include harvesting crops.
(D) They deal with baby animals.

すべての体験活動に共通することは何ですか。

(A) 午前中に開始する。
(B) 動物に触れることを伴う。
(C) 作物の収穫が含まれている。
(D) 動物の赤ちゃんを扱っている。

すべての体験活動に共通しているものは何かが問われている。体験活動に目を通すと、❷「牛の乳しぼり」、❹「子羊へ、哺乳瓶からミルクを飲ませ、羊の毛刈りを学ぶ」、❻「乗馬の基本を習得、仔馬へおやつをあげる」、❽「ひよこをなでる」、とすべての項目で動物に触れることがわかる。以上より、それを言い換えた **(B)** が正解。他の選択肢はすべてに共通しているわけではないので、いずれも不正解。

☐ harvest ～を収穫する ☐ deal with ～を扱う

★★★★★

24. How can visitors pay a lower price?

(A) By sending an e-mail
(B) By going to the farm in person
(C) By visiting with a large group
(D) By purchasing tickets online

訪問者が安い価格で支払うにはどうしたらいいですか。

(A) Eメールを送る
(B) 直接農場に行く
(C) 大人数で訪れる
(D) オンラインでチケットを購入する

訪問者が安い価格で支払うためにはどうするかが問われている。❾で「ウェブサイトからチケットを事前注文すると割引となる」と述べられているため、オンラインでの購買、つまり **(D)** が正解となる。(A) と (C) は、メールするのは大人数での申し込みの場合であり、低価格という記載がないため、不正解。

☐ in person 直接

★★☆☆☆

25. What is suggested about Folksy Farm?

(A) It is most popular on the weekends.
(B) It is located in a rural area.
(C) It posts advertisements in multiple cities.
(D) It opened last year.

Folksy Farm について何が示唆されていますか。

(A) 週末に最も人気がある。
(B) 田舎にある。
(C) 多数の都市に広告を出している。
(D) 昨年開業した。

Folksy Farm について何が示唆されているかを問う選択肢照合型問題。❿で「Folksy Farm は市から南に 1 時間程度、人口わずか 200 人の小さな町にある」と述べている。ここから、都市部から離れ、人口の少ない閑散としたエリアを a rural area と表現した **(B)** が正解となる。(A) 週末に人気がある、(C) 広告を出稿した地域、(D) いつ開業したか、については本文に記載がなく、いずれも不正解。

□ rural 田舎の　□ post（広告等）を出す、掲載する　□ multiple 多数の

問題 22 から 25 は次のウェブページに関するものです。

http://www.folksyfarm.com/whatson

Folksy Farm

トップメニュー	ふれあい動物園	農場体験活動	チケットを買う

あなたやあなたのお子さまは農業に関心がありますか？　動物が好きですか？　それなら、どうぞ Folksy Farm にお越しください。安全で心が躍る環境で、両方について学ぶことができます！今季の体験活動予定表はこちらです。

酪農―火曜日と土曜日 午前 10 時から午後 2 時
牛の乳しぼりをした後、トラクターに乗ってさまざまな種類の牛を見に行きましょう。

羊飼い―水曜日と金曜日 午前 10 時から午後 2 時
かわいらしい春の子羊に哺乳瓶からミルクを飲ませ、正しい羊の毛刈りについて学びましょう。

馬の飼育係―土曜日と日曜日 午後 1 時から午後 5 時
乗馬の基本を習得して、仔馬に大好きなおやつをあげましょう。

養鶏農家―月曜日と木曜日 午後 1 時から午後 5 時
卵狩りコンテストに参加して、ふ化室を訪れましょう。ひよこをなでることができます。

ウェブサイトからチケットを事前注文すると 10 パーセント割引となります。＊または直接農場にご来場ください。

Folksy Farm は市から南に 1 時間程度、人口わずか 200 人の小さな町 Chester Flats にあります！Highway 47 でお越しいただけます。出口 14 から降りて、左折してください。お会いできることを楽しみにしています！

＊ 大人数での来場をご検討の場合、事前に E メール（*info@folksyfarm.com*）でお問い合わせください。

GO ON
TO THE
NEXT PAGE!

Questions 26-29 refer to the following online chat discussion.

Live Chat

Neil Adams [9:13 A.M.]
Hello, everyone. I'm back from my trip. I'm sorry that I wasn't able to attend last week's meeting with Ms. Warner from Brixton's Department Stores. How did it go?

Gunther Jarvis [9:14 A.M.]
Welcome back! Did your inspections go well? I caught a cold last week, so only Leslie was able to meet with Ms. Warner.

Neil Adams [9:15 A.M.]
Yes, they went very well. The new factory will allow us to create twice the number of T-shirts that we were making before.

Leslie Mao [9:17 A.M.]
It's good to have you back, Neil. I'm happy to report that Ms. Warner wants to start selling our T-shirts at all of their west-coast stores. She said that their customers will appreciate that we specialize in luxury T-shirts only.

Neil Adams [9:18 A.M.]
Fantastic.

Gunther Jarvis [9:19 A.M.]
That's not all. Singer Christine Nomura has agreed to endorse Divinity Apparel. She'll be wearing an item from our fall line in the picture on the cover of her next album. And yesterday she praised our company's environmentally friendly production methods in an interview on *The Bob Parker Show*.

Neil Adams [9:20 A.M.]
I'm looking forward to watching it. Really great work, everyone.

26. Why did Mr. Adams miss last week's meeting?

    (A) He was on vacation.
    (B) He was sick.
    (C) He had to attend a meeting with another client.
    (D) He was inspecting a factory.

27. What is indicated about Divinity Apparel?

    (A) It runs television advertisements.
    (B) Its production capabilities are expected to increase.
    (C) It is raising the prices of its products.
    (D) Its products are sold nationwide.

28. At 9:19 A.M., what does Mr. Jarvis most likely mean when he writes, "That's not all"?

    (A) The company's products will be sold in additional stores.
    (B) They should have gotten a better deal from Ms. Warner.
    (C) A new marketing tactic has been successful.
    (D) He has more positive news to share.

29. How will most likely Ms. Nomura promote the company?

    (A) By singing a song
    (B) By wearing a T-shirt
    (C) By attending an interview
    (D) By hosting a giveaway

Single Q4

P. 126

Questions 26-29 refer to the following online chat discussion.

Live Chat

Neil Adams [9:13 A.M.]
Hello, everyone. ❶ I'm back from my trip. ❷ I'm sorry that I wasn't able to attend last week's meeting with Ms. Warner from Brixton's Department Stores. How did it go?

Gunther Jarvis [9:14 A.M.]
Welcome back! ❸ Did your inspections go well? I caught a cold last week, so only Leslie was able to meet with Ms. Warner.

Neil Adams [9:15 A.M.]
Yes, they went very well. ❹ The new factory will allow us to create twice the number of T-shirts that we were making before.

Leslie Mao [9:17 A.M.]
It's good to have you back, Neil. ❺ I'm happy to report that Ms. Warner wants to start selling our T-shirts at all of their west-coast stores. She said that their customers will appreciate that we specialize in luxury T-shirts only.

Neil Adams [9:18 A.M.]
Fantastic.

Gunther Jarvis [9:19 A.M.]
❻ That's not all. ❼ Singer Christine Nomura has agreed to endorse Divinity Apparel. ❽ She'll be wearing an item from our fall line in the picture on the cover of her next album. And yesterday she praised our company's environmentally friendly production methods in an interview on *The Bob Parker Show*.

Neil Adams [9:20 A.M.]
I'm looking forward to watching it. Really great work, everyone.

☐ trip（テーマがビジネスの場合）出張　☐ inspection 視察　☐ go well うまくいく
☐ catch a cold 風邪をひく　☐ allow A to B A が B することを可能にする　☐ create ～を製作する
☐ west-coast 西海岸の　☐ appreciate ～を高く評価する　☐ specialize in ～を専門とする　☐ luxury 高級な
☐ fantastic 素晴らしい　☐ endorse ～を支持する　☐ fall line 秋シリーズの商品　☐ praise ～を称賛する
☐ environmentally friendly 環境にやさしい　☐ method 方法

26. Why did Mr. Adams miss last week's meeting?

(A) He was on vacation.
(B) He was sick.
(C) He had to attend a meeting with another client.
(D) He was inspecting a factory.

Adams さんは、なぜ先週の会議を欠席しましたか。

(A) 休暇だった。
(B) 病気だった。
(C) 他の顧客との会議に出席しなければならなかった。
(D) 工場の視察をしていた。

Adams さんがなぜ先週の会議を欠席したかが問われている。Adams さんは❶・❷で「今出張から戻った」「先週の会議に参加できず申し訳ない」と述べ、その直後に Jarvis さんが❸で「視察は順調でしたか」と尋ねている。Adams さんはそれに対し、❹で「視察は順調で、新工場は 2 倍の T シャツを製造できる」と返答していることから、工場に視察に行っていたとわかる。よって、正解は **(D)** となる。

□ on vacation 休暇中の　□ inspect 〜を視察する

27. What is indicated about Divinity Apparel?

(A) It runs television advertisements.
(B) Its production capabilities are expected to increase.
(C) It is raising the prices of its products.
(D) Its products are sold nationwide.

Divinity Apparel 社について何が示されていますか。

(A) テレビ広告を流している。
(B) 生産能力の向上が期待できる。
(C) 製品の価格を引き上げている。
(D) 製品が全国的に売られている。

Divinity Apparel 社について示されていることが問われている。❹で Adams さんは、「新工場では、以前の 2 倍の数の T シャツを製造できる見込みだ」と述べている。これを生産能力の向上と言い換えた、**(B)** が正解となる。

□ run（広告等）を放映する　□ production capability 生産能力　□ raise 〜を引き上げる　□ nationwide 全国で

28. At 9:19 A.M., what does Mr. Jarvis most likely mean when he writes, "That's not all"?

(A) The company's products will be sold in additional stores.
(B) They should have gotten a better deal from Ms. Warner.
(C) A new marketing tactic has been successful.
(D) He has more positive news to share.

午前 9 時 19 分に、Jarvis さんは "That's not all" という発言で、何を意味していると考えられますか。

(A) 会社の製品が新たに他のお店でも売られる。
(B) Warner さんからより良い取引ができたはずである。
(C) 新しいマーケティング戦略が成功した。
(D) 共有するためのさらなる良いニュースを持っている。

意図問題。問われている❻は「それだけではない」という意味。前後を見ると、❺で「うれしいご報告ですが、Warner さんが西海岸の全店舗で当社の T シャツを売りたいと言っている。彼女は〜」とポジティブな情報を述べ、❼で「歌手の Nomura さんが Divinity Apparel 社を支持することに同意した」と、さらにポジティブな情報を述べている。つまり、❻「それだけではない」は「さらに良い情報がある」という意図があるとわかる。よって、これを言い換えた **(D)** が正解となる。意図問題は、前後にポジティブ⇔ネガティブ、ネガティブ→ネガティブというパターンもある。文脈をしっかり意識して解こう。

□ deal 取引　□ marketing tactic マーケティング戦略　□ positive 明るい兆しのある

29. How will most likely Ms. Nomura promote the company?

(A) By singing a song
(B) By wearing a T-shirt
(C) By attending an interview
(D) By hosting a giveaway

Nomura さんはどのように会社をアピールすると考えられますか。

(A) 歌を歌うことにより
(B) T シャツを着ることにより
(C) インタビューに参加することにより
(D) 賞品付きクイズ番組の司会をすることにより

Nomura さんはどのように会社をアピールするかが問われている。Nomura さんは❼から、歌手であり、話し手達の会社（Divinty Apparel 社）を支持することに同意したことがわかる。次に❽で「次のアルバムのジャケット写真で当社の秋シリーズの商品を着てくれるそうだ」と述べている。❺で、話し手達の会社は高級 T シャツを専門に扱っていると述べていることから、Nomura さんは T シャツを着ると考えられる。以上から、正解は **(B)**。(A) は、歌手とあるが、歌を歌うことが会社のアピールにつながるとは述べられていないので、不正解。

問題 26 から 29 は次のオンラインチャットの話し合いに関するものです。

Live Chat

Neil Adams [午前 9 時 13 分]
みなさん、こんにちは。出張から戻りました。先週は Brixton's Department Stores の Warner さんとの会議に参加できず、すみませんでした。手ごたえはいかがでしたでしょうか？

Gunther Jarvis [午前 9 時 14 分]
おかえりなさい！　視察は順調でしたか？　先週、私は風邪をひいてしまって、Warner さんと会えたのは Leslie さんだけなんです。

Neil Adams [午前 9 時 15 分]
はい、視察はとても順調でした。新工場では、以前の 2 倍の数の T シャツを製造できます。

Leslie Mao [午前 9 時 17 分]
Neil さん、戻ってきてくれてうれしいです。うれしいご報告ですが、Warner さんが西海岸の全店舗で当社の T シャツを売りたいと言っています。彼女は、当社が高級 T シャツのみを専門に扱っていることを、彼女のお客様たちが高く評価するだろうと言っていました。

Neil Adams [午前 9 時 18 分]
素晴らしい。

Gunther Jarvis [午前 9 時 19 分]
それだけではありません。歌手の Christine Nomura が Divinity Apparel 社を支持することに同意しました。次のアルバムのジャケット写真で当社の秋シリーズの商品を着てくれるそうです。そして昨日、*The Bob Parker Show* でのインタビューで、当社の環境に配慮した製造方法について賞賛しました。

Neil Adams [午前 9 時 20 分]
見るのが楽しみですね。みなさん、素晴らしい働きです。

Questions 30-34 refer to the following e-mail and article.

5分00秒

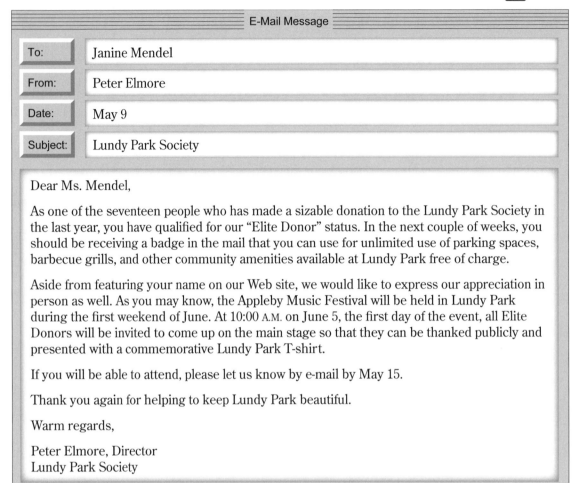

E-Mail Message

To:	Janine Mendel
From:	Peter Elmore
Date:	May 9
Subject:	Lundy Park Society

Dear Ms. Mendel,

As one of the seventeen people who has made a sizable donation to the Lundy Park Society in the last year, you have qualified for our "Elite Donor" status. In the next couple of weeks, you should be receiving a badge in the mail that you can use for unlimited use of parking spaces, barbecue grills, and other community amenities available at Lundy Park free of charge.

Aside from featuring your name on our Web site, we would like to express our appreciation in person as well. As you may know, the Appleby Music Festival will be held in Lundy Park during the first weekend of June. At 10:00 A.M. on June 5, the first day of the event, all Elite Donors will be invited to come up on the main stage so that they can be thanked publicly and presented with a commemorative Lundy Park T-shirt.

If you will be able to attend, please let us know by e-mail by May 15.

Thank you again for helping to keep Lundy Park beautiful.

Warm regards,

Peter Elmore, Director
Lundy Park Society

Appleby Music Festival Comes to Springdale

Springdale (June 7) — The annual Appleby Music Festival took place for the first time in Springdale on June 5 and 6. Held for the past decade in Trinity Park in the nearby town of Fulton, the festival organizers decided to move it to Lundy Park this year. The decision to have more space turned out to be the right one, as a record number of visitors from across the region showed up to enjoy the many musical performances.

Springdale's mayor, Rosie Harrison, stated that: "Lundy Park is one of the main reasons that so many people choose to visit our little town." Ms. Harrison joined the Lundy Park Society's president on stage to thank those who contributed more than $1,000 to recent park-improvement projects. She also helped him hand out gifts to these donors, who received warm applause from the audience.

Although next year's Appleby Music Festival is a while away, Ms. Harrison mentioned that it may be held in Springdale again. "The festival organizers reported being very happy with the turnout. We hope to welcome them back next year."

30. Why did Mr. Elmore write to Ms. Mendel?

(A) To solicit another donation from her
(B) To explain how donated funds were used
(C) To tell her about an upcoming fundraiser
(D) To recognize her contribution to an organization

31. What is true about the Appleby Music Festival?

(A) It takes place once every two years.
(B) It moved to a larger venue this year.
(C) It was first held five years ago in Trinity Park.
(D) It was free to attend for Lundy Park Society members.

32. What is suggested about Springdale?

(A) It has a smaller population than Fulton.
(B) It is a popular tourist destination.
(C) It is home to several large parks.
(D) It will host other music festivals throughout the year.

33. What is indicated about Ms. Mendel?

(A) She founded the Lundy Park Society.
(B) She recently moved to Springdale.
(C) She visited Trinity Park last year.
(D) She donated over $1,000 to the Lundy Park Society.

34. According to the article, what did Ms. Harrison most likely do on the stage?

(A) She thanked the festival organizers.
(B) She presented donors with free T-shirts.
(C) She pledged to donate her own money to the park.
(D) She talked about why she likes the town of Springdale.

 P. 132

Questions 30-34 refer to the following e-mail and article.

E-Mail Message

To:	Janine Mendel
From:	Peter Elmore
Date:	May 9
Subject:	Lundy Park Society

Dear Ms. Mendel,

❶ As one of the seventeen people who has made a sizable donation to the Lundy Park Society in the last year, you have qualified for our "Elite Donor" status. In the next couple of weeks, you should be receiving a badge in the mail that you can use for unlimited use of parking spaces, barbecue grills, and other community amenities available at Lundy Park free of charge.

Aside from featuring your name on our Web site, we would like to express our appreciation in person as well. ❷ As you may know, the Appleby Music Festival will be held in Lundy Park during the first weekend of June. At 10:00 A.M. on June 5, the first day of the event, all Elite Donors will be invited to come up on the main stage so that they can be thanked publicly and presented with a commemorative Lundy Park T-shirt.

If you will be able to attend, please let us know by e-mail by May 15.

Thank you again for helping to keep Lundy Park beautiful.

Warm regards,

Peter Elmore, Director
Lundy Park Society

Appleby Music Festival Comes to Springdale

Springdale (June 7) — ❸ The annual Appleby Music Festival took place for the first time in Springdale on June 5 and 6. ❹ Held for the past decade in Trinity Park in the nearby town of Fulton, the festival organizers decided to move it to Lundy Park this year. ❺ The decision to have more space turned out to be the right one, as a record number of visitors from across the region showed up to enjoy the many musical performances.

❻ Springdale's mayor, Rosie Harrison, stated that: "Lundy Park is one of the main reasons that so many people choose to visit our little town." ❼ Ms. Harrison joined the Lundy Park Society's president on stage to thank those who contributed more than $1,000 to recent park-improvement projects. ❽ She also helped him hand out gifts to these donors, who received warm applause from the audience.

Although next year's Appleby Music Festival is a while away, Ms. Harrison mentioned that it may be held in Springdale again. "The festival organizers reported being very happy with the turnout. We hope to welcome them back next year."

★★☆☆☆

30. Why did Mr. Elmore write to Ms. Mendel?

(A) To solicit another donation from her
(B) To explain how donated funds were used
(C) To tell her about an upcoming fundraiser
(D) To recognize her contribution to an organization

Elmore さんはなぜ Mendel さんに E メールを書きましたか。

(A) 別の寄付を募るため
(B) 寄付された資金がどのように使用されたかを説明するため
(C) 今後の募金活動について伝えるため
(D) 組織への貢献を表彰するため

🔍 Elmore さんはなぜ Mendel に E メールを出したかが問われている。1 文書目の E メールの冒頭❶で Elmore さんは Mendel さんに「昨年 Lundy Park Society に多額の寄付をされた 1 人として、当協会の "Elite Donor（貢献者）" の資格を取得した」と述べている。ここから、ある組織への寄付にした功績が認められた、ということがわかるので、それを言い換えた **(D)** が正解。recognize one's contribution で「貢献を認める・称える」という意味になる。(A)(B)(C) に関しては特に記載がなく不正解となる。

✎ □ solicit ～を懇願する　□ donated fund 寄付された資金　□ fundraiser 募金活動
□ recognize ～を認める、表彰する

★★★☆☆

31. What is true about the Appleby Music Festival?

(A) It takes place once every two years.
(B) It moved to a larger venue this year.
(C) It was first held five years ago in Trinity Park.
(D) It was free to attend for Lundy Park Society members.

Appleby Music Festival について当てはまることは何ですか。

(A) 2 年に 1 度開催される。
(B) 今年はより大きい会場に場所を移した。
(C) 5 年前に初めて Trinity Park で開催された。
(D) Lundy Park Society のメンバーは無料で参加できた。

🔍 Appleby Music Festival について当てはまることを問う選択肢照合型問題。2 文書目の記事の❸・❹・❺より、「Appleby Music Festival が毎年恒例である」「今年 Springdale で初めて開催された」「最近は Fulton の Trinity Park で開催していたが、今年はより広い Lundy Park に移動した」ということが述べられているので、本年は今までより大きな会場に変更したことがわかる。以上より、これを言い換えた **(B)** が正解。❺の "The decision to have more space" が選択肢の It moved to a larger venue に対応している。(A) は頻度、(C) は時期、が文書の内容と異なる。(D) はメンバー全員が無料、という言及がない。

✎ □ take place 開催される　□ venue 会場

32. What is suggested about Springdale?

(A) It has a smaller population than Fulton.
(B) It is a popular tourist destination.
(C) It is home to several large parks.
(D) It will host other music festivals throughout the year.

Springdale について何が示唆されていますか。

(A) Fulton よりも人口が少ない。
(B) 人気の観光地である。
(C) 大きな公園がいくつかある。
(D) その年の間ずっと、他の音楽祭を開催する。

Springdale について示唆されていることを問う選択肢照合型問題。Springdale 市長が記事の❻で「非常に多くの人々がこの小さな町を訪れることを決めた主な理由の１つは Lundy Park だ」と述べている。つまり、Lundy Park 自体は人が訪れるような理由がもともとあった、ということが示唆されているので、これを「人気の観光地」と表現した (B) が正解となる。(A) は人口数、(C) は大きな公園の有無、(D) は音楽祭開催頻度、について言及がないため不正解。

□ tourist destination 観光地　□ host ～を開催する　□ throughout ～を通じて

---

33. What is indicated about Ms. Mendel?

(A) She founded the Lundy Park Society.
(B) She recently moved to Springdale.
(C) She visited Trinity Park last year.
(D) She donated over $1,000 to the Lundy Park Society.

Mendel さんについて何が示されていますか。

(A) Lundy Park Society を設立した。
(B) 最近 Springdale に引っ越した。
(C) 昨年 Trinity Park を訪問した。
(D) Lundy Park Society に 1,000 ドル以上を寄付した。

Mendel さんについて示されていることを問う選択肢照合型問題。まず、Mendel さんは１文書目のＥメールの❶で、「Lundy Park Society に多額の寄付をしたことから、貢献者の資格を取得した」と述べている。また、❷で「Appleby Music Festival が Lundy Park で開催予定で、すべての貢献者をメインステージにお招きし、直接の感謝と Lundy Park の記念Ｔシャツをプレゼントする」と述べている。次に、２文書目の記事の❼で「Springdale 市長の Harrison さんが、Lundy Park Society の会長と共に、公園の改修プロジェクトに 1,000 ドル以上の寄付をしてくれた人々に感謝を述べた」とある。これらの情報から、Mendel さんは 1,000 ドル以上を寄付したことがわかるため、正解は (D) となる。(A)(B)(C) は、それぞれ Mendel さんが関与した記載がなく、不正解。

□ found ～を設立する

---

34. According to the article, what did Ms. Harrison most likely do on the stage?

(A) She thanked the festival organizers.
(B) She presented donors with free T-shirts.
(C) She pledged to donate her own money to the park.
(D) She talked about why she likes the town of Springdale.

記事によると、Harrison さんはステージの上でおそらく何をしましたか。

(A) フェスティバルの主催者に感謝を述べた。
(B) 寄付者たちに無料のＴシャツをプレゼントした。
(C) 自身のお金を公園に寄付することを約束した。
(D) なぜ Springdale の町が気に入っているのかについて話した。

記事から、Harrison さんはステージの上でおそらく何をしたかを問う問題。２文書目の記事の❽で「貢献者たちに贈呈品を手渡すことを手伝った」とある。１文書目のＥメールの❷で「貢献者をメインステージに招き、記念Ｔシャツをプレゼントする」と述べられているので、贈呈品はＴシャツであると推察される。よって、正解は (B) とわかる。❽の "gifts" が何を意味するのかを検索できないと解けない難問。(A) は感謝を述べているのは主催者ではなく貢献者。(C)(D) については、ステージ上で行った内容には当てはまらないため不正解。

□ thank ～に感謝する　□ organizer 主催者　□ donor 寄付者

受信者： Janine Mendel
送信者： Peter Elmore
日付： 5 月 9 日
件名： Lundy Park Society

Mendel 様

昨年 Lundy Park Society に多額の寄付をされた 17 人の内の 1 人として、あなたは当協会の"貢献者"の資格を取得されました。2 週間以内に郵便で、Lundy Park の駐車場、バーベキューグリル、その他のコミュニティー設備を無料で無制限にご利用いただけるバッジをお届けします。

ウェブサイトにお名前を掲載するだけでなく、直接感謝の意を表したいと思います。ご存じかもしれませんが、Appleby Music Festival が 6 月の最初の週末に Lundy Park で開催されます。イベントの初日である 6 月 5 日午前 10 時に、すべての貢献者をメインステージにお招きし、皆さんの前で感謝を伝え、Lundy Park の記念 T シャツをプレゼントいたします。

ご参加いただける場合は、5 月 15 日までに E メールにてご連絡ください。

Lundy Park の美観保全にご協力いただき、重ねてお礼申し上げます。

敬具

Lundy Park Society
管理者 Peter Elmore

Appleby Music Festival が Springdale にやって来た

Springdale（6 月 7 日）— 毎年恒例の Appleby Music Festival が 6 月 5 日と 6 日に、Springdale で初めて開催された。この 10 年間は近くの町である Fulton にある Trinity Park で開催されていたが、音楽祭の主催者が今年は Lundy Park に場所を移すことに決めた。より広いスペースを求めて下した決定は結果的に正解で、たくさんの音楽演奏を楽しむために地域全体から記録的な数の訪問者が来場した。

Springdale の市長である Rosie Harrison 氏は、「非常に多くの人々がこの小さな町を訪れることを選ぶ主な理由の 1 つは Lundy Park です。」と述べている。Harrison 氏は Lundy Park Society の会長と共にステージに上がり、最近行われた公園の改修プロジェクトに 1,000 ドル以上の寄付をしてくれた人々に感謝を述べた。また、聴衆から温かい拍手を受けたその寄付者たちに贈呈品を手渡すことを手伝った。

来年の Appleby Music Festival はまだ先のことであるが、Harrison さんは再度 Springdale で開催される可能性があることを述べた。「音楽祭の主催者は訪問者数にとても満足している。来年もまた戻ってきてもらいたい。」

Questions 35-39 refer to the following survey and letter.

5分00秒

Chirona Hotel Survey

Dear Valued Guest:
Please take a moment to complete this survey by checking the applicable boxes in the chart below.

	Strongly agree	Agree	Disagree	Strongly disagree	N/A
My overall experience was excellent.		✓			
The reservation process was efficient.		✓			
The check-in/check-out process was timely.	✓				
The front desk staff was courteous and helpful.	✓				
The room was clean and comfortable.		✓			
The restaurant staff was reliable and friendly.					✓
Room service was easy to use and efficient.			✓		
The fitness center was adequately furnished.		✓			

Comments:

My wife and I have been coming to Chirona Hotel for years. The staff is always very friendly, and the rooms are comfortable.

On this particular stay, the hotel felt a little bit too crowded because of the conference being held there. I also experienced a problem with my room service order. It took almost an hour to come, and the bacon and eggs were cold when they arrived.

Otherwise, everything was great.

Name:	Rewards #:	Check in:	Check out:
Jason Patterson	*894453*	*08/24*	*08/26*

Chirona Hotel
51 Crest Lane, Pearl Beach, OR 97188

September 1

Jason Patterson
9346 Western Avenue,
Portland, OR 97124

Dear Mr. Patterson,

On behalf of the staff at the Chirona Hotel, I apologize for the problem you experienced during your recent stay with us.

After reading your comments, hotel management looked into the matter right away. We found that after you placed your order, our new cook prepared your meal and set it down on a room service cart just as he had been trained to do. However, what he did not put on the cart was the order form with your name and room number on it, so other staff members did not know the meal was yours. After some time passed, another cook realized that it was meant for you, at which point it was taken to your room.

In the future, we will make sure new kitchen staff members are better trained to carry out all room service procedures properly. We are very sorry for the inconvenience. We have refunded you for the cost of the meal, and we hope you will accept the $30.00 voucher included with this letter as a form of apology. It can be redeemed for accommodation, dining, or other services at any Chirona Hotel in the country. I recommend visiting the new Chirona Hotel that opened in Cedar Falls last month. It's truly beautiful, and at the moment rooms are 25% off for rewards program members. Just provide your rewards number when booking. You'll find more details in the enclosed brochure.

Yours sincerely,

Beatrice Clark

Beatrice Clark
Guest Services Manager
Chirona Hotel

35. What does Mr. Patterson suggest in the survey?

- (A) He had difficulty reserving a hotel room.
- (B) He was unhappy about the check-in process.
- (C) He exercised during his hotel stay.
- (D) He ate dinner at the hotel's restaurant.

36. What is indicated about Mr. Patterson?

- (A) He ordered room service in the morning.
- (B) He stayed at the hotel for three nights.
- (C) He attended a conference during his stay.
- (D) He is a member of the hotel's rewards program.

37. What is the main purpose of the letter?

- (A) To explain the details of the hotel's policies
- (B) To investigate the cause of a customer's problem
- (C) To introduce the grand opening of a new hotel
- (D) To preserve a relationship with a repeat customer

38. What caused Mr. Patterson's room service experience to be unsatisfactory?

- (A) The hotel was unusually busy on the days of his stay.
- (B) His meal was sent to the wrong hotel room.
- (C) There was a communication problem among the staff.
- (D) A cook had not been trained to make modifications to meals.

39. What is included with the letter?

- (A) A receipt
- (B) A questionnaire
- (C) An invoice
- (D) A brochure

P. 138

Double

Questions 35-39 refer to the following survey and letter.

Chirona Hotel Survey

Dear Valued Guest:
Please take a moment to complete this survey by checking the applicable boxes in the chart below.

	Strongly agree	Agree	Disagree	Strongly disagree	N/A
My overall experience was excellent.		✓			
The reservation process was efficient.		✓			
The check-in/check-out process was timely.	✓				
The front desk staff was courteous and helpful.	✓				
The room was clean and comfortable.		✓			
The restaurant staff was reliable and friendly.					✓
Room service was easy to use and efficient.			✓		
❶ The fitness center was adequately furnished.		✓			

Comments:

❷ _My wife and I have been coming to Chirona Hotel for years._ _The staff is always very friendly, and the rooms are comfortable._

On this particular stay, the hotel felt a little bit too crowded because of the conference being held there. ❸ _I also experienced a problem with my room service order._ ❹ _It took almost an hour to come, and the bacon and eggs were cold when they arrived._

Otherwise, everything was great.

Name:	Rewards #:	Check in:	Check out:
Jason Patterson	_894453_	_08/24_	_08/26_

Chirona Hotel
51 Crest Lane, Pearl Beach, OR 97188

September 1

Jason Patterson
9346 Western Avenue,
Portland, OR 97124

Dear Mr. Patterson,

❺ On behalf of the staff at the Chirona Hotel, I apologize for the problem you experienced during your recent stay with us.

❻ After reading your comments, hotel management looked into the matter right away. ❼ We found that after you placed your order, our new cook prepared your meal and set it down on a room service cart just as he had been trained to do. ❽ However, what he did not put on the cart was the order form with your name and room number on it, so other staff members did not know the meal was yours. After some time passed, another cook realized that it was meant for you, at which point it was taken to your room.

❾ In the future, we will make sure new kitchen staff members are better trained to carry out all room service procedures properly. We are very sorry for the inconvenience. We have refunded you for the cost of the meal, and we hope you will accept the $30.00 voucher included with this letter as a form of apology. It can be redeemed for accommodation, dining, or other services at any Chirona Hotel in the country. ❿ I recommend visiting the new Chirona Hotel that opened in Cedar Falls last month. It's truly beautiful, and at the moment rooms are 25% off for rewards program members. ⓫ Just provide your rewards number when booking. ⓬ You'll find more details in the enclosed brochure.

Yours sincerely,

Beatrice Clark

Beatrice Clark
Guest Services Manager
Chirona Hotel

調査票
☐ applicable box 該当欄　☐ overall 全体の　☐ efficient 効率的な　☐ timely 時間がちょうどよい
☐ courteous 丁寧な　☐ comfortable 快適な　☐ reliable 信頼できる　☐ friendly 親切な
☐ easy to use 使いやすい　☐ for years 何年も　☐ this particular 特に今回の　☐ otherwise それ以外では

手紙
☐ on behalf of ～を代表して　☐ management 経営陣、幹部　☐ look into ～を調査する　☐ right away 早急に
☐ train ～を教育する　☐ pass 経過する　☐ at which point その時点で　☐ carry out ～を実行する
☐ procedure 手順　☐ properly 正しく　☐ inconvenience 不便　☐ refund ～に払い戻す
☐ voucher クーポン券　☐ redeem ～を引き換える　☐ truly 本当に　☐ at the moment 現在
☐ rewards program 報酬プログラム　☐ enclosed 同封の

★★☆☆☆

35. What does Mr. Patterson suggest in the survey?

 (A)　He had difficulty reserving a hotel room.
 (B)　He was unhappy about the check-in process.
 (C)　He exercised during his hotel stay.
 (D)　He ate dinner at the hotel's restaurant.

Patterson さんは調査表で何を示唆していますか。

 (A)　ホテルの予約に苦労した。
 (B)　チェックインの手順に不満があった。
 (C)　ホテルでの滞在中に運動した。
 (D)　ホテルのレストランで夕食をとった。

🔍 Patterson さんは調査表で何を示唆したかが問われている。調査表の項目を見ていくと、❶の「フィットネスセンター内には十分な器具が備えつけられていた」で「そう思う」にチェックを入れているため、ここから Patterson さんがホテル滞在時に運動をしたことが示唆されている。以上から、正解は **(C)**。Patterson さんはレストランに関する項目について「該当しない」にチェックを入れているため (D) は間違い、(A) に関する項目はなく、(B) は「予約手順が効率的だった」という項目で「そう思う」にチェックを入れている。

✎ ☐ have difficulty (in) doing ～するのに苦労する　☐ unhappy 不満な　☐ exercise 運動する

★★★★☆

36. What is indicated about Mr. Patterson?

 (A)　He ordered room service in the morning.
 (B)　He stayed at the hotel for three nights.
 (C)　He attended a conference during his stay.
 (D)　He is a member of the hotel's rewards program.

Patterson さんについて何が示されていますか。

 (A)　朝、ルームサービスを注文した。
 (B)　ホテルに 3 泊した。
 (C)　滞在中に協議会に出席した。
 (D)　ホテルの報酬プログラム会員である。

🔍 Patterson さんについて何が示されているかを問う選択肢照合型問題。2 文書目の手紙の❿で、ホテル側は Patterson さんに新しくに開業した Chirona Hotel を勧め、「現在は報酬プログラム会員様のみ 25 パーセント割引で提供」と述べている。そして、⓫で「予約の際に Patterson さんの報酬番号（your rewards number）をお知らせください」と述べているので、ここから Patterson さんがホテルの報酬プログラム会員になっていることがわかる。以上から、正解は **(D)**。(A) いつルームサービスを注文したか、(C) 協議会の出席、については述べられていないため、いずれも不正解。(B) は、1 文書目のチェックイン、チェックアウトの日付から 2 泊とわかる。

✎ ☐ night 晩（stay ... for ○○ nights …に○○泊する）

37. What is the main purpose of the letter?

- (A) To explain the details of the hotel's policies
- (B) To investigate the cause of a customer's problem
- (C) To introduce the grand opening of a new hotel
- **(D)** To preserve a relationship with a repeat customer

手紙の主な目的は何ですか。

- (A) ホテルの方針について詳細を説明すること
- (B) 顧客の問題の原因を調査すること
- (C) 新しいホテルのグランドオープンを紹介すること
- **(D)** リピート客との関係を維持すること

🔍 2文書目の手紙の目的が問われている。手紙のそれぞれの段落の冒頭❺・❻・❾を読むと、「先日のホテルでのご迷惑のお詫び」「運営者がすぐに問題の調査を実施した」「今後の対策」と、お客様のコメントに対するお詫びと今後は問題の再発を防ぐ旨を伝えている。そして、調査表❷・❸・❹から、これらはホテルのリピーターであるPattersonさんが遭遇した問題に対する返事だとわかる。以上から、リピーターとの良好な関係の維持が手紙の目的だとわかる。よって、正解は **(D)** となる。

✏️ ☐ detail 詳細　☐ investigate 〜を調査する　☐ cause 原因　☐ grand opening グランドオープン
☐ preserve 〜を維持する　☐ repeat customer リピート客

★★★☆☆

38. What caused Mr. Patterson's room service experience to be unsatisfactory?

- (A) The hotel was unusually busy on the days of his stay.
- (B) His meal was sent to the wrong hotel room.
- **(C)** There was a communication problem among the staff.
- (D) A cook had not been trained to make modifications to meals.

何が原因でPattersonさんのルームサービスの経験は不快なものとなりましたか。

- (A) 滞在期間はホテルが異常に忙しかったこと。
- (B) 食事が違う部屋に届けられたこと。
- **(C)** スタッフ間での意思疎通に問題があったこと。
- (D) コックは食事に変更を加える研修を受けていなかったこと。

🔍 Pattersonさんのルームサービスで不快となった原因が問われている。2文書目の手紙でPattersonさんにお詫びと発生した原因について言及があり、❼・❽で「注文時に新人コックが対応した際、ルームサービスのカートには、手順のとおり食事が置かれたが、名前と部屋番号が書かれた注文書は置かれず、誰のものかわからなかったので時間がかかった」とあるため、スタッフ間で連携が取れなかったということがわかる。以上より、正解は意思疎通に問題があったという内容の **(C)** となる。(A) の「ホテルが忙しい」というのは、この問題の原因としては述べられておらず、(B) の「届け先の間違い」、(D) の「食事の変更」は述べられていないので、いずれも不正解。

✏️ ☐ cook 調理係　☐ make modifications to 〜に変更を加える

★★★★★

39. What is included with the letter?

- (A) A receipt
- (B) A questionnaire
- (C) An invoice
- **(D)** A brochure

手紙には何が同封されていますか。

- (A) レシート
- (B) アンケート
- (C) 請求書
- **(D)** パンフレット

🔍 2文書目の手紙に同封されているものは何かが問われている。手紙の⓬で「詳細は同封のパンフレットをご覧ください」と述べられているため、手紙にはパンフレットが同封されていることがわかる。以上から、正解は **(D)**。

Chirona Hotel 調査

ご宿泊のお客様：
お手数をおかけしますが調査にご協力ください。下の表で該当する
欄にチェックを入れてください。

	とてもそう思う	そう思う	そう思わない	まったくそう思わない	該当しない
全体として素晴らしい経験だった。		✓			
予約手順が効率的だった。		✓			
チェックイン、チェックアウトにかかる時間は短かった。	✓				
フロントデスクのスタッフは丁寧で親切だった。	✓				
部屋は清潔で快適だった。		✓			
レストランのスタッフは信頼でき、親しみやすかった。					✓
ルームサービスは使いやすく効率的だった。			✓		
フィットネスセンターには十分な器具が備えつけられていた。		✓			

コメント：
妻と私は Chirona Hotel には何年も通っています。スタッフはいつもとても親しみやすく、部屋は快適です。
今回の滞在時は、協議会が行われていたためか、ホテルが少々混雑しているように感じました。ルームサービスの注文にも問題がありました。届くまでに 1 時間もかかり、届いた時にはベーコンエッグは冷めてしまっていました。
その他については問題ありませんでした。

お名前：	会員番号：	チェックイン：	チェックアウト：
Jason Patterson	894453	8 月 24 日	8 月 26 日

Chirona Hotel

51 Crest Lane, Pearl Beach, オレゴン州 97188

9 月 1 日

Jason Patterson 様
9346 Western Avenue,
Portland, オレゴン州 97124

Patterson 様

Chirona Hotel のスタッフを代表して、先日の当ホテルでのご滞在中にご迷惑をおかけしたことをお詫びいたします。

お客様のコメントを拝見し、ホテルの経営陣はすぐに問題の調査を行いました。お客様がご注文された後、当ホテルの新人コックは、研修手順のとおりにお食事を準備し、ルームサービスのカートに配置いたしました。しかし、カートにお客様の名前と部屋番号が書かれた注文書が置かれませんでしたので、他のスタッフはお食事がお客様のものだとはわかりませんでした。時間が経ってから、別のコックがお客様のものであると気づき、お食事が運ばれました。

今後は、新人の調理場のスタッフが、すべてのルームサービスの手順を適切に実行できるように研修を強化するつもりです。ご迷惑をおかけし申し訳ございませんでした。お食事代は返金いたしました。また、お詫びとして 30 ドルのクーポン券をお手紙に同封しましたので、お受け取りいただければと思います。クーポン券は、国内の Chirona Hotel でのご宿泊、お食事、その他のサービスにご利用いただけます。先月、新しく Cedar Falls に開業した Chirona Hotel に行かれることをお勧めします。とても美しく、現在、お部屋は報酬プログラム会員様のみ 25 パーセント割引で提供しております。ご予約の際に報酬番号をお知らせください。詳細は同封のパンフレットをご覧ください。

よろしくお願いいたします

Beatrice Clark

Chirona Hotel
顧客サービス部長
Beatrice Clark

To:	All Department Staff
From:	Stacy Simmons, Director
Date:	Tuesday, April 2
Subject:	Orientation and Training

Arcstone Chemical will be welcoming twenty-six new employees to the head office next week, five of whom will be joining our department. As you may remember, new hires receive a general orientation during their first week at the company. During the program, we go over basic information about Arcstone, including our policies and procedures. So, although their first day will be Monday, April 8, they will not be trained to perform their specific roles in their respective departments until the following week, starting on April 15.

Since I will be participating in the orientation next Wednesday and Friday, Eric Murphy will be supervising our department at the times I am unavailable on those days. I realize you have all been busier than usual lately; however, once our new coworkers have been trained and settle in, we will no longer be short-staffed.

Thank you in advance for your cooperation. If you have any questions about the trainees or would like to get involved in their training, please let me or Eric know.

Stacy Simmons

Arcstone Chemical General Orientation Schedule*

Date	Session	Leader
Monday, April 8		
9:00 A.M. to 11:45 A.M.	Welcome, introductions, and tour of the building	Debbie Quinn, Al Owens
1:30 P.M. to 5:00 P.M.	Overview of the company and its management structure	Al Owens
Tuesday, April 9		
9:00 A.M. to 11:30 A.M.	Review of the company's rules and regulations	Al Owens
1:00 P.M. to 5:00 P.M.	Review of the administrative procedures manual	Debbie Quinn, Al Owens
Wednesday, April 10		
9:00 A.M. to 12:30 P.M.	Security and safety at the head office and company facilities	Lloyd Estrada
2:00 P.M. to 5:30 P.M.	Overview of the company's research and development activities	Stacy Simmons
Thursday, April 11		
9:00 A.M. to 12:30 P.M.	Sales and marketing strategy at Arcstone Chemical	Gary Bower
2:00 P.M. to 5:30 P.M.	Overview of international operations and logistics management	Akiko Tanaka
Friday, April 12		
9:00 A.M. to 2:00 P.M.	Introduction to coworkers and lunch with all department directors	All orientation leaders
2:30 P.M. to 5:30 P.M.	Expectations of new employees during departmental training	Debbie Quinn, Al Owens

*All orientation sessions except for the tour and Friday lunch will take place in Conference Room B on the eighth floor. Debbie Quinn and Al Owens from the human resources department are in charge of the orientation. Sessions not conducted by them will be led by the chief directors of the departments relevant to the particular session topic.

From: Al Owens
To: Debbie Quinn
Sent: April 10, 5:52 P.M.

Debbie, I've switched Gary Bower's orientation session with the other one we have scheduled for tomorrow. He has to meet with a big customer outside the office but assured me he'll be back in time. Also, he wants to use two projectors simultaneously during his talk, so I'll need to get the one from the other conference room and set it up for him. See you tomorrow.

Send

40. What is the main purpose of the memo?

(A) To share some details about a training process for new personnel
(B) To explain why a program will begin a week later than scheduled
(C) To provide details about an upcoming department meeting
(D) To inform the staff of a department about changes to a policy

41. In which department does Ms. Simmons probably work?

(A) Administration
(B) Research and development
(C) Sales and marketing
(D) Human resources

42. What are the new hires scheduled to do on their first day at the head office?

(A) Meet Stacy Simmons and Eric Murphy in a conference room
(B) Fill out a number of forms in the human resources department
(C) Learn about the management structure of Arcstone Chemical
(D) Review a list of rules and regulations for company employees

43. What is suggested in the text message?

(A) A customer will need directions to an office building.
(B) Two conference rooms will be used at the same time.
(C) Ms. Tanaka will begin her session at 9:00 A.M.
(D) Mr. Bower's session may have to be cancelled.

44. What will Mr. Owens most likely do on April 11?

(A) Notify directors about a change to the schedule
(B) Confirm that Mr. Bower is prepared for his presentation
(C) Inform Ms. Quinn about a director's problem
(D) Take some equipment to Conference Room B

Triple

 P. 144

Questions 40-44 refer to the following memo, schedule, and text message.

To:　　All Department Staff
From:　**❶** Stacy Simmons, Director
Date:　Tuesday, April 2
Subject:　Orientation and Training

❷ Arcstone Chemical will be welcoming twenty-six new employees to the head office next week, five of whom will be joining our department. As you may remember, **❸** new hires receive a general orientation during their first week at the company. **❹** During the program, we go over basic information about Arcstone, including our policies and procedures. So, although their first day will be Monday, April 8, they will not be trained to perform their specific roles in their respective departments until the following week, starting on April 15.

Since **❺** I will be participating in the orientation next Wednesday and Friday, Eric Murphy will be supervising our department at the times I am unavailable on those days. I realize you have all been busier than usual lately; however, once our new coworkers have been trained and settle in, we will no longer be short-staffed.

Thank you in advance for your cooperation. If you have any questions about the trainees or would like to get involved in their training, please let me or Eric know.

Stacy Simmons

Arcstone Chemical General Orientation Schedule*

Date	Session	Leader
Monday, April 8		
9:00 A.M. to 11:45 A.M.	Welcome, introductions, and tour of the building	Debbie Quinn, Al Owens
1:30 P.M. to 5:00 P.M.	**❻** Overview of the company and its management structure	Al Owens
Tuesday, April 9		
9:00 A.M. to 11:30 A.M.	Review of the company's rules and regulations	Al Owens
1:00 P.M. to 5:00 P.M.	Review of the administrative procedures manual	Debbie Quinn, Al Owens
Wednesday, April 10		
9:00 A.M. to 12:30 P.M.	Security and safety at the head office and company facilities	Lloyd Estrada
2:00 P.M. to 5:30 P.M.	**❼** Overview of the company's research and development activities	Stacy Simmons
Thursday, April 11		
❽ 9:00 A.M. to 12:30 P.M.	Sales and marketing strategy at Arcstone Chemical	Gary Bower
❾ 2:00 P.M. to 5:30 P.M.	Overview of international operations and logistics management	Akiko Tanaka
Friday, April 12		
9:00 A.M. to 2:00 P.M.	Introduction to coworkers and lunch with all department directors	All orientation leaders
2:30 P.M. to 5:30 P.M.	Expectations of new employees during departmental training	Debbie Quinn, Al Owens

***❿** All orientation sessions except for the tour and Friday lunch will take place in Conference Room B on the eighth floor. Debbie Quinn and Al Owens from the human resources department are in charge of the orientation. Sessions not conducted by them will be led by the chief directors of the departments relevant to the particular session topic.

From: Al Owens
To: Debbie Quinn
⓫**Sent:** April 10, 5:52 P.M.

Debbie, ⓬ I've switched Gary Bower's orientation session with the other one we have scheduled for tomorrow. He has to meet with a big customer outside the office but assured me he'll be back in time. Also, ⓭ he wants to use two projectors simultaneously during his talk, so I'll need to get the one from the other conference room and set it up for him. See you tomorrow.

Send

連絡メモ
☐ orientation オリエンテーション ☐ head office 本社 ☐ new hire 新入社員
☐ go over (研修等で) 〜を練習・習得する ☐ procedure 手順 ☐ train 〜を教育する
☐ specific role 具体的な役割 ☐ respective それぞれの ☐ the following week 翌週
☐ participate in 〜に参加する ☐ supervise 〜を監督する ☐ at the times SV S が V する際に
☐ unavailable 不在の ☐ than usual いつもより ☐ lately 最近 ☐ settle in 定着する
☐ no longer もう〜でない ☐ short-staffed 人手不足の ☐ thank you in advance for 〜についてよろしく頼む
☐ trainee 研修生 ☐ get involved in 〜に関与する

予定表
☐ overview 概要 ☐ management structure 経営体制 ☐ review 確認
☐ administrative procedure 管理手続き ☐ research and development 研究開発 ☐ strategy 戦略
☐ logistics ロジスティクス、物流 ☐ expectations 期待されること ☐ except for 〜を除く
☐ in charge of 〜の担当で ☐ conduct 〜を行う ☐ lead 〜を進める・担当する ☐ chief director 部長
☐ relevant to 〜に関連して

テキストメッセージ
☐ switch 〜を入れ替える ☐ big customer 重要な顧客 ☐ assure 〜に保証・約束する ☐ in time 間に合って
☐ simultaneously 同時に ☐ set up 〜を準備する

40. What is the main purpose of the memo?

(A) To share some details about a training process for new personnel
(B) To explain why a program will begin a week later than scheduled
(C) To provide details about an upcoming department meeting
(D) To inform the staff of a department about changes to a policy

連絡メモの主な目的は何ですか。

(A) 新人研修の手順の詳細について、情報を伝えること
(B) プログラムが予定よりも１週間遅れて始まる理由を説明すること
(C) 今度の部会の詳細を伝達すること
(D) 方針の変更について部員に通知すること

🔍 連絡メモの目的について問われている。１文書目の連絡メモの❷・❸・❹で「Arcstone Chemical 社は、来週本社に 26 名の新入社員を迎える」「入社後最初の週に新入社員は基本オリエンテーションを受ける」「プログラムではArcstone 社の基本情報を確認する」とある。ここから、新入社員の研修内容について述べていることがわかるので、これを言い換えた **(A)** が正解となる。(B) は、❹の次の文にある「翌週の 4 月 15 日まで各部署の役割を果たせない」という内容から「遅れる」と思ってしまいそうだが、これは研修の遅れのことではないので注意しよう。(C) は部会について述べられていないので、不正解となる。

✏️ ☐ detail 詳細　☐ personnel 人員　☐ later than scheduled 予定されていたよりも遅く　☐ upcoming きたる

41. In which department does Ms. Simmons probably work?

(A) Administration
(B) Research and development
(C) Sales and marketing
(D) Human resources

Simmons さんはおそらくどの部署で働いていますか。

(A) 管理
(B) 研究開発
(C) 販売とマーケティング
(D) 人事

🔍 Simmons さんが働いている部署について問われている。１文書目の連絡メモの❶で、Simmons さんは部を統括する管理職に就いていることがわかる。そして❺で「水曜と金曜にオリエンテーションに参加する」と述べている。次に、２文書目の予定表を見ると、水曜日に❼「社の研究開発活動の概要」を担当することになっていることから、Simmons さんは、研究開発に関する仕事をしていることが推測できる。以上から、正解は **(B)** となる。

42. What are the new hires scheduled to do on their first day at the head office?

(A) Meet Stacy Simmons and Eric Murphy in a conference room
(B) Fill out a number of forms in the human resources department
(C) Learn about the management structure of Arcstone Chemical
(D) Review a list of rules and regulations for company employees

新入社員たちは、本社での初日に何をすることが予定されていますか。

(A) 会議室で Stacy Simmons と Eric Murphy に会う
(B) 人事部でいくつかの書類に記入をする
(C) Arcstone Chemical の経営体制について学ぶ
(D) 会社の従業員向けの規則と規定について確認する

🔍 新入社員が本社で初日に何をするかが問われている。予定表の❻を見ると、「会社概要と経営体制」についての講習があるため、これを言い換えた **(C)** が正解。設問に first day とあるので、予定表の初日の項目から選択肢に該当するものを検索すれば、容易に解ける問題。

✏️ ☐ conference room 会議室　☐ a number of 複数の　☐ management structure 経営体制　☐ regulation 規定

43. What is suggested in the text message?

 (A) A customer will need directions to an office building.
 (B) Two conference rooms will be used at the same time.
 (C) Ms. Tanaka will begin her session at 9:00 A.M.
 (D) Mr. Bower's session may have to be cancelled.

テキストメッセージで、何が示唆されていますか。

 (A) 顧客がオフィスビルへの道順を必要とすること。
 (B) 2つの会議室が同時に使用されること。
 (C) Tanaka さんが午前9時に講習を開始すること。
 (D) Bower さんの講習を休講にしなければならないかもしれないこと。

テキストメッセージで示唆されていることが問われている。3文書目のテキストメッセージの⓫・⓬で、4月10日に Owens さんが「Gary Bower さんのオリエンテーションの予定を、明日（4月11日）に予定されているもう一つのものと入れ替えた」とメッセージを送っている。2文書目の予定表を見ると、❽・❾と2つの講習が、4月11日に予定されている。つまり、この2つの講習の順番が入れ替わったということなので、午前9時からの講習は、午後担当予定だった Tanaka さんが行うことがわかる。よって、正解は **(C)** となる。この問題を解くカギは "switched"= 入れ替えた、"the other one we have scheduled for tomorrow"= 明日の（Bower さん担当ではない）もう1つの講習= Tanaka さんの講習、という関係を見抜くことが重要になる。

✎ □ directions 道順   □ at the same time 同時に

44. What will Mr. Owens most likely do on April 11?

 (A) Notify directors about a change to the schedule
 (B) Confirm that Mr. Bower is prepared for his presentation
 (C) Inform Ms. Quinn about a director's problem
 (D) Take some equipment to Conference Room B

Owens さんは4月11日に何をすると考えられますか。

 (A) 予定の変更について部長たちに知らせる。
 (B) Bower さんの講演の準備ができていることを確認する。
 (C) 部長の問題について Quinn さんに知らせる。
 (D) 会議室Bへ機材を持っていく。

Owens さんが4月11日に何をすると考えられるかが問われている。3文書目のテキストメッセージの⓭で、Owens さんは「彼（Gary さん）は、講演の間、2つのプロジェクターを同時に使用したいので、私は他の会議室からプロジェクターを1台持ってきて準備をする必要がある。」と述べている。次に2文書目の予定表を見ると、❿で「ツアーと昼食を除くすべてのオリエンテーションは8階の会議室Bで行われる」とある。ここから、Owens さんはプレゼンに必要な機器を会議室Bに持ち込むことが予測される。以上から、正解は **(D)** となる。会議室Bへ持ち込む根拠が複数の文書にあり、それらを参照して解く必要があることに注意。

宛先：　　すべての部員
差出人：　部長 Stacy Simmons
日付：　　4 月 2 日火曜日
件名：　　オリエンテーションと研修

Arcstone Chemical 社は来週、本社に 26 名の新入社員を迎え、その内の 5 名が当部署に加わります。ご存じのとおり、入社後最初の週に新入社員は基本オリエンテーションを受けます。プログラムでは、方針や手順を含む Arcstone 社についての基本的な情報を確認します。そのため、彼らの入社日は 4 月 8 日月曜日ですが、その翌週の 4 月 15 日までは、各部署での具体的な役割を行うために訓練は受けられません。

来週の水曜日と金曜日に、私はオリエンテーションに参加するので、私が不在の間は Eric Murphy さんが部署を監督します。皆さんがここのところ、いつも以上に忙しいことは承知していますが、新しい同僚たちが研修を受けて慣れてくれば、人手が足りないということもなくなります。

ご協力よろしくお願いいたします。新入社員たちについて質問のある方や研修に参加したい方は、私か Eric さんまでお知らせください。

Stacy Simmons

Arcstone Chemical 社基本オリエンテーション予定表 *

日付	講習	担当者
4 月 8 日月曜日		
午前 9 時から午前 11 時 45 分	はじめに、自己紹介、ビルの見学	Debbie Quinn, Al Owens
午後 1 時 30 分から午後 5 時	会社概要と経営体制	Al Owens
4 月 9 日火曜日		
午前 9 時から午前 11 時 30 分	社の規則と規定の確認	Al Owens
午後 1 時から午後 5 時	管理手続きマニュアルの確認	Debbie Quinn, Al Owens
4 月 10 日水曜日		
午前 9 時から午後 12 時 30 分	本社および会社施設の警備と安全体制	Lloyd Estrada
午後 2 時から午後 5 時 30 分	社の研究開発活動の概要	Stacy Simmons
4 月 11 日木曜日		
午前 9 時から午後 12 時 30 分	Arcstone Chemical の販売・マーケティング戦略	Gary Bower
午後 2 時から午後 5 時 30 分	国際業務と物流管理の概要	Akiko Tanaka
4 月 12 日金曜日		
午前 9 時から午後 2 時	同僚の紹介と全部長との昼食会	全担当者
午後 2 時 30 分から午後 5 時 30 分	部内研修で新入社員に求められること	Debbie Quinn, Al Owens

＊見学と金曜日の昼食を除くすべてのオリエンテーションは 8 階の会議室 B で行われます。オリエンテーションの担当は人事部の Debbie Quinn さんと Al Owens さんです。二人が担当しない講習については、それぞれの講習題目に関連する部の部長が担当します。

送信者： Al Owens
受信者： Debbie Quinn
送信日時： 4 月 10 日、午後 5 時 52 分

Debbie さん、Gary Bower さんのオリエンテーションを、明日予定されていたもう一つのものと入れ替えました。Gary Bower さんは社外で重要な顧客と会わなければならないのですが、時間までには戻ると約束してくれました。また、彼は講演中に 2 台のプロジェクターを同時に使用したいそうなので、他の会議室から 1 台持ってきて、設置する必要があります。では、また明日。

Send

CTS

COLD TRUCKING & STORAGE

667 North Grand Ave., Portland,
ME 04092, USA (Phone: 555-0194)

How do fresh food and flowers get from farms to stores without spoiling? The answer is truckers. CTS has served customers across North America for over half a century, transporting their products to locations both near and far. Moreover, our professional drivers and office staff remain dedicated to providing superior service at rates that are always competitive.

As indicated in our name, we not only offer refrigerated transport but also operate temperature and humidity-controlled warehouses, which are located in dozens of places across the United States and Canada. What's more, for this month only, any *Farmers Gazette* reader who contacts us to reserve warehouse space will be given a 15 percent discount on the price of storage. The storage period reserved can begin at any time this year and can be for any duration.

Whatever your trucking or storage needs are, you can rely on CTS. Call us between 8 A.M. and 8 P.M. any day of the week for an estimate on our transport service or to reserve warehouse space!

From: Darrell McCormick
To: Renee Burke
Date: January 19
Subject: Refrigerated Transport

Dear Ms. Burke:

A mutual friend of ours, Ben Yates, gave me your e-mail address and suggested that I get in touch with you. He and I grew up together in Augusta, and he mentioned you work for a company in Portland, Maine, with a refrigerated truck service. I have a four-acre farm near Auburn, where we mainly grow melons. This year, however, we will also have a fairly large crop of flowers, which we plan to sell to a wholesaler and retailers in Portland.

While we work with a distributor for our fruits and vegetables, we have yet to find a partner to transport our flowers. Our flower crop list and planned harvest dates are as follows. We would like to have our flowers transported no later than three days after being cut. Ideally, they would be transported the day after being harvested.

Tulips—April 15
Roses—May 31
Ranunculus—July 1
Hydrangeas—August 5

If this is something your business may be able to help us out with, I would like to discuss the particulars with you and get a price estimate. I can be reached by e-mail or phone at 555-0153.

Best regards,

Darrell McCormick
Ferguson Farm

From: Renee Burke
To: Darrell McCormick
Date: January 29
Subject: 📎 Refrigerated Transport

Dear Mr. McCormick,

Thank you for taking the time to go over your transport and storage needs with us in detail. As per our agreement, we will be transporting your first flower crop on April 16. We estimate that three trucks will be able to move the flowers to Portland. Nevertheless, we will have another truck on hand in case it is needed. At least five trucks will be required to transport the flowers in June, which is why the overall cost for that month is higher on both the attached estimate and the one I showed you during our meeting.

In addition, we were happy to hear that you saw our advertisement in the *Farmers Gazette* magazine yesterday. The attachment is a revised estimate that factors in the markdown mentioned in the ad.

Should you have any questions, please feel free to contact me anytime.

Warm regards,

Renee Burke
General Manager
Cold Trucking & Storage

45. What aspect of Cold Trucking & Storage is NOT mentioned in the advertisement?

(A) It has been operating for more than fifty years.
(B) It has some trucks that can keep shipments cool.
(C) Its staff can provide an estimate at any time of day.
(D) Its prices are lower than those of its competitors.

46. What is indicated about the advertisement?

(A) It was circulated in January.
(B) It was printed in a newspaper.
(C) It was released with incorrect information.
(D) It was issued by Mr. McCormick's business.

47. What is stated about Ms. Burke?

(A) She is a florist in Portland.
(B) She is an acquaintance of Mr. Yates.
(C) She is a resident of Augusta.
(D) She is a vegetable farmer.

48. What is implied about Ferguson Farm in the first e-mail?

(A) It will expand its flower crop from four to six acres.
(B) It received an estimate from Cold Trucking & Storage.
(C) It had a smaller than usual crop of melons last year.
(D) It has been working with a company that transports food.

49. Which of Mr. McCormick's flower crops will most likely be the largest?

(A) Tulips
(B) Roses
(C) Ranunculus
(D) Hydrangeas

 P. 152

Questions 45-49 refer to the following advertisement and e-mails.

COLD TRUCKING & STORAGE

667 North Grand Ave., Portland,
ME 04092, USA (Phone: 555-0194)

How do fresh food and flowers get from farms to stores without spoiling? The answer is truckers. ❶ CTS has served customers across North America for over half a century, transporting their products to locations both near and far. Moreover, ❷ our professional drivers and office staff remain dedicated to providing superior service at rates that are always competitive.

As indicated in our name, ❸ we not only offer refrigerated transport but also operate temperature and humidity-controlled warehouses, which are located in dozens of places across the United States and Canada. What's more, ❹ for this month only, any *Farmers Gazette* reader who contacts us to reserve warehouse space will be given a 15 percent discount on the price of storage. The storage period reserved can begin at any time this year and can be for any duration.

Whatever your trucking or storage needs are, you can rely on CTS. ❺ Call us between 8 A.M. and 8 P.M. any day of the week for an estimate on our transport service or to reserve warehouse space!

E メール（1）

From: Darrell McCormick
To: Renee Burke
Date: January 19
Subject: Refrigerated Transport

Dear Ms. Burke:

❻ A mutual friend of ours, Ben Yates, gave me your e-mail address and suggested that I get in touch with you. He and I grew up together in Augusta, and he mentioned you work for a company in Portland, Maine, with a refrigerated truck service. I have a four-acre farm near Auburn, where we mainly grow melons. This year, however, we will also have a fairly large crop of flowers, which we plan to sell to a wholesaler and retailers in Portland.

❼ While we work with a distributor for our fruits and vegetables, we have yet to find a partner to transport our flowers. ❽ Our flower crop list and planned harvest dates are as follows. ❾ We would like to have our flowers transported no later than three days after being cut. Ideally, they would be transported the day after being harvested.

Tulips—April 15
❿ Roses—May 31
Ranunculus—July 1
Hydrangeas—August 5

If this is something your business may be able to help us out with, ⓫ I would like to discuss the particulars with you and get a price estimate. I can be reached by e-mail or phone at 555-0153.

Best regards,

Darrell McCormick
Ferguson Farm

From: Renee Burke
To: Darrell McCormick
Date: January 29
Subject: 📎 Refrigerated Transport

Dear Mr. McCormick,

Thank you for taking the time to go over your transport and storage needs with us in detail. As per our agreement, we will be transporting your first flower crop on April 16. We estimate that three trucks will be able to move the flowers to Portland. Nevertheless, we will have another truck on hand in case it is needed. ⑫ At least five trucks will be required to transport the flowers in June, which is why the overall cost for that month is higher on both the attached estimate and the one I showed you during our meeting.

In addition, we were happy to hear that ⑬ you saw our advertisement in the *Farmers Gazette* magazine yesterday. ⑭ The attachment is a revised estimate that factors in the markdown mentioned in the ad.

Should you have any questions, please feel free to contact me anytime.

Warm regards,

Renee Burke
General Manager
Cold Trucking & Storage

広告
☐ spoil 傷む ☐ trucker トラック運転手 ☐ half a century 50 年 ☐ transport ～を輸送する
☐ near and far 近距離ならびに遠距離 ☐ moreover さらに ☐ dedicated to ～に貢献する
☐ superior 優れた ☐ competitive 競争力のある ☐ as indicated 示されたとおり
☐ refrigerated transport 冷凍輸送 ☐ temperature and humidity-controlled 温度や湿度が管理された
☐ dozens of たくさんの ☐ what's more さらに ☐ storage 保管 ☐ duration 期間 ☐ rely on ～に頼る
☐ estimate 見積もり

E メール（1）
☐ mutual friend 共通の友人 ☐ get in touch 連絡を取る ☐ grow up in A A で育つ
☐ mention ～に言及する ☐ four-acre 4 エーカーの ☐ fairly かなり ☐ crop 収穫高
☐ wholesaler 卸売業者 ☐ retailer 小売業者 ☐ distributor 流通業者 ☐ harvest date 収穫日
☐ as follows 以下のとおり ☐ no later than 遅くとも～以内に ☐ ideally 理想的には ☐ ranunculus キンポウゲ
☐ hydrangea アジサイ ☐ particulars 詳細 ☐ reach ～に連絡する

E メール（2）
☐ take the time to *do* 時間を取って～する ☐ go over ～を検討する ☐ in detail 詳細に
☐ as per ～により ☐ agreement 合意 ☐ estimate ～と予測する ☐ nevertheless にもかかわらず
☐ on hand 手元に ☐ in case SV S が V する場合 ☐ at least 少なくとも ☐ the overall cost 全体の費用
☐ in addition 加えて ☐ revised 修正した ☐ factor in ～を計算に入れる ☐ markdown 値下げ ☐ ad 広告
☐ Should you have もし～があるなら ☐ feel free to *do* 気軽に～する

45. What aspect of Cold Trucking & Storage is NOT mentioned in the advertisement?

(A) It has been operating for more than fifty years.

(B) It has some trucks that can keep shipments cool.

(C) Its staff can provide an estimate at any time of day.

(D) Its prices are lower than those of its competitors.

広告で言及されていないのは、Cold Trucking & Storage のどの特徴についてですか。

(A) 50 年以上も営業している。

(B) 荷物を冷やすことができるトラックを保有している。

(C) 一日中いつでも職員が見積もりを提供することができる。

(D) 競合と比べて価格が低い。

Cold Trucking & Storage の特徴について、1文書目の広告で触れられていないことが問われている。広告の❶「半世紀以上にわたりサービスを提供」が (A) に、❷の「他社に劣らぬ価格」が (D) に、❸の「当社では冷蔵輸送の提供だけでなく」が (B) に、それぞれ対応しているため、残った (C) が正解となる。(C) は❺で「午前8時から午後8時の間にお電話を」と、一日中職員が対応していないことから、事実と異なる。

□ operate 営業する　□ competitor 競合他社

46. What is indicated about the advertisement?

(A) It was circulated in January.

(B) It was printed in a newspaper.

(C) It was released with incorrect information.

(D) It was issued by Mr. McCormick's business.

広告について何が示されていますか。

(A) 1月に配布された。

(B) 新聞に掲載された。

(C) 誤った情報で公開された。

(D) McCormick さんの事業によって発行された。

広告について示されていることが問われている選択肢照合型問題。まず、1文書目の広告の❹で「今月のみ Farmers Gazette の読者が保管庫契約のために連絡すれば、保管料が 15 パーセント割引となる」とある。3文書目のEメール (2) の❸、❹を読むと、「昨日のお話にあった Farmers Gazette 誌で当社の広告を見かけた」「広告に書かれていた値下げを反映し、修正した見積もり」とあり、このメールが1月内のやりとりで行われたことがわかるので、ここから、この広告については、1月に出版流通し、市場に出回っていたことがわかる。その状況を circulate という動詞を使って言い換えた (A) が正解。(B) 新聞、(C) 誤った情報、(D)McCormick さんの事業、はいずれも記載や関連がなく、不正解。

□ circulate ～を配布する　□ incorrect 正しくない　□ issue ～を発行する

47. What is stated about Ms. Burke?

(A) She is a florist in Portland.

(B) She is an acquaintance of Mr. Yates.

(C) She is a resident of Augusta.

(D) She is a vegetable farmer.

Burke さんについて何が述べられていますか。

(A) Portland の花屋である。

(B) Yates さんの知人である。

(C) Augusta の住人である。

(D) 野菜農家である。

Burke さんについて述べられていることが問われている選択肢照合型問題。2文書目のEメール (1) の❻で、McCormick さんが Burke さん宛てに「共通の友人である Ben Yates さんにEメールアドレスをいただき、」とある。ここから Burke さんと McCormick さんは、それぞれ Yates さんと知り合いであることがわかる。以上から、知り合いを acquaintance と言い換えた (B) が正解。(A)(C) は記載がなく、(D) の野菜農家は McCormick さん（＝メロン栽培）のこと。

□ florist 花屋　□ acquaintance 知り合い、知人　□ resident 住人

48. What is implied about Ferguson Farm in the first e-mail?

- (A) It will expand its flower crop from four to six acres.
- (B) It received an estimate from Cold Trucking & Storage.
- (C) It had a smaller than usual crop of melons last year.
- **(D)** It has been working with a company that transports food.

1通目のEメールで、Ferguson Farm について何が示唆されていますか。

- (A) 花の耕作を4から6エーカーに拡大した。
- (B) Cold Trucking & Storage から見積書を受け取った。
- (C) 昨年はメロンの収穫量が通常よりも少なかった。
- **(D)** 食品を輸送する会社と協力している。

1通目のEメールで Ferguson Farm について示唆されていることが問われている、選択肢照合型問題。まず、McCormick さんはEメール (1) の最後の社名から Ferguson Farm で働いていることがわかる。次に❼で「果物や野菜については、協力している流通業者がいる」と、食べ物に関する輸送は他の会社に頼んでいることがわかる。以上から、それを言い換えた **(D)** が正解。(A) 花の耕作規模、(C) メロン収穫量については触れられておらず、また❶から、このメールで初めて見積もりをお願いしているので、(B) は事実と異なる。

✎ □ crop 収穫物　□ acre エーカー（面積の単位）　□ transport 〜を輸送する

49. Which of Mr. McCormick's flower crops will most likely be the largest?

- (A) Tulips
- **(B)** Roses
- (C) Ranunculus
- (D) Hydrangeas

McCormick さんの花の耕作量の中で最大量のものはどれであると考えられますか。

- (A) チューリップ
- **(B)** バラ
- (C) キンポウゲ
- (D) アジサイ

McCormick さんの花の耕作量の中で最大量のものが問われている。3文書目のEメール (2) を読むと、⓬で「6月の花の輸送には、少なくとも5台のトラックが必要で、総費用が他の月よりも高額」という記載がある。つまり、6月に輸送する花が最大量だとわかる。次に2文書目のEメール (1) の❽、❾で「当園の花の一覧と収穫予定日は以下のとおり」「切花後、3日以内に当園の花を輸送、理想的には収穫された翌日にお願い」と述べている。❿から、バラの収穫予定日が5月31日、つまり、6月輸送だとわかる。以上から、正解は **(B)** となる。本文では花の耕作量 "flower crops" ではなく、"truck" "transport" と輸送するモノで捉えていたため、難易度が高い問題。

COLD TRUCKING & STORAGE

667 North Grand Ave., Portland,
メイン州 04092, アメリカ合衆国 (電話番号 : 555-0194)

生鮮食品や花は品質を維持しつつ、どのようにお店に運搬されていると思われますか。答えは
トラック運転手によってです。CTS は半世紀以上にわたり、近くでも遠くでも商品を目的地
に輸送し、北米中のお客様にサービスを提供してまいりました。さらに、当社のプロのドライ
バーや職員は常に他社に劣らぬ価格でより優れたサービスを提供することに専念しています。

その名前にあるように、当社では冷蔵輸送の提供だけでなく、温度や湿度が管理された倉庫を
米国とカナダ中に何十も運営しています。さらに、今月のみ、*Farmers Gazette* の読者ならど
なたでも、保管庫のご契約のためにご連絡をいただくと、保管料が 15 パーセント割引となり
ます。保管庫のご利用はいつでも開始可能で、期間も自由です。

トラック輸送でも保管庫のご利用でも、CTS は信頼していただけます。当社の輸送サービス
のお見積もりや保管庫のご予約は、1 週間毎日、午前 8 時から午後 8 時の間にお電話ください！

E メール（1）

送信者：	Darrell McCormick
受信者：	Renee Burke
日付：	1 月 19 日
件名：	冷蔵輸送

Burke さん

共通の友人である Ben Yates さんにあなたの E メールアドレスをいただき、ご連絡することを勧められました。
Ben Yates さんと私は共に Augusta の出身で、あなたはメイン州の Portland にある冷蔵輸送サービスの会社で働い
てらっしゃるとお聞きしています。私は Auburn の近くに 4 エーカーの農場を持っていて、主にメロンを栽培して
います。しかし今年は、かなり大量の花もあり、Portland の卸売業者や小売業者に販売する予定です。

果物や野菜については、協力している流通業者がいますが、花の輸送については協力者がまだ見つかっていません。
当園の花の一覧と収穫予定日は以下のとおりです。切花後、3 日以内に当園の花を輸送していただければと思って
います。理想的には収穫された翌日にお願いできればと思います。

チューリップ―4 月 15 日
バラ―5 月 31 日
キンポウゲ―7 月 1 日
アジサイ―8 月 5 日

もし、こちらを請け負っていただけるようでしたら、詳細について話し合い、その後価格の見積もりをお願いした
いと思います。E メールか電話 555-0153 までご連絡ください。

よろしくお願いいたします。

Ferguson Farm
Darrell McCormick

E メール（2）

送信者：	Renee Burke
受信者：	Darrell McCormick
日付：	1 月 29 日
件名：	📎 冷蔵輸送

McCormick さん

わざわざ必要となる輸送と保管の詳細についてご説明いただきありがとうございます。契約に基づき、4 月 16 日に最初の花の輸送をいたします。3 台のトラックで Portland まで花を運ぶことができると考えます。しかし、必要であれば追加のトラックのご用意もできます。6 月の花の輸送には、少なくとも 5 台のトラックが必要となりますので、該当月の総費用は、添付の見積書、お会いした際に提示したもの、両方で他の月よりも高額となっています。

また、昨日のお話にあった *Farmers Gazette* 誌で当社の広告を見かけられたとのことうれしく思います。添付ファイルは、広告に書かれていた値下げを反映し修正した見積もりです。

ご不明点がありましたら、いつでもお気軽にご連絡ください。

どうぞよろしくお願いいたします。

Cold Trucking & Storage
業務部長
Renee Burke

---

http://www.ctig.org

| Register | Program | **Special Events** | Park Map |

6th Annual Crystal Thought Inventors Guild Show
April 6–9, Artemis Park, Bison Hills, VT

After the show wraps up each day, please join us for some fun activities in the evening. Only registered CTIG members may attend.

Day 1: Walking Tour of City's Old Town Area
Meet at the park's eastern gate at 6:00 P.M. Participants will be divided into four groups, each with their own guide. No fee or registration is required.

Day 2: Visit to the Auriga Planetarium
No registration is required. Bus transportation to the planetarium will be provided. Admission fee: $6. Meet in the lobby of the Artemis Park Hotel at 5:30 P.M.

Day 3: Banquet at Sandy's Seafood Restaurant
Advance registration is required. Fee per person: $85. Select from various meal options, including vegetarian, when you register.

Day 4: Reception in the Artemis Park Hotel Exhibition Hall
Enjoy complimentary snacks and beverages while listening to jazz band *The Silhouettes* and mingling with other show attendees. No need to sign up!

*To account for the large space needed for some inventors' displays, we have chosen to hold this year's event outdoors, at Artemis Park. If the snow has not melted by these dates, the event may be held from June 8–11, instead. Final dates will be posted by March 1st.

Auriga Planetarium

Welcome all CTIG Show attendees!

Because space is limited inside the planetarium, you may have to wait until the next show. Shows start every 40 minutes. While waiting, we invite you to watch our short film, *Across the Universe*, shown every 15 minutes in the theater. You are also welcome to walk through any of our exhibitions, including our collection of telescopes in Hall G.

Please be aware that our cafeteria is currently closed for renovations. Snack and drink vending machines are located on the ground floor, and there are a café and a bakery across the street from our building.

COMMENT CARD

Please let us know about your experience at the CTIG Show. Your feedback will be valuable to us as we plan for the same event next year.

Comments:
Overall, I had a great time, and I saw a lot of interesting inventions. Holding the event at Artemis Park was a great idea. It was lucky that the weather has been so warm the last few months. Some additional evening activities were added this year, which I liked because I've never had enough time to meet everybody during only the banquet. They were a lot of fun, too. I especially enjoyed the exhibits at the planetarium. I had to catch my return flight to Boston on the afternoon of the final day, so I wasn't able to attend the reception. I'm sorry I missed it, but I heard from a fellow member that the food and the band were both fantastic.

Roland Ramirez

---

50. For which event is it necessary to sign up in advance?

(A) The walking tour
(B) The visit to a planetarium
(C) The dinner at a restaurant
(D) The reception in a hall

51. What is one purpose of the notice?

(A) To announce the date a facility will reopen
(B) To notify visitors about a schedule change
(C) To explain where to get refreshments
(D) To provide details about tickets to a film

52. What can be inferred about Mr. Ramirez?

(A) He saw a collection of scientific instruments.
(B) He traveled to Boston on a bus.
(C) He prefers to eat vegetarian food.
(D) He enjoyed listening to some live music.

53. What does Mr. Ramirez suggest on the comment card?

(A) He presented one of his inventions at the show.
(B) He has attended the CTIG show in previous years.
(C) Only a small number of members attended the banquet.
(D) He was unable to attend several evening activities.

54. When most likely did Mr. Ramirez return to Boston?

(A) On April 8
(B) On April 9
(C) On June 10
(D) On June 11

Triple

 P. 160

Questions 50–54 refer to the following Web page, notice, and comment card.

---

http://www.ctig.org

Register	Program	**Special Events**	Park Map

6th Annual Crystal Thought Inventors Guild Show
* ❶ *April 6–9, Artemis Park, Bison Hills, VT*

After the show wraps up each day, please join us for some fun activities in the evening. Only registered CTIG members may attend.

Day 1: Walking Tour of City's Old Town Area
Meet at the park's eastern gate at 6:00 P.M. Participants will be divided into four groups, each with their own guide. No fee or registration is required.

Day 2: Visit to the Auriga Planetarium
No registration is required. Bus transportation to the planetarium will be provided. Admission fee: $6. Meet in the lobby of the Artemis Park Hotel at 5:30 P.M.

Day 3: Banquet at Sandy's Seafood Restaurant
❷ Advance registration is required. Fee per person: $85. Select from various meal options, including vegetarian, when you register.

❸ Day 4: Reception in the Artemis Park Hotel Exhibition Hall
Enjoy complimentary snacks and beverages while listening to jazz band *The Silhouettes* and mingling with other show attendees. No need to sign up!

*To account for the large space needed for some inventors' displays, we have chosen to hold this year's event outdoors, at Artemis Park. ❹ If the snow has not melted by these dates, the event may be held from June 8–11, instead. Final dates will be posted by March 1st.

Auriga Planctarium

Welcome all CTIG Show attendees!

Because space is limited inside the planetarium, you may have to wait until the next show. Shows start every 40 minutes. While waiting, we invite you to watch our short film, *Across the Universe*, shown every 15 minutes in the theater. ❺ You are also welcome to walk through any of our exhibitions, including our collection of telescopes in Hall G.

❻ Please be aware that our cafeteria is currently closed for renovations. ❼ Snack and drink vending machines are located on the ground floor, and there are a café and a bakery across the street from our building.

COMMENT CARD

Please let us know about your experience at the CTIG Show. Your feedback will be valuable to us as we plan for the same event next year.

Comments:

Overall, I had a great time, and I saw a lot of interesting inventions. Holding the event at Artemis Park was a great idea. **❽** <u>It was lucky that the weather has been so warm the last few months.</u> **❾** <u>Some additional evening activities were added this year, which I liked because I've never had enough time to meet everybody during only the banquet.</u> They were a lot of fun, too. **❿** <u>I especially enjoyed the exhibits at the planetarium.</u> **⓫** <u>I had to catch my return flight to Boston on the afternoon of the final day,</u> so I wasn't able to attend the reception. I'm sorry I missed it, but I heard from a fellow member that the food and the band were both fantastic.

Roland Ramirez

ウェブページ
- [ ] wrap up 終了する　[ ] divide A into B AをBに分割する　[ ] required 必要となる　[ ] transportation 輸送
- [ ] planetarium プラネタリウム　[ ] provide ～を用意する　[ ] admission fee 入場料
- [ ] advance registration 事前登録　[ ] various さまざまな　[ ] vegetarian ベジタリアン・菜食主義者向けの
- [ ] reception 懇親会　[ ] complimentary 無料の　[ ] snack 軽食　[ ] mingle with ～と交流する
- [ ] account for ～を考慮する　[ ] inventor 発明家　[ ] display 展示　[ ] melt 溶ける
- [ ] post ～を発表する・掲載する

お知らせ
- [ ] exhibition 展示　[ ] telescope 望遠鏡　[ ] be aware that SV S が V することに留意する　[ ] renovation 改装
- [ ] vending machine 自動販売機　[ ] located on ～にある　[ ] the ground floor 地上階、1 階　[ ] bakery パン屋

意見カード
- [ ] comment card 意見などを記入するカード　[ ] overall 全般的に　[ ] additional 追加の　[ ] especially 特に
- [ ] return flight 帰りの便　[ ] fellow member 他の会員　[ ] fantastic 素晴らしい

★★★★★

50. For which event is it necessary to sign up in advance?

(A) The walking tour
(B) The visit to a planetarium
(C) The dinner at a restaurant
(D) The reception in a hall

事前に申し込みが必要なのはどのイベントですか。

(A) 散策ツアー
(B) プラネタリウム
(C) レストランでの夕食
(D) ホールでのパーティー

🔍 選択肢の中で事前に申し込みが必要なイベントは何かが問われている。1 文書目のウェブページの❷を見ると、レストランの夕食に関しては事前予約が必要という記載があるため、**(C)** が正解。他の選択肢には事前登録、予約という記載はない。

- [ ] planetarium プラネタリウム

51. What is one purpose of the notice?

(A) To announce the date a facility will reopen
(B) To notify visitors about a schedule change
(C) To explain where to get refreshments
(D) To provide details about tickets to a film

お知らせの 1 つの目的は何ですか。

(A) 施設の再開日を発表すること
(B) 訪問者に日程の変更を通知すること
(C) 軽食がどこで手に入る説明すること
(D) 映画のチケットについての詳細を提示すること

お知らせの 1 つの目的は何かが問われている。2 文書目のお知らせの**❻**・**❼**から「カフェテリアは現在改装工事のため休業中」「軽食と飲み物の自動販売機は 1 階、喫茶店とパン屋は当ビルの向かいにある」と、飲食に関する情報を提供している。ここから、"Snack and drink" を refreshments と言い換えた **(C)** が正解となる。(A) 食堂施設再開等の言及はないので、ここでは不正解。

✎ □ facility 施設　□ notify 〜に知らせる　□ refreshments 軽い飲食物　□ detail 詳細

★★★★★ クロスリファレンス問題

52. What can be inferred about Mr. Ramirez?

(A) He saw a collection of scientific instruments.
(B) He traveled to Boston on a bus.
(C) He prefers to eat vegetarian food.
(D) He enjoyed listening to some live music.

Ramirez さんについて何が推測できますか。

(A) 科学機器のコレクションを見た。
(B) ボストンまでバスで移動した。
(C) 菜食主義の食事を好む。
(D) 生演奏を聴くことを楽しんだ。

Ramirez さんについて何が推測されるかという選択肢照合型問題。Ramirez さんは 3 文書目の意見カードを書いた人で、**❿**で「特にプラネタリウムの展示が良かった」と述べている。次に、2 文書目のお知らせを読むと、**❺**で「Hall G にある望遠鏡のコレクションを含む、当館の展示をどれでも見ることが可能」とある。ここから望遠鏡を "scientific instruments（科学機器）" と抽象度を高めに表現した **(A)** が正解となる。この問題は、複数の文書を参照しつつ、言い換えを見抜けるかどうかという難易度の高い問題。

✎ □ scientific instrument 科学機器

★★★☆☆

53. What does Mr. Ramirez suggest on the comment card?

(A) He presented one of his inventions at the show.
(B) He has attended the CTIG show in previous years.
(C) Only a small number of members attended the banquet.
(D) He was unable to attend several evening activities.

Ramirez さんは意見カードで何を示唆していますか。

(A) 展示会で発明の 1 つを発表した。
(B) 以前 CTIG 展示会に参加したことがある。
(C) ごく少数の会員のみが宴会に参加した。
(D) いくつかの夜のアクティビティに出席することができなかった。

Ramirez さんは意見カードで何を示唆しているかが問われている選択肢照合型問題。Ramirez さんは**❾**で「今年は夜のアクティビティが追加され、今までは宴会だけで、皆さんとお会いするだけの時間は足りませんでしたので、良かった」と述べている。ここから、CTIG のショーにはこれまでも参加していたことがわかるので、それを言い換えた **(B)** が正解となる。(A) 自分でのプレゼン有無、(C) 宴会の参加規模、(D) 夜のアクティビティ参加状況は述べられていないので、これらは不正解。

✎ □ previous 過去の

54. When most likely did Mr. Ramirez return to Boston?

(A) On April 8
(B) On April 9
(C) On June 10
(D) On June 11

Ramirez さんがボストンに戻ったのはいつだと考えられますか。

(A) 4月8日に
(B) 4月9日に
(C) 6月10日に
(D) 6月11日に

Ramirez さんがボストンに戻った日が問われている。まず 3 文書目の意見カードを見ると、❽に「この数カ月、とても天候が暖かかった」、⓫に「最終日の午後にパーティーに参加せずボストンに戻った」と書いてある。次に、1 文書目のウェブページを見ると、開催予定は❶ 4月6日～9日で、パーティーのある日は❸から最終日の 4 月 9 日だとわかる。❹に、雪解けしない場合は 6 月に順延とあるが、❽より暖かかったことがわかるので、ここから雪による順延はなかったと推測できる。以上から、正解は **(B)** となる。

問題 50 から 54 は次のウェブページ、お知らせ、意見カードに関するものです。

登録	プログラム	特別イベント	公園内地図

http://www.ctig.org

第 6 回 年次 Crystal Thought Inventors Guild 展示会
4月6日～9日, Artemis Park, Bison Hills, バーモント州

各日の展示会が終了した後には、楽しい夜のアクティビティにご参加ください。ご登録済みの CTIG の会員のみご参加いただけます。

1 日目：旧市街の散策ツアー
公園の東門に午後 6 時に集合します。参加者は 4 つのグループに分かれ、それぞれにガイドが付きます。参加費や登録は必要ありません。

2 日目：Auriga Planetarium 見学
登録は不要です。プラネタリウムまでのバスをご用意いたします。入場料：6 ドル。Artemis Park Hotel のロビーに午後 5 時半に集合です。

3 日目：Sandy's Seafood Restaurant にて宴会
事前登録が必要です。1 人あたりの料金：85 ドル。登録時に菜食主義者向けを含む、さまざまな料理からお選びいただけます。

4 日目：Artemis Park Hotel Exhibition Hall にてパーティー
ジャズバンド *The Silhouettes* の演奏を聴きながら、無料の軽食や飲み物をお楽しみいただき、他のショーの参加者たちと交流することができます。登録は必要ありません！

* 一部の発明家の展示に必要な広いスペースを考慮し、今年のイベントは野外の Artemis Park で開催することになりました。開催日までに雪が溶けていない場合、イベントは 6 月 8 日～11 日に変更となることもあります。最終的な日程は 3 月 1 日までに発表いたします。

Auriga Planetarium

CTIG の展示会へご参加の皆さまを歓迎いたします！

プラネタリウムの収容人数に限りがありますので、次の上映までお待ちいただくこともあります。上映は 40 分ごとに行われます。お待ちいただいている間、劇場で 15 分ごとに上映される短編映画 *Across the Universe* をどうぞご覧ください。Hall G の望遠鏡のコレクションを含む、当館の展示をどれでもご覧いただくこともできます。

カフェテリアは現在改装工事のため休業中ですのでご注意ください。軽食と飲み物の自動販売機は 1 階、カフェとパン屋は当ビルの向かいにあります。

意見カード

CTIG 展示会での体験について教えてください。来年も同じイベントを計画しておりますので、貴殿のご意見はとても貴重です。

コメント：
全体的にとても楽しめましたし、たくさんの興味深い発明品が見られました。Artemis Park でイベントを開催したのはとても良いアイデアでした。この数カ月、とても天候が暖かったので幸運でした。今年は夜のアクティビティが追加され、今まで宴会だけでは皆さんとお会いする十分な時間がありませんでしたので、良かったです。そして、とても楽しめました。特に良かったのはプラネタリウムでの展示品です。最終日の午後にボストンへの帰りの便に乗らなければならなかったので、パーティーには参加できませんでした。参加できず、申し訳ありません。しかし、他の会員から、食事もバンド演奏も共に素晴らしかったとお聞きしました。

Roland Ramirez

TOKIMAKURE!

Test

3

Test 3

Questions 1-2 refer to the following directory.

Welcome to Starlight Department Store

Please make use of this temporary directory to find your way around our store while it is being renovated. We are expanding Floor 5, which previously held our Home Furnishings, in order to create an eating area for our valued customers.

Floor 1: Cosmetics

Floor 2: Women's Clothing

Floor 3: Men's Clothing

Floor 4: Electronics and Technology

Floor 5: Closed for Renovations until July 10

Floor 6: Exercise Machines

---

1. Why is the Starlight Department Store being renovated?

　(A) To build a food court
　(B) To remodel extra dressing rooms
　(C) To expand a clothing department
　(D) To reorganize a shoe department

2. Where is athletic equipment most likely located?

　(A) Floor 3
　(B) Floor 4
　(C) Floor 5
　(D) Floor 6

 P. 168

Forest's Ice Cream

349 Broad Street in San Francisco
415-789-2031

Once you taste Forest's Ice Cream, you will return repeatedly. Forest's is conveniently located for the entire family. And also, we are the only Forest's Ice Cream shop in the city with many private rooms for families and babies.

We offer

· 31 flavors of ice cream, made right here in our shop with locally grown ingredients

· Many toppings such as fresh fruit and crispy cereal

· Ice cream cakes custom-made to order

· Free wireless Internet access

Business Hours: Tuesday through Friday, from 9 A.M. to 8 P.M.
              Saturday through Sunday, from 9 A.M. to 10 P.M.
Summer Hours (May through August): Open until 11 P.M.

Every Thursday is Family Day — Receive a kid-size serving of any ice cream at a reduced price of one dollar.

---

3. What is indicated about Forest's Ice Cream?

(A) It has constructed a new Internet site.
(B) Its ice cream is made on site.
(C) Its items are sold in local grocery stores.
(D) It is a family-owned business.

4. What is mentioned about Family Day?

(A) Another menu is added to the original order.
(B) Complimentary toppings are provided.
(C) It occurs every weekend.
(D) People can buy a kid-size ice cream at a discounted price.

P. 170

Questions 1-2 refer to the following directory.

Welcome to Starlight Department Store

❶ Please make use of this temporary directory to find your way around our store while it is being renovated.
❷ We are expanding Floor 5, which previously held our Home Furnishings, in order to create an eating area for our valued customers.

    Floor 1: Cosmetics
    Floor 2: Women's Clothing
    Floor 3: Men's Clothing
    Floor 4: Electronics and Technology
    Floor 5: Closed for Renovations until July 10
    ❸ Floor 6: Exercise Machines

□ directory 案内板　□ make use of ～を利用する　□ temporary 一時的な　□ renovate ～を改装する
□ expand ～を拡張する　□ previously 過去に　□ in order to *do* ～するために　□ eating area 食事場所
□ valued customer（お得意先である）大事なお客様　□ cosmetics 化粧品

★★☆☆☆

1. Why is the Starlight Department Store being renovated?

  (A) To build a food court
  (B) To remodel extra dressing rooms
  (C) To expand a clothing department
  (D) To reorganize a shoe department

Starlight Department Store が改装中なのはなぜですか。

  (A) フードコートを設けるため
  (B) 追加の試着室を改装するため
  (C) 衣料品部門を拡大するため
  (D) 靴部門を改編するため

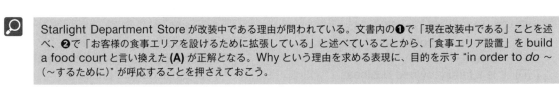

Starlight Department Store が改装中である理由が問われている。文書内の❶で「現在改装中である」ことを述べ、❷で「お客様の食事エリアを設けるために拡張している」と述べていることから、「食事エリア設置」を build a food court と言い換えた **(A)** が正解となる。Why という理由を求める表現に、目的を示す "in order to *do* ～（～するために）" が呼応することを押さえておこう。

□ remodel ～を改装する　□ extra 追加の　□ dressing room 試着室　□ reorganize ～を再編・改編する

★★★★★

2. Where is athletic equipment most likely located?

(A) Floor 3
(B) Floor 4
(C) Floor 5
(D) Floor 6

運動器具はおそらくどこにありますか。

(A) 3 階
(B) 4 階
(C) 5 階
(D) 6 階

🔍 運動器具がおそらくどこにあるかが問われている。仮の案内板を読むと、❸に「トレーニングマシーン」と記載されている。他の階には運動器具を取り扱っているような売り場が見当たらないため、**(D)** が正解となる。❸の "Exercise Machines" が、設問では athletic equipment と言い換えられている。このような言い換えをすぐ見抜けるようになろう。

✎ ☐ athletic equipment 運動器具

📝 問題 1 から 2 は次の館内案内板に関するものです。

Starlight Department Store へようこそ

店内改装中はこちらの仮の案内板で、店内の売り場をお探しください。私たちの大切なお客様のお食事エリアを設けるため、以前は家具売り場だった 5 階を拡張しています。

1 階：化粧品
2 階：婦人服
3 階：紳士服
4 階：電子機器
5 階：7 月 10 日まで改装のため休業
6 階：トレーニングマシーン

Questions 3-4 refer to the following advertisement.

Forest's Ice Cream

349 Broad Street in San Francisco
415-789-2031

Once you taste Forest's Ice Cream, you will return repeatedly. Forest's is conveniently located for the entire family. And also, we are the only Forest's Ice Cream shop in the city with many private rooms for families and babies.

❶ We offer

- ❷ 31 flavors of ice cream, made right here in our shop with locally grown ingredients
- Many toppings such as fresh fruit and crispy cereal
- Ice cream cakes custom-made to order
- Free wireless Internet access

Business Hours: Tuesday through Friday, from 9 A.M. to 8 P.M.
　　　　　　　　Saturday through Sunday, from 9 A.M. to 10 P.M.
Summer Hours (May through August): Open until 11 P.M.

❸ Every Thursday is Family Day — Receive a kid-size serving of any ice cream at a reduced price of one dollar.

□ taste 〜を飲食する □ repeatedly 繰り返して □ conveniently located 便利なところに位置している
□ entire 全体の □ private room 個室 □ locally grown ingredient 地元でとれた材料
□ topping トッピング（上に乗せる食べ物） □ such as 〜のような □ crispy サクサクの、カリカリの
□ cereal シリアル食品（穀物を主に加工した栄養食品） □ custom-made 特注の □ wireless 無線の
□ business hours 営業時間 □ kid-size 子ども用サイズの □ serving 給仕、提供
□ at a reduced price 割引価格で

★★☆☆☆

3. What is indicated about Forest's Ice Cream?

(A) It has constructed a new Internet site.
(B) Its ice cream is made on site.
(C) Its items are sold in local grocery stores.
(D) It is a family-owned business.

Forest's Ice Cream について何が示されていますか。

(A) 新しいウェブサイトを構築した。
(B) アイスクリームはその場で作られている。
(C) 商品は地元の食料品店で販売されている。
(D) 家族経営の会社である。

 Forest's Ice Cream について示されていることを問う選択肢照合型の問題。❶・❷で、Forest's Ice Cream が提供することとして「こちらの店内で作った」と述べている。ここから、アイスクリームは店の中で作られていることがわかる。よって、❷の "right here in our shop" を on site と表現した **(B)** が正解。"here in our shop" の "here" が選択肢で on site に言い換えられていることに注目。(A) 新ネットサイト構築、(C) 販売先、(D) 家族経営についてはいずれも言及がない。

□ construct 〜を構築する □ on site 現場、現地で □ grocery store 食料雑貨店 □ family-owned 家族経営の

4. What is mentioned about Family Day?

(A) Another menu is added to the original order.
(B) Complimentary toppings are provided.
(C) It occurs every weekend.
(D) People can buy a kid-size ice cream at a discounted price.

ファミリーデーについて何が言及されていますか。

(A) 注文すると別のメニューも付いてくる。
(B) 無料トッピングが提供される。
(C) 毎週末に行われる。
(D) 子ども向けサイズのアイスクリームは割引価格で購入できる。

ファミリーデーについて言及されていることを問う選択肢照合型の問題。❸で「毎週木曜日はファミリーデーで、子ども用サイズ（のアイス）を 1 ドルの割引価格で提供」と述べられている。ここから、この割引価格を discounted price と表現した **(D)** が正解。(A) 他メニューの追加、(B) トッピング無料、には言及がなく、(C) ファミリーデーは木曜日で週末ではない。

□ be added to ～に加えられる　□ original もともとの　□ complimentary 無料の　□ discounted 割引された

問題 3 から 4 は次の広告に関するものです。

Forest's Ice Cream

サンフランシスコ　349 Broad Street
415-789-2031

一度 Forest's Ice Cream のアイスクリームを食べてみれば、きっと何度でも食べにきたくなることでしょう。Forest's は家族の皆さんにとって便利な場所にあります。また、当店は市内にある Forest's Ice Cream では唯一の、ご家族や赤ん坊のための多くの個室を備えた店舗です。

当店でご提供しているもの
・地元産の食材を使い、こちらの店内で作った 31 種類のアイスクリーム
・新鮮な果物やカリカリのシリアルなどのたくさんのトッピング
・特注のアイスクリームケーキ
・無料の無線インターネット接続

営業時間：火曜日から金曜日まで、午前 9 時から午後 8 時
　　　　　　土曜日から日曜日まで、午前 9 時から午後 10 時
夏季期間（5 月から 8 月まで）：午後 11 時まで営業

毎週木曜日はファミリーデー … どのアイスクリームでも、子ども用サイズは 1 ドルの割引価格で提供

Recycling Paper Goods

To: All Employees
From: Team Leader of the Material Department
Subject: Paper recycling program

You might have heard that about 20 million pieces of used paper are thrown into the landfills of our city every year. This will become a serious environmental problem in the near future.

Now we are able to help reduce the amount of used paper by selling it!

Our company is supposed to start a paper recycling program with ROCL Inc. in an effort to preserve and protect our priceless natural resources.

ROCL bears the cost of carrying used paper from our location to their workplace. In addition, they will pay for this, though it is very little for every reusable paper which we save and send them. This money from reusable paper will be donated to such organizations as social services, charities, or hospitals.

Please DO NOT dump any used paper. Please forward to me any questions you may have. I hope that everyone cooperates with us to keep our environment safe. Play your part in helping us to preserve a clean and green future.

5. What is the main purpose of the paper recycling program?

(A) To make a profit
(B) To protect natural resources
(C) To donate money to charity
(D) To keep offices clean

6. What are the employees asked to do?

(A) Throw away used paper
(B) Contribute to the hospital
(C) Sell used pieces of paper individually
(D) Participate in a program

P. 174

Questions 7-8 refer to the following text-message chain.

 1分30秒

Isabella Swenson 2:29 P.M.
I'm enjoying a cup of coffee at the coffee shop. I have a table near the window. Are you on your way?

Dylan Harwood 2:31 P.M.
Yes, sorry. I'm nearby but I'm looking for a place to park my car.

Isabella Swenson 2:32 P.M.
There's a parking lot on Dunham Street. I think the charge is $3.00 an hour.

Dylan Harwood 2:32 P.M.
Thanks. I'll be there soon.

Isabella Swenson 2:35 P.M.
Do you want me to order you something to drink? They have good lattes here.

Dylan Harwood 2:36 P.M.
That sounds great. Okay. See you soon.

---

7. What can be suggested about Ms. Harwood?

(A) She will meet Ms. Swenson for the first time.
(B) She is driving to the coffee shop.
(C) She made a last-minute cancellation.
(D) She got lost on the way to the coffee shop.

8. At 2:36 P.M., what does Ms. Harwood mean when she writes, "That sounds great"?

(A) She agrees to meet at a different time.
(B) She thinks the business has fair prices.
(C) She wants Ms. Swenson to order a drink for her.
(D) She will go to Dunham Street.

P. 176

Questions 5-6 refer to the following memo.

Recycling Paper Goods

To: All Employees
From: Team Leader of the Material Department
Subject: Paper recycling program

You might have heard that about 20 million pieces of used paper are thrown into the landfills of our city every year. This will become a serious environmental problem in the near future.

Now we are able to help reduce the amount of used paper by selling it!

❶ Our company is supposed to start a paper recycling program with ROCL Inc. in an effort to preserve and protect our priceless natural resources.

ROCL bears the cost of carrying used paper from our location to their workplace. In addition, they will pay for this, though it is very little for every reusable paper which we save and send them. This money from reusable paper will be donated to such organizations as social services, charities, or hospitals.

❷ Please DO NOT dump any used paper. Please forward to me any questions you may have. ❸ I hope that everyone cooperates with us to keep our environment safe. ❹ Play your part in helping us to preserve a clean and green future.

□ paper goods 紙製品　□ Material Department 資材部　□ used papers 古紙　□ throw into ～を ～に捨てる
□ landfill ごみ埋め立て地　□ environmental problem 環境問題　□ in the near future 近い将来に　□ amount 量
□ be supposed to *do* ～することになっている　□ effort 努力　□ preserve ～を保存する
□ protect ～を保護する　□ priceless 貴重な　□ natural resource 自然資源、天然資源
□ bear the cost of ～の費用を負担する　□ carry ～を運搬する　□ workplace 職場　□ in addition 加えて
□ though ～だけれども　□ reusable 再生可能な　□ donate A to B　A を B に寄付する　□ charity 慈善団体
□ dump ～を捨てる　□ forward to ～に送付する　□ cooperate with ～と協働する
□ keep ... safe …を安全な状態に保つ　□ play one's part in *do*ing ～する際の役割を果たす
□ green future 緑豊かな未来

★★☆☆☆

5. What is the main purpose of the paper recycling program?

(A) To make a profit
(B) To protect natural resources
(C) To donate money to charity
(D) To keep offices clean

紙のリサイクルプログラムの主な目的は何ですか。

(A) 利益を出すこと
(B) 自然資源を守ること
(C) 慈善団体にお金を寄付すること
(D) 事務所を清潔に保つこと

紙のリサイクルプログラムの主な目的が問われている。❶で紙のリサイクルプログラムについて触れられており、「貴重な自然資源を保護し、守る取り組みによるプログラム」だと説明しているので、**(B)** が正解となる。

□ make a profit 利益を上げる　□ keep ... clean …を清潔に保つ

6. What are the employees asked to do?　　　　従業員は何をするように頼まれていますか。

(A) Throw away used paper　　　　　　　　　(A) 古紙を捨てる
(B) Contribute to the hospital　　　　　　　(B) 病院に寄付をする
(C) Sell used pieces of paper individually　　(C) 個別に古紙を売る
(D) Participate in a program　　　　　　　　**(D)** プログラムに参加する

従業員が何をするように頼まれているかが問われている。最終段落の❷・❸・❹で「古紙を捨てないようにすること」「環境を安全に保つための協力」「清潔で緑豊かな未来を守るための役割を果たすこと」といった、紙のリサイクル活動が呼び掛けられていることがわかる。よって、これらの活動を program と表現した **(D)** が正解となる。(A) は❷に反し、(B) は寄付を従業員にお願いしているわけではない。(C) も個別に売ることを求められていない。

□ throw away 〜を捨てる　□ contribute to 〜に寄付をする　□ individually 個別に

問題5から6は次のメモに関するものです。

紙製品のリサイクル

宛先：　全従業員
差出人：資材部チームリーダー
件名：　紙のリサイクルプログラム

毎年約 2000 万枚の古紙が市のごみ埋め立て地に捨てられていると聞いたことがあるでしょう。近い将来、それは深刻な環境問題を引き起こしかねません。

今、当社は販売を通して、その大量の古紙を減らす手伝いをすることができます！

当社は ROCL 社と共に、貴重な自然資源を保護し、守る取り組みによる紙のリサイクルプログラムを始めました。

ROCL 社は当社から彼らの作業場までの古紙の運送費用を持ちます。さらに、当社が蓄え送る再利用可能な紙は非常に少ないですが、その費用も支払うことになっています。この再利用可能な紙から出た利益は、社会団体、慈善団体、病院などに寄付されます。

古紙を捨てないようにしましょう。不明な点があれば、お気軽にお問い合わせください。われわれの環境を安全に保つため、皆さんのご協力をお願いします。清潔で緑豊かな未来を守るため、あなたの役割を果たしましょう。

Questions 7-8 refer to the following text-message chain.

Isabella Swenson 2:29 P.M.
❶ I'm enjoying a cup of coffee at the coffee shop. I have a table near the window. Are you on your way?

Dylan Harwood 2:31 P.M.
Yes, sorry. ❷ I'm nearby but I'm looking for a place to park my car.

Isabella Swenson 2:32 P.M.
There's a parking lot on Dunham Street. I think the charge is $3.00 an hour.

Dylan Harwood 2:32 P.M.
Thanks. I'll be there soon.

Isabella Swenson 2:35 P.M.
❸ Do you want me to order you something to drink? ❹ They have good lattes here.

Dylan Harwood 2:36 P.M.
❺ That sounds great. Okay. See you soon.

☐ nearby 近くの　☐ park ～を駐車する　☐ parking lot 駐車場　☐ charge 料金
☐ latte ラテ（牛乳入り飲料、通常ミルク入りコーヒーを指す）

★★★☆☆

7. What can be suggested about
Ms. Harwood?

   (A) She will meet Ms. Swenson for the first
      time.
   (B) She is driving to the coffee shop.
   (C) She made a last-minute cancellation.
   (D) She got lost on the way to the coffee
      shop.

Harwood さんについて何が示唆されていますか。

   (A) Swenson さんと初めて会う。
   (B) 喫茶店に向かって運転している。
   (C) 直前に取りやめた。
   (D) 喫茶店へ行く途中で道に迷った。

🔍 Harwood さんについて示唆されていることを問う選択肢照合型の問題。冒頭の❶で、Swenson さんが喫茶店でコーヒーを飲みながら、Harwood さんにメッセージを送ったところ、❷で「近くにいて車を止める場所を探している」と返答している。ここから、Harwood さんは車で喫茶店へ向かっていることがわかるため、正解は **(B)** となる。道に迷っているわけではないので (D) は不正解。

✎ ☐ for the first time 初めて ☐ last-minute cancellation 直前の中止 ☐ get lost 道に迷う ☐ on the way 途中で

★★★★★ 意図問題

8. At 2:36 P.M., what does Ms. Harwood mean
when she writes, "That sounds great"?

   (A) She agrees to meet at a different time.
   (B) She thinks the business has fair prices.
   (C) She wants Ms. Swenson to order a
      drink for her.
   (D) She will go to Dunham Street.

午後 2 時 36 分に、Harwood さんは "That sounds
great" という発言で、何を意味していますか。

   (A) 別の機会に会うことに同意する。
   (B) 店の価格設定は妥当だと思う。
   (C) Swenson さんに飲み物を注文してほしい。
   (D) Dunham Street に行く。

🔍 意図問題。問われている❺は「それはいいですね」と前の発言に同意している意味。直前の❸・❹を見ると、Swenson さんが「何か飲み物を注文しておきましょうか」「この店はカフェラテがおいしいですよ」とお勧めの飲み物を提案していることがわかるので、これに同意していると考えられる。以上より、正解は **(C)**。同意や反対をしている場合は、直前の表現が正解のヒントとなる。

✎ ☐ fair price 妥当な価格

📝 問題 7 から 8 は次のテキストメッセージのやりとりに関するものです。

Isabella Swenson 午後 2 時 29 分
喫茶店でコーヒーを飲みながらくつろいでいます。窓際のテーブルです。こちらに向かっていますか？

Dylan Harwood 午後 2 時 31 分
はい、すみません。近くにいますが、車を止める場所を探しているところです。

Isabella Swenson 午後 2 時 32 分
Dunham Street に駐車場がありますよ。利用料は 1 時間 3 ドルだったと思います。

Dylan Harwood 午後 2 時 32 分
ありがとうございます。間もなくそちらに着きます。

Isabella Swenson 午後 2 時 35 分
何か飲み物を注文しておきましょうか。このお店はカフェラテがおいしいですよ。

Dylan Harwood 午後 2 時 36 分
それはいいですね。それでは、後ほどお会いしましょう。

Questions 9-11 refer to the following article.

Ottawa (April 1)—Beginning on April 15, the Theatre Department at Carleton University will be performing a series of modern plays in the children's ward at Ottawa General Hospital. These plays have been adapted for children and will be acted and directed by enrolled students.

Sarenna Tarley, Head Performance Arts Lecturer at Carleton University, said yesterday that the performances will be included in the students' final grades. "Theatre is about the interaction between the audience and the actors," she said during an interview yesterday. "The space may be difficult to work in, but making adjustments for different venues is just part of the challenge of becoming a successful performer." The plays chosen include *The Wizard of Oz* by Frank Baum and *Mary Poppins* by Pamela Lyndon Travers, etc.

"This really is a meaningful project," said Children's Ward Director Allison Underwood yesterday. "Many children cannot leave the hospital, so being able to bring the stage to these special patients is a real bonus. They are really excited about it."

The project is made possible through support from the university itself and the Ottawa Drama Centre, resulting in sufficient funding for a run of one performance for each play. But, with further donations from the residents, the run can be extended to make sure that all under 17 have a chance to see each play at least once. Contributions can be made through www.ottawadp.edu. Individuals calling the hospital about donations will be directed to this site.

9. What is the article about?

    (A) A traveling student musical group
    (B) A hospital benefit concert for patients
    (C) A university performing arts examination
    (D) A charity drama project for sick children

10. According to the article, what is indicated about Carleton University?

    (A) It will host an event to attract temporary students.
    (B) It will perform only one show.
    (C) It will be supporting an event financially.
    (D) It will donate its talent to a hospital building project.

11. Which of the following is NOT true about the performances?

    (A) They have received funding from a local arts group.
    (B) They will be proper for younger audiences to watch.
    (C) They will be modified for an unusual performance space.
    (D) They are based on the life of two playwrights.

P. 180

Questions 9-11 refer to the following article.

Ottawa (April 1)—❶ Beginning on April 15, the Theatre Department at Carleton University will be performing a series of modern plays in the children's ward at Ottawa General Hospital. ❷ These plays have been adapted for children and will be acted and directed by enrolled students.

Sarenna Tarley, Head Performance Arts Lecturer at Carleton University, said yesterday that the performances will be included in the students' final grades. "Theatre is about the interaction between the audience and the actors," she said during an interview yesterday. ❸ "The space may be difficult to work in, but making adjustments for different venues is just part of the challenge of becoming a successful performer." The plays chosen include *The Wizard of Oz* by Frank Baum and *Mary Poppins* by Pamela

Lyndon Travers, etc.

"This really is a meaningful project," said Children's Ward Director Allison Underwood yesterday. ❹ "Many children cannot leave the hospital, so being able to bring the stage to these special patients is a real bonus. They are really excited about it."

❺ The project is made possible through support from the university itself and the Ottawa Drama Centre, resulting in sufficient funding for a run of one performance for each play. ❻ But, with further donations from the residents, the run can be extended to make sure that all under 17 have a chance to see each play at least once. ❼ Contributions can be made through www.ottawadp.edu. Individuals calling the hospital about donations will be directed to this site.

✎
☐ a series of 一連の、さまざまな ☐ modern 現代的な ☐ play 劇 ☐ adapt for (~を) ~に合うようにする
☐ direct ~を監督・演出する ☐ enrolled student 在校生 ☐ final grade 最終評価
☐ interaction between A and B AとBの交流 ☐ work in ~で上演する ☐ adjustment 調整 ☐ venue 会場
☐ meaningful 意義のある ☐ children's ward 小児科病棟 ☐ patient 患者 ☐ be made possible 可能となる
☐ result in 結果として~となる ☐ sufficient 十分な ☐ funding 資金提供 ☐ run 上演、公演 ☐ donation 寄付
☐ extend ~を延長する ☐ under ~歳未満の ☐ contribution 寄付 ☐ individuals 個人
☐ direct A to B AをBへ導く

★★★☆☆

9. What is the article about?

(A) A traveling student musical group
(B) A hospital benefit concert for patients
(C) A university performing arts examination
(D) A charity drama project for sick children

何についての記事ですか。

(A) 巡業している学生の音楽グループ
(B) 患者のための病院慈善演奏会
(C) 大学の舞台芸術の試験
(D) 病気の子どもたちのための慈善演劇プロジェクト

🔍 この記事が何に関するものかが問われている。❶で「小児病棟で演劇が行われる」とあり、❹や最終段落の❺・❻・❼で、この演劇が病院の子どもに向けたもので、公演のための寄付を募っていることがわかる。よって、正解は **(D)**。情報が分散しているので、注意して読み取る必要がある。(A) は上演する学生が巡業公演しているわけではないので不正解。(B) は演奏会ではなく劇（play, drama）であれば正解となる。

✎ ☐ travel 巡業する ☐ benefit concert 慈善演奏会 ☐ charity drama 慈善演劇

★★★☆☆

10. According to the article, what is indicated about Carleton University?

(A) It will host an event to attract temporary students.
(B) It will perform only one show.
(C) It will be supporting an event financially.
(D) It will donate its talent to a hospital building project.

記事によると、Carleton 大学について何が示唆されていますか。

(A) 短期間在籍する学生を集めるためのイベントを主催する。
(B) 1 回だけ公演を行う。
(C) イベントの金銭的な支援を行う。
(D) 病院建設プロジェクトに才能のある人材を送る。

⭐⭐⭐☆☆ NOT 問題

11. Which of the following is NOT true about the performances?

(A) They have received funding from a local arts group.

(B) They will be proper for younger audiences to watch.

(C) They will be modified for an unusual performance space.

(D) They are based on the life of two playwrights.

上演する劇について正しくないことはどれですか。

(A) 地元の芸術グループから資金の提供を受けている。

(B) 若い観客が見るのに適切なものになる。

(C) 普段とは違う上演会場に向けに変更される。

(D) 2 人の劇作家の人生に基づいている。

📝 問題 9 から 11 は次の記事に関するものです。

オタワ（4 月 1 日）— 4 月 15 日より、Ottawa General Hospital の小児病棟でさまざまな現代演劇が Carleton 大学の舞台芸術学部により上演される。演劇は子ども向けにアレンジされており、在校生たちによって演技・演出が行われる。

Carleton 大学の舞台芸術の主任講師である Sarenna Tarley は昨日、この舞台は学生たちの最終的な成績評価の対象になると述べた。「演劇は観客と役者との交流です」と昨日のインタビューの中で語っている。「たやすく上演を行える場所ではないかもしれませんが、会場に合わせて調整することは演者として成功するための挑戦の一部に過ぎません。」選ばれた演劇には、Frank Baum の オズの魔法使い や Pamela Lyndon Travers の 風にのってきたメアリー・ポピンズ などがある。

小児病棟の部長である Allison Underwood は昨日、「これは本当に意味のあるプロジェクトです」と語った。「子どもたちの多くは病院を離れることができませんので、演劇をこれら特定の患者の方々に提供できるのはとても素晴らしいことです。子どもたちは本当にわくわくしています。」

このプロジェクトは、大学と Ottawa Drama Centre の支援により実現し、演目ごとの 1 回の上演に十分な資金が提供されるに至った。しかし、住民からさらに寄付が集まれば、17 歳未満のすべての患者が各演目を少なくとも 1 回必ず観られるように、上演を延長することができる。寄付は www.ottawadp.edu を通じて行うことができる。個人が病院へ寄付について問い合わせをした場合も、このサイトを紹介される。

Questions 12-14 refer to the following article.

 2分45秒

New Student Dormitory for Goodwin University
by Garret Kent, Campus Reporter

June 15—A ground-breaking ceremony was convened last Friday at the intersection of Vine Street and Aldrich Avenue in Atlanta. Now, Goodwin University is constructing its new student dormitory, Thomas Hall. Evan Harrison, university president, lifted the first shovelful of soil at the site, located three blocks south of the main campus. — [1] —.

Thomas Hall is a joint project between the university, a state-run institution, and the Moore Group, a local property development agency. It will consist of eight full-service buildings. Each will have retail space on the first floor, recreational space on the second floor, and private student living quarters on the third, fourth, and fifth floors. The Moore Group will develop the site and run the retail businesses. — [2] —.

Recently the school has noticed a drastic rise in the number of applicants who request housing on campus. The twelve-story on-campus apartment building built last fall has helped accommodate some of the demands. But, when this project is completed, the university will be in a much better position to meet students' needs.

Some business owners have already expressed interest in renting space in the structure, including a number of retail shops and eateries. — [3] —. Sally Carter, the Moore Group's head partner, said that she has approached a large grocery store chain in the area about opening a small shop. — [4] —.

12. Who is Mr. Harrison?

(A) A city official
(B) A land owner
(C) A university administrator
(D) A real estate agent

13. What business does the Moore Group hope to attract to Thomas Hall?

(A) A clothing store
(B) A laundry
(C) A coffee shop
(D) A supermarket

14. In which of the positions marked [1], [2], [3], and [4] does the following sentence best belong?

"According to Mr. Harrison, until the last few years, most of our students have been commuters."

(A) [1]
(B) [2]
(C) [3]
(D) [4]

P. 182

Questions 12-14 refer to the following article.

New Student Dormitory for Goodwin University
by Garret Kent, Campus Reporter

June 15—A ground-breaking ceremony was convened last Friday at the intersection of Vine Street and Aldrich Avenue in Atlanta. Now, Goodwin University is constructing its new student dormitory, Thomas Hall. ❶ Evan Harrison, university president, lifted the first shovelful of soil at the site, located three blocks south of the main campus. — [1] —.

❷ Thomas Hall is a joint project between the university, a state-run institution, and the Moore Group, a local property development agency. ❸ It will consist of eight full-service buildings. Each will have retail space on the first floor, recreational space on the second floor, and private student living quarters on the third, fourth, and fifth floors. ❹ The Moore Group will develop the site and run the retail businesses. — [2] —.

❺ Recently the school has noticed a drastic rise in the number of applicants who request housing on campus. The twelve-story on-campus apartment building built last fall has helped accommodate some of the demands. But, when this project is completed, the university will be in a much better position to meet students' needs.

Some business owners have already expressed interest in renting space in the structure, including a number of retail shops and eateries. — [3] —. ❻ Sally Carter, the Moore Group's head partner, said that she has approached a large grocery store chain in the area about opening a small shop. — [4] —.

□ dormitory 寮 □ ground-breaking ceremony 起工式 □ convene (会議等) を開催、召集する
□ intersection 交差点 □ lift ～を持ち上げる、すくい上げる □ shovelful シャベル1杯 □ soil 土 □ site 現場
□ located (～に) 位置する □ joint project between A and B AとBとの共同プロジェクト
□ state-run institution 州立機関 □ property development agency 不動産開発機関 □ consist of ～で構成される
□ retail 小売りの □ recreational レクリエーションの □ drastic rise 劇的な上昇・増加 □ applicant 申込者
□ housing 住居 □ -story - 階建ての □ accommodate demand 需要を満たす
□ express interest in ～に関心を示す □ structure 建物 □ eatery 飲食店

★★☆☆☆

12. Who is Mr. Harrison?

(A) A city official
(B) A land owner
(C) A university administrator
(D) A real estate agent

Harrison さんとは誰ですか。

(A) 市の職員
(B) 土地の所有者
(C) 大学の管理者
(D) 不動産業者

🔍 Harrison さんは誰かが問われている。❶から、Harrison さんが大学の学長とわかるので、「学長＝管理者」と言い換えている **(C)** が正解となる。人物の直後にカンマに狭まれた肩書や役職がある場合は、その人物が何者なのかを指している。試験でよく狙われる箇所なので、確実に正解できるようにしておこう。

★★★☆☆

13. What business does the Moore Group hope to attract to Thomas Hall?

(A) A clothing store
(B) A laundry
(C) A coffee shop
(D) A supermarket

Moore Group 社は Thomas Hall にどんな店を誘致したいと考えていますか。

(A) 衣料品店
(B) クリーニング店
(C) 喫茶店
(D) スーパーマーケット

Moore Group 社は Thomas Hall にどんな店を誘致したいかが問われている。❻で Moore Group 社の経営者である Sally Carter さんが「地域の大型食料品店チェーンに小規模な店舗を出店することについて打診した」と述べていることから、"grocery store" を言い換えた **(D)** が正解だとわかる。

★★★★☆ 文挿入位置問題

14. In which of the positions marked [1], [2], [3], and [4] does the following sentence best belong?

"According to Mr. Harrison, until the last few years, most of our students have been commuters."

(A) [1]
(B) [2]
(C) [3]
(D) [4]

次の文は [1]、[2]、[3]、[4] のどの位置に最もよく当てはまりますか。

「Harrison 氏によると、ここ数年までは、ほとんどの学生が通学者だった」

(A) [1]
(B) [2]
(C) [3]
(D) [4]

適切な文の位置を問う問題。問われている文は、「(学長の) Harrison さんによると、学生の大半が通学者である」という内容だ。「学生が通学者」という箇所に注目しよう。学生寮の Thomas Hall について❷・❸・❹で「小売スペース、レクリエーションスペース、学生が生活する個室がある」と述べられている。そして次の段落の❺で「大学構内に居住を希望する学生が増えている」とあるため、ここに文を入れると文意が成立する。以上より、正解は **(B)** となる。

□ last few years 過去数年 □ commuter 通勤者、通学者

問題 12 から 14 は次の記事に関するものです。

Goodwin University の新学生寮
キャンパス記者 Garret Kent による報告

6 月 15 日 — 先週金曜日にアトランタの Vine Street と Aldrich Avenue の交差点で起工式が行われた。現在、Goodwin University はその場所に新しい学生寮 Thomas Hall を建設中である。大学の学長 Evan Harrison 氏は主要キャンパスから南に 3 区画離れた現場で、最初のシャベルいっぱいの土をすくい上げた。—[1]—

Thomas Hall は州営機関である大学と地元の不動産開発機関である Moore Group 社との共同プロジェクトである。8 棟のフルサービスのビルからなる。それぞれ 1 階に小売スペース、2 階にレクリエーションスペース、そして 3、4、5 階に学生が生活する個室がある。Moore Group 社が開発を行い、小売店を運営する。—[2]— Harrison 氏によると、ここ数年までは、ほとんどの学生が通学者だった。

近年、大学ではキャンパス内の住居を希望する学生の数が劇的に増えてきていることがわかった。昨年の秋に当校に建てられた 12 階建てのキャンパス内アパートは、需要の一部に対応することができた。しかし、今回のプロジェクトが完了した際には、大学はもっと容易に学生のニーズを満たすことができるだろう。—[3]—

多くの小売店や飲食店など、すでに建物のスペースを借りることに関心を示している事業者もいる。Moore Group 社の主な共同経営者である Sally Carter 氏は、地域の大型食料品店チェーンに小規模な店舗を出店することについて打診したと語った。—[4]—

Questions 15-17 refer to the following form.

2分45秒

Cindy Clothing Co.
Annual Employee Review

Employee's Name: Richard Kay **Director's Name:** Jenny Manning
Title: Visual Assistant Designer **Title:** Design Head Director
Department: Design
Length of time you have supervised the employee: 2 years

	Very Bad	Bad	Average	Good	Very Good
Originality in creations					O
Fulfilling obligations			O		
Software handling skills		O			
Artistic ability				O	

Director's Comments: Though Mr. Kay sometimes tends to slack off and fails to finish his assignment until its deadline, he has shown excellent talent and created very innovative and original designs. His designs are what our company requires the most and therefore makes him an incomparable asset to our firm. Most other workers prefer their work to be done electronically, but Mr. Kay finishes all of his work manually. I think that his work speed can be greatly improved if he learns to use some of our design software. I recommend that he register for courses on this software at the company's expense.

Employee: Richard Kay	Signature: *Richard Kay*
Director: Jenny Manning	Signature: *Jenny Manning*
Reviewer: Ryan Fenton	Signature: *Ryan Fenton*

15. What is the purpose of the form?

    (A) To ask for funding for a special training session
    (B) To assess an employee's performance
    (C) To admire a company member for his achievements
    (D) To persuade an employee into receiving training

16. What does Ms. Manning say about Mr. Kay?

    (A) He arrives at work late at times.
    (B) He majored in visual design at university.
    (C) He prefers doing work electronically.
    (D) He has been part of the company for over a year.

17. In what skill area does Mr. Kay need to develop the most?

    (A) Computer knowledge
    (B) Creativeness
    (C) Work obligations
    (D) Artistic value

P. 188

Questions 15-17 refer to the following form.

Cindy Clothing Co.
❶ Annual Employee Review

❷ **Employee's Name:** Richard Kay   ❸ **Director's Name:** Jenny Manning
Title: Visual Assistant Designer   **Title:** Design Head Director
Department: Design
❹ **Length of time you have supervised the employee:** 2 years

	Very Bad	❺ Bad	Average	Good	Very Good
Originality in creations					O
Fulfilling obligations			O		
❺ Software handling skills		❺ O			
Artistic ability				O	

Director's Comments: Though Mr. Kay sometimes tends to slack off and fails to finish his assignment until its deadline, he has shown excellent talent and created very innovative and original designs. His designs are what our company requires the most and therefore makes him an incomparable asset to our firm. ❻ Most other workers prefer their work to be done electronically, but Mr. Kay finishes all of his work manually. I think that his work speed can be greatly improved if he learns to use some of our design software. ❼ I recommend that he register for courses on this software at the company's expense.

Employee: Richard Kay	Signature: *Richard Kay*
Director: Jenny Manning	Signature: *Jenny Manning*
Reviewer: Ryan Fenton	Signature: *Ryan Fenton*

☐ employee review 従業員評価 ☐ title 役職、肩書 ☐ length of time 期間 ☐ supervise ～を監督する
☐ originality 独特さ ☐ creation 創造 ☐ fulfill ～を履行する ☐ obligation 義務、責任 ☐ artistic 芸術的な
☐ slack off 義務を怠る ☐ fail to *do* ～し損ねる ☐ assignment 業務、任務 ☐ deadline 締め切り
☐ talent 才能 ☐ innovative 革新的な ☐ therefore それゆえ ☐ incomparable 比較することのできない
☐ asset 財産となる人材 ☐ electronically 電子的に ☐ register for ～に登録する ☐ reviewer 確認者

★☆☆☆☆

15. What is the purpose of the form?

(A) To ask for funding for a special training session
(B) To assess an employee's performance
(C) To admire a company member for his achievements
(D) To persuade an employee into receiving training

書式の目的は何ですか。

(A) 特別研修会のために資金を調達すること
(B) 従業員の仕事に対する評価をすること
(C) 会社員の功績を称賛すること
(D) 研修を受けるように従業員を説得すること

この書式の目的が問われている。❶で「従業員評価」とあり、その後に被評価者である従業員名・評価者である管理者名、および項目ごとの評価表とコメントが続いているため、従業員の実績を評価するためのものだとわかる。以上から、正解は「従業員評価」を言い換えた **(B)**。

☐ ask for ～を求める ☐ funding for ～への資金提供 ☐ training session 研修会 ☐ assess ～を評価する
☐ performance 実績 ☐ admire ～を称賛する ☐ achievement 功績
☐ persuade A into doing A を～するように説得する

★★☆☆☆

16. What does Ms. Manning say about Mr. Kay?

(A) He arrives at work late at times.
(B) He majored in visual design at university.
(C) He prefers doing work electronically.
(D) He has been part of the company for over a year.

Manning さんは Kay さんについて何と言っていますか。

(A) 時々遅れて出社する。
(B) 大学でビジュアルデザインを専攻した。
(C) コンピューターで仕事をすることを好む。
(D) 1 年以上会社に勤めている。

Manning さんは Kay さんについて何と言っているかが問われている。❷・❸より Manning さんは管理者（つまり、評価者）で、Kay さんは従業員（つまり、被評価者）であることがわかる。そして、❹で監督した期間が 2 年と述べている。ここから Kay さんは少なくとも 2 年間はこの会社にいることがわかり、これを「1 年以上会社に勤めている」と言い換えている **(D)** が正解となる。(C) は❻から Kay さんではない他の社員についてだとわかるため不正解。

✎ ☐ at times 時折 ☐ major in 〜を専攻する

★★★☆☆

17. In what skill area does Mr. Kay need to develop the most?

(A) Computer knowledge
(B) Creativeness
(C) Work obligations
(D) Artistic value

Kay さんはどの分野を最も向上させる必要がありますか。

(A) コンピューターの知識
(B) 創造性
(C) 仕事の責任
(D) 芸術的な価値

Kay さんはどの分野を最も向上させる必要があるかが問われている。評価表の❺で、「ソフトウェアを扱う力」が悪い評価となっており、❼で「会社の費用でソフトウェアのコースに登録することをお勧めする」と述べていることから、間接的にコンピューターの知識の向上を必要としていることがわかる。よって、正解は **(A)**。

 問題 15 から 17 は次の書式に関するものです。

Cindy Clothing Co.
年次従業員評価

従業員名：Richard Kay　　　　　　　　管理者名：Jenny Manning
役職：ビジュアルデザイナーアシスタント　　役職：デザイン担当役員
部署：デザイン部
従業員を監督した期間：2 年

	とても悪い	悪い	平均的	良い	とても良い
独創性					O
義務の履行			O		
ソフトウェアを扱う能力		O			
芸術性				O	

管理者のコメント：Kay さんは時に気が緩み、期限までに割り当てられた業務を終えられないことがありますが、優れた才能があり、非常に革新的で独創的なデザインを生み出しています。彼のデザインは当社が最も必要としているものであり、したがって、彼は当社にとって、比類のない財産になっています。他の社員はほとんどがコンピューターを使った作業を好みますが、Kay さんはすべての作業を手作業で行います。もし彼が当社のデザインソフトウェアを使えるようになれば、作業速度は大いに向上することと思います。会社の費用で、彼がこのソフトウェアのコースに登録することをお勧めします。

従業員：Richard Kay	署名：Richard Kay
管理者：Jenny Manning	署名：Jenny Manning
確認者：Ryan Fenton	署名：Ryan Fenton

4分 00秒

AMBO ENTERTAINMENT SECTION

"Dolomino's Strings"
by John Doily, Reviewer

"Dolomino's Strings", the new musical composed by Patricia Johnson, was performed as part of the Hortensen Musical Service's annual summer program last Tuesday. The musical is based on the life of a cello player who overcame many obstacles throughout his life to become an internationally well-known musician.

Aaron Burnard, who achieved worldwide recognition for his beautiful performance in the movie "Looking for the Dream", is very believable as the famous cello player, Roberto Wi. A Hortensen Musical Service regular, Noelle Ibarra, also gives an amazing performance as Mr. Wi's supportive wife, Annabelle Diaz.

"Dolomino's Strings" is much more dramatic and suspenseful than the light-hearted comedies that Hortensen Musical Service has frequently shown. Even with a running time of one and a half hours, the performers draw the audience into the world of the musical. The sparse decorations and low-key wardrobe help the audience get lost in the musical as well.

Frank Briggs, the National Musical Award-winner who grew up in Ambo, is the director of "Dolomino's Strings."

The theater box office can be reached at 408-757-7512 for ticket sales and show time information.

18. According to the review, who wrote the play?

(A) Aaron Burnard
(B) Frank Briggs
(C) Patricia Johnson
(D) Noelle Ibarra

19. How does "Dolomino's Strings" differ from the Hortensen Musical Service's usual entertainment?

(A) It contains a full orchestra.
(B) It features a world-famous person's life.
(C) It uses an entirely local cast.
(D) It is more dramatic and serious.

20. How can information about the show times be obtained?

(A) By forwarding an e-mail
(B) By phoning the ticket office
(C) By picking up a booklet
(D) By visiting a theater

21. What can be suggested about "Dolomino's Strings"?

(A) The musical recently won an award.
(B) All actors are vividly dressed.
(C) It is being shown during the summer.
(D) The musical is performed by trained actors.

P. 192

Questions 18-21 refer to the following review.

AMBO ENTERTAINMENT SECTION

"Dolomino's Strings"
by John Doily, Reviewer

❶ "Dolomino's Strings", the new musical composed by Patricia Johnson, was performed as part of the Hortensen Musical Service's annual summer program last Tuesday. The musical is based on the life of a cello player who overcame many obstacles throughout his life to become an internationally well-known musician.

Aaron Burnard, who achieved worldwide recognition for his beautiful performance in the movie "Looking for the Dream", is very believable as the famous cello player, Roberto Wi. A Hortensen Musical Service regular, Noelle Ibarra, also gives an amazing performance as Mr. Wi's supportive wife, Annabelle Diaz.

❷ "Dolomino's Strings" is much more dramatic and suspenseful than the light-hearted comedies that Hortensen Musical Service has frequently shown. Even with a running time of one and a half hours, the performers draw the audience into the world of the musical. ❸ The sparse decorations and low-key wardrobe help the audience get lost in the musical as well.

Frank Briggs, the National Musical Award-winner who grew up in Ambo, is the director of "Dolomino's Strings."

❹ The theater box office can be reached at 408-757-7512 for ticket sales and show time information.

□ compose ～を創作する、作曲する　□ as part of ～の一部として　□ based on ～に基づいて
□ overcome ～に打ち勝つ　□ obstacle 障害　□ well-known よく知られた、有名な　□ achieve ～を達成する
□ recognition 認知、認識　□ believable 信じることのできる　□ supportive 献身的な　□ dramatic 劇的な
□ suspenseful サスペンスに満ちた　□ light-hearted 愉快な　□ frequently 頻繁に　□ running time 上演時間
□ sparse わずかな　□ decoration 装飾　□ low-key 控えめな　□ wardrobe 衣装　□ get lost 没頭する
□ as well 同様に　□ box office チケット売り場

★★★★★

18. According to the review, who wrote the play?

(A) Aaron Burnard
(B) Frank Briggs
(C) Patricia Johnson
(D) Noelle Ibarra

レビューによると、演劇を制作したのは誰ですか。

(A) Aron Burnard
(B) Frank Briggs
(C) Patricia Johnson
(D) Noelle Ibarra

演劇を制作したのは誰かが問われている。❶で「Patricia Johnson が作曲した新作ミュージカル "Dolomino's Strings"」と述べている。ここから正解は **(C)**。設問の wrote と文書の❶の "composed" が言い換えとなっていることもチェックしておこう。

19. How does "Dolomino's Strings" differ from the Hortensen Musical Service's usual entertainment?

(A) It contains a full orchestra.
(B) It features a world-famous person's life.
(C) It uses an entirely local cast.
(D) It is more dramatic and serious.

"Dolomino's Strings" は Hortensen Musical Service のいつもの演劇とどのように違いますか。

(A) フルオーケストラが含まれている。
(B) 世界的に有名な人物の人生を取り上げている。
(C) 全員が地元の演者である。
(D) より劇的で堅い内容である。

Dolomino's Strings が Hortensen Musical Service の通常の演劇とどう違うかが問われている。❷で「"Dolomino's Strings" は Hortensen Musical Service が上演してきたコメディーに比べて、ドラマチックでサスペンスに満ちている」と述べている。ここから "suspenseful" を serious に言い換えた **(D)** が正解。❷の "much more ... than frequently shown" が「いつも上演するものより…だ」という意味で、設問では differ from に言い換えられていることにも注目しておこう。

□ differ from ～と異なる　□ usual いつもの　□ contain ～を含む　□ orchestra オーケストラ
□ feature ～を大きく取り上げる　□ entirely 完全に　□ cast 出演者　□ dramatic 劇的な

20. How can information about the show times be obtained?

(A) By forwarding an e-mail
(B) By phoning the ticket office
(C) By picking up a booklet
(D) By visiting a theater

上演時間についての情報は、どうすれば得られますか。

(A) E メールを転送する
(B) チケット窓口に電話をする
(C) 冊子をもらう
(D) 劇場を訪れる

上演時間についての情報の取得方法が問われている。❹に「チケット売り場に電話をかける」と記載があるため、これを言い換えた **(B)** が正解。be reached at ○○（電話番号）で「○○に電話をかけると繋がる」という意味になるので、すぐに言い換えとして識別できるようにしておこう。

□ obtain ～を得る　□ forward ～を転送する、送付する　□ booklet 冊子

21. What can be suggested about "Dolomino's Strings"?

(A) The musical recently won an award.
(B) All actors are vividly dressed.
(C) It is being shown during the summer.
(D) The musical is performed by trained actors.

"Dolomino's Strings" について何が示唆されていますか。

(A) ミュージカルは最近賞を受賞した。
(B) すべての演者が鮮やかな衣装を着ている。
(C) 夏の間上演されている。
(D) ミュージカルは、ベテランの俳優が演じている。

演劇 "Dolomino's Strings" について何が示唆されているかが問われている。まず冒頭❶で、「"Dolomino's Strings" が夏のプログラムの一環として上演された」とわかる。次に❹で、このチケットが今販売されていることから、この劇自体は今も上演中であることがわかるため、受け身の進行形を使っている **(C)** が正解となる。(B) は❸で、鮮やかではなく控えめな衣装、と言っている。(A) 受賞、(D) ベテラン俳優、等も記載がなく、ここではいずれも不正解。

□ win（賞など）を獲得する　□ vividly 鮮やかに　□ trained ベテランの、習熟した

Ambo エンターテインメント部門

"Dolomino's Strings"
評論家　John Doily

Patricia Johnson が作曲した新作ミュージカル "Dolomino's Strings" が Hortensen Musical Service の毎年恒例の夏のプログラムの一環として、先週火曜日に上演された。このミュージカルは、数々の困難を乗り越えて国際的に有名な音楽家となったあるチェロ奏者の人生に基づいたものである。

映画 "Looking for the Dream" での素晴らしい演技で世界的に認められた Aaron Burnard 氏は、有名なチェロ奏者 Roberto Wi を忠実に演じている。Hortensen Musical Service の常連である Noelle Ibarra 氏もまた、Wi の献身的な妻 Annabelle Diaz として圧巻の演技を見せている。

"Dolomino's Strings" は Hortensen Musical Service がしばしば上演してきた陽気なコメディーに比べて、よりドラマチックでサスペンスに満ちている。1 時間半という上演時間にもかかわらず、演者たちは観客をミュージカルの世界に引き込む。乏しい装飾や控えめな衣装もまた観客がミュージカルに没頭させることに役立っている。

Ambo で育った National Musical Award の受賞者 Frank Briggs 氏が、Dolomino's Strings の演出家である。

劇場のチケット窓口 408-757-7512 では、チケットの販売や上演時間の情報を提供している。

GO ON TO THE NEXT PAGE!

Dellinger (October 5)—Our city of Dellinger has seven major sports complexes, and is renovating and expanding three of them. These renovations have cost the city $850,000 until now, which is equal to the amount that the Dellinger City Hall spends each year on operations and maintenance for all the sports complexes under its management. An extra $300,000 is supposed to be spent before the renovation plan is ended next month, making the total cost about $1,150,000. —— [1] ——.

But many financial demands will not hurt the city budget, because the renovation plan is paid for by the Dellinger City Hall. In the past few years, the city's sports complexes have brought in increasingly more visitors, including local residents and out-of-town tourists. Therefore, this has led to a steady increase in profits coming from ballpark and swimming pool admission fees, concession stand sales, rental fees of sports complexes, and other related sources; in fact, last year's profits totaled $ 2,000,000. —— [2] ——. So, at present the Dellinger City Hall is one of only a few city agencies in the state that can honestly claim to be financially independent.

—— [3] ——. The current plan is the result of a lengthy study conducted last summer by the Dellinger City Hall that concentrated on the quality and conditions of the area's sports complexes. As part of the study, a survey was sent to 5,000 local residents who frequently go to the sports complexes. Among other things, the participants were asked to evaluate the condition of the sports complexes and to suggest improvements. —— [4] ——. After careful thought, the mayor approved the implementation of the renovation program of the Dellinger City Hall.

22. How much does it cost the Dellinger City Hall yearly to operate and maintain the city's sports complexes?

(A) $300,000
(B) $850,000
(C) $1,150,000
(D) $2,000,000

23. According to the article, what will most likely happen in November?

(A) New City Hall officials will be named.
(B) Surveys will be mailed out.
(C) A new facility will open.
(D) Renovations will be finished.

24. How is the Dellinger City Hall different from other similar agencies?

(A) It manages the largest government agency in the state.
(B) It is staffed mostly by the elected officials.
(C) It can pay for all operation expenses from its annual profits.
(D) It supplies several different kinds of activities.

25. In which of the positions marked [1], [2], [3], and [4] does the following sentence best belong?

"Then the result along with a proposed plan was given to the mayor's office."

(A) [1]
(B) [2]
(C) [3]
(D) [4]

P. 198

Questions 22-25 refer to the following article.

Dellinger (❶ October 5)—Our city of Dellinger has seven major sports complexes, and is renovating and expanding three of them. ❷ These renovations have cost the city $850,000 until now, which is equal to the amount that the Dellinger City Hall spends each year on operations and maintenance for all the sports complexes under its management. ❸ An extra $300,000 is supposed to be spent before the renovation plan is ended next month, making the total cost about $1,150,000. — [1] —.

❹ But many financial demands will not hurt the city budget, because the renovation plan is paid for by the Dellinger City Hall. In the past few years, the city's sports complexes have brought in increasingly more visitors, including local residents and out-of-town tourists. Therefore, this has led to a steady increase in profits coming from ballpark and swimming pool admission fees, concession stand sales, rental fees of sports complexes, and other related sources; in fact, last year's profits totaled $ 2,000,000. — [2] —. ❺ So, at present the Dellinger City Hall is one of only a few city agencies in the state that can honestly claim to be financially independent.

— [3] —. The current plan is the result of a lengthy study conducted last summer by the Dellinger City Hall that concentrated on the quality and conditions of the area's sports complexes. ❻ As part of the study, a survey was sent to 5,000 local residents who frequently go to the sports complexes. Among other things, the participants were asked to evaluate the condition of the sports complexes and to suggest improvements. — [4] —. ❼ After careful thought, the mayor approved the implementation of the renovation program of the Dellinger City Hall.

✎
- ☐ sports complex 運動施設 ☐ until now 今まで ☐ equal to ～に等しい ☐ amount 金額 ☐ extra 追加の
- ☐ be supposed to *do* ～するはずである ☐ total cost 総額 ☐ financial demand 費用の負担
- ☐ hurt ～に影響を与える ☐ increasingly 増加して ☐ out-of-town 市外の ☐ lead to ～に至る
- ☐ steady 堅調な ☐ ballpark 球場 ☐ admission fee 入場料 ☐ concession stand 売店
- ☐ total 合計～となる ☐ at present 現在 ☐ honestly 正直に ☐ claim ～を主張する ☐ independent 独立した
- ☐ lengthy 長期にわたる ☐ concentrate on ～に焦点を当てる ☐ as part of ～の一環として
- ☐ among other things とりわけ ☐ evaluate ～を評価する ☐ careful thought 慎重な考察
- ☐ implementation 実行

★★★☆☆

22. How much does it cost the Dellinger City Hall yearly to operate and maintain the city's sports complexes?

(A) $300,000
(B) $850,000
(C) $1,150,000
(D) $2,000,000

Dellinger 市当局が、市の運動施設の運営や維持をするために、毎年いくら費用がかかりますか。

(A) 30万ドル
(B) 85万ドル
(C) 115万ドル
(D) 200万ドル

🔍 Dellinger 市当局が、市の運動施設の運営や維持をするための毎年の費用が問われている。❷で「今まで改修に費やした 85万ドルは、Dellinger 市当局の管理下にあるすべての運動施設の運営と維持に毎年費やしている金額と等しい」と述べられているため、**(B)** が正解となる。❷の "be equal to（～に等しい）" という語が解答のポイントとなる。

✎ ☐ yearly 毎年

23. According to the article, what will most likely happen in November?

(A) New City Hall officials will be named.
(B) Surveys will be mailed out.
(C) A new facility will open.
(D) Renovations will be finished.

記事によると、11月に何が起こると考えられますか。

(A) 新たな市当局の職員が任命される。
(B) アンケートが一度に発送される。
(C) 新施設が開業する。
(D) 改修工事が終了する。

11月に何が起こるかが問われている。❸で「来月に改修計画が終了」と述べられており、❶からこの記事が書かれたのは10月であるとわかるため、11月に改修（工事）計画が終了すると考えられる。以上から、正解は **(D)**。記事冒頭の日付は解答のヒントになることもあるので、押さえておくクセをつけておこう。

....

24. How is the Dellinger City Hall different from other similar agencies?

(A) It manages the largest government agency in the state.
(B) It is staffed mostly by the elected officials.
(C) It can pay for all operation expenses from its annual profits.
(D) It supplies several different kinds of activities.

Dellinger市当局は他の同様の機関と何が違いますか。

(A) 州で最も大きな政府機関を管理している。
(B) 働いているのは、ほとんどが選ばれた役人である。
(C) 毎年の利益によってすべての運営費を支払うことができる。
(D) さまざまな種類の活動をいくつか実施している。

Dellinger市当局は他の同様の機関と何が違うのかが問われている。第2段落の❹で「改修計画の費用はDellinger市当局によって負担されているため、財政的負担が市の予算に影響を与えることはない」、❺で「現在、Dellinger市当局は（収益性があり）財政的に独立していると堂々と主張できる州内でも数少ない市の機関である」ことが述べられている。ここから、毎年の利益で運営費を賄えているくらい、財政状況が安定していることがわかる。以上から、これを言い換えた **(C)** が正解となる。(D) は、第2段落に複数の活動が書かれているが、他の同様の機関と違うかどうかはわからないので不正解。

☐ elected 選出された　☐ expense 支出、費用

....

 文挿入位置問題

25. In which of the positions marked [1], [2], [3], and [4] does the following sentence best belong?

"Then the result along with a proposed plan was given to the mayor's office."

(A) [1]
(B) [2]
(C) [3]
(D) [4]

次の文は [1]、[2]、[3]、[4] のどの位置に最もよく当てはまりますか。

「その後、その結果は提案された計画とともに市長室に提出された」

(A) [1]
(B) [2]
(C) [3]
(D) [4]

適切な文の位置を問う問題。問われている文は「その後、その結果は提案された計画とともに市長室に提出された」なので、この文の前には「提案、調査などの何かを実施したという内容」が書かれていると予想できる。[4] の前の❻に「この調査の一環として、アンケートが送られた」とあり、後には❼「慎重な調査の結果、実施を承認した」とある。よって、**(D)** が正解となる。

☐ along with ～とともに　☐ proposed 提案された

Dellinger（10 月 5 日）— 私たちが暮らす Dellinger 市には 7 つの大きな運動施設があり、そのうち 3 つの改修及び拡張を行っている最中である。これらの改修は現在までに、市に 85 万ドルを費やさせており、これは Dellinger 市当局の管理下にあるすべての運動施設の運営と維持に毎年費やしている金額に等しい。来月の改修計画終了までに、追加で 30 万ドルを費やすことになっているため、総額は約 115 万ドルとなる。—[1]—

しかし、改修計画の費用は Dellinger 市当局によって負担されているため、財政的負担が市の予算に影響を与えることはない。ここ数年間で、市内の複合スポーツ施設には、地元住民や市外からの観光客など、多くの人が訪れている。そのため、球場や水泳施設の入場料、売店での売り上げ、運動施設の貸出料などの収益が順調伸びており、実際に昨年の収益は合計で 200 万ドルとなった。—[2]— つまり、現在、Dellinger 市当局は財政的に独立していると堂々と主張できる州内でも数少ない市の機関の一つである。

—[3]— 現在の計画は、Dellinger 市当局が昨年の夏に行った、地域の運動施設の品質と状態に焦点を当てた、長期にわたる調査の結果である。この調査の一環として、運動施設に頻繁に行く地元住民 5,000 人にアンケートが送られた。とりわけ参加者（アンケートの回答者）には、運動施設の状態を評価することと改善点をあげることが求められた。—[4]— その後、その結果は提案された計画とともに市長室に提出された。慎重な検討の結果、市長は Dellinger 市当局による改修プログラムの実施を承認した。

Questions 26-29 refer to the following online chat discussion.

 4分00秒

Wally Penn [2:14 P.M.]
I've received an inquiry about our web designing service from Tollington Inc. I want your ideas before I meet with them.

Zullo Lee [2:15 P.M.]
That's one of the largest advertising firms in our state, isn't it?

Wally Penn [2:17 P.M.]
Right! They're telling us that they'd like a more user-friendly Web site than the current one that was created by the Cove Agency.

Tom Anderson [2:19 P.M.]
Our competitor? I know a great deal about their Web site templates. One of their drawbacks is the organization of their links. Theirs are a little challenging to use.

Wally Penn [2:24 P.M.]
That's good to know. Tom, can you write a brief summary of their drawbacks and get it to me?

Tom Anderson [2:26 P.M.]
Of course. I'll start on it right after this.

Zullo Lee [2:27 P.M.]
Maybe, I can make a slide show for the presentation. I'm good at that.

Wally Penn [2:29 P.M.]
That would be very helpful.

Tom Anderson [2:31 P.M.]
Zullo, I'll send you the summary, too.

Wally Penn [2:32 P.M.]
I think we're all set!

26. What kind of business do the writers work at?

(A) A web design firm
(B) An advertising agency
(C) A computer repair store
(D) A legal office

27. What is mentioned about the Cove Agency?

(A) Its sales are much higher than the writers'.
(B) It specializes in online advertising campaigns.
(C) It is a rival to the writers' company.
(D) It failed to secure an agreement with Tollington Inc.

28. What will Mr. Anderson most likely do next?

(A) Make a presentation
(B) Design a Web site
(C) Contact a client
(D) Start preparing a summary

29. At 2:32 P.M., what does Mr. Penn mean when he writes, "I think we're all set"?

(A) He is satisfied with the outcome of the discussion.
(B) He will write a summary with Mr. Anderson.
(C) He will leave to attend a meeting.
(D) He does not expect to hear ideas from the others.

P. 204

Questions 26-29 refer to the following online chat discussion.

Wally Penn [2:14 P.M.]
❶ I've received an inquiry about our web designing service from Tollington Inc. I want your ideas before I meet with them.

Zullo Lee [2:15 P.M.]
That's one of the largest advertising firms in our state, isn't it?

Wally Penn [2:17 P.M.]
❷ Right! They're telling us that they'd like a more user-friendly Web site than the current one that was created by the Cove Agency.

Tom Anderson [2:19 P.M.]
❸ Our competitor? I know a great deal about their Web site templates. One of their drawbacks is the organization of their links. Theirs are a little challenging to use.

Wally Penn [2:24 P.M.]
That's good to know. ❹ Tom, can you write a brief summary of their drawbacks and get it to me?

Tom Anderson [2:26 P.M.]
❺ Of course. I'll start on it right after this.

Zullo Lee [2:27 P.M.]
Maybe, I can make a slide show for the presentation. I'm good at that.

Wally Penn [2:29 P.M.]
That would be very helpful.

Tom Anderson [2:31 P.M.]
Zullo, I'll send you the summary, too.

Wally Penn [2:32 P.M.]
❻ I think we're all set!

☐ inquiry 問い合わせ ☐ advertising firm 広告代理店 ☐ user-friendly 使いやすい ☐ competitor 競合他社
☐ drawback 欠点 ☐ challenging 難しい ☐ That's good to know それはいいことを聞いた ☐ brief 簡潔な
☐ right after 〜の後すぐに ☐ slide show（プレゼンの）スライドショー ☐ be good at 〜が得意である
☐ all set 準備ができている

26. What kind of business do the writers work at?

(A) A web design firm
(B) An advertising agency
(C) A computer repair store
(D) A legal office

書き手たちはどのような会社で働いていますか。

(A) ウェブデザインの会社
(B) 広告代理店
(C) コンピューター修理店
(D) 法律事務所

このオンラインチャットの書き手たちがどのような会社に勤めているかが問われている。冒頭の❶で、「Tollington 社から当社のウェブデザインサービスについての問い合わせがあった」と述べている。ここから、彼らがウェブデザインの仕事を行っていることがわかる。以上より正解は **(A)**。"our ○○ company" と述べている場合、○○に注目すると正解が得られやすい。

---

27. What is mentioned about the Cove Agency?

(A) Its sales are much higher than the writers'.
(B) It specializes in online advertising campaigns.
(C) It is a rival to the writers' company.
(D) It failed to secure an agreement with Tollington Inc.

Cove Agency 社について何が言及されていますか。

(A) 書き手たちの会社よりもはるかに売り上げが多い。
(B) オンライン広告キャンペーンに特化している。
(C) 書き手たちの会社のライバルである。
(D) Tollington 社との契約を維持できなかった。

Cove Agency 社について何が言及されているかを問う選択肢照合型の問題。Penn さんと Anderson さんが❷・❸で、「Cove Agency 社が制作した…」➡「当社の競合相手の？」というやりとりをしている。ここから、Cove Agency 社はこの書き手たちの競合会社であることがわかる。以上から、これを rival と言い換えた **(C)** が正解。

□ specialize in ～に特化している　□ rival 競合相手、ライバル　□ fail to *do* ～し損ねる　□ secure ～を確保する

---

28. What will Mr. Anderson most likely do next?

(A) Make a presentation
(B) Design a Web site
(C) Contact a client
(D) Start preparing a summary

Anderson さんは次に何をすると考えられますか。

(A) プレゼンテーションを行う
(B) ウェブサイトをデザインする
(C) 顧客に連絡をする
(D) 要約の準備を始める

Anderson さんは次に何をするかが問われている。Anderson さんは❺で「この後すぐにそれに取り掛かる」と述べている。この直前の❹を見ると、Penn さんが Anderson さんに「競合相手の欠点について簡単な要約を書いて、送ってほしい」と依頼しているため、これに取り掛かると考えられる。以上から、**(D)** が正解。次の行動は、"I'll ..." 等の未来を表す表現が含まれた文の指示語をもとに導き出そう。

★★★★★ 意図問題

29. At 2:32 P.M., what does Mr. Penn mean when he writes, "I think we're all set"?

- **(A)** He is satisfied with the outcome of the discussion.
- (B) He will write a summary with Mr. Anderson.
- (C) He will leave to attend a meeting.
- (D) He does not expect to hear ideas from the others.

午後 2 時 32 分に、Penn さんは "I think we're all set" という発言で、何を意味していますか。

- **(A)** 話し合いの結果に満足している。
- (B) Anderson さんと一緒に要約を書く。
- (C) 会議に出席するために外出する。
- (D) 他の人からアイデアをもらうことを想定していない。

意図問題。問われている❻は、チャット最後の「準備は万全ですね」という Penn さんの発言だ。ここでいう「準備」とは、冒頭の❶で Penn さんが発言した「クライアントから受けた問い合わせに対するアイデアが欲しい」に関することだ。❶の後は、競合他社が制作したウェブサイトを改善したいというクライアントの依頼内容→他社のテンプレートに欠点があること→その欠点の要約やプレゼン資料の準備、などの議論がなされている。これらの議論の後に❻が述べられていることから、「このチャットでの議論によって、クライアントの問い合わせに対する準備ができそうだ」という意図が含まれていると考えられる。以上より、正解は **(A)**。意図問題は、問われている前後の意味を取りながら解く問題が多いが、今回のように最後の発言が問われたときは、チャット全体を把握する必要があることを留意しておこう。

☐ outcome 結果

Wally Penn ［午後 2 時 14 分］
Tollington 社から当社のウェブデザインサービスについての問い合わせがありました。彼らに会う前に皆さんのアイデアが欲しいです。

Zullo Lee ［午後 2 時 15 分］
そこは私たちの州で最大の広告会社の一つですよね。

Wally Penn ［午後 2 時 17 分］
そうです！　Cove Agency 社が制作した現在のウェブサイトを、より使い勝手の良いものにしたいとのことです。

Tom Anderson ［午後 2 時 19 分］
当社の競合相手の？　彼らのウェブサイトのテンプレートについてはとてもよく知っています。彼らの欠点の一つはリンクの構成です。彼らのものを使うのは少し難しいのです。

Wally Penn ［午後 2 時 24 分］
それはいいことを聞きました。Tom さん、彼らの欠点について簡単な要約を書いて、私に送ってもらえませんか。

Tom Anderson ［午後 2 時 26 分］
もちろんです。この後すぐに取り掛かりますね。

Zullo Lee ［午後 2 時 27 分］
おそらく、私はプレゼンテーションのためのスライドショーを作れると思います。それが得意なので。

Wally Penn ［午後 2 時 29 分］
それはとても助かります。

Tom Anderson ［午後 2 時 31 分］
Zullo さんにも要約を送りますね。

Wally Penn ［午後 2 時 32 分］
準備は万全ですね！

Questions 30-34 refer to the following article and review.

Bramwell (December 16)—Blake Nelson, the management expert, has written a book about effective employee relations in today's modern companies. The title of his book is *The Growing Power of Employees*. This book is a very timely examination of what it takes to get the most from your employees, especially within a big company, and he reviews the psychology and dynamics of extremely large work groups. Thereafter he applies his conclusions to today's companies. His basic view that the workers are very important to the success or failure of a big company is supported by evidence from the international market. According to his detailed analysis of many company case histories, he reveals the company behavior patterns common to firms that succeed and fail. His well-founded conclusions may surprise even the most experienced human resource supervisors as well as the company's operators. I think they will provide immense benefit to these professionals.

Author biography: A professor at Linwood Business Community Center, Blake Nelson has conducted extensive research into company dynamics and behavior. He has bachelor's degrees in both business and psychology, and he serves on the board of directors for three multi-national companies. His previous book, *A Shortcut to Success in Business*, was bestseller.

Weekly Book Review
by Audrey Sanchez

The Growing Power of Employees
Written by Blake Nelson

This book is a scholarly investigation into the subject of employee dynamics within a big company. The book is well organized. It is clear where the research descriptions and the writer's conclusions can be found. But the book is not easy to read. Nelson's writing is both boring and extremely long-winded.

The title of the book indicates that there will be some suggestions that human resource supervisors may use on the job. Actually, the suggestions given are very ambiguous and high-level. The readers are left to figure out for themselves how to execute them in an actual business environment.

As a graduate student who recently took Mr. Nelson's classes, I can see that this book may work well as a university textbook. But I don't think it's of value to company operators.

30. What did Mr. Nelson use to reach his conclusions?

(A) Private work experience
(B) Interviews with the workers
(C) Books about company policy
(D) Case studies from businesses

31. According to the article, who will benefit from reading *The Growing Power of Employees*?

(A) Corporate recruitment directors
(B) Business degree professors
(C) Human resource managers
(D) Corporate marketing specialists

32. What is NOT mentioned about Mr. Nelson?

(A) He arranges the contents of his book well.
(B) He has conducted business research.
(C) He has already written a book.
(D) He used to work in human resources.

33. What does Ms. Sanchez say about Mr. Nelson?

(A) His book offers useful on-site advice.
(B) He lacks professional knowledge.
(C) His writing style is uninteresting.
(D) He has published many business-related textbooks.

34. What is implied about Ms. Sanchez?

(A) She attended a business school.
(B) She worked for a magazine company.
(C) She did research on company management.
(D) She was responsible for a personnel department.

Double

 P. 210

Questions 30-34 refer to the following article and review.

Bramwell (December 16)—Blake Nelson, the management expert, has written a book about effective employee relations in today's modern companies. The title of his book is *The Growing Power of Employees*. This book is a very timely examination of what it takes to get the most from your employees, especially within a big company, and he reviews the psychology and dynamics of extremely large work groups. Thereafter he applies his conclusions to today's companies. His basic view that the workers are very important to the success or failure of a big company is supported by evidence from the international market. ❶ According to his detailed analysis of many company case histories, he reveals the company behavior patterns common to firms that succeed and fail. ❷ His well-founded conclusions may surprise even the most experienced human resource supervisors as well as the company's operators. I think they will provide immense benefit to these professionals.

Author biography: ❸ A professor at Linwood Business Community Center, Blake Nelson has conducted extensive research into company dynamics and behavior. He has bachelor's degrees in both business and psychology, and he serves on the board of directors for three multi-national companies. ❹ His previous book, *A Shortcut to Success in Business*, was bestseller.

Weekly Book Review
by Audrey Sanchez

The Growing Power of Employees
Written by Blake Nelson

This book is a scholarly investigation into the subject of employee dynamics within a big company. ❺ The book is well organized. It is clear where the research descriptions and the writer's conclusions can be found. But the book is not easy to read. ❻ Nelson's writing is both boring and extremely long-winded.

The title of the book indicates that there will be some suggestions that human resource supervisors may use on the job. Actually, the suggestions given are very ambiguous and high-level. The readers are left to figure out for themselves how to execute them in an actual business environment.

❼ As a graduate student who recently took Mr. Nelson's classes, I can see that this book may work well as a university textbook. But I don't think it's of value to company operators.

記事
- [ ] management expert 経営専門家　[ ] relation 関係　[ ] modern 現代の　[ ] timely 時流に合った
- [ ] examination 考察　[ ] review ～を検証する　[ ] psychology 心理(学)　[ ] dynamic 活動力
- [ ] extremely 極めて　[ ] thereafter その後　[ ] apply A to B A を B に適用する　[ ] conclusion 結論
- [ ] basic view 基本的な考え　[ ] failure 失敗　[ ] evidence 証拠　[ ] detailed 詳細な　[ ] case history 事例の歴史
- [ ] reveal ～を明らかにする　[ ] behavior pattern 行動様式　[ ] common to ～に共通する　[ ] firm 会社
- [ ] well-founded しっかりとした　[ ] experienced 経験のある　[ ] human resources 人事部　[ ] immense 大きな
- [ ] benefit 利益　[ ] professional 専門家　[ ] biography 経歴　[ ] conduct extensive research 幅広い研究を行う
- [ ] bachelor's degree 学士号　[ ] serve on ～を務めている　[ ] board of directors 取締役
- [ ] multi-national company 多国籍企業

書評
- [ ] scholarly investigation 学術的な調査　[ ] subject テーマ、題目　[ ] well organized よく整理されている
- [ ] description 描写　[ ] easy to read 読みやすい　[ ] boring 退屈な　[ ] long-winded 冗長な、くどい
- [ ] ambiguous あいまいな　[ ] be left to *do* ～することを委ねられる　[ ] figure out ～を理解する
- [ ] execute ～を実行する　[ ] business environment ビジネス環境　[ ] textbook 教科書　[ ] of value 価値のある

30. What did Mr. Nelson use to reach his conclusions?

(A) Private work experience
(B) Interviews with the workers
(C) Books about company policy
(D) Case studies from businesses

Nelson 氏は結論にたどり着くために何を使いましたか。

(A) 個人的な仕事の経験
(B) 労働者とのインタビュー
(C) 企業の方針に関する本
(D) 企業の事例研究

Nelson 氏が自分の調査の結論にたどり着くために何を使ったかが問われている。記事の❶に、「多くの企業での事例の歴史に対する著者の詳細な分析から、著者（= Nelson 氏）が企業の傾向を明らかにしている」とあるため、企業の事例を使ったことがわかる。よって、「事例研究」を case studies と表現した **(D)** が正解。(C) は企業方針に関する本を使ったかもしれないが、本文には触れられていないため、不正解。

□ company policy 会社の方針　□ case study 事例研究

31. According to the article, who will benefit from reading *The Growing Power of Employees*?

(A) Corporate recruitment directors
(B) Business degree professors
(C) Human resource managers
(D) Corporate marketing specialists

記事によると、*The Growing Power of Employees* を読むことによって利益を得られるのは誰ですか。

(A) 法人の採用責任者
(B) ビジネス課程の教授
(C) 人事担当者
(D) 企業マーケティングの専門家

記事から、『The Growing Power of Employees』を読むことによって誰が利益を得るかが問われている。記事の❷で、「しっかりと根拠に基づいた（この本の）結論は、最も経験を持つ人事担当者や会社の経営者でさえも驚かせるかもしれない」と述べられている。ここから、**(C)** が正解となる。

□ corporate 企業の　□ recruitment 採用　□ specialist 専門家

NOT 問題

32. What is NOT mentioned about Mr. Nelson?

(A) He arranges the contents of his book well.
(B) He has conducted business research.
(C) He has already written a book.
(D) He used to work in human resources.

Nelson 氏について言及されていないことは何ですか。

(A) 自著の内容をよくまとめている。
(B) ビジネスの調査を行った。
(C) すでに本を書いている。
(D) 以前は人事の仕事をしていた。

NOT 問題。Nelson 氏について述べられていないことが問われている。記事の❸から、過去に企業研究を行ったことがわかるので (B) が当てはまり、同じく記事の❹で過去に書いた本について述べられているので (C) が当てはまる。そして、書評の❺で、本の内容がとてもよく整理されていることがわかるので (A) が該当する。以上より、**(D)** が正解。ダブルパッセージの NOT 問題は 2 つの文書に根拠があると思って読み進めよう。

□ contents 内容

★★★★☆

33. What does Ms. Sanchez say about Mr. Nelson?

- (A) His book offers useful on-site advice.
- (B) He lacks professional knowledge.
- **(C)** His writing style is uninteresting.
- (D) He has published many business-related textbooks.

Sanchez さんは Nelson 氏について何と言っていますか。

- (A) 本には現場で有用なアドバイスが書かれている。
- (B) 専門知識が不足している。
- **(C)** 文体が興味をそそらない。
- (D) 多くのビジネス関連の教科書を出版した。

🔍 Sanchez さんが Nelson 氏について何と言っているかが問われている。書評の❺で、「Nelson 氏の文体は退屈でくどい」とネガティブなコメントをしているため、あまり興味がないことがわかる。よって、これを言い換えた **(C)** が正解となる。言い換えは少し難しいレベルだが、全体的にネガティブなコメントであることから、言い換えが探せなかった場合でも推測して正解を導ける場合もある。

✏️ □ on-site 現場の　□ professional 専門的な　□ uninteresting 興味のない、つまらない　□ business-related ビジネスに関連した

★★★★☆ クロスリファレンス問題

34. What is implied about Ms. Sanchez?

- **(A)** She attended a business school.
- (B) She worked for a magazine company.
- (C) She did research on company management.
- (D) She was responsible for a personnel department.

Sanchez さんについて何が示唆されていますか。

- **(A)** ビジネススクールに通っていた。
- (B) 雑誌社で働いていた。
- (C) 会社の経営に関する研究をした。
- (D) 人事部の責任者だった。

🔍 Sanchez さんについて何が示唆されているかを問う選択肢照合型の問題。2 文書目の書評の❼より、Sanchez さんは、「Nelson 氏の授業を受けた大学院生」とある。次に、1 文書目の記事の❸から、Nelson 氏は「Linwood Business Community Center の教授で、企業研究を行ってきた」ことがわかる。よって、Sanchez さんは、ビジネスに関する教育機関に通っていたことがわかるので、**(A)** が正解となる。複数文書から根拠を探すクロスリファレンス問題だ。

✏️ □ attend（学校等）に通う

Bramwell（12 月 16 日）— 経営専門家の Blake Nelson 氏が、今日の現代企業における効果的な従業員との関係についての本を書いた。著書のタイトルは *The Growing Power of Employees* である。この本は、特に大企業において、従業員から最大の成果を得るためには何が必要なのかをとてもタイムリーに考察しており、著者は極めて大規模な作業グループの心理と活動力を検証している。そして、その結論を今日の企業に当てはめている。労働者たちが大企業の成功や失敗にとって非常に重要であるという著者の基本的な考え方は、国際市場からの証拠によって裏付けられている。多くの企業での事例史に対する著者の詳細な分析によって、著者は成功を収める企業と失敗をする企業に共通する、会社としての行動とパターンを明らかにしている。しっかりと根拠に基づいた結論は、最も経験を持つ人事担当者や会社の経営者でさえも驚かせるかもしれない。これらの情報はこのような専門家に多大な利益をもたらすだろう。

著者の経歴：Linwood Business Community Center の教授である Blake Nelson 氏は企業の活動力と行動についての広範な研究を行ってきた。ビジネスと心理学の両方で学士号を取得しており、3 社の多国籍企業で取締役を務めている。前の著書である *A Shortcut to Success in Business* はベストセラーとなった。

今週の書評

Audrey Sanchez

The Growing Power of Employees
Blake Nelson 著

本書は、大企業内における従業員の活動力をテーマにした学術的な調査である。本書はよく整理されている。研究の説明や著者の結論がどこに書いてあるかが明確になっている。しかし、容易に読める本ではない。Nelson 氏の文体は退屈で極めてくどい。

本のタイトルは、人事担当者が仕事で使えるような提案が書かれていることを示している。だが、実際は書かれている提案はとても曖昧でレベルが高い。読者は実際のビジネス環境でそれらを実行する方法を自分自身で考える必要がある。

最近 Nelson 氏の授業を受けた大学院生として、私はこの本が大学の教科書としては非常によいものであるとわかる。しかし、企業の経営者にとって十分な価値があるとは思わない。

Questions 35-39 refer to the following e-mail and budget.

5分00秒

To: Sean Patel, Chief Financial Officer <sean0727@lomaindustries.com>
From: Jason Adachi, Marketing Director <jadachi@lomaindustries.com>
Subject: RE: Department Budget
Date: April 1
Attachment: 📎 Marketing Budget

Dear Mr. Patel,

I'm writing to you to ask for an increase in budget for the Marketing Department. Please find attached a detailed statement of the marketing budget for the period of May through August. As you know, our expenses have steadily risen over the past few months because of increased focus on advertising. For instance, as we started advertising our old HY4 monitors on social media sites last month to prepare for releasing a new model in June, our online advertising costs went up to $13,000.

We have still managed to stay within our monthly budget of $46,000. However, our expenses will continue to rise from May until August. Therefore, I would be grateful if you could approve revising the budget to a sum of $50,000 per month for the May-August period, which will ensure that we have enough funds to cover all expenses.

If you would like to speak about the expenses or my request for additional funds, please don't hesitate to contact me. I have meetings all day on Thursday, but I'll be free on Friday.

Thanks,

Jason Adachi
Marketing Director
Loma Industries

Marketing Department

	May	June	July	August	Total
Print Media Advertising	$6,000	$9,000	$9,000	$8,000	$32,000
Social Media Advertising	$13,000	$13,000	$13,000	$13,000	$52,000
Research & Surveys	$11,000	$0	$0	$0	$11,000
Staff Wages	$19,000	$22,000	$23,000	$26,000	$90,000
Total	$49,000	$44,000	$45,000	$47,000	$185,000

35. What is the purpose of the e-mail?

(A) To request a budget increase
(B) To advise ways to reduce expenses
(C) To solve an overspending problem
(D) To arrange a meeting schedule

36. Why did Mr. Adachi most likely concentrate on online advertising recently?

(A) To satisfy the customers
(B) To sell the inventory
(C) To advertise a new product
(D) To decrease marketing expenses

37. What is suggested about Mr. Adachi?

(A) He will not be available on Thursday.
(B) He is planning a business trip in June.
(C) He is requesting more stores.
(D) He will try to reduce office expenses.

38. According to the budget, when will most likely the investigation be conducted?

(A) In May
(B) In June
(C) In July
(D) In August

39. Which of the following is most likely the cause of their revising the budget?

(A) Offline Advertising
(B) Online Advertising
(C) Research and Surveys
(D) Employee Salaries

P. 216

Double

Questions 35-39 refer to the following e-mail and budget.

To: Sean Patel, Chief Financial Officer <sean0727@lomaindustries.com>
From: Jason Adachi, Marketing Director <jadachi@lomaindustries.com>
Subject: RE: Department Budget
Date: April 1
Attachment: Marketing Budget

Dear Mr. Patel,

❶ I'm writing to you to ask for an increase in budget for the Marketing Department. Please find attached a detailed statement of the marketing budget for the period of May through August. As you know, our expenses have steadily risen over the past few months because of increased focus on advertising. ❷ For instance, as we started advertising our old HY4 monitors on social media sites last month to prepare for releasing a new model in June, our online advertising costs went up to $13,000.

We have still managed to stay within our monthly budget of $46,000. ❸ However, our expenses will continue to rise from May until August. ❹ Therefore, I would be grateful if you could approve revising the budget to a sum of $50,000 per month for the May-August period, which will ensure that we have enough funds to cover all expenses.

If you would like to speak about the expenses or my request for additional funds, please don't hesitate to contact me. ❺ I have meetings all day on Thursday, but I'll be free on Friday.

Thanks,

Jason Adachi
Marketing Director
Loma Industries

Marketing Department

	❻ May	June	July	August	Total
Print Media Advertising	$6,000	$9,000	$9,000	$8,000	$32,000
Social Media Advertising	$13,000	$13,000	$13,000	$13,000	$52,000
❼ Research & Surveys	$11,000	$0	$0	$0	$11,000
❽ Staff Wages	$19,000	$22,000	$23,000	$26,000	$90,000
Total	$49,000	$44,000	$45,000	$47,000	$185,000

E メール
☐ ask for ～を求める ☐ detailed 詳細な ☐ statement 明細 ☐ steadily 堅実に ☐ increased 増加した
☐ social media site ソーシャルメディアサイト（インターネット上の情報交換ツール） ☐ release ～を発売する
☐ go up to ～まで上昇する ☐ manage to *do* 何とかして～する ☐ stay 留まる ☐ sum 額

予算
☐ research & surveys 研究調査 ☐ wage 賃金

35. What is the purpose of the e-mail?

    (A) To request a budget increase
    (B) To advise ways to reduce expenses
    (C) To solve an overspending problem
    (D) To arrange a meeting schedule

Eメールの目的は何ですか。

    (A) 予算増額の要請をすること
    (B) 費用削減の方法を勧めること
    (C) 浪費の問題を解決すること
    (D) 会議の予定を調整すること

1文書目のEメールの目的が問われている。Eメールの冒頭❶で「追加予算を要請するために連絡した」と述べているため、**(A)** が正解となる。❶の冒頭の "I'm writing to you to" は文書の目的を示す際によく使われる書き出しの表現なので、特に注意しよう。

✎ □ overspending 浪費、費用の使い過ぎ

....

36. Why did Mr. Adachi most likely concentrate on online advertising recently?

    (A) To satisfy the customers
    (B) To sell the inventory
    (C) To advertise a new product
    (D) To decrease marketing expenses

Adachi さんが最近インターネット広告に専念していたのはなぜだと考えられますか。

    (A) 顧客を満足させるため
    (B) 在庫を売り切るため
    (C) 新製品を宣伝するため
    (D) マーケティング費用を削減するため

Eメールの送信者である Adachi さんが最近インターネット広告に専念した理由が問われている。Adachi さんは❷で「6月に発売する新モデルの準備のため、先月はソーシャルメディアで旧モデル商品の宣伝を開始した」とある。ここから、商品の入れ替えで旧モデル商品の在庫を売る目的でネット広告に専念したことがわかるため、在庫を inventory と **(B)** が正解。

✎ □ inventory 在庫品（全体）

....

37. What is suggested about Mr. Adachi?

    (A) He will not be available on Thursday.
    (B) He is planning a business trip in June.
    (C) He is requesting more stores.
    (D) He will try to reduce office expenses.

Adachi さんについて何が推測できますか。

    (A) 木曜日は都合が悪い。
    (B) 6月に出張を計画している。
    (C) 店を増やすことを要求している。
    (D) 事務所経費の削減をするつもりである。

Adachi さんについて何が推測されるかを問う選択肢照合型の問題。Adachi さんはEメールで、予算を増額してほしいことについて触れ、最終段落で「打ち合わせがしたい場合は連絡をください」と伝えながら、❺で「木曜日は終日会議がありますが、金曜日は時間があります」と、空いている日を伝えている。よって、これを言い換えた **(A)** が正解。

✎ □ office expense 事務所経費

38. According to the budget, when will most likely the investigation be conducted?

(A) In May
(B) In June
(C) In July
(D) In August

予算案によると、調査はいつ行われると考えられますか。

(A) 5 月
(B) 6 月
(C) 7 月
(D) 8 月

調査がいつ行われると考えられるかが問われている。予算案を見ると、❼に研究・調査の予算が記載されており、❻の 5 月のみ割り当てられている。ここから予算が割り当てられている 5 月に調査が行われると考えられるため、正解は **(A)** となる。設問の investigation が予算案の "research & surveys" を言い換えているものだと気づけば、比較的容易に解ける。

★★★★★ クロスリファレンス問題

39. Which of the following is most likely the cause of their revising the budget?

(A) Offline Advertising
(B) Online Advertising
(C) Research and Surveys
(D) Employee Salaries

予算を修正した原因として考えられるのは次のうちどれですか。

(A) オンライン以外の広告
(B) オンライン広告
(C) 研究と調査
(D) 従業員の給与

予算を修正した原因はおそらく何かが問われている。Adachi さんは 1 文書目の E メールの❸・❹で「5 月から 8 月にかけて経費が増えるので、予算の増額をしてほしい」と述べている。次に 2 文書目の予算案を見ると、❽の従業員賃金が増え続けていることがわかる。以上から、"wages" を salaries と言い換えた **(D)** が正解。1 文書目の❸・❹から、2 文書目の❽を見て解くというクロスリファレンス問題であることを理解して解くようにしよう。

受信者：	Sean Patel、最高財務責任者〈sean0727@lomaindustries.com〉
送信者：	Jason Adachi、マーケティング管理者〈jdadachi@lomaindustries.com〉
件名：	Re：部署の予算
日付け：	4月1日
添付ファイル：	マーケティング部 予算案

Patel 様

マーケティング部の追加予算を要請するためにご連絡いたしました。5月から8月までの期間のマーケティング予算の明細を添付いたしました。ご存じのとおり、広告に力を入れるようになり、この数カ月で経費は確実に増加しています。例えば、6月に発売する新モデルの準備のため、先月はソーシャルメディアで旧モデルの HY4 モニターの宣伝を開始したことにより、オンライン広告費用は 13,000 ドルになりました。

今のところ月額予算である 46,000 ドル以内に抑えることができています。しかしながら、5月から8月にかけて経費は増加します。したがって、5月から8月までの間、毎月 50,000 ドルの予算に修正することをご承認いただければ、すべての経費を賄うための十分な資金を確保できます。

費用やこの追加資金の要請について打ち合わせを希望される場合は、遠慮なくご連絡ください。木曜日は終日会議がありますが、金曜日は時間があります。

よろしくお願いいたします。

Jason Adachi
マーケティング管理者
Loma Industries

マーケティング部

	5月	6月	7月	8月	合計
紙媒体の広告	6,000 ドル	9,000 ドル	9,000 ドル	8,000 ドル	32,000 ドル
ソーシャルメディアの広告	13,000 ドル	13,000 ドル	13,000 ドル	13,000 ドル	52,000 ドル
研究・調査	11,000 ドル	0 ドル	0 ドル	0 ドル	11,000 ドル
従業員賃金	19,000 ドル	22,000 ドル	23,000 ドル	26,000 ドル	90,000 ドル
合計	49,000 ドル	44,000 ドル	45,000 ドル	47,000 ドル	185,000 ドル

Questions 40-44 refer to the following Web page, e-mail, and evaluation form. 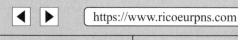 5分30秒

◀ ▶ | https://www.ricoeurpns.com | ▶

| **Home** | **Customer Profiling** | **Location** | **Gallery** |

Ricoeur Products & Services
Evaluation Underscores How Our Company Can Become Better

To improve our service, the department of customer satisfaction has come into contact with 10,000 regular customers, who often make a purchase at our store. We asked them to fill in the evaluation form including some questions about the current services and suggestions to improve our services. They provided some very helpful feedback.

What we've determined from the result of the evaluation is that most of our customers are quite satisfied with our service. Just over 75 percent of them said that their order always arrives on time. But only 10 percent said they had returned a product to us, because it had a flaw. In this particular case, we have been willing to provide full refunds to customers. The suggestion that the majority of customers had made was for us to offer monthly sales on various products. We will follow this suggestion in order to increase customer satisfaction. A small number of customers also suggested that we offer a complimentary shipping option.

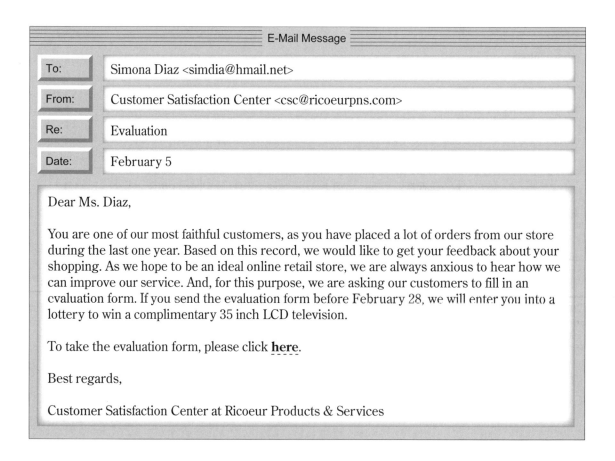

	E-Mail Message
To:	Simona Diaz <simdia@hmail.net>
From:	Customer Satisfaction Center <csc@ricoeurpns.com>
Re:	Evaluation
Date:	February 5

Dear Ms. Diaz,

You are one of our most faithful customers, as you have placed a lot of orders from our store during the last one year. Based on this record, we would like to get your feedback about your shopping. As we hope to be an ideal online retail store, we are always anxious to hear how we can improve our service. And, for this purpose, we are asking our customers to fill in an evaluation form. If you send the evaluation form before February 28, we will enter you into a lottery to win a complimentary 35 inch LCD television.

To take the evaluation form, please click **here**.

Best regards,

Customer Satisfaction Center at Ricoeur Products & Services

EVALUATION FORM

Thank you for choosing Ricoeur Products & Services. We greatly value your opinion. Please take a moment to complete the evaluation form. The results of this evaluation will be used to improve our products and services.

1-1. Is Ricoeur Products & Services online retail store the one you use most frequently?
√ Yes   ___ No

1-2. If yes, how often do you use Ricoeur Products & Services online retail store?
___ Once a year   ___ Twice to five times a year   ___ Six to ten times a year
___ More than ten times a year   √ More than twenty times a year

2. How do you feel about Ricoeur Products & Services?
___ Very dissatisfied   ___ Dissatisfied   ___ Fair
√ Satisfied   ___ Very Satisfied

3. How often do your orders arrive on time?
___ Never   ___ Seldom   ___ Sometimes   ___ Often   √ Always

4-1. Have you ever returned items because they were damaged during shipping?
√ Yes   ___ No

4-2. If yes, how often does this happen?
√ Seldom   ___ Sometimes   ___ Often   ___ Always

5. Are there any ways we can improve our service?
There should be a paid membership plan that contains a complimentary delivery service. I purchase many items from Ricoeur Products & Services, but I always have to pay shipping fees.

Name: *Simona Diaz*
Date: *February 20*

---

40. According to the Web page, what will Ricoeur Products & Services do for its customer satisfaction?

(A) Promise timely deliveries
(B) Provide a free shipping service
(C) Found a customer support center
(D) Offer routine discounts on items

41. What is indicated about Ricoeur Products & Services?

(A) It is constructing a product review Web site.
(B) It is a domestic chain store.
(C) It now collects opinions from its customers.
(D) It is trying to move its headquarters.

42. What can be inferred about Ms. Diaz?

(A) She does not use Ricoeur Products & Services often.
(B) She sometimes does not receive orders on time.
(C) She began using Ricoeur Products & Services six months ago.
(D) She will be entered into a raffle.

43. What did Ricoeur Products & Services most likely offer to Ms. Diaz?

(A) A gift certificate
(B) A full refund
(C) Free shipping
(D) A discount

44. Which of the following is Ms. Diaz most likely to be satisfied with?

(A) The delivery date
(B) The price of products
(C) The quality of service
(D) The solidity of packing

 P. 222

Questions 40-44 refer to the following Web page, e-mail, and evaluation form.

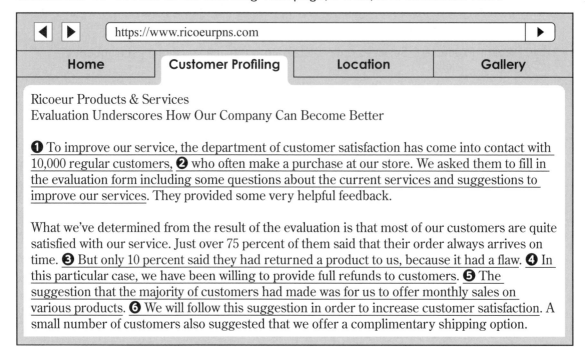

https://www.ricoeurpns.com

| Home | Customer Profiling | Location | Gallery |

Ricoeur Products & Services
Evaluation Underscores How Our Company Can Become Better

❶ To improve our service, the department of customer satisfaction has come into contact with 10,000 regular customers, ❷ who often make a purchase at our store. We asked them to fill in the evaluation form including some questions about the current services and suggestions to improve our services. They provided some very helpful feedback.

What we've determined from the result of the evaluation is that most of our customers are quite satisfied with our service. Just over 75 percent of them said that their order always arrives on time. ❸ But only 10 percent said they had returned a product to us, because it had a flaw. ❹ In this particular case, we have been willing to provide full refunds to customers. ❺ The suggestion that the majority of customers had made was for us to offer monthly sales on various products. ❻ We will follow this suggestion in order to increase customer satisfaction. A small number of customers also suggested that we offer a complimentary shipping option.

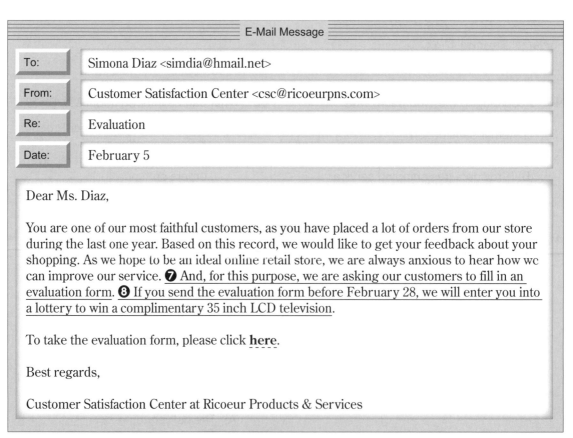

E-Mail Message

To: Simona Diaz <simdia@hmail.net>

From: Customer Satisfaction Center <csc@ricoeurpns.com>

Re: Evaluation

Date: February 5

Dear Ms. Diaz,

You are one of our most faithful customers, as you have placed a lot of orders from our store during the last one year. Based on this record, we would like to get your feedback about your shopping. As we hope to be an ideal online retail store, we are always anxious to hear how we can improve our service. ❼ And, for this purpose, we are asking our customers to fill in an evaluation form. ❽ If you send the evaluation form before February 28, we will enter you into a lottery to win a complimentary 35 inch LCD television.

To take the evaluation form, please click **here**.

Best regards,

Customer Satisfaction Center at Ricoeur Products & Services

EVALUATION FORM

Thank you for choosing Ricoeur Products & Services. We greatly value your opinion. Please take a moment to complete the evaluation form. The results of this evaluation will be used to improve our products and services.

1-1. Is Ricoeur Products & Services online retail store the one you use most frequently?
_√_ Yes   ___ No

1-2. If yes, how often do you use Ricoeur Products & Services online retail store?
___ Once a year   ___ Twice to five times a year   ___ Six to ten times a year
___ More than ten times a year   _√_ More than twenty times a year

2. How do you feel about Ricoeur Products & Services?
___ Very dissatisfied   ___ Dissatisfied   ___ Fair
_√_ Satisfied   ___ Very Satisfied

❾ 3. How often do your orders arrive on time?
___ Never   ___ Seldom   ___ Sometimes   ___ Often   _√_ Always

❿ 4-1. Have you ever returned items because they were damaged during shipping?
_√_ Yes   ___ No

4-2. If yes, how often does this happen?
_√_ Seldom   ___ Sometimes   ___ Often   ___ Always

5. Are there any ways we can improve our service?
There should be a paid membership plan that contains a complimentary delivery service. I purchase many items from Ricoeur Products & Services, but I always have to pay shipping fees.

⓫ Name: *Simona Diaz*
Date: *February 20*

ウェブページ
□ customer profiling 顧客調査　□ underscore 〜を明確にする　□ customer satisfaction 顧客満足
□ come into contact with 〜と連絡する　□ regular customer 常連のお客様　□ fill in 〜に記入する
□ evaluation form 評価用紙　□ current 現在の　□ suggestion 提案、提言　□ helpful 役立つ
□ feedback 評価、感想　□ determine 〜を決定する　□ be satisfied with 〜に満足する　□ quite とても
□ on time 時間どおりに　□ flaw 欠陥、不具合　□ be willing to *do* 進んで〜する　□ full refund 全額払い戻し
□ majority of 多数の　□ offer sales on 〜で特売をする　□ various さまざまな
□ in order to *do* 〜するために　□ a small number of ごくわずかな　□ complimentary shipping 送料無料

Eメール
□ faithful 忠実な　□ based on 〜に基づいて　□ ideal 理想的な　□ retail store 小売店舗
□ anxious to *do* 〜することを切望して　□ by the time 〜する時までに　□ enter 人 into 人を〜に登録する
□ lottery くじ　□ win（賞や抽選など）を勝ち取る

評価用紙
□ greatly とても　□ value one's opinion 人の意見を大事にする　□ take a moment to *do* 時間を取って〜する
□ complete 〜に記入する　□ frequently 頻繁に　□ dissatisfied 不満足な
□ paid membership plan 有料会員プラン　□ contain 〜を含む
□ complimentary delivery service 無料配送サービス　□ shipping fee 送料

40. According to the Web page, what will Ricoeur Products & Services do for its customer satisfaction?

(A) Promise timely deliveries
(B) Provide a free shipping service
(C) Found a customer support center
(D) Offer routine discounts on items

ウェブページによると、顧客が満足するように Ricoeur Products & Services 社は今後何をしますか。

(A) タイミングのいい配送を約束する
(B) 送料無料サービスを提供する
(C) 顧客サポートセンターを創設する
(D) 定期的に商品の割引を行う

🔍 ウェブページから、Ricoeur Products & Services 社が顧客満足のために今後何をするかが問われている。ウェブページの❺に「多くのお客様から、月ごとのセールを行うという提案があった」、❻に「これに従う」とあるため、ここからセールを discounts と言い換えた **(D)** が正解。(A) 配送遅延、(B) 無料サービスに関しても若干意見はあるが、これに対して新しく何かをする、という記載はないので不正解。

✏️ ☐ timely タイミングの良い　☐ free shipping 送料無料

41. What is indicated about Ricoeur Products & Services?

(A) It is constructing a product review Web site.
(B) It is a domestic chain store.
(C) It now collects opinions from its customers.
(D) It is trying to move its headquarters.

Ricoeur Products & Services 社について何が示されていますか。

(A) 商品評価のためのウェブサイトを構築中である。
(B) 国内のチェーン店である。
(C) 現在顧客から意見を収集している。
(D) 本社を移転しようとしている。

🔍 Ricoeur Products & Services 社について示されていることを問う選択肢照合型の問題。ウェブページの❶・❷で「顧客満足部門が常連客に連絡して、評価用紙の記入をお願いした」という記載があるため、これを言い換えた **(C)** が正解。2文書目の E メールの❼にも類似の記載があるため、この部分を解答根拠にしても OK。(A) ウェブサイトの構築、(B) 国内チェーン店、(D) 本社移転は記載がなく、ここでは不正解。

✏️ ☐ construct ～を構築する　☐ product review 商品の感想　☐ domestic 国内の　☐ chain store チェーン店
☐ headquarters 本社

★★★★★ クロスリファレンス問題

42. What can be inferred about Ms. Diaz?

   (A) She does not use Ricoeur Products & Services often.
   (B) She sometimes does not receive orders on time.
   (C) She began using Ricoeur Products & Services six months ago.
   (D) She will be entered into a raffle.

Diaz さんについて何が推測できますか。

   (A) Ricoeur Products & Services 社をあまり利用しない。
   (B) 予定どおりに商品を受け取れないことが時々ある。
   (C) 6 カ月前から Ricoeur Products & Services 社を利用し始めた。
   (D) 抽選に参加することになる。

 Diaz さんについて推測できることを問う選択肢照合型の問題。2 文書目の E メールの❽で、Ricoeur Products & Services 社が Diaz さん宛てに「2 月 28 日前に評価用紙を送ってくれれば、大型テレビが無料で当たる抽選に登録する」と述べている。次に、Diaz さんは 3 文書目の評価用紙の⓫に記載があるため、「常連のお客様で、2 月 20 日に評価内容を記載した」とわかる。以上より、Diaz さんは、商品が当たる抽選に登録されたことが推測できるため、この抽選くじを raffle と言い換えた **(D)** が正解となる。2 文書目と 3 文書目の情報を参照するクロスリファレンス問題に加え、lottery=raffle の言い換えが少し難しいので、しっかりと解答根拠を押さえておこう。

✎ □ **raffle** 抽選（くじ）

 ★★★★★ クロスリファレンス問題

43. What did Ricoeur Products & Services most likely offer to Ms. Diaz?

   (A) A gift certificate
   (B) A full refund
   (C) Free shipping
   (D) A discount

Ricoeur Products & Services 社は Diaz さんに何を提供したと考えられますか。

   (A) 商品券
   (B) 全額返金
   (C) 送料無料
   (D) 値引き

 Ricoeur Products & Services 社が Diaz さんにおそらく何を提供したかが問われている。Diaz さんは 3 文書目の調査用紙の❿で、「配送中に破損した商品を返品したことがあるか」に対して "Yes" にチェックしている。次に 1 文書目のウェブページの❸・❹では、「欠陥による返品の経験者が若干おり、そのような場合はお客様に全額返金を提供するようにしていた」と述べられている。つまり、欠陥商品を返品したことのある Diaz さんには返金が提供されたことが考えられる。以上より、正解は **(B)**。これも 1 文書目と 3 文書目を参照して解く、クロスリファレンス問題となっている。

✎ □ **gift certificate** 商品券

 ★★★★★

44. Which of the following is Ms. Diaz most likely to be satisfied with?

   (A) The delivery date
   (B) The price of products
   (C) The quality of service
   (D) The solidity of packing

Diaz さんが最も満足していると考えられることは次のどれですか。

   (A) 配送日
   (B) 商品の価格
   (C) サービスの質
   (D) しっかりとした包装

 Diaz さんが最も満足していると考えられることについて問われている。3 文書目の調査用紙の❾で、「注文品が予定どおりに届く頻度」については、"Always（いつも）" にチェックを入れている。ここから、配送のタイミングに関する満足度は高いと推測できるため、これに該当する **(A)** が正解となる。

✎ □ **solidity** しっかりとしていること

https://www.ricoeurpns.com			
トップページ	**顧客調査**	**所在地**	**写真**

Ricoeur Products & Services
評価が当社の改善点を明らかにします

当社のサービス改善のため、顧客満足部門は、いつも当店でお買い物をしてくださっている 1 万人の常連のお客さまにご連絡しました。現在のサービスに関する質問やサービス改善のためのご提案などを含んだ評価用紙のご記入をお願いしました。皆さまはとても有益なご意見をくださいました。

評価の結果からわかっていることは、ほとんどのお客様が当社のサービスを非常に満足してくださっているということです。75 パーセント強のお客様が注文品は予定どおりに届くとお答えになっています。一方、欠陥があったために商品を返品したことがあると答えられたのは、わずか 10 パーセントでした。このような特殊な場合は、お客様へ全額返金を行っています。多くのお客様からご提案いただいたのは、当社がさまざまな商品で月ごとのセールを行うというものです。お客様にさらにご満足いただくため、このご提案を実施いたします。一部のお客様からは無料配送についてご提案をいただきました。

受信者:	Simona Diaz <simdia@hmail.net>
送信者:	顧客満足センター <csc@ricoeurpns.com>
件名:	評価
日付:	2 月 5 日

Diaz 様

お客様には過去 1 年間の間に当店にたくさんご注文いただき、非常にごひいきにしていただいております。この記録に基づいて、お買い物に関するご意見をいただきたいと存じます。私どもは理想的なオンラインショップを目指しているため、サービスを改善する方法を常に模索しております。そのため、お客様に評価用紙のご記入をお願いしております。2 月 28 日までに評価用紙を送っていただければ、35 インチの液晶テレビが当たる抽選にご参加いただけます。

評価用紙の入手は**こちら**をクリックしてください。

よろしくお願いいたします。

Ricoeur Products & Services 顧客満足センター

評価用紙

Ricoeur Products & Services をご利用いただきありがとうございます。当社はお客様のご意見をとても重視しております。お手数をおかけいたしますが、評価用紙のご記入をお願いいたします。この評価の結果は商品とサービスの改善のために活用いたします。

1-1. 最も頻繁に利用するオンラインショップは Ricoeur Products & Services ですか？
✓はい　__いいえ

1-2. 答えがはいの場合、Ricoeur Products & Services のオンラインショップをどのくらいの頻度で利用していますか？
__年に1回　__年に2～5回　__年に6～10回　__年に10回を超える　✓年に20回を超える

2. Ricoeur Products & Services についてどのように感じていますか？
__非常に不満である　__不満である　__普通　✓満足である　__非常に満足である

3. 注文品が予定どおりに届く頻度はどのくらいですか？
__まったくない　__めったにない　__時々届く　__しばしば届く　✓常に届く

4-1. 配送中に破損した商品を返品したことはありますか？
✓はい　__いいえ

4-2. 答えがはいの場合、どの程度の頻度でそれは起こりますか？
✓めったにない　__時々起きる　__しばしば起きる　__常に起きる

5. 当社のサービスを向上させる方法はありますか？
送料が無料になる有料の会員サービスがあればいいと思います。Ricoeur Products & Services ではたくさんの商品を購入していますが、毎回送料が掛かりますので。

名前：Simona Diaz
日付：2月20日

Questions 45-49 refer to the following article, schedule, and flyer. 5分30秒

Exciting New Comedy Movie
Opens in Theaters
February 10

"The Secret Life of My House" is going to play on screens throughout the country, starting tomorrow. Comedy movie addicts will love this movie, which is a remake of "SCREAM AND LIVE."

Starring Arthur Gage and Natalia Beckley, the movie has a background setting in the 1970s and explores the legacy of the real-life Pacino family through the eyes of Gage, who plays the youngest son. Ms. Beckley plays her love for this story of honor.

Over $30 million was spent in making the movie, which was directed by a famous veteran in the field, Tyler Greiner. Mr. Greiner is well-known especially for his comedy movies. Until now, he has directed over 20 movies, and he has said that "The Secret Life of My House" is one of the best movies he has ever made.

"When I read the script, immediately I knew that I had to direct this movie. I've wanted to make a comedy movie based on a true story for a long time, so it was a great opportunity for me. Arthur and Natalia are the perfect couple for the main characters and everyone worked really hard to produce this wonderful work."

The premiere of "The Secret Life of My House" is being held tonight and the movie will start playing tomorrow in theaters nationwide.

The Secret Life of My House
Promotional Activities Schedule

Date	Place	Staff Attending	Activity
Feb. 8	Seattle Public Theater Seattle	Natalia Beckley & Tyler Greiner	Newspaper Interview
Feb. 10	Sunrise Theater San Diego	All	Opening Night
Feb. 12	Chinese News Studio Los Angeles	All	Moving Screening
Feb. 16	Reno Theater San Francisco	Arthur Gage	Radio Interview
Feb. 18	Delgado Studios San Francisco	Natalia Beckley & Tyler Greiner	Q & A Session

The Secret Life of My House
ADMIT ONE
Join us for movie night

When: March 5
Where: 554 Juniper Drive, San Francisco
Time: 8 P.M.

RSVP to contact 980-813-9213

Fans loving comedy movies will be happy with "The Secret Life of My House."
Tyler Greiner's new movie "The Secret Life of My House" has opened.

Review:

The movie offers a fascinating insight into the life of the Pacino family. The Pacinos were a typical 1970s American family living in Boston and Philadelphia.

The leading roles are played by popular actors Arthur Gage and Natalia Beckley. She plays her character convincingly. Some people may feel that Mr. Gage's accent slightly annoying. But it's occurred because of his excellent performance. He admitted this might be a topic in an interview with Topanga Everdine on February 16.

The movie was shot on location in Boston, and many of the city's landmarks are highlighted during the family scenes which take place during the day.

An excellent soundtrack adds to the movie with many famous songs from the 1970s.

At over two hours, the movie may be slightly too long for some audiences, and it would have been better if it had been shorter by 30 minutes.

45. What can be inferred about "The Secret Life of My House"?

(A) It was filmed in various countries.
(B) It includes some elements of romance.
(C) It isn't appropriate for young children.
(D) It is based on a novel.

46. What is suggested about Mr. Greiner?

(A) He cannot attend the movie premiere.
(B) He has starred in many movies.
(C) He has gotten some awards for his work.
(D) He is an experienced director.

47. Where is the movie premiere being held?

(A) San Diego
(B) Los Angeles
(C) San Francisco
(D) Seattle

48. Who most likely is Ms. Everdine?

(A) A television host
(B) An actress
(C) A radio presenter
(D) A newspaper journalist

49. What was the reviewer dissatisfied with about the movie?

(A) Its setting
(B) Its music
(C) Its film distributor
(D) Its running time

P. 230

Questions 45-49 refer to the following article, schedule, and flyer.

Exciting New Comedy Movie
Opens in Theaters
❶ February 10

"The Secret Life of My House" is going to play on screens throughout the country, starting tomorrow. Comedy movie addicts will love this movie, which is a remake of "SCREAM AND LIVE."

Starring Arthur Gage and Natalia Beckley, the movie has a background setting in the 1970s and explores the legacy of the real-life Pacino family through the eyes of Gage, who plays the youngest son. ❷ Ms. Beckley plays her love for this story of honor.

Over $30 million was spent in making the movie, which was directed by a famous veteran in the field, Tyler Greiner. ❸ Mr. Greiner is well-known especially for his comedy movies. Until now, he has directed over 20 movies, and he has said that "The Secret Life of My House" is one of the best movies he has ever made.

"When I read the script, immediately I knew that I had to direct this movie. I've wanted to make a comedy movie based on a true story for a long time, so it was a great opportunity for me. Arthur and Natalia are the perfect couple for the main characters and everyone worked really hard to produce this wonderful work."

❹ The premiere of "The Secret Life of My House" is being held tonight and the movie will start playing tomorrow in theaters nationwide.

The Secret Life of My House
Promotional Activities Schedule

Date	Place	Staff Attending	Activity
Feb. 8	Seattle Public Theater Seattle	Natalia Beckley & Tyler Greiner	Newspaper Interview
❺ Feb. 10	Sunrise Theater San Diego	All	Opening Night
Feb. 12	Chinese News Studio Los Angeles	All	Moving Screening
❻ Feb. 16	Reno Theater San Francisco	Arthur Gage	Radio Interview
Feb. 18	Delgado Studios San Francisco	Natalia Beckley & Tyler Greiner	Q & A Session

The Secret Life of My House
ADMIT ONE
Join us for movie night

When: March 5
Where: 554 Juniper Drive, San Francisco
Time: 8 P.M.

RSVP to contact 980-813-9213

Fans loving comedy movies will be happy with "The Secret Life of My House."
Tyler Greiner's new movie "The Secret Life of My House" has opened.

Review:

The movie offers a fascinating insight into the life of the Pacino family. The Pacinos were a typical 1970s American family living in Boston and Philadelphia.

The leading roles are played by popular actors Arthur Gage and Natalia Beckley. She plays her character convincingly. ❼ Some people may feel that Mr. Gage's accent slightly annoying. ❽ But it's occurred because of his excellent performance. ❾ He admitted this might be a topic in an interview with Topanga Everdine on February 16.

The movie was shot on location in Boston, and many of the city's landmarks are highlighted during the family scenes which take place during the day.

An excellent soundtrack adds to the movie with many famous songs from the 1970s.

❿ At over two hours, the movie may be slightly too long for some audiences, ⓫ and it would have been better if it had been shorter by 30 minutes.

記事
☐ play on screen 上映される ☐ comedy 喜劇、コメディー ☐ addict 愛好者 ☐ remake リメイク（改作）
☐ star ～を主演させる ☐ background setting 背景設定 ☐ explore ～を探究する ☐ legacy 遺産
☐ real-life 実在の ☐ play ～を演じる ☐ honor 名誉 ☐ direct ～の監督をする ☐ veteran 熟練者
☐ well-known 有名な ☐ script 脚本 ☐ immediately すぐに ☐ based on ～に基づく ☐ opportunity 機会
☐ premiere 初演、封切り ☐ nationwide 全国で

予定表
☐ promotional activities schedule 宣伝活動予定表 ☐ staff attending 参加スタッフ

チラシ
☐ RSVP（Répondez s'il vous plaît）返事を下さい ☐ contact ～に連絡をする ☐ fascinating 魅力的な
☐ insight 洞察 ☐ typical 典型的な ☐ leading role 主役 ☐ character 登場人物
☐ convincingly 説得力をもって ☐ accent アクセント、話し方 ☐ slightly やや ☐ annoying いらいらさせる
☐ occur 起こる ☐ admit ～と認める ☐ shot shoot（～を撮影する）の過去・過去分詞形 ☐ landmark 観光名所
☐ highlight ～を強調する ☐ take place 起こる ☐ soundtrack サウンドトラック（映画等に収録された音楽）

★★★☆☆

45. What can be inferred about "The Secret Life of My House"?

(A) It was filmed in various countries.
(B) It includes some elements of romance.
(C) It isn't appropriate for young children.
(D) It is based on a novel.

"The Secret Life of My House" について何が推測できますか。

(A) さまざまな国で撮影された。
(B) 恋愛の要素が含まれている。
(C) 小さい子ども向けではない。
(D) 小説が原作である。

映画 "The Secret Life of My House" について、何が推測できるかを問う選択肢照合型の問題。1 文書目の記事の❷で、「Beckley さんが、このストーリーで自分の恋愛（感情）を演じている」とあるので、この映画には恋愛に関する要素も含まれていることがわかる。以上より、❷の "love" を romance と言い換えた **(B)** が正解。TOEIC では、恋愛、結婚に関する具体的な話題が出題されることはあまりないが、このように分野・ジャンルに関するものは時折出題されることもあるので押さえておこう。

□ various さまざまな　□ element 要素　□ novel 小説

★★★☆☆

46. What is suggested about Mr. Greiner?

(A) He cannot attend the movie premiere.
(B) He has starred in many movies.
(C) He has gotten some awards for his work.
(D) He is an experienced director.

Greiner さんについて何が示されていますか。

(A) 映画の封切りに参加できない。
(B) 多くの映画で主役を務めた。
(C) 作品で賞を受賞したことがある。
(D) 経験豊富な監督である。

Greiner さんについて示されていることを問う選択肢照合型の問題。1 文書目の記事の❸で、「コメディ映画では特に有名で、これまで 20 本以上の映画の監督をしてきた」とあるため、これを "experienced（経験のある）" と言い換えた **(D)** が正解。

□ star 主役を務める　□ award 賞　□ experienced 経験のある

★★★★☆ クロスリファレンス問題

47. Where is the movie premiere being held?

(A) San Diego
(B) Los Angeles
(C) San Francisco
(D) Seattle

映画の初日はどこで開催されますか。

(A) サンディエゴ
(B) ロサンゼルス
(C) サンフランシスコ
(D) シアトル

映画の初日はどこで行われているかが問われている。1 文書目の記事は❶から 2 月 10 日付の記事だとわかり、❹で「"The Secret Life of My House" は今晩封切りされる」と書かれている。次に 2 文書目の予定表を見ていくと、❺から「2 月 10 日のイベントは San Diego で開催」だとわかる。以上から、正解は **(A)**。

48. Who most likely is Ms. Everdine?

(A) A television host
(B) An actress
(C) A radio presenter
(D) A newspaper journalist

Evedine さんとはおそらく誰ですか。

(A) テレビ番組の司会者
(B) 女優
(C) ラジオの司会者
(D) 新聞記者

Evedine さんはおそらく誰かが問われている。Evedine さんは、3 文書目のチラシの中にあるレビューに登場し、❼・❽・❾から、「2 月 16 日に Gage さんとインタビューをした人物」ということがわかる。次に 2 文書目の予定表を見ていくと、❻で、2 月 16 日にラジオインタビューをしていることがわかる。つまり、Evedine さんは、ラジオで Gage さんにインタビューに携わることのできる人物であると考えられるため、**(C)** が正解だとわかる。most likely が含まれた設問の場合、このように情報から推測することが重要で、今回はその情報が 2 つの文書に書かれていたことに注意しておこう。

□ host 主催者、司会者　□ presenter (テレビ、ラジオの)司会者

....

★★★☆☆

49. What was the reviewer dissatisfied with about the movie?

(A) Its setting
(B) Its music
(C) Its film distributor
(D) Its running time

映画について評論家が気に入らなかったことは何ですか。

(A) 設定
(B) 音楽
(C) 配給会社
(D) 上映時間

映画について、評論家が気に入らなかったことが問われている。3 文書目のチラシの中に評論家のレビューがあり、❿で「時間が少し長すぎた」、⓫で「30 分くらい短い方がよかった」と述べている。以上より、上映時間について気に入っていないことがわかる。これを running time と言い換えた **(D)** が正解。

□ setting 設定

ワクワクする新作コメディー映画
劇場公開
2月10日

"The Secret Life of My House" は明日から全国の映画館で上映される。コメディー映画愛好家なら "SCREAM AND LIVE" のリメイクであるこの映画がとても気に入ることだろう。

Arthur Gage さんと Natalia Beckley さんが主演するこの映画は、1970年代を背景に、末っ子を演じた Gage さんの視点から、実際の Pacino 一家の遺産を探究する。Beckley さんはこの名誉の物語のために自分の恋愛を演じている。

映画の製作には3千万ドル以上が掛かり、この分野の有名な大御所である Tyler Greiner さんが監督を務めた。Greiner さんは特にコメディー映画で有名である。現在までに20本以上の映画で監督を務め、"The Secret Life of My House" はこれまでで最高の映画の一つであると述べた。

「脚本を読んですぐに、私がこの映画の監督をやらなければと思いました。実話を基にしたコメディー映画を長年作りたかったので、とても良い機会をいただきました。Arthur さんと Natalia さんは主要な登場人物として完璧な夫婦ですし、全員がこの素晴らしい作品を作るために一生懸命に仕事をしました。」

"The Secret Life of My House" は今晩封切りされ、全国の劇場での上映は明日から始まる。

The Secret Life of My House
宣伝活動予定表

日程	場所	参加者	活動内容
2月8日	シアトル市シアトル公立図書館	Natalia Beckley さんと Tyler Greiner さん	新聞インタビュー
2月10日	サンディエゴ市 Sunrise Theater	全員	公開初日
2月12日	ロサンゼルス市 Chinese News studio	全員	移動上映会
2月16日	サンフランシスコ市 Reno Theater	Arthur Gage さん	ラジオインタビュー
2月18日	サンフランシスコ市 Delgado Studios	Natalia Beckley さんと Tyler Greiner さん	質疑応答

The Secret Life of My House
1 名入場可能
夜の映画上映会にお越しください。

日付：3 月 5 日
場所：554 Juniper Drive サンフランシスコ市
時間：午後 8 時

980-813-9213 まで出欠のお返事をお願いいたします。

コメディー映画が好きなら、"The Secret Life of My House" をお楽しみいただけます。
Tyler Greiner さんの新作映画 "The Secret Life of My House" が始まりました。

レビュー：

映画は、Pacino 一家の生活に鋭く切り込んでいきます。Pacino 一家は、ボストンやフィラデルフィアで暮らす、典型的な 1970 年代のアメリカの家族でした。

主役は人気俳優 Arthur Gage さんと Natalia Beckley さんです。Natalia Beckley さんは登場人物を説得力を持って演じています。人によっては、Gage さんの話し方が少々耳障りだと感じるかもしれません。しかし、それは彼の優れた演技力のために起きたことです。2 月 16 日の Topanga Everdine さんとのインタビューで、このことが話題になるかもしれないと認めています。

映画のロケはボストンで行われ、昼間の家族のシーンで、街の名所がたくさん見られることが印象深いです。

1970 年代の有名な曲を多く使った素晴らしいサウンドトラックが映画を彩っています。

2 時間を超えるのは長すぎると感じる観客もいるでしょうから、30 分ほど短ければもっとよかったかもしれません。

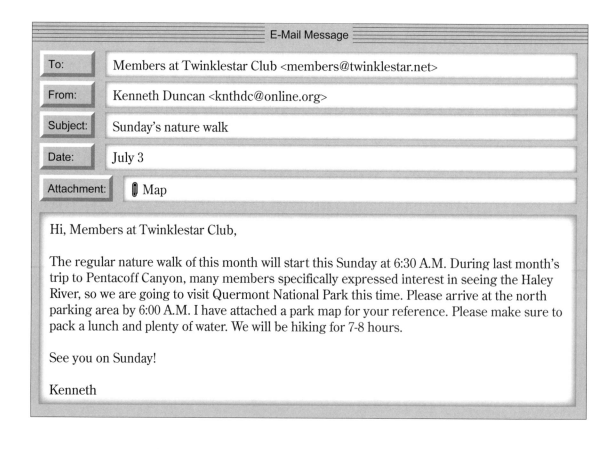

QUERMONT NATIONAL PARK TRAILS GUIDANCE

Name of Trail	Length	Highlights
Gemma Falls Trail	3.6 km	Beginning behind the main pavilion, this easy trail course extends through the Olathe Forest and ends at Gemma Falls. Picnic and barbeque areas can be found along the way.
Geotron Mohail Glen Trail	7.5 km	This trail course stretches along the banks of the Haley River. The flat trail begins at the north parking area and ends at Atlantic Torres Park.
Applewood Cove Trail	6.8 km	Trek up the steep and sharp side of Applewood Ridge. This difficult trail features rocky terrain and an intermittent steep slope with views of Atlantic Torres Valley. The trailhead can be found 200 meters south of the ranger station.
West Brim Trail	9.3 km	You can enjoy beautiful scenery of the Haley River from the top of the ridge, followed by a clear trail that loops back and descends into the north parking area.

E-Mail Message

To: Members at Twinklestar Club <members@twinklestar.net>

From: Kenneth Duncan <knthdc@online.org>

Subject: Sunday's nature walk

Date: July 3

Attachment: Map

Hi, Members at Twinklestar Club,

The regular nature walk of this month will start this Sunday at 6:30 A.M. During last month's trip to Pentacoff Canyon, many members specifically expressed interest in seeing the Haley River, so we are going to visit Quermont National Park this time. Please arrive at the north parking area by 6:00 A.M. I have attached a park map for your reference. Please make sure to pack a lunch and plenty of water. We will be hiking for 7-8 hours.

See you on Sunday!

Kenneth

Policy Statement
Friday, July 8

In Twinklestar Club Trails, we are guided by our policies. One of the main roles of the board of Twinklestar Club is to develop a policy that helps govern our operations. The Twinklestar Club Trails Policy has been organized utilizing the state safety regulations.

Because the recent rainstorms have flooded the Haley River, Geotron Mohail Glen Trail is closed until further notice. Please avoid this trail and any areas near the bank of the Haley River until the floodwaters lessen. Floodwaters have also damaged the north parking area, which is now being repaired. Please park in the east parking area and follow the Bluff Path to reach the trailheads.

50. How long is the trail that goes up Applewood Ridge?

(A) 3.6 km
(B) 6.8 km
(C) 7.5 km
(D) 9.3 km

51. Where will Twinklestar Club members likely hike?

(A) On West Brim Trail
(B) On Applewood Cove Trail
(C) On Geotron Mohail Glen Trai
(D) On Gemma Falls Trail

52. What can be inferred about Quermont National Park?

(A) It offers food to purchasers.
(B) It opens at 6:30 A.M.
(C) It provides guided nature walks.
(D) It has several parking lots.

53. In the notice, the word "utilizing" in paragraph 1, line 3, is closest in meaning to

(A) featuring
(B) accompanying
(C) using
(D) preceding

54. What will Twinklestar Club members likely do after they arrive at the park?

(A) Buy a trip map
(B) Walk along Bluff Path
(C) Watch Haley Falls
(D) Eat at the pavilion

Triple

P. 238

Questions 50-54 refer to the following brochure, e-mail, and notice.

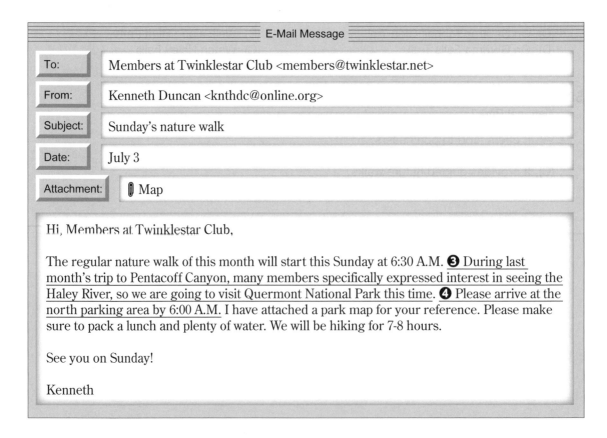

Name of Trail	Length	Highlights
Gemma Falls Trail	3.6 km	Beginning behind the main pavilion, this easy trail course extends through the Olathe Forest and ends at Gemma Falls. Picnic and barbeque areas can be found along the way.
Geotron Mohail Glen Trail	7.5 km	This trail course stretches along the banks of the Haley River. The flat trail begins at the north parking area and ends at Atlantic Torres Park.
❶ Applewood Cove Trail	6.8 km	Trek up the steep and sharp side of Applewood Ridge. This difficult trail features rocky terrain and an intermittent steep slope with views of Atlantic Torres Valley. The trailhead can be found 200 meters south of the ranger station.
❷ West Brim Trail	9.3 km	You can enjoy beautiful scenery of the Haley River from the top of the ridge, followed by a clear trail that loops back and descends into the north parking area.

QUERMONT NATIONAL PARK TRAILS GUIDANCE

E-Mail Message

To: Members at Twinklestar Club <members@twinklestar.net>

From: Kenneth Duncan <knthdc@online.org>

Subject: Sunday's nature walk

Date: July 3

Attachment: 📎 Map

Hi, Members at Twinklestar Club,

The regular nature walk of this month will start this Sunday at 6:30 A.M. ❸ During last month's trip to Pentacoff Canyon, many members specifically expressed interest in seeing the Haley River, so we are going to visit Quermont National Park this time. ❹ Please arrive at the north parking area by 6:00 A.M. I have attached a park map for your reference. Please make sure to pack a lunch and plenty of water. We will be hiking for 7-8 hours.

See you on Sunday!

Kenneth

Policy Statement
Friday, July 8

In Twinklestar Club Trails, we are guided by our policies. One of the main roles of the board of Twinklestar Club is to develop a policy that helps govern our operations. ❺ The Twinklestar Club Trails Policy has been organized utilizing the state safety regulations.

Because the recent rainstorms have flooded the Haley River, Geotron Mohail Glen Trail is closed until further notice. Please avoid this trail and any areas near the bank of the Haley River until the floodwaters lessen. ❻ Floodwaters have also damaged the north parking area, which is now being repaired. Please park in the east parking area and ❼ follow the Bluff Path to reach the trailheads.

パンフレット
☐ trail ハイキングコース　☐ highlight 見どころ　☐ pavilion 休憩所　☐ extend 伸びる、広がる　☐ stretch 伸びる
☐ bank 土手　☐ flat 平らな　☐ trek up 〜に登る　☐ steep 険しい、急な　☐ feature 〜を特徴としている
☐ terrain 地形　☐ intermittent 断続的に発生する　☐ slope 坂　☐ trailhead 登山口
☐ ranger station 警備隊の拠点　☐ scenery 景色　☐ ridge 尾根　☐ followed by 続いて〜がある
☐ loop back ループ（輪）になって戻る　☐ descend 下りる

E メール
☐ specifically 特に　☐ express interest in 〜に関心を示す　☐ attach 〜を添付する
☐ for your reference ご参考まで　☐ plenty of 多量の

お知らせ
☐ guided by 〜に沿って　☐ role 役割　☐ develop a policy 方針を策定する　☐ govern 〜を統括する
☐ organize 〜をまとめる　☐ utilize 〜を利用する　☐ rainstorm 暴風雨　☐ flood 〜を氾濫させる
☐ until further notice 次の知らせまで　☐ avoid 〜を避ける　☐ floodwaters 氾濫した水　☐ lessen 減少する、引く

★★★★★

50. How long is the trail that goes up Applewood Ridge?

(A) 3.6 km
(B) 6.8 km
(C) 7.5 km
(D) 9.3 km

Applewood Ridge を登るコースの長さはどれくらいですか。

(A) 3.6 km
(B) 6.8 km
(C) 7.5 km
(D) 9.3 km

Applewood Ridge を登るコースの長さが問われている。1 文書目のパンフレットの❶に、Applewood Cove コースについての記載があり、ここから正解は **(B)** とわかる。このような検索すれば正解できる問題は、確実に取れるようになっておこう。

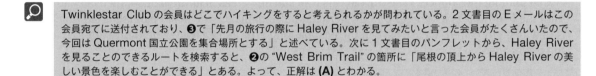

★★★☆☆ クロスリファレンス問題

51. Where will Twinklestar Club members likely hike?

(A) On West Brim Trail
(B) On Applewood Cove Trail
(C) On Geotron Mohail Glen Trai
(D) On Gemma Falls Trail

Twinklestar Club の会員はどこでハイキングをすると考えられますか。

(A) West Brim コースで
(B) Applewood Slope Cove コースで
(C) Geotron Mohail Glen コースで
(D) Gemma Falls コースで

Twinklestar Club の会員はどこでハイキングをすると考えられるかが問われている。2 文書目の E メールはこの会員宛てに送付されており、❸で「先月の旅行の際に Haley River を見てみたいと言った会員がたくさんいたので、今回は Quermont 国立公園を集合場所とする」と述べている。次に 1 文書目のパンフレットから、Haley River を見ることのできるルートを検索すると、❷の "West Brim Trail" の箇所に「尾根の頂上から Haley River の美しい景色を楽しむことができる」とある。よって、正解は **(A)** とわかる。

★★★★★ クロスリファレンス問題

52. What can be inferred about Quermont National Park?

(A) It offers food to purchasers.
(B) It opens at 6:30 A.M.
(C) It provides guided nature walks.
(D) It has several parking lots.

Quermont 国立公園について何が推測できますか。

(A) 買い物をした人に食料を提供している。
(B) 午前 6 時半に開園する。
(C) ガイド付き自然ウォーキングを催行している。
(D) 複数の駐車場がある。

Quermont 国立公園について何が推測できるかを問う選択肢照合型の問題。2 文書目の E メールの❸で、クラブメンバー宛てに、「Quermont 国立公園に行くこと」、❹で「午前 6 時に北駐車場に集合」という案内を出している。次に、3 文書目のお知らせを見ると、❻から、「洪水により、北駐車場も被害を受けたため、車は東駐車場に止めるように」と述べている。つまり、Haley River を見るために集まる Quermont 国立公園には、北と東に駐車場があることが推測できるため、これを言い換えた **(D)** が正解となる。厳密にいうと、この公園に 2 つの駐車場があると断定してはいないが、代わりに止める駐車場があるという情報から推測（infer）することは十分に可能。複数文書から情報をしっかり読み取ろう。

✏ ☐ purchaser 購入者 ☐ guided ガイド付きの

★★★☆☆ 同義語問題

53. In the notice, the word "utilizing" in paragraph 1, line 3, is closest in meaning to

(A) featuring
(B) accompanying
(C) using
(D) preceding

お知らせの、第 1 段落・3 行目にある "utilizing" に最も意味が近いのは

(A) ～を呼び物にし
(B) ～に同行し
(C) ～を利用して
(D) ～に先立って

同義語問題。問われている箇所は、3 文書目のお知らせの❺「（州の安全規制）を活用して」で、「～を利用、活用する」という意味の動詞が動名詞の形となっている。以上から、これと同じ意味となるのは **(C)**。utilize は、use のフォーマルなカタチとして覚えておこう。(A) はどちらかというと、include（含める）、show（見せる）という意味合いと同義になるため、ここでは不正解。

54. What will Twinklestar Club members likely do after they arrive at the park?

   (A) Buy a trip map
   (B) Walk along Bluff Path
   (C) Watch Haley Falls
   (D) Eat at the pavilion

Twinklestar Club の会員は、公園到着後に何をすると考えられますか。

   (A) 道順の案内図を買う
   (B) Bluff Path に沿って歩く
   (C) Haley Falls を見る
   (D) 休憩所で食事をする

Twinklestar Club の会員は公園到着後に何をすると考えられるかが問われている。3 文書目のお知らせの❼で、「登山口まで Bluff Path に沿っていくように」と書かれている。以上から、**(B)** が正解となる。

□ walk along ～に沿って歩く

問題 50 から 54 は次のパンフレット、E メール、お知らせに関するものです。

Quermont 国立公園 ハイキングコースガイド

コース名	長さ	見どころ
Gemma Falls コース	3.6 km	休憩所の裏からスタート、この難易度の低いコースは Olathe Forest を通り、Gemma Falls が終着点となります。途中にピクニックとバーベキューができる場所があります。
Geotron Mohail Glen コース	7.5 km	このハイキングコースは Haley River の土手に沿って伸びています。この平坦なコースは北駐車場から始まり、Atlantic Torres Park が終着地です。
Applewood Cove コース	6.8 km	Applewood Ridge の険しい急斜面を登って行きましょう。この難易度の高いハイキングコースは岩の多い地形と断続的に続く急な斜面が特徴で、Atlantic Torres Valley を眺めることができます。登山口は警備隊の拠点から南に 200 メートルのところにあります。
West Brim コース	9.3 km	尾根の頂上から Haley River の美しい景色を楽しんだら、輪を描いて戻る足場の良いコースをたどり、北駐車場まで下って行けます。

受信者：	Twinklestar Club の会員〈members@twinklestar.net〉
送信者：	Kenneth Duncan〈knthdc@online.org〉
件名：	日曜日の自然ウォーキング
日付：	7月3日
添付ファイル：	地図

Twinklestar Club 会員の皆さま

今月の定例自然ウォーキングは今週の日曜日の午前6時半開始です。先月の Pentacoff Canyon の旅行の際、Haley River を見てみたいと言った会員がたくさんいたので、今回は Quermont 国立公園を訪れることにします。午前6時までに北駐車場に集まってください。参考のために公園の地図を添付しました。昼食と十分な水を用意するのをお忘れなく。ハイキングは7～8時間かかります。

では、日曜日に会いましょう！

Kenneth

方針について
7月8日（金）

Twinklestar Club Trails の会員はクラブの方針に従って活動します。Twinklestar Club 理事会の主な役割の一つは、活動が統括しやすくなるような方針を策定することです。Twinklestar Club Trails の方針は州の安全規制を活用して制定されています。

Haley River を氾濫させた先日の暴風雨の影響で、Geotron Mohail Glen コースはさらなる通知があるまで閉鎖となっています。水が引くまで、このコースや Haley River の土手の近くには一切立ち入らないでください。洪水の水により、北駐車場も被害を受けたため、現在復旧を行っています。車は東駐車場に止め、登山口までは Bluff Path に沿っていってください。

Test 4

Questions 1-2 refer to the following coupon.

 1分30秒

Please accept this coupon with our compliments in order to celebrate the change of the proprietor at MoonBay Coffee Shop.

This coupon can be used toward one of the following:
▶ Purchase one coffee, and obtain three free biscuits
▶ Receive 20% off fresh milk
▶ Purchase one tea, and obtain another at half price

Expires September 30

Valid at our three locations: 237 Hilson Avenue, 3009 Glendale Park Road, and 450 Post Street

1. What has recently altered at MoonBay Coffee Shop?

   (A) Someone new has become the owner.
   (B) A third location has been opened.
   (C) The selection has increased.
   (D) Free items are distributed.

2. What is indicated on the coupon?

   (A) The coffee can be ordered in advance.
   (B) Free biscuits are available with each purchase.
   (C) The coupon is good for a single offer.
   (D) Guests can purchase two teas for the price of one.

 P. 246

Questions 3-4 refer to the following advertisement. 1分30秒

Garrison Consulting Institution is performing research in the field of macroeconomics.

Garrison Consulting Institution is a high level world consulting organization that has successfully undertaken many projects since 1990. And also, we are researching the correlation between financial flows and economic growth. The task is intellectually difficult. However, at the same time, it will be satisfactory to us. We are trying to find an expert with experience in the following areas:

- Comparative study of macroeconomic data between developed and developing countries

- Analysis of economic and financial statistics

- Writing reports for both economists and non-economists

The applicant should have a bachelor degree or more in economics and also at least seven years' experience. Great computer skills and data analytical and numerical abilities are imperative.

Applications with résumé should be sent to:

Erin Riordan, Manager of Garrison Consulting Institution
7910 Westchester Avenue
Pensacola, FL 52456

3. What is NOT a requirement for this position?

(A) Ability to analyze data
(B) More than seven years' experience
(C) Knowledge of a foreign language
(D) A degree in economics

4. According to the advertisement, what is the advantage of this job?

(A) It is challenging but worthwhile.
(B) It is well-suited for active people.
(C) It is creative and innovative.
(D) It is intellectually predictable.

P. 248

Questions 1-2 refer to the following coupon.

❶ Please accept this coupon with our compliments in order to celebrate the change of the proprietor at MoonBay Coffee Shop.

❷ This coupon can be used toward one of the following:
▶ Purchase one coffee, and obtain three free biscuits
▶ Receive 20% off fresh milk
▶ Purchase one tea, and obtain another at half price

Expires September 30

Valid at our three locations: 237 Hilson Avenue, 3009 Glendale Park Road, and 450 Post Street

□ compliment 感謝の気持ち　□ in order to *do* ~するために　□ celebrate ~を祝う　□ proprietor 経営者
□ following 以下の事項　□ obtain ~を獲得する　□ at half price 半額で　□ expire 期限切れとなる
□ valid 有効である

★★☆☆☆

1. What has recently altered at MoonBay Coffee Shop?

(A) Someone new has become the owner.
(B) A third location has been opened.
(C) The selection has increased.
(D) Free items are distributed.

MoonBay Coffee Shop で最近何が変わりましたか。

(A) オーナーが新しくなった。
(B) 3 店舗目が開業した。
(C) 選択が増えた。
(D) 無料の商品が配布されている。

MoonBay Coffee Shop で最近何が変わったかが問われている。冒頭❶で「MoonBay Coffee Shop のオーナー交代を祝して、このクーポン券をお受け取りください」と述べているので、所有者が交代したことがわかる。これを「オーナーが新しくなった」と言い換えた **(A)** が正解。クーポン券を無料で配布しているが、商品を無料では配布していないので (D) は不正解。

□ alter 変わる　□ distribute ~を配る

★★★☆☆

2. What is indicated on the coupon?

　(A) The coffee can be ordered in advance.
　(B) Free biscuits are available with each purchase.
　(C) The coupon is good for a single offer.
　(D) Guests can purchase two teas for the price of one.

クーポン券に何が記載されていますか。

　(A) コーヒーは事前に注文できる。
　(B) 購入ごとに無料のビスケットが付いてくる。
　(C) クーポン券は 1 つの注文に利用できる。
　(D) 客は 2 杯のお茶を 1 杯分の価格で購入できる。

クーポン券に何が記載されているかが問われている。❷から「このクーポン券は次のいずれかに利用できる」とあり、3 つの項目があることから、このクーポンは 3 つの項目のどれか 1 つのサービスに使うことができる。よって、これを a single offer（1 つの注文）と言い換えた **(C)** が正解。(B) は商品がコーヒーと指定されており、(D) は「1 杯分の価格で 2 杯提供」ではなく、「1 杯購入すると 2 杯目が半額」が正しいので、いずれも不正解。

□ in advance 事前に　□ be good for ～に対して有効である
□ two ○○ for the price of one 1 つ分の価格で 2 つの○○

問題 1 から 2 は次のクーポン券に関するものです。

MoonBay Coffee Shop のオーナー交代を祝し、当店からの感謝のしるしとして、クーポン券を進呈いたします。どうぞお受け取りください。

このクーポン券は次のいずれかにご利用いただけます。
▶ コーヒーを 1 杯ご購入いただくと、ビスケットを 3 枚無料で進呈いたします
▶ 新鮮なミルクが 20%引きとなります
▶ お茶を 1 杯ご購入いただくと、もう 1 杯を半額でご提供いたします

9 月 30 日まで有効

3 店舗で利用可能：237 Hilson Avenue、3009 Glendale Park Road、450 Post Street

Questions 3-4 refer to the following advertisement.

Garrison Consulting Institution is performing research in the field of macroeconomics.

Garrison Consulting Institution is a high level world consulting organization that has successfully undertaken many projects since 1990. And also, we are researching the correlation between financial flows and economic growth. ❶ The task is intellectually difficult. However, at the same time, it will be satisfactory to us. We are trying to find an expert with experience in the following areas:

　- Comparative study of macroeconomic data between developed and developing countries
　- Analysis of economic and financial statistics
　- Writing reports for both economists and non-economists

❷ The applicant should have a bachelor degree or more in economics and also ❸ at least seven years' experience. ❹ Great computer skills and data analytical and numerical abilities are imperative.

Applications with résumé should be sent to:

Erin Riordan, Manager of Garrison Consulting Institution
7910 Westchester Avenue
Pensacola, FL 52456

✏️ ☐ perform ～を行う　☐ in the field of ～の分野において　☐ macroeconomics マクロ経済の
☐ high level 高水準の　☐ consulting organization コンサルティング機関　☐ successfully 成功のうちに
☐ undertake ～を引き受ける　☐ correlation 相関　☐ financial flow 金融フロー、資金の流れ
☐ economic growth 経済成長　☐ task 任務　☐ intellectually 知的に　☐ at the same time 同時に
☐ satisfactory 満足な　☐ expert 専門家　☐ following 以下の　☐ comparative study 比較研究
☐ developed and developing countries 先進国と発展途上国　☐ financial statistics 財務統計
☐ bachelor degree 学士号　☐ in economics 経済学の　☐ at least 少なくとも　☐ numerical 数字に関する
☐ imperative 不可欠である

★★★☆☆ NOT 問題

3. What is NOT a requirement for this position?

(A) Ability to analyze data
(B) More than seven years' experience
(C) Knowledge of a foreign language
(D) A degree in economics

この仕事の必要条件でないものは何ですか。

(A) データを分析する能力
(B) 7 年以上の経験
(C) 外国語の知識
(D) 経済学の学位

🔍 NOT 問題。求人の要件ではないものが問われている。文書中盤より下に応募要件が書かれており、❷の専門学位に関することが (D) に、❸の最低経験年数が (B) に、❹にある「データ分析力」が (A) にそれぞれ該当する。よって、記載のない **(C)** が正解となる。

✏️ ☐ degree 学位

4. According to the advertisement, what is the advantage of this job?

(A) It is challenging but worthwhile.
(B) It is well-suited for active people.
(C) It is creative and innovative.
(D) It is intellectually predictable.

広告によると、この仕事の利点とは何ですか。

(A) 難しいが、やりがいがある。
(B) 活動的な人に向いている。
(C) 創造的かつ革新的である。
(D) 知的に予測ができる。

この求人の仕事の利点について問われている。❶で「知的に難しいが、我々にとって満足のいくものになる」と、大変だがやりがいがあることを述べている。よって、それを言い換えた **(A)** が正解。challenging は「困難（だがやりがいのある）」、worthwhile は「やりがいのある」という意味で、❶の "...difficult. However,...satisfactory..." の言い換えになっている。

□ advantage 利点　□ challenging 困難な　□ worthwhile やりがいのある　□ well-suited 適合している
□ active 行動的な　□ predictable 予測ができる

問題 3 から 4 は次の広告に関するものです。

Garrison Consulting Institution は、マクロ経済の分野で研究を行っています。

Garrison Consulting Institution は 1990 年以来、多くのプロジェクトを成功に導いた高水準の世界的コンサルティング機関です。また、金融フローと経済成長の予測との相関関係を研究しています。作業には知的な困難さがありますが、それと同時に満足することでしょう。当社は以下の分野での経験を持つ専門家を求めています。

- 先進国と発展途上国のマクロ経済データの比較研究
- 経済統計および財務統計の分析
- 経済学者と非経済学者、両方に向けたレポート作成

応募者は、経済学の学士号以上の学士号を持っていることと、最低 7 年間の経験が求められます。優れたコンピュータースキルとデータ分析力、数値を扱う能力が不可欠です。

応募用紙と履歴書をこちらにお送りください：

Garrison Consulting Institution 所長 Erin Riordan
7910 Westchester Avenue
Pensacola, フロリダ州 52456

Make It Yourself Supply

Policy of Shipping and Returns

Shipping: Make It Yourself Supply is offering the highest quality automotive parts and equipment all over the globe. You can choose among various delivery options: overnight, two-day, weekend options and so on. Please contact one of our sales associates for shipping prices. When you make purchases online, shipping fees are automatically added to your total amount at the time of purchase.

Returns: All purchases can be returned within 30 days of purchase and you must include the original receipt for a full refund to be processed. Items purchased at a store may be returned to any of our locations. Purchases made by phone or through our Web site may be brought back to or mailed to our main distribution center in Los Angeles. Any item that was sent to you in a sealed wrap can be returned for a full refund only if its wrapping has not been removed. We do not refund shipping costs.

5. What is true about Make It Yourself Supply?

(A) It supplies customized motorcycles.
(B) It fixes computers at an affordable price.
(C) It carries automobile parts internationally.
(D) It distributes gasoline nationwide.

6. According to the information, which of the following is Make It Yourself Supply's return policy?

(A) Refunds generally include shipping costs.
(B) Returned items should not be accompanied by a receipt.
(C) Some items can only be returned in their original condition.
(D) Items must be returned to the original place of purchase.

P. 252

John Hence 4:48 p.m.

Hey, Kate. This message is to tell you that I am leaving my office right now. I had a conference that was supposed to finish at 3:55, but it continued until 4:25.

Kate Silva 4:51 p.m.

Oh, no problem. I'm almost at the Timber Drama Center. Do you want me to wait for you out front, or shall I go inside?

John Hence 4:53 p.m.

It's usually pretty busy on a Friday night. Perhaps you had better go ahead and buy our tickets.

Kate Silva 4:55 p.m.

Good idea. So, we decided to see "A Winter Fairy" at 6:00, right?

John Hence 4:57 p.m.

Yes. All of the magazine reviews say the movie is excellent and has some amazing performances and cinematography.

Kate Silva 4:58 p.m.

Can't wait. I'll grab some drinks and popcorn for us as well. How about diet cola and salted popcorn?

John Hence 4:59 p.m.

Perfect. I'll pay you back upon my arrival. See you soon.

---

7. What can be inferred about Mr. Hence?

(A) He has visited Timber Drama Center before.
(B) He has bought tickets for a concert.
(C) He will be delayed by one hour.
(D) He has already seen "A Winter Fairy."

8. At 4:58 P.M., what does Ms. Silva mean when she writes, "Can't wait"?

(A) She wants to read a magazine review right now.
(B) She should wait for Mr. Hence inside the drama center.
(C) She would like to have a big dinner.
(D) She is looking forward to seeing the movie.

 P. 254

Questions 5-6 refer to the following information.

Make It Yourself Supply

Policy of Shipping and Returns

Shipping: ❶ Make It Yourself Supply is offering the highest quality automotive parts and equipment all over the globe. You can choose among various delivery options: overnight, two-day, weekend options and so on. Please contact one of our sales associates for shipping prices. When you make purchases online, shipping fees are automatically added to your total amount at the time of purchase.

Returns: All purchases can be returned within 30 days of purchase and you must include the original receipt for a full refund to be processed. Items purchased at a store may be returned to any of our locations. Purchases made by phone or through our Web site may be brought back to or mailed to our main distribution center in Los Angeles. ❷ Any item that was sent to you in a sealed wrap can be returned for a full refund only if its wrapping has not been removed. We do not refund shipping costs.

☐ policy 規約 ☐ shipping and returns 配送と返品 ☐ the highest quality 最高品質の
☐ automotive parts and equipment 自動車部品と機器 ☐ all over the globe 世界中で ☐ various さまざまな
☐ delivery option 配送手段 ☐ overnight 翌日配達の ☐ and so on ～など ☐ sales associate 販売員
☐ shipping fee 送料 ☐ automatically 自動的に ☐ total amount 総額 ☐ at the time of ～の際に
☐ original receipt レシート（領収書）原本 ☐ full refund 全額払い戻し ☐ process ～の処理をする
☐ bring back to ～に持ち込む ☐ mail to ～に郵送する ☐ distribution center 配送センター
☐ sealed wrap 密閉された包装状態

★★★☆☆

5. What is true about Make It Yourself Supply?

(A) It supplies customized motorcycles.
(B) It fixes computers at an affordable price.
(C) It carries automobile parts internationally.
(D) It distributes gasoline nationwide.

Make It Yourself Supply 社について正しいことは何ですか。

(A) 特別注文のオートバイを提供している。
(B) 手ごろな価格でコンピューターを修理する。
(C) 国際的に自動車部品を販売している。
(D) ガソリンを全国で販売している。

Make It Yourself 社について正しいことは何かを問う選択肢照合型の問題。❶で、この会社が「自動車部品と機器を世界中で提供している」と述べている。この「世界中で」を internationally と表現し、また "offer（～を提供する）" を carry（～を取り扱う）と言い換えた **(C)** が正解。(A) 特別注文のバイク、(B) パソコン修理、(D) ガソリンの全国販売は記載がないので、それぞれ不正解。

☐ customized 特別注文された ☐ motorcycle オートバイ ☐ fix ～を修理する
☐ at an affordable price 手ごろな価格で ☐ carry （商品）を扱う ☐ internationally 国際的に
☐ distribute ～を供給する ☐ gasoline ガソリン ☐ nationwide 全国的に

6. According to the information, which of the following is Make It Yourself Supply's return policy?

(A) Refunds generally include shipping costs.
(B) Returned items should not be accompanied by a receipt.
(C) Some items can only be returned in their original condition.
(D) Items must be returned to the original place of purchase.

情報によると、Make It Yourself Supply 社の返品規約は次のどれですか。

(A) 返金額には送料が通常含まれる。
(B) 返品する品物にレシートを添付してはいけない。
(C) 一部の品物は元の状態でのみ返品が可能である。
(D) 品物は購入した場所に返品しなければならない。

🔍 Make It Yourself Supply 社の返品規約が選択肢はどれかが問われている。❷で「密封された状態で配送した商品は、包装が外されていない場合のみ全額返金が可能」と述べているので、返品の場合は元の状態のまま返送される必要があるということがわかる。これを original condition（元の状態）と表現した **(C)** が正解となる。(A) は本文に記載がなく、(B) は返品にはレシートが必要、(D) はどの店舗でも返品が可能となっているので、それぞれ不正解。

✎ □ generally 一般的に　□ shipping cost 送料　□ be accompanied by ～を添付している
　 □ original condition 元の状態　□ original place of purchase 元々の購入場所

📖 問題 5 から 6 は次の情報に関するものです。

Make It Yourself Supply 社

配送と返品の規約

配送：Make It Yourself Supply 社は最も高品質な自動車部品と機器を世界中で提供しています。配送にはさまざまな選択肢があります（翌日配達、2日配達、週末配達など）。送料については店舗の販売員にお問合せください。オンラインでお買い物をされた際、配送料はご購入時に合計金額へ自動的に追加されます。

返品：ご購入いただいたすべての商品は30日以内の返品が可能です。全額払い戻しの処理をするために、領収書の原本を一緒にお持ちいただく必要があります。店舗で購入された商品は当社のどの店舗でもご返品いただけます。お電話もしくはウェブサイトで購入された商品はロサンゼルスにある当社の主要配送センターに直接お持ちになるか、ご郵送ください。密封された状態でお届けした商品は、包装が外されていない場合のみ全額返金が可能です。送料の返金はいたしません。

---

7. (A) 8. (D)

Questions 7-8 refer to the following text-message chain.

John Hence 4:48 p.m.
Hey, Kate. This message is to tell you that I am leaving my office right now. I had a conference that was supposed to finish at 3:55, but it continued until 4:25.

Kate Silva 4:51 p.m.
Oh, no problem. I'm almost at the Timber Drama Center. Do you want me to wait for you out front, or shall I go inside?

John Hence 4:53 p.m.
❶ It's usually pretty busy on a Friday night. ❷ Perhaps you had better go ahead and buy our tickets.

Kate Silva 4:55 p.m.
Good idea. So, we decided to see "A Winter Fairy" at 6:00, right?

John Hence 4:57 p.m.
Yes. ❸ All of the magazine reviews say the movie is excellent and has some amazing performances and cinematography.

Kate Silva 4:58 p.m.
❹ Can't wait. I'll grab some drinks and popcorn for us as well. How about diet cola and salted popcorn?

John Hence 4:59 p.m.
Perfect. I'll pay you back upon my arrival. See you soon.

□ right now 今から　□ conference 会議　□ be supposed to *do* 〜することになっている
□ almost ほぼ、ほとんど　□ out front 建物の前で　□ pretty とても　□ perhaps たぶん
□ you had better 〜したほうがよい　□ go ahead 先に行く　□ review 感想、批評　□ amazing 素晴らしい
□ performance 演技　□ cinematography 撮影技術　□ grab 〜をサッと手に入れる　□ as well 同様に
□ salted 塩味の　□ upon one's arrival 到着したらすぐに

★★★★★

7. What can be inferred about Mr. Hence?

(A) He has visited Timber Drama Center before.
(B) He has bought tickets for a concert.
(C) He will be delayed by one hour.
(D) He has already seen "A Winter Fairy."

Hence さんについて何が推測できますか。

(A) Timber Drama Center に以前行ったことがある。
(B) コンサートのチケットを購入した。
(C) 1時間遅刻する。
(D) 『A Winter Fairy』をすでに見た。

🔍 Hence さんについて何が推測できるかを問う選択肢照合型の問題。Hence さんは❶・❷で「(これから映画を観ようとしている Timber Drama Center は)金曜の夜はいつも混むので、早目にチケットを買う方がいい」と Silva さんにメッセージを送っている。Hence さんが、この映画館は金曜の夜は混むと知っていることから、前にもこの映画館を訪れたことがあると推測できる。以上より、**(A)** が正解となる。

□ before 以前に　□ delay 〜を遅らせる

254

8. At 4:58 P.M., what does Ms. Silva mean when she writes, "Can't wait"?

(A) She wants to read a magazine review right now.
(B) She should wait for Mr. Hence inside the drama center.
(C) She would like to have a big dinner.
(D) She is looking forward to seeing the movie.

午後 4 時 58 分に、Silva さんは "Can't wait" という発言で、何を意味していますか。

(A) 雑誌の批評を今すぐに読みたい。
(B) Timber Drama Center の中で Hence さんを待つべきである。
(C) 豪華な夕食を食べたい。
(D) 映画を観ることが楽しみである。

意図問題。問われている表現❹は「待つことができない」という表現なので、これから起こることが待てないことを示唆している。この直前の❸を見ると、Hence さんがこれから観る映画について、「どの雑誌の批評でも、この映画は素晴らしくて、演技も撮影技術も圧巻だと書かれている」と、映画に関するポジティブな情報を提供していることから、この映画を早く観たいという意図で発言したことがわかる。以上から、正解は **(D)** となる。

□ right now 今から　□ look forward to ～を楽しみにする

 問題 7 から 8 は次のテキストメッセージのやりとりに関するものです。

John Hence 午後 4 時 48 分
やぁ、Kate！　オフィスを今出ることを知らせるためのメッセージだよ。会議があって、3 時 55 分に終わる予定だったのに、4 時 25 分まで延びてしまったよ。

Kate Silva 午後 4 時 51 分
あぁ、気にしないで。私はもうすぐ Timber Drama Center に到着するよ。建物の前で待っていた方がいいかな、それとも中で待っておこうか。

John Hence 午後 4 時 53 分
金曜日の夜はいつもかなり混雑しているから。できれば先に入ってチケットを買う方がいいだろうね。

Kate Silva 午後 4 時 55 分
いい考えね。ええと、6 時の『A Winter Fairy』を見るということだったよね。

John Hence 午後 4 時 57 分
そうだよ。どの雑誌の批評でも、この映画は素晴らしく、演技も撮影技術も圧巻だと書いていたよ。

Kate Silva 午後 4 時 58 分
待ちきれないわ。飲み物とポップコーンも買っておくね。ダイエットコーラと塩味のポップコーンはどう？

John Hence 午後 4 時 59 分
完璧だよ。到着したら君にお金を渡すね。じゃあ、あとで。

Questions 9-11 refer to the following article.

 2分45秒

New Restaurant In Hartport
By Sophie Lee—Hartport Newspaper Staff Journalist

Hartport—Rangel's Café is going to open on Friday, April 15. Rangel's is a welcome addition to the many wonderful eating establishments around Hartport's lakefront district. Head Chef Nayeli Rangel said, "Rangel's specializes in traditional Mexican cuisine. This delicious yet highly unique cuisine is where we differ from other restaurants nearby. Customers can expect to taste various dishes made with the best quality meats, seafood, and fresh vegetables. Our mission is to please our customers and keep them returning for more."

Ms. Rangel, formerly head chef at Trundle Restaurant, began developing a plan to open her own restaurant in Hartport six years ago. She toured some properties around the city but was set on a lakefront location. She sought the former shirt factory building and had it renovated. Ms. Rangel says, "I worked with construction workers and renovation experts to make sure that many of the original architectural elements were preserved in order to pay tribute to the rich history of this city."

Rangel's is beautiful inside and out. We'll have to wait and see if the residents of Hartport will like the food. Rangel's Café will be open Tuesdays through Sundays for lunch and dinner. The menu items are very affordable; the average price of dishes is less than that of other restaurants in the area.

9. What is the purpose of the article?

(A) To inspect a particular type of cuisine
(B) To advertise a building for sale
(C) To report the opening of a new business
(D) To search for employees for a new establishment

10. According to the article, what is NOT true about Rangel's Café?

(A) It is located in a remodeled building.
(B) Its menu items are reasonably priced.
(C) It is owned by Trundle Restaurant.
(D) It is near to many other eating establishments.

11. What can be inferred about Sophie Lee?

(A) She is good at remodeling buildings.
(B) She previously worked at Trundle Restaurant.
(C) She has spoken with Ms. Rangel.
(D) She enjoys Mexican food very much.

P. 258

Questions 9-11 refer to the following article.

New Restaurant In Hartport
By Sophie Lee—Hartport Newspaper Staff Journalist

Hartport—❶ Rangel's Café is going to open on Friday, April 15. ❷ Rangel's is a welcome addition to the many wonderful eating establishments around Hartport's lakefront district. ❸ Head Chef Nayeli Rangel said, "Rangel's specializes in traditional Mexican cuisine. This delicious yet highly unique cuisine is where we differ from other restaurants nearby. Customers can expect to taste various dishes made with the best quality meats, seafood, and fresh vegetables. Our mission is to please our customers and keep them returning for more."

Ms. Rangel, formerly head chef at Trundle Restaurant, began developing a plan to open her own restaurant in Hartport six years ago. She toured some properties around the city but was set on a lakefront location. ❹ She sought the former shirt factory building and had it renovated. ❺ Ms. Rangel says, "I worked with construction workers and renovation experts to make sure that many of the original architectural elements were preserved in order to pay tribute to the rich history of this city."

Rangel's is beautiful inside and out. We'll have to wait and see if the residents of Hartport will like the food. Rangel's Café will be open Tuesdays through Sundays for lunch and dinner. ❻ The menu items are very affordable; the average price of dishes is less than that of other restaurants in the area.

☐ addition 追加 ☐ eating establishment 飲食店 ☐ traditional 伝統的な ☐ cuisine 料理
☐ A yet B AでありそれでいてBである ☐ highly unique とても個性的な ☐ differ from ～と異なる
☐ taste ～を味わう ☐ various さまざまな ☐ mission 使命 ☐ formerly かつて、以前は
☐ develop a plan 計画を策定する ☐ property 不動産 ☐ set on ～に定める ☐ sought (seek「～を探す」の過去形)
☐ former 過去の ☐ renovate ～を改装する ☐ construction worker 建築作業員
☐ architectural element 建築要素 ☐ preserve ～を保存する ☐ pay tribute to ～に敬意を表する
☐ inside and out 内装や外装において ☐ affordable お手ごろ価格の ☐ less than ～よりも安い

★★★☆☆

9. What is the purpose of the article?

(A) To inspect a particular type of cuisine
(B) To advertise a building for sale
(C) To report the opening of a new business
(D) To search for employees for a new establishment

記事の目的は何ですか。

(A) 特定の種類の料理を検査すること
(B) 売り出し中の建築物を宣伝すること
(C) 新規開業を知らせること
(D) 新しい施設の従業員を募集すること

🔍 記事の目的が問われている。第1段落の冒頭❶に「Rangel's Caféが4月15日（金）に営業を開始する」とあり、以降はこの店に関する詳細が述べられているため、ある事業のオープンについて述べられていることがわかる。よって **(C)** が正解。(A)(D) は、料理の検査や求人に関する記載が本文にはないため、いずれも不正解となる。

☐ inspect ～を検査する ☐ a particular type of 特定の種類の～ ☐ for sale 売り出し中の
☐ search for ～を探す・募集する ☐ establishment 会社、施設

10. According to the article, what is NOT true about Rangel's Café?

(A) It is located in a remodeled building.
(B) Its menu items are reasonably priced.
(C) It is owned by Trundle Restaurant.
(D) It is near to many other eating establishments.

記事によると、Rangel's Café について正しくないことは何ですか。

(A) 改装された建物にある。
(B) メニューの品目は手ごろな価格である。
(C) Trundle Restaurant が所有している。
(D) 他の多くの飲食店の近くにある。

NOT 問題。Rangel's Café について正しくないものは何かが問われている。❷の「同地区（Harport）のレストランとして加わる」が (D) に、❹の「シャツ工場だったビルを改装した」が (A) に、❻の「メニューにある商品はどれもお手ごろ価格」が (B) に、それぞれ言い換えられている。残った **(C)** の記載が本文にはないため、これが正解となる。第 2 段落の冒頭で、Trundle Restaurant は Rangel's Café の主任シェフの以前の勤務先と述べられており、この店の所有者ではない。NOT 問題では、正しくないものを探すのではなく、正しいものを 3 つ探し、残ったものを正解としてマークするようにすれば、NOT true に惑わされずに済むだろう。

☐ located in 〜にある ☐ remodeled 改装された ☐ reasonably priced 手ごろな価格の ☐ near to 〜に近い

11. What can be inferred about Sophie Lee?

(A) She is good at remodeling buildings.
(B) She previously worked at Trundle Restaurant.
(C) She has spoken with Ms. Rangel.
(D) She enjoys Mexican food very much.

Sophie Lee さんについて何が推測できますか。

(A) 建物の改装を得意としている。
(B) 以前 Trundle Restaurant で働いていた。
(C) Rangel さんと話したことがある。
(D) メキシコ料理がとても好きである。

Sophie Lee さんについて何が推測できるかを問う選択肢照合型の問題。タイトルの下の記者名から、Lee さんはこの記事を書いた人物だとわかる。❸・❺で、主任シェフの Rangel さんがこの店について❸「〜と語った」、❺「〜と語る」と述べていることから、この記事の書き手の Lee さんが Rangel さんを直接取材し、記事にしていると推測される。よって **(C)** が正解。Lee さんが、(A) 建物の改装が得意、(D) メキシコ料理が好きだ、という根拠となる箇所はなく、(B) の Trundle Restaurant で働いていたのは Rangel さんであるため、いずれも不正解となる。

☐ be good at 〜が得意である ☐ previously 過去に

問題 9 から 11 は次の記事に関するものです。

Hartport に新しいレストラン
Sophie Lee — Hartport Newspaper 所属記者

Hartport — Rangel's Café が 4 月 15 日（金）に営業を開始する。Rangel's は Hartport 湖畔地区周辺の多くの素晴らしい飲食店にとっても歓迎される店だ。主任シェフの Nayeli Rangel は、「Rangel's は伝統的なメキシコ料理の専門店です。おいしいうえに個性的なこの料理が地域の他のレストランと異なるところです。お客さまは最高品質の肉、海鮮、新鮮な野菜で作ったさまざまなのメニューをお召し上がりになれます。当店の使命はお客様にお喜びいただき、より頻繁にご利用いただけるようにすることです。」と語った。

Trundle Restaurant でかつて主任シェフを務めた Rangel さんは、6 年前、Hartport に自身のレストランを開く計画を練り始めた。彼女は町中のいくつかの物件を見て回ったが、湖畔地区に決めた。かつてシャツの工場だったビルを探し出し、改装を行った。Rangel さんは、「この町の豊かな歴史に敬意を表すため、元からの建築要素の多くを確実に保持するように、建設業者や改装の専門家と協力をしました」と語る。

Rangel's は内装も外装も美しい。Hartport の住民がここの食事を気に入るかどうかは様子を見なくてはいけない。Rangel's Café は火曜日から日曜日の昼食と夕食時に開店する予定だ。メニューの商品はお手ごろ価格で、料理の平均価格はその地域の他のレストランよりも安くなっている。

Questions 12-14 refer to the following survey.

2分45秒

A recent survey reports that most workers do not want to be in managerial positions. Managers who are concerned about workers trying to occupy their positions should relax. According to this survey, 65 percent of workers do not want to be in charge. Moreover, 60 percent of respondents said that they maybe could not do a better job than their current superiors.

The survey was carried out by Employment & Job, an independent research company that provides the services of management consultants to executives. The survey included 1,000 men and women over the age of 31 working in a professional environment.

Workers were asked:

1. "Would you like to do your superior's job?"
        Responses: Yes   20%
                      No   65%
                      Don't know 15%

2. "Do you think you could do a better job than your superior?"
        Responses: Yes   30%
                      No   60%
                      Don't know 10%

"A superior or manager can be the target of workplace humor," said Beth Wilkins, general manager of Employment & Job. "However, it can be demanding to become the superior and many workers acknowledge this fact, even though they might not always agree with their manager's decisions."

12. What is Employment & Job?

    (A) A provider of staffing services
    (B) An organization of administrative professionals
    (C) A research firm
    (D) A government employment agency

13. According to the survey, what percentage of employees want their superiors' job?

    (A) 5
    (B) 20
    (C) 60
    (D) 65

14. What does Ms. Wilkins say about most workers?

    (A) They know that being a manager is not easy.
    (B) They usually do not agree with their supervisors.
    (C) They do not think much about their presidents.
    (D) They are satisfied with their managers.

P. 262

Questions 12-14 refer to the following survey.

A recent survey reports that most workers do not want to be in managerial positions. Managers who are concerned about workers trying to occupy their positions should relax. According to this survey, 65 percent of workers do not want to be in charge. Moreover, 60 percent of respondents said that they maybe could not do a better job than their current superiors.

❶ The survey was carried out by Employment & Job, an independent research company that provides the services of management consultants to executives. The survey included 1,000 men and women over the age of 31 working in a professional environment.

Workers were asked:

1. ❷ **"Would you like to do your superior's job?"**
   ❸ Responses: Yes   20%
                 No   65%
                 Don't know   15%

2. **"Do you think you could do a better job than your superior?"**
   Responses: Yes   30%
                 No   60%
                 Don't know   10%

"A superior or manager can be the target of workplace humor," said Beth Wilkins, general manager of Employment & Job. ❹ "However, it can be demanding to become the superior and many workers acknowledge this fact, even though they might not always agree with their manager's decisions."

□ managerial position 管理職 □ be concerned about ～について懸念している
□ occupy one's position ～の役職に就く □ be in charge 責任を負う、担当している □ respondent 回答者
□ superior 上司 □ carry out ～を実行する □ independent research company 独立した調査会社
□ executives 経営者 □ professional environment プロフェッショナル（職業的）な環境
□ target of workplace humor 職場の笑いのネタ □ demanding 厳しい □ acknowledge ～を認めている

★★☆☆☆

12. What is Employment & Job?

(A) A provider of staffing services
(B) An organization of administrative
    professionals
(C) A research firm
(D) A government employment agency

Employment & Job 社とは何ですか。

(A) 人材派遣会社
(B) 経営のプロの組織
(C) 調査会社
(D) 政府の人材紹介会社

Employment & Job 社とは何かが問われている。❶に「独立した調査会社である Employment & Job 社」とあるため、ここから調査会社だとわかる。以上から、正解は company を firm と言い換えた **(C)**。

□ employment agency 人材紹介会社

★★☆☆☆

13. According to the survey, what percentage of employees want their superiors' job?

(A) 5
(B) 20
(C) 60
(D) 65

調査によると、何パーセントの従業員が自分の上司の役職に就きたいですか。

(A) 5
(B) 20
(C) 60
(D) 65

🔍 何パーセントの従業員が自分の上司の役職に就きたいかが問われている。❷・❸に、この内容の質問と回答があり、「はい」と回答した人が 20 パーセントいることから、正解は **(B)** となる。

- -

★★★★☆

14. What does Ms. Wilkins say about most workers?

(A) They know that being a manager is not easy.
(B) They usually do not agree with their supervisors.
(C) They do not think much about their presidents.
(D) They are satisfied with their managers.

Wilkins さんはほとんどの労働者について何と言っていますか。

(A) 管理職に就くことは容易ではないと理解している。
(B) 通常、上司には同意できない。
(C) 社長についてはあまり考えない。
(D) 自身の上司について満足している。

🔍 Wilkins さんがほとんどの労働者について何と言っているかが問われている。Wilkins さんの発言は文書の最後にある。❹で「上司になることは厳しいものであり、多くの労働者はそれを理解している」述べている。これを言い換えた **(A)** が正解となる。

✎ □ supervisor 上司、監督者

📝 問題 12 から 14 は次の調査に関するものです。

最近の調査が、ほとんどの労働者は管理職につくことを望んでいないと報じている。自身の役職に就くことを部下が狙っていることについて不安を感じている管理職は気を楽にしていいだろう。この調査によれば、労働者の 65 パーセントは責任を負いたくない。さらに、回答者の 60 パーセントは現在の上司よりも良い仕事はできないだろうと答えた。

この調査は、独立した調査会社である Employment & Job 社が実施したもので、経営者を対象とした経営コンサルタントのサービスを提供している。調査対象は、プロフェッショナルな環境で働く 31 歳以上の男女 1,000 名である。

労働者への質問：

1. 「上司の仕事をやりたいと思いますか？」
　　　　回答：　　　はい　　　　　　　　20 パーセント
　　　　　　　　　　いいえ　　　　　　　65 パーセント
　　　　　　　　　　わからない　　　　　15 パーセント

2. 「上司よりも良い仕事ができると思いますか？」
　　　　回答：　　　はい　　　　　　　　30 パーセント
　　　　　　　　　　いいえ　　　　　　　60 パーセント
　　　　　　　　　　わからない　　　　　10 パーセント

「上司や管理職は職場でのユーモアの対象となる可能性があります。」と Employment & Job 社の業務部長である Beth Wilkins 氏は語る。「しかし、上司になることは厳しいものであり、たとえ管理職の決定に常に同意できないとしても、多くの労働者はそれを理解しています。」

Lexington's Heating & Cooling

HOME	SERVICES	**REVIEWS**	SCHEDULE APPOINTMENT	E-MAIL US

What our customers are saying.
Rating: ★★★★☆
Date of service: 10 July
Type of service: Installation of new air conditioner unit

A few days ago, I found that my air conditioner in my property was out of order and did not blow cool air. I remembered that an advertisement for Lexington's Heating & Cooling was posted in my local building supply store, so I rang Lexington's up. Although it was Saturday and the business is usually not open on that day, the owner, Jack Lexington, came there within 2 hours after receiving my phone call. He examined my air conditioner and said to me that I would need to either get a new one or order several new parts to have it mended. Because it was a really old model, I decided to get a new one. Mr. Lexington showed me a catalog with some different air conditioner models, and chose an energy-efficient one. I thought it would take a couple of days to order the model and have it installed. But, Mr. Lexington found one and installed it on the very same day. —[1]—. He didn't even charge me extra for working on a weekend. —[2]—. One of his employees rang me up the next day to ask whether the new unit was working properly or not. —[3]—. The whole process demonstrates the exceptional customer service offered by Lexington's Heating & Cooling. —[4]—.

Martha Usman

15. Why has the information most likely been included on the Web site?

    (A) To describe an installation procedure
    (B) To attract new customers
    (C) To advertise the latest model
    (D) To explain a business policy

16. What is indicated about Mr. Lexington?

    (A) He mended a broken air conditioner on July 10.
    (B) He charges an additional fee for working on certain types of air conditioner.
    (C) He finished the work for Ms. Usman on the same day she contacted him.
    (D) He advertises in a business magazine that Ms. Usman subscribes to.

17. In which of the positions marked [1], [2], [3], and [4] does the following sentence best belong?

    "I will definitely use this business's service in the future."

    (A) [1]
    (B) [2]
    (C) [3]
    (D) [4]

P. 266

Questions 15-17 refer to the following information on a web site.

◀ ▶ http://www.lexingtonaircon.org ▶

Lexington's Heating & Cooling

HOME	SERVICES	❶ REVIEWS	SCHEDULE APPOINTMENT	E-MAIL US

❷ What our customers are saying.
❸ Rating: ★★★★☆
Date of service: 10 July
Type of service: Installation of new air conditioner unit

A few days ago, I found that my air conditioner in my property was out of order and did not blow cool air. I remembered that an advertisement for Lexington's Heating & Cooling was posted in my local building supply store, so I rang Lexington's up. Although ❹ it was Saturday and the business is usually not open on that day, the owner, Jack Lexington, came there within 2 hours after receiving my phone call. He examined my air conditioner and said to me that I would need to either get a new one or order several new parts to have it mended. Because it was a really old model, I decided to get a new one. Mr. Lexington showed me a catalog with some different air conditioner models, and chose an energy-efficient one. I thought it would take a couple of days to order the model and have it installed. But, ❺ Mr. Lexington found one and installed it on the very same day. —[1]—. ❻ He didn't even charge me extra for working on a weekend. —[2]—. ❼ One of his employees rang me up the next day to ask whether the new unit was working properly or not. —[3]—. ❽ The whole process demonstrates the exceptional customer service offered by Lexington's Heating & Cooling. —[4]—.

Martha Usman

☐ rating 評価 ☐ installation 設置 ☐ unit 設備・装置一式 ☐ property 物件、所有地
☐ out of order 故障している ☐ blow ～を吹く ☐ post ～を掲示・掲載する
☐ building supply store 建築資材店 ☐ ring up ～に電話をかける ☐ examine ～を点検する
☐ either A or B A か B のいずれか ☐ part 部品 ☐ mend ～を修理する
☐ energy-efficient 省エネの、エネルギー効率の良い ☐ charge ～に請求する ☐ work properly 正しく動作する
☐ whole 全体の ☐ exceptional 優れた

15. Why has the information most likely been included on the Web site?

(A) To describe an installation procedure
(B) To attract new customers
(C) To advertise the latest model
(D) To explain a business policy

ウェブサイトにこの情報が掲載されているのはなぜだと考えられますか。

(A) 取り付けの工程について説明ため
(B) 新しい顧客を獲得するため
(C) 最新のモデルを宣伝するため
(D) 事業方針について説明するため

ウェブサイトにこの情報が掲載されているのはおそらくなぜかが問われている。❶から「この文章はレビュー（評価）」であること、❷・❸から「顧客の意見と評価が記載されていること」がわかる。レビューは、良質なサービス・対応について書かれているため、新たな顧客を引き付けようとしていることが考えられる。よって、正解は **(B)** となる。(A)は「取り付けた」という記述はあるが、工程については書かれていない。(C) 最新機種広告、(D) 事業方針については記載がないため、それぞれ不正解となる。ウェブサイトのタブがヒントになることも多いので、細かい点もしっかり見ておこう。

✎ □ procedure 手順　□ latest 最新の

---

16. What is indicated about Mr. Lexington?

(A) He mended a broken air conditioner on July 10.
(B) He charges an additional fee for working on certain types of air conditioner.
(C) He finished the work for Ms. Usman on the same day she contacted him.
(D) He advertises in a business magazine that Ms. Usman subscribes to.

Lexington さんについて何が示唆されていますか。

(A) 7月10日に壊れたエアコンを修理した。
(B) ある種類のエアコンの作業には追加料金を請求する。
(C) Usman さんが連絡をしたその日に作業を終わらせた。
(D) Usman さんが購読しているビジネス雑誌に広告を載せている。

Lexington さんについて示唆されていることを問う選択肢照合型問題。❹から、Lexington さんはエアコンの修理会社のオーナーだとわかる。そして❺に「Lexington さんは、（連絡した）その日のうちにその機種を調達して、取り付けてくれた」とあるため、お客である Usman さんが電話した当日に作業をエアコンを取り付けてくれたことがわかる。以上より、正解はこれを言い換えた **(C)**。(A) は、サービスは7月10日に行ったが、「修理」ではなく「新品手配と取り付け」のため不正解。

✎ □ mend ～を修理する　□ subscribe to ～を定期購読する

17. In which of the positions marked [1], [2], [3], and [4] does the following sentence best belong?

"I will definitely use this business's service in the future."

(A) [1]
(B) [2]
(C) [3]
(D) [4]

次の文は [1]、[2]、[3]、[4] のどの位置に最もよく当てはまりますか。

「今後もこちらの会社のサービスをぜひ利用したいと思います」

(A) [1]
(B) [2]
(C) [3]
(D) [4]

🔍 適切な文の位置を求める問題。問われている文は「今後もこちらの会社のサービスをぜひ利用したい」なので、「またサービスを利用したくなるほど素晴らしい」といった内容が前にくることが考えられる。ウェブサイトの後半を読んでいくと、❺「当日調達と設置」、❻「週末作業の追加料金なし」、❼「翌日のアフターフォロー」があり、❽で「一連の作業全体が素晴らしいサービスだ」と述べている。以上から、この❽の後ろの [4] に問われている文を入れると文意が通る。よって、正解は **(D)** となる。

✎ □ definitely 間違いなく、ぜひ

📝 問題 15 から 17 は次のウェブサイトの情報に関するものです。

http://www.lexingtonaircon.org

Lexington's Heating & Cooling

トップページ	サービス	レビュー（評価）	スケジュール・予約	メール

お客様のご意見
評価：★★★★☆
サービス実施日：7 月 10 日
サービスの種類：新しいエアコン設備の設置

数日前、私の物件のエアコンが故障し、冷気が出てきていないことに気がつきました。Lexington's Heating & Cooling の広告が近所の建築資材店に掲示されていたことを思い出し、Lexington's に電話をかけました。その日は土曜日で通常は営業をしていない日でしたが、オーナーの Jack Lexington 氏は電話を受けてから 2 時間以内に来てくださいました。彼はエアコンを点検し、新品を購入するか、いくつかの部品を注文して修理を行う必要があると言いました。とても古いモデルだったので、新しいものを購入することに決めました。Lexington さんにいくつかのエアコンが掲載されたカタログを見せてもらい、エネルギー効率の良いものを選んでもらいました。注文をしてから取り付けをしてもらうまで、数日かかると思っていました。しかし、Lexington さんは、その日のうちにその機種を調達して、取り付けてくれました。 —[1]— 週末の作業に対する追加料金の請求もありませんでした。 —[2]— 従業員の方が翌日電話をかけてきて、新しい機器が正常に動作しているかどうか気にかけてくれました。 —[3]— 一連の工程が Lexington's Heating & Cooling の素晴らしい顧客サービスを証明しています。 —[4]— 今後もこちらの会社のサービスをぜひ利用したいと思います。

Martha Usman

AVA FLIES THINKS ABOUT CHINA

At first, Ava Flies commenced its flight service to the warm resort cities of the Philippines. At present, Ava Flies is considering flights to the north. According to a representative of its Financial Department, Annie Newfarm, this kind of low price airline has to try to research the feasibility of expanding its service to some Asian cities.

"We're not staying at the point of listing destinations or making a timetable," said Ms. Newfarm during an interview, "but we're interested in expanding our presence in China."

Hera Constant, one of the industry analysts in the Wheaton Group, agrees that China is a suitable place for Ava Flies. She said "Ava Flies already has three bases on the edges of Asia: Beijing, Seoul and Tokyo. It will be easy to expand into Asia."

Ava Flies commenced its low-price service to the Philippines two years ago. At that time, Ava Flies started its operations in some cities in the Philippines such as Manila and Cebu.

Ms. Constant said, "Asia regularly offers a steady flow of traffic to the Philippines, Ava Flies could occupy a big part of the large potential market in the near future."

Ava Flies serves 30 destinations in 15 Asian cities, and also two cities in the Philippines.

18. Which of the following is true about Ava Flies?

    (A) It has recently bought new planes.
    (B) It has been in business for three years.
    (C) It is based in Singapore.
    (D) It specializes in low cost fares.

19. What is Ava Flies considering?

    (A) Dropping its service to Beijing, Seoul and Tokyo
    (B) Adding a service to China
    (C) Acquiring a rival airline
    (D) Replacing its older airplanes

20. Who is most likely Hera Constant?

    (A) An airline industry analyst
    (B) An Ava Flies spokesperson
    (C) A magazine reporter
    (D) An airline executive

21. The word "potential" in paragraph 5, line 2, is closest in meaning to

    (A) public
    (B) viable
    (C) promising
    (D) usable

P. 272

Questions 18-21 refer to the following article.

AVA FLIES THINKS ABOUT CHINA

At first, Ava Flies commenced its flight service to the warm resort cities of the Philippines. At present, Ava Flies is considering flights to the north. ❶ According to a representative of its Financial Department, Annie Newfarm, this kind of low price airline has to try to research the feasibility of expanding its service to some Asian cities.

"We're not staying at the point of listing destinations or making a timetable," said Ms. Newfarm during an interview, "but ❷ we're interested in expanding our presence in China."

❸ Hera Constant, one of the industry analysts in the Wheaton Group, agrees that China is a suitable place for Ava Flies. She said "Ava Flies already has three bases on the edges of Asia: Beijing, Seoul and Tokyo. It will be easy to expand into Asia."

Ava Flies commenced its low-price service to the Philippines two years ago. At that time, Ava Flies started its operations in some cities in the Philippines such as Manila and Cebu.

Ms. Constant said, "Asia regularly offers a steady flow of traffic to the Philippines, Ava Flies could occupy a big part of the large ❹ potential market in the near future."

Ava Flies serves 30 destinations in 15 Asian cities, and also two cities in the Philippines.

☐ commence ～を開始する ☐ at present 現在のところ ☐ representative 代表者 ☐ low price 低価格
☐ feasibility 実現可能性 ☐ expand ～を拡大する ☐ at the point of ～の段階に ☐ destination 目的地
☐ timetable 時刻表 ☐ be interested in ～に興味がある ☐ presence 存在感 ☐ industry 産業
☐ analyst アナリスト、分析家 ☐ suitable 適切な ☐ base 拠点 ☐ such as ～といったような
☐ regularly 定期的に ☐ steady 堅調な ☐ occupy ～を占める ☐ potential 潜在的な
☐ in the near future 近い将来に

18. Which of the following is true about Ava Flies?

   (A) It has recently bought new planes.
   (B) It has been in business for three years.
   (C) It is based in Singapore.
   (D) It specializes in low cost fares.

Ava Flies 社について正しいことは次のどれですか。

   (A) 最近、新しい航空機を購入した。
   (B) 創業から3年が経った。
   (C) シンガポールを拠点としている。
   (D) 低価格の運賃に特化している。

Ava Flies 社について正しいことを問う選択肢照合型の問題。❶に「低価格航空会社」とあるため、ここから **(D)** が正解。(A) の新しい飛行機を購入したという記載はなく、(B) は第1段落の1文目と第4段落の1文目から、2年前に創業とわかる。(C) は、第3段落に複数の拠点が述べられているが、シンガポールはないため不正解。

□ be in business 事業をしている　□ based in 〜を拠点としている　□ specialize in 〜を専門としている
□ fare 運賃

19. What is Ava Flies considering?

   (A) Dropping its service to Beijing, Seoul and Tokyo
   (B) Adding a service to China
   (C) Acquiring a rival airline
   (D) Replacing its older airplanes

Ava Flies 社が検討していることは何ですか。

   (A) 北京、ソウル、東京への運航を停止する
   (B) 中国への運航を増やす
   (C) ライバルの航空会社を買収する
   (D) 古い航空機を入れ替える

Ava Flies 社が検討していることが問われている。❷で「中国での存在感を拡大していくことに興味がある」と述べられており、ここから **(B)** が正解とわかる。(A) は拠点名であり、運航停止の候補ではないため不正解。

□ acquire 〜を買収する　□ replace 〜を入れ替える

20. Who is most likely Hera Constant?

   (A) An airline industry analyst
   (B) An Ava Flies spokesperson
   (C) A magazine reporter
   (D) An airline executive

Hera Constant は誰だと考えられますか。

   (A) 航空業界アナリスト
   (B) Ava Flies 社の広報担当者
   (C) 雑誌記者
   (D) 航空会社の幹部

Hera Constant さんが誰かが問われている。❸で Hara Constant さんについて記載があり、「Wheaton Group の業界アナリストの一人で、中国が Ava Flies 社にとって最適の場所であるという主張に同意している」と、航空会社である Ava Flies 社について意見を述べていることから、航空関係の業界アナリストであると考えられる。よって、正解は **(A)**。

□ spokesperson 広報担当者　□ executive 経営幹部

21. The word "potential" in paragraph 5, line 2, is closest in meaning to

(A) public
(B) viable
(C) promising
(D) usable

第5段落・2行目にある "potential" に最も意味が近いのは

(A) 公共の
(B) 実行可能な
(C) 見込みのある
(D) 使うことができる

同義語問題。問われている❹は、「将来の大きな（潜在的可能性のある）市場」という意味である。この意味に近い「隠れた可能性」という意味を持つのは **(C)**。(B) も「可能な」という意味があるが、これは計画等が実行可能という意味で、潜在可能性とは意味合いが異なるため、ここでは不正解。**(C)** は少し語彙レベルが難しいが、語彙の意味がわからない場合は、解答時間を考慮しながら、他の3つを消去して解く必要がある。

問題 18 から 21 は次の記事に関するものです。

Ava Flies 社が中国を視野にいれる

Ava Flies 社は、まずフィリピンの温暖なリゾート地へのフライト便から開始した。現在、Ava Flies 社は北へのフライトに目をむけている。財務部代表の Annie Newfarm によると、このような低価格航空会社はアジアの都市へのサービス拡大の実現可能性について調査をしようとするものだという。

インタビューで「当社はまだ就航地のリストや時刻表を作成する段階には至っていません。」と Newfarm さんは語った。「しかし、中国における当社の存在感をもっと大きくしたいとは考えています。」

Wheaton Group の業界アナリストの一人である Hera Constant さんは、中国が Ava Flies 社にとって最適な場所であるという主張に同意している。「Ava Flies 社はすでに、アジアの端にある、北京、ソウル、東京という3つの拠点を有しています。アジアへさらに進出するのは容易でしょう。」と語った。

Ava Flies 社はフィリピン行きの低価格のフライトを2年前に開始した。その時点で、Ava Flies 社はマニラとセブなど、フィリピンの都市での業務を始めた。

Constant さんは「アジアからフィリピンへは一定の人や物の流れがあります。Ava Flies 社は近い将来、大きな潜在的市場の大きな部分を占めるかもしれません。」と語った。

Ava Flies 社はアジア 15 都市の 30 カ所の行先とフィリピンの2都市に就航している。

GO ON TO THE NEXT PAGE!

Angela Bass [4:31 p.m.]
Hi. I want some information on the Riverside Well-being Center. Will the work be completed on schedule?

Ella Lancaster [4:34 p.m.]
I doubt it. The problem is that the lawn is basically frozen because of the freezing temperatures we've been having. We cannot remove the shrubs and bushes we'll be using for the job.

Kai Dunshea [4:36 p.m.]
That'll put us behind schedule. Do you have any solution? I got the impression that our client wants us to hurry up and end the project.

Isabelle Tonga [4:38 p.m.]
Oh, I heard that Eva Denberg had a similar problem a few years ago. She worked something out.

Angela Bass [4:40 p.m.]
Isabelle, would you mind asking her how to solve a problem like this one?

Isabelle Tonga [4:43 p.m.]
Of course not. I think that she said she poured warm water on the plants to thaw out the ground. She was careful not to get the water hot enough to damage the plant roots.

Kai Dunshea [4:47 p.m.]
There's another choice. If we can't do that, we should ask a garden center from a warmer area. It may take some time to look for the types of shrubs the client is wanting to shield the balcony view from outside.

Angela Bass [4:48 p.m.]
Either way, those are good ideas!

Isabelle Tonga [4:50 p.m.]
I'll give Ms. Denberg a call right now.

Kai Dunshea [4:52 p.m]
I'll also try what I mentioned. So, business will get back to normal.

22. At 4:34 P.M., what does Ms. Lancaster mean when she writes, "I doubt it"?

(A) She is not happy about the finished job.
(B) She is happy with her upcoming vacation.
(C) She thinks that the work will be behind schedule.
(D) She has already finished the project.

23. What kind of business do the writers work in?

(A) A landscaping service
(B) A garden center
(C) A moving company
(D) A construction firm

24. What can be inferred about Ms. Denberg?

(A) She will attend the online discussion soon.
(B) She was recently hired at the company.
(C) She works at the Riverside Well-being Center.
(D) She might know how to solve their problem.

25. What will Mr. Dunshea most likely do next?

(A) Call a different supplier
(B) Leave work
(C) Arrange an appointment
(D) Meet the client

P. 278

Questions 22-25 refer to the following online chat discussion.

Angela Bass [4:31 p.m.]
Hi. I want some information on the Riverside Well-being Center. ❶ Will the work be completed on schedule?

Ella Lancaster [4:34 p.m.]
❷ I doubt it. ❸ The problem is that the lawn is basically frozen because of the freezing temperatures we've been having. ❹ We cannot remove the shrubs and bushes we'll be using for the job.

Kai Dunshea [4:36 p.m.]
That'll put us behind schedule. Do you have any solution? ❺ I got the impression that our client wants us to hurry up and end the project.

Isabelle Tonga [4:38 p.m.]
Oh, ❻ I heard that Eva Denberg had a similar problem a few years ago. ❼ She worked something out.

Angela Bass [4:40 p.m.]
Isabelle, would you mind asking her how to solve a problem like this one?

Isabelle Tonga [4:43 p.m.]
Of course not. I think that she said she poured warm water on the plants to thaw out the ground. She was careful not to get the water hot enough to damage the plant roots.

Kai Dunshea [4:47 p.m.]
❽ There's another choice. ❾ If we can't do that, we should ask a garden center from a warmer area. It may take some time to look for the types of shrubs the client is wanting to shield the balcony view from outside.

Angela Bass [4:48 p.m.]
Either way, those are good ideas!

Isabelle Tonga [4:50 p.m.]
I'll give Ms. Denberg a call right now.

Kai Dunshea [4:52 p.m]
❿ I'll also try what I mentioned. So, business will get back to normal.

☐ on schedule 予定どおりに ☐ I doubt it. そう思わない。 ☐ basically 基本的に、概ね ☐ frozen 凍っている
☐ freezing temperatures 氷点下の気温 ☐ shrub 低木 ☐ bush (庭の) 茂み
☐ behind schedule 予定より遅れて ☐ solution 解決法 ☐ impression 印象、感じ ☐ hurry up 急ぐ
☐ solve ～を解決する ☐ pour ～を注ぐ ☐ thaw out (凍ったもの等) を溶かす ☐ root 根
☐ shield ～を覆い隠す ☐ right now すぐに ☐ get back to normal 元に戻る

22. At 4:34 P.M., what does Ms. Lancaster mean when she writes, "I doubt it"?

(A) She is not happy about the finished job.
(B) She is happy with her upcoming vacation.
(C) She thinks that the work will be behind schedule.
(D) She has already finished the project.

午後 4 時 34 分に、Lancaster さんは "I doubt it" という発言で、何を意味していますか。

(A) 終了した仕事に満足していない。
(B) 間もなく来る休暇を喜んでいる。
(C) 仕事が予定よりも遅れてしまうと感じている。
(D) プロジェクトはすでに終わらせた。

意図問題。❷の "I doubt it" は、問われたことに対して「そうは思わない、わからない」という意味。チャットを見てみると、❶で「作業が予定どおりに終わるのか？」という質問がされており、「予定どおり終わらなそうだ」という意図で返答していることがわかる。以上から、予定より遅れていることを behind schedule と表現した **(C)** が正解。

✎ □ pleasant 満足して　□ finished job 終了した仕事　□ upcoming きたる　□ behind time 予定より遅れて

----

23. What kind of business do the writers work in?

(A) A landscaping service
(B) A garden center
(C) A moving company
(D) A construction firm

書き手たちはどのような会社で働いていますか。

(A) 造園サービス
(B) 園芸用品店
(C) 引っ越し会社
(D) 建設会社

書き手がどのような会社で働いているのかが問われている。Lancaster さんが、❸・❹で「芝生が常に凍っている」「仕事に使用する低木や茂み」と述べている。そして、Dunshea さんが、❺で「クライアントが早くしてほしそうだ」とも言っていることから、造園サービス関係の仕事であることがわかる。以上より正解は **(A)**。(B) は❾で他の園芸店に聞いてみる等の発言をしているため、ここでは不正解。

✎ □ landscaping 造園　□ moving company 引っ越し会社

----

24. What can be inferred about Ms. Denberg?

(A) She will attend the online discussion soon.
(B) She was recently hired at the company.
(C) She works at the Riverside Well-being Center.
(D) She might know how to solve their problem.

Denberg さんについて何が推測できますか。

(A) オンラインでの話し合いにもうすぐ参加する。
(B) 最近会社に雇われた。
(C) Riverside Well-being Center で働いている。
(D) 問題を解決する方法を知っているかもしれない。

Denberg さんについて何が推測できるかを問う選択肢照合型の問題。Denberg さんについて、Tonga さんが❻・❼で言及しており、「数年前同じような問題を抱えていたと聞いた」、「どうにか解決したようだ」と述べている。ここから、今回の問題について解決方法を知っている可能性があることがわかる。以上より、正解は **(D)**。(A) もうすぐチャットに加わる、(B) 最近雇われた、(C)Riverside Well-being Center で働いている、は根拠となる箇所がないため、いずれも不正解。

25. What will Mr. Dunshea most likely do next?

 (A) Call a different supplier
 (B) Leave work
 (C) Arrange an appointment
 (D) Meet the client

Dunshea さんは次に何をすると考えられますか。

 (A) 別の供給業者に電話をする
 (B) 仕事を辞める
 (C) 会う約束をする
 (D) 顧客と会う

> Dunshea さんがおそらく取る次の行動について問われている。Dunshea さんは、チャットの最後の発言❿で、「言ったことを試してみる」と述べている。つまり、「言及したこと」を見ていくと、❽・❾で別の提案をしており、「もう一つの選択肢がある」「暖かい地域にある園芸店に問い合わせてみるといい」と述べている。この園芸店は、彼らに園芸の材料を供給する業者と考えられる。以上より、供給業者に連絡を取る手段である **(A)** が正解。

📝 問題 22 から 25 は次のオンラインチャットの話し合いに関するものです。

Angela Bass [午後 4 時 31 分]
こんにちは。Riverside Well-being Center についての情報がほしいのですが。作業は予定どおりに終えられそうですか？

Ella Lancaster [午後 4 時 34 分]
おそらく無理ですね。このところの氷点下の気温のせいで、芝生が常に凍ってしまっているのが問題です。仕事に使用する低木や茂みを取り除くことができません。

Kai Dunshea [午後 4 時 36 分]
それではスケジュールが遅れてしまいますね。何か解決策はありますか？　クライアントは早くこのプロジェクトを終わらせてほしいようです。

Isabelle Tonga [午後 4 時 38 分]
そういえば、数年前に Eva Denberg さんが同じような問題を抱えていたと聞きました。どうにか解決したようですが。

Angela Bass [午後 4 時 40 分]
Isabelle さん、このような問題を解決する方法を彼女に尋ねてもらえませんか？

Isabelle Tonga [午後 4 時 43 分]
もちろんです。彼女は地面を溶かすために温水を植物にかけたと言っていたと思います。植物の根を傷つけるほどお湯が熱くならないように注意していました。

Kai Dunshea [午後 4 時 47 分]
もう一つの選択肢があります。それができなければ、暖かい地域にある園芸店に問い合わせてみるといいですよ。バルコニーを外部の目から隠すために、クライアントが求めている種類の低木を見つけるには、少々時間がかかるかもしれません。

Angela Bass [午後 4 時 48 分]
いずれにしても、どちらもいいアイデアですね！

Isabelle Tonga [午後 4 時 50 分]
Denberg さんに今すぐに電話してみます。

Kai Dunshea [午後 4 時 52 分]
私が提案したことも試してみます。それで、仕事がまた回り出すでしょう。

Questions 26-29 refer to the following e-mail.

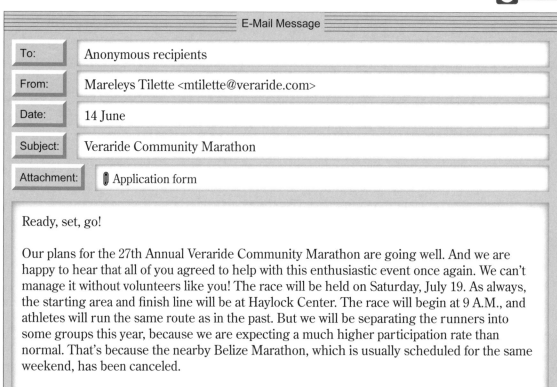

E-Mail Message

To:	Anonymous recipients
From:	Mareleys Tilette <mtilette@veraride.com>
Date:	14 June
Subject:	Veraride Community Marathon
Attachment:	📎 Application form

Ready, set, go!

Our plans for the 27th Annual Veraride Community Marathon are going well. And we are happy to hear that all of you agreed to help with this enthusiastic event once again. We can't manage it without volunteers like you! The race will be held on Saturday, July 19. As always, the starting area and finish line will be at Haylock Center. The race will begin at 9 A.M., and athletes will run the same route as in the past. But we will be separating the runners into some groups this year, because we are expecting a much higher participation rate than normal. That's because the nearby Belize Marathon, which is usually scheduled for the same weekend, has been canceled.

—[1]—. Please complete the form and return it to me by e-mail by June 26. —[2]—. You will all be given a complimentary Veraride Community Marathon T-shirt to wear during the event. —[3]—. Of course, this is yours to keep as a token of our appreciation. If you have any questions about your jobs, don't hesitate to contact me. I'll be controlling the water station setup, the marking of the route, and post-event cleanup. The other event coordinator, Keiran Perdomo, will be in charge of greeting athletes when they get to the site and directing them to the right place, as well as awarding the prizes. It'll be great working together with all of you again. —[4]—.

Best regards!

Mareleys Tilette

26. Which of the following is NOT true about the recipients of the e-mail?

    (A) They will get a free clothing item.
    (B) They have volunteered at a race in previous years.
    (C) They are athletes who competed in a race.
    (D) They can ask Ms. Tilette further questions.

27. According to Ms. Tilette, how will the event be different from last year's event?

    (A) It will be held at a different location.
    (B) It will feature famous athletes.
    (C) It will have more participants than usual.
    (D) It will be in competition this year.

28. What is Mr. Perdomo's job?

    (A) Overseeing the arrival of athletes
    (B) Keeping a site clean
    (C) Installing a station to serve water
    (D) Buying prizes for the winners

29. In which of the positions marked [1], [2], [3], and [4] does the following sentence best belong?

"In this e-mail, I have attached an application form, on which you can indicate where you would like to work."

    (A) [1]
    (B) [2]
    (C) [3]
    (D) [4]

Single Q4

P. 284

Questions 26-29 refer to the following e-mail.

E-Mail Message

To:	Anonymous recipients
From:	Mareleys Tilette <mtilette@veraride.com>
Date:	14 June
Subject:	Veraride Community Marathon
Attachment:	📎 Application form

Ready, set, go!

Our plans for the 27th Annual Veraride Community Marathon are going well. ❶ And we are happy to hear that all of you agreed to help with this enthusiastic event once again. We can't manage it without volunteers like you! The race will be held on Saturday, July 19. As always, the starting area and finish line will be at Haylock Center. The race will begin at 9 A.M., and athletes will run the same route as in the past. ❷ But we will be separating the runners into some groups this year, because we are expecting a much higher participation rate than normal. That's because the nearby Belize Marathon, which is usually scheduled for the same weekend, has been canceled.

—[1]—. ❸ Please complete the form and return it to me by e-mail by June 26. —[2]—. ❹ You will all be given a complimentary Veraride Community Marathon T-shirt to wear during the event. —[3]—. Of course, this is yours to keep as a token of our appreciation. ❺ If you have any questions about your jobs, don't hesitate to contact me. I'll be controlling the water station setup, the marking of the route, and post-event cleanup. ❻ The other event coordinator, Keiran Perdomo, will be in charge of greeting athletes when they get to the site and directing them to the right place, as well as awarding the prizes. It'll be great working together with all of you again. —[4]—.

Best regards!

Mareleys Tilette

☐ anonymous 匿名の ☐ recipient 受信者 ☐ go well うまくいく ☐ enthusiastic 熱狂的な
☐ once again 今一度 ☐ race 競走 ☐ as always いつものように ☐ starting area スタート地点
☐ finish line ゴールライン ☐ as in the past 過去と ☐ Separate A into B A を B に分ける
☐ participation rate 参加率 ☐ normal 通常 ☐ nearby 近隣の ☐ complimentary 無料の
☐ a token of one's appreciation 感謝のしるし ☐ control ～を管理する ☐ setup 設置 ☐ marking 表示
☐ route 走行順路 ☐ post-event イベント後の ☐ cleanup 清掃 ☐ coordinator 調整、まとめ役
☐ be in charge of ～を担っている ☐ greet ～を迎える ☐ award prizes 賞を贈呈する

26. Which of the following is NOT true about the recipients of the e-mail?

(A) They will get a free clothing item.
(B) They have volunteered at a race in previous years.
(C) They are athletes who competed in a race.
(D) They can ask Ms. Tilette further questions.

E メールの受信者について正しくないものは次のどれですか。

(A) 無料の衣料品を受け取る。
(B) 前年までのレースでボランティアをしたことがある。
(C) レースに出場したことのある選手である。
(D) Tilette さんにさらに質問することができる。

NOT 問題。この E メールの受信者について正しくないことは何かが問われている。❶の「再びこのイベントにご助力いただけることになり」が (B) に、❹の「イベント中に着る T シャツを無料で支給」が (A) に、そして、❺の「質問があれば遠慮なく私（E メール送信者の Tilette さん）に連絡を」が (D) に該当する。残った **(C)** レース出場経験は記載がないため、これが正解。❺の "contact（連絡する）" が (D) では ask に言い換えられている。

---

27. According to Ms. Tilette, how will the event be different from last year's event?

(A) It will be held at a different location.
(B) It will feature famous athletes.
(C) It will have more participants than usual.
(D) It will be in competition this year.

Tilette さんによると、今年のイベントは昨年とどのような違いがありますか。

(A) 別の場所で開催される。
(B) 有名選手が招待される。
(C) 例年よりも多くの参加者がいる。
(D) 今年は競争することになる。

E メール送信者である Tilette さんが、今年のイベントが昨年とどう違うと述べているかが問われている。Tilette さんは❷で、「例年よりもはるかに多くの参加者が見込まれる」と述べている。ここから、❷の "a much higher participation rate than normal" を more participants than usual と言い換えた **(C)** が正解。それ以外の選択肢は、昨年と異なったこととして述べられていないため、いずれも不正解。

□ in competition 競争して

---

28. What is Mr. Perdomo's job?

(A) Overseeing the arrival of athletes
(B) Keeping a site clean
(C) Installing a station to serve water
(D) Buying prizes for the winners

Perdomo さんの仕事は何ですか。

(A) 選手の到着に対応すること
(B) 会場を清潔に保つこと
(C) 給水する場所を設置すること
(D) 勝者に授与する賞品を購入すること

Perdomo さんの仕事が何かについて問われている。❻に Perdomo さんの役割についての記載があり、「会場に到着した選手の応対、正しい位置への誘導、そして賞の授与を担当」とあるため、この中の「会場へ到着した選手の応対」を oversee を使って表現した **(A)** が正解となる。(C) は Tilette さんの役割となるため、混同しないように注意しよう。

□ oversee 〜を管理・監督する　□ arrival 到着　□ prize 賞品

29. In which of the positions marked [1], [2], [3], and [4] does the following sentence best belong?

"In this e-mail, I have attached an application form, on which you can indicate where you would like to work."

(A) [1]
(B) [2]
(C) [3]
(D) [4]

次の文は [1]、[2]、[3]、[4] のどの位置に最もよく当てはまりますか。

「このEメールに申込書を添付いたしました。活動を希望される場所をご記入ください」

(A) [1]
(B) [2]
(C) [3]
(D) [4]

適切な文の位置を求める問題。問われている文は「このメールに申込書を添付しており、そこにボランティアを希望する場所を記入できる」とある、つまり、申込書やボランティア場所に関連した内容の前後にこの文が入ることがわかる。文書を見ていくと、❸で「6月26日までに、それ（it）にすべて記入し、私まで返送を」とある。この代名詞 it に、挿入文にある application form を当てはめると意味が通る。つまり、この❸の前に挿入文を入れると文意が成立する。以上から、正解は **(A)**。位置問題や Part 6 の文選択問題は、こういった代名詞が何を指すか考えることで正解を絞り込むことができるので、チェックしておこう。

□ application form 申込書

 問題 26 から 29 は次のEメールに関するものです。

受信者：	匿名の受信者
送信者：	Mareleys Tilette <mtilette@veraride.com>
日付：	6月14日
件名：	Veraride 市民マラソン
添付ファイル：	申込書

位置について、用意、ドン！

第27回 Veraride 市民マラソンの計画は順調に進んでいます。また、皆さまに再びこの一大イベントにご助力いただけることになり、感謝いたします。皆さまのようなボランティアの方がいなければ、これを遂行することはできません！ レースは7月19日土曜日に開催されます。スタート地点とゴール地点はいつもと同じ Haylock Center です。レースは午前9時に開始し、選手は以前と同じコースを走ります。しかし、今年は走者をいくつかのグループに分けます。例年よりもはるかに多くの参加者が見込まれるからですが、それは通常同じ週末に開催されている近隣のベリーズマラソンが中止となったためです。

―[1]― このEメールに申込書を添付いたしました。活動を希望される場所をご記入ください。すべてご記入のうえ、6月26日までに私宛てにご返送ください。―[2]― 皆さまにイベント期間中にご着用いただく Veraride 市民マラソンのTシャツを無料で支給いたします。―[3]― もちろん、私どもの感謝の印としてお持ち帰りいただけます。お仕事についてご質問があれば、ご遠慮なくご連絡ください。私は給水所の設置、コースの表示、イベント後の清掃の管理を担当いたします。もう1人のイベントのまとめ役、Keiran Perdomo 氏が、会場に到着した選手の応対、正しい位置への誘導、そして賞の授与を担当いたします。皆さまとまた一緒に働けることをうれしく思います。―[4]―

よろしくお願いいたします！

Mareleys Tilette

GO ON TO THE NEXT PAGE!

Harper Healthcare Center
136 Hillcrest Ave., Harrisburg, PA 16803
878-610-7722

Information for New Clients

Thanks for visiting the Harper Healthcare Center (HHC). For the past 25 years, we've been helping Harrisburg and nearby counties to be healthier by giving advice on diet and lifestyle to our patients and clients. Additionally, we provide culinary classes, which are taught by the cook at Brigham Garden, Daniel Hammond, to help clients improve their eating habits with delicious and healthy food.

You can enroll in a class by visiting our Web site at www.harperhc.net/event. For information on events happening in the area, including our events, or for resources about living a healthier life, make sure to visit the online bulletin board. Moreover, you can sign up for the HHC Saving Card, which you can also use to get discounts of up to 20% at participating restaurants and retailers in Harrisburg and the nearby counties.

If you have any questions, don't hesitate to contact HHC's supervisor, Leila Baler.

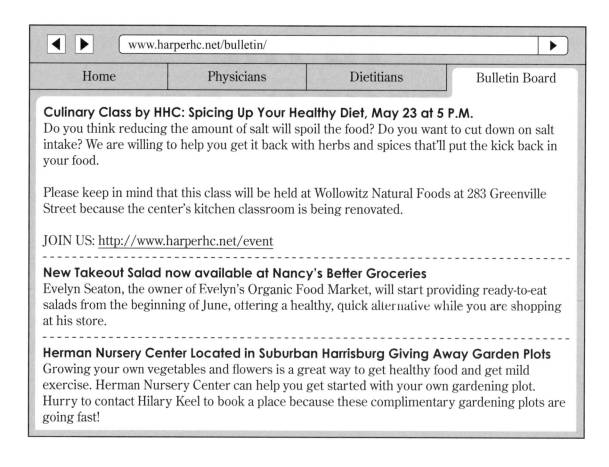

www.harperhc.net/bulletin/

| Home | Physicians | Dietitians | Bulletin Board |

Culinary Class by HHC: Spicing Up Your Healthy Diet, May 23 at 5 P.M.
Do you think reducing the amount of salt will spoil the food? Do you want to cut down on salt intake? We are willing to help you get it back with herbs and spices that'll put the kick back in your food.

Please keep in mind that this class will be held at Wollowitz Natural Foods at 283 Greenville Street because the center's kitchen classroom is being renovated.

JOIN US: http://www.harperhc.net/event
- -
New Takeout Salad now available at Nancy's Better Groceries
Evelyn Seaton, the owner of Evelyn's Organic Food Market, will start providing ready-to-eat salads from the beginning of June, offering a healthy, quick alternative while you are shopping at his store.
- -
Herman Nursery Center Located in Suburban Harrisburg Giving Away Garden Plots
Growing your own vegetables and flowers is a great way to get healthy food and get mild exercise. Herman Nursery Center can help you get started with your own gardening plot. Hurry to contact Hilary Keel to book a place because these complimentary gardening plots are going fast!

30. According to the advertisement, what is available at Harper Healthcare Center?

(A) Various herbs and spices for purchase
(B) General vitamin supplements at discounted prices
(C) Tips on making better diet selections
(D) Complimentary community exercise classes

31. How can HHC clients get a discount at restaurants?

(A) By presenting a card issued by HHC
(B) By frequently using Evelyn's Organic Food Market
(C) By joining the membership of the discounted club
(D) By attending a restaurant's grand opening

32. Who will lead a session at Wollowitz Natural Foods?

(A) Leila Baker
(B) Evelyn Seaton
(C) Daniel Hammond
(D) Hilary Keel

33. Where will the event take place in June?

(A) At Brigham Garden restaurant
(B) At Nancy's Better Groceries
(C) At Evelyn's Organic Food Market
(D) At Herman Nursery Center

34. What is suggested about the Herman Nursery Center's garden plots?

(A) They are popular with Harrisburg citizens.
(B) They are used to grow flowers for local businesses.
(C) They can be leased for a nominal charge.
(D) They can be used exclusively for growing vegetables.

Double

P. 290

Questions 30-34 refer to the following advertisement and Web page.

Harper Healthcare Center
136 Hillcrest Ave., Harrisburg PA, 16803
878-610-7722

Information for New Clients

Thanks for visiting the Harper Healthcare Center (HHC). ❶ For the past 25 years, we've been helping Harrisburg and nearby counties to be healthier by giving advice on diet and lifestyle to our patients and clients. ❷ Additionally, we provide culinary classes, which are taught by the cook at Brigham Garden, Daniel Hammond, to help clients improve their eating habits with delicious and healthy food.

You can enroll in a class by visiting our Web site at www.harperhc.net/event. For information on events happening in the area, including our events, or for resources about living a healthier life, make sure to visit the online bulletin board. ❸ Moreover, you can sign up for the HHC Saving Card, which you can also use to get discounts of up to 20% at participating restaurants and retailers in Harrisburg and the nearby counties.

If you have any questions, don't hesitate to contact HHC's supervisor, Leila Baler.

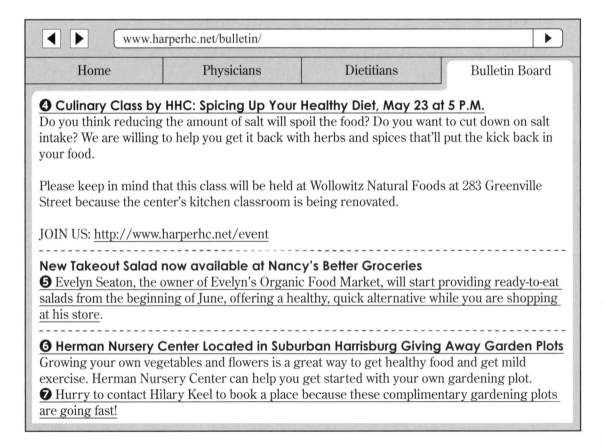

www.harperhc.net/bulletin/

| Home | Physicians | Dietitians | Bulletin Board |

❹ Culinary Class by HHC: Spicing Up Your Healthy Diet, May 23 at 5 P.M.
Do you think reducing the amount of salt will spoil the food? Do you want to cut down on salt intake? We are willing to help you get it back with herbs and spices that'll put the kick back in your food.

Please keep in mind that this class will be held at Wollowitz Natural Foods at 283 Greenville Street because the center's kitchen classroom is being renovated.

JOIN US: http://www.harperhc.net/event

New Takeout Salad now available at Nancy's Better Groceries
❺ Evelyn Seaton, the owner of Evelyn's Organic Food Market, will start providing ready-to-eat salads from the beginning of June, offering a healthy, quick alternative while you are shopping at his store.

❻ Herman Nursery Center Located in Suburban Harrisburg Giving Away Garden Plots
Growing your own vegetables and flowers is a great way to get healthy food and get mild exercise. Herman Nursery Center can help you get started with your own gardening plot. ❼ Hurry to contact Hilary Keel to book a place because these complimentary gardening plots are going fast!

★★★☆☆

30. According to the advertisement, what is available at Harper Healthcare Center?

(A) Various herbs and spices for purchase
(B) General vitamin supplements at discounted prices
(C) Tips on making better diet selections
(D) Complimentary community exercise classes

広告によると、Harper Healthcare Center では何を提供していますか。

(A) 販売用のさまざまな香草や香辛料
(B) 割引価格の一般的なビタミン剤
(C) より適切に食事する方法のヒント
(D) 地域の無料の体操教室

🔍 広告から、Harper Healthcare Center で何を提供しているのかが問われている。広告の❶で「当センターは 25 年間、食事と生活習慣に関するアドバイスを通して、周辺地域の皆さまの健康のサポートを行ってきた」と述べている。ここから、食事に関するアドバイスを言い換えた **(C)** が正解。tips が❶の "giving advice" の言い換えになっていることに気づくことがポイント。

✎ □ various さまざまな　□ supplement サプリメント（栄養補助食品）　□ at discounted price 割引価格で
□ tip アドバイス　□ community 地域の

★★★★☆

31. How can HHC clients get a discount at restaurants?

(A) By presenting a card issued by HHC
(B) By frequently using Evelyn's Organic Food Market
(C) By joining the membership of the discounted club
(D) By attending a restaurant's grand opening

HHC の顧客はレストランで割引を受けるために何をしたらいいですか。

(A) HHC から発行されたカードを提示する
(B) Evelyn's Organic Food Market を頻繁に利用する
(C) 割引クラブの会員になる
(D) レストランの開店式に出席する

🔍 HHC の顧客がレストランで割引を受けるためにすべきことが問われている。広告の❸で、「HHC Saving Card に申し込み、このカードを使用すると、周辺の提携レストランや商店で割引を受けられる」と述べられているので、HHC で発行されたカードを提示することで割引されることがわかる。以上より、"use" を present を使って表現した **(A)** が正解。

✎ □ issue ～を発行する　□ frequently 頻繁に　□ grand opening グランドオープン

32. Who will lead a session at Wollowitz Natural Foods?

(A) Leila Baker
(B) Evelyn Seaton
(C) Daniel Hammond
(D) Hilary Keel

Wollowitz Natural Food での講習会を進行するのは誰ですか。

(A) Lelia Baker
(B) Evelyn Seaton
(C) Daniel Hammond
(D) Hilary Keel

 Wollowitz Natural Foods での講習会を進めるのは誰かが問われている。この講習会は、ウェブページの❹から「健康的な食生活を送るための料理教室」だとわかる。次に広告を見ると、❷に食生活の改善に関する料理教室の記載があり、Daniel Hammond さんによって行われることがわかる。加えて、❷及び、❹のイベントの申込先が同じウェブサイトアドレスであることから、これらが同一の料理教室だとわかる。以上より、正解は **(C)**。それぞれの文書の関連箇所を読み取って解く、クロスリファレンスの問題であることに注意しよう。

★★★☆☆

33. Where will the event take place in June?

(A) At Brigham Garden restaurant
(B) At Nancy's Better Groceries
(C) At Evelyn's Organic Food Market
(D) At Herman Nursery Center

6 月の HHC のイベントはどこで開催されますか。

(A) Brigham Garden レストランで
(B) Nancy's Better Groceries で
(C) Evelyn's Organic Food Market で
(D) Herman Nursery Center で

 6 月の HHC のイベントはどこで開催されるかが問われている。ウェブページの❺に 6 月のイベントの記載があり、「Evelyn's Organic Food Market の店主 Evelyn Seaton さんは、6 月初旬より、サラダの販売を店内で開始する」とある。ここから、正解は **(C)** とわかる。この問題は、❺の "at his store（店内で）" という記載に注目して、「Seaton さんの店＝ Evelyn's Organic Food Market」であることを見抜くのがポイント。

★★★★★

34. What is suggested about the Herman Nursery Center's garden plots?

(A) They are popular with Harrisburg citizens.
(B) They are used to grow flowers for local businesses.
(C) They can be leased for a nominal charge.
(D) They can be used exclusively for growing vegctables.

Herman Nursery Center の菜園について何が示唆されていますか。

(A) ハリスバーグ市民に人気がある。
(B) 地元企業のために花を育てるのに使われている。
(C) わずかな料金で借りることができる。
(D) 野菜を育てるためにのみ使用できる。

 Herman Nursery Center の菜園について示唆されていることを問う選択肢照合型の問題。ウェブページの❻に「Herman Nursery Center が菜園を提供」という記載があるため、ここを見ていくと、❼で「無料の菜園はすぐに埋まってしまいますので、場所を確保するには Hilary Keel まで至急連絡を」と呼び掛けている。ここから、ハリスバーグ市民にとって、すぐに埋まるほどのイベント＝人気のあることがうかがえる。これを popular と言い換えた **(A)** が正解。(B) 地元企業のための花、(C) レンタル料金、に関しては具体的な記載がなく、(D) 育てる作物は、❻の直後で「野菜や花」となっているため、いずれも不正解。

 ☐ nominal charge わずかな料金　☐ exclusively for ～に対してのみ

Harper Healthcare Center
136 Hillcrest Ave. ハリスバーグ市，ペンシルベニア州 16803
878-610-7722

新規のお客様へのご案内

Harper Healthcare Center（HHC）をご利用いただきありがとうございます。当センターは 25 年間にわたり、患者様とお客様への食事と生活習慣に関するアドバイスを通して、ハリスバーグと周辺の郡の皆さまの健康のサポートを行ってきました。さらに、おいしくて健康的な食事によってお客様の食生活の改善をお手伝いすべく、Brigham Garden の料理人である Daniel Hammond による料理教室を開講しております。

ウェブサイト www.harperhc.net/event にアクセスすることで、クラスへの登録を行うことができます。地域のイベント情報や、より健康的な生活を送るための情報については、インターネットの掲示板をご覧ください。さらに HHC Saving Card に申し込むこともできます。このカードを使用すると、ハリスバーグと周辺の郡にある提携レストランや商店で最大 20 パーセントの割引を受けることができます。

ご質問があれば、HHC の責任者 Leila Baler まで遠慮なくお問い合わせください。

---

www.harperhc.net./bulletin/

メインページ	医師	栄養士	掲示板

HHC 料理教室：健康的な食生活に刺激を　5 月 23 日午後 5 時
塩分を減らすことが食事を台無しにするとお考えですか？　塩分の摂取量を減らしたいとお考えですか？　私たちが、あなたの料理に刺激を与えるハーブやスパイスで、それを取り戻すお手伝いをいたします。

当センターの調理用教室は改装中のため、このクラスは 283 Greenville Street の Wollowitz Natural Foods で開催しますのでご注意ください。

参加はこちら：http://www.harperhc.net/event

- -

新しいテイクアウト用サラダは現在 Nancy's Better Groceries でご購入いただけます
Evelyn's Organic Food Market の店主 Evelyn Seaton さんは、6 月初旬より、調理済みサラダの販売を開始し、店で買い物をしながら健康的で手軽な食品を提供します。

- -

ハリスバーグ市郊外の Herman Nursery Center が菜園をご提供
自分で野菜や花を育てると、健康的な食品を手に入れられ、簡単な運動にもなります。Herman Nursery Center は、ご自身の菜園で始めることをお手伝いいたします。無料の菜園はすぐに埋まってしまいますので、場所を確保するには Hilary Keel まで至急ご連絡ください！

To: publicrelations@supercopa.net
From: Malee Suarez <maleesu@forvo.org>
Date: September 9
Subject: Inquiry

To Whom It May Concern,

I want to ask about how to qualify for a press card that will enable me to interview a team at the seventh annual Supercopa Football Cup in October. I have been commissioned by *Liga Deporte*, a Spanish newspaper, to write about the match featuring the national teams of Spain and Brazil. I know this match is gaining a great deal of attention in the two nations, and also the rest of the world, so you are receiving a lot of inquiries.

I am a freelance sports journalist and review various types of sports events for Spanish organizations and publications such as FICHAS and COPES. Actually, the former has commissioned my latest piece, covering the performance of a Spanish player in the Taiwan Swinging Forest Golf match.

Please inform me of your decision at your earliest convenience.

Best regards,

Malee Suarez

To: Malee Suarez <maleesu@forvo.org>
From: Pierre Ramirez <pierrepr@supercopa.net>
Date: September 9
Subject: RE > Inquiry

Dear Ms. Suarez,

I sincerely appreciate your interest in the Supercopa Football Cup. The Supercopa Group, the organizer of the contest, welcomes all active reporters of the news and press media to report on the final match between Spain and Brazil.

As you mentioned, the match is drawing international attention. Any journalists with the necessary credentials are qualified, but because of the overwhelming inquiries about the journalist passes, we have decided to issue them on a first-come, first-served basis. If you are seeking to get the pass, you should show us your credentials with a letterhead issued by an officially recognized publisher or organization. Our committee will confirm all of your documents; as soon as approved, you will be contacted by e-mail. There will be a pass in the attached file of the e-mail.

Thank you,

Pierre Ramirez
Public Relations, Supercopa Football Cup

35. Why did Ms. Suarez write the first e-mail?

(A) To ask about a currently empty position
(B) To learn about guidelines for players
(C) To buy a ticket to a sports event
(D) To inquire about special access to a sports match

36. For what organization did Ms. Suarez most recently write an assignment?

(A) Liga Deporte
(B) The Supercopa Group
(C) FICHAS
(D) COPES

37. What does Mr. Ramirez indicate Mr. Suarez do?

(A) Submit a document issued by the newspaper
(B) Read the credentials carefully before sending them
(C) Put forward a representative from the affiliated company
(D) Send an e-mail to the committee for additional information

38. What is NOT indicated about the Supercopa Football Cup?

(A) It has the attention of international media.
(B) It invites multiple national teams.
(C) It is held by a Brazilian company.
(D) It only has its last match remaining.

39. How will Mr. Suarez receive a pass?

(A) By a fax
(B) By an e-mail
(C) By a delivery man
(D) By an express mail

P. 296

Double

Questions 35-39 refer to the following e-mails.

Eメール（1）

To: publicrelations@supercopa.net
From: Malee Suarez <maleesu@forvo.org>
Date: September 9
Subject: Inquiry

To Whom It May Concern,

❶ I want to ask about how to qualify for a press card that will enable me to interview a team at the seventh annual Supercopa Football Cup in October. ❷ I have been commissioned by *Liga Deporte*, a Spanish newspaper, to write about ❸ the match featuring the national teams of Spain and Brazil. I know this match is gaining a great deal of attention in the two nations, and also the rest of the world, so you are receiving a lot of inquiries.

❹ I am a freelance sports journalist and review various types of sports events for Spanish organizations and publications such as FICHAS and COPES. ❺ Actually, the former has commissioned my latest piece, covering the performance of a Spanish player in the Taiwan Swinging Forest Golf match.

Please inform me of your decision at your earliest convenience.

Best regards,

Malee Suarez

Eメール（2）

To: Malee Suarez <maleesu@forvo.org>
From: Pierre Ramirez <pierrepr@supercopa.net>
Date: September 9
Subject: RE > Inquiry

Dear Ms. Suarez,

I sincerely appreciate your interest in the Supercopa Football Cup. ❻ The Supercopa Group, the organizer of the contest, welcomes all active reporters of the news and press media to report on the final match between Spain and Brazil.

❼ As you mentioned, the match is drawing international attention. ❽ Any journalists with the necessary credentials are qualified, but because of the overwhelming inquiries about the journalist passes, we have decided to issue them on a first-come, first-served basis. ❾ If you are seeking to get the pass, you should show us your credentials with a letterhead issued by an officially recognized publisher or organization. ❿ Our committee will confirm all of your documents; as soon as approved, you will be contacted by e-mail. ⓫ There will be a pass in the attached file of the e-mail.

Thank you,

Pierre Ramirez
Public Relations, Supercopa Football Cup

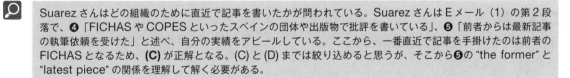

Eメール（1）
- [ ] inquiry 問い合わせ　[ ] To Whom It May Concern ご担当者様宛　[ ] qualify for ～を得る資格がある
- [ ] press card 取材許可証、プレスカード　[ ] commission ～に委託する　[ ] match 試合
- [ ] feature ～を呼び物にする　[ ] gain ～を獲得する　[ ] a great deal of たくさんの
- [ ] freelance フリーランスの、個人契約の　[ ] organization 組織、機関　[ ] publication 出版物　[ ] former 前者
- [ ] latest 最新の　[ ] piece 記事　[ ] cover ～を報道する
- [ ] at one's earliest convenience ～の一番早く都合のつくときに

Eメール（2）
- [ ] interest in ～に対する興味　[ ] organizer 組織運営者　[ ] active 現役の　[ ] as you mentioned お話ししたとおり
- [ ] draw attention 注目を引く　[ ] credential 証明書　[ ] overwhelming 圧倒するほど多数の
- [ ] issue ～を発行する　[ ] on a first-come, first-served basis 先着順で　[ ] seek to *do* ～しようとする
- [ ] letterhead レターヘッド　[ ] committee 委員会　[ ] confirm ～を確認する

★★★☆☆

35. Why did Ms. Suarez write the first e-mail?

(A) To ask about a currently empty position
(B) To learn about guidelines for players
(C) To buy a ticket to a sports event
(D) To inquire about special access to a sports match

Suarez さんはなぜ1通目のEメールを書きましたか。

(A) 現在欠員となっている職について尋ねるため
(B) 選手のためのガイドラインについて学ぶため
(C) スポーツイベントのチケットを買うため
(D) スポーツの試合会場への特別な入場について問い合わせるため

Suarez さんがなぜ1文書目のEメール（1）を書いたかが問われている。Eメール（1）の❶で「10月の Supercopa Football Cup でチームにインタビューをするための取材許可証を取得する方法について尋ねている」ことがわかる。ここから、インタビューするための会場への入場許可証を special access と言い換えた **(D)** が正解。TOEIC の場合、access は「ある場所への入室・立ち入りやインターネットへの接続」を表すことが多い。

- [ ] empty position 欠員となっている職　[ ] access to ～への入場

★★★★★

36. For what organization did Ms. Suarez most recently write an assignment?

(A) Liga Deporte
(B) The Supercopa Group
(C) FICHAS
(D) COPES

Suarez さんはどの組織のために直近で記事を書きましたか。

(A) Liga Deporte
(B) The Supercopa Group
(C) FICHAS
(D) COPES

Suarez さんはどの組織のために直近で記事を書いたかが問われている。Suarez さんはEメール（1）の第2段落で、❹「FICHAS や COPES といったスペインの団体や出版物で批評を書いている」、❺「前者からは最新記事の執筆依頼を受けた」と述べ、自分の実績をアピールしている。ここから、一番直近で記事を手掛けたのは前者の FICHAS となるため、**(C)** が正解となる。(C) と (D) までは絞り込めると思うが、そこから❺の "the former" と "latest piece" の関係を理解して解く必要がある。

37. What does Mr. Ramirez indicate Mr. Suarez do?

    (A) Submit a document issued by the newspaper
    (B) Read the credentials carefully before sending them
    (C) Put forward a representative from the affiliated company
    (D) Send an e-mail to the committee for additional information

Ramirez さんは、Suarez さんは何をすべきであると示唆していますか。

    (A) 新聞社が発行する書類を提出する
    (B) 送信前に証明書を注意深く読む
    (C) 関連会社から代理の人物を推薦する
    (D) 追加情報としてEメールを委員会に送る

Ramirez さんは、Suarez さんが何をすべきであると示唆しているかが問われている。Eメール（1）で、Suarez さんがインタビューのための取材許可証の取得方法を問い合わせたのに対し、Ramirez さんはEメール（2）の❾で「記者証取得を希望の場合、公式に認められた出版社や団体が発行したレターヘッド付き証明書の提示が必要」と返答している。Eメール（1）の❷を見ると、Ramirez さんは新聞社からこのインタビューを依頼されていることがわかる。以上から、Ramirez さんは依頼を受けた新聞社のレターヘッド付き証明書を提示する必要があるので、正解は **(A)** となる。2つの文書に書かれていることを交互に読んで解く、少し難しめの問題だ。

☐ representative 代表者　☐ affiliated 関連の

---

38. What is NOT indicated about the Supercopa Football Cup?

    (A) It has the attention of international media.
    (B) It invites multiple national teams.
    (C) It is held by a Brazilian company.
    (D) It only has its last match remaining.

Supercopa Football Cup について示されていないことは何ですか。

    (A) 国際的な報道機関に注目されている。
    (B) トーナメントに複数の国の代表チームを招待する。
    (C) ブラジルの会社によって開催される。
    (D) 最終試合のみが残っている。

NOT 問題。Supercopa Football Cup について示されていないことが問われている。❸の「スペイン代表とブラジルの代表チームの試合」という記載が (B) に、❻の後半にある "the final match（決勝戦）" という表現が (D) に、❼・❽の「この試合は国際的な注目を集めている」「記者証について問い合わせが殺到している」という記載が (A) に、それぞれ該当する。よって、残った **(C)** が正解。大会の組織団体がどこの国の会社なのかは記載がない。この NOT 問題は両方の文書に根拠がまたがっているため、しっかり読んで、根拠と選択肢を一致できるようにしておこう。

☐ last match 決勝戦、最終戦　☐ remaining 残っている

---

39. How will Mr. Suarez receive a pass?

    (A) By a fax
    (B) By an e-mail
    (C) By a delivery man
    (D) By an express mail

Suarez さんはどのようにして許可証を受け取りますか。

    (A) ファックスで
    (B) Eメールで
    (C) 配達員によって
    (D) 速達で

Suarez さんが許可証を受け取る方法が問われている。Eメール（2）の❿・⓫で「（許可証要請が）承認され次第、Eメールで連絡する」「記者証はそのEメールに添付されている」とあるため、Eメールにて送付されることがわかる。以上より、正解は **(B)**。"mail" という表現につられて、拙速に (D) を選ばないように気を付けよう。

☐ express mail 速達郵便

Ｅメール（1）

受信者：	publicrelations@supercopa.net
送信者：	Malee Suarez <maleesu@forvo.org>
日付：	9 月 9 日
件名：	問い合わせ

ご担当者様

10 月の第 7 回年次 Supercopa Football Cup でチームにインタビューをするための取材許可証を取得するにはどうすればいいかお尋ねします。私はスペインの新聞 *Super Deporte* から、スペインとブラジルの代表チームの試合の記事を書くように依頼を受けています。この試合は、両国はもちろん、その他の国々からも大きな注目を集めていますので、多くの問い合わせを受けていらっしゃることでしょう。

私はフリーのスポーツ記者であり、Fichajes や COPE といったスペインの団体や出版物で、さまざまな種類のスポーツイベントの批評を書いています。実際に、前者からは Taiwan Swinging Skirts Golf の試合におけるスペイン人選手の活躍を取材する最新記事の執筆依頼を受けました。

ご都合つき次第、回答をお知らせいただけますか。

よろしくお願いいたします。

Malee Suarez

Ｅメール（2）

受信者：	Malee Suarez <maleesu@forvo.org>
送信者：	Pierre Ramirez <pierrepr@supercopa.net>
日付：	9 月 9 日
件名：	RE ＞ 問い合わせ

Suarez 様

Supercopa Football Cup に関心をお寄せいただき、誠にありがとうございます。競技会の主催者である The Supercopa Group は、スペイン対ブラジルの決勝戦を報道するために、ニュースや報道機関の現役記者の皆さまを歓迎いたします。

ご存じのとおり、この試合は国際的な注目を集めています。必要な証明書をお持ちの記者の方であれば誰でも資格がありますが、記者証について膨大な問い合わせのため、先着順で記者証を発行とすることといたしました。記者証の取得をご希望の場合は、公式に認められた出版社や団体が発行したレターヘッド付きの証明書をご提示いただく必要があります。当委員会がすべての文書の確認をいたします。承認され次第、Ｅメールにてご連絡いたします。記者証はそのＥメールに添付のファイルの中にあります。

よろしくお願いいたします。

Pierre Ramirez
Supercopa Football Cup 広報

Questions 40-44 refer to the following e-mail, letter, and calendar.

🕐 5分30秒

To: Mac Tailor <mtailor@billysf.com>
From: Maria Cloudia <maria77@billysf.com>
Date: August 6
Subject: Re: Company Credit Card

Dear Mr. Tailor,

You have requested a company credit card. In order to issue a card to you, I need at least one of the following items of proof.
▶ Five or more international and domestic business trips for this year
▶ Signed documentation from a supervisor indicating that you are asked to entertain company customers
▶ Expected business-related expenses of $500 or more

As you wait for your card, please keep in mind that you should review our expense and travel policies on pages 67-83 of the handbook for workers. Here are highlights from those policies.
▶ All transportation such as airline, train and bus, also hotel reservations should be made through the company travel division.
▶ Car rentals should be approved by your supervisor before requesting a rental through the company travel division.
▶ Meals are covered by the firm as far as they do not pass daily allowances (refer to section 18, page 59).

Best regards,

Maria Cloudia
Company Travel Division, Billy Skill Firm

The Skill and Method Association (SMA)

Mac Tailor
Billy Skill Firm
213 Queen Avenue
Seattle, WA 98122

Dear Mac Tailor,

You have successfully enrolled in the SMA Conference in Buenos Aires, Argentina. Your payment of $550 has been approved.

For a comfortable trip, SMA recommends that you should make arrangements for transportation and accommodation. We have established discounted rates for conference attendees at Hotel Duhau, which is the conference site. Rooms at Hotel Duhau are booked for SMA members only. We will be offering a free breakfast from 6:30 to 8:30 A.M. as well as coffee and tea from 1 to 6 P.M. every day, both in the hotel lobby. Attendees are in charge of all other meals.

For more information, don't hesitate to contact us at help@smaconference.net.

Truly,

SMA Conference Committee

Calendar for Mac Tailor: Week from 4 to 8 October		
Day	Time	Description
4 Oct. (Mon)	9:00 A.M.	Depart: Seattle, WA (flight BW006)
	8:00 P.M.	Arrive: Buenos Aires, Argentina Transportation to Hotel Duhau via Taxi (late check-in confirmed by hotel manager)
5 Oct. (Tue)	9:00 A.M.	Conference Sessions
	4:30 P.M.	Take a Rest
	5:00 P.M.	Rashard Beltran: Job Interview
6 Oct. (Wed)	9:00 A.M.	Conference Sessions
	3:30 P.M.	Take a Rest
	4:00 P.M.	Rashard Beltran: Presentation (Conference Room)
7 Oct. (Thu)	9:00 A.M.	Conference Sessions
	5:00 P.M.	Take a Rest
	6:00 P.M.	Closing Ceremony and Reception (Crystal Ballroom)
8 Oct. (Fri)	9:00 A.M.	Transportation to Airport via Hotel Shuttle
	11:15 A.M.	Depart: Buenos Aires, Argentina (flight BW202)
	10:00 P.M.	Arrive: Seattle, WA

40. What qualifies Mr. Tailor to receive a corporate credit card?

(A) He will be traveling for more than five days.
(B) He will be entertaining customers on his business trip.
(C) His upcoming travel is international.
(D) His registration fee is over $500.

41. What expense policy does NOT apply to Mr. Tailor's trip?

(A) The policy about food costs
(B) The policy about hotel reservations
(C) The policy about booking flights
(D) The policy about renting cars

42. Why is the letter written?

(A) To confirm a registration
(B) To describe about the SMA
(C) To provide a conference information
(D) To share the reviews of restaurants

43. What does the SMA Conference Committee NOT offer to participants?

(A) Breakfast
(B) Manuals for the attendees
(C) Hotel room discount
(D) Answers to questions

44. What can be inferred about Mr. Tailor?

(A) He couldn't secure enough rest time.
(B) He used a different airline.
(C) He is leaving the conference early.
(D) He has a meeting with Mr. Beltran.

Triple

P. 302

Questions 40-44 refer to the following e-mail, letter, and calendar.

To: Mac Tailor <mtailor@billysf.com>
From: Maria Cloudia <maria77@billysf.com>
Date: August 6
Subject: Re: Company Credit Card

Dear Mr. Tailor,

You have requested a company credit card. In order to issue a card to you, I need at least one of the following items of proof.
▶ Five or more international and domestic business trips for this year
▶ Signed documentation from a supervisor indicating that you are asked to entertain company customers
▶ ❶ Expected business-related expenses of $500 or more

As you wait for your card, please keep in mind that you should review our expense and travel policies on pages 67-83 of the handbook for workers. Here are highlights from those policies.
▶ ❷ All transportation such as airline, train and bus, also hotel reservations should be made through the company travel division.
▶ Car rentals should be approved by your supervisor before requesting a rental through the company travel division.
▶ ❸ Meals are covered by the firm as far as they do not pass daily allowances (refer to section 18, page 59).

Best regards,

Maria Cloudia
Company Travel Division, Billy Skill Firm

The Skill and Method Association (SMA)

Mac Tailor
Billy Skill Firm
213 Queen Avenue
Seattle, WA 98122

Dear Mac Tailor,

❹ You have successfully enrolled in the SMA Conference in Buenos Aires, Argentina. Your payment of $550 has been approved.

For a comfortable trip, SMA recommends that you should make arrangements for transportation and accommodation. ❺ We have established discounted rates for conference attendees at Hotel Duhau, which is the conference site. Rooms at Hotel Duhau are booked for SMA members only. ❻ We will be offering a free breakfast from 6:30 to 8:30 A.M. as well as coffee and tea from 1 to 6 P.M. every day, both in the hotel lobby. ❼ Attendees are in charge of all other meals.

❽ For more information, don't hesitate to contact us at help@smaconference.net.

Truly,
SMA Conference Committee

Calendar for Mac Tailor: Week from 4 to 8 October		
Day	Time	Description
4 Oct. (Mon)	9:00 A.M.	Depart: Seattle, WA (❾ flight BW006)
	8:00 P.M.	Arrive: Buenos Aires, Argentina ❿ Transportation to Hotel Duhau via Taxi (late check-in confirmed by hotel manager)
5 Oct. (Tue)	9:00 A.M.	Conference Sessions
	4:30 P.M.	Take a Rest
	5:00 P.M.	⓫ Rashard Beltran: Job Interview
6 Oct. (Wed)	9:00 A.M.	Conference Sessions
	3:30 P.M.	Take a Rest
	4:00 P.M.	Rashard Beltran: Presentation (Conference Room)
7 Oct. (Thu)	9:00 A.M.	Conference Sessions
	5:00 P.M.	Take a Rest
	6:00 P.M.	Closing Ceremony and Reception (Crystal Ballroom)
8 Oct. (Fri)	9:00 A.M.	Transportation to Airport via Hotel Shuttle
	11:15 A.M.	Depart: Buenos Aires, Argentina (⓬ flight BW202)
	10:00 P.M.	Arrive: Seattle, WA

Eメール
- [ ] in order to *do* ～するために　[ ] issue ～を発行する　[ ] following 以下の　[ ] proof 証拠、証明
- [ ] domestic 国内の　[ ] signed documentation 署名入り文書　[ ] indicate ～を示す　[ ] entertain ～をもてなす
- [ ] expected 予定された　[ ] business-related 業務関連の　[ ] expense 支出　[ ] or more もしくはそれを超える
- [ ] keep in mind that ～に留意しておく　[ ] highlight 要点　[ ] transportation 交通手段　[ ] cover ～を賄う
- [ ] firm 会社　[ ] as far as ～である限り　[ ] pass ～を超過する　[ ] daily allowance 日当　[ ] refer to ～を参照する

手紙
- [ ] successfully 問題なく　[ ] enroll in ～に登録する　[ ] comfortable 快適な　[ ] make arrangement 手配する
- [ ] discounted rate 割引料金　[ ] attendee 出席者　[ ] book ～を予約する
- [ ] in charge of ～を責任もって対応する

日程表
- [ ] depart 出発する　[ ] via ～経由で　[ ] late check-in 遅いチェックイン　[ ] confirm ～を確認する
- [ ] shuttle 往復運行の乗り物

40. What qualifies Mr. Tailor to receive a corporate credit card?

(A) He will be traveling for more than five days.
(B) He will be entertaining customers on his business trip.
(C) His upcoming travel is international.
(D) His registration fee is over $500.

Tailor さんが法人クレジットカードを受け取る要件は何ですか。

(A) 5 日以上旅行をする。
(B) 出張で顧客を接待する。
(C) 次の旅行は海外旅行である。
(D) 参加料が 500 ドルを超える。

Tailor さんが法人クレジットカードを受け取る要件が問われている。まず 1 文書目の E メールには、カード付与の条件がいくつか並べられており、このうち 1 点を満たすことが必要だとわかる。次に、2 文書目の手紙では、今回の協議会参加費用が 550 ドルであり、500 ドル以上であることがわかる。ここから、E メールに書かれているカード付与条件の❶「500 ドル以上の業務上の支出の予定」に合致する。よって、正解は **(D)**。証明する条件がどこに該当するか、複数の文書を読んで手掛かりを見つける必要があり、少し難易度の高い問題。

□ qualify 〜に資格を与える　□ upcoming きたる

---

41. What expense policy does NOT apply to Mr. Tailor's trip?

(A) The policy about food costs
(B) The policy about hotel reservations
(C) The policy about booking flights
(D) The policy about renting cars

Tailor さんの出張に適用されない経費の規定は何ですか。

(A) 食費に関する規定
(B) ホテルの予約に関する規定
(C) 飛行機の予約に関する規定
(D) レンタカーに関する規定

NOT 問題。Tailor さんの出張に適用されない経費規定について問われている。まず、1 文書目の E メール❷の「交通手段とホテルに関する予約の規定」が、3 文書目の日程表の❿及び、❾・⓬のホテルとフライトの手配に関連するので (B)(C) が該当する。次に❸の「食事に関する規定」が、手紙の❼に関連するため (A) が該当することがわかる。**(D)** のレンタカーに関する規定は、今回適用する予定が記載されていないため、これが正解となる。規定内容に関わる（＝適用される）箇所を複数文書から探していく必要があるので、注意して解こう。

---

42. Why is the letter written?

(A) To confirm a registration
(B) To describe about the SMA
(C) To provide a conference information
(D) To share the reviews of restaurants

手紙はなぜ書かれますか。

(A) 登録の確認をするため
(B) SMA について説明するため
(C) 協議会の情報を提供するため
(D) レストランの評価を伝えるため

2 文書目の手紙がなぜ書かれたかが問われている。手紙の冒頭❹で「協議会への参加登録が完了した」と、ある登録が終了したことを述べている。よって、それを言い換えた **(A)** が正解となる。

□ registration 登録　□ describe 〜を述べる・説明する

★★★★☆ NOT 問題

43. What does the SMA Conference Committee NOT offer to participants?

(A) Breakfast
(B) Manuals for the attendees
(C) Hotel room discount
(D) Answers to questions

SMA 協議会の委員会が出席者に提供しないものは次のどれですか。

(A) 朝食
(B) 出席者向けの手引き
(C) ホテルの宿泊割引
(D) 質問への回答

 NOT 問題。SMA 協議会が提供しないものが問われている。2 文書目の手紙を見ていくと、❺の使用ホテルの割引が (C)、❻の無料の朝食提供が (A) に、そして、❽の追加情報等に関しての連絡先が (D) にそれぞれ該当する。よって **(B)** が正解となる。**(B)** の manual は 1 文書目の E メールにある規定とは異なり、協議会参加者へのマニュアルということになり、文書には特に登場していない。しっかり情報を整理して正解を導こう。

★★★☆☆

44. What can be inferred about Mr. Tailor?

(A) He couldn't secure enough rest time.
(B) He used a different airline.
(C) He is leaving the conference early.
(D) He has a meeting with Mr. Beltran.

Tailor さんについて何が推測できますか。

(A) 十分な休憩時間を確保できなかった。
(B) 違う航空会社を利用した。
(C) 協議会から早く退出する。
(D) Beltran さんと面会する。

 Tailor さんについて推測できることを問う選択肢照合型問題。3 文書目の日程表より、⓫で Rashard Beltran さんと面接を行うことがわかる。以上より、**(D)** が正解となる。日程表の冒頭に、「Tailor さんの予定」だと明記されているので、ここからしっかりキーワードを引き出して解くようにしよう。

 □ secure 〜を確保する　□ rest time 休憩時間

受信者： Mac Tailor <mtailor@billysf.com>
送信者： Maria Cloudia <maria77@billysf.com>
日付： 8月6日
件名： Re：会社のクレジットカード

Tailor 様

会社名義のクレジットカードを申請されましたが、カードの発行には、次のいずれか1点を証明するものが必要です。
▶ 今年の海外と国内の出張の予定が5回以上あること
▶ 当社の顧客接待を任されていることを証明する上司の署名入りの文書
▶ 500ドル以上の業務上の支出の予定があること

カードが届くまでの間、従業員のための手引きの67～83ページにある、当社の経費と出張に関する規定のご確認をお願いいたします。以下は規定の要点です。
▶ 飛行機、電車、バスなどすべての交通手段やホテルの予約は出張部門を通して行ってください。
▶ 出張部門にレンタカーの依頼をする前に上司の承認を得てください。
▶ 日当を超えない限り、食費は会社が負担します（59ページ18項を参照）。

よろしくお願いいたします。

Maria Cloudia
Billy Skill Firm 出張部門

The Skill and Method Association (SMA)

Mac Tailor 様
Billy Skill Firm 社
213 Queen Avenue
シアトル，ワシントン州 98122

Mac Tailor 様

アルゼンチンのブエノスアイレスで開催される SMA 協議会への参加お申込みが完了しました。550ドルの支払いが承認されました。

快適な旅のため、SMA では交通手段と宿泊施設の手配をしておくことをお勧めしています。当協会では協議会への出席者向けに協議会会場である Hotel Duhau の割引宿泊料金を設定しています。Hotel Duhau の客室は SMA の会員以外は予約できません。毎日午前6時半から午前8時半まで無料の朝食、午後1時から午後6時までコーヒーやお茶を、ホテルのロビーにて提供いたします。その他の食事については、出席者ご自身でご用意ください。

その他の情報につきましては、当協会 help@smaconference.net までお気軽にお問い合わせください。

よろしくお願いいたします。

SMA 協議会委員会

Mac Tailor さんの日程表：10 月 4 日から 8 日までの週		
日付	時間	内容
10 月 4 日（月）	午前 9:00	ワシントン州シアトル出発（フライト BW006）
	午後 8:00	アルゼンチン、ブエノスアイレス到着 タクシーにて Hotel Duhau まで移動 （チェックインが遅くなることはホテルの支配人の了承済み）
10 月 5 日（火）	午前 9:00	協議会出席
	午後 4:30	休憩
	午後 5:00	Rashard Beltran さん：採用面接
10 月 6 日（水）	午前 9:00	協議会出席
	午後 3:30	休憩
	午後 4:00	Rashard Beltran さん：発表（会議室にて）
10 月 7 日（木）	午前 9:00	協議会出席
	午後 5:00	休憩
	午後 6:00	閉会式と懇親会（Crystal Ballroom にて）
10 月 8 日（金）	午前 9:00	ホテルの送迎車にて空港まで移動
	午前 11:15	アルゼンチン、ブエノスアイレス出発（フライト BW202）
	午後 10:00	ワシントン州シアトル到着

Questions 45-49 refer to the following article, book review, and interview transcript. 5分30秒

July 3—Bonnie Ricci's sequel to the best seller *Raising Myself*, which so many readers have long anticipated, has finally arrived. The very popular *Raising Myself* chronicled the ups and downs that Ms. Ricci underwent as she moved from job to job as a youth, working as everything from a construction worker and sailor, to a store clerk and fitness advisor.

The new publication starts again where the previous book left off, with Ms. Ricci having just arrived in Los Angeles. We follow her rise from copywriter to the director of an R&D department, at a highly successful marketing agency. Written in the entertaining, informative style that has made Ms. Ricci's marketing campaigns so successful over the years, the book shares stories of client case histories and makes public how she developed her most successful marketing campaigns. The book is now available online and in bookstores everywhere across the country.

Book Review: *My Motto in Marketing*
By Michael Green

Considering that it took fifteen years for Bonnie Ricci to publish her second book, *My Motto in Marketing*, the impression I got as a reader is that she forgot to edit her work. I thoroughly enjoyed Ms. Ricci's previous book, but this sequel is made up of dull, complicated sentences that make reading it a bore. There's no argument about her abilities as a marketing executive, but the stories about her life in the marketing business are much less engaging than those earlier stories that almost jumped off the pages. For instance, nothing matches the earlier book's crystal-clear descriptions like her unpredictable adventures as a store clerk in southern Colorado. This is one book you should skip.

Monthly Marketing Journal

A minute with Marketing specialist Bonnie Ricci
This interview will be conducted by Anna Tate of the *Monthly Marketing Journal*.

Anna Tate: It's a very long time since you wrote your first book. Now you have come back with your second book. Why did it take so long?

Bonnie Ricci: It's interesting. I've always considered my copywriting to be what I do. However, long pieces of writing, like manuscripts, are very difficult for me, so I take my time to edit them carefully. But I'm very proud of the end result — it's easy to read and highly enjoyable, just like my first book.

Anna Tate: You've experienced so many jobs, like sailor and fitness advisor. Why do you keep doing this job now?

Bonnie Ricci: I'm not so sure it does suit me. My belief is to be open to any chance that comes my way. Marketing came my way, but I'm rather sure it's not the last thing I'll try my hand at. And you never know, I might go to another occupation.

---

45. In the article, the word "underwent" in paragraph 1, line 5, is closest in meaning to

(A) experienced
(B) relocated
(C) overcame
(D) enhanced

46. What is indicated about *Raising Myself*?

(A) It is out of print.
(B) It includes pictures.
(C) It has been made into a TV drama.
(D) It was published fifteen years ago.

47. In the book review, what is suggested about Ms. Ricci's time as a store clerk?

(A) She met some marketing executives.
(B) She wrote a draft in the evenings.
(C) She experienced some surprising incidents.
(D) She traveled throughout Colorado.

48. On what point do Ms. Ricci and Mr. Green disagree?

(A) The reason *Raising Myself* is popular
(B) The quality of the writing in *My Motto in Marketing*
(C) Ms. Ricci's effectiveness as a marketing executive
(D) Ms. Ricci's attitude toward reading for pleasure

49. What does Ms. Ricci imply in the interview transcript?

(A) She learned the most from her job as a fitness advisor.
(B) She may change her profession again.
(C) She is searching for a new publisher.
(D) She has recently purchased a new fishing boat.

P. 310

Triple

Questions 45-49 refer to the following article, book review, and interview transcript.

July 3— ❶ Bonnie Ricci's sequel to the best seller *Raising Myself*, which so many readers have long anticipated, has finally arrived. ❷ The very popular *Raising Myself* chronicled the ups and downs that Ms. Ricci underwent as she moved from job to job as a youth, working as everything from a construction worker and sailor, to a store clerk and fitness advisor.

The new publication starts again where the previous book left off, with Ms. Ricci having just arrived in Los Angeles. We follow her rise from copywriter to the director of an R&D department, at a highly successful marketing agency. Written in the entertaining, informative style that has made Ms. Ricci's marketing campaigns so successful over the years, the book shares stories of client case histories and makes public how she developed her most successful marketing campaigns. The book is now available online and in bookstores everywhere across the country.

Book Review: *My Motto in Marketing*
By Michael Green

❸ Considering that it took fifteen years for Bonnie Ricci to publish her second book, *My Motto in Marketing*, the impression I got as a reader is that she forgot to edit her work. ❹ I thoroughly enjoyed Ms. Ricci's previous book, but this sequel is made up of dull, complicated sentences that make reading it a bore. There's no argument about her abilities as a marketing executive, but the stories about her life in the marketing business are much less engaging than those earlier stories that almost jumped off the pages. ❺ For instance, nothing matches the earlier book's crystal-clear descriptions like her unpredictable adventures as a store clerk in southern Colorado. This is one book you should skip.

Monthly Marketing Journal

A minute with Marketing specialist Bonnie Ricci
This interview will be conducted by Anna Tate of the *Monthly Marketing Journal*.

Anna Tate: It's a very long time since you wrote your first book. Now you have come back with your second book. Why did it take so long?

Bonnie Ricci: It's interesting. I've always considered my copywriting to be what I do. However, long pieces of writing, like manuscripts, are very difficult for me, so I take my time to edit them carefully. ❻ But I'm very proud of the end result — it's easy to read and highly enjoyable, just like my first book.

Anna Tate: You've experienced so many jobs, like sailor and fitness advisor. Why do you keep doing this job now?

Bonnie Ricci: I'm not so sure it does suit me. My belief is to be open to any chance that comes my way. Marketing came my way, but I'm rather sure it's not the last thing I'll try my hand at. ❼ And you never know, I might go to another occupation.

📝

記事
- ☐ sequel 続編　☐ anticipate ～を楽しみに待つ　☐ chronicle ～を時系列で記録する・記録に留める
- ☐ ups and downs 上り坂と下り坂、浮き沈み　☐ undergo ～を経験する　☐ youth 若者、青年　☐ sailor 船乗り
- ☐ store clerk 店員　☐ publication 出版物　☐ leave off 終了する　☐ rise 昇進
- ☐ entertaining わくわくして楽しませる　☐ informative 有用な　☐ case history 事例
- ☐ make public ～を公表する

書評
- ☐ motto モットー、主義　☐ considering that ～と考えると　☐ impression 印象　☐ edit ～を編集する
- ☐ thoroughly 徹底的に　☐ A is made up of B A は B で構成されている　☐ dull つまらない
- ☐ complicated 複雑な　☐ bore 退屈なもの　☐ argument 議論　☐ executive 幹部　☐ engaging 魅力がある
- ☐ jump off the page 本の内容が自然と目に飛び込んでくるくらい面白い　☐ for instance 例えば
- ☐ match ～に匹敵する　☐ crystal-clear 明快な　☐ description 描写　☐ unpredictable 予測できない
- ☐ adventure 冒険

インタビューの筆記録
- ☐ minute 短い時間　☐ conduct ～を実行する　☐ copywriting コピーライティング（広告・宣伝の表現を考えること）
- ☐ long piece 長編作品　☐ manuscript 原稿　☐ be proud of ～を誇りに思う
- ☐ highly enjoyable とても楽しめる　☐ suit ～に適している　☐ belief 信条　☐ try one's hand at ～をやってみる
- ☐ occupation 職業

★★★☆☆ 同義語問題

45. In the article, the word "underwent" in paragraph 1, line 5, is closest in meaning to

(A) experienced
(B) relocated
(C) overcame
(D) enhanced

記事の、第 1 段落・5 行目にある "underwent" に最も意味が近いのは

(A) 動詞 experience「～を経験する」の過去形
(B) 動詞 relocate「～を移転させる」の過去形
(C) 動詞 overcome「～に打ち勝つ」の過去形
(D) 動詞 enhance「～を高める」の過去形

🔍 同義語問題。問われている箇所は、1 文書目の記事❷にある「(Ricci さんが) 経験した」で、「経験、体験をした」という意味で使用されている。以上から **(A)** が正解。"underwent" は undergo「経験・体験をする」という意味で、experience との言い換えができるようにしておこう。

★★★★★ クロスリファレンス問題

46. What is indicated about *Raising Myself*?

(A) It is out of print.
(B) It includes pictures.
(C) It has been made into a TV drama.
(D) It was published fifteen years ago.

Raising Myself について何が示されていますか。

(A) 絶版である。
(B) 写真が載っている。
(C) テレビドラマ化された。
(D) 15 年前に出版された。

🔍 Raising Myself について何が示されているかを問う選択肢照合型の問題。1 文書目の記事の❶に、「Bonnie Ricci さんのベストセラー Raising Myself の続編がついに出版された」とあり、最新作の前作であることがわかる。次に 2 文書目の書評の❸で、「2 冊目の本 My Motto in Marketing を出版するまでに 15 年が経過」とあるため、ここから前作は 15 年前に出版されたことがわかる。以上から、正解は **(D)**。最新作のタイトルが My Motto in Marketing とわかれば容易に解けるが、それに至るまで、複数文書を参照して解く必要がある。

📝 ☐ out of print 絶版になって

47. In the book review, what is suggested about Ms. Ricci's time as a store clerk?

(A) She met some marketing executives.
(B) She wrote a draft in the evenings.
(C) She experienced some surprising incidents.
(D) She traveled throughout Colorado.

書評では、Ricci さんの店員時代について何が示唆されていますか。

(A) マーケティング担当役員と会った。
(B) 夜に原稿を書いた。
(C) 驚くべき出来事を経験した。
(D) コロラド州内を旅した。

2文書目の書評から、Ricci さんの店員時代について示唆されていることが問われている。書評の❺では「Ricchi さんがコロラド州南部で店員をしていたときの予測不可能な冒険」と述べている。これを「Ricchi さんが驚くべき出来事を経験した」と言い換えている **(C)** が正解。ここでの "adventure" は、端的な和訳では「冒険」だが、「ありふれていない、わくわくするような出来事を経験する」といった意味で使われており、**(C)** の surprising incidents と言い換えになっている。実際に旅行したわけではないので、**(D)** は不正解。

□ draft ドラフト、原稿草案　□ surprising 驚くべき　□ incident 出来事、事件

クロスリファレンス問題

48. On what point do Ms. Ricci and Mr. Green disagree?

(A) The reason *Raising Myself* is popular
(B) The quality of the writing in *My Motto in Marketing*
(C) Ms. Ricci's effectiveness as a marketing executive
(D) Ms. Ricci's attitude toward reading for pleasure

Ricci さんと Green さんの意見が合わない点は何ですか。

(A) *Raising Myself* が人気がある理由
(B) *My Motto in Marketing* の文章の質
(C) Ricci さんのマーケティング担当役員としての力
(D) 娯楽としての読書に対する Ricci さんの態度

Ricci さんと Green さんの意見が合わない点について問われている。まず、2文書目の E メールの❹で Green さんは、Ricci さんの新作について「前作は非常に楽しめたが、この続編はつまらなく、退屈だ」と酷評している。一方で、著者の Ricci さんは、3文書目のインタビューの筆記録の❻で「出来上がったものは誇りに思っていて、最初の本と同様、読みやすく楽しめる」と述べており、この本の内容の質について意見が合っていない。以上より、それを言い換えた **(B)** が正解。複数の文書から、異なる点を探し出して矛盾点を見つけることがポイントとなる。

□ effectiveness 能力があること　□ attitude 態度　□ for pleasure 娯楽として

---

49. What does Ms. Ricci imply in the interview transcript?

(A) She learned the most from her job as a fitness advisor.
(B) She may change her profession again.
(C) She is searching for a new publisher.
(D) She has recently purchased a new fishing boat.

Ricci さんはインタビューの筆記録で何を暗示していますか。

(A) フィットネスアドバイザーとしての仕事から最も多くを学んだ。
(B) 仕事をまた変えるかもしれない。
(C) 新たな出版社を探している。
(D) 先日、新しい漁船を購入した。

Ricci さんがインタビューの筆記録で暗示していることが問われている。Ricci さんは、インタビューの筆記録の❼で、「わからないが、また、他の職業に就くかもしれない」と述べている。つまり、職業を変える可能性があることを示唆していることがわかるため、"go to another occupation" を change her profession と言い換えた **(B)** が正解となる。

□ profession 職業　□ search for 〜を探す　□ fishing boat 釣り用の船

7月3日 — 非常に多くの読者が待ちに待った Bonnie Ricci さんのベストセラー *Raising Myself* の続編がついに出版された。大変よく読まれた *Raising Myself* は、建設作業員や船乗りから店員にフィットネスアドバイザーまで、若いころ、次から次に仕事を変えた Ricci さんが経験した、山あり谷ありの人生の記録だった。

新作は、前作が終わったところから始まる。Ricci さんはロサンゼルスに到着する。コピーライターから、大手のマーケティング会社の研究開発部の部長に昇進するまでを追っている。同書は Ricci さんのマーケティングキャンペーンを長年にわたり成功に導いてきた、面白く情報として役立つ文体で書かれ、本の中では顧客の事例や最も成功したマーケティングキャンペーンを考案した方法を公開している。
この本は現在オンライン書店と全国の書店で入手可能である。

書評：*My Motto in Marketing* について
Michael Green

Bonnie Ricci さんが2冊目の本 *My Motto in Marketing* を出版するまでに15年が経過していることを考えると、読者の一人として、著者が本を編集するのを忘れてしまったような印象を受けた。Ricci さんの前作は非常に楽しめたが、この続編はつまらない複雑な文章で書かれており、読んでいると退屈してしまう。マーケティング担当役員としての能力についての議論はないが、マーケティングビジネスにかけた人生の話は、とても面白かった前作の話と比べるとはるかに魅力がない。例えば、コロラド州南部で店員をしていたときの予測不可能な冒険のような、前作にあった明快な描写に匹敵するものはない。この本は読まない方が無難だ。

Monthly Marketing Journal

マーケティング専門家 Bonnie Ricci との短い対談
このインタビューは *Monthly Marketing Journal* の Anna Tate が行います。

Anna Tate: 最初の本をお書きになってから、だいぶ経ちました。ついに2冊目の本を携えて戻っていらっしゃいましたが、なぜこんなに時間がかかったのでしょうか？

Bonnie Ricci: これが面白いんですよ。私は今まで、コピーライターの仕事こそ自分の仕事だと考えてきました。しかし、原稿のように長い物を書くのは私にとって非常に難しいので、時間をかけて丁寧に編集することにしたのです。でも、出来上がったものは、とても誇りに思っています。最初の本と同様、読みやすく、非常に楽しめます。

Anna Tate: 船乗りやフィットネスアドバイザーなど、さまざまな仕事の経験がおありですが、なぜ今、この仕事を続けているのですか？

Bonnie Ricci: これが自分に合っているどうかはわかりません。私の信念は自分に訪れるどのような機会も見逃さないことです。マーケティングに出合いはしましたが、これが自分自身で取り組むべき最後のことではないという確信はあります。わかりませんよ、また、他の職業に就くかもしれません。

Questions 50-54 refer to the following notice, e-mail, and floor plan.

5分30秒

Swansea Arts and Culture News
Written by: Jane Milton

This year Swansea city hall granted permission for various art programmes to be held at Swansea City Art Centre. As it comes to the end of this year, it is time that we have to decide on the list of programmes for next year's courses here at the Swansea City Art Centre.

Same as this year, we are going to separate the year into quarters and offer a variety of programmes that our citizens are able to attend throughout the year. Until now, the classes we are considering are oriental painting, oil painting, photography, sequentially listed. According to what we discussed at the conference, the last spot will be taken by the programme with the greatest number of attendees this year.

After all courses are approved by the city council, we will first have to hire instructors for the courses before accepting registrations. But I will be responsible for that because I personally know a couple of people who are interested in leading the painting classes. Lastly, even if I probably say this again later, we do not accept reservations. Seats will be given out in the order in which the applications were submitted until the maximum number we can hold is reached.

E-Mail Message

To:	Jane Milton <janemn@scac.org>
From:	Stan Kovar <stankovar@addinternational.net>
Subject:	Photography Class
Date:	July 2

Dear Ms. Milton,

I heard that a course that was well received last year was being offered again. Through your Web site, I learned that it offers a photography class, which I really would like to take part in. But it seems the registration was closed before I tried to send my application. I've found out the class may have already been filled up, but I would like to know whether there is a spot available or not, perhaps because someone's enrollment has been revoked by any chance.

Best regards,

Stan Kovar

Floor Plan of Swansea City Art Centre

The Swansea City Art Centre invites the citizens of Swansea City to various art programmes.
Registration is open one month before the following quarter starts.
For questions, contact Jane Milton at janemn@scac.org.

Floor	Course Name	Instructor	Course Schedule	Class Size
1F	Oriental Painting	David Harrison	January–March	50
2F	Oil Painting	Brigit Bedford	April–June	40
3F	Photography	Greta Briggs	July–September	45
4F	Ceramics	Bradley Usman	October–December	60

50. Why was the notice written?

(A) To review last year's events
(B) To fix up a change in a plan
(C) To explain the progress of a project
(D) To distribute tasks to workers

51. What does Ms. Milton say must happen first?

(A) Compose a timetable to be applied at the art centre
(B) Open a part of a Web site to receive applications
(C) Recruit experts to instruct attendees in the courses
(D) Check a set of programmes with an organization

52. Why did Mr. Kovar send an e-mail to Ms. Milton?

(A) To revise a message
(B) To get information
(C) To respond to a question
(D) To inform her of a change

53. What is indicated about the ceramics class?

(A) It was a popular program.
(B) The application deadline is closed.
(C) It will be taught by a different instructor from last year's.
(D) It will take place in the third quarter.

54. What is suggested about Ms. Bedford?

(A) She has previously instructed a class at the art centre.
(B) She is acquainted with Ms. Milton.
(C) She is a well-known artist in Swansea City.
(D) She teaches painting at a university.

Triple

 P. 316

Questions 50-54 refer to the following notice, e-mail, and floor plan.

Swansea Arts and Culture News
Written by: Jane Milton

❶ This year Swansea city hall granted permission for various art programmes to be held at Swansea City Art Centre. ❷ As it comes to the end of this year, it is time that we have to decide on the list of programmes for next year's courses here at the Swansea City Art Centre.

Same as this year, we are going to separate the year into quarters and offer a variety of programmes that our citizens are able to attend throughout the year. Until now, the classes we are considering are oriental painting, oil painting, photography, sequentially listed. ❸ According to what we discussed at the conference, the last spot will be taken by the programme with the greatest number of attendees this year.

❹ After all courses are approved by the city council, we will first have to hire instructors for the courses before accepting registrations. ❺ But I will be responsible for that because I personally know a couple of people who are interested in leading the painting classes. Lastly, even if I probably say this again later, we do not accept reservations. Seats will be given out in the order in which the applications were submitted until the maximum number we can hold is reached.

E-Mail Message

To:	Jane Milton <janemn@scac.org>
From:	Stan Kovar <stankovar@addinternational.net>
Subject:	Photography Class
Date:	July 2

Dear Ms. Milton,

I heard that a course that was well received last year was being offered again. Through your Web site, I learned that it offers a photography class, which I really would like to take part in. But it seems the registration was closed before I tried to send my application. I've found out the class may have already been filled up, but ❻ I would like to know whether there is a spot available or not, perhaps because someone's enrollment has been revoked by any chance.

Best regards,

Stan Kovar

Floor Plan of Swansea City Art Centre

The Swansea City Art Centre invites the citizens of Swansea City to various art programmes.
Registration is open one month before the following quarter starts.
For questions, contact Jane Milton at janemn@scac.org.

Floor	Course Name	Instructor	Course Schedule	Class Size
1F	Oriental Painting	David Harrison	January–March	50
❼ 2F	Oil Painting	Brigit Bedford	April–June	40
3F	Photography	Greta Briggs	July–September	45
❽ 4F	Ceramics	Bradley Usman	October–December	60

お知らせ
□ city hall 市役所　□ grant ～を承諾する　□ various さまざまな　□ same as ～と同じように
□ separate ～を分ける　□ quarter 四半期　□ a variety of 多様な　□ citizen 市民　□ oriental 東洋の
□ oil painting 油絵　□ sequentially 順次　□ spot 場所、地点　□ the greatest number of 最多の
□ attendee 出席者　□ instructor 講師　□ registration 登録　□ lastly 最後に　□ order 順番
□ maximum 最大の

E メール
□ be informed of ～を知る　□ take part in ～に参加する　□ fill up ～を満員・満杯に達する　□ enrollment 登録
□ revoke ～を取り消す　□ by any chance ひょっとして

案内板
□ one month before ～の 1 カ月前　□ following 次の

★★★☆☆

50. Why was the notice written?

(A) To review last year's events
(B) To fix up a change in a plan
(C) To explain the progress of a project
(D) To distribute tasks to workers

お知らせはなぜ書かれましたか。

(A) 昨年のイベントについて振り返るため
(B) 予定の変更を決定するため
(C) プロジェクトの進行状況について説明するため
(D) 作業員たちに仕事を分配するため

1 文書目のお知らせが書かれた理由について問われている。❶で「スウォンジー市役所が Swansea City Art Centre で芸術のプログラムを実施することを許可した」、❷で「来年のコースのプログラムリストを決める時期となった」と、ある芸術プログラムの進行について触れている。ここから、この芸術プログラムを project と言い換えて、「進行状況について説明する」と表現した **(C)** が正解。何かお題を上げて取り組むこと全般を project と表現できることを押さえておこう。

□ review ～を振り返る　□ fix up ～を決定する　□ progress 進捗　□ distribute ～を分配する・配る
□ task 業務、任務

51. What does Ms. Milton say must happen first?

(A) Compose a timetable to be applied at the art centre
(B) Open a part of a Web site to receive applications
(C) Recruit experts to instruct attendees in the courses
(D) Check a set of programmes with an organization

Milton さんは、まず何をするべきだと言っていますか。

(A) 芸術センターで使用する時間割表を作成する
(B) ウェブサイトの一部を公開し、申し込みを受け付ける
(C) コースの参加者を指導する専門家を採用する
(D) 一連のプログラムについて団体に確認する

お知らせの書き手である Milton さんは、まず何をするべきだと言っているかが問われている。お知らせの❹で「まずコースの講師を雇わなければならない」と述べているので、これを "recruit experts" と言い換えた **(C)** が正解。❹にある "first" がキーワードだな、と思って読み進めて解こう。

□ compose 〜を作る　□ timetable 時間割表　□ apply 〜を適用する　□ application 申し込み
□ recruit 〜を採用する　□ expert 専門家　□ a set of 一連の　□ organization 組織、団体

---

52. Why did Mr. Kovar send an e-mail to Ms. Milton?

(A) To revise a message
(B) To get information
(C) To respond to a question
(D) To inform her of a change

Kovar さんはなぜ Milton さんに E メールを送りましたか。

(A) メッセージを訂正するため
(B) 情報を得るため
(C) 質問に答えるため
(D) 変更を通知するため

Kovar さんが Milton さんに E メールを送付した理由が問われている。Kovar さんは 2 文書目の E メールの❻で、「空きがあるかどうかを知りたい」と述べている。ここから、「空きの有無」＝「情報」と抽象度高く表現した **(B)** が正解となる。(C) は、質問に対する返答、と逆の立場になっているので不正解。お互いの立場をしっかり認識して解くようにしよう。

□ revise 〜を修正する・変更する

---

53. What is indicated about the ceramics class?

(A) It was a popular program.
(B) The application deadline is closed.
(C) It will be taught by a different instructor from last year's.
(D) It will take place in the third quarter.

陶芸のクラスについて何が示されていますか。

(A) 人気があったプログラムである。
(B) 申し込みは締め切られている。
(C) 昨年とは違う講師が教える。
(D) 第 3 四半期に開催される。

陶芸のクラスについて示されていることを問う選択肢照合型の問題。1 文書目のお知らせの❸で今年参加者数が最も多かったプログラムが最後の 1 つとなる、と述べられており、そこから 3 番目の案内板の❽を見ると、陶芸のクラスに該当する。つまり 1 番人気のあったクラスということがわかる。よって、正解は **(A)** となる。

□ take place 開催される

54. What is suggested about Ms. Bedford?

    (A) She has previously instructed a class at the art centre.
    (B) She is acquainted with Ms. Milton.
    (C) She is a well-known artist in Swansea City.
    (D) She teaches painting at a university.

Bedford さんについて何が示唆されていますか。

    (A) 芸術センターで以前クラスを指導したことがある。
    (B) Milton さんと知り合いである。
    (C) スウォンジー市ではよく知られた芸術家である。
    (D) 大学で絵画を教えている。

Bedford さんについて示唆されていることを問う選択肢照合型の問題。Bedford さんは3文書目の案内版の❼から、油絵の講師となっていることがわかる。次に1文書目のお知らせの❺で、Milton さんが、「絵画のクラスを担当することに興味のある人材数名の心当たりがあるので、私が講師確保の責任者だ」と述べている。以上から、Milton さんと Bedford さんは知り合いであることがわかる。よって、正解は知り合いであることを be acquainted with と表現した **(B)**。

□ previously 過去に　□ instruct 〜を教える　□ be acquainted with 〜と知り合いである　□ well-known 有名な

問題 50 から 54 は次のお知らせ、Eメール、案内板に関するものです。

Swansea アート・カルチャーニュース
Jane Milton　記

今年、スウォンジー市役所は Swansea City Art Centre にて、さまざまな芸術のプログラムを実施することを許諾した。今年も終わりに近づき、ここ Swansea City Art Center の来年のコースのプログラムリストを決める時期となった。

今年と同様、1年を四半期に分け、市民が年間を通じて参加できるさまざまなプログラムを提供する。現在のところ、検討されている講座は、順に、東洋絵画、油絵、写真だ。協議会で話し合った結果、残る一つには今年参加者数が最も多かったプログラムが採用されることになる。

すべてのコースが市議会の承認を得た後、申し込みの受付を開始する前に、まずコースの講師を雇わなければならない。だが、絵画のクラスを担当することに興味のある数名の人材に心当たりがあるので、私が講師確保の責任者となる。最後に、おそらく後でまた同じことを言うだろうが、予約は受け付けていない。座席の確保は申し込み順となり、受講可能最大人数に達するまで受け付ける。

受信者： Jane Milton <janemn@scac.org>
送信者： Stan Kovar <stankovar@addinternational.net>
件名： 写真のクラス
日付： 7月2日

Milton 様

昨年好評だったコースが再び提供されるとお聞きしました。ウェブサイトで写真のクラスが開講されることを知り、ぜひ受講したいと思いました。しかし、私が申し込み用紙を送ろうとする前に、登録は締め切られたようです。クラスはすでに満席となっているのかもしれませんが、もしかしたらどなたかの登録がキャンセルされているかもしれませんので、空きがあるかどうかを教えていただけませんか。

よろしくお願いいたします。

Stan Kovar

Swansea City Art Centre フロア案内

The Swansea City Art Centre では、スウォンジー市民の皆さんにさまざまな芸術プログラムを提供しています。
お申込みの受付は次の四半期が始まる1カ月前から開始します。
ご質問は、Jane Milton (janemn@scac.org) までご連絡ください。

階	コース名	講師	コース開催期間	クラス人数
1階	東洋絵画	David Harrison	1月から3月	50
2階	油絵	Brigit Bedford	4月から6月	40
3階	写真	Greta Briggs	7月から9月	45
4階	陶芸	Bradley Usman	10月から12月	60

Test

5

Test 5

Questions 1-2 refer to the following description information.

HOUSTON COMPUTER SHOP

Order Number: TA31916
Customer Name: Sandra Worthwood
Device Model: OYU Gold 3
Ready By: March 21

Drop-off Date: March 15
Contact Number: (713) 355-1849
Requested Service: Monitor repair
Service Assigned To: Donna Martin

Notes: Warranty covers 75% of the total payment. Device will be picked up by Andy Stein.

---

1. Who most likely is Ms. Martin?

    (A) Ms. Worthwood's secretary
    (B) A retail sales person
    (C) An expert technician
    (D) An assembly line worker

2. According to the document, what will Ms. Worthwood most likely do?

    (A) She will deliver her device to Houston Computer Shop.
    (B) She will come back to the shop on March 21.
    (C) She will buy a new monitor.
    (D) She will pay a quarter of the total cost.

Questions 3-4 refer to the following letter.

 1分 30秒

Dear Customer,

We would like to apologize for the fact that the newest carpet you ordered is out of stock. The last one in stock was sold to a walk-in customer before we received your order via our online store. We contacted our providers about this product.

They told us that they no longer have this product in stock. We apologize for the inconvenience and confusion caused by this unexpected situation. We are taking steps to process a full refund. You will receive full refund confirmation from our support center as soon as possible. We regret that we couldn't complete your order. As this seems to be an isolated incident, we hope to have your continued patronage.

Please contact us if you need some help.

Sincerely,
Stock Mall.com

---

3. Why is the letter written?

(A) To make a reservation
(B) To ask for further information
(C) To inform inventory status
(D) To place an order

4. According to the letter, how much of a refund will the customer receive?

(A) Less than 20%
(B) More than 30%
(C) A minimum of 70%
(D) A full refund

P. 326

Questions 1-2 refer to the following description information.

HOUSTON COMPUTER SHOP

Order Number: TA31916
❶ Customer Name: Sandra Worthwood
Device Model: OYU Gold 3
Ready By: March 21

Drop-off Date: March 15
Contact Number: (713) 355-1849
❷ Requested Service: Monitor repair
❸ Service Assigned To: Donna Martin

Notes: **❹** Warranty covers 75% of the total payment. Device will be picked up by Andy Stein.

☐ drop-off date (配送の) 受取日　☐ contact number 連絡先電話番号
☐ device model 装置・部品の型式　☐ requested ご要望の　☐ service assigned to 担当者名
☐ notes 注意・留意事項　☐ warranty 保証　☐ cover (費用) を負担する　☐ payment 支払い
☐ pick up 〜を引き取る

★★☆☆☆

1. Who most likely is Ms. Martin?

   (A) Ms. Worthwood's secretary
   (B) A retail sales person
   (C) An expert technician
   (D) An assembly line worker

Martin さんはおそらくどのような人物ですか。

   (A) Worthwood さんの秘書
   (B) 小売販売員
   (C) 専門技術者
   (D) 組立ラインの作業員

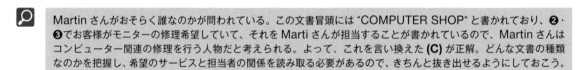

Martin さんがおそらく誰なのかが問われている。この文書冒頭には "COMPUTER SHOP" と書かれており、❷・❸でお客様がモニターの修理希望していて、それを Marti さんが担当することが書かれているので、Martin さんはコンピューター関連の修理を行う人物だと考えられる。よって、これを言い換えた **(C)** が正解。どんな文書の種類なのかを把握し、希望のサービスと担当者の関係を読み取る必要があるので、きちんと抜き出せるようにしておこう。

☐ retail 小売りの　☐ expert technician 専門技術者　☐ assembly line 組立ライン

★★★★☆

2. According to the document, what will Ms. Worthwood most likely do?

(A) She will deliver her device to Houston Computer Shop.
(B) She will come back to the shop on March 21.
(C) She will buy a new monitor.
(D) She will pay a quarter of the total cost.

文書によると、Worthwood さんは何をすると考えられますか。

(A) 自分のデバイスを Houston Computer Shop へ届ける。
(B) 3 月 21 日に再度来店する。
(C) 新しいモニターを購入する。
(D) 総額の 4 分の 1 を支払う。

文書から Worthwood さんが何をすると考えられるかが問われている。まず Worthwood さんは、❶から、この店のサービスを受ける顧客だとわかる。次に❹で「保証が支払い総額の 75 パーセントを負担する」と書かれている。ここから Worthwood さんは残りの 25 パーセントを支払う必要があるため、残金を a quarter（4 分の 1）、つまり、25 パーセントと言い換えた **(D)** が正解。(A) は彼女自身が届けるかは記載がなく、(B) は修理した装置を取りに来るのは Andy さんであるため、いずれも不正解。

□ quarter 4 分の 1　□ total cost 総額

問題 1 から 2 は次の明細情報に関するものです。

HOUSTON COMPUTER SHOP

注文番号：TA31016
お客様のお名前：Sandra Worthwood
装置のモデル：OYU Gold 3
修理完了日：3 月 21 日

お預かり日：3 月 15 日
連絡先電話番号 ：（713）355-1849
ご要望のサービス：モニターの修理
サービス担当者：Donna Martin

注意事項：保証が支払い総額の 75 パーセントを負担します。装置の受取人は Andy Stein さんです。

Questions 3-4 refer to the following letter.

Dear Customer,

❶ We would like to apologize for the fact that the newest carpet you ordered is out of stock. The last one in stock was sold to a walk-in customer before we received your order via our online store. We contacted our providers about this product.

They told us that they no longer have this product in stock. We apologize for the inconvenience and confusion caused by this unexpected situation. ❷ We are taking steps to process a full refund. ❸ You will receive full refund confirmation from our support center as soon as possible. We regret that we couldn't complete your order. As this seems to be an isolated incident, we hope to have your continued patronage.

Please contact us if you need some help.

Sincerely,
Stock Mall.com

□ apologize for 〜について謝罪する □ the fact that SV S が V であるという事実 □ out of stock 在庫切れである
□ walk-in 予約なしで入った □ via 〜を介して □ provider 供給会社 □ no longer もはや〜ではない
□ have ○○ in stock ○○の在庫がある □ inconvenience 不便 □ confusion 混乱 □ caused by 〜によって生じた
□ unexpected 予期しない □ take steps to *do* 段階を踏んで〜する □ process 〜を処理する
□ full refund 全額払い戻し □ confirmation from 確認書式 □ regret that 〜を申し訳なく思う
□ complete one's order 〜の注文を行う □ isolated 一過性の、連続していない □ incident 事案
□ continued 継続した □ patronage ご愛顧、お得意先

★★★☆☆

3. Why is the letter written?

(A) To make a reservation
(B) To ask for further information
(C) To inform inventory status
(D) To place an order

手紙はなぜ書かれましたか。

(A) 予約をするため
(B) より詳しい情報を尋ねるため
(C) 在庫状況を知らせるため
(D) 注文するため

この手紙がなぜ書かれたかが問われている。冒頭❶で「（お客様が）注文した最新のカーペットが在庫切れとなっており、申し訳ない」と伝えているので、在庫状況の伝達と謝罪が目的だとわかる。このうちの前者に相当する **(C)** が正解となる。本文の "out of stock" が inventory status となることを押さえておこう。

□ further さらなる □ inventory status 在庫状況 □ place an order 注文する

4. According to the letter, how much of a refund will the customer receive?

(A) Less than 20%
(B) More than 30%
(C) A minimum of 70%
(D) A full refund

手紙によると、顧客はどのくらいの額の返金を受け取りますか。

(A) 20 パーセントより少ない
(B) 30 パーセントより多い
(C) 少なくとも 70 パーセント
(D) 全額返金

手紙から顧客はどのくらいの額の返金を受け取るかが問われている。第 2 段落で返金について書かれており、❷で「当社から全額払い戻しの手続きをする」、❸で「全額返金の確認書を（お客様宛てに）送付する」と述べている。ここから全額返金されることがわかるため、正解は **(D)** となる。

□ less than ～より少ない　□ more than ～より多い　□ a minimum of 最低～

問題 3 から 4 は次の手紙に関するものです。

お客様

　ご注文いただきました最新のカーペットが在庫切れとなりましたことをお詫びいたします。在庫の最後の 1 点は、当社のオンラインストアでお客様のご注文を受ける前に、来店されたお客様に販売しておりました。この商品に関して仕入れ業者に連絡をいたしました。

　業者からは、この商品の在庫はないとの回答でございました。この予期せぬ事態に関し、ご不便とご迷惑をおかけいたしまして、誠に申し訳ございません。当社から全額払い戻しの手続きをいたします。速やかに当社のサポートセンターから全額返金のご確認書をお送りいたします。ご注文にお応えできず、申し訳ありません。今回の件は一過性のものと思われますので、今後ともご愛顧のほどよろしくお願いいたします。

　ご不明な点がございましたら、お問い合わせください。

　よろしくお願いいたします。
　Stock Mall.com

Notice

15 November

The president of our company has announced this morning that Julia Adler will leave her job as the finance manager of the company on 23 November. The directors showed gratitude for her great involvement in the company during the past ten years and wished her happiness in her new workplace.

We are happy to inform everyone that Lindsey Stevens will fill the position of finance manager on 24 November. Lindsey Stevens is a competent accountant. She graduated from the Faculty of Business Administration at Emory University, and for the past 14 years has worked in investment banking, and is currently with the Spandex Investment Corporation.

5. What is this notice about?

(A) The merger of the two companies
(B) Personnel changes
(C) A strategy proposal
(D) A job offer

6. What is mentioned about Lindsey Stevens?

(A) She is one of the most qualified accountants at Spandex Investment Corporation.
(B) She is admired for her contribution to the company.
(C) She is working for Spandex Investment Corporation at the moment.
(D) She will start working for this company from 23 November.

Questions 7-8 refer to the following text-message chain.

1分30秒

Single Q2

MICHAEL BENABOU 10:41 A.M.
I'm in the office supply shop to purchase copier paper. There's a big discount only for today. It's 30 percent off! Do you want me to buy several boxes? We'd save a whole bunch of money.

JEAN CAMPBELL 10:42 A.M.
Fantastic, but I'm not sure how much room we have in the supply cabinet.

MICHAEL BENABOU 10:44 A.M.
So, should I just buy what we need right now?

JEAN CAMPBELL 10:45 A.M.
Hold on. I'll check with the supervisor.

JEAN CAMPBELL 10:50 A.M.
He says to buy twice as much as we planned. We'll find a place to store all of it.

MICHAEL BENABOU 10:53 A.M.
Great. I'll be back to the office in 30 minutes.

JEAN CAMPBELL 10:54 A.M.
It'll probably take me at least that long to make some room in the cabinet.

---

7. What does Mr. Benabou suggest?

(A) Asking for a price quote
(B) Shopping at a different store
(C) Negotiating for better shipping rates
(D) Taking advantage of a sale

8. At 10:45 A.M., what does Ms. Campbell mean when she writes, "Hold on"?

(A) She will make room to store some supplies.
(B) She needs time to ask about the issue.
(C) She disagrees with a recommendation.
(D) She would like to check on the location of a cabinet.

P. 332

Questions 5-6 refer to the following notice.

Notice

15 November

❶ The president of our company has announced this morning that Julia Adler will leave her job as the finance manager of the company on 23 November. The directors showed gratitude for her great involvement in the company during the past ten years and wished her happiness in her new workplace.

We are happy to inform everyone that Lindsay Stevens will fill the position of finance manager on 24 November. Lindsay Stevens is a competent accountant. ❷ She graduated from the Faculty of Business Administration at Emory University, and for the past 14 years has worked in investment banking, ❸ and is currently with the Spandex Investment Corporation.

□ president 社長 □ leave one's job 仕事を辞める □ finance manager 財務責任者
□ director 取締役、経営幹部 □ show gratitude for ～に対して感謝を示す □ involvement 関与
□ wish one's happiness ～の幸運を願う □ workplace 職場 □ fill the position 職務を果たす
□ competent 有能な □ accountant 会計士 □ graduate from ～を卒業する
□ investment banking 投資銀行

★★☆☆☆

5. What is this notice about?

(A) The merger of the two companies
(B) Personnel changes
(C) A strategy proposal
(D) A job offer

これは何についてのお知らせですか。

(A) ２つの会社の合併
(B) 人事異動
(C) 戦略の提案
(D) 求人

この文書が何についてのお知らせなのかが問われている。❶で「Julia Adler さんが財務責任者を辞任することを社長が発表した」と述べた後、その後任者について触れていることから、人事異動だとわかる。よって **(B)** が正解となる。

□ merger 企業の合併 □ personnel changes 人事異動 □ strategy 戦略 □ proposal 提案 □ job offer 求人

6. What is mentioned about Lindsey Stevens?

(A) She is one of the most qualified accountants at Spandex Investment Corporation.

(B) She is admired for her contribution to the company.

(C) She is working for Spandex Investment Corporation at the moment.

(D) She will start working for this company from 23 November.

Lindsay Stevens さんについて何が言及されていますか。

(A) Spandex Investment Corporation で最も適任の会計士の一人である。

(B) 会社への貢献が称賛されている。

(C) 現在 Spandex Investment Corporation で働いている。

(D) 11 月 23 日からこの会社で働き始める。

Lindsay Stevens さんについて何を述べられているかを問う選択肢照合型の問題。❷で Lindsay Stevens さんの経歴が書かれており、❸で「現在は Spandex Investment Corporation に所属している」と述べられているため、**(C)** が正解となる。❸の "is currently with" が **(C)** では at the moment と言い換えられていることにも注目。(A) 最も適任、(B) 会社への貢献、については触れられておらず、(D) は 23 日ではなく 24 日に働き始めるので、それぞれ不正解。

□ qualified 適任の   □ admire ～を称賛する   □ contribution to ～への貢献   □ at the moment 現在

問題 5 から 6 は次のお知らせに関するものです。

お知らせ

11 月 15 日

当社の社長が、11 月 23 日に、Julia Adler さんが財務責任者の職を辞任することを今朝発表しました。取締役会は、彼女の過去 10 年間における会社への多大な関与に感謝し、新しい職場での成功を願っていると述べました。

11 月 24 日に Lindsay Stevens さんが財務責任者に着任することを皆さんにお知らせします。Lindsay Stevens は有能な会計士です。彼女は Emory 大学の経営学部を卒業し、14 年間投資銀行で勤務、現在は Spandex Investment Corporation に所属しています。

Questions 7-8 refer to the following text-message chain.

MICHAEL BENABOU 10:41 A.M.
I'm in the office supply shop to purchase copier paper. ❶ There's a big discount only for today. It's 30 percent off! ❷ Do you want me to buy several boxes? We'd save a whole bunch of money.

JEAN CAMPBELL 10:42 A.M.
Fantastic, but I'm not sure how much room we have in the supply cabinet.

MICHAEL BENABOU 10:44 A.M.
❸ So, should I just buy what we need right now?

JEAN CAMPBELL 10:45 A.M.
❹ Hold on. ❺ I'll check with the supervisor.

JEAN CAMPBELL 10:50 A.M.
He says to buy twice as much as we planned. We'll find a place to store all of it.

MICHAEL BENABOU 10:53 A.M.
Great. I'll be back to the office in 30 minutes.

JEAN CAMPBELL 10:54 A.M.
It'll probably take me at least that long to make some room in the cabinet.

☐ office supply 事務用品　☐ several 複数のもの　☐ a whole bunch of 非常に多くの　☐ fantastic 素晴らしい
☐ I'm not sure わからない　☐ supply cabinet 備品棚　☐ right now 今、現時点で　☐ hold on 待つ
☐ supervisor 監督者、上司　☐ twice as much as ～の2倍の量　☐ at least 少なくとも
☐ that long それくらい長く

★★☆☆☆

7. What does Mr. Benabou suggest?

(A) Asking for a price quote
(B) Shopping at a different store
(C) Negotiating for better shipping rates
(D) Taking advantage of a sale

Benabou さんは何を提案していますか。

(A) 価格の見積もりの依頼をすること
(B) 別の店で買い物をすること
(C) 配送料を値切るように交渉すること
(D) セールを有効に利用すること

Benabou さんは何を提案しているかが問われている。Benabou さんは❶・❷で「コピー用紙が割引されているので、数箱か買おうか」とセール品への対応を提案している。以上より、このセール品への対応を take advantage of で表現した **(D)** が正解となる。

☐ ask for ～を求める　☐ price quote 価格見積もり　☐ negotiate for ～を交渉する　☐ shipping rate 配送料金
☐ take advantage of ～有効利用する

8. At 10:45 A.M., what does Ms. Campbell mean when she writes, "Hold on"?

 (A) She will make room to store some supplies.
 (B) She needs time to ask about the issue.
 (C) She disagrees with a recommendation.
 (D) She would like to check on the location of a cabinet.

午前 10 時 45 分に、Campbell さんは "Hold on" という発言で、何を意味していますか。

 (A) 備品を収納するための場所を確保する。
 (B) 案件について問うための時間が必要である。
 (C) 推奨に同意しない。
 (D) 棚の位置を確認したい。

意図問題。問われている表現❹は「待ってほしい」とお願いしている表現。その前後❸・❺も含めてみてみると、❸「必要なものを買うか？」→❹「待ってほしい」→❺「上司に確認する」と、問われている案件について、「他の人に尋ねるので少し時間がかかるから待ってほしい」という意図で伝えていることがわかる。以上より、現在の案件を "issue" と言い換えた **(B)** が正解となる。意図問題は、問われている表現の前後でどういう状況かを把握しながら解く必要がある。

☐ make room 余裕を作る   ☐ supply 備品   ☐ issue 課題   ☐ disagree with ～に反対する

問題 7 から 8 は次のテキストメッセージのやりとりに関するものです。

MICHAEL BENABOU 午前 10 時 41 分
事務用品店にコピー用紙を買いに来ています。店が今日だけ大安売りをしています。30 パーセント引です！ 数箱買っていきましょうか？ かなりの金額の節約になります。

JEAN CAMPBELL 午前 10 時 42 分
とてもいいと思いますが、備品棚にどのくらいスペースの余裕があるかが心配です。

MICHAEL BENABOU 午前 10 時 44 分
では、今必要なぶんだけ買うことにしましょうか？

JEAN CAMPBELL 午前 10 時 45 分
少し待ってください。上司に確認します。

JEAN CAMPBELL 午前 10 時 50 分
「予定の 2 倍買ってください」とのことです。全部収納する場所は確保します。

MICHAEL BENABOU 午前 10 時 53 分
了解しました。30 分後に事務所に戻ります。

JEAN CAMPBELL 午前 10 時 54 分
こちらも棚にスペースを空けるのに、少なくともそのくらいの時間がかかると思います。

Questions 9-11 refer to the following article.

 2分45秒

Sydney (February 14)—Beginning three years ago, Courtney Mart started its new strategic effort to open 30 marts in previously unopened markets. Until now, customer response to Courtney Mart in international markets has been much better than in its home country of Australia. In fact, the number of new membership applications within the first six months of a shop's opening has been much larger abroad than in Australia. One reason may be the excitement generated when a new commercial concept is introduced to foreign consumers.

—[1]—. By offering superior merchandise at affordable prices, Courtney Mart is also managing to preserve these new members effectively. Its international membership renewal rate has grown to an impressive 89.2%. —[2]—. Rising membership retention rates are also contributing to an increase in overall net sales at Courtney Mart's international stores. —[3]—. Net sales in Oceania markets are growing at an average of 9% per year, while domestic net sales are growing at an average of 6.1%. —[4]—.

9. What is the article about?

(A) A company's global expansion
(B) A mart's relocation
(C) A successful advertising campaign
(D) An effort to increase foreign exports

10. According to the article, what is NOT true about Courtney Mart?

(A) It is experiencing financial growth.
(B) Its domestic sales are decreasing.
(C) It keeps the majority of its members.
(D) It carries cheaply priced products.

11. In which of the positions marked [1], [2], [3], and [4] does the following sentence best belong?

"This is clear evidence that Courtney Mart's plan to break into international markets is rapidly driving the company's growth."

(A) [1]
(B) [2]
(C) [3]
(D) [4]

P. 336

Questions 9-11 refer to the following article.

Sydney (February 14)—❶ Beginning three years ago, Courtney Mart started its new strategic effort to open 30 marts in previously unopened markets. ❷ Until now, customer response to Courtney Mart in international markets has been much better than in its home country of Australia. In fact, the number of new membership applications within the first six months of a shop's opening has been much larger abroad than in Australia. One reason may be the excitement generated when a new commercial concept is introduced to foreign consumers.

—[1]—. ❸ By offering superior merchandise at affordable prices, ❹ Courtney Mart is also managing to preserve these new members effectively. ❺ Its international membership renewal rate has grown to an impressive 89.2%. —[2]—. ❻ Rising membership retention rates are also contributing to an increase in overall net sales at Courtney Mart's international stores. —[3]—. ❼ Net sales in Oceania markets are growing at an average of 9% per year, while domestic net sales are growing at an average of 6.1%. —[4]—.

☐ strategic effort 戦略的な取り組み　☐ mart 店舗　☐ previously 過去に　☐ unopened 開業していない
☐ much（比較級を強調して）ずっと　☐ home country 母国　☐ membership application 会員申請
☐ abroad 海外で　☐ excitement 興奮　☐ generate ～をもたらす　☐ commercial 商業的な　☐ concept 概念
☐ superior 優れた　☐ merchandise 商品　☐ at affordable prices 手ごろな価格で
☐ manage to do 何とかして～する　☐ preserve ～を保存する　☐ effectively 効果的に　☐ renewal rate 更新費用
☐ impressive 顕著な　☐ rising 上昇している　☐ retention rates 維持率　☐ contribute to ～に貢献する
☐ increase in ～の増加　☐ overall 全体の　☐ domestic 国内の　☐ net sales 純売上高

★★★★★

9. What is the article about?

(A) A company's global expansion
(B) A mart's relocation
(C) A successful advertising campaign
(D) An effort to increase foreign exports

何についての記事ですか。

(A) 会社の海外展開
(B) 店舗の移転
(C) 成功した広告キャンペーン
(D) 外国からの輸出を増やす努力

何についての記事かが問われている。❶で、「Courtney Mart 社は未開拓市場に新たに出店」、❷で「同社の国際市場における顧客の反応は母国より好意的」とあるため、ある会社が海外へ進出していく記事であることがわかる。よって正解は (A)。新規出店であり移転ではないため、(B) は不正解。

☐ expansion 拡大、展開　☐ relocation 移転　☐ export 輸出

★★★☆☆ NOT 問題

10. According to the article, what is NOT true about Courtney Mart?

(A) It is experiencing financial growth.
(B) Its domestic sales are decreasing.
(C) It keeps the majority of its members.
(D) It carries cheaply priced products.

記事によると、Courtney Mart 社について正しくないものはどれですか。

(A) 経済的な成長を遂げている。
(B) 国内の販売が減少している。
(C) 会員の大半を維持している。
(D) 低価格の製品を取り扱っている。

NOT 問題。Courtney Mart 社について正しくないものが問われている。❸の「手ごろな価格で優良商品を提供」が (D) に、❹・❺の「新規会員保持」と「海外会員更新率の高さ」が (C) に、❻の「会員維持率が海外店舗全体の売上高に貢献」が (A) にそれぞれ該当する。よって、残った (B) が正解。「国内の販売が減少」という記載はない。

☐ financial growth 経済成長　☐ majority 大多数　☐ carry ～を取り扱う　☐ cheaply priced 安い価格の

11. In which of the positions marked [1], [2], [3], and [4] does the following sentence best belong?

"This is clear evidence that Courtney Mart's plan to break into international markets is rapidly driving the company's growth."

(A) [1]
(B) [2]
(C) [3]
(D) [4]

次の文は [1]、[2]、[3]、[4] のどの位置に最もよく当てはまりますか。

「これは、Courtney Mart 社の国際市場参入計画が会社の成長を推進していることの明白な証拠である」

(A) [1]
(B) [2]
(C) [3]
(D) [4]

適切な文の位置を問う問題。問われている文は「これは、Courtney Mart 社の国際市場参入計画が急速に会社の成長につながっている明確な証拠である」という意味である。つまり、「この明確な証拠（＝急速な会社の成長）」がこの文の直前にあると、論理的な文意となることがわかる。記事を見ると、❼で「オセアニア市場と国内の売上高に関する年平均成長率」という具体的な成長指標が挙げられているため、これが国際市場に参入する明確な証拠だとわかる。よって正解は **(D)**。

□ evidence 証拠　□ break into ～に参入する　□ rapidly 急速に

📝 問題 9 から 11 は次の記事に関するものです。

シドニー（2 月 14 日）— 3 年前から、Courtney Mart 社は未開拓市場に新たに 30 店を出店するために新しい戦略的取り組みを始めた。これまでの Courtney Mart 社に対する国際市場における顧客の反応は、母国のオーストラリアよりもはるかに好意的である。事実、店舗が開店してからの最初の 6 カ月における新規会員申請の数は、オーストラリアよりも海外の方がはるかに多い。その理由の一つには、海外の消費者に新たな商業概念がもたらされた時の興奮があるのかもしれない

—[1]— 優れた商品を手ごろな価格で提供することにより、Courtney Mart 社は新しい会員を効果的に囲い込むこともできている。海外会員の更新率は 89.2 パーセントと顕著な伸びを見せている。—[2]— 会員維持率の上昇も Courtney Mart 社の海外店舗全体の純売上高の増加に貢献している。—[3]— オセアニア市場における純売上高は年間平均 9 パーセントの成長を遂げている一方で、国内の純売上高は平均で 6.1 パーセントの成長である。—[4]— これは、Courtney Mart 社の国際市場参入計画が会社の成長を推進していることの明白な証拠である。

Ivy Textiles Company
9900 Manchester Drive
Beaumont, TX 58414

August 2

Mr. Kevin Crisman
10 Ottinger Lane
Longview, TX 56871

Dear Mr. Crisman,

Ivy Textiles Company is pleased to offer you a job at our main Beaumont factory. If you agree to work for us, you would be a junior accounts manager and would report directly to Kathleen Zini, director of sales. You would start on September 1, and your office hours would be 7 A.M. to 4 P.M. Your monthly salary would be $2,800, to be paid weekly. After one year of employment, you would be granted two paid weeks of vacation each year.

If the terms stated above are acceptable, please sign and return the enclosed contract to my secretary, Ms. Mary Cooper, at the corporate office in Beaumont, by August 16. We suggest that you keep a copy of this letter and all other documents for your personal use.

While we do not reimburse moving expenses, our relocation consultant Mr. Nathan Ackerman would be happy to assist you in locating a place to live that suits your needs and can help you contact moving services. You can contact Mr. Ackerman at n.ackerman@ivytextiles.com.

If you have any questions, please feel free to contact me at (870) 555-8215.

We know that you will be an asset to our company, and we look forward to you joining us!

Sincerely,

Kurt Bernard
Personnel Manager

12. Why was the letter written?

(A) To describe the business of Ivy Textiles Company
(B) To advise Mr. Crisman that his salary amount will change
(C) To go over details regarding joining a company
(D) To confirm the date of Mr. Crisman's job interview

13. What does Mr. Bernard recommend that Mr. Crisman do?

(A) Tour the factory in Beaumont
(B) Schedule an appointment with Ms. Cooper
(C) Retain a copy of the documents
(D) Make vacation plans in advance

14. What is suggested about Mr. Ackerman?

(A) He is familiar with the housing market in Beaumont.
(B) He is not an employee of Ivy Textiles Company.
(C) He is Mr. Bernard's secretary.
(D) He arranges reimbursement of relocation expenses for new employees.

P. 340

Questions 12-14 refer to the following letter.

Ivy Textiles Company
9900 Manchester Drive
Beaumont, TX 58414

August 2

Mr. Kevin Crisman
10 Ottinger Lane
Longview, TX 56871

Dear Mr. Crisman,

Ivy Textiles Company is pleased to offer you a job at our main Beaumont factory. If you agree to work for us, you would be a junior accounts manager and would report directly to Kathleen Zini, director of sales. You would start on September 1, and your office hours would be 7 A.M. to 4 P.M. Your monthly salary would be $2,800, to be paid weekly. After one year of employment, you would be granted two paid weeks of vacation each year.

❶ If the terms stated above are acceptable, please sign and return the enclosed contract to my secretary, Ms. Mary Cooper, at the corporate office in Beaumont, by August 16. ❷ We suggest that you keep a copy of this letter and all other documents for your personal use.

❸ While we do not reimburse moving expenses, our relocation consultant Mr. Nathan Ackerman would be happy to assist you in locating a place to live that suits your needs and can help you contact moving services. You can contact Mr. Ackerman at n.ackerman@ivytextiles.com.

If you have any questions, please feel free to contact me at (870) 555-8215.

We know that you will be an asset to our company, and we look forward to you joining us!

Sincerely,

Kurt Bernard
Personnel Manager

☐ junior ～の職の補佐   ☐ account 顧客   ☐ report directly to ～の直属となる   ☐ monthly salary 月給
☐ grant ～を付与する   ☐ term 条件   ☐ above 上述の   ☐ enclosed 同封された   ☐ corporate office 本社
☐ personal use 個人的使用   ☐ reimburse ～を払い戻す   ☐ moving expense 引っ越し費用
☐ relocation 移転   ☐ asset 貴重なもの（人材、技術）   ☐ look forward to ～を楽しみにしている

12. Why was the letter written?

(A) To describe the business of Ivy Textiles Company
(B) To advise Mr. Crisman that his salary amount will change
(C) To go over details regarding joining a company
(D) To confirm the date of Mr. Crisman's job interview

この手紙はなぜ書かれたのですか。

(A) Ivy Textiles Company の事業内容を説明するため
(B) Crisman さんの給与額が変更になることを通知するため
(C) 入社に関する詳細を確認するため
(D) Crisman さんの面接の日程を確認するため

🔍 どうしてこの手紙が書かれたのかが問われている。この文書は第1段落で仕事のオファーを出し、その後の第2段落の❶で「条件に同意したら、同封の契約書に署名し、期日まで返送してほしい」とお願いしている。つまり、入社に同意するか諸条件を検討してほしいということを知らせる手紙だとわかるので、正解はそれを言い換えた **(C)** となる。通常、目的は第1段落にくることが多いが、この手紙は第2段落に目的を記載しているため、注意して読んでいこう。

✎ ☐ amount 額　☐ go over 〜を検討する　☐ detail 詳細　☐ regarding 〜に関して　☐ confirm 〜を確認する

13. What does Mr. Bernard recommend that Mr. Crisman do?

(A) Tour the factory in Beaumont
(B) Schedule an appointment with Ms. Cooper
(C) Retain a copy of the documents
(D) Make vacation plans in advance

Bernard さんは Crisman さんに何をするように勧めていますか。

(A) Beaumont の工場を見学する
(B) Cooper さんとの面会を計画する
(C) 書類のコピーを保管する
(D) 事前に休暇の計画を立てる

🔍 Bernard さんが Crisman さんに勧めていることが問われている。手紙の差出人である Bernard さんは Crisman さんに❷で「この手紙とその他の書類は、個人的に使用するためにコピーを取っておくことを勧める」と述べている。ここから、それを言い換えた **(C)** が正解となる。❷の "suggest" が設問では recommend に言い換えられている。この言い換えに気づいていることがカギとなる。

✎ ☐ tour 〜を見学する　☐ retain 〜を保持・保有する　☐ in advance 前もって

14. What is suggested about Mr. Ackerman?

(A) He is familiar with the housing market in Beaumont.
(B) He is not an employee of Ivy Textiles Company.
(C) He is Mr. Bernard's secretary.
(D) He arranges reimbursement of relocation expenses for new employees.

Ackerman 氏について示唆されていることは何ですか。

(A) 彼は Beaumont の住宅市場に精通している。
(B) 彼は Ivy Textiles Company の社員ではない。
(C) 彼は Bernard さんの秘書である。
(D) 彼は新入社員の移転費用の払い戻しを手配している。

Ackerman 氏について示唆されていることを問う選択肢照合型の問題。第 3 段落で Ackerman 氏に関する記載があり、❸で「当社の移転コンサルタントである Ackerman 氏が、要望に合った住居を探し、引っ越しサービスの手伝いをする」とある。ここから、Ackerman 氏が、この周辺である Beaumont 地区の、住居探しや引っ越しに精通しているのを示唆していることがわかる。以上より正解は **(A)** となる。「業務経験がある＝精通している可能性がある」というように読み解こう。

☐ be familiar with ～に精通している　☐ housing market 住宅市場　☐ reimbursement 払い戻し
☐ relocation expense 移転費用

Ivy Textiles Company
9900 Manchester Drive
Beaumont, TX 58414

8 月 2 日

Kevin Crisman 氏
10 Ottinger Lane
Longview, TX 56871

Crisman さんへ

Ivy Textiles Company は、あなたに Beaumont の本社工場での仕事を提供したいと考えています。あなたが当社で働くことに同意された場合、あなたは顧客管理補佐として、営業部長の Kathleen Zini に直属することになります。仕事は 7 月 1 日に始まり、勤務時間は午前 7 時から午後 4 時です。月給は 2,800 ドルで、週払いです。入社 1 年後には、毎年 2 週間の有給休暇が与えられます。

上記の条件に同意いただけましたら、同封の契約書にご署名の上、8 月 16 日までに Beaumont の本社にいる私の秘書、Mary Cooper さんにご返送ください。この手紙とその他の書類は、個人的に使用するためにコピーを取っておくことをお勧めします。

当社では引っ越し費用の払い戻しは行っておりませんが、当社の移転コンサルタントである Nathan Ackerman 氏が、あなたの要望に合った住居を探し、引っ越しサービスに連絡するお手伝いをいたします。Ackerman 氏への連絡先は、n.ackerman@ivytextiles.com です。

何か質問がありましたら、(870) 555-8215 へお気軽にお問い合わせください。

あなたが当社の財産になることを確信しており、あなたの入社を楽しみにしています！

敬具

Kurt Bernard
人事部長

Questions 15-17 refer to the following schedule.

 2分45秒

Event Calendar for Melbourne Performing Arts Centre (MPAC) in Melbourne, Victoria.	
The Gareth Theatre Association presents *The Blue Sheba* **Wednesday, August 6, 6:00 p.m.** **Admission: $20 ~ $30** In response to the demands of a large number of fans, the dance team is coming back to repeat their wonderful performance at MPAC. The seats for the performance sold out immediately, in Sydney, Perth, Brisbane and Canberra, and Hilda Simonski of the Midland Express called this the most entertaining dance company of the last few decades.	**The Kent Tap Troupe presents** *Vivid Dreams* **Friday, August 22, to Monday, August 25, 6:30 p.m.** This comical play realizes the interesting idea that an ancient prophet appears in modern times. The playwright, Tim O'Connell, was chosen this year for the prestigious Mariana Award for Best New Comedy. Performances are made possible by generous monetary donations from Deluca Clinic and Bailey Bus Lines.
Monique Larson's "Old English" Tour **Wednesday, August 13, to Saturday, August 16, 6:00 p.m.** **Admission: $20** The show boasts a famous line-up of Melissa Rodriguez, Anthony Ritolo and Evan Harris. These British comedians will help you laugh until you cry.	**12th Annual MPAC Festival Sponsored by West Preece Drive** **Monday, August 25, 9:00 a.m. to 6:00 p.m.** **Admission: adult $10 children $5** Come and hear your favourite local musical groups including the Erica Lewis Band and Patricia Leigh.

Event tickets can be bought at the MPAC ticket window or online at www.mpac.net. More details about our autumn events, which begin November 1, will be posted on our Web site on September 12.

15. According to the schedule, what is true about MPAC?

    (A) It is now only featuring performers from Victoria.
    (B) It will be closed for remodeling in September.
    (C) It holds events that receive financial backing from businesses.
    (D) It provides multiple events that are open to everyone at no cost.

16. What is suggested about the Gareth Theatre Association?

    (A) It has performed in Melbourne before.
    (B) It recently recruited a new choreographer.
    (C) It is now hiring new dancers.
    (D) Its performances have received bad reviews.

17. Who will NOT perform at an MPAC event in August?

    (A) A dance group
    (B) A musical group
    (C) A comedy group
    (D) An acrobatic group

P. 346

Questions 15-17 refer to the following schedule.

❶ Event Calendar for Melbourne Performing Arts Centre (MPAC) in Melbourne, Victoria.	
❷ **The Gareth Theatre Association presents** *The Blue Sheba* **Wednesday, August 6, 6:00 p.m.** **Admission: $20 ~ $30** ❸ In response to the demands of a large number of fans, the dance team is coming back to repeat their wonderful performance at MPAC. The seats for the performance sold out immediately, in Sydney, Perth, Brisbane and Canberra, and Hilda Simonski of the Midland Express called this the most entertaining ❹ dance company of the last few decades.	❺ **The Kent Tap Troupe presents** *Vivid Dreams* **Friday, August 22, to Monday, August 25, 6:30 p.m.** This comical play realizes the interesting idea that an ancient prophet appears in modern times. The playwright, Tim O'Connell, was chosen this year for the prestigious Mariana Award for Best New Comedy. ❻ Performances are made possible by generous monetary donations from Deluca Clinic and Bailey Bus Lines.
Monique Larson's "Old English" Tour **Wednesday, August 13, to Saturday, August 16, 6:00 p.m.** **Admission: $20** The show boasts a famous line-up of Melissa Rodriguez, Anthony Ritolo and Evan Harris. These British ❼ comedians will help you laugh until you cry.	**12th Annual MPAC Festival Sponsored by West Preece Drive** **Monday, August 25, 9:00 a.m. to 6:00 p.m.** **Admission: adult $10 children $5** Come and hear your favourite local ❽ musical groups including the Erica Lewis Band and Patricia Leigh.

Event tickets can be bought at the MPAC ticket window or online at www.mpac.net. More details about our autumn events, which begin November 1, will be posted on our Web site on September 12.

□ in response to ～に応えるために □ demand 要求 □ a large number of たくさんの □ immediately すぐに
□ call Ａ Ｂ ＡをＢと呼ぶ・評価する □ the last few decades 最近数十年 □ comical play 喜劇
□ ancient 古代の □ prophet 預言者 □ modern times 現代 □ playwright 脚本家、劇作家
□ prestigious 権威ある □ generous 惜しみない □ monetary donation 寄付金 □ boast ～を自慢する
□ line-up 顔ぶれ □ ticket window チケット売り場・窓口 □ detail 詳細 □ post ～を掲載する

15. According to the schedule, what is true about MPAC?

(A) It is now only featuring performers from Victoria.
(B) It will be closed for remodeling in September.
(C) It holds events that receive financial backing from businesses.
(D) It provides multiple events that are open to everyone at no cost.

予定表によると、MPAC に関して、正しいこととは何ですか。

(A) 現在、ビクトリア州出身の演者のみが出演している。
(B) 9 月に改装のため休館する。
(C) 企業から財政的援助を受けたイベントを開催する。
(D) 誰でも無料で参加できるイベントを多数用意している。

MPAC に関して正しいことが何かを問う選択肢照合型の問題。❺の "The Kent Tap Troupe presents Vivid Dreams" の欄を見ていくと、❻で「公演はある会社団体からの寄付により実現」とあるため、これを言い換えた **(C)** が正解。**(C)** backing とは「支援、援助」という意味。(A) ビクトリア出身者の演者のみ出演、(B) 9 月改装、はそれぞれ記載がない。(D) 無料イベントは、4 つのイベントのうち金額記載のないものが 1 つしかなく、多数とは言えないため、いずれも不正解となる。

☐ feature 〜を出演させる　☐ remodeling 改装　☐ financial backing 資金支援　☐ multiple 多数の
☐ open to 〜に公開する　☐ at no cost 無料で

16. What is suggested about the Gareth Theatre Association?

(A) It has performed in Melbourne before.
(B) It recently recruited a new choreographer.
(C) It is now hiring new dancers.
(D) Its performances have received bad reviews.

Gareth Theatre Association について何が示唆されていますか。

(A) 以前メルボルンで公演を行ったことがある。
(B) 最近、新しい振付師を採用した。
(C) 現在、新しいダンサーを採用している。
(D) 公演は悪い評価を受けている。

❷の欄に記載がある Gareth Theatre Association について何が推測されるかを問う選択肢照合型問題。❸で、この団体が「多数のファンの要望に応え、MPAC でパフォーマンスを再び披露するため帰ってくる」とある。次に、❶から MPAC がメルボルンで開催されることがわかる。以上から、この団体はかつてメルボルンでパフォーマンスを行ったことがわかる。よって正解は **(A)**。根拠となる情報が分散しているため注意して読んでいこう。(B) 振付師の採用、(C) ダンサーの採用、(D) 悪い感想については、それぞれ記載がないため不正解。

☐ recruit 〜を採用する　☐ choreographer 振付師　☐ review 感想、批評

17. Who will NOT perform at an MPAC event in August?

(A) A dance group
(B) A musical group
(C) A comedy group
(D) An acrobatic group

8月に MPAC のイベントに出演しないのは誰ですか。

(A) ダンスグループ
(B) 音楽グループ
(C) コメディーグループ
(D) 曲芸グループ

NOT 問題。8月の MPAC イベントに出演しないのは誰かが問われている。❹が (A) に、❼が (C) に、❽が (B) に、それぞれ当てはまる。残った **(D)** に該当する記載がないため、これが正解。❺のイベントの説明文の最初に "comical play" という表現もあるため、これが (C) に該当すると捉えても OK。

☐ comedy 喜劇　☐ acrobatic 曲芸の

問題 **15** から **17** は次の予定表に関するものです。

Melbourne Performing Arts Centre (MPAC) イベントカレンダー　ビクトリア州メルボルン	
Gareth Theatre Association による *The Blue Sheba* 8月6日水曜日、午後6時 入場料：20ドルから30ドル 大勢のファンの要望に応えて、MPAC での素晴らしいパフォーマンスを再び披露するため、ダンスチームが帰ってきます。シドニー、パース、ブリスベン、キャンベラでの公演の座席はすぐに完売し、Midland Express の Hilda Simonski 氏は、このチームはこの数十年間で最も見ごたえのあるダンス集団であると評しました。	Kent Tap Troupe による *Vivid Dreams* 8月22日金曜日から8月25日月曜日、午後6時半 この喜劇は、古代の預言者が現代に現れるという面白いアイデアを具現化しています。この劇作家の Tim O'Connell は権威ある Mariana Award で今年の最優秀新人コメディー賞に選ばれました。公演は、Deluca Clinic と Bailey Bus Lines からの多額の寄付により実現しています。
Monique Larson による "Old English" ツアー 8月13日水曜日から8月16日土曜日、午後6時 入場料：20ドル このショーは Melissa Rodriguez、Anthony Ritolo、Evan Harris という有名な顔ぶれが自慢です。これらのイギリス人コメディアンはあなたが涙を流すほど笑わせてくれるでしょう。	West Preece Drive 主催による第12回年次 MPAC Festival 8月25日月曜日、午前9時から午後6時まで 入場料：大人10ドル 子ども5ドル Erica Lewis Band や Patricia Leigh など、お気に入りの地元の音楽グループの演奏を聴きにご来場ください。

イベントのチケットは MPAC のチケット窓口かオンライン www.mpac.net で購入できます。11月1日から始まる秋のイベントに関する詳細な情報は、9月12日にウェブサイトに掲載されます。

Questions 18-21 refer to the following online chat discussion.

4分00秒

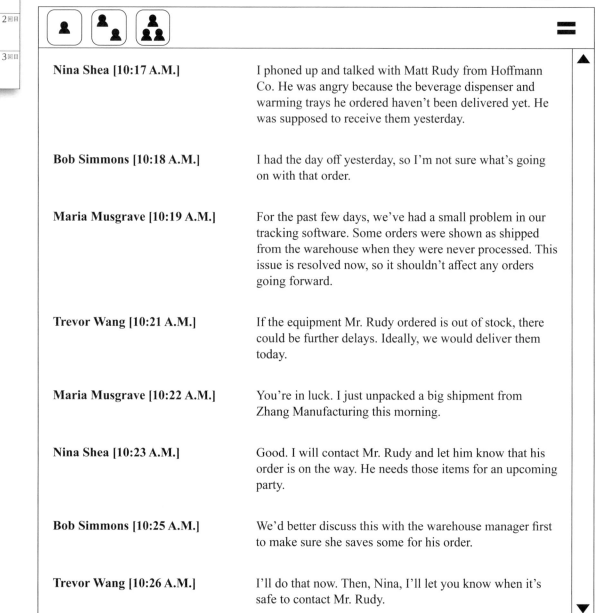

Nina Shea [10:17 A.M.]	I phoned up and talked with Matt Rudy from Hoffmann Co. He was angry because the beverage dispenser and warming trays he ordered haven't been delivered yet. He was supposed to receive them yesterday.
Bob Simmons [10:18 A.M.]	I had the day off yesterday, so I'm not sure what's going on with that order.
Maria Musgrave [10:19 A.M.]	For the past few days, we've had a small problem in our tracking software. Some orders were shown as shipped from the warehouse when they were never processed. This issue is resolved now, so it shouldn't affect any orders going forward.
Trevor Wang [10:21 A.M.]	If the equipment Mr. Rudy ordered is out of stock, there could be further delays. Ideally, we would deliver them today.
Maria Musgrave [10:22 A.M.]	You're in luck. I just unpacked a big shipment from Zhang Manufacturing this morning.
Nina Shea [10:23 A.M.]	Good. I will contact Mr. Rudy and let him know that his order is on the way. He needs those items for an upcoming party.
Bob Simmons [10:25 A.M.]	We'd better discuss this with the warehouse manager first to make sure she saves some for his order.
Trevor Wang [10:26 A.M.]	I'll do that now. Then, Nina, I'll let you know when it's safe to contact Mr. Rudy.

18. What kind of business most likely is Hoffmann Co.?

    (A) A catering company
    (B) An insurance planner
    (C) A courier service
    (D) A packaging manufacturer

19. What has caused a delay?

    (A) A late payment
    (B) A software malfunction
    (C) Some damaged merchandise
    (D) Some absent staff

20. At 10:22 A.M., what does Ms. Musgrave mean when she writes, "You're in luck"?

    (A) Some repairs have been made.
    (B) She is free to work overtime.
    (C) Some items are available.
    (D) She found a missing order.

21. What will Mr. Wang most likely do next?

    (A) Issue a refund
    (B) Close the warehouse
    (C) Contact a customer
    (D) Call the warehouse manager

Single Q4

P. 352

Questions 18-21 refer to the following online chat discussion.

Nina Shea [10:17 A.M.]	I phoned up and talked with Matt Rudy from Hoffmann Co. ❶ He was angry because the beverage dispenser and warming trays he ordered haven't been delivered yet. He was supposed to receive them yesterday.
Bob Simmons [10:18 A.M.]	I had the day off yesterday, so I'm not sure what's going on with that order.
Maria Musgrave [10:19 A.M.]	❷ For the past few days, we've had a small problem in our tracking software. Some orders were shown as shipped from the warehouse when they were never processed. This issue is resolved now, so it shouldn't affect any orders going forward.
Trevor Wang [10:21 A.M.]	If the equipment Mr. Rudy ordered is out of stock, there could be further delays. ❸ Ideally, we would deliver them today.
Maria Musgrave [10:22 A.M.]	❹ You're in luck. ❺ I just unpacked a big shipment from Zhang Manufacturing this morning.
Nina Shea [10:23 A.M.]	❻ Good. I will contact Mr. Rudy and let him know that his order is on the way. ❼ He needs those items for an upcoming party.
Bob Simmons [10:25 A.M.]	❽ We'd better discuss this with the warehouse manager first to make sure she saves some for his order.
Trevor Wang [10:26 A.M.]	❾ I'll do that now. Then, Nina, I'll let you know when it's safe to contact Mr. Rudy.

☐ phone up ～に電話をする　☐ beverage dispenser 飲料抽出器具、ドリンクディスペンサー　☐ warming 保温用
☐ be supposed to *do* ～する予定になっている　☐ day off 休暇　☐ tracking software 追跡ソフト
☐ resolve ～を解決する　☐ affect ～に影響する　☐ go forward 今後に進む　☐ out of stock 在庫切れである
☐ further さらなる　☐ ideally 理想的には　☐ unpacked ～を開梱する　☐ upcoming 今度の
☐ we'd better *do* ～した方がよい　☐ first to *do* まず～するために

★★★★☆

18. What kind of business most likely is Hoffmann Co.?

(A) A catering company
(B) An insurance planner
(C) A courier service
(D) A packaging manufacturer

Hoffmann 社はどんな会社であると考えられますか。

(A) ケータリング会社
(B) 保険プランナー
(C) 宅配便
(D) 包装資材メーカー

Hoffmann 社はおそらくどんな会社かが問われている。冒頭❶で、Hoffmann 社の担当者に関連した話題を切り出し、「注文したドリンクディスペンサーと保温トレー」と述べている。そして❼で「今度のパーティーに使用」とある。ドリンクを提供し、保温トレーをパーティーに使用するということから、**(A)** が正解と考えられる。設問の most likely は、はっきりとした根拠は明示されていないが、推測して読み解く問題だ。今回のように手掛かりが離れている場合は、注意して解いていこう。

✎ ☐ courier service 宅配サービス　☐ packaging manufacturer 包装資材メーカー

....

★★★☆☆

19. What has caused a delay?

(A) A late payment
(B) A software malfunction
(C) Some damaged merchandise
(D) Some absent staff

遅延の原因は何ですか。

(A) 支払いの遅延
(B) ソフトウェアの誤作動
(C) 破損した商品
(D) 休んでいる従業員

Q 遅延の原因が問われている。Musgrave さんが、❷で「この数日、追跡ソフトウェアに小さな問題があった」「注文が処理の前に出荷されたことになっていた」と述べている。よって、ソフトウェアに問題があったことを言い換えている **(B)** が正解。

✎ ☐ late payment 支払い遅延　☐ malfunction 故障、誤作動　☐ absent 欠席の、休んでいる

....

★★★☆☆ 意図問題

20. At 10:22 A.M., what does Ms. Musgrave mean when she writes, "You're in luck"?

(A) Some repairs have been made.
(B) She is free to work overtime.
(C) Some items are available.
(D) She found a missing order.

午前 10 時 22 分に、Musgrave さんは "You're in luck" という発言で、何を意味していますか。

(A) 修理が行われた。
(B) 残業を自由にすることができる。
(C) いくつかの商品は在庫がある。
(D) 行方不明だった注文品を見つけた。

意図問題。問われている❹は「運がいい」という意味。どういう意図か前後を見ていくと、❸～❻で、❸「本日品物を届けたい」→❹「運がいい」＋❺「ちょうど大きな荷物を開けたところだ」→❻「よかった」という流れになっている。つまり、「不具合で届けられなかった品物が手に入りそうだ」という意図で述べたことがわかる。以上から、正解は **(C)**。

✎ ☐ be free to *do* 自由に～できる　☐ missing 行方不明の

★★★☆☆

21. What will Mr. Wang most likely do next?

    (A) Issue a refund
    (B) Close the warehouse
    (C) Contact a customer
    (D) Call the warehouse manager

Wang さんは次に何をすると考えられますか。

    (A) 返金を行う
    (B) 倉庫を閉める
    (C) 顧客に連絡をする
    (D) 倉庫の管理者に電話をする

Wang さんが次に何をするかが問われている。Wang さんはチャットの最後の❾で、「私が今それをやる」と述べている。そのため、この直前を見ると、❽で Simmons さんが「手配注文用の取り置きのために、先に倉庫の管理者に相談したほうがいい」と述べているので、Wang さんはこれに対応することが考えられる。よって、連絡手段を電話という表現に変えた **(D)** が正解。

□ refund 払い戻し

問題 18 から 21 は次のオンラインチャットの話し合いに関するものです。

Nina Shea［午前 10 時 17 分］
Hoffmann 社の Matt Rudy 様にお電話をし、お話ししました。彼は注文したドリンクディスペンサーと保温トレーがまだ配達されていないことにお怒りでした。昨日受け取ることになっていました。

Bob Simmons［午前 10 時 18 分］
私は昨日は休暇をとっていたので、その注文がどうなっているのかわかりません。

Maria Musgrave［午前 10 時 19 分］
この数日、追跡ソフトウェアに小さな問題がありました。一部の注文は処理されていないのに、倉庫から出荷されたと表示されていました。この問題は今は解決しているので、今後の注文には影響がないはずです。

Trevor Wang［午前 10 時 21 分］
Rudy 様が注文した機器が在庫切れの場合、さらに遅れが生じる可能性があります。理想を言えば、今日お届けしたいと思っています。

Maria Musgrave［午前 10 時 22 分］
運がいいですね。今朝、ちょうど Zhang Manufacturing 社からの大きな荷物を開けました。

Nina Shea［午前 10 時 23 分］
よかったです。Rudy 様に連絡して、注文品が配達中だと伝えますね。今度のパーティーでその品物を必要とされています。

Bob Simmons［午前 10 時 25 分］
彼の注文用にいくつか取り置かれることを確認するために、先に倉庫の管理者に相談したほうがいいと思います。

Trevor Wang［午前 10 時 26 分］
私が今すぐにやります。そのあと、Nina さん、Rudy 様に連絡しても差し支えないとわかったらお知らせしますね。

GO ON
TO THE
NEXT PAGE!

By Samuel DeGenero

At last, after a long absence, Le Fiero has come back to Bordeaux, and it will give you one of the most impressive eating experiences in your life. At present, Le Fiero occupies a spot on the second floor of the Golden Tulip Hotel and takes full advantage of its more spacious and elegant surroundings.

The concept of Le Fiero is to focus on the meal itself. To begin with, you enter the dining room of Le Fiero through the heavy black curtains and then will find your seat. After about five minutes, you are about to enjoy a five-course meal with minimal lightning without the sound. Mobile phones and other electronic devices are kept securely in the reception area.

—[1]—. Obviously, it would be pointless to have menus in the dining room, so diners must select among the Asian, Mediterranean, and Mystery five-course menus before they are led to their table. —[2]—. When each dish arrives, you have absolutely no idea what it is, and this forces you to use only your senses of smell and taste to identify it. At several points during the meal, the members of my dining party debated what ingredients they could taste. I can wholeheartedly tell you that the food is delicious, but to discuss it in detail here would ruin the surprise! —[3]—. Reservations can be made at www.lefiero.net. —[4]—.

22. Where would this review most likely be found?

(A) In a hotel guide
(B) In a restaurant magazine
(C) In a traffic guide
(D) In a tire company guide

23. What can be inferred about Le Fiero?

(A) It is located opposite the Golden Tulip Hotel.
(B) It has several locations within Bordeaux.
(C) It recently hosted a grand opening event.
(D) It previously operated in different premises.

24. What does Mr. DeGenero suggest about the menu?

(A) It should be chosen in advance.
(B) It changes on a regular basis.
(C) It is a buffet-style menu.
(D) It contains several uncommon types of food.

25. In which of the positions marked [1], [2], [3], and [4] does the following sentence best belong?

"I would highly recommend experiencing Le Fiero for yourself."

(A) [1]
(B) [2]
(C) [3]
(D) [4]

Single Q4

P. 358

Questions 22-25 refer to the following review.

By Samuel DeGenero

❶ At last, after a long absence, Le Fiero has come back to Bordeaux, and it will give you one of the most impressive eating experiences in your life. ❷ At present, Le Fiero occupies a spot on the second floor of the Golden Tulip Hotel and takes full advantage of its more spacious and elegant surroundings.

The concept of Le Fiero is to focus on the meal itself. To begin with, you enter the dining room of Le Fiero through the heavy black curtains and then will find your seat. After about five minutes, you are about to enjoy a five-course meal with minimal lightning without the sound. Mobile phones and other electronic devices are kept securely in the reception area.

—[1]—. ❸ Obviously, it would be pointless to have menus in the dining room, so diners must select among the Asian, Mediterranean, and Mystery five-course menus before they are led to their table. —[2]—. When each dish arrives, you have absolutely no idea what it is, and this forces you to use only your senses of smell and taste to identify it. At several points during the meal, the members of my dining party debated what ingredients they could taste. ❹ I can wholeheartedly tell you that the food is delicious, but to discuss it in detail here would ruin the surprise! —[3]—. Reservations can be made at www.lefiero.net. —[4]—.

□ at last ついに □ absence 不在 □ impressive 感動的な □ occupy ～に位置する □ spot 場所
□ take full advantage of ～を十分に活用する □ spacious 広々とした □ elegant 優雅な
□ surrounding 環境 □ five-course meal 5品のコース料理 □ minimal 最低限の □ lightening 照明
□ electronic device 電子機器 □ securely 安全に □ reception area 受付 □ obviously 明らかに
□ pointless 価値がない □ Mediterranean 地中海の（料理） □ mystery 不可解な、なぞの
□ absolutely 絶対に □ have no idea わからない □ force A to *do* Aに強制的に～させる
□ senses of smell and taste 嗅覚と味覚 □ identify ～を特定する □ debate ～について議論する
□ ingredient 材料 □ wholeheartedly 心から □ ruin ～を台無しにする

★★☆☆☆

22. Where would this review most likely be found?

   (A) In a hotel guide
   (B) In a restaurant magazine
   (C) In a traffic guide
   (D) In a tire company guide

このレビューは何に掲載されていると考えられますか。

   (A) ホテルガイド
   (B) レストラン雑誌
   (C) 交通ガイド
   (D) タイヤ会社の案内

このレビューがおそらく何に掲載されているかを問う推測問題。❶で「この店はあなたに人生で最も感動的な食事体験を提供する」と述べられているため、食事を提供する施設についてのレビューだとわかる。ここから **(B)** のレストラン雑誌へのレビュー掲載と考えられるため、これが正解。

23. What can be inferred about Le Fiero?

- (A) It is located opposite the Golden Tulip Hotel.
- (B) It has several locations within Bordeaux.
- (C) It recently hosted a grand opening event.
- **(D)** It previously operated in different premises.

Le Fiero について何が推測できますか。

- (A) Golden Tulip Hotel の向かいにある。
- (B) ボルドーに何店かある。
- (C) 先日、開店記念イベントを開催した。
- **(D)** 以前は別の建物で営業していた。

Le Fiero について何が推測できるかを問う選択肢照合型問題。❶・❷で「Le Fiero が久々にボルドーに戻ってきて、現在はより広く、優雅な環境を活用」とあるので、今までより広く、優雅な環境下で食事を提供していることがわかる。ここから、過去は他の場所で営業していたことが推測されるため、正解は **(D)**。正解の根拠は❷の比較級で、「以前より広く、優雅な」という箇所を見抜くのがポイント。他の選択肢については推測される箇所がないので、いずれも不正解。

□ opposite 〜の向かい側に　□ grand opening グランドオープン　□ premises 建物の敷地、場所

24. What does Mr. DeGenero suggest about the menu?

- **(A)** It should be chosen in advance.
- (B) It changes on a regular basis.
- (C) It is a buffet-style menu.
- (D) It contains several uncommon types of food.

DeGenero さんはメニューについて何を示唆していますか。

- **(A)** 先に選択すべきである。
- (B) 定期的に変更される。
- (C) ビュッフェ形式のメニューである。
- (D) 珍しい種類の食べ物がいくつかある。

レビュー記載者の DeGenero さんがメニューについて何を示唆しているかが問われている。❸で「客はテーブルに案内される前にいくつかのコースメニューの中から選択する必要がある」と述べている。ここから、客が事前にメニューを選ぶ必要があるとわかるため、正解は **(A)**。(C) はコース料理であり、ビュッフェ形式ではない。また (B) 定期的な変更、(D) 珍しい食材に関しては記載がないので、いずれも不正解。

□ in advance 事前に　□ on a regular basis 定期的に　□ buffet-style ビュッフェ形式の　□ contain 〜を含む
□ uncommon 珍しい

25. In which of the positions marked [1], [2], [3], and [4] does the following sentence best belong?

"I would highly recommend experiencing Le Fiero for yourself."

(A)　[1]
(B)　[2]
(C)　[3]
(D)　[4]

次の文は [1]、[2]、[3]、[4] のどの位置に最もよく当てはまりますか。

「Le Fiero を自分自身で体験することを強くお勧めする」

(A)　[1]
(B)　[2]
(C)　[3]
(D)　[4]

適切な文の位置を問う問題。問われている文は、「Le Fiero を自分自身で体験することを強く勧める」とある。つまり、この文の前に体験を強く勧める理由があることがわかる。その視点で文書を読んでいくと、❹に「食事はおいしいが、ここで詳しく論じると、この驚きが台無しになる」と、敢えて自身の体験を伏せており、間接的に読者に体験を勧めていることがわかる。よって正解は **(C)** となる。

□ highly recommend ～を強く勧める

問題 22 から 25 は次のレビューに関するものです。

Samuel DeGenero 記

長期間の不在の末、ついに Le Fiero がボルドーに戻ってきた。この店はあなたに人生で最も感動的な食事体験を提供してくれるだろう。現在、Le Fiero は Golden Tulip Hotel の 2 階に位置し、より広く、優雅な環境を最大限に活用している。

Le Fiero のコンセプトは、「食事そのもの」だ。まず、重厚な黒いカーテンをくぐって Le Fiero のダイニングルームに入ると、自分の席を見つける。約 5 分後には、音楽のない中で、最小限の照明で 5 品のコース料理を楽しむことができる。携帯電話やその他の電子機器は受付で安全に保管される。

—[1]— 当然のことだが、ダイニングにメニューを置くことは意味がないので、客はテーブルに案内される前にアジア、地中海、おまかせ（ミステリー）の 5 品のコースメニューの中から選択する必要がある。 —[2]— それぞれの料理が運ばれてきても、それが何なのか見当がつかないので、嗅覚と味覚を使ってそれが何であるのかを判別しなければならない。食事中に何度か一緒に食事をしている人たちで、どの食材の味がするか議論を行った。食事は心からおいしいと断言できるが、ここで詳しく論じると、この驚きが台無しになってしまう！ —[3]— Le Fiero を自分自身で体験することを強くお勧めする。予約は www.lefiero.net から行うことができる。 —[4]—

4分00秒

Job Opening: Public Relations Supervisor

The outstanding hospital in the state, Columbus Medical Center, is looking for a public relations supervisor to work in Macon. Candidates must be willing to travel to the Brunswick office and to Columbus's smaller medical clinics in Augusta and Marrieta. The public relations supervisor will be in charge of communicating hospital announcements to media outlets.

Candidates should have not only a strong background in public speaking and journalism but also excellent communication ability. A master's degree is mandatory; knowledge in the area of hospital administration is a plus. Priority will be given to candidates who have at least five years of experience working with the media. We offer high pay and a comprehensive benefits package.

Please mail an application, which can be downloaded from our website, along with names and contact numbers of references and a résumé by June 22 to:

Adam Tyler, Personnel Manager, Columbus Medical Center
3166 Napier Ave., Macon, GA 31204

No phone applications, please.

26. Where is the job location?

    (A) Macon
    (B) Augusta
    (C) Brunswick
    (D) Marrieta

27. According to the advertisement, what is NOT a requirement of the job?

    (A) Willingness to take trips
    (B) Communication skills
    (C) A master's degree
    (D) Experience in administration

28. What must the applicant submit by June 22?

    (A) A résumé
    (B) A letter of self-introduction
    (C) A medical license
    (D) A gift certificate

29. How should a candidate apply for the position?

    (A) By visiting Columbus Medical Center
    (B) By sending a mail
    (C) By completing the online form
    (D) By calling the Personnel Manager

Single Q4

P. 364

Questions 26-29 refer to the following advertisement.

Job Opening: Public Relations Supervisor

❶ The outstanding hospital in the state, Columbus Medical Center, is looking for a public relations supervisor to work in Macon. ❷ Candidates must be willing to travel to the Brunswick office and to Columbus's smaller medical clinics in Augusta and Marrieta. The public relations supervisor will be in charge of communicating hospital announcements to media outlets.

❸ Candidates should have not only a strong background in public speaking and journalism but also excellent communication ability. ❹ A master's degree is mandatory; ❺ knowledge in the area of hospital administration is a plus. Priority will be given to candidates who have at least five years of experience working with the media. We offer high pay and a comprehensive benefits package.

❻ Please mail an application, which can be downloaded from our website, along with names and contact numbers of references and a résumé by June 22 to:

Adam Tyler, Personnel Manager, Columbus Medical Center
3166 Napier Ave., Macon, GA 31204

❼ No phone applications, please.

□ job opening 仕事の求人　□ public relations 広報宣伝部　□ supervisor 監督者、管理者
□ outstanding 優れた、素晴らしい　□ be willing to *do* ～する気がある　□ be in charge of ～を担当する
□ media outlet メディア支局　□ strong background 豊富な経験　□ journalism 報道
□ master's degree 修士号　□ mandatory 必須としている　□ administration 管理部門　□ plus 採用の優遇対象
□ priority 優先　□ comprehensive 包括的な　□ benefits package 福利厚生プラン　□ reference 身元照会先
□ résumé 履歴書　□ no phone applications 電話での応募は受け付けていない

★★☆☆☆

26. Where is the job location?

    (A) Macon
    (B) Augusta
    (C) Brunswick
    (D) Marrieta

勤務地はどこですか。

    (A) Macon
    (B) Augusta
    (C) Brunswick
    (D) Marietta

求人文書の勤務地はどこになるかが問われている。冒頭❶で「Macon での勤務が可能な広報担当者を募集」とあるので、**(A)** が正解。それ以外は、出張先の場所として、❷に書かれているので、不正解。

27. According to the advertisement, what is NOT a requirement of the job?

(A) Willingness to take trips
(B) Communication skills
(C) A master's degree
(D) Experience in administration

広告によると、仕事の要件ではないものは何ですか。

(A) 出張をする意欲
(B) コミュニケーション能力
(C) 修士号
(D) 管理の経験

 NOT 問題。仕事の要件ではないものは何かが問われている。求人の要件を見ていくと、❷の「診療所に出張」という記載が (A) に、❸の「優れたコミュニケーション能力」が (B) に、❹の「修士号は必須」という記載が (C) に、それぞれ該当するため、残った **(D)** が正解。(D) は❺で "a plus" とあるが、これは「必須ではないがあると望ましい」という表現。また、❸で "not only A but also B" とあるが、これは「A も B も必要」という意味。not があるからといって、すぐ飛びつかないようにしよう。

 □ willingness to *do* ～する意欲

---

28. What must the applicant submit by June 22?

(A) A résumé
(B) A letter of self-introduction
(C) A medical license
(D) A gift certificate

6 月 22 日までに応募者は何を提出する必要がありますか。

(A) 履歴書
(B) 自己紹介文
(C) 医療免許
(D) 商品券

 6 月 22 日までに応募者が何を提出する必要があるかが問われている。❻に「会社ウェブサイトからダウンロードできる応募用紙に、身元照会先の名前と連絡先電話番号、履歴書を添えて 6 月 22 日までに郵送を」とあるため、これに該当する **(A)** が正解。

 □ self-introduction 自己紹介

---

29. How should a candidate apply for the position?

(A) By visiting Columbus Medical Center
(B) By sending a mail
(C) By completing the online form
(D) By calling the Personnel Manager

志願者はどのように仕事に応募する必要がありますか。

(A) Columbus Medical Center を訪れる
(B) 郵便を送る
(C) オンラインフォームを入力する
(D) 人事担当者に電話をする

志願者はどのように仕事に応募する必要があるかが問われている。❻に「応募書類を郵送で」とあるので、これを言い換えた **(B)** が正解。mail は「郵送する」という意味で、E メールで送ることではないので注意しよう。また (D) は❼で「電話応募は受け付けていない」という記載があるため、不正解。

□ apply for ～に申し込む

求人：広報担当者

州内で最も優れた病院である Columbus Medical Center は、Macon での勤務が可能な広報担当者を募集しています。Brunswick の事務所と Augusta と Marietta にある Columbus の小規模な診療所に出張することができる方に限ります。広報担当者は外部メディアに対し病院の告知を伝えることを担当します。

志願者はスピーチや報道での豊富な経験だけでなく、優れたコミュニケーション能力も必要です。修士号は必須で、病院管理の分野での知識があれば好ましいです。メディアでの最低 5 年間の職務経験がある志願者を優先いたします。高額な給与と包括的な福利厚生プランを提供いたします。

当社のウェブサイトからダウンロードできる応募用紙に、身元照会先の名前と連絡先電話番号、履歴書を添えて 6 月 22 日までに下記へ郵送してください。

Adam Tyler、人事担当、Columbus Medical Center
3166 Napier Ave.、Macon 市、ジョージア州 31204

お電話での応募は受け付けておりません。

GO ON TO THE NEXT PAGE!

Announcement about the Tour in our Factory

We are now providing the chance for the employees of our partner company to visit our factory in Los Angeles directly to get knowledge of the high-tech products that are made by our well-trained technicians. We believe that this kind of visit will be more profitable to support our business for your better understanding of our merchandise. It could be a very valuable experience for you, and also it will help you to answer difficult questions from potential customers.

Those interested in the tour should sign up as soon as possible due to the fact that we need to prepare transportation. The price of this program is $50 and this includes return transportation and lunch, and will be charged to your division. Please complete the attached participation form, signed and approved by your division manager, and give it to me for confirmation.

Lunch will be provided during this tour. Also two coffee breaks will be offered.

Here is the schedule list as below:

8:20 a.m.	Meet at the front gate
8:35 a.m.	Departure by bus
10:10 a.m.	Reach factory
10:25 a.m.	Morning factory tour by Michael Mason
12:00 p.m.	Lunch at a restaurant
1:00 p.m.	Afternoon factory tour by Michael Mason
4:30 p.m.	Conference hosted by Michael Mason and sales director Cindy Miskel (including Q&A session)
5:00 p.m.	Leave the factory
5:30 p.m.	Arrive back at the head office

Eric Parker
Human Resources
ACC Manufacturing Inc.

Participation Form to Visit Factory at ACC Manufacturing Inc.

Name: Brian Pence
Division: The Marketing and Advertising Department
E-mail: brianpence@hmail.net

I would like to join the plant visit on April 5.

Staff's Signature: *Brian Pence*

I allow Brian Pence to join the program with the participation fee charged to the division.

Manager's Signature: *Dylan Maddox*

Date: *March 10*

---

30. According to the announcement, what is the purpose of the factory tour?

(A) To have a conference with Michael Mason and Cindy Miskel
(B) To improve the staff members' knowledge of ACC's products
(C) To provide a substitute worker with extra staff training
(D) To allow customers to ask sales staff questions

31. Who should the form be submitted to?

(A) Dylan Maddox
(B) Cindy Miskel
(C) Michael Mason
(D) Eric Parker

32. Who will cover Mr. Brian's $50 fee?

(A) The Marketing and Advertising Department
(B) The Human Resources Department
(C) The ACC factory
(D) Michael Mason

33. When will the visitors be able to ask questions during the tour?

(A) After the morning tour with Mr. Mason
(B) Before lunch
(C) During the conference
(D) Upon arrival at Head Office

34. When will the tour be held?

(A) On March 5
(B) On March 10
(C) On April 5
(D) On April 10

P. 370

Questions 30-34 refer to the following announcement and form.

Announcement about the Tour in our Factory

We are now providing the chance for the employees of our partner company to visit our factory in Los Angeles directly to get knowledge of the high-tech products that are made by our well-trained technicians. ❶ We believe that this kind of visit will be more profitable to support our business for your better understanding of our merchandise. It could be a very valuable experience for you, and also it will help you to answer difficult questions from potential customers.

Those interested in the tour should sign up as soon as possible due to the fact that we need to prepare transportation. ❷ The price of this program is $50 and this includes return transportation and lunch, and will be charged to your division. ❸ Please complete the attached participation form, signed and approved by your division manager, and give it to me for confirmation.

Lunch will be provided during this tour. Also two coffee breaks will be offered.

Here is the schedule list as below:

8:20 a.m.	Meet at the front gate
8:35 a.m.	Departure by bus
10:10 a.m.	Reach factory
10:25 a.m.	Morning factory tour by Michael Mason
12:00 p.m.	Lunch at a restaurant
1:00 p.m.	Afternoon factory tour by Michael Mason
4:30 p.m.	❹ Conference hosted by Michael Mason and sales director Cindy Miskel (including Q&A session)
5:00 p.m.	Leave the factory
5:30 p.m.	Arrive back at the head office

❺ Eric Parker
Human Resources
ACC Manufacturing Inc.

Participation Form to Visit Factory at ACC Manufacturing Inc.

Name: Brian Pence
❻ **Division:** The Marketing and Advertising Department
E-mail: brianpence@hmail.net

❼ I would like to join the plant visit on April 5.

Staff's Signature: *Brian Pence*

❽ I allow Brian Pence to join the program with the participation fee charged to the division.

Manager's Signature: *Dylan Maddox*

Date: *March 10*

お知らせ
□ directly 直接　□ get knowledge of ～の知識を得る　□ well-trained 十分に訓練された、熟練の
□ profitable 収益性の高い　□ better understanding of ～に関するより良い理解　□ valuable 価値ある
□ potential customer 将来顧客となってくれる人　□ those interested in ～に興味のある人
□ sign up 申し込む、登録する　□ due to ～が原因で、　□ the fact that SV S が V であるという事実
□ transportation 移動手段　□ participation form 参加申込書　□ division 部署　□ confirmation 確認
□ as below 以下のとおり

書式
□ participation fee 参加費用

★★★☆☆

30. According to the announcement, what is the purpose of the factory tour?

(A) To have a conference with Michael Mason and Cindy Miskel
(B) To improve the staff members' knowledge of ACC's products
(C) To provide a substitute worker with extra staff training
(D) To allow customers to ask sales staff questions

お知らせによると、工場見学ツアーの目的は何ですか。

(A) Michael Mason さん と Cindy Miskel さんとの協議会を行うこと
(B) ACC 製品に対するスタッフの知識を深めること
(C) 代理の労働者に臨時の従業員研修を受けさせること
(D) 顧客が営業スタッフに質問するのを許可すること

お知らせから、工場見学ツアーの目的が問われている。お知らせの冒頭で、パートナー企業の従業員に向けた工場見学について触れた後、❶で「このような訪問は彼らの当社の商品に対する理解を深める」とある。ここでいう「彼ら」はパートナー企業の従業員のことで、「当社の商品」は❺から ACC 社の商品を指すことがわかる。よって、それぞれを言い換えた **(B)** が正解となる。

□ conference 会議、協議会　□ substitute 代わりとなる

★★★☆☆

31. Who should the form be submitted to?

(A) Dylan Maddox
(B) Cindy Miskel
(C) Michael Mason
(D) Eric Parker

書式は誰に提出されなければなりませんか。

(A) Dylan Maddox
(B) Cindy Miskel
(C) Michael Mason
(D) Eric Parker

書式の提出先について問われている。お知らせの❸で「添付の参加申込書にご記入いただき、私へ、確認のために提出してほしい」とある。このお知らせの差出人は、❺から Eric Parker さんだとわかるので、ここでいう「私」は Eric Parker さんのことである。よって、正解は **(D)**。この問題は正解の根拠が 2 カ所になっており、❸の代名詞が何を指すかしっかり読み取ることがポイントとなる。

32. Who will cover Mr. Brian's $50 fee?

   (A) The Marketing and Advertising
        Department
   (B) The Human Resources Department
   (C) The ACC factory
   (D) Michael Mason

Brian さんの費用 50 ドルは誰が支払いますか。

   (A) マーケティング広報部
   (B) 人事部
   (C) ACC の工場
   (D) Michael Mason

 Brian さんの 50 ドルの費用を誰が負担するかが問われている。まず、この 50 ドルの費用は、1 文書目のお知らせの❷に「工場見学プログラムの参加費用で、所属部署へ請求される」とあるので、参加者の所属部署がこの費用を負担することがわかる。次に 2 文書目の書式の❺を見ると、今回参加を希望する従業員の所属部署が "The Marketing and Advertising Department" であるとわかる。また、❽で承認された内容もある。以上より、正解は **(A)**。50 ドルの費用が参加費用ということを 1 文書目から読み取り、2 文書目で負担先を探す、という両文書を参照する問題。

---

33. When will the visitors be able to ask
     questions during the tour?

   (A) After the morning tour with Mr. Mason
   (B) Before lunch
   (C) During the conference
   (D) Upon arrival at Head Office

訪問者はツアーの間、いつ質問をすることができますか。

   (A) Mason さんとの午前のツアーの後で
   (B) 昼食の前に
   (C) 協議会中に
   (D) 本社に到着して

 （工場）訪問者が、ツアー中のどのタイミングで質問できるかが問われている。お知らせに書かれているスケジュール表の❹を見ると、協議会開催中に質疑の時間が設けられていることがわかる。以上から、正解は **(C)**。選択肢はどれも、質問をしようと思えばできそうだが、Part 7 は本文で明らかとなっている部分を探すことが重要なので、主観で解かないように気を付けよう。

 □ upon arrival 到着後

---

34. When will the tour be held?

   (A) On March 5
   (B) On March 10
   (C) On April 5
   (D) On April 10

ツアーはいつ行われますか。

   (A) 3 月 5 日
   (B) 3 月 10 日
   (C) 4 月 5 日
   (D) 4 月 10 日

 ツアーがいつ行われるかが問われている。書式の❼で「4 月 5 日の工場見学に参加を希望」とあるので、4 月 5 日に開催されることがわかる。以上より、正解は **(C)**。設問の the tour は、1 文書目のお知らせの文脈から、工場見学を指すということがわかる。2 文書目の❼の "the plant visit" のような多少言い換えた表現でも、the tour のことだと客観的に読むことができることを押さえておこう。

工場見学ツアーのお知らせ

現在、パートナー企業の従業員の方々へ、ロサンゼルスにある当社の工場を直接訪問し、当社の熟練した技術者によって作られたハイテク製品の知識を得る機会を提供しています。このような訪問は彼らの当社の商品に対する理解を深め、パートナー企業の従業員の方々にとって非常に貴重な経験になり、また、潜在的な顧客からの難しい質問に答えるのにも役に立つため、当社のビジネスをサポートするうえでより有益であると考えています。

ツアーに興味がある方は、送迎の準備が必要なため、なるべく早い段階でのお申込みをお願いいたします。このプログラムの参加費用は 50 ドルで往復の送迎と昼食が含まれており、所属している部署に請求されます。添付の参加申込書にご記入いただき、所属長の署名と承認を得たうえで、私へ、確認のために提出をお願いいたします。

ツアーでは昼食が提供されます。また、短いコーヒー休憩も 2 回あります。

予定は下記のとおりです：

午前 8 時 20 分	正門に集合
午前 8 時 35 分	バスで出発
午前 10 時 10 分	工場に到着
午前 10 時 25 分	Michael Mason さんによる午前の工場ツアー
午後 12 時 00 分	レストランにて昼食
午後 1 時 00 分	Michael Mason さんによる午後の工場ツアー
午後 4 時 30 分	Michael Mason さんと営業部長 Cindy Miskel さんの司会による協議会（質疑応答の時間を含む）
午後 5 時 00 分	工場を出発
午後 5 時 30 分	本社に戻る

Eric Parker
人事部
ACC Manufacturing 社

ACC Manufacturing 社 工場見学参加申込書

名前： Brian Pence
部署： マーケティング広報部
E メール： brianpence@hmail.net

4 月 5 日の工場見学に参加を希望します。

従業員署名： Brian Pence

部署へ請求される参加費と Brian Pence のプログラムへの参加を承認します。

部長署名： Dylan Maddox

日付： 3 月 10 日

Questions 35-39 refer to the following Web page and review.

5分00秒

---

http://www.townsendonc.org ▶

| Home | About | Store Locations | What's New |

Your online office and computer equipment store

Townsend Office & Computer Equipment is the best store to purchase everything for your office. This week only, we are offering discounts on the following items:

▶ Markright black gel ink pens, 20-pack, $10 each
▶ Madigan brand reams of white copy paper, $3 and up depending on quantity ordered
▶ Edge color ink cartridges, $35

Get a complimentary box of staples when you buy a Front Force stapler, now on sale for $25. Our customer support employees are available to help you at custsupp@townsendonc.org

---

Business Savings

All the Office & Computer Equipment You will Ever Want

Business Savings: Today's featured business

Townsend Office & Computer Equipment is a welcome option to many more popular supply stores. It makes its own brand of items, called Edge, on which it often offers discounts. The range of products at Townsend Office & Computer Equipment is vast, consisting of everything from pencils to fax machines. The quality of all the products may not be the best, but for offices that consume a great deal of supplies, it is worth considering. Townsend Office & Computer Equipment will definitely save you money.

Townsend Office & Computer Equipment offers complimentary shipping for orders over $100, but some items can take up to four weeks to arrive. The discounts are advertised only on the business's Web page, http://www.townsendonc.org. Look for discounted items there. It holds new sales every week but they sell out quickly, so you'll have to order now to purchase them.

35. Which of the following is produced by Townsend Office & Computer Equipment?

(A) Staplers
(B) Gel ink pens
(C) Ink cartridges
(D) Copy paper

36. According to the Web page, who will most likely the customer support employees assist?

(A) Potential buyers
(B) Web designers
(C) Stapler makers
(D) Reviewers

37. What is suggested about Townsend Office & Computer Equipment?

(A) It is popular in the office supplies industry.
(B) It has many store locations.
(C) It limits the quantity of items that can be ordered online.
(D) It can be a good alternative for a business.

38. In the review, the word "definitely" in paragraph 1, line 6, is closest in meaning to

(A) exactly
(B) certainly
(C) justly
(D) eventually

39. What does the reviewer consider a disadvantage of Townsend Office & Computer Equipment?

(A) The price of its products
(B) The limited selection of items
(C) The time it takes to receive some goods
(D) The quality of its customer support

P. 376

Double

Questions 35-39 refer to the following Web page and review.

◀ ▶ | http://www.townsendonc.org | ▶

| Home | About | Store Locations | What's New |

Your online office and computer equipment store

Townsend Office & Computer Equipment is the best store to purchase everything for your office. This week only, we are offering discounts on the following items:

▶ Markright black gel ink pens, 20-pack, $10 each
▶ Madigan brand reams of white copy paper, $3 and up depending on quantity ordered
▶ ❶ Edge color ink cartridges, $35

Get a complimentary box of staples when you buy a Front Force stapler, now on sale for $25.
❷ Our customer support employees are available to help you at custsupp@townsendonc.org

---

Business Savings

All the Office & Computer Equipment You will Ever Want

Business Savings: Today's featured business

❸ Townsend Office & Computer Equipment is a welcome option to many more popular supply stores. ❹ It makes its own brand of items, called Edge, on which it often offers discounts. The range of products at Townsend Office & Computer Equipment is vast, consisting of everything from pencils to fax machines. The quality of all the products may not be the best, but for offices that consume a great deal of supplies, it is worth considering. Townsend Office & Computer Equipment will ❺ definitely save you money.

Townsend Office & Computer Equipment offers complimentary shipping for orders over $100, but ❻ some items can take up to four weeks to arrive. The discounts are advertised only on the business's Web page, http://www.townsendonc.org. Look for discounted items there. It holds new sales every week but they sell out quickly, so you'll have to order now to purchase them.

....

✎ ウェブページ
□ computer equipment コンピューター機器　□ gel ink ゲルインク　□ reams of 大量の〜
□ depending on quantity ordered 注文量に応じて　□ complimentary 無料の
□ staple ステープラー（ホッチキス）の針　□ stapler ステープラー（ホッチキス）

レビュー
□ featured 注目の　□ range 範囲　□ vast 広大である　□ consist of 〜で構成されている
□ consume 〜を消費する　□ a great deal of 大量の〜　□ worth *doing* 〜する価値がある
□ definitely 間違いなく　□ sell out 売り切れる

35. Which of the following is produced by Townsend Office & Computer Equipment?

(A) Staplers
(B) Gel ink pens
(C) Ink cartridges
(D) Copy paper

Townsend Office & Computer Equipment 社の製品は次のどれですか。

(A) ステープラー
(B) ゲルインクペン
(C) インクカートリッジ
(D) コピー用紙

Townsend Office & Computer Equipment 社の製品が選択肢のうちどれかが問われている。選択肢はどれもウェブページに製品として記載がある。2文書目のレビューを見ていくと、❹で「(Townsend Office & Computer Equipment 社は) Edge という自社ブランド商品を製造している」と述べられている。これを手掛かりにウェブページを見ていくと、❶に Edge ブランドの製品がある。以上より、正解は **(C)**。自社製品と取り扱っている他のブランドで混同したかもしれないが、しっかり手掛かりを見極めて解こう。

---

36. According to the Web page, who will most likely the customer support employees assist?

(A) Potential buyers
(B) Web designers
(C) Stapler makers
(D) Reviewers

ウェブページによると、顧客サポートの従業員は誰を手伝うと考えられますか。

(A) 潜在的な顧客
(B) ウェブデザイナー
(C) ステープラー製造業者
(D) 評論家

ウェブページから、顧客サポートの従業員は誰を手伝うと考えられるかが問われている。ウェブページを見ると、この内容自体が「割引品の紹介とステープラー購入時の無料サービスの記載」であり、締めくくりに❷で、「当社のお客様サポート担当従業員がお手伝いする」と述べている。つまり、このウェブページは購入する意思のある人か、ひょっとしたら購入するかもしれない人が見るページであることがわかる。よって後者を「潜在的な顧客」と言い換えた **(A)** が正解となる。

---

37. What is suggested about Townsend Office & Computer Equipment?

(A) It is popular in the office supplies industry.
(B) It has many store locations.
(C) It limits the quantity of items that can be ordered online.
(D) It can be a good alternative for a business.

Townsend Office & Computer Equipment 社について何が示唆されていますか。

(A) オフィス用品業界で人気がある。
(B) 店舗数が多い。
(C) オンラインで注文できる商品の数に限りがある。
(D) 企業にとって良い選択肢となり得る。

Townsend Office & Computer Equipment 社について示唆されていることを問う選択肢照合型問題。2文書目のレビューの❸で、「Townsend Office & Computer Equipment 社は他の多くの人気のある消耗品店と比べても歓迎される選択肢だ」と述べている。以上より、正解は「歓迎される選択肢（a welcome option）」を a good alternative と言い換えた **(D)** が正解。(A) オフィス業界で人気、(B) 店舗数、はそれぞれ該当する記載がなく不正解。また、(C) オンラインで限りがある、はレビューの第2段落で在庫が切れる可能性について触れられているものの、発注する商品の数は記載されていない。

□ alternative 代わりとなる選択肢

38. In the review, the word "definitely" in paragraph 1, line 6, is closest in meaning to

(A) exactly
(B) certainly
(C) justly
(D) eventually

レビューの、第1段落・6行目にある "definitely" に最も意味が近いのは

(A) 厳密に
(B) 確かに
(C) 正当に
(D) 結局は

 同義語問題。問われている❺は「間違いなく、確実に」という意味で使われており、「間違いなく節約する」となっている。以上より、同様の意味となるのは **(B)**。"definitely" と certainly はともに「疑いの余地がない」という意味があり、言い換えとしてよく用いられるので押さえておこう。

---

39. What does the reviewer consider a disadvantage of Townsend Office & Computer Equipment?

(A) The price of its products
(B) The limited selection of items
(C) The time it takes to receive some goods
(D) The quality of its customer support

評論家は Townsend Office & Computer Equipment の欠点は何であると考えていますか。

(A) 製品の価格
(B) 商品の種類の少なさ
(C) 商品受け取りまでにかかる時間
(D) 顧客サポートの質

 評論家の考える、Townsend Office & Computer Equipment 社の欠点について問われている。2文書目のレビューの第2段落の❻で、「Townsend Office & Computer Equipment 社は100ドルを超える注文で送料無料となるが、到着までに最大4週間を要する商品もある」と述べている。つまり、送料無料というメリットの一方で、時間がかかるというデメリット・欠点も指摘している。以上から、これを言い換えた **(C)** が正解。

□ limited selection of 限られた品揃えの〜

http://www.townsendonc.org			
トップページ	当店について	店舗所在地	新着情報

オフィス・コンピューター用品のオンラインショップ

Townsend Office & Computer Equipment はお客様のオフィスのためのすべてのものを購入するのに最適な店です。今週に限り、次の品物を割引で提供します。

▶ Markright の黒色ゲルインクペン、20 本入り、1 点につき 10 ドル
▶ Madigan ブランドの白色コピー用紙（500 枚入り）、注文数量に応じて 3 ドルから
▶ Edge カラーインクカートリッジ、35 ドル

25 ドルで販売中の Front Force 社のステープラーをご購入のお客様に、無料でステープラーの針を 1 箱お付けいたします。当社のお客様サポート担当従業員が custsupp@townsendonc.org にてお手伝いいたします。

企業の節約

欲しかったすべてのオフィス・コンピューター用品がある

企業の節約：本日の注目企業

Townsend Office & Computer Equipment は他の多くの人気のある消耗品店と比べても歓迎される選択肢である。Edge という名の自社ブランド商品を製造しており、しばしば割引を提供している。Townsend Office & Computer Equipment の製品は、鉛筆からファックスまで幅広く取り揃えている。すべての品物の品質が最高ではないかもしれないが、多くの消耗品を消費するオフィスにとっては検討に値する。Townsend Office & Computer Equipment は間違いなく経費を節約してくれるだろう。

Townsend Office & Computer Equipment では 100 ドルを超える注文に対し送料が無料となるが、中には到着までに最大 4 週間を要する商品もある。割引は同社のウェブページ http://www.townsendonc.org でのみ告知されている。このページで割引商品を探してみるとよい。毎週新しいセールが行われているが、すぐに売り切れとなるので、購入するためにはすぐに注文しなければならない。

Questions 40-44 refer to the following information, e-mail, and customer review. ⏱ 5分30秒

◀ ▶ | https://www.acfordings.info | ▶

Enjoy a Cool Summer with Fording's Air Conditioners !!!

INFORMATION

Description of our Units

Fording's is a company that provides wall-mounted air conditioning. The units can be installed without existing pipes or ducts, so they're ideal for all types of homes and offices. We will visit your site free of charge to measure the area and give advice to you. All of our employees have been working in the field for at least ten years, so you can trust their expertise. We also guarantee our work — both the installation itself and the devices — for five years. Check our reasonable prices below, and then contact us at 777-5582 to reserve an appointment.

Code of Units	Materials Costs	Labor Costs	Total
ABN3	$3,500	$1,990	$5,490
SSR5	$4,600	$1,500	$6,100
OCM7	$4,000	$1,700	$5,700
EDN9	$5,200	$1,990	$7,190

We require a minimum of 3 units for installation. If you need 8 plus units, please call us about a bulk discount. Basic recommendation: 1 unit in each bedroom, 1 unit in the kitchen, and 1 unit in the living room.

To: Fording's Air Conditioners <info@fordingsair.com>
From: Riley Baxter <ribaxter@allemail.net>
Date: June 30
Subject: Client Inquiry

Dear Fording's Air Conditioners,

I'd like to buy air conditioners for my home. There is no other system to remove or replace, because my home was built long before air conditioning was commonly used. I want to know more about the services you offer and how long it would take to finish the installation, because I also have renovations planned for later in the summer. My home has one kitchen, one living room and some bedrooms. Thank you in advance for your information.

Best regards,

Riley Baxter

Written by Riley Baxter
July 29

I was really happy with the service provided by Fording's. I wrote my inquiry online and was surprised that they were able to reserve an appointment for the very next day. The technician, Ricky Shire, was very kind and skillful at the job. He recommended that the equipment with the lowest charge for installation would be appropriate and made helpful suggestions about where to place each unit to maximize the efficiency of the system. I ended up getting 7 units in total, using the basic recommendation from the Web site. A work crew visited my home the following week, and the installation only took a few hours. I've been using the system for about three weeks, and I'm completely satisfied with it. I wish I'd had air conditioning in my home much sooner.

40. What is NOT indicated about Fording's services?

(A) It provides a free initial consultation.
(B) Its services are performed by experienced employees.
(C) Its work and products are guaranteed for five years.
(D) It is one of the largest companies of its kind in the area.

41. What is suggested about Ms. Baxter's home?

(A) It is recently used for business.
(B) It has partially been renovated.
(C) It is an old structure.
(D) It was decorated again.

42. What units did Mr. Shire recommend to Ms. Baxter?

(A) ABN3
(B) SSR5
(C) OCM7
(D) EDN9

43. How many bedrooms does Ms. Baxter's home most likely have?

(A) Four
(B) Five
(C) Six
(D) Seven

44. How long was Fording's preparing for the installation?

(A) For a few hours
(B) For a day
(C) For a week
(D) For a month

Triple

 P. 382

Questions 40-44 refer to the following information, e-mail, and customer review.

https://www.acfordings.info

Enjoy a Cool Summer with Fording's Air Conditioners !!!

INFORMATION

Description of our Units

Fording's is a company that provides wall-mounted air conditioning. The units can be installed without existing pipes or ducts, so they're ideal for all types of homes and offices. ❶ We will visit your site free of charge to measure the area and give advice to you. ❷ All of our employees have been working in the field for at least ten years, so you can trust their expertise. ❸ We also guarantee our work — both the installation itself and the devices — for five years. Check our reasonable prices below, and then contact us at 777-5582 to reserve an appointment.

Code of Units	Materials Costs	Labor Costs	Total
ABN3	$3,500	$1,990	$5,490
❹ SSR5	$4,600	$1,500	$6,100
OCM7	$4,000	$1,700	$5,700
EDN9	$5,200	$1,990	$7,190

We require a minimum of 3 units for installation. If you need 8 plus units, please call us about a bulk discount. ❺ Basic recommendation: 1 unit in each bedroom, 1 unit in the kitchen, and 1 unit in the living room.

To: Fording's Air Conditioners <info@fordingsair.com>
From: Riley Baxter <ribaxter@allemail.net>
Date: June 30
Subject: Client Inquiry

Dear Fording's Air Conditioners,

I'd like to buy air conditioners for my home. ❻ There is no other system to remove or replace, because my home was built long before air conditioning was commonly used. I want to know more about the services you offer and how long it would take to finish the installation, because I also have renovations planned for later in the summer. ❼ My home has one kitchen, one living room and some bedrooms. Thank you in advance for your information.

Best regards,

Riley Baxter

Written by Riley Baxter
July 29

I was really happy with the service provided by Fording's. ❽ I wrote my inquiry online and was surprised that they were able to reserve an appointment for the very next day. The technician, Ricky Shire, was very kind and skillful at the job. ❾ He recommended that the equipment with the lowest charge for installation would be appropriate and made helpful suggestions about where to place each unit to maximize the efficiency of the system. ❿ I ended up getting 7 units in total, using the basic recommendation from the Web site. ⓫ A work crew visited my home the following week, and the installation only took a few hours. I've been using the system for about three weeks, and I'm completely satisfied with it. I wish I'd had air conditioning in my home much sooner.

情報
- [ ] description 説明　[ ] unit（設備・装置）一式　[ ] wall-mounted 壁側設置式の　[ ] existing 既存の
- [ ] pipe 配管　[ ] duct ダクト　[ ] ideal 理想的な　[ ] site 現場　[ ] free of charge 無料で
- [ ] measure ～を測定する　[ ] field 分野　[ ] trust ～を信用する　[ ] expertise 専門技術
- [ ] guarantee ～を保証する　[ ] device 装置　[ ] reasonable お手ごろな　[ ] material 原材料　[ ] labor cost 人件費
- [ ] require ～を要求する　[ ] a minimum of 最低～の　[ ] bulk 大量の

E メール
- [ ] inquiry 問い合わせ　[ ] replace ～を交換する　[ ] commonly used 一般的になる、おなじみになる
- [ ] later 後の方で　[ ] in advance 事前に

顧客レビュー
- [ ] very next day まさにその翌日　[ ] skillful 技術力のある　[ ] equipment 装置、設備　[ ] appropriate 適切な
- [ ] suggestion 提言、提案　[ ] where to *do* どこに～するか　[ ] maximize ～を最大化する
- [ ] efficiency 効果、効率　[ ] ended up *do*ing 最終的に～する　[ ] in total 合計　[ ] completely すっかり、完全に
- [ ] I wish I'd had ～があったらよかったのにと思う　[ ] much sooner もっと早く

★★★★☆ NOT 問題

40. What is NOT indicated about Fording's services?

(A) It provides a free initial consultation.
(B) Its services are performed by experienced employees.
(C) Its work and products are guaranteed for five years.
(D) It is one of the largest companies of its kind in the area.

Fording's 社のサービスとして示されていないことは何ですか。

(A) 無料の初回相談を提供する。
(B) サービスは経験豊富な従業員が行う。
(C) 作業や製品は 5 年間保証される。
(D) その分野において地域で最も大きな会社の一つである。

NOT 問題。Fording's 社のサービスとして示されていないことが問われている。1 文書目の情報にある❶の無料相談が (A) に、❷の「現場経験 10 年以上の専門的に信頼できる社員」が (B) に、❸の「5 年保証」が (C) にそれぞれ該当する。残った **(D)** が本文に記載がなく正解となる。(A) は、無料の初回相談、とは本文に書かれていないが、❶から初回でも 2 回目でも無料となるため、初回は当然含まれることがあると解釈しよう。

- [ ] initial 初回の　[ ] experienced 経験豊富な

41. What is suggested about Ms. Baxter's home?

(A) It is recently used for business.
(B) It has partially been renovated.
(C) It is an old structure.
(D) It was decorated again.

Baxter さんの家について何が示唆されていますか。

(A) 最近、ビジネスで使用されている。
(B) 部分的に改装された。
(C) 古い建築物である。
(D) 再び装飾が施された。

🔍 Baxter さんの家について何が示唆されているかを問う選択肢照合型の問題。2 文書目の E メールの❻で、Baxter さんは自分の家について「エアコンの使用が一般化するよりもかなり前に建てられたので、撤去や取り換えが必要なシステムは設置されていない」と述べている。ここから、ずいぶん前に建築されたことを示唆している。よって、これを old structure と言い換えた **(C)** が正解。

✏️ □ for business 業務用に　□ partially 部分的に　□ structure 建築物

··

42. What units did Mr. Shire recommend to Ms. Baxter?

(A) ABN3
(B) SSR5
(C) OCM7
(D) EDN9

Shire さんが Baxter さんに勧めた製品は何ですか。

(A) ABN3
(B) SSR5
(C) OCM7
(D) EDN9

🔍 Shire さんが Baxter さんに勧めた製品について問われている。3 文書目の顧客レビューに Baxter さんのコメントがあり、❾で「料金が最も安い機器が適切であると勧めてくれた」とある。次に 1 文書目の情報を見ると❹から、設置費用が一番安いのが SSR5 だとわかる。よって **(B)** が正解となる。この問題は❾に "recommended" という設問と同じ動詞が使われているため、「設置料金が最も安い＝作業費が最も安い」という視点で、"the lowest charge for installation" と 1 文書目の❹の "labor cost" が結び付けられるか、が解答のポイントとなる。

··

43. How many bedrooms does Ms. Baxter's home most likely have?

(A) Four
(B) Five
(C) Six
(D) Seven

Baxter さんの家には寝室がいくつあると考えられますか。

(A) 4 室
(B) 5 室
(C) 6 室
(D) 7 室

🔍 Baxter さんの家にある寝室の数が問われている。Baxter さんは、3 文書目の顧客レビューの❿で「ウェブサイトにある基本的な推奨構成を基に、最終的に 7 台購入した」と記載している。次に 1 文書目の情報を見ると、❺に基本的な推奨構成が書かれており、「各寝室に 1 台、キッチンに 1 台、リビングに 1 台」と記載がある。また、Baxter さんは 2 文書目の E メールの❼で、「家にはキッチンとリビングが 1 つずつと寝室が複数ある」と述べている。つまり、7 台購入したエアコンは、キッチンとリビングを除いた 5 つの寝室に設置したことがわかる。よって、正解は **(B)**。

44. How long was Fording's preparing for the installation?

    (A) For a few hours
    (B) For a day
    (C) For a week
    (D) For a month

Fording's 社は設置の準備にどのくらいかけていましたか。

    (A) 数時間
    (B) 1 日
    (C) 1 週間
    (D) 1 カ月間

Fording's 社の設置のための準備期間が問われている。3 文書目の顧客レビューの❽で「問い合わせをした翌日に予約を受けた」、⓫で「その翌週には顧客の家に訪問し、数時間で取り付けた」という記載があるため、Fording's 社は最初の接触から約 1 週間かけていたことがわかる。以上より、正解は **(C)**。選択肢をヒントに、期間に関わる表現を本文から探し、整理して読み解こう。

📝 問題 40 から 44 は次の情報、E メール、顧客レビューに関するものです。

---

https://www.acfordings.info

Fording's 社のエアコンで涼しい夏をお過ごしください！！！

インフォメーション

当社製品の説明

Fording's 社は壁に設置するエアコンを販売している会社です。本体はパイプやダクトがなくても設置できるため、どんな家や事務所にも合います。寸法計測と相談のための出張は無料です。従業員は全員 10 年以上、現場の経験がありますので、専門知識が豊富でお任せいただけます。また、商品設置作業と機器本体には 5 年間の保証をお付けします。下記の手ごろな価格をご確認の上、ご予約は 777-5582 までご連絡ください。

型式	機材費	人件費	合計
ABN3	3,500 ドル	1,990 ドル	5,490 ドル
SSR5	4,600 ドル	1,500 ドル	6,100 ドル
OCM7	4,000 ドル	1,700 ドル	5,700 ドル
EDN9	5,200 ドル	1,990 ドル	7,190 ドル

設置は 3 台から承ります。8 台以上をご希望の場合の一括購入割引については、お電話でお問い合せください。
基本的な推奨構成：各寝室に 1 台、キッチンに 1 台、リビングに 1 台

受信者：	Fording's Air Conditioners <info@fordingsair@com>
送信者：	Riley Baxter <ribaxter@allemail.net>
日付：	6月30日
件名：	顧客の問い合わせ

Fording's Air Conditioners 御中

家庭用のエアコンを購入したいと思います。私の家はエアコンの使用が一般化するよりもかなり前に建てられたので、撤去や取り換えが必要なシステムは設置されていません。この夏の間に他の改修をする予定もありますので、貴社が提供されているサービス内容と、設置完了までどのくらいの時間がかかるのかについて詳しく教えていただけますか。私の家には、キッチン、リビングが1つずつと寝室が複数あります。ご回答をお待ちしております。

よろしくお願いいたします。

Riley Baxter

---

https://www.acfordings.review

記載者　Riley Baxter
7月29日

Fording's 社のサービスにとても満足しました。オンラインで問い合わせをしたところ、翌日には予約を入れてくれたので驚きました。技術者の Ricky Shire さんは非常に親切で仕事が上手な方でした。彼は設置に掛かる料金が最も安い機器が適切であると勧め、システムの効率を最大化するために各製品をどこに設置すればいいかについて参考になる提案をしてくださいました。ウェブサイトに載っている基本的な推奨構成を基に、最終的には全部で7台買うことにしました。翌週、作業員が私の家を訪れ、設置には数時間しかかかりませんでした。システムを使い始めて3週間になりますが、非常に満足しています。もっと早く家にエアコンを設置すればよかったと思っています。

GO ON
TO THE
NEXT PAGE!

TIMKO AUDITORIUM

Come and enjoy the wonderful shows at Timko Auditorium !!!

Timko Auditorium, the most well-known theater in the country, has hosted various performances by some of the most popular performers in the country.

Timko Auditorium has been providing audiences with many award-winning musicals, moving dramatic plays, arts festivals, and more. Every afternoon, we permit visitors to look around the auditorium with a guide, going backstage and finding out more about the auditorium's rich history.

We're also raising money for next year's renovation project. Donate to the project and get a Golden Membership, which offers 30% off all ticket purchases to you (up to eight tickets per show). Don't miss what's playing this month at Timko Auditorium:

Duration	Contents
May 1-7	Eastmon Philharmonic Orchestra, playing classical music by Haydn
May 8-19	Non-commercial Film Festival, new showings every night
May 20-23	Pan-Am Ballet Championships, dancers competing from across the country
May 24-31	Comedy by Jose Bolivar, humorous comedy that'll keep you laughing

---

Dear Ms. Martin,

I was told that you are going to visit us from May 7 to 9. It will be my great pleasure to meet you in person after having some discussions over the phone. We are in the final stages of installing the production machinery for manufacturing our microchips on-site, and it will be helpful to have you examine everything to make sure there are no issues.

On a lighter note, after a hard day of work, you have an evening of entertainment to look forward to, as my coworker Pitt Jackson and I will be taking you to the Timko Auditorium on your first night here.

I look forward to seeing you!

Drew Hess

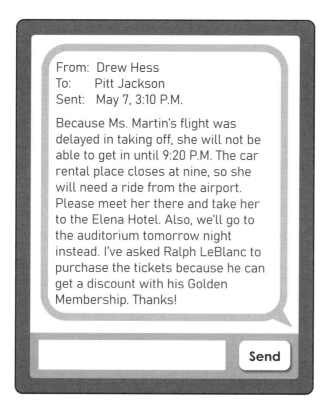

From: Drew Hess
To: Pitt Jackson
Sent: May 7, 3:10 P.M.

Because Ms. Martin's flight was delayed in taking off, she will not be able to get in until 9:20 P.M. The car rental place closes at nine, so she will need a ride from the airport. Please meet her there and take her to the Elena Hotel. Also, we'll go to the auditorium tomorrow night instead. I've asked Ralph LeBlanc to purchase the tickets because he can get a discount with his Golden Membership. Thanks!

Send

45. What is stated about Timko Auditorium?

(A) It was recently purchased by new investors.
(B) Its architecture won an award.
(C) It offers behind-the-scene tours.
(D) It is now under renovation.

46. Why will Ms. Martin visit Mr. Hess' company?

(A) To inspect some equipment
(B) To sign a contract
(C) To introduce new equipment
(D) To educate staff members

47. What kind of event did Mr. Hess initially plan to take Ms. Martin to?

(A) A musical performance
(B) A dance competition
(C) A comedy show
(D) A film festival

48. What is Mr. Jackson asked to do?

(A) Make a reservation in advance
(B) Take a visitor to dinner
(C) Confirm a flight time
(D) Pick up Ms. Martin

49. What can be inferred about Mr. LeBlanc?

(A) He will join the group for dinner.
(B) He made a donation to Timko Auditorium.
(C) He has met Ms. Martin before.
(D) He works at the Elena Hotel.

P. 390

Triple

Questions 45-49 refer to the following information, letter, and text message.

TIMKO AUDITORIUM

Come and enjoy the wonderful shows at Timko Auditorium !!!

Timko Auditorium, the most well-known theater in the country, has hosted various performances by some of the most popular performers in the country.

Timko Auditorium has been providing audiences with many award-winning musicals, moving dramatic plays, arts festivals, and more. ❶ Every afternoon, we permit visitors to look around the auditorium with a guide, going backstage and finding out more about the auditorium's rich history.

We're also raising money for next year's renovation project. ❷Donate to the project and get a Golden Membership, which offers 30% off all ticket purchases to you (up to eight tickets per show). Don't miss what's playing this month at Timko Auditorium:

Duration	Contents
❸ May 1-7	❸ Eastmon Philharmonic Orchestra, playing classical music by Haydn
May 8-19	Non-commercial Film Festival, new showings every night
May 20-23	Pan-Am Ballet Championships, dancers competing from across the country
May 24-31	Comedy by Jose Bolivar, humorous comedy that'll keep you laughing

---

Dear Ms. Martin,

❹ I was told that you are going to visit us from May 7 to 9. It will be my great pleasure to meet you in person after having some discussions over the phone. ❺ We are in the final stages of installing the production machinery for manufacturing our microchips on-site, and it will be helpful to have you examine everything to make sure there are no issues.

❻ On a lighter note, after a hard day of work, you have an evening of entertainment to look forward to, as my coworker Pitt Jackson and I will be taking you to the Timko Auditorium on your first night here.

I look forward to seeing you!

Drew Hess

From: Drew Hess
To: Pitt Jackson
Sent: May 7, 3:10 P.M.

Because Ms. Martin's flight was delayed in taking off, she will not be able to get in until 9:20 P.M. The car rental place closes at nine, so she will need a ride from the airport. ❼ Please meet her there and take her to the Elena Hotel. Also, we'll go to the auditorium tomorrow night instead. ❽ I've asked Ralph LeBlanc to purchase the tickets because he can get a discount with his Golden Membership. Thanks!

情報
□ auditorium 講堂、ホール、公会堂　□ well-known 有名な　□ host 〜を主催・開催する
□ award-winning 賞を獲得した　□ dramatic play 演劇　□ look around 〜を見て回る　□ backstage 舞台裏
□ raise 〜を稼ぐ・獲得する　□ donate to 〜に寄付をする　□ per 〜あたり　□ duration 期間　□ content 内容
□ non-commercial 非商業的な、非営利の

手紙
□ in person 直接　□ over the phone 電話で　□ production machinery 製造機械
□ manufacture 〜を製造する　□ microchip マイクロチップ　□ on-site 現場で　□ examine 〜を調査する
□ issue 課題　□ on a lighter note 軽い話題に変えますが

テキストメッセージ
□ take off 離陸する　□ instead 代わりに

★★★★☆

45. What is stated about Timko Auditorium?

(A) It was recently purchased by new investors.
(B) Its architecture won an award.
(C) It offers behind-the-scene tours.
(D) It is now under renovation.

Timko Auditorium について何が述べられていますか。

(A) 最近、新しい投資家に購入された。
(B) 建築物が賞を受賞した。
(C) 舞台裏のツアーを催行している
(D) 現在、改装中である。

Timko Auditorium について述べられていることを問う選択肢照合型の問題。1 文書目の情報の❶で、「訪問者をガイド付きで舞台裏を見て回ることを許可している」とあるため、ここから舞台裏を見て回ることを behind-the-scene tour と言い換えた **(C)** が正解。言い換えがわからない場合は、保留にして、他の 3 つの選択肢の記載がない、という手掛かりで解いても OK。

□ investor 投資家　□ architecture 建築物　□ win an award 賞を勝ち取る
□ behind-the-scene 舞台裏の、内密の　□ under renovation 改装中の

★★★★☆

46. Why will Ms. Martin visit Mr. Hess' company?

(A) To inspect some equipment
(B) To sign a contract
(C) To introduce new equipment
(D) To educate staff members

Martin さんはなぜ Hess さんの会社を訪れますか。

(A) 機械の検査をするため
(B) 契約を締結するため
(C) 新しい機械を導入するため
(D) 職員を教育するため

Martin さんはなぜ Hess さんの会社を訪れるかが問われている。Hess さんは 2 文書目の手紙の❺で、Martin さんに、「マイクロチップ製造設備導入の最終段階のため、問題ないかすべて点検してもらえると助かる」と述べている。ここから Martin さんがある設備点検のために訪問することがわかるので、点検を inspect、機械設備を equipment と言い換えた **(A)** が正解。

□ sign (契約等) を締結する　□ educate 〜を教育する

★★★★☆

47. What kind of event did Mr. Hess initially plan to take Ms. Martin to?

(A) A musical performance
(B) A dance competition
(C) A comedy show
(D) A film festival

Hess さんは当初どのようなイベントに Martin さんを連れていく予定でしたか。

(A) 音楽の演奏
(B) ダンス競技会
(C) コメディーショー
(D) 映画祭

Hess さんは当初 Martin さんをどんなイベントに連れていく予定だったかが問われている。2 文書目の手紙を見ると、Hess さんは Martin さんに対し、❹で「5 月 7 日から 9 日にかけて当社にお越しになる」、❻で「最初の晩、Timko Auditorium に案内する」と述べている。ここから 1 文書目の情報の❸を見ると、最初の晩である 5 月 7 日に該当しているイベントは演奏会だとわかる。よって、正解は **(A)**。

□ competition 競技会

....

★★★☆☆

48. What is Mr. Jackson asked to do?

(A) Make a reservation in advance
(B) Take a visitor to dinner
(C) Confirm a flight time
(D) Pick up Ms. Martin

Jackson さんは何をするように求められていますか。

(A) あらかじめ予約をする
(B) 訪問客を夕食に連れていく
(C) 飛行機の時間を確認する
(D) Matin さんを迎えに行く

Jackson さんは何をするように求められているかが問われている。Jackson さんは 3 文書目のテキストメッセージの❼で、「Martin さんに会ってホテルまで送ってほしい」と頼まれている。つまり、Martin さんを迎えに行くことがわかる。以上から、正解は **(D)**。❼の代名詞 her が Ms. Martin さんを指していることを、この文書の冒頭の宛名から把握することがポイントとなる。

□ in advance 事前に　□ fight time 飛行時間

....

★★★★★

49. What can be inferred about Mr. LeBlanc?

(A) He will join the group for dinner.
(B) He made a donation to Timko Auditorium.
(C) He has met Ms. Martin before.
(D) He works at the Elena Hotel.

LeBlanc さんについて何が推測できますか。

(A) 夕食のためにグループに加わる。
(B) Timko Auditorium に寄付をした。
(C) 以前、Martin さんに会ったことがある。
(D) Elena Hotel で働いている。

LeBlanc さんについて何が推測できるかが問われている。3 文書目のテキストメッセージの❽で、「Ralph LeBlanc さんは Golden Membership を持っていて割引が受けられるので、チケットの購入を頼んだ」と述べている。次に、1 文書目の情報の❷で、「(Timko Auditorium の) プロジェクトに寄付をすると、Golden Membership が取得でき、チケットはすべて 30 パーセント割引となる」ことがわかる。つまり、すでに Golden Membership を持っている LeBlanc さんは、Timko Auditorium のプロジェクトに寄付をした、ということがわかる。以上から正解は **(B)**。ある条件で割引になる、というのはどういうことか、という視点で別の文書を参照して解く少し難しい問題。

□ make a donation 寄付をする　□ before 以前

TIMKO AUDITORIUM

Timko Auditorium で素晴らしいショーをご堪能ください！！！

国内で最高の知名度を誇る劇場である Timko Auditorium では、国内で大人気のパフォーマーがさまざまなパフォーマンスを披露してきました。

Timko Auditorium では、数々の賞を受賞したミュージカル、感動的な劇、芸術祭などを観客の皆さまに提供してきました。毎日午後には、ガイドと一緒に公会堂を見学して、舞台裏に行ったり、公会堂の興味深い歴史について学ぶことができます。

また、当館では来年の改修プロジェクトのための資金も集めています。プロジェクトに寄付をすると、Golden Membership が取得でき、チケットはすべて 30 パーセント割引でお求めになれます（1 つのショーにつき 8 枚まで）。Timko Auditorium の今月の演目をお見逃しなく：

期間	内容
5 月 1 日から 7 日	Eastmon Philharmonic Orchestra、ハイドンの古典音楽の演奏
5 月 8 日から 19 日	Non-commercial Film Festival、毎晩違う映画を上演
5 月 20 日から 23 日	Pan-Am Ballet Championships、全国からのダンサーの競演
5 月 24 日から 31 日	Comedy by Jose Bolivar、笑いが止まらない、ユーモアにあふれるコメディー

Martin 様

5 月 7 日から 9 日にかけて当社にお越しになるとお聞きしました。お電話で話し合った後で、直接お会いできることをとてもうれしく思います。マイクロチップを製造するための生産設備を現地に設置する最終段階ですので、問題がないか確認するため、すべて点検していただけると助かります。

話は変わりますが、忙しい一日が終わったら、同僚の Pitt Jackson さんと私が Timko Auditorium にご案内しますので、こちらでの最初の晩、夜のエンターテイメントをお楽しみください。

お会いできるのを楽しみにしております！

Drew Hess

送信者： Drew Hess
受信者： Pitt Jackson
送信時間： 5 月 7 日、午後 3 時 10 分

Martin さんのフライトは離陸が遅れたため、到着が午後 9 時 20 分以降になります。レンタカーの窓口は 9 時に閉まりますので、空港からの送迎が必要となります。Martin さんを迎えに行って、Elena Hotel まで送ってください。また、公会堂へ行くのは明日の夜に変更します。Ralph LeBlanc さんは Golden Membership を持っていて割引が受けられるので、チケットの購入を頼みました。よろしくお願いいたします！

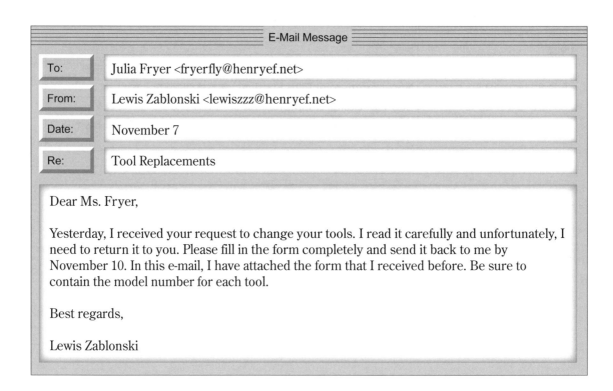

We are informing you of the procedure for replacing tools. All maintenance workers should remember that they need to order all replacements at this time. Our maintenance budget allocates money to replace tools with purchase costs less than $300, such as pliers, wrenches, screwdrivers, and hammers to be replaced every three years. Tools that cost $300 or more will be sent for repair unless the repair cost exceeds the purchase price. If you are unsure of the repair or replacement costs, please ask an employee of the ordering department.

I have attached a tool replacement request form for you to list the tools you need to replace. You may make copies of the form as you need. A supervisor's signature is required on each document. You should fill in the tool replacement request form completely. Forms must be returned to Lewis Zablonski, Ordering Department, Suite 347, before November 10.

E-Mail Message

To:	Julia Fryer <fryerfly@henryef.net>
From:	Lewis Zablonski <lewiszzz@henryef.net>
Date:	November 7
Re:	Tool Replacements

Dear Ms. Fryer,

Yesterday, I received your request to change your tools. I read it carefully and unfortunately, I need to return it to you. Please fill in the form completely and send it back to me by November 10. In this e-mail, I have attached the form that I received before. Be sure to contain the model number for each tool.

Best regards,

Lewis Zablonski

Henry Environmental Facility

Tool Replacement Request

- Employee's Name: Julia Fryer
- Employee's Number: 24811
- E-mail Address: fryerfly@henryef.net

Tool	Model Number	Replacement cost
Slip Joint Pliers		$80
Torque Wrench	TWC81134	$120
Cordless Drill	CDL12460	$329

Approved by Georgina Goodman

Signature: *Georgina Goodman*

---

50. Why is the notice written?

(A) To decide on how the prices of tools are researched
(B) To inform employees of a budget decrease for tool purchases
(C) To explain how maintenance equipment will be inventoried
(D) To review how to order new tools

51. In the notice, the word "allocates" in paragraph 1, line 3, is closest in meaning to

(A) acquires
(B) distributes
(C) establishes
(D) composes

52. What can be inferred about the cordless drill?

(A) Its warranty expires in one year.
(B) It is not compatible with the company's new system.
(C) Purchasing a new one would cost less than repairing it.
(D) It is no longer available for order.

53. Why most likely did Mr. Zablonski send his e-mail to Ms. Fryer?

(A) Because she listed the wrong tools
(B) Because she did not turn in the document
(C) Because she missed the required information
(D) Because Ms. Goodman did not sign the form

54. Who most likely is Ms. Goodman?

(A) A supervisor
(B) An ordering agent
(C) An executive assistant
(D) A maintenance employee

P. 396

Questions 50-54 refer to the following notice, e-mail, and form.

❶ We are informing you of the procedure for replacing tools. All maintenance workers should remember that they need to order all replacements at this time. ❷ Our maintenance budget allocates money to replace tools with purchase costs less than $300, such as pliers, wrenches, screwdrivers, and hammers to be replaced every three years. ❸ Tools that cost $300 or more will be sent for repair unless the repair cost exceeds the purchase price. If you are unsure of the repair or replacement costs, please ask an employee of the ordering department.

I have attached a tool replacement request form for you to list the tools you need to replace. You may make copies of the form as you need. ❹ A supervisor's signature is required on each document. You should fill in the tool replacement request form completely. Forms must be returned to Lewis Zablonski, Ordering Department, Suite 347, before November 10.

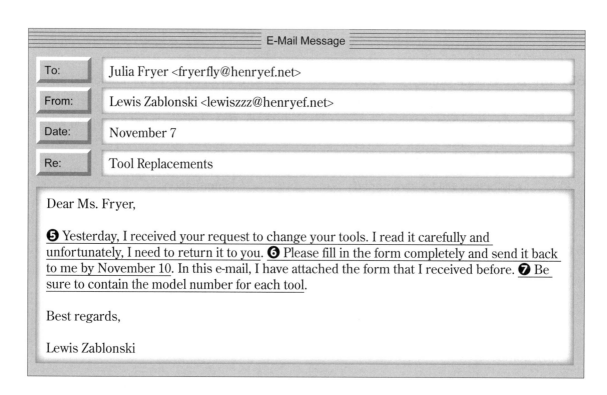

E-Mail Message

To:	Julia Fryer <fryerfly@henryef.net>
From:	Lewis Zablonski <lewiszzz@henryef.net>
Date:	November 7
Re:	Tool Replacements

Dear Ms. Fryer,

❺ Yesterday, I received your request to change your tools. I read it carefully and unfortunately, I need to return it to you. ❻ Please fill in the form completely and send it back to me by November 10. In this e-mail, I have attached the form that I received before. ❼ Be sure to contain the model number for each tool.

Best regards,

Lewis Zablonski

Henry Environmental Facility

Tool Replacement Request

- Employee's Name: Julia Fryer
- Employee's Number: 24811
- E-mail Address: fryerfly@henryef.net

Tool	Model Number	Replacement cost
Slip Joint Pliers		$80
Torque Wrench	TWC81134	$120
❽ Cordless Drill	CDL12460	$329

Approved by Georgina Goodman

Signature: ❾ *Georgina Goodman*

お知らせ
☐ inform A of B AにBのことを知らせる　☐ procedure 手順　☐ maintenance worker 整備員
☐ replacement 交換品　☐ at this time 今回　☐ allocate ～を割り当てる・配分する　☐ such as ～のような
☐ pliers ペンチ、プライヤー　☐ wrench レンチ　☐ screwdriver （ねじ回しの）ドライバー　☐ hammer ハンマー
☐ exceed ～を超える　☐ purchase price 購入価格　☐ unsure of ～が不明・わからない
☐ ordering department 発注部門　☐ attach ～を添付する　☐ replacement request form 交換申請書
☐ as you need 必要に応じて　☐ require ～を必要とする　☐ fill in ～を記入する

E メール
☐ send A back to B AをBに返送する　☐ contain ～を含める　☐ model number 型番

用紙
☐ slip joint スリップジョイント式（支柱接合の一種）　☐ torque wrench トルクレンチ　☐ cordless コードレスの

★★★☆☆

50. Why is the notice written?

(A) To decide on how the prices of tools are researched
(B) To inform employees of a budget decrease for tool purchases
(C) To explain how maintenance equipment will be inventoried
(D) To review how to order new tools

お知らせはなぜ書かれましたか。

(A) 工具の価格の調査方法を決定するため
(B) 工具購入に関する予算の削減について従業員に周知するため
(C) 整備器具の一覧表を作成する方法を説明するため
(D) 新しい工具の注文方法を確認するため

お知らせがなぜ書かれたかが問われている。1 文書目のお知らせの❶で、「工具交換の手順を知らせる」と述べ、その後には費用の割り当て等の記載があるため、新規に工具を購入して古いものと交換するための手順だとわかる。よって、そのことを To review how to order ... と表現している **(D)** が正解。価格の調査まで決定するわけではないので、(A) は不正解。

☐ decide on ～を決定する　☐ decrease 減少　☐ inventory ～の一覧表を作成する

397

51. In the notice, the word "allocates" in paragraph 1, line 3, is closest in meaning to

(A) acquires
(B) distributes
(C) establishes
(D) composes

お知らせの、第1段落・3行目にある "allocates" に最も意味が近いのは

(A) ～を習得する
(B) ～を分配する
(C) ～を設立する
(D) ～を構成する

同義語問題。問われている1文書目のお知らせの❷にある "allocates" は、「(予算が工具交換金額を)割り当て・分配している」、という意味で使われている。以上より、同じ意味となるのは **(B)**。(D) は「(要素・部品を)構成している」という意味で使われており、ここでは文意に合わない。

---

52. What can be inferred about the cordless drill?

(A) Its warranty expires in one year.
(B) It is not compatible with the company's new system.
(C) Purchasing a new one would cost less than repairing it.
(D) It is no longer available for order.

コードレスドリルについて何が推測できますか。

(A) 保証が1年後に切れる。
(B) 会社の新しいシステムと一緒に使えない。
(C) 新品を購入するほうが修理するよりも安い。
(D) 注文できなくなった。

コードレスドリルについて何が推測できるかが問われている。1文書目のお知らせの❸で、「300ドル以上の工具は、修理費用が購入額を超えない限り修理対象として送られる」と述べられている。次に3文書目の用紙を見ると、表内の❽で、コードレスドリルの交換費用が300ドルを超過しており、このお知らせ文書の対象工具であることがわかる。つまり、このコードレスドリルは、修理費用よりも購入費用が安かった、ということが推測できる。以上から **(C)** が正解。ここは事実ではないが、交換申請に出されている、ということは、推測として考えることができる、と判断しよう。

☐ expire 期限が切れる　☐ compatible 互換性がある　☐ no longer もはや～ではない

---

53. Why most likely did Mr. Zablonski send his e-mail to Ms. Fryer?

(A) Because she listed the wrong tools
(B) Because she did not turn in the document
(C) Because she missed the required information
(D) Because Ms. Goodman did not sign the form

Zablonski さんはなぜ Fryer さんに E メールを送ったと考えられますか。

(A) 間違った工具を一覧に載せたため
(B) 書類を提出していなかったため
(C) 必要情報の記入漏れがあったため
(D) Goodman さんが用紙に署名をしていなかったため

Zablonski さんが Fryer さんに E メールを送った理由が問われている。Zablonski さんは Fryer さんに2文書目の E メールの❺で、「工具変更についての申請書を受け取り、確認したが、戻さなければいけない」と切り出し、❻で「申請書に漏れなく記入して、期日まで返送してほしい」、❼で「それぞれの工具の型番号を必ず書いてほしい」と伝えている。つまり、必要情報に記入漏れがあったことが考えられる。以上から、正解は **(C)**。

☐ list ～を一覧表にする　☐ turn in ～を提出する　☐ miss ～を見落とす

54. Who most likely is Ms. Goodman?

(A) A supervisor
(B) An ordering agent
(C) An executive assistant
(D) A maintenance employee

Goodman さんとはどんな人物であると考えられますか。

(A) 部門長
(B) 発注係
(C) 管理職の補佐
(D) 整備員

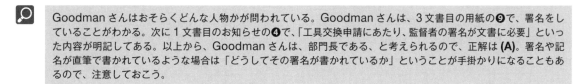

Goodman さんはおそらくどんな人物かが問われている。Goodman さんは、3 文書目の用紙の❾で、署名をしていることがわかる。次に 1 文書目のお知らせの❹で、「工具交換申請にあたり、監督者の署名が文書に必要」といった内容が明記してある。以上から、Goodman さんは、部門長である、と考えられるので、正解は **(A)**。署名や記名が直筆で書かれているような場合は「どうしてその署名が書かれているか」ということが手掛かりになることもあるので、注意しておこう。

□ agent 担当者　□ executive assistant 管理補佐

工具交換の手順をお知らせします。全整備員は、今回すべての交換物品を注文する必要があることを忘れないでください。当社の整備予算は、ペンチ、プライヤー、ドライバー、ハンマーなどの3年ごとに取り換えられる、購入費用が300ドル未満の工具を交換するための費用として割り当てられています。購入費用が300ドル以上の工具に関しては、修理費が購入価格を超えない限りは修理に回されます。修理又は交換費用がわからない場合は、発注部門の担当者にお問い合わせください。

交換が必要な工具の一覧を作るための工具交換申請書を添付しました。必要に応じてコピーをとっておいてください。どの書類にも部門長の署名が必要です。工具交換申請書には記入漏れがないようにしてください。申請書は、347号室の発注部門 Lewis Zablonski さん宛てに11月10日までに返送をお願いいたします。

受信者： Julia Fryer <fryerfly@henryef.net>
送信者： Lewis Zablonski <lewiszzz@henryef.net>
日付： 11月7日
件名： 工具交換

Fryer さん

昨日、工具変更についての申請書を受け取りました。入念に確認させていただきましたが、あいにくお戻ししなければなりません。申請書に漏れなく記入して、11月10日までに私宛てに返送してください。このEメールに、送っていただいた申請書を添付しました。それぞれの工具の型番号を必ず書いてください。

よろしくお願いいたします。

Lewis Zablonski

Henry Environmental Facility

工具交換申請書

- 従業員の名前：Julia Fryer
- 従業員番号：24811
- Eメールアドレス：fryerfly@henryef.net

工具	型番号	交換費用
スリップジョイントプライヤー		80ドル
トルクレンチ	TWC81134	120ドル
コードレスドリル	CDL12460	329ドル

決済者：Georgina Goodman

署名：Georgina Goodman

Test

TOKIMAKURE!

6

Test 6

Questions 1-2 refer to the following job statement.

JOB STATEMENT

Hurley's job is to provide electricity and natural gas in a dependable, effective, reasonable, and environmentally sound manner. We try to do the best in the public utilities industry and are committed to achieving operational excellence, supreme customer satisfaction, and a strong financial performance for our investors.

Hurley Company

---

1. What kind of business is Hurley Company?

(A) An accounting firm
(B) A utility firm
(C) A financial company
(D) An investment bank

2. According to the document, what is NOT true of Hurley Company?

(A) It is environmentally conscious.
(B) It tries to make its customers happy.
(C) It is now expanding its business internationally.
(D) It aims to make money for its shareholders.

P. 404

Questions 3-4 refer to the following article.

 1分30秒

Daily Riversdale, September 5—The Municipal Council of Riversdale has recently invited local major land developers to participate in building an industrial park on the south side of the city, on a 20,000 square foot plot of land.

The industrial park will be located just off of Ford Drive, on the land that used to house many Riversdale companies such as the bottling firm, the lawn mower plant and the textiles factory. The new buildings will incorporate cutting-edge technology and ecologically friendly practices. In addition, the city plans to develop a small residential neighborhood across the road from the site within ten years.

"We are very excited about this chance to bring new businesses to our area," said City Council member Emma Campbell. "The new industrial park will be in a perfect location, near a major freeway, and close to many commercial venues and eateries." She added that space will be allocated according to occupants' needs after the initial design phase is finished.

A great deal of the development activity in Riversdale has been prompted by the recent expansion of the international airport which is located thirteen miles away from Riversdale.

3. What is implied about the southern part of Riversdale?

(A) It is important to an international airport.
(B) There is now a housing area.
(C) Lawn mowers were once produced there.
(D) A bottling plant will be relocated.

4. Which of the following is NOT mentioned as the features of the new industrial park?

(A) Increased job opportunities
(B) Nearness to dining establishments
(C) Environmentally conscious design
(D) Proximity to a major expressway

P. 406

Questions 1-2 refer to the following job statement.

JOB STATEMENT

Hurley's job is to provide electricity and natural gas in a dependable, effective, reasonable, and ❶ environmentally sound manner. ❷ We try to do the best in the public utilities industry and are committed to achieving operational excellence, ❸ supreme customer satisfaction, and ❹ a strong financial performance for our investors.

Hurley Company

✏️ ☐ provide ～を供給する ☐ natural gas 天然ガス ☐ dependable 信頼のできる ☐ effective 効果的な
☐ reasonable 理にかなった ☐ environmentally 環境的に ☐ in a sound manner 健全な方法で
☐ public utilities industry 公共事業業界 ☐ be committed to *do*ing ～することに取り組んでいる
☐ achieve ～を達成する ☐ operational 経営の ☐ excellence 卓越性、優秀さ ☐ supreme 圧倒的な
☐ customer satisfaction 顧客満足 ☐ financial performance 財務実績 ☐ investor 投資家

★★☆☆☆

1. What kind of business is Hurley Company?

  (A) An accounting firm
  (B) A utility firm
  (C) A financial company
  (D) An investment bank

Hurley Company の業種は何ですか。

  (A) 会計事務所
  (B) 公益事業会社
  (C) 金融会社
  (D) 投資銀行

🔍 Hurley Company の業種が何かが問われている。❷で Hurley Company を "we" と表現し、「私たちは公共事業の業界の中で最善を尽くしている」と述べていることから、公益事業会社であるとわかる。よって、これを言い換えた **(B)** が正解。company と firm の言い換えは頻繁にあるので瞬時に判別できるようにしておこう。

★★★☆☆ NOT 問題

2. According to the document, what is NOT true of Hurley Company?

  (A) It is environmentally conscious.
  (B) It tries to make its customers happy.
  (C) It is now expanding its business internationally.
  (D) It aims to make money for its shareholders.

文書によると、Hurley Company に当てはまらないことは何ですか。

  (A) 環境に配慮している。
  (B) 顧客を幸福にすることに尽力している。
  (C) 現在、国際的に事業を拡大している。
  (D) 株主のためにお金を儲けることを目的としている。

🔍 NOT 問題。Hurley Company に当てはまらないことが問われている。❶の「環境に配慮した健全な方法」が (A) に、❸の「圧倒的な顧客満足」が (B) に、❹の「投資家への強力な財務実績」が (D) にそれぞれ当てはまる。残った **(C)** については述べられていないため、これが正解となる。

✏️ ☐ conscious 意識して、配慮して ☐ expand ～を拡大・拡張する ☐ internationally 国際的に
☐ aim to *do* ～するのを目的とする ☐ shareholder 株主

問題1から2は次の事業内容に関するものです。

事業内容

Hurley 社の事業は電力と天然ガスを、信頼できるやり方で、効果的かつ合理的に、そして環境に配慮した健全な形で提供することです。私たちは公益事業の業界の中で最善を尽くし、経営の卓越性、圧倒的な顧客満足、そして投資家の皆さまとって優れた財務実績の達成に取り組んでいます。

Hurley Company

Questions 3-4 refer to the following article.

Daily Riversdale, September 5—❶ The Municipal Council of Riversdale has recently invited local major land developers to participate in building an industrial park on the south side of the city, on a 20,000 square foot plot of land.

❷ The industrial park will be located just off of Ford Drive, on the land that used to house many Riversdale companies such as the bottling firm, the lawn mower plant and the textiles factory. ❸ The new buildings will incorporate cutting-edge technology and ecologically friendly practices. In addition, the city plans to develop a small residential neighborhood across the road from the site within ten years.

"We are very excited about this chance to bring new businesses to our area," said City Council member Emma Campbell. ❹ "The new industrial park will be in a perfect location, near a major freeway, and close to many commercial venues and eateries." She added that space will be allocated according to occupants' needs after the initial design phase is finished.

A great deal of the development activity in Riversdale has been prompted by the recent expansion of the international airport which is located thirteen miles away from Riversdale.

✏️
- ☐ municipal council 市議会　☐ land developer 土地開発会社　☐ participate in ～に参加する
- ☐ industrial park 工業団地　☐ square 平方　☐ foot フィート（複数形は feet）　☐ plot of land 1 区画
- ☐ just off of ～から少し離れたところに　☐ house ～を収容する　☐ such as ～のような　☐ bottling firm 瓶詰会社
- ☐ lawn mower 芝刈り機　☐ textiles factory 繊維工場　☐ incorporate A and B A と B を組み込む
- ☐ cutting-edge 最新鋭の　☐ ecologically friendly 環境に配慮した　☐ practice 実践、仕組み
- ☐ residential neighborhood 住宅街　☐ freeway 高速道路　☐ close to ～に近い　☐ commercial venue 商業施設
- ☐ eatery 食堂、レストラン　☐ allocate ～を割り当てる　☐ according to ～に応じて　☐ occupant 入居者、入居団体
- ☐ needs ニーズ、需要　☐ initial 初期の　☐ phase 段階　☐ a great deal of 多くの　☐ prompt ～を促進する
- ☐ expansion 拡張

★★★★☆

3. What is implied about the southern part of Riversdale?

(A) It is important to an international airport.
(B) There is now a housing area.
(C) Lawn mowers were once produced there.
(D) A bottling plant will be relocated.

Riversdale の南部について何が示唆されていますか。

(A) 国際空港にとって重要である。
(B) 現在、住宅地がある。
(C) かつて芝刈り機がそこで生産されていた。
(D) 瓶詰工場が移転してくる。

・・

★★★☆☆ NOT 問題

4. Which of the following is NOT mentioned as the features of the new industrial park?

(A) Increased job opportunities
(B) Nearness to dining establishments
(C) Environmentally conscious design
(D) Proximity to a major expressway

新しい工業団地の特徴として言及されていないものは、次のうちどれですか。

(A) 雇用機会の増加
(B) 飲食店への近さ
(C) 環境に配慮したデザイン
(D) 主要高速道路への隣接

📝 問題 3 から 4 は次の記事に関するものです。

Daily Riversdale、9 月 5 日 — Riversdale 市議会は先日、地元の主要な土地開発会社に、市の南側にある 20,000 平方フィートの土地での工業団地の建設に参加することを要請した。

工業団地は Ford Drive の少し先にある、かつて瓶詰会社や芝刈り機工場、繊維工場といった Riversdale の多くの企業があった場所にできる予定である。新しい建物には最先端の技術と環境に配慮した仕組みが採用される。さらに、敷地から道路を挟んだ場所に小さな住宅街を 10 年以内に開発する予定である。

市議会議員 Emma Campbell 氏は、「地域に新たな企業を誘致するこのチャンスにとても期待しています。」と述べた。「新しい工業団地は、主要な高速道路から近く、また多くの商業施設やレストランからも近い、申し分のない場所になるでしょう。」また、初めの設計段階が終了した後、入居企業の要望に応じて区域が割り当てられると加えた。

多くの Riversdale の開発活動は、Riversdale から 13 マイル先にある国際空港の最近の拡張をきっかけに促進されている。

A few days ago, you requested us to send *Monthly Stat Fund* to your new address. To ensure *Monthly Stat Fund* reaches you on a regular and timely basis, please take the time to check your name and new address as mentioned below. Remember to confirm the postal code, and add an apartment number if you have one. Additionally, this is a perfect time to extend your *Monthly Stat Fund* subscription for a year or two more. You will be protected from all increasing rates and ensured flexible delivery. And you can consider *Monthly Stat Fund* as a present to your best friends or colleagues. Your thoughtfulness will be remembered through the year.

Old address:
Brian O'Connor
59213 West 54th Avenue
New York, NY 10057

Check new address: Yes / No (fill in correction below)
Brian O'Connor
20184 West 54th Avenue, Apt. 6A
New York, NY 10057

Correct new address:
Name:
Address:
City: State: Postal code:

Extend my subscription for:
1 year (12 issues, $44) / 2 years (24 issues, $76)

Send a gift subscription of *Monthly Stat Fund* for:
1 year (12 issues, $44) / 2 years (24 issues, $76)

To:
Name:
Address:
City: State: Postal code:

---

5. Why is this form sent to Mr. O'Connor?

(A) He sent a past due payment for a subscription.
(B) He recently changed his address.
(C) He complained about irregular service.
(D) His subscription is expiring soon.

6. What kind of benefit would Mr. O'Connor gain from renewing his subscription now?

(A) A reduced rate for a gift subscription
(B) A guarantee against future price increases
(C) A free calendar
(D) A second year at half price

P. 410

Questions 7-8 refer to the following text-message chain.

 1分30秒

Janice Perez 2:21 P.M.

Are you carrying the materials for today's presentation?

Patrick Miller 2:23 P.M.

Yes, I have them with me. However, I'm afraid I might be a little late.

Janice Perez 2:24 P.M.

Really? How come?

Patrick Miller 2:26 P.M.

I'm stuck in a traffic jam. There's been an accident further up the road.

Janice Perez 2:27 P.M.

Unfortunately, we have to start the meeting at 3:30. I could give the presentation by myself, but I need those materials you have.

Patrick Miller 2:28 P.M.

I see. Why don't you ask to move our meeting time to 4:00?

Janice Perez 2:31 P.M.

I'll try. But as you know, there are other guests who are supposed to meet us at 3:00.

Patrick Miller 2:32 P.M.

Oh, that's right. I'm so sorry. Please apologize to them on my behalf. I'll be there as soon as possible.

---

7. Why cannot Mr. Miller make it on time?

   (A) He is sick now.
   (B) He is caught in heavy traffic.
   (C) He forgot to bring some materials.
   (D) He was involved in a car accident.

8. At 2:31 P.M., what does Ms. Perez mean when she writes, "I'll try"?

   (A) She will drive faster to get there on time.
   (B) She will request the delay of the meeting.
   (C) She will give the presentation by herself.
   (D) She will take notes during the presentation.

P. 412

Questions 5-6 refer to the following information.

❶ A few days ago, you requested us to send *Monthly Stat Fund* to your new address. To ensure *Monthly Stat Fund* reaches you on a regular and timely basis, please take the time to check your name and new address as mentioned below. Remember to confirm the postal code, and add an apartment number if you have one. Additionally, this is a perfect time to extend your *Monthly Stat Fund* subscription for a year or two more. ❷ You will be protected from all increasing rates and ensured flexible delivery. And you can consider *Monthly Stat Fund* as a present to your best friends or colleagues. Your thoughtfulness will be remembered through the year.

Old address:
Brian O'Connor
59213 West 54th Avenue
New York, NY 10057

Check new address: Yes / No (fill in correction below)
Brian O'Connor
20184 West 54th Avenue, Apt. 6A
New York, NY 10057

Correct new address:
Name:
Address:
City: State: Postal code:

Extend my subscription for:
1 year (12 issues, $44) / 2 years (24 issues, $76)

Send a gift subscription of *Monthly Stat Fund* for:
1 year (12 issues, $44) / 2 years (24 issues, $76)

To:
Name:
Address:
City: State: Postal code:

□ ensure ～を確実にする □ reach ～のところに届ける
□ on a regular and timely basis 定期的かつ遅れることがないように □ take the time to *do* 時間を取って～する
□ as mentioned below 下記のとおり □ remember to *do* 忘れずに～する □ confirm ～を確認する
□ postal code 郵便番号 □ additionally 加えて □ perfect time ふさわしい時 □ extend ～を延長する
□ subscription 定期購読 □ protect ～を保護する □ flexible 融通の利く □ thoughtfulness 配慮、心遣い

★★★☆☆

5. Why is this form sent to Mr. O'Connor?

(A) He sent a past due payment for a subscription.
(B) He recently changed his address.
(C) He complained about irregular service.
(D) His subscription is expiring soon.

なぜこの用紙が O'Connor さんに送られますか。

(A) 支払い期限を過ぎた定期購読料を送金したため。
(B) 最近、住所を変更したため。
(C) 通常とは違うサービスについて苦情を申し立てたため。
(D) もうすぐ定期購読の期限が終わるため。

なぜこの用紙が O'Connor さんのところに送付されたのかが問われている。冒頭の❶で「新住所への送付依頼を承った」と述べているため、ここから O'Connor さんの住所が変わったことがわかる。よって、これを changed his address と言い換えた **(B)** が正解となる。

□ due payment 支払い期限 □ complain 苦情を言う □ irregular 不定期な □ expire 期限が切れる

6. What kind of benefit would Mr. O'Connor gain from renewing his subscription now?

(A) A reduced rate for a gift subscription
(B) A guarantee against future price increases
(C) A free calendar
(D) A second year at half price

今、定期購読契約を更新すると O'Connor さんはどんな特典をもらえますか。

(A) 定期購読のギフトのための割引料金
(B) 将来の値上げに対する保証
(C) 無料のカレンダー
(D) 2 年目は半額

O'Connor さんが今、定期購読契約を更新することでどんな特典をもらえるかが問われている。❷で「値上げの際も料金は据え置きで、融通が利く配送を保証する」と持ち掛けられていることから、前者に相当する **(B)** が正解となる。値下げや景品については触れられていないため、その他の選択肢はいずれも不正解。

□ reduced rate 割引価格　□ guarantee 保証　□ price increase 値上げ　□ at half price 半額で

問題 5 から 6 は次の情報に関するものです。

Monthly Stat Fund の新しい住所への送付依頼を数日前に承りました。*Monthly Stat Fund* を定期的かつ遅延のないように確実にお届けするため、下記のお名前と新しい住所の確認をお願いいたします。郵便番号をご確認いただき、お部屋番号がある場合はご記入ください。また、この機会に *Monthly Stat Fund* の定期購読の 1 ～ 2 年の延長を、ぜひご検討ください。値上げの際も料金は据え置きで、融通が利く配送を保証いたします。*Monthly Stat Fund* を親しいお友達や同僚の方への贈り物とすることも可能です。また 1 年間ご愛顧いただければ幸いです。

旧住所：
Brian O'Connor 様
59213 West 54th Avenue
ニューヨーク市、ニューヨーク州 10057

新住所の確認：正しい　/　間違っている（下に正しいものをご記入ください。）
Brian O'Connor 様
20184 West 54th Avenue, 部屋番号 6A
ニューヨーク市、ニューヨーク州 10057

正しい新住所：
お名前：
ご住所：
市：　　　　　　　　　　　州：　　　　　　　　郵便番号：

ご購読を延長する：
1 年間（12 号分、44 ドル）/　2 年間 (24 号分、76 ドル)

***Monthly Stat Fund* の定期購読のギフトを贈る：**
1 年間（12 号分、44 ドル）/　2 年間 (24 号分、76 ドル)

送り先：
お名前：
ご住所：
市：　　　　　　　　　　　州：　　　　　　　　郵便番号：

Questions 7-8 refer to the following text-message chain.

Janice Perez 2:21 P.M.

Are you carrying the materials for today's presentation?

Patrick Miller 2:23 P.M.

Yes, I have them with me. However, ❶ I'm afraid I might be a little late.

Janice Perez 2:24 P.M.

Really? ❷ How come?

Patrick Miller 2:26 P.M.

❸ I'm stuck in a traffic jam. There's been an accident further up the road.

Janice Perez 2:27 P.M.

Unfortunately, ❹ we have to start the meeting at 3:30. I could give the presentation by myself, but I need those materials you have.

Patrick Miller 2:28 P.M.

I see. ❺ Why don't you ask to move our meeting time to 4:00?

Janice Perez 2:31 P.M.

❻ I'll try. But as you know, there are other guests who are supposed to meet us at 3:00.

Patrick Miller 2:32 P.M.

Oh, that's right. I'm so sorry. Please apologize to them on my behalf. I'll be there as soon as possible.

□ carry 〜を運ぶ　□ material 資料　□ I'm afraid すまないが…　□ How come? なぜですか？
□ stuck in a traffic jam 交通渋滞の中にいて動けない　□ further up the road この先を行ったところで
□ be supposed to *do* 〜するはずになっている　□ apologize to 〜に謝罪する　□ on one's behalf 〜の代わりに
□ as soon as possible できるだけ早く

★★☆☆☆

7. Why cannot Mr. Miller make it on time?

(A) He is sick now.
(B) He is caught in heavy traffic.
(C) He forgot to bring some materials.
(D) He was involved in a car accident.

Miller さんが時間どおりに来れないのはなぜですか。

(A) 今、病気である。
(B) 交通渋滞に巻き込まれている。
(C) 資料を持ってくるのを忘れた。
(D) 自動車事故に巻き込まれた。

> Miller さんが時間どおりに来れないのはなぜかが問われている。Miller さんは❶で「ちょっと遅れるかもしれない」と述べ、Perez さんが❷でその理由を尋ねたところ、❸で「交通渋滞で身動きが取れない」と返事をしている。以上から、その状況を caught in heavy traffic と言い換えた **(B)** が正解となる。

 □ make it 来る　□ on time 時間どおり　□ sick 病気である　□ be involved in 〜に関与している・巻き込まれている

8. At 2:31 P.M., what does Ms. Perez mean when she writes, "I'll try"?

(A) She will drive faster to get there on time.
(B) She will request the delay of the meeting.
(C) She will give the presentation by herself.
(D) She will take notes during the presentation.

午後 2 時 31 分に、Perez さんは "I'll try" という発言で、何を意味していますか。

(A) 送れずに着くように速く運転する。
(B) 会議を遅らせることをお願いする。
(C) 発表を一人で行う。
(D) 発表中にメモを取る。

意図問題。問われている❻は「やってみます」なので、前のやりとりを受けて試してみる旨を返答していると考えられる。この直前の❺を見ると、「会議を4時に変更するようにお願いしてみてはどうか？」と言っている。❹より、本来3時30分に打ち合わせをスタートさせる予定だったことがわかるので、「会議時間を遅らせることをやってみる」という意味になる。以上から、正解は **(B)** となる。

□ take note メモを取る

問題 7 から 8 は次のテキストメッセージのやりとりに関するものです。

Janice Perez 午後 2 時 21 分
今日の発表の資料は持ってきていますか？

Patrick Miller 午後 2 時 23 分
はい、ここにあります。ただ、少し遅れるかもしれません。

Janice Perez 午後 2 時 24 分
本当に？　どうしましたか？

Patrick Miller 午後 2 時 26 分
交通渋滞に巻き込まれているのです。この先のほうで事故が起きています。

Janice Perez 午後 2 時 27 分
あいにく、3時半には会議を始めなければいけません。私一人で発表をすることもできますが、そちらにある資料が必要です。

Patrick Miller 午後 2 時 28 分
そうですか。会議の時間を4時に変更するようにお願いしてみるのはどうでしょう？

Janice Perez 午後 2 時 31 分
やってみます。しかし、ご存じのとおり、3時に会う予定の他のお客様がいらっしゃいます。

Patrick Miller 午後 2 時 32 分
あぁ、そうでした。すみません。私に代わってお客様にお詫びをしてもらえますか。できるだけ早く着くようにします。

2分45秒

No more complimentary parking in Phoenix
November 22
By Robert Seeley

As an attempt to reduce the traffic congestion in downtown Phoenix, the municipal council has announced changes to parking regulations in the city.

—— [1] ——. "Our streets tend to be at their busiest in the evening hours," said David Miller, a member of the Phoenix City Council. —— [2] ——. "That's because both residents and nonresidents come to an entertainment district near our downtown area to enjoy our restaurants, theaters, and concert halls. —— [3] ——. They drive around looking for free street parking and this increases traffic congestion." —— [4] ——.

Now, payment for parking is requested only from 9 A.M. until 5 P.M. and no parking fees are charged past 5 o'clock. "This rule should be changed," Mr. Miller said. "We'd like to observe the example of other cities, where payment is required all day long."

If the proposed change takes effect, it will be the second one in recent months. In August, new parking meters that accept coins and credit cards as well as special Phoenix parking cards were installed. The cards, which became available in September, can be bought from any markets or shopping malls in Phoenix.

9. What is implied about Phoenix?

   (A) Its residents can park their cars anywhere free of charge.
   (B) Its roads are under construction.
   (C) It raises public awareness about the lack of roads.
   (D) The traffic gets heavy at a certain time.

10. What is the city council considering?

   (A) Increasing the hourly rate for parking
   (B) Introducing evening parking fees
   (C) Expanding existing parking lots
   (D) Looking for new parking areas

11. In which of the positions marked [1], [2], [3], and [4] does the following sentence best belong?

   "Drivers tend to avoid parking spaces that charge a substantial fee."

   (A) [1]
   (B) [2]
   (C) [3]
   (D) [4]

P. 416

Questions 9-11 refer to the following article.

No more complimentary parking in Phoenix
November 22
By Robert Seeley

❶ As an attempt to reduce the traffic congestion in downtown Phoenix, the municipal council has announced changes to parking regulations in the city.

— [1] —. ❷ "Our streets tend to be at their busiest in the evening hours," said David Miller, a member of the Phoenix City Council. — [2] —. "That's because both residents and nonresidents come to an entertainment district near our downtown area to enjoy our restaurants, theaters, and concert halls. — [3] —. ❸ They drive around looking for free street parking and this increases traffic congestion." — [4] —.

❹ Now, payment for parking is requested only from 9 A.M. until 5 P.M. and no parking fees are charged past 5 o'clock. ❺ "This rule should be changed," Mr. Miller said. "We'd like to observe the example of other cities, where payment is required all day long."

If the proposed change takes effect, it will be the second one in recent months. In August, new parking meters that accept coins and credit cards as well as special Phoenix parking cards were installed. The cards, which became available in September, can be bought from any markets or shopping malls in Phoenix.

☐ attempt 試み ☐ reduce ～を減らす ☐ traffic congestion 交通渋滞 ☐ downtown 繁華街
☐ municipal council 市議会 ☐ regulation 規則 ☐ tend to *do* ～する傾向がある ☐ nonresident 非居住者
☐ entertainment district 歓楽街 ☐ observe ～を観察する ☐ all day long 1日中 ☐ proposed 提案された
☐ take effect 施行する ☐ accept ～を利用可能とする ☐ A as well as B B同様にAも ☐ install ～を設置する

★★★☆☆

9. What is implied about Phoenix?

(A) Its residents can park their cars anywhere free of charge.
(B) Its roads are under construction.
(C) It raises public awareness about the lack of roads.
(D) The traffic gets heavy at a certain time.

フェニックスについて何が示唆されていますか。

(A) 居住者は市内の駐車場に無料で駐車できる。
(B) 道路が建設中である。
(C) 道路の不足に対する市民の意識を高めている。
(D) ある時間になると交通量が増える。

フェニックスについて示唆されていることを問う選択肢照合型の問題。冒頭の❶で「フェニックス都心部の交通渋滞緩和対策として、市議会が市内の駐車規則の変更を発表した」とある。また、❷で「この町の道路は夕方の時間帯に最も混雑する傾向がある」と述べられている。ここから、フェニックスでは対応が必要なほど交通渋滞が発生していることがわかるため、正解は **(D)** となる。(A) 居住者の無料駐車、(B) 道路建設、(C) 市民への道路不足への気づき、はいずれも記載がないので不正解。

☐ anywhere どこでも ☐ free of charge 無料で ☐ under construction 建設中の ☐ raise ～を高める
☐ public awareness 公共の意識 ☐ lack of ～の不足

10. What is the city council considering?

    (A) Increasing the hourly rate for parking
    (B) Introducing evening parking fees
    (C) Expanding existing parking lots
    (D) Looking for new parking areas

市議会は何を検討していますか。

    (A) 駐車場の時間貸し料金を上げること
    (B) 夜間の駐車料金を導入すること
    (C) 既存の駐車場を拡大すること
    (D) 新たな駐車場を探すこと

市議会が検討していることが問われている。まず、第3段落の❹から「現在、駐車料金の支払いは午前9時から午後5時までで、それ以降は駐車料金が掛からない」ことがわかる。次に❺で、「この規則を変更するべき」と市議会議員の Miller 氏が語り、「駐車料金が終日掛かる他の都市の例を見たい」と述べている。ここから、夜間も駐車料金を取るようにする変更を加えることがわかる。よって、正解は **(B)**。

□ the hourly rate 時間当たり料金　□ existing 既存の　□ parking lot 駐車場

11. In which of the positions marked [1], [2], [3], and [4] does the following sentence best belong?

"Drivers tend to avoid parking spaces that charge a substantial fee."

    (A) [1]
    (B) [2]
    (C) [3]
    (D) [4]

次の文は [1]、[2]、[3]、[4] のどの位置に最もよく当てはまりますか。

「車で来る人は、高い料金が掛かる駐車場を避ける傾向があります」

    (A) [1]
    (B) [2]
    (C) [3]
    (D) [4]

適切な文の位置を問う問題。問われている文は「車で来る人は、高い料金が掛かる駐車場を避ける傾向にある」という意味になっている。文書の中に、運転手が有料駐車場を避けるような行動について述べているところがないかを探していくと、❸に「無料駐車場を探し回っていて、これが渋滞を引き起こしている」という記載がある。この❸の直前に置けば "They" という代名詞が Drivers を指すことになり、文意が成立する。よって、正解は **(C)**。

□ avoid 〜を避ける　□ charge 〜を課す　□ substantial かなりの　□ fee 手数料

問題 9 から 11 は次の記事に関するものです。

フェニックスにおける無料駐車場の廃止
11 月 22 日
Robert Seeley による報告

フェニックスの都心部における交通渋滞緩和への試みとして、市議会は市内の駐車規則の変更を発表した。

—[1]— 「この町の道路は夕方の時間帯に最も混雑する傾向があります。」とフェニックス市議会議員の David Miller 氏は語った。 —[2]— 「それは居住者と非居住者の両方がレストランや劇場、コンサートホールで楽しむために都心部近くの繁華街へ来るからです。—[3]— 車で来る人は、高い料金がかかる駐車場を避ける傾向があります。無料の路上駐車場を探すためぐるぐると運転し、交通渋滞を増やしています。」—[4]—

現在、駐車料金の支払いは午前9時から午後5時までの間のみとされており、5時を過ぎると駐車料金は掛からない。「この規則は変更するべきです。」と Miller 氏は語る。「駐車料金が終日掛かる他の都市の例を見ていきたいと思っています。」

もし提案された変更が実施されれば、この数カ月で2つ目となる。8月には、硬貨、クレジットカード、そして、特別なフェニックス駐車カードが利用できる、新しいパーキングメーターが導入された。9月に販売が開始されたこのカードは、フェニックスにあるどのマーケットやショッピングモールでも購入できる。

NOTICE

Trenton International Airport is happy to inform all the passengers that a wireless Internet system has been established throughout all the terminals. Our wireless service provides easy-to-use access so you can use the Internet and send or receive e-mail throughout the day. The service is free. All you need to get connected to the Internet is a computer.

If you do not have a computer but would like to access the Internet, computer stations are located throughout Terminal D for your convenience and are marked by green signs. This service is available at the nominal charge of 5 dollars per one hour and is accessible 7 days a week from 6 A.M. to 11 P.M.

If you require technical support or more information or if you are dissatisfied with the service, come to our 24 hour Help Desk, located at Gate 14 in Terminal C. We are always doing our best to offer a better service to you. Thank you!

12. What is the purpose of this notice?

    (A) To advertise merchandise
    (B) To ask for assistance
    (C) To inform people of directions
    (D) To publicize a service

13. What does the notice state about the computer station?

    (A) It is available free of charge.
    (B) It is indicated by a certain sign.
    (C) It is available all day long.
    (D) It is located in Terminal C.

14. What are the users asked to do when they need help?

    (A) Call the computer manager
    (B) Contact the computer service center
    (C) Go to Gate 14
    (D) Forward their e-mail to the airport manager

P. 420

Questions 12-14 refer to the following notice.

NOTICE

❶ Trenton International Airport is happy to inform all the passengers that a wireless Internet system has been established throughout all the terminals. Our wireless service provides easy-to-use access so you can use the Internet and send or receive e-mail throughout the day. The service is free. All you need to get connected to the Internet is a computer.

❷ If you do not have a computer but would like to access the Internet, computer stations are located throughout Terminal D for your convenience and are marked by green signs. This service is available at the nominal charge of 5 dollars per one hour and is accessible 7 days a week from 6 A.M. to 11 P.M.

❸ If you require technical support or more information or if you are dissatisfied with the service, come to our 24 hour Help Desk, located at Gate 14 in Terminal C. We are always doing our best to offer a better service to you. Thank you!

✎ ☐ wireless 無線の ☐ establish ～を確立する・設立する ☐ terminal (空港・駅の) ターミナル
☐ easy-to-use 利用しやすい ☐ access 接続 ☐ get connected to ～に接続する
☐ for one's convenience 都合に合わせて ☐ marked by green signs 緑色のしるしで示された
☐ nominal わずかな ☐ accessible 使用できる ☐ require ～を要求する ☐ be dissatisfied with ～に不満である

★★☆☆☆

12. What is the purpose of this notice?

(A) To advertise merchandise
(B) To ask for assistance
(C) To inform people of directions
(D) To publicize a service

このお知らせの目的は何ですか。

(A) 商品を宣伝すること
(B) 支援を求めること
(C) 行きかたについて教えること
(D) サービスについて周知すること

🔍 このお知らせの目的が問われている。❶で、「Trenton International Airport は、搭乗客にターミナル全域で無線インターネットが利用可能となったことを知らせる」とあるので、あるサービスを知らせる目的だとわかる。この「知らせる」を "publicize" を用いて言い換えた **(D)** が正解となる。

✎ ☐ advertise ～を広告に出す ☐ publicize ～を周知する・宣伝する

★☆☆☆☆

13. What does the notice state about the computer station?

(A) It is available free of charge.
(B) It is indicated by a certain sign.
(C) It is available all day long.
(D) It is located in Terminal C.

お知らせにはコンピューターステーションについて何が記載されていますか。

(A) 無料で利用できる。
(B) ある表示で示されている。
(C) 一日中利用できる。
(D) ターミナルCにある。

🔍 コンピューターステーションについて何が記載されているかが問われている。❷で「ターミナルDのあらゆる場所に緑色のしるしで示されたコンピューターステーションが設置されている」とある。よって、正解は **(B)** となる。

✎ ☐ free of charge 無料で ☐ all day long 一日中 ☐ be located in ～にある

★★☆☆☆

14. What are the users asked to do when they need help?

- (A) Call the computer manager
- (B) Contact the computer service center
- **(C)** Go to Gate 14
- (D) Forward their e-mail to the airport manager

利用者はサポートが必要な場合、何をするように求められていますか。

- (A) コンピューターの管理者に電話をする
- (B) コンピューターサービスセンターに連絡する
- **(C)** 搭乗口 14 に行く
- (D) E メールを空港管理者に転送する

 利用者がサポートが必要な場合、何をするように求められているかが問われている。❸で「技術的サポートが必要な場合、ターミナル C 搭乗口 14 にある当空港の 24 時間相談窓口まで来るように」と述べている。よって、正解は **(C)** となる。

 □ forward A to B A を B に送付・転送する

 問題 12 から 14 は次のお知らせに関するものです。

お知らせ

Trenton International Airport は、ご搭乗のすべてのお客様に、すべてのターミナル全域で無線インターネットが利用可能となったことをお知らせいたします。当空港の無線インターネットサービスへのアクセスは利用しやすいものとなっていますので、一日中インターネットを使ったり、E メールを送受信したりできます。サービスは無料です。インターネットに接続するのに必要なものはパソコンだけです。

パソコンをお持ちでない方で、インターネットにアクセスされたい場合、ご都合の良いように、ターミナル D のあらゆる場所に緑色のしるしで示されたコンピューターステーションが設置されています。このサービスは 1 時間あたりわずか 5 ドルで利用可能で、週 7 日間、午前 6 時から午後 11 時までご使用いただけます。

技術的なサポートやより詳しい情報が必要な場合、またはサービスにご不満がある場合は、ターミナル C 搭乗口 14 にある当空港の 24 時間相談窓口までお越しください。より良いサービスをご提供できるよう、いかなる時でも最善を尽くしております。よろしくお願いいたします！

THE RECYCLING CITY HERE FOR THE YEAR

COLLECTION SCHEDULE

10 A.M. – 2 P.M. ON THE FOLLOWING DATES
MAY 14, JULY 16, SEPTEMBER 15, NOVEMBER 20

Item	Price	Explanation
Tires	$4	Remove rims, please. Less than 17 inches
Furniture	$32	More than 40 kg, Pay $22
Large size machines	$12	Microwave, washers, ovens, and so on
Electronic goods	$12	Computer bodies, monitors, DVD and video players, stereos, and so on (no cell phones)
Fax machines, printers, copiers	$22	
Televisions	$32	Up to 30-inch screen size
Televisions	$42	32-inch and more

Dispose of your old stuff at Recycling City, 500 Arabesque Street, Potomac, MD 20447. For detailed information contact (340)777-6482 or visit www.recyclingcity.net.

Volunteers needed on collection days!

15. At which of the following dates and times would it be possible to recycle goods at the Recycling City?

    (A) At 9 A.M. May 14
    (B) At 3 P.M. July 16
    (C) At 4 P.M. September 15
    (D) At 11 A.M. November 20

16. Which of the following electronic items would NOT be included in recycling?

    (A) Computer bodies
    (B) Mobile phones
    (C) DVD players
    (D) Stereos

17. What is a limitation on recycling tires at the Recycling City?

    (A) They must be smaller than 17 inches.
    (B) They must be delivered before noon.
    (C) They must weigh no more than 30 kg each.
    (D) They must have no punctures.

Single Q3

P. 424

Questions 15-17 refer to the following schedule.

THE RECYCLING CITY HERE FOR THE YEAR

COLLECTION SCHEDULE

❶ 10 A.M. – 2 P.M. ON THE FOLLOWING DATES
MAY 14, JULY 16, SEPTEMBER 15, NOVEMBER 20

Item	Price	Explanation
❷ Tires	$4	Remove rims, please. ❸ Less than 17 inches
Furniture	$32	More than 40 kg, Pay $22
Large size machines	$12	Microwave, washers, ovens, and so on
❹ Electronic goods	$12	❺ Computer bodies, monitors, DVD and video players, stereos, and so on (no cell phones)
Fax machines, printers, copiers	$22	
Televisions	$32	Up to 30-inch screen size
	$42	32-inch and more

Dispose of your old stuff at Recycling City, 500 Arabesque Street, Potomac, MD 20447. For detailed information contact (340)777-6482 or visit www.recyclingcity.net.

Volunteers needed on collection days!

☐ collection schedule 回収予定　☐ rim 枠　☐ microwave 電子レンジ　☐ and so on ～など
☐ electronic good 電子機器　☐ body 本体　☐ up to 上限～まで　☐ dispose of ～を捨てる　☐ stuff もの
☐ detailed 詳細な

★★★★★

15. At which of the following dates and times would it be possible to recycle goods at the Recycling City?

(A) At 9 A.M. May 14
(B) At 3 P.M. July 16
(C) At 4 P.M. September 15
(D) At 11 A.M. November 20

Recycling City で品物をリサイクルできるのは、次のどの日時ですか。

(A) 5 月 14 日 午前 9 時
(B) 7 月 16 日 午後 3 時
(C) 9 月 15 日 午後 4 時
(D) 11 月 20 日 午前 11 時

Recycling City で品物をリサイクルできる日時が問われている。❶に回収予定日が複数あり、5 月 14 日、7 月 16 日、9 月 15 日、11 月 20 日と、いずれの選択肢も該当する。しかし、2 行目の時間帯を見ていくと、「午前 10 時から午後 2 時まで」とある。以上より、この時間帯に該当する **(D)** が正解。

16. Which of the following electronic items would NOT be included in recycling?

    (A) Computer bodies
    (B) Mobile phones
    (C) DVD players
    (D) Stereos

次の電子機器のうち、リサイクルの対象にならないものはどれですか。

    (A) コンピューター本体
    (B) 携帯電話
    (C) DVD プレーヤー
    (D) ステレオ

NOT 問題。電子機器のうちリサイクルされないものが問われている。電子機器は❹の欄にあり、❺に詳細が述べられている。これを見ると、(A) のコンピューター本体、(C) の DVD プレイヤー、(D) のステレオが対象となっており、**(B)** の携帯電話は除くとある。よって、正解は **(B)** だとわかる。"cell phone" が mobile phone に言い換えられていることも押さえておこう。

□ body 本体

---

17. What is a limitation on recycling tires at the Recycling City?

    (A) They must be smaller than 17 inches.
    (B) They must be delivered before noon.
    (C) They must weigh no more than 30 kg each.
    (D) They must have no punctures.

Recycling City でタイヤをリサイクルする際の制限は何ですか。

    (A) 17 インチよりも小さくなければならない。
    (B) 正午までに配達されなければならない。
    (C) 1 本につき 30 kg を超えてはならない。
    (D) パンクがあってはならない。

Recycling City でタイヤをリサイクルする際の制限について問われている。タイヤの項目である❷を見ていくと、❸に「17 インチ未満」という制限がある。よって、"less than" を smaller than と言い換えた **(A)** が正解となる。

□ weigh 〜の重量がある　□ no more than 〜未満の　□ puncture (タイヤの) パンク

問題 15 から 17 は次の予定表に関するものです。

今年の THE RECYCLING CITY

回収の予定

以下の日程で、午前 10 時から午後 2 時まで
5 月 14 日、7 月 16 日、9 月 15 日、11 月 20 日

品目	価格	補足
タイヤ	4 ドル	タイヤの枠を取り外してください。17 インチ未満。
家具	32 ドル	40 キロを超える場合は、22 ドルをお支払いください。
大型機械	12 ドル	電子レンジ、洗濯機、オーブンなど
電子機器	12 ドル	コンピューター本体、モニター、DVD プレーヤーやビデオデッキ、ステレオなど（携帯電話を除く）
ファックス、プリンター、コピー機	22 ドル	
テレビ	32 ドル	30 インチの画面サイズまで
	42 ドル	32 インチ以上

古くなったものは Recycling City（500 Arabesque Street, Potomac 市，メリーランド州　郵便番号 20447）で処分しましょう。詳しい情報は (340)777-6482 までお電話いただくか、www.recyclingcity.net をご覧ください。

回収日のボランティアを募集しています！

Commercial News in Pirello Island City

Pirello Island City (March 27)—The tourism director of Pirello Island City confirmed this morning that the last construction phase of Fantasy Pirello would be completed on June 30.

Victor Napoli told *Pirello Island News*, "Forty additional employees were hired for the guest house, beach area, pools and spas, and all other amenities will be finished well before the beginning of the busy tourist season. Many tourists have booked the guest house at the resort. Fantasy Pirello will be a huge boost to our island's economy."

This construction of Pirello Island's first business resort began four years ago, and is part of an important development project that is hoped to increase tourist visits to the island. In addition to Fantasy Pirello, the project contains an enlarged port area to accommodate more boats and the island's first airline, Pirello Flies, which has already begun running flights to nearby Italy. Five new restaurants will soon open very close to Fantasy Pirello.

Mr. Napoli said he is working diligently to publicize Fantasy Pirello along with the other tourist attractions on the island. At an international travel expert convention in Lisbon last month, he showed a video, Holidays in Pirello, which he said got many favorable comments. He told me that the video's production costs were contained in the development project's marketing budget.

When Ariana Vallone appointed Mr. Napoli to be the island's tourism director five years ago, she challenged him to increase the number of tourists to the island by 50%. Mr. Napoli said, "At first, the mayor's assignment appeared to be an impossible task. However, I think Fantasy Pirello is going to take us closer to this aim."

18. What is the purpose of the article?

(A) To inform the travelers about Pirello Island's attractions
(B) To report on the status of a building project
(C) To ask for applications for resort work
(D) To inform the clients of a new marketing campaign for Pirello Island

19. Which of the following is NOT mentioned as being a part of the development project?

(A) A new airline
(B) A promotional movie
(C) A public parking lot
(D) An expanded seaport

20. According to the article, who is Ms. Vallone?

(A) The leader of a construction crew
(B) The mayor of Pirello Island City
(C) The manager of tourism in Pirello Island City
(D) The owner of a hotel

21. What is indicated about Mr. Napoli?

(A) He is planning a business trip to Lisbon.
(B) He believes that the number of tourists visiting Pirello Island will increase.
(C) He will hire many construction employees from Italy.
(D) He is concerned that the construction of Fantasy Pirello may not be completed by June 30.

P. 428

Questions 18-21 refer to the following article.

Commercial News in Pirello Island City

Pirello Island City (March 27)—❶ The tourism director of Pirello Island City confirmed this morning that the last construction phase of Fantasy Pirello would be completed on June 30.

Victor Napoli told *Pirello Island News*, "Forty additional employees were hired for the guest house, beach area, pools and spas, and all other amenities will be finished well before the beginning of the busy tourist season. Many tourists have booked the guest house at the resort. Fantasy Pirello will be a huge boost to our island's economy."

This construction of Pirello Island's first business resort began four years ago, and is part of an important development project that is hoped to increase tourist visits to the island. ❷ In addition to Fantasy Pirello, the project contains an enlarged port area to accommodate more boats and the island's first airline, Pirello Flies, which has already begun running flights to nearby Italy. Five new restaurants will soon open very close to Fantasy Pirello.

Mr. Napoli said he is working diligently to publicize Fantasy Pirello along with the other tourist attractions on the island. At an international travel expert convention in Lisbon last month, he showed a video, Holidays in Pirello, which he said got many favorable comments. ❸ He told me that the video's production costs were contained in the development project's marketing budget.

❹ When Ariana Vallone appointed Mr. Napoli to be the island's tourism director five years ago, she challenged him to increase the number of tourists to the island by 50%. ❺ Mr. Napoli said, "At first, the mayor's assignment appeared to be an impossible task. ❻ However, I think Fantasy Pirello is going to take us closer to this aim."

☐ tourism 観光（局） ☐ confirm ～を確認・承認する ☐ last construction phase 最終建築段階 ☐ spa 温泉、スパ
☐ amenity 設備 ☐ tourist season 観光シーズン ☐ book ～を予約する ☐ huge 巨大な ☐ boost 上昇
☐ development 開発 ☐ in addition to ～に加えて ☐ contain ～を含む ☐ enlarged 拡張した
☐ port area 湾岸エリア ☐ accommodate ～を収容する ☐ nearby 近隣の ☐ close to ～の近くに
☐ diligently 勤勉に ☐ publicize ～を広報宣伝する ☐ along with ～とともに ☐ tourist attraction 観光名所
☐ convention 会議 ☐ favorable 好意的な ☐ production cost 制作費 ☐ appoint A to be B A を B に任命する
☐ tourism 観光、観光局 ☐ challenge A to *do* A に～するように挑戦させる ☐ assignment 業務
☐ appear ～のように見える ☐ task 任務 ☐ aim 目標

★★☆☆☆

18. What is the purpose of the article?

(A) To inform the travelers about Pirello Island's attractions
(B) To report on the status of a building project
(C) To ask for applications for resort work
(D) To inform the clients of a new marketing campaign for Pirello Island

記事の目的は何ですか。

(A) Pirello Island の魅力について旅行客に知らせること
(B) 建設プロジェクトの状況について知らせること
(C) リゾートでの仕事の応募用紙を請求すること
(D) Pirello Island の新しいマーケティングキャンペーンについて顧客に知らせること

🔍 記事の目的が問われている。冒頭の❶で「観光局長が今朝、Fantasy Pirello の最後の建設段階が 6 月 30 日に完了することを確認した」とあるため、ある建設に関するプロジェクトの状況を報告していることがわかる。よって正解は **(B)**。

✎ ☐ status 状況 ☐ ask for ～を求める ☐ application 申込書 ☐ inform A of B A に B のことを知らせる

19. Which of the following is NOT mentioned as being a part of the development project?

(A) A new airline
(B) A promotional movie
(C) A public parking lot
(D) An expanded seaport

開発プロジェクトの一部として言及されていないのは次のうちどれですか。

(A) 新しい航空会社
(B) 販売促進用の映画
(C) 公共駐車場
(D) 拡張された港

NOT 問題。開発プロジェクトの一部として言及されていないものが問われている。❷の「拡大された港湾エリア」が (D) に、「島で初めての航空会社」が (A) に、それぞれ合致する。また第 4 段落で、観光名所の宣伝について触れており、❸でこれに関するビデオ制作について言及していることが (B) に合致する。残った **(C)** の記載は文書にないので、これが正解となる。

□ promotional 販売促進用の　□ parking lot 駐車場　□ expand ～を拡張する　□ seaport 港

★★★★☆

20. According to the article, who is Ms. Vallone?

(A) The leader of a construction crew
(B) The mayor of Pirello Island City
(C) The manager of tourism in Pirello Island City
(D) The owner of a hotel

記事によると、Vallone さんとは誰ですか。

(A) 建設工事スタッフのリーダー
(B) Pirello Island City の市長
(C) Pirello Island City の観光局長
(D) ホテルのオーナー

Vallone さんは誰かが問われている。❹で Vallone さんが登場し、「5 年前に島の観光局長として Napoli 氏を指名し、観光客の増加目標を課した」人物だとわかる。次に Napoli さんが❺で、「当初、市長に命じられた任務は不可能そうだった」と述べているので、この任務は市長により命じられたことだとわかる。以上により、Vallone さんは市長だと考えられるため、正解は **(B)** となる。登場人物と行動、指示代名詞をしっかりと把握する必要があるので注意しよう。

★★★☆☆

21. What is indicated about Mr. Napoli?

(A) He is planning a business trip to Lisbon.
(B) He believes that the number of tourists visiting Pirello Island will increase.
(C) He will hire many construction employees from Italy.
(D) He is concerned that the construction of Fantasy Pirello may not be completed by June 30.

Napoli さんについて何が示されていますか。

(A) リスボンに出張を計画している。
(B) Pirello Island の観光客が増加すると信じている。
(C) イタリアから多くの建設労働者を雇用する。
(D) Fantasy Pirello の建設が 6 月 30 日までに終わらないかもしれないと懸念している。

Napoli さんについて示されていることを問う選択肢照合型問題。Napoli さんは❻で「その目標に近いところまで行けると思う」と述べている。そしてその目標とは、同じ段落の❹にある「観光客の増加目標」だとわかる。以上から正解は **(B)**。(A) のリスボンへの出張は、第 4 段落で触れられているが、先月すでに終了しており、計画しているとも書かれていないため不正解。

□ be concerned that ～のことを心配する

Pirello Island City 商業ニュース

Pirello Island City（3月27日）—Pirello Island City の観光局長は今朝、Fantasy Pirello の最後の建設段階が6月30日に完了することを確認した。

Victor Napoli 氏は Pirello Island News で、「ゲストハウス、ビーチエリア、プール、スパのために40人の従業員が追加で雇用され、その他のすべての設備は観光の繁忙期が始まる前には完成するでしょう。多くの観光客がこのリゾートのゲストハウスを予約しています。Fantasy Pirello は島の経済の大きな後押しとなるでしょう。」と語った。

Pirello Island で初めての商業リゾートの建設は4年前に始まり、島を訪問する観光客を増やすことが期待される重要な開発プロジェクトの一部である。Fantasy Pirello に加え、プロジェクトには、より多くのボートを停泊するために拡大された港湾エリアや、島で初めての航空会社であり、すでに近隣のイタリアに就航を開始している Pirello Flies が含まれる。間もなく Fantasy Pirello のすぐ近くに5つの新しいレストランが開業する。

Napoli 氏は Fantasy Pirello や島のその他の観光名所を宣伝するために懸命に取り組んでいると語った。先月のリスボンでの国際旅行専門家会議では Holidays in Pirello というビデオを公開し、多くの好意的なコメントが得られたと語っている。ビデオの制作費用は開発プロジェクトのマーケティング予算に含まれていたと語った。

Ariana Vallone 氏が5年前に島の観光局長として Napoli 氏を指名したとき、島への観光客を50パーセント増加するという目標を課した。Napoli 氏は「当初、市長に命じられた任務は不可能な仕事のように見えました。しかし Fantasy Pirello により、その目標に近いところまで行けるのではと思います。」と述べた。

GO ON
TO THE
NEXT PAGE!

Business Magazine in Brampton

Written by Carla Hyde

June 21—The spokesperson of Brampton City Business Community has issued a report on the current state of business. The report includes details on the fastest growing industries, occupations and declining ones. The report is released quarterly, to ensure that the information reflects the existing business market in Brampton City and the surrounding districts.

Obviously, the greatest job growth is expected for surgeons, dentists, nursing resources, and health-care providers over the following year. Each of these categories is expected to grow more than 7 percent this year. — [1] —. On the one hand, moderate growth is anticipated for almost all positions in the accommodation sector. — [2] —. This is because the tourism and hospitality industry continues to grow and the holiday season is about to start. — [3] —. However, on the other hand, domestic sales of IT items are continually decreasing. — [4] —.

For more information, visit www.bramptonbusiness.org, where you can read forecasts for the various industries.

22. According to the article, what is discussed in the report?

(A) Amendments to manufacturers' strategies
(B) Future jobs in Brampton City and the nearby areas
(C) Workplace safety concerns
(D) Changes in local salaries

23. How often is the report published?

(A) Every month
(B) Twice a year
(C) Four times a year
(D) Every year

24. What industries will grow the most next year?

(A) The accommodation sector
(B) The hospitality industry
(C) The health care related industries
(D) The tourism

25. In which of the positions marked [1], [2], [3], and [4] does the following sentence best belong?

"As a result of this, positions in manufacturing are expected to decline by 12 percent."

(A) [1]
(B) [2]
(C) [3]
(D) [4]

P. 434

Questions 22-25 refer to the following article.

Business Magazine in Brampton

Written by Carla Hyde

June 21—The spokesperson of Brampton City Business Community has issued a report on the current state of business. ❶ The report includes details on the fastest growing industries, occupations and declining ones. ❷ The report is released quarterly, to ensure that the information reflects the existing business market in Brampton City and the surrounding districts.

❸ Obviously, the greatest job growth is expected for surgeons, dentists, nursing resources, and health-care providers over the following year. Each of these categories is expected to grow more than 7 percent this year. —— [1] ——. On the one hand, moderate growth is anticipated for almost all positions in the accommodation sector. —— [2] ——. This is because the tourism and hospitality industry continues to grow and the holiday season is about to start. —— [3] ——. ❹ However, on the other hand, domestic sales of IT items are continually decreasing. —— [4] ——.

For more information, visit www.bramptonbusiness.org, where you can read forecasts for the various industries.

- □ spokesperson 広報担当者 □ issue ~を発行する □ growing industry 成長している業界
- □ occupation 職業 □ declining 減少・衰退している □ quarterly 四半期ごとに □ reflect ~を反映する
- □ existing 既存の □ surrounding district 周辺地域 □ obviously 当然ながら □ surgeon 外科医
- □ nursing resource 看護資源となる人、看護師 □ health-care provider 医療提供者 □ the following year 翌年
- □ category 領域 □ on the one hand 一方で □ moderate 緩やかな □ anticipated 期待される
- □ accommodation sector 宿泊施設部門 □ hospitality industry サービス業、接客業
- □ domestic sales 国内売り上げ □ continually 継続して □ forecast 予測 □ various さまざまな

★★★★☆

22. According to the article, what is discussed in the report?

(A) Amendments to manufacturers' strategies
(B) Future jobs in Brampton City and the nearby areas
(C) Workplace safety concerns
(D) Changes in local salaries

記事によると、報告書では何が論じられていますか。

(A) メーカーの戦略の修正について
(B) ブランプトン市と周辺地域における将来の仕事について
(C) 仕事場の安全に関する懸念について
(D) 地域の給与の変動について

記事から報告書では何が論じられているのかが問われている。❶から、報告書では「最も急成長している産業と職業、および衰退しているものについて」触れていることがわかる。つまり、急成長している企業、今後新たに就くかもしれない職業を特集している、ということがわかる。以上から、正解は **(B)**。"growing" が future に繋がっている、ということに注目しておこう。

□ strategy 戦略 □ workplace safety 職場安全 □ concern 懸念

23. How often is the report published?

(A) Every month
(B) Twice a year
(C) Four times a year
(D) Every year

報告書はどのくらいの頻度で発行されますか。

(A) 毎月
(B) 年に 2 回
(C) 年に 4 回
(D) 毎年

 この報告書の発行頻度について問われている。❷で「報告書が四半期ごとに発表される」と述べられているため、四半期に 1 回、つまり年 4 回発行していることがわかる。以上から、正解は "quarterly" を「年に 4 回」と言い換えた **(C)** が正解。

---

24. What industries will grow the most next year?

(A) The accommodation sector
(B) The hospitality industry
(C) The health care related industries
(D) The tourism

来年最も成長する産業とは何ですか。

(A) 宿泊施設部門
(B) 接客業
(C) 医療関連の産業
(D) 観光業

 来年最も成長する産業について問われている。❸で「医療関係の雇用が来年最も増加が見込まれる」とあるため、これを "health care related（医療関連）" と表現した **(C)** が正解。(B) の hospitality industry（接客業）は、"hospital industry（病院業界）" と見た目が少し似ているので、早とちりして間違えないように注意しよう。

---

25. In which of the positions marked [1], [2], [3], and [4] does the following sentence best belong?

"As a result of this, positions in manufacturing are expected to decline by 12 percent."

(A) [1]
(B) [2]
(C) [3]
(D) [4]

次の文は [1]、[2]、[3]、[4] のどの位置に最もよく当てはまりますか。

「その結果、製造業の職種は 12 パーセント衰退すると予想されている」

(A) [1]
(B) [2]
(C) [3]
(D) [4]

 適切な文の位置を求める問題。問われている文は「この結果として、製造業の職業は 12 パーセントほど低くなる見込みだ」とある。つまり、この "this" が指す箇所を探す必要がある。文書を見ていくと、❹に「IT 系商品の国内の売り上げは下がり続けている」とある。この後ろに入れると、これ（IT 系商品の国内売り上げが悪いという結果）により、製造業の雇用が減るという因果関係が成立し、文意が通る。よって、正解が **(D)** となる。

ブランプトン市のビジネス誌
Carla Hyde 記

6月21日 — ブランプトン市商業組合の広報官によって、現在のビジネスの状況について報告書が発行された。報告書には、最も急成長している産業と職業、および衰退しているものについて詳しく書かれている。報告書は、ブランプトン市と周辺地域における現在のビジネス市場が、書かれている情報に確実に表れるように、四半期ごとに発表される。

当然のことながら、外科医、歯科医、看護師、および医療提供者の雇用は、来年最も増加が見込まれている。これらの職種は、それぞれ今年7パーセント超の成長が見込まれている。—[1]— 一方、宿泊施設部門に関わるすべての職種は、緩やかな成長が予想されている。—[2]— これは観光業と接客業が成長を続け、長期休暇のシーズンも間もなく始まるからである。—[3]— しかし他方では、IT系商品の国内の売り上げは下がり続けている。—[4]— その結果、製造業の職種は12パーセント衰退すると予想されている。

さらに詳しい情報は www.bramptonbusiness.org で閲覧可能である。そこでは多くの産業の先行きの予想を読むことができる。

GO ON
TO THE
NEXT PAGE!

Questions 26-29 refer to the following online chat discussion.

4分00秒

3:12 P.M. VANCE, MARY
Did you hear that the supervisor plans to open the office on Saturdays?

3:14 P.M. RHODES, LUCY
Yes, and it was very surprising. To make matters worse, there was no mention of the company hiring additional staff!

3:15 P.M. VANCE, MARY
Right! She plans to implement a shift schedule. All employees, including us, will need to work from 9 to 5, one Saturday per month. She thinks we can increase our overall productivity.

3:17 P.M. COOPER, PHILL
I get that. However, the thing is, it won't work.

3:19 P.M. RHODES, LUCY
Why do you say that?

3:22 P.M. COOPER, PHILL
All employees will be so disappointed to be working on the weekend that I doubt there'll be any increase in work efficiency. Actually, I think it will have the opposite effect.

3:23 P.M. VANCE, MARY
I'm with you on this one. I would like to speak with the supervisor myself and let her know how everyone feels.

3:25 P.M. RHODES, LUCY
Well, let me know if you do. I'd be happy to join you and lend some support.

26. What is the supervisor planning to do?

    (A) Open an additional office
    (B) Decrease daily office hours
    (C) Extend the work week
    (D) Hire some new employees

27. What disadvantage does Mr. Cooper say there will be?

    (A) The deadlines will be shortened.
    (B) The employees will be less productive.
    (C) The customers will be less pleased.
    (D) The profits will begin to increase.

28. At 3:17 P.M., what does Mr. Cooper mean when he writes, "I get that"?

    (A) He was already informed about a new rule.
    (B) He thinks a proposed change will be positive.
    (C) He has gotten a copy of a work schedule.
    (D) He understands the supervisor's motivations.

29. What can be suggested about Ms. Vance?

    (A) She has arranged a meeting with the supervisor.
    (B) She would like to meet with Mr. Cooper.
    (C) She would prefer that Ms. Rhodes contact the supervisor.
    (D) She is in agreement with Mr. Cooper.

Single Q4

P. 440

Questions 26-29 refer to the following online chat discussion.

3:12 P.M. VANCE, MARY
❶ Did you hear that the supervisor plans to open the office on Saturdays?

3:14 P.M. RHODES, LUCY
Yes, and it was very surprising. To make matters worse, there was no mention of the company hiring additional staff!

3:15 P.M. VANCE, MARY
Right! She plans to implement a shift schedule. All employees, including us, will need to work from 9 to 5, one Saturday per month. ❷ She thinks we can increase our overall productivity.

3:17 P.M. COOPER, PHILL
❸ I get that. ❹ However, the thing is, it won't work.

3:19 P.M. RHODES, LUCY
Why do you say that?

3:22 P.M. COOPER, PHILL
❺ All employees will be so disappointed to be working on the weekend that I doubt there'll be any increase in work efficiency. Actually, I think it will have the opposite effect.

3:23 P.M. VANCE, MARY
❻ I'm with you on this one. I would like to speak with the supervisor myself and let her know how everyone feels.

3:25 P.M. RHODES, LUCY
Well, let me know if you do. I'd be happy to join you and lend some support.

□ on Saturdays 毎週土曜日に　□ surprising 驚くべきことだ　□ to make matters worse さらに悪いことに
□ no mention of ～に関する言及・記載がない　□ implement ～を実行する　□ overall 全体の
□ productivity 生産性　□ I get that 理解した　□ the thing is 問題は、事態は
□ it won't work うまくいかないだろう　□ disappointed がっかりする　□ doubt ～ではないと思う
□ work efficiency 作業効率　□ opposite effect 逆効果　□ I'm with you あなたに賛成である

★★★★★

26. What is the supervisor planning to do?

   (A) Open an additional office
   (B) Decrease daily office hours
   (C) Extend the work week
   (D) Hire some new employees

主任は何をしようとしていますか。

   (A) 追加の事務所を開く
   (B) 1 日の勤務時間を短縮する
   (C) 1 週間の労働時間を延長する
   (D) 新しい従業員を何人か雇う

主任が何をしようとしているのかが問われている。チャットの冒頭❶で、「主任が毎週土曜日に事務所を開けるつもりだということを聞いたか？」と切り出している。そして❺では "to be working" という表現を用いて「全従業員は、週末に働くことに対してがっかりするだろう」と述べている。以上より、主任が今後毎週土曜日も仕事をさせるつもりだということがわかる。よって、これを「1 週間の労働時間延長」と言い換えた **(C)** が正解となる。

 □ decrease ～を減少させる　□ extend ～を延長する

★★★★☆

27. What disadvantage does Mr. Cooper say there will be?

(A) The deadlines will be shortened.
(B) The employees will be less productive.
(C) The customers will be less pleased.
(D) The profits will begin to increase.

Cooper さんはどんな不利益があると言っていますか。

(A) 締め切りが短くなる。
(B) 従業員の生産性が低下する。
(C) 顧客の満足度が低下する。
(D) 収益が増え始める。

Cooper さんはどんな不利益があると言っているかが問われている。Cooper さんは、❺で「全従業員が、週末に働かされることに対してがっかりするため、作業効率が上がるとは思えない。実際には逆効果だ」と述べている。ここから、生産性が低下すると言い換えている **(B)** が正解。"less+ 形容詞 " で、性質が低下する、逆になるという意味になることを押さえておこう。(C) は customers の箇所が employees であれば、❺の "disappointed" との言い換えになる。惑わされないようにしょう。

✎ □ disadvantage 不利な点　□ profit 利益

- -

★★★☆☆ 意図問題

28. At 3:17 P.M., what does Mr. Cooper mean when he writes, "I get that"?

(A) He was already informed about a new rule.
(B) He thinks a proposed change will be positive.
(C) He has gotten a copy of a work schedule.
(D) He understands the supervisor's motivations.

午後 3 時 17 分に、Cooper さんは "I got that" という発言で、何を意味していますか。

(A) 新しい規則についてすでに知らされていた。
(B) 提案された変更は好ましいと考えている。
(C) すでに就労予定表のコピーを受け取った。
(D) 主任の動機を理解している。

意図問題。問われている❸は Cooper さんの「理解している」という表現だ。何を理解しているかを探すため、その前後を見ていくと、❷で Vance さんが「彼女（主任）は全体の生産性が高まると思っている」と述べ、その後 Cooper さんが❸・❹で「理解している」「でもうまくいかないだろう」と返答している。ここから、Cooper さんは、主任が生産性が上がると期待しているのを理解していることがわかるので、その期待を motivations と表現した **(D)** が正解となる。

✎ □ positive（物事が）前向きで好ましい　□ motivation 動機、モチベーション

29. What can be suggested about Ms. Vance?

- (A) She has arranged a meeting with the supervisor.
- (B) She would like to meet with Mr. Cooper.
- (C) She would prefer that Ms. Rhodes contact the supervisor.
- **(D)** She is in agreement with Mr. Cooper.

Vance さんについて何が示唆されていますか。

- (A) 主任との面談を手配した。
- (B) Cooper さんと会いたがっている。
- (C) Rhodes さんが主任に連絡をすることを望んでいる。
- **(D)** Cooper さんに同意している。

Vance さんについて何が示唆されているかを問う選択肢照合型の問題。Vance さんは、Cooper さんが❺で「週末に働くことは逆に生産性を低下させる」と述べたことに対し、❻で「あなたに賛成だ」と返答している。ここから、Cooper さんに同意していることがわかるので、正解は **(D)**。"be with you" は、いろいろな意味があるが、ここでは「あなたに同意している、味方となっている」という意味で使われていることも押さえておこう。(A) は「主任と話す」とは言っているが、面談の手配を完了したとは言及していない。(B)(C) は該当する箇所がないため、いずれも不正解。

□ prefer that ～ということを望んでいる　□ in agreement with ～に同意して

問題 **26** から **29** は次のオンラインチャットの話し合いに関するものです。

午後 3 時 12 分　VANCE, MARY
主任が毎週土曜日に事務所を開けるつもりだということを聞きましたか？

午後 3 時 14 分　RHODES, LUCY
はい、とても驚きました。さらに困ったことに、会社が追加の従業員を雇うことについて、まったく知らされていませんでした！

午後 3 時 15 分　VANCE, MARY
そのとおりです！　彼女は交替制を施行するようです。私たちを含めたすべての従業員が月に 1 度、土曜日に 9 時から 5 時まで働かなければいけなくなります。彼女は全体の生産性が高まると思っているようです。

午後 3 時 17 分　COOPER, PHILL
それはわかります。しかし、それではうまくいかないでしょう。

午後 3 時 19 分　RHODES, LUCY
どうしてそう言えますか？

午後 3 時 22 分　COOPER, PHILL
すべての従業員は、週末に働かされることに対してがっかりするでしょうから、作業効率が上がるとは思えません。実際には、逆効果だと思います。

午後 3 時 23 分　VANCE, MARY
これについては私も同感です。主任と話してみんながどのように感じているのか伝えたいと思います。

午後 3 時 25 分　RHODES, LUCY
そうですね、そのときは教えてください。喜んで手助けをさせていただきます。

GO ON
TO THE
NEXT PAGE!

To: Paula Malone <paulama@zmail.net>
From: Kenny Bilecki <kbilecki@athertoncruise.com>
Subject: RE: Confirmation
Date: May 13

Dear Paula Malone,

This is to confirm that we have received the articles below and that we plan to include them in the next four issues of *Atherton Cruise* magazine. The payment dates that we discussed are listed in the chart below. Please expect to receive a check for each article within fifteen business days of the publication date.

Title	Amount	Date
Airfare Package	$390	June 10
Tips for Selecting the Right Cabin	$370	July 10
Web Resources for Planning Cruises	$435	August 10
Kid-Friendly Cruises	$305	September 10

Thank you very much for sending articles for our magazine. Our popular publication is aimed at high-class travelers. It has been in print without interruption for the last 30 years. We appreciate your cooperation as one of our team of guest writers. We invite you to submit proposals for future articles by e-mail or fax. And also, we welcome you to bring your proposals to us in person.

Please do not hesitate to contact me if you have any questions before you send a proposal.

Best regards,

Kenny Bilecki, Managing Editor

To: Kenny Bilecki <kbilecki@athertoncruise.com>
From: Paula Malone <paulama@zmail.net>
Subject: Check
Date: July 31

Dear Mr. Bilecki,

I am writing to inform you that three weeks have passed since the payment day that we agreed upon. To my regret, I have not received payment for my article. Could you please let me know why I have not received it, and tell me when I should expect to get it?

Yours truly,

Paula Malone

30. What did Mr. Bilecki receive from Ms. Malone?

(A) Subscription forms
(B) Magazine articles
(C) Print advertisements
(D) Paychecks

31. What is true about the *Atherton Cruise* magazine?

(A) It is available in multiple languages.
(B) It is written for travel professionals.
(C) It has been published for three decades.
(D) It is no longer accepting submissions.

32. Which of the following is NOT mentioned as a way to send proposals?

(A) By e-mail
(B) By fax
(C) By visiting the Atherton Cruise magazine office
(D) By an agent

33. Why does Ms. Malone send the second e-mail to Mr. Bilecki?

(A) To ask about a missing payment
(B) To send an article
(C) To request an interview
(D) To inquire about the subscription price

34. How much should Ms. Malone receive from the *Atherton Cruise* magazine?

(A) $305
(B) $370
(C) $390
(D) $435

Double

P. 446

Questions 30-34 refer to the following e-mails.

E メール（1）

> To: Paula Malone <paulama@zmail.net>
> From: Kenny Bilecki <kbilecki@athertoncruise.com>
> Subject: RE: Confirmation
> Date: May 13

> Dear Paula Malone,
>
> ❶ This is to confirm that we have received the articles below and that we plan to include them in the next four issues of *Atherton Cruise* magazine. The payment dates that we discussed are listed in the chart below. Please expect to receive a check for each article within fifteen business days of the publication date.
>
> | Title | Amount | Date |
> |---|---|---|
> | Airfare Package | $390 | June 10 |
> | ❷ Tips for Selecting the Right Cabin | $370 | July 10 |
> | Web Resources for Planning Cruises | $435 | August 10 |
> | Kid-Friendly Cruises | $305 | September 10 |
>
> Thank you very much for sending articles for our magazine. Our popular publication is aimed at high-class travelers. ❸ It has been in print without interruption for the last 30 years. We appreciate your cooperation as one of our team of guest writers. ❹ We invite you to submit proposals for future articles by e-mail or fax. And also, ❺ we welcome you to bring your proposals to us in person.
>
> Please do not hesitate to contact me if you have any questions before you send a proposal.
>
> Best regards,
>
> Kenny Bilecki, Managing Editor

E メール（2）

> To: Kenny Bilecki <kbilecki@athertoncruise.com>
> From: Paula Malone <paulama@zmail.net>
> Subject: Check
> ❻ Date: July 31

> Dear Mr. Bilecki,
>
> ❼ I am writing to inform you that three weeks have passed since the payment day that we agreed upon. ❽ To my regret, I have not received payment for my article. ❾ Could you please let me know why I have not received it, and tell me when I should expect to get it?
>
> Yours truly,
>
> Paula Malone

E メール（1）
□ confirm ～を確認する　□ below 下記にある　□ issue（雑誌等の）号　□ payment date 支払い期日
□ list ～をリスト化する　□ check 小切手　□ publication date 出版日
□ be aimed at ～を目的・ターゲットとしている　□ high-class 上流階級の、高級志向の　□ be in print 発行する
□ without interruption 休刊なく　□ in person 直接（の持ち込み）

E メール（2）
□ agreed upon ～に同意する　□ to my regret 残念なことに

★★★☆☆

30. What did Mr. Bilecki receive from Ms. Malone?

(A) Subscription forms
(B) Magazine articles
(C) Print advertisements
(D) Paychecks

Bilecki さんは Malone さんから何を受け取りましたか。

(A) 定期購読の申込書
(B) 雑誌の記事
(C) 印刷広告
(D) 給与

Bilecki さんが Malone さんから受け取ったものが問われている。Bilecki さんは、1 文書目の E メール（1）の❶で「以下の記事を受領したことと、Atherton Cruise 誌の次の 4 つの号に掲載する予定について確認の連絡」と述べている。ここから雑誌の記事を受け取ったことがわかるため、正解は **(B)**。(D) は労働者が受け取る定期的な給与だが、実際受け取るのは check（小切手）である。また、小切手を受け取るのは Malone さんなので不正解。

□ subscription form 定期購読申込書　□ paycheck 給与

....

★★★☆☆

31. What is true about the *Atherton Cruise* magazine?

(A) It is available in multiple languages.
(B) It is written for travel professionals.
(C) It has been published for three decades.
(D) It is no longer accepting submissions.

Atherton Cruise 誌について正しいことは何ですか。

(A) 多数の言語で読むことができる。
(B) 旅行の専門家向けに書かれている。
(C) 30 年間発行され続けている。
(D) 投稿の受付を取りやめた。

Atherton Cruise 誌について正しいことは何かを問う選択肢照合型の問題。E メール（1）の❸に「この 30 年間休刊することなく発行を続けている」とあるので、ここから 30 年間を for three decades と言い換えた **(C)** が正解。(A) 多言語対応、(D) 投稿の受付中止、はいずれも記載がなく、(B) は専門家向けではなく、高級志向の旅行者向けであるため、いずれも不正解。

□ multiple 多数の　□ professional 専門家　□ no linger もはや～ではない

32. Which of the following is NOT mentioned as a way to send proposals?

   (A) By e-mail
   (B) By fax
   (C) By visiting the Atherton Cruise magazine office
   (D) By an agent

提案を送る方法として言及されていないものは次のどれですか。

   (A) E メールによる方法
   (B) ファックスによる方法
   (C) Atherton Cruise 誌のオフィスを訪問する方法
   (D) 代理人を通す方法

NOT 問題。提案を送る方法として言及されていないものが問われている。E メール（1）の❹・❺で提出方法について言及されている。❹の「E メール、ファックスでお願いできればと思います」が (A) と (B) に、❺の「直接のお持ちいただいても結構です」が (C) に該当する。残った **(D)** 代理人については記載がないため、これが正解となる。❺の bring ○○ in person は、「○○を直接持ち込む」という意味で、visit と言い換えが可能な表現であることを押さえておこう。

   □ as a way to *do* ～する方法として   □ agent 代理人

---

33. Why does Ms. Malone send the second e-mail to Mr. Bilecki?

   (A) To ask about a missing payment
   (B) To send an article
   (C) To request an interview
   (D) To inquire about the subscription price

Malone さんはなぜ Bilecki さんに 2 通目の E メールを送っていますか。

   (A) 未払い金について尋ねるため
   (B) 記事を送るため
   (C) インタビューを申し込むため
   (D) 定期購読料金について問い合わせるため

Malone さんが Bilecki さんに E メールを送っている理由が問われている。Malone さんは E メール（2）の❽で「未だに原稿料をお支払いいただいていない」、❾で「未送付の理由、いつ送付されるのかが知りたい」と述べている。以上より、未払いの件についての情報を求めているとわかる。この未払いを a missing payment と表現した **(A)** が正解。(B) の記事送付については、メール（1）で、すでに受領されていると書かれているため不正解。

   □ missing 行方不明の   □ subscription price 定期購読料金

---

34. How much should Ms. Malone receive from the *Atherton Cruise* magazine?

   (A) $305
   (B) $370
   (C) $390
   (D) $435

Malone さんは *Atherton Cruise* 誌からいくら受け取らなければなりませんか。

   (A) 305 ドル
   (B) 370 ドル
   (C) 390 ドル
   (D) 435 ドル

Malone さんが Atherton Cruise 誌からいくら受け取らなくてはいけないかが問われている。まず、2 文書目の E メール（2）の❻・❼より「7 月 31 日付けで、3 週間支払いがない」ということがわかる。よって、未払いの対象は 7 月 10 日に支払われる予定の記事だとわかる。1 文書目の E メール（1）を見ると、❷より 7 月 10 日の支払日に相当する金額は 370 ドルだとわかる。よって、正解は **(B)**。時系列として、支払い期日がいつで、支払われなかったのはいつから起算しているか、を 2 つの文書から正しく導こう。

問題 30 から 34 は次の 2 通の E メールに関するものです。

E メール（1）

受信者：Paula Malone 〈paulama@zmail.net〉
送信者：Kenny Bilecki 〈kbilecki@athertoncruise.com〉
件名：　RE：確認
日付：　5 月 13 日

Paula Malone 様

以下の記事を受領したことと、Atherton Cruise 誌の次の 4 つの号に掲載する予定について確認のためのご連絡です。相談した支払い期日は次の表のとおりです。各記事への小切手は出版日から 15 営業日以内にお受け取りいただけるとお考えください。

題名	価格	期日
航空運賃パッケージ	390 ドル	6 月 10 日
適切な客室を選ぶためのヒント	370 ドル	7 月 10 日
クルーズ計画のためのウェブ上の情報源	435 ドル	8 月 10 日
子どもに優しいクルーズ	305 ドル	9 月 10 日

当誌へ記事を送っていただき、ありがとうございます。当社の人気刊行物は主に高級志向の旅行者を対象としています。この 30 年間休刊することなく発行を続けています。当社の非専属のライターチームの一員としてご協力いただきありがとうございます。今後の記事のご提案は、E メールかファックスでお願いできればと思います。また、ご提案を直接お持ちいただいても結構です。

ご提案をお送りいただく前に質問があれば、どうぞお気軽にご連絡ください。

よろしくお願いいたします。

Kenny Bilecki　編集長

E メール（2）

受信者：Kenny Bilecki 〈kbilecki@athertoncruise.com〉
送信者：Paula Malone 〈paulama@zmail.net〉
件名：　小切手
日付：　7 月 31 日

Bilecki 様

お約束の支払い日から 3 週間が経過したことをお知らせいたします。残念ながら、未だに原稿料をお支払いいただいておりません。お送りいただけていない理由や、いつお送りいただけるのかを教えていただけますか。

よろしくお願いいたします。

Paula Malone

5分00秒

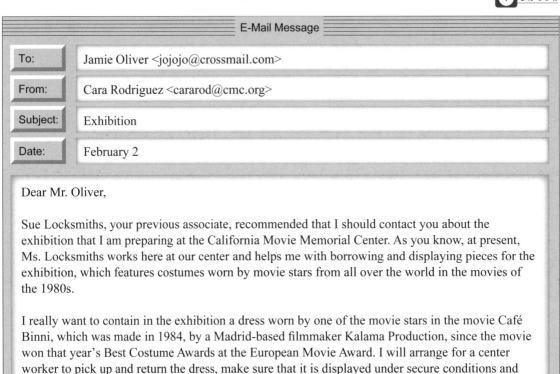

=== E-Mail Message ===

To:	Jamie Oliver <jojojo@crossmail.com>
From:	Cara Rodriguez <cararod@cmc.org>
Subject:	Exhibition
Date:	February 2

Dear Mr. Oliver,

Sue Locksmiths, your previous associate, recommended that I should contact you about the exhibition that I am preparing at the California Movie Memorial Center. As you know, at present, Ms. Locksmiths works here at our center and helps me with borrowing and displaying pieces for the exhibition, which features costumes worn by movie stars from all over the world in the movies of the 1980s.

I really want to contain in the exhibition a dress worn by one of the movie stars in the movie Café Binni, which was made in 1984, by a Madrid-based filmmaker Kalama Production, since the movie won that year's Best Costume Awards at the European Movie Award. I will arrange for a center worker to pick up and return the dress, make sure that it is displayed under secure conditions and have it professionally cleaned by a specialist before it is sent back to you. Thank you in advance for your help.

Best regards,

Cara Rodriguez

Movie Costumes from the 1980s. p.25

The dress shown in the photograph was worn by the Spanish actress Alba Lozano, who made her debut in the 1984 blockbuster movie Café Binni. The hand-beaded dress was designed by David Kranmer, who has created costumes for Kalama Production for two decades. He continues to work for the company as a costume consultant. For this dress, he embellished a classically styled gown with tiny crystal beads. The high leg slit added a modern touch to the outfit — perfect for Ms. Lozano, who had many dance scenes as Jonny Horge in Café Binni.

35. Why was the e-mail written?

(A) To inquire about a movie star's availability for a movie
(B) To describe a movie from the 1980's
(C) To advertise new works at a memorial center
(D) To request to borrow a piece worn by a famous actress

36. Who is helping Ms. Rodriguez to organize the exhibition?

(A) Sue Locksmiths
(B) Jonny Horge
(C) Alba Lozano
(D) David Kranmer

37. What does Ms. Rodriguez offer to do?

(A) Pay for a cloth to be designed
(B) Arrange for Mr. Kranmer to travel to California
(C) Offer more information about the exhibit
(D) Make sure that a dress is cleaned by a specialist

38. What is NOT true about the movie Café Binni?

(A) It will be shown at the California Movie Memorial Center.
(B) The costume was designed by Mr. Kranmer.
(C) It was created by a European production company.
(D) A beaded dress was worn in the movie.

39. What can be inferred about Mr. Kranmer?

(A) He would like to manage his own business in Madrid.
(B) He has had a long career at a movie making company.
(C) He appeared in the movie Café Binni.
(D) He dropped the idea of making costumes in the past.

P. 452

Double

Questions 35-39 refer to the following e-mail and report.

E-Mail Message

To:	Jamie Oliver <jojojo@crossmail.com>
From:	Cara Rodriguez <cararod@cmc.org>
Subject:	Exhibition
Date:	February 2

Dear Mr. Oliver,

Sue Locksmiths, your previous associate, recommended that I should contact you about the exhibition that I am preparing at the California Movie Memorial Center. As you know, at present, ❶ Ms. Locksmiths works here at our center and helps me with borrowing and displaying pieces for the exhibition, which features costumes worn by movie stars from all over the world in the movies of the 1980s.

❷ I really want to contain in the exhibition a dress worn by one of the movie stars in ❸ the movie Café Binni, which was made in 1984, by a Madrid-based filmmaker Kalama Production, since the movie won that year's Best Costume Awards at the European Movie Award. ❹ I will arrange for a center worker to pick up and return the dress, make sure that it is displayed under secure conditions and have it professionally cleaned by a specialist before it is sent back to you. Thank you in advance for your help.

Best regards,

Cara Rodriguez

Movie Costumes from the 1980s. p.25

❺ The dress shown in the photograph was worn by the Spanish actress Alba Lozano, who made her debut in the 1984 blockbuster movie Café Binni. ❻ The hand-beaded dress was designed by David Kranmer, ❼ who has created costumes for Kalama Production for two decades. ❽ He continues to work for the company as a costume consultant. For this dress, he embellished a classically styled gown with tiny crystal beads. The high leg slit added a modern touch to the outfit — perfect for Ms. Lozano, who had many dance scenes as Jonny Horge in Café Binni.

E メール
- [ ] exhibition 展示（会） □ associate 同僚 □ recommend that S should V S が V するように勧める
- [ ] at present 現在のところ □ feature 〜を特集する □ costume 衣装
- [ ] worn wear（〜を着る・身に付ける）の過去分詞 □ -based 〜に本社がある □ filmmaker 映画制作会社
- [ ] pick up 〜を取りに行く □ secure 安全な □ professionally 専門的に □ specialist 専門家
- [ ] thank you in advance for 〜についてよろしくお願いします

報告書
- [ ] debut デビュー、初出演 □ blockbuster 大ヒット作 □ hand-beaded 手作業でビーズを縫い付けた
- [ ] decade 10 年 □ embellish A with B A に B を装飾する □ classically styled クラシックスタイルの
- [ ] gown ガウン □ tiny とても小さな □ crystal bead クリスタルビーズ □ touch 要素 □ outfit 衣装、装い

35. Why was the e-mail written?

(A) To inquire about a movie star's availability for a movie
(B) To describe a movie from the 1980's
(C) To advertise new works at a memorial center
(D) To request to borrow a piece worn by a famous actress

Eメールはなぜ書かれましたか。

(A) 映画スターが映画に出演できるかどうかを問い合わせるため
(B) 1980年代の映画について説明するため
(C) 新しい作品を記念館で宣伝するため
(D) 有名な女優が着用していた作品の貸し出しを依頼するため

Eメールが書かれた理由が問われている。第1段落でEメールを書いた背景を説明し、第2段落の❷で「映画出演者の一人が着ていたドレスを展覧会で使用したい」ことを切り出している。以上より、これを borrow a piece for ... と言い換えている **(D)** が正解。❷のI really want to を含む一文が、Eメールの目的となっている。こういう表現が出てきたら注意して読み進めるようにしましょう。

☐ availability 予定の空き　☐ describe 〜を説明する　☐ memorial center 記念館

---

36. Who is helping Ms. Rodriguez to organize the exhibition?

(A) Sue Locksmiths
(B) Jonny Horge
(C) Alba Lozano
(D) David Kranmer

展覧会を開催するために Rodriguez さんに力を貸しているのは誰ですか。

(A) Sue Locksmiths
(B) Jonny Horge
(C) Alba Lozano
(D) David Kranmer

展覧会を開催するために Rodriguez さんに力を貸しているのは誰かが問われている。Eメールの第1段落の❶で、「Rodriguez さんが展示品を借りてきて陳列するときに、Locksmiths さんの力を借りている」と述べている。よって、正解は **(A)**。

---

37. What does Ms. Rodriguez offer to do?

(A) Pay for a cloth to be designed
(B) Arrange for Mr. Kranmer to travel to California
(C) Offer more information about the exhibit
(D) Make sure that a dress is cleaned by a specialist

Rodriguez さんは何をすることを申し出ていますか。

(A) デザインをしてもらうために生地の費用を支払うこと
(B) Kranmer さんのカリフォルニアへの旅行を手配すること
(C) 展示についてさらに情報を提供すること
(D) ドレスを専門家にクリーニングしてもらうようにすること

Rodriguez さんが申し出ていることが問われている。Rodriguez さんはEメールで、衣装の借用を切り出し、❹で「ドレスの展示の安全対策と、返却の前に専門的なクリーニングを行う」と申し出ている。以上から、後者に相当する言い換えの **(D)** が正解。

☐ cloth 服の生地

38. What is NOT true about the movie Café Binni?

- **(A)** It will be shown at the California Movie Memorial Center.
- (B) The costume was designed by Mr. Kranmer.
- (C) It was created by a European production company.
- (D) A beaded dress was worn in the movie.

映画 Café Binni について正しくないものは何ですか。

- **(A)** California Movie Memorial Center で上映される。
- (B) 衣装は Kranmer さんによってデザインされた。
- (C) ヨーロッパの制作会社によって作られた。
- (D) 映画の中でビーズのついたドレスを着ていた。

NOT 問題。映画 Café Binni について正しくないものが問われている。❸の「マドリートに本社のある制作会社によって作られた」が (C) に、❺・❻の「David Kranmer さんによりデザインされた衣装」が (B) に、❼の「映画制作会社 Kalama Production に作られた衣装（ビーズ付きは❻から読み取れる）」が (D) に該当することがわかる。以上より、残った **(A)** が正解。California Movie Memorial Center で上映されるかは言及がない。

□ production company 制作会社　□ beaded ビーズ付きの

---

39. What can be inferred about Mr. Kranmer?

- (A) He would like to manage his own business in Madrid.
- **(B)** He has had a long career at a movie making company.
- (C) He appeared in the movie Café Binni.
- (D) He dropped the idea of making costumes in the past.

Kranmer さんについて何が推測できますか。

- (A) マドリードで自身の企業を経営したいと思っている。
- **(B)** 映画制作会社で長いキャリアがある。
- (C) 映画 Café Binni に出演した。
- (D) 過去に衣装を作ることを諦めた。

Kranmer さんについて推測できることを問う選択肢照合型の問題。Kranmer さんについては、報告書の❻〜❽に言及があり、「20 年にわたって（映画制作会社の）Kalama Production のために衣装を作ってきた。現在は同社の衣装顧問を務め続けている」と述べられている。つまり、映画制作会社で長年にわたってキャリアを築いていることがわかる。これを a long career と表現した **(B)** が正解。

□ appear in 〜に登場する

受信者：　Jamie Oliver <jojojo@crossmail.com>
送信者：　Cara Rodriguez <cararod@cmc.org>
件名：　　展覧会
日付け：　2 月 2 日

Oliver 様

かつて Oliver さんとご一緒に働いていらっしゃった Sue Locksmiths さんから、私が準備している California Movie Memorial Center での展覧会について、Oliver さんに連絡することをお勧めいただきました。ご存じのとおり、Locksmiths さんは現在当センターで勤務なさっていて、私は展示品を借りてきて陳列するときに、Locksmiths さんのお力をお借りしています。展覧会では主に 1980 年代の映画で世界中の映画スターが着ていた衣装を展示します。

映画 Café Binni で出演者の一人が着ていたドレスを、ぜひ展覧会で展示したいと思っています。映画はマドリードを拠点とする映画制作会社 Kalama Production により 1984 年に作られたもので、映画が同年の European Movie Awards にて最優秀衣装賞を受賞したため、展示したいと思います。センターの者が受け取りと返却にお伺いします。ドレスは安全対策を講じて展示し、返却前には職人による専門的なクリーニングを行います。どうぞお力添えをお願いいたします。

よろしくお願いいたします。

Cara Rodriguez

1980 年代の映画の衣装　25 ページ

写真の衣装は 1984 年の大ヒット映画 Café Binni でデビューしたスペインの女優 Alba Lozano さんが着用したものです。手作業でビーズを縫い付けたドレスは、20 年にわたって、Kalama Production のために衣装を作ってきた David Kranmer さんによりデザインされました。彼は同社の衣装顧問を務め続けています。このドレスは古典的なスタイルのガウンに極小のクリスタルビーズが装飾されています。深いスリットが装いに現代的な要素を加えており、Café Binni で Jonny Horge 役として多くのダンスシーンを演じた Lozano さんに非常に似合っています。

http://www.greenville.go.nz

Frank Lake Park to Receive Upgrade

The Greenville Park and Recreation Department would like to announce that it has a budget of over $100,000 and is planning to renovate Frank Lake Park in a few months. At first, the funds were designated for building an outdoor stage on a plot of land along Bramwell Avenue. But because of noise pollution concerns from many residents, the project was postponed several times, eventually being called off altogether.

Instead, some alternative projects being considered for the site are removing debris from the lake, building a changing area and concession stand, expanding the parking space, and adding a jogging trail around the lake. A committee has been set up to hear suggestions from the residents at City Hall about which projects are most positively favored. The residents and the representatives from community groups may present their ideas on June 28 and June 30, respectively. Opinions will also be accepted by e-mail until June 7. These can be directed to gpnrd@greenville.go.nz.

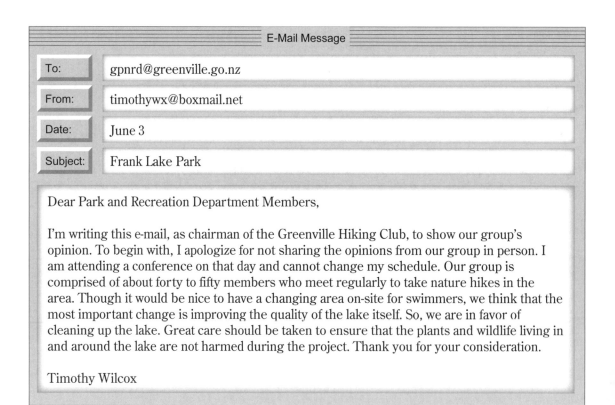

E-Mail Message

To:	gpnrd@greenville.go.nz
From:	timothywx@boxmail.net
Date:	June 3
Subject:	Frank Lake Park

Dear Park and Recreation Department Members,

I'm writing this e-mail, as chairman of the Greenville Hiking Club, to show our group's opinion. To begin with, I apologize for not sharing the opinions from our group in person. I am attending a conference on that day and cannot change my schedule. Our group is comprised of about forty to fifty members who meet regularly to take nature hikes in the area. Though it would be nice to have a changing area on-site for swimmers, we think that the most important change is improving the quality of the lake itself. So, we are in favor of cleaning up the lake. Great care should be taken to ensure that the plants and wildlife living in and around the lake are not harmed during the project. Thank you for your consideration.

Timothy Wilcox

E-Mail Message

To: gpnrd@greenville.go.nz

From: ninaoneal@outlook.net

Date: July 5

Subject: Suggestions for park project

To Whom It May Concern,

It is my honor to have a chance to participate in the issue: Upgrades around Frank Lake Park. In my opinion, the largest portion of the money should be spent on building a jogging trail around the lake. There are already some dirt paths, but I think the site would get more use if it had a high-quality surface for walking and jogging. Because it is so easy to get to the lake using city bus 168, that is the preferred method for most residents to go to the lake. So, there is no need for extra parking, and I would strongly advise against a new parking lot. Whichever project you choose, I hope you will take the environmental surroundings into account and take the necessary precautions to ensure that there is no damage to the vegetation, soil, or animals there.

Best regards,

Nina O'Neal

---

40. How can the cost of repairing Frank Lake Park be funded?

(A) By applying for a city grant
(B) By imposing taxes on local residents
(C) By hosting a community fundraising event
(D) By using funds from a canceled project

41. In the Web page, the word "eventually" in paragraph 1, line 5, is closest in meaning to

(A) relatively
(B) subsequently
(C) ultimately
(D) crucially

42. When did Mr. Wilcox attend a conference?

(A) On June 28
(B) On June 30
(C) On July 3
(D) On July 4

43. What does Ms. O'Neal indicate about Frank Lake Park?

(A) Many residents have complained about some noise produced there.
(B) Most of its visitors use public transportation.
(C) It is the site of community jogging competitions.
(D) The surface of its parking space is poor.

44. Which of the following does Mr. Wilcox's and Ms. O'Neal's opinion have in common?

(A) The workers should be careful of the environment.
(B) The city should try to complete the work quickly.
(C) The changing area should be the first project completed.
(D) The funds should be used for more than one project.

Triple

 P. 458

457

Questions 40-44 refer to the following Web page and e-mails.

http://www.greenville.go.nz

Frank Lake Park to Receive Upgrade

❶ The Greenville Park and Recreation Department would like to announce that it has a budget of over $100,000 and is planning to renovate Frank Lake Park in a few months. ❷ At first, the funds were designated for building an outdoor stage on a plot of land along Bramwell Avenue. ❸ But because of noise pollution concerns from many residents, the project was postponed several times, eventually being called off altogether.

Instead, some alternative projects being considered for the site are removing debris from the lake, building a changing area and concession stand, expanding the parking space, and adding a jogging trail around the lake. A committee has been set up to hear suggestions from the residents at City Hall about which projects are most positively favored. ❹ The residents and the representatives from community groups may present their ideas on June 28 and June 30, respectively. Opinions will also be accepted by e-mail until June 7. These can be directed to gpnrd@greenville.go.nz.

E メール（1）

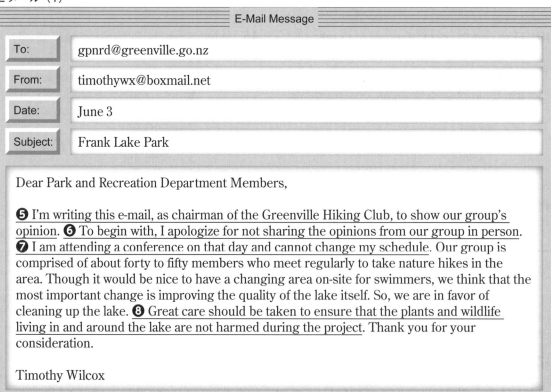

E-Mail Message

To:	gpnrd@greenville.go.nz
From:	timothywx@boxmail.net
Date:	June 3
Subject:	Frank Lake Park

Dear Park and Recreation Department Members,

❺ I'm writing this e-mail, as chairman of the Greenville Hiking Club, to show our group's opinion. ❻ To begin with, I apologize for not sharing the opinions from our group in person. ❼ I am attending a conference on that day and cannot change my schedule. Our group is comprised of about forty to fifty members who meet regularly to take nature hikes in the area. Though it would be nice to have a changing area on-site for swimmers, we think that the most important change is improving the quality of the lake itself. So, we are in favor of cleaning up the lake. ❽ Great care should be taken to ensure that the plants and wildlife living in and around the lake are not harmed during the project. Thank you for your consideration.

Timothy Wilcox

E メール（2）

To:	gpnrd@greenville.go.nz
From:	ninaoneal@outlook.net
Date:	July 5
Subject:	Suggestions for park project

To Whom It May Concern,

It is my honor to have a chance to participate in the issue: Upgrades around Frank Lake Park. In my opinion, the largest portion of the money should be spent on building a jogging trail around the lake. There are already some dirt paths, but I think the site would get more use if it had a high-quality surface for walking and jogging. ❾ Because it is so easy to get to the lake using city bus 168, that is the preferred method for most residents to go to the lake. So, there is no need for extra parking, and I would strongly advise against a new parking lot. Whichever project you choose, ❿ I hope you will take the environmental surroundings into account and take the necessary precautions to ensure that there is no damage to the vegetation, soil, or animals there.

Best regards,

Nina O'Neal

ウェブページ
☐ upgrade 改良、更新　☐ renovate 〜を改修する　☐ fund 資金、基金　☐ designate 〜を指定する
☐ plot 土地、地点　☐ noise pollution 騒音　☐ concern 懸念　☐ eventually 最終的に　☐ call off 〜を中止する
☐ altogether 完全に　☐ instead 代わりに　☐ alternative 代替の　☐ debris がれき　☐ concession stand 売店
☐ expand 〜を拡張する　☐ jogging trail ジョギングコース　☐ set up 〜を設定する　☐ suggestion 提言
☐ positively 積極的に　☐ favored 好意を持たれている　☐ representative 代表者　☐ respectively それぞれ
☐ be directed to 〜に向けられている

E メール（1）
☐ chairman 会長　☐ in person 直接　☐ be comprised of 〜で構成されている　☐ regularly 定期的に
☐ nature hike 自然の中でのハイキング　☐ on-site 現地で　☐ be in favor of 〜に賛成している　☐ care 注意
☐ ensure that 〜を確認する　☐ wildlife 野生生物　☐ harm 〜に害を与える
☐ thank you for your consideration ご検討いただきありがとうございます

E メール（2）
☐ To Whom It May Concern ご担当者様宛　☐ honor 光栄　☐ participate in 〜に参加する　☐ issue 課題、問題
☐ in one's opinion 自分の意見として　☐ portion 部分　☐ dirt path 未舗装の道　☐ surface 表面
☐ preferred method 推奨方法　☐ there is no need for 〜は必要ない
☐ strongly advise against 〜しないことを強く助言する　☐ environmental 環境的な　☐ surrounding 周辺
☐ take A into account A を考慮に入れる　☐ precaution 予防措置　☐ vegetation 植物（の生育）　☐ soil 土壌

40. How can the cost of repairing Frank Lake Park be funded?

- (A) By applying for a city grant
- (B) By imposing taxes on local residents
- (C) By hosting a community fundraising event
- **(D)** By using funds from a canceled project

Frank Lake Park の改修費はどうすれば工面できますか。

- (A) 市の補助金を申請する
- (B) 住民に追加の税金を課す
- (C) 地域の募金イベントを主催する
- **(D)** 中止になったプロジェクトの資金を使用する

🔍 Frank Lake Park の改修費をどうすれば工面できるかが問われている。1 文書目のウェブページの冒頭❶で「10万ドル以上の費用で、数カ月をかけて Frank Lake Park の改修を計画」と発表し、直後の❷・❸で、「当初、この資金は野外ステージの建設用だったが、最終的には建設が中止となった」と述べている。ここから、中止になったプロジェクト資金を利用していることがわかる。以上から、正解は **(D)**。❸の called off が、**(D)** で canceled に言い換えられていることも押さえておこう。

✏️ □ apply for ～に申し込む　□ grant 補助金　□ impose ～を課す　□ fundraising event 募金イベント

41. In the Web page, the word "eventually" in paragraph 1, line 5, is closest in meaning to

- (A) relatively
- (B) subsequently
- **(C)** ultimately
- (D) crucially

ウェブページの、第 1 段落・5 行目にある "eventually" に最も意味が近いのは

- (A) 比較的
- (B) その後
- **(C)** 最後に
- (D) 決定的に

🔍 同義語問題。問われている 1 文書目のウェブページの❸は「最終的に（中止になった）」という意味で使われている。この「最終的に、結局」と同じ意味で使われるのは **(C)**。(B) も似たような意味だと思って選んだ人もいるかもしれないが、(B) は前後のつながりとして、「その後」と次に起こる時系列的なニュアンスがあるのに対し、eventually と ultimately は、「長い年月をかけ、検討し、最終的に出す結論・結果として」というニュアンスになるため、不正解となる。

42. When did Mr. Wilcox attend a conference?

- (A) On June 28
- **(B)** On June 30
- (C) On July 3
- (D) On July 4

Wilcox さんはいつ協議会に出席しましたか。

- (A) 6 月 28 日
- **(B)** 6 月 30 日
- (C) 7 月 3 日
- (D) 7 月 4 日

🔍 Wilcox さんが協議会に出席した日が問われている。Wilcox さんは 2 文書目の E メール（1）の差出人。❺で「自分のグループの意見表明のために、この E メールを書いている」と切り出し、❻・❼で、直接会って意見できない理由を「その日は協議会に出席するつもりで、予定を変更できない」と述べている。「その日」というのは、1 文書目のウェブページの❹にある「住民と地域団体の代表者が意見を述べるのが、それぞれ 6 月 28 日と 30 日」のこと。❺で「自分のグループの意見表明」とあるため、地域団体の代表者としての参加、つまり、6 月 30 日であることがわかる。以上から、正解は **(B)**。この問題は、参照する 1 番目の文書の "respectively（それぞれ）" が、住民と地域団体代表の意見を述べる日を規定しているため、この語の意味をくみ取って解く必要がある。"respectively" は、よく正解のヒントとして登場するので、今回のような問題の解き方を押さえておこう。

★★★★★

43. What does Ms. O'Neal indicate about Frank Lake Park?

(A) Many residents have complained about some noise produced there.
(B) Most of its visitors use public transportation.
(C) It is the site of community jogging competitions.
(D) The surface of its parking space is poor.

O'Neal さんは Frank Lake Park について何を示していますか。

(A) 住民の多くが、騒音がすることに対して不満を述べている。
(B) 訪問者のほとんどが公共交通機関を利用する。
(C) 地域のジョギング競技会の会場である。
(D) 駐車場の地面が整備されていない。

O'Neal さんは Frank Lake Park について何を示しているかを問う選択肢照合型の問題。3 文書目の E メール(2) の❾で、O'Neal さんは Frank Lake Park について「湖へは市バスでとても簡単に行くことができるので、湖へ行く住民のほぼ全員が利用している」と述べている。ここから、この公園を利用する人は公共交通機関を利用していることがわかるので、これを言い換えた **(B)** が正解。resident ≒ visitor と必ずしも言い切れないという考えもあるが、O'Neal さんは、❾の直後で、「だから駐車場はこれ以上必要ない」と、訪問者が増えることもないという主張をしている。つまり、O'Neal さんは resident ≒ visitor と考えていると捉えることができる。

□ site 現場、会場　□ competition 大会、協議会

★★★★★ クロスリファレンス問題

44. Which of the following does Mr. Wilcox's and Ms. O'Neal's opinion have in common?

(A) The workers should be careful of the environment.
(B) The city should try to complete the work quickly.
(C) The changing area should be the first project completed.
(D) The funds should be used for more than one project.

Wilcox さんと O'Neal さんの意見が一致していることは次のどれですか。

(A) 作業する人は環境に配慮する必要がある。
(B) 市は工事を迅速に完了するよう努めるべきである。
(C) 更衣室は最初に完了すべきプロジェクトである。
(D) 資金は 2 つ以上のプロジェクトに使用されるべきである。

Wilcox さんと O'Neal さんの意見が一致していることは何かが問われている。それぞれの E メールの主張を見ていくと、Wilcox さんは E メール（1）の❽で「プロジェクトの進行中に、湖やその周辺の植物・生物に危害がないように配慮を」と述べ、O'Neal さんは E メール（2）の❿で「周辺環境を考慮し、植物、土壌、動物に被害が出ないように対策を」と周辺環境に関する対応を訴えていることがわかる。以上から、対応する作業者を "workers" と表現し、環境に配慮すべき、と述べた **(A)** が共通意見として正解。

□ changing area 更衣室

461

http://www.greenville.go.nz

Frank Lake Park の改良

Greenville 市公園レジャー局は 10 万ドル以上の費用で、数カ月をかけて Frank Lake Park の改修を計画していることをお知らせします。当初、この資金は Bramwell Avenue 沿いの土地に野外ステージを建設するためのものでした。しかし、多くの住民から騒音公害の懸念が表明され、プロジェクトは何度か延期し、最終的には完全に中止となりました。

その代わりとして、同地に検討されている代替えプロジェクトは、湖からがれきを取り除くこと、更衣室や売店の設置、駐車場の拡張、湖の周りへのジョギングコースの追加です。どのプロジェクトが最も好意的な支持を得られるかについて住民からの意見を聞くため、市役所に委員会が設置されています。住民は 6 月 28 日に、地域団体の代表者は 6 月 30 日に、それぞれ意見を述べることができます。ご意見は 6 月 7 日まで E メールでも受け付けています。送信先は、gpnrd@greenville.go.nz です。

E メール（1）

受信者： gpnrd@greenville.go.nz
送信者： timothywx@boxmail.net
日付： 6 月 3 日
件名： Frank Lake Park

公園レジャー局員の皆さま

Greenville Hiking Club の会長として、私たちの意見をお伝えするためこの E メールを書いています。まずはじめに、直接お会いして、私たちの意見をお伝えできないことをお詫びいたします。その日は協議会に出席しており、予定を変更できませんでした。私たちのグループは約 40 から 50 人の会員で構成されており、その地域の自然の中でハイキングするために定期的に集まっています。泳ぐ人のために、現地に着替える場所を設けるのは良い案だと思いますが、最も重要な変更は湖自体の水質を改善することだと考えます。そのため、私たちは湖の清掃に賛成します。プロジェクトの進行中に、湖やその周辺に生息する植物や野生生物が危害を加えられないように細心の注意を払う必要があるでしょう。ご検討ください。

Timothy Wilcox

E メール（2）

受信者： gpnrd@greenville.go.nz
送信者： ninaoneal@outlook.net
日付： 7 月 5 日
件名： 公園のプロジェクトに対する提案

ご担当者様

Frank Lake Park 周辺の改良に関する議論に参加する機会をいただき、光栄です。私は、この資金の大部分を湖の周りにジョギングコースを作ることに費やすべきだと思います。未舗装の道は、すでにいくつかありますが、ウォーキングやジョギングのための質の高い路面の道があれば、もっと利用されると思います。湖へは 168 番の市バスでとても簡単に行くことができるので、湖へ行く住民のほとんど全員が利用しています。ですから、駐車場はこれ以上必要ありませんし、新たな駐車場には強く反対します。どのプロジェクトを選択するにしても、周辺環境を考慮し、植物、土壌、動物に被害が出ないように、必要な予防策が講じられることを望みます。

よろしくお願いいたします。

Nina O'Neal

Questions 45-49 refer to the following Web page, letter, and article.

 5分30秒

◀ ▶   http://www.easternbc.org   ▶

| Home | About Us | Event | Contact Us |

Event for New Members

As we welcome new members to our committee, we are preparing a fantastic banquet at Hinkle Conference Hall in Atlanta, Georgia, on June 30. Doors will open at 6:00 P.M., and dinner will be served at 6:30 P.M. We extend the invitation to this banquet to all members who have joined in the past six months. Click here to register.

Dear Mr. Goodwin,

Do you know the Eastern Business Committee (EBC)? I joined the EBC three months ago. If not, you'd better closely read the following. Our goal is to construct connections between companies that can assist each other. This is especially important in a newly established company such as Braud Co.

Joining the EBC is easy and can be done online for a nominal fee. If you become a member, you will be able to attend EBC events, providing your employees with a platform in which they can make contact with other professionals in the field. You will be listed in the EBC online business directory, which has a steady stream of visitors. This would be a way for us to promote your business without any marketing costs. Moreover, you will receive a monthly newsletter with the latest data on local government regulations that may affect your business and municipal grants that you may be eligible for.

The EBC is a relatively new committee with just forty companies as members. But its mission for the third quarter is to double in size through a big recruitment campaign. Let's take this opportunity to get in on the ground floor.

Best regards,

Silvia Veidt

Eastern Business Committee Constructs Strong Member Base

July 5—Since its establishment, the Eastern Business Committee (EBC) has mainly accepted as its members companies in construction fields such as builders and property developers. The officials of EBC recently decided to expand the membership criteria to include realtors, a complementary business to the construction industry. One such business eligible under the new rules is Braud Co. A spokesperson for Braud Co., Jay Louden, reported high satisfaction with joining the committee. "I think being an EBC member will help to give our company the continuous steadiness that we are seeking," stated Mr. Louden. The EBC continues to bring in new members, and at the monthly meeting on July 2, founder Mark Ralston reported that the committee had met its third-quarter recruitment goal. "With a larger membership, we can host more events and serve our members even better," Mr. Ralston said.

45. What can be inferred about Ms. Veidt?

(A) Her suggestion was met with resistance.
(B) Her office is located in Atlanta, Georgia.
(C) Her job mainly involves recruitment.
(D) She was invited to a formal dinner.

46. What is the purpose of setting up the EBC?

(A) To encourage consumers to patronize local companies
(B) To build mutually beneficial business relationships among companies
(C) To offer training for business owners of newly formed companies
(D) To promote fair employment

47. What is NOT mentioned as a benefit of joining the EBC?

(A) Receiving ongoing advertising on a Web site
(B) Accessing a database of government
(C) Having access to professional networking opportunities
(D) Getting up-to-date information about public funding

48. What did Mr. Louden get from the EBC?

(A) The qualifications required by the new rules
(B) The change of membership
(C) The longer-term stability of a company
(D) The information in construction fields

49. What is indicated about the EBC after its July meeting?

(A) It has at least eighty companies as members.
(B) It has moved its head office.
(C) It has increased its membership fees.
(D) It has promised a minimum number of events.

Triple

P. 466

Questions 45-49 refer to the following Web page, letter, and article.

◀ ▶   http://www.easternbc.org   ▶

| Home | About Us | Event | Contact Us |

Event for New Members

As we welcome new members to our committee, we are preparing a fantastic banquet at Hinkle Conference Hall in Atlanta, Georgia, on June 30. Doors will open at 6:00 P.M., and dinner will be served at 6:30 P.M. ❶ We extend the invitation to this banquet to all members who have joined in the past six months. Click here to register.

Dear Mr. Goodwin,

Do you know the Eastern Business Committee (EBC)? ❷ I joined the EBC three months ago. If not, you'd better closely read the following. ❸ Our goal is to construct connections between companies that can assist each other. This is especially important in a newly established company such as Braud Co.

Joining the EBC is easy and can be done online for a nominal fee. If you become a member, you will be able to attend EBC events, ❹ providing your employees with a platform in which they can make contact with other professionals in the field. ❺ You will be listed in the EBC online business directory, which has a steady stream of visitors. ❻ This would be a way for us to promote your business without any marketing costs. ❼ Moreover, you will receive a monthly newsletter with the latest data on local government regulations that may affect your business and municipal grants that you may be eligible for.

❽ The EBC is a relatively new committee with just forty companies as members. But its mission for the third quarter is to double in size through a big recruitment campaign. Let's take this opportunity to get in on the ground floor.

Best regards,

Silvia Veidt

Eastern Business Committee Constructs Strong Member Base

July 5—Since its establishment, the Eastern Business Committee (EBC) has mainly accepted as its members companies in construction fields such as builders and property developers. The officials of EBC recently decided to expand the membership criteria to include realtors, a complementary business to the construction industry. One such business eligible under the new rules is Braud Co. A spokesperson for Braud Co., Jay Louden, reported high satisfaction with joining the committee. ❾ "I think being an EBC member will help to give our company the continuous steadiness that we are seeking," stated Mr. Louden. ❿ The EBC continues to bring in new members, and at the monthly meeting on July 2, founder Mark Ralston reported that the committee had met its third-quarter recruitment goal. "With a larger membership, we can host more events and serve our members even better," Mr. Ralston said.

★★★★★ クロスリファレンス問題

45. What can be inferred about Ms. Veidt?

(A) Her suggestion was met with resistance.
(B) Her office is located in Atlanta, Georgia.
(C) Her job mainly involves recruitment.
(D) She was invited to a formal dinner.

Veidt さんについて何が推測できますか。

(A) 提案に反対意見があった。
(B) 事務所はジョージア州のアトランタにある。
(C) 主な仕事は採用に関することである。
(D) フォーマルな夕食会に招待された。

Veidt さんについて何が推測できるかが問われている。Veidt さんは、2 文書目の手紙の❷で、「3 カ月前に EBC に入会した」と述べている。そして、1 文書目のウェブページの❶で、「過去 6 カ月以内に入会した会員を（EBC）晩餐会に招待する」と述べられている。以上から、Veidt さんは晩餐会に招かれたことがわかる。よって "banquet" を a formal dinner と言い換えた **(D)** が正解。1 文書目が EBC のものかどうかは、ウェブページのアドレスから推測することができる。このようにウェブページのアドレス、メールアドレスの拡張子（アドレスの @ 以下）に解答根拠があることもあるので、注意して読んでいこう。

★★★★★

46. What is the purpose of setting up the EBC?

(A) To encourage consumers to patronize local companies
(B) To build mutually beneficial business relationships among companies
(C) To offer training for business owners of newly formed companies
(D) To promote fair employment

EBC 創設の目的は何ですか。

(A) 消費者に地域の企業の常連客になるように促すこと
(B) 企業間で相互に有益なビジネス関係を構築すること
(C) 設立されて間もない会社の事業主たちに研修を提供すること
(D) 公正な雇用を促進すること

EBC 創設の目的は何かが問われている。2 文書目の手紙の❸に、「互いに支援する会社の関係を構築すること」という目的が書かれている。以上から、これを言い換えた **(B)** が正解。"each other" を mutually と言い換えていることにも注目しよう。

47. What is NOT mentioned as a benefit of joining the EBC?

   (A) Receiving ongoing advertising on a Web site

   (B) Accessing a database of government

   (C) Having access to professional networking opportunities

   (D) Getting up-to-date information about public funding

EBC に入会することの利点として述べられていないこととは何ですか。

   (A) ウェブサイトで継続的な広告掲載が受けられること

   (B) 政府のデータベースにアクセスできること

   (C) 専門的な人脈作りの機会が持てること

   (D) 公的資金に関する最新情報を手に入れられること

NOT 問題。EBC に入会することの利点として述べられていないことが問われている。2 文書目の手紙の❹の「その分野の他の専門家と交流できるプラットホーム提供」が (C) に、❺・❻の「多くが訪問するビジネス住所録に登録することで販売促進できる」が (A) に、❼の「補助金に関する最新情報を定期的に受け取る」が (D) に、それぞれ一致する。残った **(B)** が本文に述べられておらず、これが正解。それぞれの言い換えが難解なので、一致する表現を押さえておこう。

✎ □ ongoing 継続的な　□ access to ～への接続・接触　□ up-to-date 最新の　□ public funding 公的資金

---

48. What did Mr. Louden get from the EBC?

   (A) The qualifications required by the new rules

   (B) The change of membership

   (C) The longer-term stability of a company

   (D) The information in construction fields

Louden さんは EBC から何を得ましたか。

   (A) 新たな規則で必要とされる資格

   (B) 会員権の変更

   (C) 会社の長期的な安定性

   (D) 建設業界の情報

Louden さんが EBC から何を得たかが問われている。3 文書目の記事に Louden さんの談話があり、❾で「EBC の会員になれたので、当社が求めている継続的な安定を得られるだろう」と、会社の長期にわたる安定が得られると述べていることがわかる。以上より、これを言い換えた **(C)** が正解。

✎ □ qualification 資格　□ longer-term 長期間にわたる

---

49. What is indicated about the EBC after its July meeting?

   (A) It has at least eighty companies as members.

   (B) It has moved its head office.

   (C) It has increased its membership fees.

   (D) It has promised a minimum number of events.

7 月の会議の後の EBC について何が示されていますか。

   (A) 少なくとも 80 社が会員である。

   (B) 本社を移転した。

   (C) 会費を引き上げた。

   (D) 最小限のイベントを開催することを約束した。

7 月の会議の後の EBC について示されていることが問われている。2 文書目の手紙の❽で、Veidt さんが「第 3 四半期の目標は大規模な新会員募集キャンペーンを行って、規模を 2 倍に拡大することだ」と述べている。❽の前半に現在の会員は 40 社とあるので、この 2 倍の 80 社が目標であるとわかる。次に 3 文書目の記事の❿を見ると、「EBC は、7 月 2 日の月例会議で、創設者の Mark Ralston 氏が、委員会が第 3 四半期の入会者数の目標を達成したことを報告した。」とあるため、目標の会員規模である 80 社に達した、ということがわかる。以上から、これを言い換えた **(A)** が正解。EBC の目標達成／第 3 四半期というキーワードで 2 つの文書から根拠を探し出して解こう。

 □ head office 本社　□ a minimum number of 最小限の

http://www.easternbc.org			
トップページ	当委員会について	イベント	連絡先

新会員向けイベント

当委員会へ新たな会員の方々を迎えるので、6月30日にジョージア州アトランタの Hinkle Conference Hall にて素敵な歓迎会を準備しています。開場は午後6時、夕食は午後6時半に提供されます。過去6カ月間に入会された会員の皆さまを、この歓迎会にご招待いたします。お申し込みはこちらをクリックしてください。

Goodwin さんへ

Eastern Business Committee (EBC) をご存じですか？　私は3カ月前、EBC に入会しました。もしご存じでなければ、これから書くことをよく読んでみてください。委員会の目的は企業が相互に助け合うためのつながりを構築することです。これは Braud Co. のような新しく設立された会社にとって特に重要です。

EBC への入会は簡単で、わずかな費用を払えばオンラインで行うことができます。会員になると、EBC のイベントに参加することができ、貴社の従業員たちにこの分野の他の専門家と交流できるプラットフォームを提供することができます。一定の訪問者数がある EBC のオンライン商工名鑑に貴社が掲載されます。これによって、マーケティング費用をかけずに貴社の知名度を上げられるでしょう。さらに、貴社の仕事に影響を与える可能性のある、地方自治体の規制や給付の条件に当てはまる可能性のある地域助成金に関する最新のデータが載ったニュースレターが毎月届きます。

EBC は会員がわずか40社の比較的新しい委員会です。しかし、第3四半期の目標は大規模な新会員募集キャンペーンを行って、規模を2倍に拡大することです。始まったばかりのこの委員会に、この機会に入会しませんか。

よろしくお願いいたします。

Silvia Veidt

Eastern Business Committee が会員獲得の強固な基盤を構築

7月5日—創設以来、Eastern Business Committee (EBC) は主に建設業者や不動産開発業者などの建設分野の企業を会員として受け入れてきた。EBC 当局は先日、会員の範囲を拡張し、建設業界を補完する事業である不動産仲介業者を含めることを決定した。新規程の下で入会が可能となった企業の一つが、Braud Co. である。Braud Co. の広報の Jay Louden は、委員会に入会して非常に満足していると述べた。「EBC の会員になれたので、当社が求めている継続的な安定を得られることでしょう」と Louden 氏は述べた。EBC は引き続き新会員を募っており、7月2日の月例会議で、創設者の Mark Ralston 氏が、委員会が第3四半期の入会者数の目標を達成したことを報告した。「会員数が増えれば、私たちはさらに多くのイベントを主催し、会員にさらに良いものを提供することができます」と Ralston 氏は語った。

Dear Colleagues,

As we opened the new premises last week, the management has made the decision to hire four new members. If you know an individual who you think would be a good addition to our organization, please send his or her name to me. For your information, I have attached a draft of our job listing that will be published online, at www.employmentforum.com, on 15 September.

I appreciate your help.

Tom Stimson

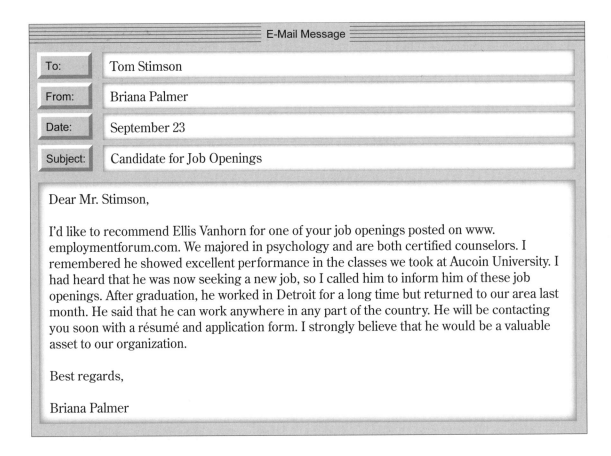

E-Mail Message

To:	Tom Stimson
From:	Briana Palmer
Date:	September 23
Subject:	Candidate for Job Openings

Dear Mr. Stimson,

I'd like to recommend Ellis Vanhorn for one of your job openings posted on www.employmentforum.com. We majored in psychology and are both certified counselors. I remembered he showed excellent performance in the classes we took at Aucoin University. I had heard that he was now seeking a new job, so I called him to inform him of these job openings. After graduation, he worked in Detroit for a long time but returned to our area last month. He said that he can work anywhere in any part of the country. He will be contacting you soon with a résumé and application form. I strongly believe that he would be a valuable asset to our organization.

Best regards,

Briana Palmer

JOB OPENINGS

As it has opened a new facility in this city, a famous government-run youth center is seeking new personnel for the four positions as follows.

Behavioral Therapist	Offers plenty of counseling services, behavior management programs, and other support services. After hiring, they will be sent to different local community centers throughout the state.
Nurse	Works in a free clinic treating patients with non-life-threatening illnesses. Will make referrals to the hospital or a physician when necessary. A bachelor's degree in nursing is mandatory.
Security Guard	Keeps the facility safe and secure. Must work at night on a rotating basis. Above-average communication skills are preferred. A degree in criminology or a related field is required. Moreover, one must have at least three years of experience in the security field.
Activities Coordinator	Assists professionals like nurses or coordinators to plan educational activities and events for local youth. A high school diploma is a minimum requirement and some experience is preferred.

For more details or to apply for one of these positions, please sign in to your account or phone us at 777-9934 with your registration number.

50. Who most likely is Mr. Stimson?

(A) A personnel manager
(B) A college faculty member
(C) A job advisor
(D) A medical staff member

51. What position is Mr. Vanhorn most suitable for?

(A) Nurse
(B) Activities Coordinator
(C) Security Guard
(D) Behavioral Therapist

52. What is NOT indicated about Ms. Palmer?

(A) She is a coworker of Mr. Stimson.
(B) She has contacted Mr. Vanhorn about the job.
(C) She attended the same school as Mr. Vanhorn.
(D) She worked with Mr. Vanhorn in Detroit.

53. What will most likely Mr. Vanhorn need to apply?

(A) His photo
(B) His registration number
(C) His bank account number
(D) His certificate of job career

54. What is NOT required for the security guard job?

(A) Three years of relevant work experience
(B) Willingness to work at night
(C) A degree in a related field
(D) The skill to coordinate activity programs

P. 472

Questions 50-54 refer to the following letter, e-mail and advertisement.

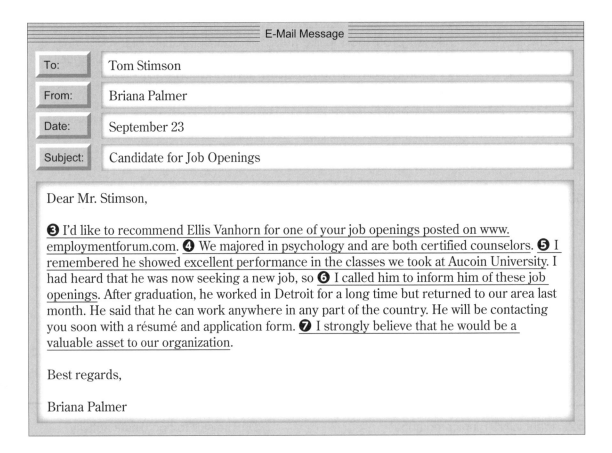

Dear Colleagues,

❶ As we opened the new premises last week, the management has made the decision to hire four new members. ❷ If you know an individual who you think would be a good addition to our organization, please send his or her name to me. For your information, I have attached a draft of our job listing that will be published online, at www.employmentforum.com, on 15 September.

I appreciate your help.

Tom Stimson

E-Mail Message

To:	Tom Stimson
From:	Briana Palmer
Date:	September 23
Subject:	Candidate for Job Openings

Dear Mr. Stimson,

❸ I'd like to recommend Ellis Vanhorn for one of your job openings posted on www.employmentforum.com. ❹ We majored in psychology and are both certified counselors. ❺ I remembered he showed excellent performance in the classes we took at Aucoin University. I had heard that he was now seeking a new job, so ❻ I called him to inform him of these job openings. After graduation, he worked in Detroit for a long time but returned to our area last month. He said that he can work anywhere in any part of the country. He will be contacting you soon with a résumé and application form. ❼ I strongly believe that he would be a valuable asset to our organization.

Best regards,

Briana Palmer

JOB OPENINGS

As it has opened a new facility in this city, a famous government-run youth center is seeking new personnel for the four positions as follows.

❽ Behavioral Therapist	❽ Offers plenty of counseling services, behavior management programs, and other support services. After hiring, they will be sent to different local community centers throughout the state.
Nurse	Works in a free clinic treating patients with non-life-threatening illnesses. Will make referrals to the hospital or a physician when necessary. A bachelor's degree in nursing is mandatory.
Security Guard	Keeps the facility safe and secure. ❾ Must work at night on a rotating basis. Above-average communication skills are preferred. ❿ A degree in criminology or a related field is required. ⓫ Moreover, one must have at least three years of experience in the security field.
Activities Coordinator	Assists professionals like nurses or coordinators to plan educational activities and events for local youth. A high school diploma is a minimum requirement and some experience is preferred.

⓬ For more details or to apply for one of these positions, please sign in to your account or phone us at 777-9934 with your registration number

50. Who most likely is Mr. Stimson?

(A) A personnel manager
(B) A college faculty member
(C) A job advisor
(D) A medical staff member

Stimson さんとはどんな人物であると考えられますか。

(A) 人事部長
(B) 大学教員
(C) 職業アドバイザー
(D) 医療機関の職員

> 🔍 Stimson さんはおそらくどんな人物かが問われている。1 文書目の手紙❶で「経営陣は 4 人の新しい人員を雇用することを決定した」、❷で「適していると思う人を知っていたら私に名前を知らせてほしい」と述べている。つまり、採用に関わる仕事に就いていると考えられるので、**(A)** が正解となる。

✎ □ faculty member 教員

---

51. What position is Mr. Vanhorn most suitable for?

(A) Nurse
(B) Activities Coordinator
(C) Security Guard
(D) Behavioral Therapist

Vanhorn さんは何の仕事に最も適任ですか。

(A) 看護師
(B) 活動コーディネーター
(C) 警備員
(D) 行動療法士

> 🔍 Vanhorn さんは何の仕事に最も適任かが問われている。Vanhorn さんは、2 文書目の E メール冒頭の❸に登場し、その後の❹で、「認定カウンセラーだ」と述べられている。次に、3 文書目の広告を見ると、❽で「カウンセリングサービスを提供する仕事」と述べられている欄があり、行動療法士が適任と考えられる。以上から正解は **(D)**。

---

52. What is NOT indicated about Ms. Palmer?

(A) She is a coworker of Mr. Stimson.
(B) She has contacted Mr. Vanhorn about the job.
(C) She attended the same school as Mr. Vanhorn.
(D) She worked with Mr. Vanhorn in Detroit.

Palmer さんについて示されていないことは何ですか。

(A) Stimson さんの同僚である。
(B) Vanhorn さんに仕事の件で連絡をした。
(C) Vanhorn さんと同じ学校に通っていた。
(D) Vanhorn さんと一緒にデトロイトで仕事をした。

> 🔍 NOT 問題。Palmer さんについて示されていないことが問われている。2 文書目の Palmer さんの書いた E メールを見ると、❺の「私たち（Palmer さんと Vanhorn さん）が Aucoin 大学で受けた授業」が (C) に、❻の「この求人のことを知らせるために、彼（Vanhorn さん）に連絡した」が (B) に、❼の「私たちの団体にとって貴重な人財となる」が、メール受信者である Stimson さんと働いていることを示し (A) に、それぞれ該当する。よって、記載がない **(D)** が正解となる。

✎ □ coworker 同僚　□ attend（学校）に通う

53. What will most likely Mr. Vanhorn need to apply?

   (A) His photo
   (B) His registration number
   (C) His bank account number
   (D) His certificate of job career

Vanhorn さんが応募する際に必要なものは何だと考えられますか。

   (A) 写真
   (B) 登録便号
   (C) 銀行口座番号
   (D) 職務経歴証明書

🔍 Vanhorn さんが応募する際におそらく必要なもの、が問われている。3 文書目の広告に募集要項が書いており、⓬ で「応募は、自身のアカウントにログインするか、登録番号を用意した上で電話を」と述べられている。よって、後者に相当する **(B)** が正解となる。

✏️ □ bank account 銀行口座　□ certificate 証明書

NOT 問題

54. What is NOT required for the security guard job?

   (A) Three years of relevant work experience
   (B) Willingness to work at night
   (C) A degree in a related field
   (D) The skill to coordinate activity programs

警備員の仕事に必須でないものとは何ですか。

   (A) 関連性のある仕事の 3 年間の職務経験
   (B) 夜勤ができること
   (C) 関連分野の学位
   (D) 活動プログラムを調整する能力

🔍 NOT 問題。警備員の仕事に必須でないものが問われている。3 文書目の広告に警備員の仕事の必須要件が記載されており、❾の「夜間勤務」が (B) に、❿の「関連分野の学位」が (C) に、⓫の「警備関係で少なくとも 3 年の職務経験」が (A) に、それぞれ該当する。以上から、残った **(D)** が正解。

✏️ □ willingness to *do* ～する意思

同僚の皆さまへ

先週、新しい施設を開業した際に、経営陣は 4 人の新しい人員を雇用することを決定しました。私たちの団体に適していると思われる方をどなたかご存じでしたら、私にお名前をお知らせください。参考までに、9 月 15 日に www.employmentforum.com へオンラインで公開される求人情報の下書きを同封しました。

ご協力に感謝します。

Tom Stimson

受信者： Tom Stimson
送信者： Briana Palmer
日付： 9 月 23 日
件名： 求人の候補者

Stimson 様

www.employmentforum.com に掲載した求人の 1 つに Ellis Vanhorn さんを推薦します。私たちは心理学を専攻し、2 人とも認定カウンセラーです。Aucoin 大学で受けた授業で、彼が優れた成績を収めていたことを思い出しました。彼は現在新しい仕事を探していると聞いていましたので、この求人のことを知らせるために彼に連絡しました。卒業後、彼は長い間デトロイトで働いていましたが、先月この地域へ戻ってきました。国内のどこでも働くことができると言っていました。すぐに本人から履歴書と応募用紙が送られてくると思います。私たちの団体にとって必ず貴重な人材になるでしょう。

よろしくお願いいたします。

Briana Palmer

求人情報

市内の新たな施設の開設に伴い、有名な公営の青少年センターが次の 4 つの職種で新たな人材を募集しています。

行動療法士	カウンセリングサービス、行動管理プログラム、その他の補助サービスを豊富に提供する仕事です。採用後は、州内のさまざまな地域コミュニティセンターに派遣されます。
看護師	無料診療所で命に関わらない病気の患者を治療する仕事です。必要に応じて病院や医師への紹介を行います。看護学士号が必須です。
警備員	施設の安全と安心を守る仕事です。交替制で夜間勤務があります。平均以上のコミュニケーション能力があることが望ましいです。犯罪学または関連分野の学位が必要です。また、警備関係で少なくとも 3 年の職務経験が必要です。
活動コーディネーター	地域の若者向けの教育活動やイベントを企画するため、看護師やコーディネーターなどの専門家を補助する仕事です。高校を卒業していることが最低要件で、いくらか職務経験があることが望ましいです。

詳細のお問合せや求人へのご応募は、ご自身のアカウントにログインするか、登録番号を用意した上で、777-9934 までお電話ください。

TOKIMAKURE!

Test 7

Test 7

Questions 1-2 refer to the following flyer.

SAVE YOUR FARES !!!

Jin Flight

Groups of 10 or more flying with Jin Flight are able to save 30% on economy class air fares. Families with four or more can save 10%. To do so, you should take flights between March and April.

Please remember that these fares can NOT be obtained at the ticket desk on the day of your flight. In order to buy a flight ticket at the discounted fares, you must reserve flights in advance. To ensure that your group gets the discounts, you must buy tickets on our web site, www.jinflight.net, at least two weeks prior to the flight. More information on flights, fares, and luggage restrictions can be found on our home page.

---

1. According to the flyer, what is true of Jin Flight?

(A) It charges for additional luggage.
(B) It is discounting fares for families.
(C) It flies to over 20 cities.
(D) It will plan fewer flights in March.

2. What does Jin Flight recommend readers to do?

(A) Ask about discounts at the ticket desk
(B) Buy tickets before the day of a flight
(C) Avoid flying during the peak seasons
(D) Pay in cash

P. 480

Questions 3-4 refer to the following letter.

 1分30秒

Jimmy & Jerry Medical Goods
51 Golden Street
Oakland 4435

Ms. Lisa Norris
891 Rison Drive
Oakland 4457

July 25

Dear Ms. Norris,

We regret to tell you that one of the items you placed an order for on July 20 is out of stock. Unfortunately, this item is no longer manufactured.

      Item #903 Gwen hospital sheets (single size), Qty: 100, $13.50/ea

In our inventory, we are able to replace the item indicated above with a similar product, which is listed below.

      Item #7938 Tony hospital sheets (single size), $15.70/ea

The only difference between the new sheets and the old ones is that the new ones are made of slightly better quality cotton. If you want us to change your order to include the new item, please contact us at 824-777-2332. All of the other items listed on your original order form are still available and will be shipped as planned.

Thank you for your patronage.

Deborah Watanabe
Customer Support Agent

---

3. What is the problem with Ms. Norris' order?

(A) Her credit card has expired.
(B) Her shipping address is wrong.
(C) An item she ordered has been discontinued.
(D) A product has been delivered in unsatisfactory condition.

4. According to the letter, why should Ms. Norris call Jimmy & Jerry Medical Goods?

(A) To approve a change to her order
(B) To ask for a renewed catalog
(C) To provide a billing address
(D) To get authorization for an item refund

P. 482

Questions 1-2 refer to the following flyer.

SAVE YOUR FARES !!!

Jin Flight

Groups of 10 or more flying with Jin Flight are able to save 30% on economy class air fares.
❶ Families with four or more can save 10%. To do so, you should take flights between March and April.

Please remember that these fares can NOT be obtained at the ticket desk on the day of your flight.
❷ In order to buy a flight ticket at the discounted fares, you must reserve flights in advance. To ensure that your group gets the discounts, you must buy tickets on our web site, www.jinflight.net, at least two weeks prior to the flight. More information on flights, fares, and luggage restrictions can be found on our home page.

☐ flyer チラシ ☐ fare 運賃 ☐ economy class 等級が安い座席、エコノミークラス ☐ obtain ～を獲得する
☐ in order to *do* ～するために ☐ discounted 割引された ☐ reserve ～を予約する ☐ in advance 事前に
☐ ensure that ～を確実にする ☐ discount 割引 ☐ at least 少なくても ☐ prior to ～に先立って
☐ restriction 制限

★★☆☆☆

1. According to the flyer, what is true of Jin Flight?

(A) It charges for additional luggage.
(B) It is discounting fares for families.
(C) It flies to over 20 cities.
(D) It will plan fewer flights in March.

チラシによると、Jin Flight 社に関して当てはまることは何ですか。

(A) 追加の荷物は有料である。
(B) 家族向けに運賃を割り引きしている。
(C) 20 都市以上に就航している。
(D) 3 月に減便を予定している。

Jin Flight 社について当てはまることを問う選択肢照合型の問題。❶に「4 人以上の家族は 10 パーセント割引」という記載があるため、正解は **(B)** となる。(A) 追加の荷物、(C) 就航都市の数、(D) 減便の計画については、いずれもチラシに記載がないので不正解。

☐ charge for ～に金額を課す ☐ additional 追加の ☐ fewer より少ない

2. What does Jin Flight recommend readers to do?

(A) Ask about discounts at the ticket desk
(B) Buy tickets before the day of a flight
(C) Avoid flying during the peak seasons
(D) Pay in cash

Jin Flight 社は、読み手に対して何をすることを勧めていますか。

(A) チケットカウンターで割引について尋ねること
(B) 搭乗日より前に航空券を購入すること
(C) 繁忙期には飛行機の利用を避けること
(D) 現金で支払うこと

Jin Flight 社が読み手に対して勧めていることが問われている。❷で「割引運賃で航空券を購入するためには、事前予約が必要」と述べているため、搭乗日より前の購入を勧めていることがわかる。よって、これを言い換えた **(B)** が正解。

□ avoid ～を避ける　□ peak season 繁忙期

問題 1 から 2 は次のチラシに関するものです。

航空運賃を節約しましょう !!!

Jin Flight 社

Jin Flight 社を 10 人以上のグループでご利用になる場合、エコノミークラスの航空運賃が 30 パーセント割引となります。4 人以上のご家族の場合は、10 パーセント割引になります。割引は 3 月から 4 月の間に搭乗した場合に適用されます。

この運賃は、ご搭乗当日のチケットカウンターではお取り扱いしておりませんので、ご注意ください。割引運賃で航空券を購入されるには、飛行機を事前予約する必要があります。グループ割引を確実に受けるには、当社のウェブサイト www.jinflight.net で、最低でもご搭乗の 2 週間前までに航空券を購入する必要があります。フライト、運賃、荷物の制限に関する、より詳しい情報については、ホームページでご確認ください。

Questions 3-4 refer to the following letter.

Jimmy & Jerry Medical Goods
51 Golden Street
Oakland 4435

Ms. Lisa Norris
891 Rison Drive
Oakland 4457

July 25

Dear Ms. Norris,

❶ We regret to tell you that one of the items you placed an order for on July 20 is out of stock. ❷ Unfortunately, this item is no longer manufactured.

      Item #903 Gwen hospital sheets (single size), Qty: 100, $13.50/ea

In our inventory, we are able to replace the item indicated above with a similar product, which is listed below.

      Item #7938 Tony hospital sheets (single size), $15.70/ea

The only difference between the new sheets and the old ones is that the new ones are made of slightly better quality cotton. ❸ If you want us to change your order to include the new item, please contact us at 824-777-2332. All of the other items listed on your original order form are still available and will be shipped as planned.

Thank you for your patronage.

Deborah Watanabe
Customer Support Agent

□ regret to tell you that 残念なことに〜をお伝えする □ no longer manufactured 製造終了となっている
□ inventory 在庫 □ replace 〜を交換する □ indicated above 上記に示されている
□ listed below 下記の □ slightly わずかに □ quality 品質の高い □ original order もともとの注文
□ ship 〜を送付する □ as planned 予定どおり □ patronage ご愛顧

★★☆☆☆

3. What is the problem with Ms. Norris' order?

(A) Her credit card has expired.
(B) Her shipping address is wrong.
(C) An item she ordered has been discontinued.
(D) A product has been delivered in unsatisfactory condition.

Norris さんの注文の問題点は何ですか。

(A) クレジットカードが有効期限切れである。
(B) 配送先住所が間違っている。
(C) 注文した商品が製造中止になっている。
(D) 製品が不完全な状態で配送されている。

★★☆☆☆

4. According to the letter, why should Ms. Norris call Jimmy & Jerry Medical Goods?

(A) To approve a change to her order
(B) To ask for a renewed catalog
(C) To provide a billing address
(D) To get authorization for an item refund

手紙によると、Norris さんが Jimmy & Jerry Medical Goods に電話をする必要があるのはなぜですか。

(A) 注文品の変更を承認するため
(B) 新しくなったカタログを請求するため
(C) 請求先住所を知らせるため
(D) 商品の払い戻しの承認を得るため

問題3から4は次の手紙に関するものです。

Jimmy & Jerry Medical Goods
51 Golden Street
オークランド 4435

Lisa Norris 様
891 Rison Drive
オークランド 4457

7 月 25 日

Norris 様

申し訳ございませんが、7 月 20 日にご注文頂いた商品のうちの一つが在庫切れでございます。残念なことに、こちらの商品は製造終了となりました。

　　　　　商品番号 903 Gwen 病院シーツ（シングルサイズ）、個数：100、1 点につき 13.50 ドル

当店の在庫商品の中で、上記の商品を下記の類似商品に交換できます。

　　　　　商品番号 7938 Tony 病院シーツ（シングルサイズ）、1 点につき 15.70 ドル

新しいシーツとご注文商品の違いは、新しいものはやや上質な綿で作られているということだけです。この新しい商品を含むご注文の変更をご希望の場合は、当店 824-777-2332 までご連絡ください。元の注文票に記載されていた他の商品に関しましては、すべて在庫がございますので、予定どおりに発送されます。

ご愛顧いただき、誠にありがとうございます。

Deborah Watanabe
顧客サポート担当

Questions 5-6 refer to the following announcement.

 1分30秒

PROVISIONS & CONDITIONS OF MWP ENTRANCE TICKET

No responsibility will be imposed on Marine World Polynesia (MWP) in respect to unintentional accidents or wounds. MWP is not liable for injury or loss of belongings while on the premises except when the staff of MWP caused the problem. Nor will compensation be offered for inconveniences or disadvantages due to the malfunction of equipment.

▶ Bring food or drinks and smoking are banned within this Aquarium.

▶ Taking pictures is banned in a few places with signs, "Do Not Take Pictures." However, where there is no sign, visitors are free to take pictures.

▶ This ticket is applicable for just one entry.

---

5. What is Marine World Polynesia responsible for?

(A) Loss caused by the staff of Marine World Polynesia
(B) Injuries by accident on the premises
(C) Conditions for sales and delivery
(D) Compensation for disobedience of contract

6. What are visitors allowed to do in Marine World Polynesia?

(A) Use a previous admission ticket
(B) Drink beverages
(C) Eat snacks
(D) Shoot photos in some areas

 P. 486

484

Questions 7-8 refer to the following text-message chain.

1分30秒

Single Q2

Phillip Janssen 12:05
Hello, I'm on my way to the conference. However, the flight I was on was postponed owing to a system error, so I missed my connecting plane in San Jose.

Phillip Janssen 12:06
So I will have to take another flight arriving in Phoenix at 3 P.M.

Margaret Edmond 12:11
Good. What airline?

Phillip Janssen 12:12
Still Dreams Airlines. It'll be arriving late.

Margaret Edmond 12:13
But still in time for the conference.

Phillip Janssen 12:18
Okay. I'll do my best.

Margaret Edmond 12:19
Do you have any checked luggage?

Phillip Janssen 12:25
Yes. Could you pick me up at the exit next to the quarantine station?

Margaret Edmond 12:27
Definitely. I'll be right there and find you.

Phillip Janssen 12:29
Thank you for your help. See you.

7. What is most likely true about Mr. Janssen?

(A) He is currently working in Phoenix.
(B) He has a meeting in San Jose.
(C) He is on business trip.
(D) He works for Dreams Airlines.

8. At 12:27, what does Ms. Edmond mean when she writes, "Definitely"?

(A) She thinks her colleague cannot pass through the quarantine station.
(B) She will meet one of her colleagues.
(C) She has confirmed Phillip's arrival time.
(D) She agrees to wait near the quarantine station.

P. 488

Questions 5-6 refer to the following announcement.

PROVISIONS & CONDITIONS OF MWP ENTRANCE TICKET

No responsibility will be imposed on Marine World Polynesia (MWP) in respect to unintentional accidents or wounds. ❶ MWP is not liable for injury or loss of belongings while on the premises except when the staff of MWP caused the problem. Nor will compensation be offered for inconveniences or disadvantages due to the malfunction of equipment.

▶ Bring food or drinks and smoking are banned within this Aquarium.

▶ Taking pictures is banned in a few places with signs, "Do Not Take Pictures." However, ❷ where there is no sign, visitors are free to take pictures.

▶ This ticket is applicable for just one entry.

□ provisions and conditions 規定と条件 □ entrance ticket 入場券 □ responsibility 責任
□ impose A on B A を B に課す □ in respect to ～に関して
□ unintentional accidents or wounds 不慮の事故や負傷 □ liable for ～に対しての法的責任がある
□ injury or loss 損害または紛失 □ belongings 所持品 □ premises 構内 □ except when ～でない限り
□ cause the problem 問題を引き起こす □ compensation 補償 □ inconvenience 不都合、不便
□ disadvantage 不利益 □ due to ～による □ banned 禁止されている □ aquarium 水族館
□ sign 看板、標識 □ be free to *do* 自由に～できる □ applicable for ～に適用される
□ just one entry 1 度限りの入場

★★★★☆

5. What is Marine World Polynesia responsible for?

(A) Loss caused by the staff of Marine World Polynesia
(B) Injuries by accident on the premises
(C) Conditions for sales and delivery
(D) Compensation for disobedience of contract

Marine World Polynesia はどんな責任を負いますか。

(A) Marine World Polynesia のスタッフが原因で発生した紛失
(B) 館内での事故による損害
(C) 販売と配送の条件
(D) 契約違反の補償

🔍 Marine World Polynesia（MWP）がどんな責任を負うのかが問われている。❶で「MWP のスタッフによる問題以外の滞在中の損害、所持品の紛失については責任を負わない」と述べている。つまり、MWP スタッフが引き起こしてしまった損害や紛失については責任を負うということとなる。よって、**(A)** が正解となる。❶にある "except when（～ではない限り）" という意味を理解して解く必要がある。他の選択肢は、スタッフが引き起こしたかどうかが不明のため、いずれも不正解となる。

□ loss 紛失 □ caused by ～が原因で引き起こされる □ injury 負傷 □ compensation for ～の補償
□ disobedience of contract 契約違反

6. What are visitors allowed to do in Marine World Polynesia?

(A) Use a previous admission ticket
(B) Drink beverages
(C) Eat snacks
(D) Shoot photos in some areas

来館者は Marine World Polynesia で何をすることが許可されていますか。

(A) 以前の入場券を使用する
(B) 飲料を飲む
(C) 軽食を食べる
(D) いくつかの場所で写真を撮る

来館者が Marine World Polynesia で許可されていることが問われている。❷に「看板がない場所では自由に撮影可能」とあるので、**(D)** が正解。(A) 入場券は１度限りであり、(B) と (C) は飲食ＯＫという記載がないため、いずれも不正解となる。

□ previous 過去の　□ admission ticket 入場券　□ snack 軽食

問題５から６は次のお知らせに関するものです。

MWP 入場券の規定と条件

Marine World Polynesia（MWP）は、不慮の事故や負傷については一切の責任を負いません。MWP のスタッフによる問題以外の滞在中の損害、所持品の紛失については責任を負いません。また、設備の故障による不都合や不利益についても補償いたしません。

▶水族館内は飲食物の持ち込み、喫煙は禁止とさせていただきます。
▶写真撮影は、「写真撮影禁止」の看板がある場所では禁止されていますが、看板がない場所ではご自由にお撮りください。
▶このチケットは１回のみの入場でご利用いただけます。

Questions 7-8 refer to the following text-message chain.

Phillip Janssen 12:05
❶ Hello, I'm on my way to the conference. However, the flight I was on was postponed owing to a system error, so I missed my connecting plane in San Jose.

Phillip Janssen 12:06
So. I will have to take another flight arriving in Phoenix at 3 P.M.

Margaret Edmond 12:11
Good. What airline?

Phillip Janssen 12:12
Still Dreams Airlines. It'll be arriving late.

Margaret Edmond 12:13
But still in time for the conference.

Phillip Janssen 12:18
Okay. I'll do my best.

Margaret Edmond 12:19
Do you have any checked luggage?

Phillip Janssen 12:25
Yes. ❷ Could you pick me up at the exit next to the quarantine station?

Margaret Edmond 12:27
❸ Definitely. ❹ I'll be right there and find you.

Phillip Janssen 12:29
Thank you for your help. See you.

□ on my way to ～の途中で　□ conference 会議　□ owing to ～が原因で　□ system error システム不具合
□ miss ～を逃す　□ connecting plane 乗り継ぎの便（飛行機）　□ airline 航空会社
□ checked luggage 預け入れ手荷物　□ pick up ～を迎えに行く　□ exit 出口　□ next to ～の隣に
□ quarantine station 検疫所　□ definitely もちろん

★★★☆☆

7. What is most likely true about Mr. Janssen?

(A) He is currently working in Phoenix.
(B) He has a meeting in San Jose.
(C) He is on business trip.
(D) He works for Dreams Airlines.

Janssen さんについておそらく正しいことは何ですか。

(A) 現在、フェニックスで働いている。
(B) サンノゼで会議がある。
(C) 出張中である。
(D) Dreams Airlines で働いている。

Janssen さんについて正しいことは何かを問う選択肢照合型の問題。Janssen さんは冒頭❶で「会議に向かう途中、乗っていた飛行機が遅延して、乗り継ぎ便に乗れなかった」と述べている。ここから飛行機で会議に向かっていると わかるので、Janssen さんは今、業務で移動していると考えられる。以上により、**(C)** が正解となる。(B) の San Jose は会議が行われる場所ではなく乗継便に乗る場所のため不正解。

□ business trip 出張

8. At 12:27, what does Ms. Edmond mean when she writes, "Definitely"?

    (A) She thinks her colleague cannot pass through the quarantine station.
    (B) She will meet one of her colleagues.
    (C) She has confirmed Phillip's arrival time.
    (D) She agrees to wait near the quarantine station.

12 時 27 分に、Edmond さんは "Definitely" という発言で、何を意味していますか。

    (A) 同僚は検疫所を通過できないと考えている。
    (B) 同僚の一人に会う。
    (C) Phillip さんの到着時刻を確認した。
    (D) 検疫所近くで待っていることに同意している。

意図問題。問われている❸は「もちろん」という意味で、前の発言を受けて賛同している表現のため、それより前の内容を確認する。直前の❷を見ると、Phillip さんが「検疫所の横の出口のところまで迎えに来てもらえるか？」と依頼をしている。❸はそれに対する返答になっており、その後の❹で「そこで待っている」と続けている。以上より、Edmond さんは検疫所近くで Phillip さんを待っているという意図があることがわかるので、正解は **(D)** となる。

□ pass through ～を通過する   □ arrival time 到着時刻

問題 7 から 8 は次のテキストメッセージのやりとりに関するものです。

Phillip Janssen 12 時 5 分
こんにちは、会議に向かっている途中なのですが、システムに不具合があったせいで乗っていた飛行機が遅延になり、サンノゼで乗り継ぎの飛行機に乗れませんでした。

Phillip Janssen 12 時 6 分
そのため、フェニックスに午後 3 時に到着する別の便に乗らなければならなくなりました。

Margaret Edmond 12 時 11 分
了解しました。どの航空会社ですか？

Phillip Janssen 12 時 12 分
Dreams Airlines のままです。到着が遅くなります。

Margaret Edmond 12 時 13 分
それでも会議には間に合う時間ですね。

Phillip Janssen 12 時 18 分
はい。最善を尽くします。

Margaret Edmond 12 時 19 分
預け入れ手荷物はありますか？

Phillip Janssen 12 時 25 分
はい。検疫所の横の出口のところまで迎えに来てもらえますか？

Margaret Edmond 12 時 27 分
もちろんです。そこで待っていますので、落ち合いましょう。

Phillip Janssen 12 時 29 分
ご協力ありがとうございます。ではまた後で。

Questions 9-11 refer to the following article.

2分45秒

Peter Mart Secure a Stake in North America

Peter Mart Inc., one of the largest retailers in the world, is buying a one-fourth stake in North American Shop Co. from Russian retailer Super Ox and could eventually become the main owner. The terms of the transaction announced on Tuesday were not revealed.

North American Shop Co. is the fourth-largest retailer in the region, and it has 42 supermarkets in North America, mainly Canada. This firm has 1,300 employees and had sales last year that were just short of $900 million.

The agreement indicated that Peter Mart Inc. will buy a large stake in the company so that it could be a major shareholder. Super Ox—which contains Canadian grocery chains Sobey's—formed the North American firm, then known as Dalhberg, as a joint venture in 2017.

9. According to the article, what is announced about Peter Mart Inc.?

(A) It plans to sell its stake to North American Shop Co.
(B) It is now owned by Super Ox.
(C) It will purchase a fourth of North American Shop Co.
(D) It has opened its 42nd store in North America.

10. The word "terms" in paragraph 1, line 3, is closest in meaning to

(A) payments
(B) contracts
(C) relationships
(D) conditions

11. What is true about Super Ox?

(A) It operates grocery stores in Canada.
(B) Its main business is oil and gas exploration.
(C) Its largest profits are from sales at Sobey's.
(D) It is based in Canada.

P. 492

Questions 9-11 refer to the following article.

Peter Mart Secure a Stake in North America

❶ Peter Mart Inc., one of the largest retailers in the world, is buying a one-fourth stake in North American Shop Co. from Russian retailer Super Ox and could eventually become the main owner. The ❷ terms of the transaction announced on Tuesday were not revealed.

North American Shop Co. is the fourth-largest retailer in the region, and it has 42 supermarkets in North America, mainly Canada. This firm has 1,300 employees and had sales last year that were just short of $900 million.

The agreement indicated that Peter Mart Inc. will buy a large stake in the company so that it could be a major shareholder. ❸ Super Ox—which contains Canadian grocery chains Sobey's—formed the North American firm, then known as Dalhberg, as a joint venture in 2017.

☐ stake 株、株式 ☐ retailer 小売業者 ☐ eventually 最終的に ☐ term 条件 ☐ transaction 取引、商取引
☐ reveal ～を明らかにする ☐ region 地域 ☐ firm 会社 ☐ short of ～に達しない、不足している
☐ agreement 合意 ☐ shareholder 株主 ☐ grocery 食料品店 ☐ form ～を設立する
☐ known as ～として知られる ☐ joint venture 合弁事業

★★☆☆☆

9. According to the article, what is announced about Peter Mart Inc.?

(A) It plans to sell its stake to North American Shop Co.
(B) It is now owned by Super Ox.
(C) It will purchase a fourth of North American Shop Co.
(D) It has opened its 42nd store in North America.

記事によると、Peter Mart 社について何が発表されていますか。

(A) 自社の株式を North American Shop 社に売却する予定である。
(B) 現在 Super Ox 社が所有している。
(C) North American Shop 社の4分の1を購入する。
(D) 北米に 42 番目の店舗を開店した。

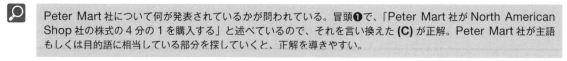

Peter Mart 社について何が発表されているかが問われている。冒頭❶で、「Peter Mart 社が North American Shop 社の株式の4分の1を購入する」と述べているので、それを言い換えた **(C)** が正解。Peter Mart 社が主語もしくは目的語に相当している部分を探していくと、正解を導きやすい。

☐ a fourth of ～の4分の1

10. The word "terms" in paragraph 1, line 3, is closest in meaning to

(A) payments
(B) contracts
(C) relationships
(D) conditions

第1段落・3行目にある "terms" に最も意味が近いのは

(A) 支払い額
(B) 契約
(C) 関係
(D) 条件

同義語問題。問われている❷の部分は、「(取引の) 条件」という意味である。よって、**(D)** が正解。この "terms" は contract（契約）や transaction（取引）などに関連した文書によく出てきて、「(契約・取引などの) 条件、諸条件、条項」という意味になる。

★★★☆☆

11. What is true about Super Ox?

(A) It operates grocery stores in Canada.
(B) Its main business is oil and gas exploration.
(C) Its largest profits are from sales at Sobey's.
(D) It is based in Canada.

Super Ox 社について正しいことは何ですか。

(A) カナダで食料品店を運営している。
(B) 主要な事業は石油とガスの探査である。
(C) 最大の利益は Sobey's の売り上げである。
(D) カナダを拠点としている。

Super Ox 社について正しいことを問う選択肢照合型の問題。文書後半の❸に Super Ox 社に関する記載があり、「カナダの食料品店チェーンの Sobey's を持つ」と述べているので、これに該当する **(A)** が正解。社名後の—はダッシュ（Dash）といって、文の間に入って、直前の語句を説明する表現。これは問題として狙われやすいのでしっかりチェックしておこう。(D) は記載がなく、(B)(C) も根拠となる情報が本文にないため不正解。

□ exploration 探査　□ be based in 〜を拠点とする

問題 9 から 11 は次の記事に関するものです。

Peter Mart 社が北米での株式を取得

世界最大の小売業者の一つである Peter Mart 社が、ロシアの小売業者 Super Ox 社から North American Shop 社の株式の4分の1を購入し、最終的に主要オーナーとなる可能性がある。火曜日に発表された取引の条件は明らかにされなかった。

North American Shop 社は地域で4番目の規模を誇る小売業者であり、北米、主にカナダに42店舗のスーパーマーケットがある。この企業は1300人の従業員を抱え、昨年の販売実績は9億ドルにわずかに届かなかった。

この合意は Peter Mart 社が大株主になれるように、大量の株を購入することを示している。カナダの食料品店チェーンの Sobey's を持つ Super Ox 社は、Dalhberg として知られている北米の企業を2017年に合弁事業として設立した。

Questions 12-14 refer to the following advertisement.

2分45秒

Aha Market Membership Card

Today, everyone is welcome to sign up for the Aha Market Membership Card. It's quick and easy and you'll begin saving without delay. Members enjoy some benefits including:

▷ Exclusive savings

▷ Special discounts on certain items

▷ A yearly coupon book for Aha Market products

In addition to these benefits, members also receive points on every purchase. If enough points have been accumulated, shoppers get additional discounts on their purchases. Our membership is the largest nationwide with hundreds of Aha Market locations to choose from.

And, we would like to make our customers aware that Aha Market is committed to protecting your personal information and we will never sell or share any membership card information with a company outside of our Aha Market. Membership is complimentary so there is no reason for not becoming a member. You can ask for a membership card application at any participating location or sign up online at www.ahamarket.net/membership.

Aha Market, Your Friendly Member Grocery Store

12. Which of the following is NOT mentioned as a benefit of the Aha Market Membership Card?

    (A) Reward points on the purchase
    (B) A discount with each selected product
    (C) Annual coupons
    (D) A monthly brochure

13. According to the advertisement, what can be inferred about Aha Market?

    (A) It can share the customer's purchasing information with other companies.
    (B) It gives free delivery service to the online shoppers.
    (C) Its accumulated points can be used at any time.
    (D) It has a strict personal information protection policy.

14. How can a customer sign up for the Aha Market Membership Card?

    (A) By buying an item
    (B) By going to a Web site
    (C) By sending an e-mail
    (D) By calling Aha Market

P. 496

Questions 12-14 refer to the following advertisement.

Aha Market Membership Card

Today, everyone is welcome to sign up for the Aha Market Membership Card. It's quick and easy and you'll begin saving without delay. Members enjoy some benefits including:

▷ Exclusive savings
▷ ❶ Special discounts on certain items
▷ ❷ A yearly coupon book for Aha Market products

In addition to these benefits, ❸ members also receive points on every purchase. If enough points have been accumulated, shoppers get additional discounts on their purchases. Our membership is the largest nationwide with hundreds of Aha Market locations to choose from.

❹ And, we would like to make our customers aware that Aha Market is committed to protecting your personal information and we will never sell or share any membership card information with a company outside of our Aha Market. Membership is complimentary so there is no reason for not becoming a member. ❺ You can ask for a membership card application at any participating location or sign up online at www.ahamarket.net/membership.

Aha Market, Your Friendly Member Grocery Store

✏️ □ sign up for ～に登録する・申し込む □ without delay 遅延なく □ benefit 特典 □ exclusive 特別な、優待の
□ yearly 毎年の □ in addition to ～に加えて □ accumulate ～を集める □ nationwide 全国で
□ be committed to *do*ing ～することに注力している □ personal information 個人情報
□ outside of ～の外部へ □ complimentary 無料の

 ★★★☆☆ NOT 問題

12. Which of the following is NOT mentioned as a benefit of the Aha Market Membership Card?

(A) Reward points on the purchase
(B) A discount with each selected product
(C) Annual coupons
(D) A monthly brochure

Aha Market 会員カードの特典として言及されていないのは次のうちどれですか。

(A) 購入に対して付与されるポイント
(B) 特定の製品の割引
(C) 年に１度のクーポン
(D) 月に１度の小冊子

🔍 NOT 問題。Aha Market 会員カードの特典として言及されていないものが問われている。❶の「特定商品の割引」が (B) に、❷の「年に１回のクーポンブック」が (C) に、そして、❸の「お買い物ごとのポイント」が (A) に、それぞれ言い換えられている。よって、残った **(D)** が正解となる。(A) の reward point とは、何かをしたときにもらえる報酬としてのポイントを意味する。**(D)** の brochure は、パンフレットと訳されることが多いが、「情報・広告・クーポン等の情報が入った冊子」のことも指すので押さえておこう。

 □ reward 報酬 □ brochure 小冊子、パンフレット

13. According to the advertisement, what can be inferred about Aha Market?

(A) It can share the customer's purchasing information with other companies.
(B) It gives free delivery service to the online shoppers.
(C) Its accumulated points can be used at any time.
(D) It has a strict personal information protection policy.

広告によると、Aha Market について何が推測できますか。

(A) 顧客の購入情報を他社と共有することがある。
(B) オンラインで買い物をした客に無料配送を提供している。
(C) ためたポイントはいつでも利用できる。
(D) 厳格な個人情報保護の方針がある。

Aha Market について何が推測できるかを問う選択肢照合型の問題。❹で、Aha Market は「お客様の個人情報の保護に努め、会員カードの情報を他社に売ったり、共有したりはしない」と述べている。ここから、これを言い換えた **(D)** が正解。❹の "is committed to protecting" や "never sell" という表現が **(D)** の strict と対応していることに注目しよう。(A) は「共有する」が間違い。(B)(C) は該当する記載がないため不正解。

□ accumulated たまった、集まった　□ at any time いつでも　□ strict 厳しい
□ personal information protection 個人情報保護

14. How can a customer sign up for the Aha Market Membership Card?

(A) By buying an item
(B) By going to a Web site
(C) By sending an e-mail
(D) By calling Aha Market

客はどうしたら Aha Market 会員カードに申し込むことができますか。

(A) 商品を購入する
(B) ウェブサイトを訪れる
(C) E メールを送る
(D) Aha Market に電話をする

客が Aha Market 会員カードに申し込むためにはどうすればいいかが問われている。❺に「会員カードの申込書は参加店舗でもらうか、オンラインで申し込みができる」とある。ここから **(B)** が正解だとわかる。

問題 12 から 14 は次の広告に関するものです。

Aha Market 会員カード

本日、どなたでも Aha Market 会員カードにお申し込みいただけます。簡単なお手続きで、すぐにお得なサービスをご利用いただけます。会員の皆さまには次のような特典をご利用いただけます：

▷ 優待割引
▷ 特定の商品の特別割引
▷ 年 1 回の Aha Market 製品のクーポンブック

これらの特典に加えて、会員の方にはお買い物ごとにポイントをお受け取りいただけます。ポイントが十分に貯まると、お買い物の際にさらに割引をいたします。当社の会員数は全国で最大規模であり、数百もの Aha Market の店舗でご利用いただけます。

また、Aha Market はお客様の個人情報の保護に努めており、会員カードの情報を Aha Market 以外の会社に売ったり、共有したりすることは決してないことをお知らせいたします。お申し込みは無料ですので、会員にならない理由はありません。会員カードの申込書は参加店舗でお求めいただくか、オンライン www.ahamarket.net/membership でお申し込みいただけます。

Aha Market、皆さまの身近な食料品店

Peyton Municipal Council Hosts April Meeting

— [1] —. Peyton Municipal Council, at its monthly meeting last night, received a proposal to build a 50 foot mobile phone base station tower in the southeastern part of Cumberland Park. The tower would offer better mobile phone coverage in the area by boosting the network signal. Supporters of the tower say it will benefit Bateman Services Inc. users greatly.

— [2] —. But people living in the neighborhood are concerned about health problems caused by the tower, as this form of technology has not been in existence long enough to provide evidence of the safety to people through long-term exposure.

— [3] —. Those who attended the meeting expressed their opinions to the council, whose members were split about fifty-fifty on the decision. Council members decided that further discussion is needed and they are inviting more options from the community. A debate on the topic has been scheduled for April 24 at 6:30 P.M. at the Peyton Municipal Center, and participation is open to all citizens. Bateman Services Inc. has been recommended to seek different locations in the meantime in case the proposal is voted down by the council.

— [4] —. The next regular council meeting is scheduled for May 4.

15. According to the press release, what is the purpose of the construction project?

    (A) To enhance the appearance of a park
    (B) To make more local jobs
    (C) To improve a communication service
    (D) To increase profits for investors

16. What are the citizens worried about?

    (A) Adverse health effects
    (B) Increased tax rates
    (C) Disruptive construction noise
    (D) Severe air pollution

17. In which of the positions marked [1], [2], [3], and [4] does the following sentence best belong?

"No other new business was discussed at the council meeting."

    (A) [1]
    (B) [2]
    (C) [3]
    (D) [4]

P. 500

Questions 15-17 refer to the following press release.

Peyton Municipal Council Hosts April Meeting

— [1] —. ❶ Peyton Municipal Council, at its monthly meeting last night, received a proposal to build a 50 foot mobile phone base station tower in the southeastern part of Cumberland Park. ❷ The tower would offer better mobile phone coverage in the area by boosting the network signal. Supporters of the tower say it will benefit Bateman Services Inc. users greatly.

— [2] —. But ❸ people living in the neighborhood are concerned about health problems caused by the tower, as this form of technology has not been in existence long enough to provide evidence of the safety to people through long-term exposure.

— [3] —. Those who attended the meeting expressed their opinions to the council, whose members were split about fifty-fifty on the decision. Council members decided that further discussion is needed and they are inviting more options from the community. A debate on the topic has been scheduled for April 24 at 6:30 P.M. at the Peyton Municipal Center, and participation is open to all citizens. Bateman Services Inc. has been recommended to seek different locations in the meantime in case the proposal is voted down by the council.

— [4] —. The next regular council meeting is scheduled for May 4.

☐ municipal council 市議会　☐ host 〜を開催する　☐ foot フィート（長さの単位：1 フィート＝約 0.3 メートル）
☐ coverage 範囲　☐ boost 〜を増強する　☐ network signal 回線信号　☐ benefit 〜に恩恵がある
☐ neighborhood 近隣　☐ caused by 〜によって引き起こされる　☐ in existence 存在して
☐ long-term exposure 長時間さらされること　☐ those who 〜する人　☐ split（2 つに）割れた、分かれた
☐ debate 討論　☐ open to 〜に公開されている　☐ in the meantime その間
☐ in case SV S が V である場合に備えて　☐ vote down 〜を否決する

★★★★☆

15. According to the press release, what is the purpose of the construction project?

(A) To enhance the appearance of a park
(B) To make more local jobs
(C) To improve a communication service
(D) To increase profits for investors

プレスリリースによると、この建設プロジェクトの目的とは何ですか。

(A) 公園の外観をより良くすること
(B) 地域により多くの仕事をもたらすこと
(C) 通信サービスを改善すること
(D) 投資家の利益を増やすこと

この建設プロジェクトの目的は何かが問われている。❶で「携帯電話基地局のタワーを建設する提案を受けた」とあり、❷で「このタワーが携帯電話のサービスエリアを向上させることになる」と述べている。ここから、「携帯電話のサービスエリア」を「通信サービス」、「〜を向上させる」を「〜を改善すること」と言い換えた **(C)** が正解となる。

☐ enhance 〜を強化する　☐ appearance 外観　☐ profit 利益　☐ investor 投資家

★★★☆☆

16. What are the citizens worried about?

    (A) Adverse health effects
    (B) Increased tax rates
    (C) Disruptive construction noise
    (D) Severe air pollution

市民は何について懸念していますか。

    (A) 健康への悪影響
    (B) 税率の上昇
    (C) 建設の騒音
    (D) 深刻な大気汚染

市民が懸念していることが問われている。第2段落の❸に近隣住民が懸念を示している記載があり、「タワー建設により、(携帯電話サービス技術の充実によっておこるかもしれない)健康被害を懸念している」とある。ここから、「健康に悪影響を及ぼす」と言い換えた **(A)** が正解。❸の "be concerned about" と設問の be worried about が言い換えになっている。この部分に反応して読めば、解きやすい問題だ。

□ adverse ～に悪影響及ぼす　□ disruptive 問題を起こしそうな　□ severe 深刻な　□ air pollution 大気汚染

★★★★★ 文挿入位置問題

17. In which of the positions marked [1], [2], [3], and [4] does the following sentence best belong?

"No other new business was discussed at the council meeting."

    (A) [1]
    (B) [2]
    (C) [3]
    (D) [4]

次の文は [1]、[2]、[3]、[4] のどの位置に最もよく当てはまりますか。

「市議会で他に話し合われた新しい議題はない」

    (A) [1]
    (B) [2]
    (C) [3]
    (D) [4]

適切な文の位置を求める問題。文の意味は「市議会で他に話し合われた新しい議題はない」という意味。そのため、これより前には、何かの議題について述べられていると考えられる。それぞれの段落を見ると、第1～第3段落にかけて「市のタワー建設による携帯電話サービスエリア向上」→「タワー建設による住民の健康不安」→「市議会委員も意見が割れているため、討論会を開催」と、タワー建設の是非に関する議論に集中していることがわかる。よって、最終段落の冒頭にこの文を入れると、次回の予定を述べている文にも合う。以上より、正解は **(D)**。

□ business 議題、課題

問題 15 から 17 は次のプレスリリースに関するものです。

Peyton 市議会が 4 月の会議を開催

―[1]― Peyton 市議会は、昨晩の月例会議で、Cumberland Park の南東部に 50 フィートの携帯電話基地局のタワーを建設する提案を受けた。このタワーは回線信号を増強し、携帯電話のサービスエリアを向上することとなる。タワー建設の支持者たちは、これが Bateman Services 社の利用者たちに利益をもたらすだろうと述べている。

―[2]― しかし、この種の技術ができてから、長期にわたり人間がさらされ続けても安全だという証拠を示すのに必要な期間が経過していないという理由で、近隣の住民はタワーによる健康被害を懸念している。

―[3]― 会議に出席した人々は、決定を下すにあたり、市議会議員が半々に割れている中、意見を表明した。市議会議員は、更なる議論が必要であるとし、地域から更なる選択肢を求めることにした。議題についての討論は 4 月 24 日午後 6 時半に Peyton Municipal Center で予定されており、すべての市民が自由に参加することができる。なお、Bateman Services 社には、提案が議会によって否決された場合に備え、他の場所を検討することを勧められた。

―[4]― 市議会で他に話し合われた新しい議題はない。次回の定例会議は 5 月 4 日の予定である。

Elliot Chemical Inc. to Undergo Transition

December 12—Jack Vogel, the successful entrepreneur who established Elliot Chemical Inc. fifteen years ago, said he would not be able to continue as president of the company, and handed over the management rights to the vice president, Chris Hendley.

A spokesperson for Elliot Chemical Inc. said Mr. Vogel formally resigned on Monday last week and strongly asked the board to choose Mr. Hendley as his successor. And also, the spokesperson said, "Mr. Vogel has been appointed as the chairperson of the board, and Mr. Hendley will be officially announced as the new president later this month."

Mr. Vogel has been on leave since April, and Mr. Hendley was widely regarded to be the leading candidate to take the role of the president. He has twelve years of experience at Elliot Chemical Inc., and has covered for Mr. Vogel whenever necessary over the last few years.

Many workers at Elliot Chemical Inc. and customers idolize Mr. Vogel, listening carefully to all of his words at trade shows and firmly defending him and his products when they are criticized. Former workers say he encouraged a unique culture of innovation and creativity within the company. Right after the announcement last Monday, many employees shared their disappointment online and the news quickly spread. Many sites were overwhelmed with traffic and temporarily went offline until Tuesday morning.

Mr. Hendley previously worked for Highbrook Physical Co. and is famous for his tough business approach. Upon joining Elliot Chemical Inc., he played an important role in founding the firm's distribution networks in Canada. Since then, he has risen through the ranks, becoming the vice president two years ago. Additionally, he has shown his leadership qualities during Mr. Vogel's recent absences.

18. What is the article mainly about?

(A) A change of leadership
(B) A company expansion
(C) A search for an executive
(D) A new business direction

19. What can be inferred about Mr. Vogel?

(A) He was formerly the vice president of Elliot Chemical Inc.
(B) He has worked with Mr. Hendley for fifteen years.
(C) He has great respect for Mr. Hendley.
(D) He will retire from Elliot Chemical Inc. to start a new business.

20. The word "carefully" in paragraph 4, line 2, is closest in meaning to

(A) readily
(B) graciously
(C) promptly
(D) attentively

21. According to the article, what happened during last week?

(A) A press conference was convened at Elliot Chemical Inc.
(B) Mr. Hendley was officially appointed as the president.
(C) Some of the websites were out of order for a while.
(D) The workers at Elliot Chemical Inc. met with the board members.

P. 504

Questions 18-21 refer to the following article.

❶ Elliot Chemical Inc. to Undergo Transition

December 12—❷ Jack Vogel, the successful entrepreneur who established Elliot Chemical Inc. fifteen years ago, said he would not be able to continue as president of the company, and handed over the management rights to the vice president, Chris Hendley.

❸ A spokesperson for Elliot Chemical Inc. said Mr. Vogel formally resigned on Monday last week and strongly asked the board to choose Mr. Hendley as his successor. And also, the spokesperson said, "Mr. Vogel has been appointed as the chairperson of the board, and Mr. Hendley will be officially announced as the new president later this month."

Mr. Vogel has been on leave since April, and Mr. Hendley was widely regarded to be the leading candidate to take the role of the president. ❹ He has twelve years of experience at Elliot Chemical Inc., and has covered for Mr. Vogel whenever necessary over the last few years.

Many workers at Elliot Chemical Inc. and customers idolize Mr. Vogel, listening ❺ carefully to all of his words at trade shows and firmly defending him and his products when they are criticized. Former workers say he encouraged a unique culture of innovation and creativity within the company. ❻ Right after the announcement last Monday, many employees shared their disappointment online and the news quickly spread. Many sites were overwhelmed with traffic and temporarily went offline until Tuesday morning.

Mr. Hendley previously worked for Highbrook Physical Co. and is famous for his tough business approach. Upon joining Elliot Chemical Inc., he played an important role in founding the firm's distribution networks in Canada. Since then, he has risen through the ranks, becoming the vice president two years ago. Additionally, he has shown his leadership qualities during Mr. Vogel's recent absences.

✎
- ☐ undergo ～を経験する ☐ transition 移行、変遷期 ☐ entrepreneur 起業家
- ☐ hand over A to B A を B へ手渡す ☐ management right 経営権 ☐ spokesperson 広報担当者
- ☐ formally 正式に ☐ resign 辞任する ☐ strongly 強く ☐ successor 後継者
- ☐ be appointed as ～として任命される ☐ chairperson 会長 ☐ board 取締役、役員 ☐ officially 公式に
- ☐ on leave 休暇中で ☐ widely regarded 広く見られている ☐ leading candidate 最有力候補
- ☐ take the role of ～の役割を担う ☐ cover for ～の代理を担う ☐ whenever necessary 必要な場合はいつでも
- ☐ idolize ～を慕う ☐ trade show 展示会 ☐ firmly しっかりと ☐ defend ～を擁護する
- ☐ criticize ～を批判する ☐ former 以前の ☐ encourage ～を奨励する ☐ innovation 革新技術
- ☐ creativity 創造性 ☐ disappointment 失望 ☐ spread 拡がる ☐ overwhelm ～を圧倒する
- ☐ temporarily 一時的に ☐ go offline （インターネットが）オフラインでつながらなくなる ☐ previously 以前に
- ☐ be famous for ～として有名である ☐ tough 厳しい ☐ business approach 事業手法 ☐ found ～を設立する
- ☐ distribution network 物流網、流通ネットワーク ☐ absence 不在

★★★☆☆

18. What is the article mainly about?

   (A) A change of leadership
   (B) A company expansion
   (C) A search for an executive
   (D) A new business direction

主に何についての記事ですか。

   (A) 指導者の変更
   (B) 会社の拡大
   (C) 役員の選定
   (D) 新しいビジネスの方向性

🔍 何についての記事かが問われている。タイトルの❶と冒頭の❷から「Elliot Chemical 社がある転換期を迎えていること」、「社長が経営権を譲ること」がわかる。よって、❷の "president of the company" を leadership と表現した **(A)** が正解となる。

✎ ☐ expansion 拡大　☐ executive 経営幹部　☐ business direction 事業の方向性

- -

★★★★★

19. What can be inferred about Mr. Vogel?

   (A) He was formerly the vice president of Elliot Chemical Inc.
   (B) He has worked with Mr. Hendley for fifteen years.
   (C) He has great respect for Mr. Hendley.
   (D) He will retire from Elliot Chemical Inc. to start a new business.

Vogel 氏について何が推測できますか。

   (A) 以前、Elliot Chemical 社の副社長だった。
   (B) Hendley 氏と 15 年間共に働いた。
   (C) Hendley 氏をとても尊敬している。
   (D) Elliot Chemical 社を退職し、新しいビジネスを始める。

🔍 Vogel 氏について推測されることを問う選択肢照合型問題。❸で「Vogel 氏は自分の後任に Hendley 氏を選ぶよう取締役会に強く求めた」とあり、また❹で「Hendley 氏がここ数年は必要に応じて Vogel 氏の代理を務めてきた」とある。以上から、後任を託せたいと願うほど Hendley さんを尊敬していることが推測できる。よって、正解は **(C)**。(B) は、❷よりこの会社の創業は 15 年とわかるが、❹で Hendley 氏の経験は 12 年間だと書かれているため不正解。

✎ ☐ respect 尊敬

- -

★★★☆☆ 同義語問題

20. The word "carefully" in paragraph 4, line 2, is closest in meaning to

   (A) readily
   (B) graciously
   (C) promptly
   (D) attentively

第 4 段落・2 行目にある "carefully" に最も意味が近いのは

   (A) 容易く
   (B) 丁重に
   (C) 即座に
   (D) 注意深く

🔍 同議語問題。問われている❺は「その言葉すべてに（注意深く）耳を傾け」「注意深く」という意味になる。この意味と同義なのは **(D)**。正解以外の選択肢も頻出語彙なので、意味がわからなかった場合はしっかりと復習しておこう。

★★★☆☆

21. According to the article, what happened during last week?

    (A) A press conference was convened at Elliot Chemical Inc.

    (B) Mr. Hendley was officially appointed as the president.

    (C) Some of the websites were out of order for a while.

    (D) The workers at Elliot Chemical Inc. met with the board members.

記事によると、先週何が起こりましたか。

    (A) Elliot Chemical 社で記者会見が行われた。

    (B) Hendley 氏が正式に社長に任命された。

    (C) いくつかのサイトがしばらく利用不可能となった。

    (D) Elliot Chemical 社の社員が取締役会のメンバーと面会した。

記事から、先週何が起こったかが問われている。❻で「先週の月曜日の（Vogel 氏辞任の）発表直後は、たくさんの人が多くのサイトにアクセスしたため、一時的につながらない状態になった」とある。正解はこれを言い換えた **(C)**。(A) は会見の場所は発表されておらず、(B) は新社長の正式任命は今月末だと第 2 段落にあるため、いずれも不正解。

☐ convene 〜を開催する　☐ out of order 故障する　☐ for a while しばらく

問題 18 から 21 は次の記事に関するものです。

Elliot Chemical 社が変遷期を迎える

12 月 12 日 ― 15 年前に Elliot Chemical 社を創設し、大成功を収めた起業家の Jack Vogel 氏は、社長を続けることはできないと語り、経営権を副社長の Chris Hendley 氏に譲り渡した。

Elliot Chemical 社の広報担当者は、Vogel 氏が先週の月曜日に正式に辞任し、後任には Hendley 氏を選ぶよう取締役会に強く求めたと述べた。また、広報担当者は、「Vogel 氏は取締役会の議長に任命されており、今月末に Hendley 氏が新社長として正式に発表される。」とも語った。

Vogel 氏は 4 月以降休暇をとっており、Hendley 氏が社長の役目を担う有力な候補として見られていた。彼は Elliot Chemical 社で 12 年間の経験があり、ここ数年は必要に応じて Vogel 氏の代理を務めてきた。

Elliot Chemical 社の社員の多くや顧客は、Vogel 氏を慕っており、展示会ではその言葉すべてに注意深く耳を傾け、また、製品が批判を受けたときには Vogel 氏と製品をしっかりと擁護した。かつての社員は、Vogel 氏は革新と創造性という独特な文化を社内で奨励していたという。先週月曜日の発表の直後は、多くの従業員がその失望をオンラインで共有し、その知らせはあっという間に拡散した。多くのサイトにアクセスが殺到し、火曜日の朝まで一時的につながらない状態になった。

Hendley 氏は以前、Highbrook Physical 社で勤務しており、厳しい仕事への取り組み方でよく知られている。Elliot Chemical 社に入社してすぐ、カナダにおける同社の流通ネットワークの設立に重要な役割を果たした。それ以来昇級を重ね、2 年前に副社長となった。さらに最近の Vogel 氏の不在中には指導者としての資質を示した。

GO ON TO THE
NEXT PAGE!

Questions 22-25 refer to the following online chat discussion.

4分00秒

Dora Ramirez [2:29 P.M.]	Hi, everyone. Is our plan going well?
Stephanie Myers [2:30 P.M.]	We should come up with an idea for our Oakland Seaside restaurants by Tuesday. We have a shortlist of seven new menu items. Narrowing them down was difficult.
Rob Fischer [2:30 P.M.]	The items are unique, but the flavors aren't that popular with the target groups.
Dora Ramirez [2:32 P.M.]	That's really not a big deal. It will only be offered for two weeks. It is just meant to be interesting new items that will get us some attention.
Garvin Whittaker [2:36 P.M.]	Actually, we don't want negative attention because of items that don't taste good.
Stephanie Myers [2:38 P.M.]	You bet. Many people love the pizza that's combined with Hawaiian toppings. It got a lot of good feedback during the tests.
Dora Ramirez [2:39 P.M.]	It tastes good. However, I think it isn't new or different. We want a really unique combination.
Rob Fischer [2:43 P.M.]	Well, the idea that the customers who we surveyed appeared to like the most was called the French-fried hamburger. If you don't mind, I will try to create my own recipe.
Dora Ramirez [2:50 P.M.]	That sounds like just what we're looking for! We'll definitely get a lot of attention from it. Be sure to send a plan to me before the due date.

22. What most likely is the Mr. Fischer's job?

(A) A waiter
(B) A marketing employee
(C) A cook
(D) A critic

23. What does Mr. Whittaker express his concern about?

(A) Going over a department's budget
(B) Protecting the company's fame
(C) Establishing a sales goal
(D) Meeting a due date

24. At 2:38 P.M., what does Ms. Myers mean when she writes, "You bet"?

(A) She likes to play a game.
(B) She wants some numerical data.
(C) She thinks that the job will be more difficult.
(D) She believes that the taste of food is significant.

25. What does Ms. Ramirez think most important?

(A) Developing a campaign slogan
(B) Bringing attention to the company's items
(C) Decreasing the price of less popular products
(D) Looking for many regular customers

P. 510

Questions 22-25 refer to the following online chat discussion.

Dora Ramirez [2:29 P.M.]	Hi, everyone. Is our plan going well?
Stephanie Myers [2:30 P.M.]	❶ We should come up with an idea for our Oakland Seaside restaurants by Tuesday. ❷ We have a shortlist of seven new menu items. ❸ Narrowing them down was difficult.
Rob Fischer [2:30 P.M.]	❹ The items are unique, but the flavors aren't that popular with the target groups.
Dora Ramirez [2:32 P.M.]	That's really not a big deal. It will only be offered for two weeks. It is just meant to be interesting new items that will get us some attention.
Garvin Whittaker [2:36 P.M.]	❺ Actually, we don't want negative attention because of items that don't taste good.
Stephanie Myers [2:38 P.M.]	❻ You bet. Many people love the pizza that's combined with Hawaiian toppings. It got a lot of good feedback during the tests.
Dora Ramirez [2:39 P.M.]	It tastes good. However, I think it isn't new or different. We want a really unique combination.
Rob Fischer [2:43 P.M.]	Well, the idea that the customers who we surveyed appeared to like the most was called the French-fried hamburger. If you don't mind, ❼ I will try to create my own recipe.
Dora Ramirez [2:50 P.M.]	❽ That sounds like just what we're looking for! We'll definitely get a lot of attention from it. Be sure to send a plan to me before the due date.

🖊 □ go well うまくいく □ come up with ~を思いつく □ shortlist 候補リスト □ narrow down ~を絞り込む
□ unique 独特である □ flavor 風味 □ target group 標的集団、ターゲットグループ □ a big deal 大した事
□ attention 注目 □ negative 否定的な □ You bet. そのとおりである。 □ combined with ~と組み合わさって
□ feedback 評価、フィードバック □ appear to *do* ~するように見える □ recipe レシピ、料理法
□ definitely 間違いなく □ due date 締め切り日

22. What most likely is the Mr. Fischer's job?

(A) A waiter
(B) A marketing employee
(C) A cook
(D) A critic

Fischer さんの仕事は何だと考えられますか。

(A) 給仕係
(B) マーケティング担当
(C) 料理人
(D) 批評家

🔍 Fischer さんの仕事はおそらく何かが問われている。❶〜❹で新しいメニューについての会話がなされている。その後、Fischer さんが❼で「私なりのレシピを生み出してみる」と言っているので、料理を作る仕事をしていると推察できる。以上から、正解は **(C)**。

✏️ ☐ critic 批評家

----

23. What does Mr. Whittaker express his concern about?

(A) Going over a department's budget
(B) Protecting the company's fame
(C) Establishing a sales goal
(D) Meeting a due date

Whittaker さんは何についての懸念を示していますか。

(A) 部の予算を精査すること
(B) 会社の名声を守ること
(C) 販売目標を設定すること
(D) 期日を守ること

🔍 Whittaker さんが懸念していることが問われている。Whittaker さんは❺で「おいしくない商品のために悪い注目を集めたくない」と述べている。つまり「会社自体が悪い評判を受けたくない＝会社の名声を守りたい」という考えがあることがわかる。よって、「名声」を fame と表した **(B)** が正解。

✏️ ☐ express one's concern 懸念を示す　☐ fame 名声　☐ due date 締め切り日

----

24. At 2:38 P.M., what does Ms. Myers mean when she writes, "You bet"?

(A) She likes to play a game.
(B) She wants some numerical data.
(C) She thinks that the job will be more difficult.
(D) She believes that the taste of food is significant.

午後 2 時 38 分に、Myers さんは "You bet" という発言で、何を意味していますか。

(A) ゲームをすることが好きである。
(B) 数値のデータが欲しい。
(C) 仕事はもっと難しくなると考えている。
(D) 料理の味が重要だと思っている。

🔍 意図問題。問われている❻は「そのとおり」という意味。直前の発言を見ると、❺で「おいしくない商品で悪い注目を集めたくない」と述べている。❻はこれに対する同意を表しているため、Myers さんは料理の味が重要だと考えていることがわかる。以上から、正解は significant という表現を使ってこれを表した **(D)** となる。

✏️ ☐ numerical 数値の　☐ significant 重要な、意義のある

25. What does Ms. Ramirez think most important?

   (A) Developing a campaign slogan
   (B) Bringing attention to the company's items
   (C) Decreasing the price of less popular products
   (D) Looking for many regular customers

Ramirez さんは何が最も重要であると考えていますか。

   (A) キャンペーンのスローガンを作成すること
   (B) 会社の商品に注目させること
   (C) 不人気の製品の価格を下げること
   (D) 多くの常連客を獲得すること

Ramirez さんは何が最も重要と考えているかが問われている。Ramirez さんは❽で、「それこそまさに私たちが求めていたものですね！　間違いなく注目をたくさん浴びるでしょう」と述べており、この直前の「調査で最もお客さんに人気のあったアイデアを具現化してみる」という Fischer さんの発言に大賛成している。ここから、新商品を作って注目を浴びることが最も重要だと考えていることがわかる。よって、新商品を the company's item に言い換えた **(B)** が正解。

□ slogan 標語、スローガン

📝 問題 22 から 25 は次のオンラインチャットの話し合いに関するものです。

Dora Ramirez [午後 2 時 29 分]	皆さん、こんにちは。計画は順調ですか？
Stephanie Myers [午後 2 時 30 分]	火曜日までに当社の Oakland Seaside のレストランについてのアイデアを出さなければなりません。7 つの新メニューの候補リストがあります。絞り込むことは困難でした。
Rob Fischer [午後 2 時 30 分]	メニューは独創的ですが、その味はターゲットのグループに人気がありません。
Dora Ramirez [午後 2 時 32 分]	それは大した問題ではありません。2 週間しか提供しませんので。これはただ面白い新メニューとして私たちに注目を集めるためです。
Garvin Whittaker [午後 2 時 36 分]	実際のところ、おいしくない商品のために悪い注目を集めたくはありません。
Stephanie Myers [午後 2 時 38 分]	そのとおりですね。ハワイアンスタイルの具を載せたピザは多くの人に愛されています。試作でも高評価をたくさんもらいました。
Dora Ramirez [午後 2 時 39 分]	おいしいですが、新しさや独特さはないと思います。私たちには本当に独創的な組み合わせが必要です。
Rob Fischer [午後 2 時 43 分]	当社が行った調査でお客様に最も人気があったアイデアは、French-Fried Hamburger というものでした。もしよければ、私なりのレシピを生み出してみます。
Dora Ramirez [午後 2 時 50 分]	それこそまさに私たちが求めているものですね！　間違いなく注目をたくさん浴びるでしょう。締め切り日までに必ず案を私に送ってください。

GO ON TO THE NEXT PAGE!

Questions 26-29 refer to the following article.

 4分00秒

Economic News in the Cosmetics Industry

By Edward Otani

September 15—Fresh Rose Cosmetics has finally managed to make a name for itself in the Australian market. For the last five years, the New Zealand-based cosmetics company has competed in the country, but in the last one year, the company has significantly increased its sales throughout Australia. By August, the company had already surpassed its yearly average. — [1] —.

The remarkable sales figures can be attributed to the effects of increased manufacturing capacity and new stores. A year ago, Fresh Rose Cosmetics opened up a new production plant in Sydney, which helped the business increase its production by almost 50 percent. Then, last fall, Fresh Rose Cosmetics doubled its number of retail stores in Australia to better handle the additional quantities of products. — [2] —.

Industry analysts also believe that the success of Fresh Rose Cosmetics is, in part, because of the lack of forward-thinking of its main competitor, Akira Elegance. Since Akira Elegance introduced its popular cosmetics line, Richwood Make-Up, a few years ago, it has not opened any new production facilities. Its makeup base became a favorite among young women. However, since then Akira Elegance has not been able to keep up with the demand for the item. — [3] —.

Without an adequate number of facilities to meet production deadlines, the business repeatedly failed to deliver orders, causing customer dissatisfaction. Market experts said that this has driven many women to start buying the items of Fresh Rose Cosmetics. The change in consumer trends is managing to help the longstanding interests of Fresh Rose Cosmetics in the Australian market. Therefore, the plan of Fresh Rose Cosmetics is to increase its production in Australia. Fresh Rose Cosmetics will move forward with the construction of a new facility in Australia. — [4] —.

26. What did Fresh Rose Cosmetics do last year?

(A) It hired a new company director.
(B) It opened up a new production plant in Melbourne.
(C) It opened more stores in Australia.
(D) It introduced a new line of make-up base.

27. According to the article, what is suggested about Akira Elegance?

(A) It made a popular make-up item.
(B) It opened a large marketing branch.
(C) It recently operated another production plant.
(D) It is based in New Zealand.

28. What will Fresh Rose Cosmetics probably do in the near future?

(A) Introduce a new make-up base
(B) Postpone a marketing campaign in New Zealand
(C) Move the business's headquarters
(D) Build another plant in Australia

29. In which of the positions marked [1], [2], [3], and [4] does the following sentence best belong?

"And also, market experts predict groundbreaking sales to continue for at least the next year."

(A) [1]
(B) [2]
(C) [3]
(D) [4]

P. 516

Questions 26-29 refer to the following article.

Economic News in the Cosmetics Industry

By Edward Otani

September 15—Fresh Rose Cosmetics has finally managed to make a name for itself in the Australian market. For the last five years, the New Zealand-based cosmetics company has competed in the country, but in the last one year, the company has significantly increased its sales throughout Australia. ❶ By August, the company had already surpassed its yearly average. — [1] —.

The remarkable sales figures can be attributed to the effects of increased manufacturing capacity and new stores. A year ago, Fresh Rose Cosmetics opened up a new production plant in Sydney, which helped the business increase its production by almost 50 percent. ❷ Then, last fall, Fresh Rose Cosmetics doubled its number of retail stores in Australia to better handle the additional quantities of products. — [2] —.

Industry analysts also believe that the success of Fresh Rose Cosmetics is, in part, because of the lack of forward-thinking of its main competitor, Akira Elegance. ❸ Since Akira Elegance introduced its popular cosmetics line, Richwood Make-Up, a few years ago, it has not opened any new production facilities. ❹ Its makeup base became a favorite among young women. However, since then Akira Elegance has not been able to keep up with the demand for the item. — [3] —.

Without an adequate number of facilities to meet production deadlines, the business repeatedly failed to deliver orders, causing customer dissatisfaction. Market experts said that this has driven many women to start buying the items of Fresh Rose Cosmetics. The change in consumer trends is managing to help the longstanding interests of Fresh Rose Cosmetics in the Australian market. Therefore, the plan of Fresh Rose Cosmetics is to increase its production in Australia. ❺ Fresh Rose Cosmetics will move forward with the construction of a new facility in Australia. — [4] —.

- ☐ cosmetics 化粧品 ☐ make a name for itself 名を残す ☐ compete in ～で競争する
- ☐ -based ～に本社を置く ☐ significantly 大きく ☐ surpass ～を超える ☐ yearly 1 年の
- ☐ remarkable 著しい ☐ sales figures 売上高 ☐ A be attributed to B A は B によるものである
- ☐ manufacturing capacity 製造能力 ☐ open up ～を開設する ☐ retail store 小売店舗
- ☐ handle ～を取り扱う ☐ quantity 量 ☐ forward-thinking 前向きな・将来性のある考え
- ☐ competitor 競合他社 ☐ makeup base 化粧下地 ☐ keep up with ～に追いつく ☐ adequate 十分な
- ☐ deadline 納期 ☐ fail to *do* ～し損ねる ☐ cause ～を引き起こす ☐ dissatisfaction 不満足
- ☐ longstanding 長期にわたる ☐ interest 利益 ☐ move forward with ～を進める

★★☆☆☆

26. What did Fresh Rose Cosmetics do last year?

(A) It hired a new company director.
(B) It opened up a new production plant in Melbourne.
(C) It opened more stores in Australia.
(D) It introduced a new line of make-up base.

Fresh Rose Cosmetics 社は昨年何を行いましたか。

(A) 新たな取締役を雇った。
(B) メルボルンに新しい生産工場を開設した。
(C) オーストラリアでさらに多くの店舗を開業した。
(D) 新たな化粧下地のシリーズを発売した。

Fresh Rose Cosmetics 社は昨年何を行ったかが問われている。❷に「昨年の秋、Fresh Rose Cosmetics はオーストラリアにおける販売店の数を 2 倍に増やした」とあり、この "Fresh Rose Cosmetics doubled its number of retail stores" を It opened more stores に言い換えた **(C)** が正解。(D) は、化粧下地については Akira Elegance の商品に関する記載はあるが、Fresh Rose Cosmetics の商品としての記載はないので不正解。

☐ line （取り扱い商品の）品目

★★★☆☆

27. According to the article, what is suggested about Akira Elegance?

(A) It made a popular make-up item.
(B) It opened a large marketing branch.
(C) It recently operated another production plant.
(D) It is based in New Zealand.

記事によると、Akira Elegance 社について何が示唆されていますか。

(A) 人気の化粧品を作った。
(B) 大規模なマーケティング支部を開設した。
(C) 最近もう一つの生産工場を稼働した。
(D) ニュージーランドを拠点としている。

記事から、Akira Elegance 社について何が示唆されているかを問う選択肢照合型の問題。❸・❹から「Akira Elegance 社が数年前に人気の化粧品を発表し、人気となった」ということがわかる。よって、正解は **(A)**。(C)(D) は、Fresh Rose Cosmetic 社のことのため不正解。

 □ branch 支店　□ based in ～を拠点として

★★★☆☆

28. What will Fresh Rose Cosmetics probably do in the near future?

(A) Introduce a new make-up base
(B) Postpone a marketing campaign in New Zealand
(C) Move the business's headquarters
(D) Build another plant in Australia

近い将来、Fresh Rose Cosmetics 社は何をすると考えられますか。

(A) 新しい化粧下地を発表する
(B) ニュージーランドにおけるマーケティングキャンペーンを延期する
(C) 本社を移転する
(D) オーストラリアにもう一つの工場を建設する

近い将来 Fresh Rose Cosmetics 社が何をすると考えられるかが問われている。❺で、「Fresh Rose Cosmetics 社はオーストラリアで新たな施設の建設を進める予定だ」と述べられているため、もっと工場を増やすと考えられる。以上から、**(D)** が正解となる。

□ headquarters 本社

★★★★☆ 文挿入位置問題

29. In which of the positions marked [1], [2], [3], and [4] does the following sentence best belong?

"And also, market experts predict groundbreaking sales to continue for at least the next year."

(A) [1]
(B) [2]
(C) [3]
(D) [4]

次の文は [1]、[2]、[3]、[4] のどの位置に最もよく当てはまりますか。

「また、市場の専門家はその突出した売り上げが少なくとも来年まで続くと予想している」

(A) [1]
(B) [2]
(C) [3]
(D) [4]

適切な文の位置を求める問題。文の意味は「また、市場の専門家はその突出した売り上げが少なくとも来年まで続くと予測している」とある。つまり、この文の前には「突出した売り上げが立っている」という内容が述べられていると考えられる。文書を読むと、❶で「8月までに Fresh Rose Cosmetics 社は年間売上の平均を超えた」という突出した売り上げについて述べられており、この直後に入れると文意が成立する。よって、正解は **(A)**。この問題はそれぞれの段落に空所選択肢があるため、それぞれの段落の内容をしっかりつかんで解くようにしよう。

 □ groundbreaking 革新的な

化粧品産業 経済ニュース

Edward Otani 記

9 月 15 日 — Fresh Rose Cosmetics 社がついにオーストラリア市場でその名を知られるようになった。この 5 年間、ニュージーランドを拠点とするこの化粧品会社は国内で競争してきたが、この 1 年間で同社はオーストラリア全土での売り上げを大幅に増加させた。8 月までに同社は年間売り上げの平均を超えたのだ。 —[1]— また、市場の専門家はその突出した売り上げが最低でも来年まで続くと予想している。

その驚異的な売上高は、生産能力の拡大と新規店舗の効果によるものと考えられる。1 年前、Fresh Rose Cosmetics 社はシドニーに新しい生産工場を開設し、同社の生産量をほぼ 50 パーセント増加させた。そして、昨年の秋、Fresh Rose Cosmetics 社はさらに多くの製品を円滑に販売するため、オーストラリアにおける販売店の数を 2 倍に増やした。 —[2]—

また、業界アナリストは、Fresh Rose Cosmetics 社の成功は主な競合相手である Akira Elegance 社の先見性のなさが理由の一端であると考えている。Akira Elegance 社は数年前に人気の化粧品シリーズである Richwood Make-Up を発表して以来、新たな生産施設を開設していない。その化粧下地は、若い女性の間で人気を博した。しかし、それ以来 Akira Elegance 社は商品の需要に追いつけていない。 —[3]—

生産期限に間に合わせるための十分な数の施設がないので、注文を受けても納品できないことが繰り返され、顧客の不満を招いた。市場の専門家は、これにより多くの女性たちが Fresh Rose Cosmetics 社の商品を買い始めたと述べている。消費者動向の変化が、Fresh Rose Cosmetics 社のオーストラリア市場での長期に渡る利益をうまく支えている。そのため、Fresh Rose Cosmetics 社がオーストラリアでの生産を増やす計画を立てた。Fresh Rose Cosmetics 社はオーストラリアで新たな施設の建設を進める予定だ。 —[4]—

GO ON TO THE NEXT PAGE!

1回目

2回目

3回目

Questions 30-34 refer to the following information and e-mail.

5分00秒

DEEPSKIN
OLIVEIRA BODYWORKS ACADEMY
PRESENTS

If you would like to build a successful career in the massage industry, Oliveira Bodyworks Academy (OBA), Hudson's highest-rated massage school, could be helpful. DEEPSKIN is our yearly trial class that offers students the chance to explore the field of massage.

Pick from one of the courses listed below, each consisting of six class sessions (information about the content of each class is posted on our Web site www.hudsonoba.edu/deepskin):

Course 1: Aromatherapy Massage Course Dates: July 9 Tue – 19 Fri Class days: Tuesdays, Thursdays, & Fridays Day Class Times: 9:00 A.M. – 12:00 P.M.	Course 2: Touch-In Massage Course Dates: August 5 Mon – 16 Fri Class Days: Mondays, Wednesdays, & Fridays Day Class Times: 2:00 P.M. – 5:00 P.M.

To participate in the DEEPSKIN program, a sign-up fee of $50 and a course materials fee of $30 are required. Should you have any concerns, contact Brock Lohan, our class coordinator, at brock@oba.edu or at (276) 888-2355 for more information.

If you're unable to attend the July and August program this year, you don't have to be disappointed. OBA will also offer the DEEPSKIN program in April from next year.

OBA has an information session on the details about its twelve-month certification programs. It will be held on Tuesday, September 3. Come to the session to find out more.

To: Brock Lohan <brock@oba.edu>
From: Tatiana Zhang <tazha@tmail.net>
Date: July 4
Subject: Question

Dear Mr. Lohan,

I recently signed up for the DEEPSKIN program; however I could not pay the fee. Could you please advise me on what I should do?

I'm fairly sure that I will be registering for the twelve-month programs and so, in addition to the Aromatherapy Massage course, I want to practice on my own. For that reason, I want to know if I could buy all the materials made available to students in the twelve-month program in advance. Please inform me of what options are available to me. I hope to hear from you soon.

Sincerely,

Tatiana Zhang

30. For whom is the information intended?

(A) Professional massage instructors
(B) Registration office employees
(C) Future massage technicians
(D) OBA staff

31. What is indicated about the DEEPSKIN program?

(A) It is being provided for the first time.
(B) It is prerequisite for the twelve-month program.
(C) It is broadcast online.
(D) It will be offered again in the future.

32. When will the programs that lead to professional licensing be discussed?

(A) On July 9
(B) On August 3
(C) On August 14
(D) On September 3

33. In the e-mail, the word, "fairly" in paragraph 2, line 1, is closest in meaning to

(A) reasonably
(B) similarly
(C) brightly
(D) justifiably

34. What is indicated about Ms. Zhang?

(A) She will not be required to pay a registration fee.
(B) She wants to take classes in the morning.
(C) She had previously contacted the academy.
(D) She wants to change her class.

Double

P. 522

Questions 30-34 refer to the following information and e-mail.

DEEPSKIN
OLIVEIRA BODYWORKS ACADEMY
PRESENTS

❶ If you would like to build a successful career in the massage industry, Oliveira Bodyworks Academy (OBA), Hudson's highest-rated massage school, could be helpful. DEEPSKIN is our yearly trial class that offers students the chance to explore the field of massage.

Pick from one of the courses listed below, each consisting of six class sessions (information about the content of each class is posted on our Web site www.hudsonoba.edu/deepskin):

❷ Course 1: Aromatherapy Massage Course Dates: July 9 Tue – 19 Fri Class days: Tuesdays, Thursdays, & Fridays ❸ Day Class Times: 9:00 A.M. – 12:00 P.M.	Course 2: Touch-In Massage Course Dates: August 5 Mon – 16 Fri Class Days: Mondays, Wednesdays, & Fridays Day Class Times: 2:00 P.M. – 5:00 P.M.

To participate in the DEEPSKIN program, a sign-up fee of $50 and a course materials fee of $30 are required. Should you have any concerns, contact Brock Lohan, our class coordinator, at brock@oba.edu or at (276) 888-2355 for more information.

If you're unable to attend the July and August program this year, you don't have to be disappointed. ❹ OBA will also offer the DEEPSKIN program in April from next year.

❺ OBA has an information session on the details about its twelve-month certification programs. ❻ It will be held on Tuesday, September 3. Come to the session to find out more.

To: Brock Lohan <brock@oba.edu>
From: Tatiana Zhang <tazha@tmail.net>
Date: July 4
Subject: Question

Dear Mr. Lohan,

I recently signed up for the DEEPSKIN program; however I could not pay the fee. Could you please advise me on what I should do?

❼ I'm fairly sure that I will be registering for the twelve-month programs and so, in addition to the Aromatherapy Massage course, I want to practice on my own. For that reason, I want to know if I could buy all the materials made available to students in the twelve-month program in advance. Please inform me of what options are available to me. I hope to hear from you soon.

Sincerely,

Tatiana Zhang

□ highest-rated 非常に高い評価の　□ trial class 体験授業　□ explore 〜を探求する　□ field 分野
□ post 〜を掲載する　□ sign-up fee 登録料、申し込み料　□ materials fee 材料費　□ require 〜を要求する
□ Should you have any concerns ご懸念がある場合　□ detail 詳細　□ certification 認定

E メール
□ sign up for 〜に申し込む・登録する　□ register for 〜に登録する　□ in addition to 〜に加えて
□ on one's own 自分自身で　□ for that reason その理由により　□ in advance 事前に　□ option 選択肢

★★★★★

30. For whom is the information intended?

(A) Professional massage instructors
(B) Registration office employees
(C) Future massage technicians
(D) OBA staff

この案内は誰のためのものですか。

(A) プロのマッサージ指導者
(B) 登録事務所の従業員
(C) 将来のマッサージ技術者
(D) OBA スタッフ

この案内が誰に向けたものかが問われている。1 文書目の案内の❶で、「マッサージ業界で成功したキャリアを築きたい方には、ハドソンで最高ランクのマッサージスクールである OBA が役立つ」と述べているため、将来マッサージ技術者を目指している人向けのお知らせだとわかる。以上より正解は **(C)**

□ instructor 指導者

★★★★★

31. What is indicated about the DEEPSKIN program?

(A) It is being provided for the first time.
(B) It is prerequisite for the twelve-month program.
(C) It is broadcast online.
(D) It will be offered again in the future.

DEEPSKIN プログラムについて何が示されていますか。

(A) 初めて提供されるものである。
(B) 12 カ月間のプログラムの前提条件である。
(C) オンラインで配信されている。
(D) 将来的には再び提供される予定である。

DEEPSKIN プログラムについて何が示されているかが問われている。案内の❹で「来年から 4 月にも DEEPSKIN プログラムを開催する予定だ」と述べられているので、今後また開催することがわかる。以上より、正解は **(D)**。

□ provide 〜を提供する　□ prerequisite 前提条件の　□ broadcast 〜を放映する　□ in the future 将来

★★★☆☆

32. When will the programs that lead to professional licensing be discussed?

(A) On July 9
(B) On August 3
(C) On August 14
(D) On September 3

免許取得につながるプログラムはいつ説明がありますか。

(A) 7月9日
(B) 8月3日
(C) 8月14日
(D) 9月3日

🔍 免許取得につながるプログラムはいつ説明されるかが問われている。案内の❺で「OBA では、12 カ月間の認定プログラムの詳細について説明会を開催する」とある。この❺の "certification" が設問の professional licensing と言い換えられている。そして❻より、この説明会が「9月3日（火）に開催される」とある。以上より正解は **(D)**。

✏️ □ professional licensing プロの資格供与

★★★★☆ 同義語問題

33. In the e-mail, the word, "fairly" in paragraph 2, line 1, is closest in meaning to

(A) reasonably
(B) similarly
(C) brightly
(D) justifiably

Eメールの、第2段落・1行目にある "fairly" に最も意味が近いのは

(A) かなり
(B) 同様に
(C) 明るく
(D) 正当に

🔍 同義語問題。問われている表現は2文書目のEメールの❼の「（私は～のことを）かなり（確信している）」で、「かなり」という意味で使われている。これと同じ意味になるのは **(A)**。"reasonably" は「完ぺきではないが相当の」という意味で、fairly の他に quite と同じ意味として言い換えられる。

★★★☆☆ クロスリファレンス問題

34. What is indicated about Ms. Zhang?

(A) She will not be required to pay a registration fee.
(B) She wants to take classes in the morning.
(C) She had previously contacted the academy.
(D) She wants to change her class.

Zhang さんについて何が示されていますか。

(A) 彼女は登録料を支払う必要はない。
(B) 彼女は午前中に授業を受けたいと思っている。
(C) 彼女は以前にアカデミーに連絡したことがある。
(D) 彼女はクラスの変更を求めている。

🔍 Zhang さんについて何が示されているかを問う選択肢照合型の問題。Zhang さんが2文書目のEメールの❼で「私は12 カ月のプログラムにも登録することを決めているので、アロマテラピーマッサージコースに加えて…」と述べていることから、アロマテラピーマッサージコースを申し込んでいることがわかる。次に1文書目の案内の❷・❸を見ると、アロマテラピーマッサージコースは午前中に開催されることがわかる。以上から、正解は **(B)** となる。この問題は両方の文書を見て解く必要がある。(A) は支配う必要がないのではなく、支払いをすることができなかったため、(C) の以前連絡を取った、(D) のクラス変更の要求、はいずれも本文に記載がないため、それぞれ不正解。

DEEPSKIN
OLIVEIRA BODYWORKS ACADEMY
主催

マッサージ業界で成功したキャリアを築きたい方には、ハドソンで最高ランクのマッサージスクールである Oliveira Bodyworks Academy (OBA) がお役に立てるでしょう。DEEPSKIN は、毎年行われている体験クラスで、マッサージの分野を探求する機会を提供しています。

以下のコースから 1 つを選択してください。各コースは 6 回で構成されています。各クラスの内容については、ウェブサイト（www.hudsonoba.edu/deepskin）に掲載されています。

コース 1：アロマテラピーマッサージ	コース 2：タッチインマッサージ
コース日程：7 月 9 日（火）～ 19 日（金）	コース日程：8 月 5 日（月）～ 16 日（金）
授業日：火曜、木曜、金曜	授業日：月曜日、水曜日、金曜日
授業時間：午前 9:00– 正午	授業時間：午後 2 時～午後 5 時

DEEPSKIN プログラムへの参加には、登録料 50 ドルと教材費 30 ドルが必要です。ご不明な点がございましたら、詳細なクラス・コーディネーターの Brock Lohan（brock@oba.edu または (276) 888-2355）までお問い合わせください。

今年、7 月と 8 月のプログラムに参加できない方も、がっかりしないでください。来年からは 4 月にも DEEPSKIN プログラムを開催する予定です。

OBA では、12 カ月間の認定プログラムの詳細について説明会を開催します。9 月 3 日（火）に開催されます。詳しくは説明会にお越しください。

受信者：Brock Lohan <brock@oba.edu>
送信者：Tatiana Zhang <tazha@tmail.net>
日付：　7 月 4 日
件名：　質問

Lohan 様

私は最近、DEEPSKIN プログラムに申し込みましたが、その料金を支払うことができませんでした。どうしたらいいかアドバイスをいただけませんか？

私は 12 カ月のプログラムにも登録することを決めているので、アロマテラピーマッサージコースに加えて、自分でも練習したいと思っています。そのために、12 カ月プログラムの生徒に提供されるすべての教材を事前に購入できるかどうかを知りたいのです。どのような選択肢があるのか教えてください。ご連絡をお待ちしております。

よろしくお願いします。

Tatiana Zhang

Questions 35-39 refer to the following e-mail and document.

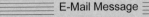 5分00秒

E-Mail Message

To:	Client Service <csmanager@acertownbank.com>
From:	Tina Gray <tngray@online.net>
Date:	September 13
Subject:	Account Questions

To Whom It May Concern

I am writing this e-mail because I don't know why an extra charge was put on my detailed statement. I think this is a mistake.

Unlike my detailed statement I received on August 30, I actually spent $40 on 12 August. You must investigate the cause of this error and credit $20 to my account. I would like you to send me a corrected one again.

I would like to resolve this problem immediately. If you need any other proof, I will send you the purchase receipt. The best way is to e-mail me at tngray@online.net, but if necessary, you may also leave me a message at 615-888-4121 and I will get back to you as quickly as possible.

Best regards,

Tina Gray

ACERTOWN Bank Credit Card Detailed Statement
30 August
Tina Gray
Account number: 875400
Card number: 4978-5321-7452-0808

Description	Date	Amount
Greengage Restaurant	08/11	$120.00
Porter Art	08/12	$60.00
Caspian Tour	08/15	$270.00
Misty Bakery	08/20	$40.00
Wendy's Set	08/25	$60.00
Monthly Service Charge		$25.00
Total		$575.00

Payment will be deducted from account number 875400 on 10 September.
The last payment was made on 10 August.

35. Why did Ms. Gray send her e-mail to the bank?

(A) She would like to pay the creditor $20.
(B) She wanted a total refund for a purchase.
(C) There was an inconsistency on her billing statement.
(D) She was undercharged on her billing statement.

36. What does Ms. Gray ask the bank to do for her?

(A) Pay the difference to her and send a new statement
(B) Charge $40 on her account
(C) Cancel her credit card
(D) Loan $20 to her and send a revised statement

37. According to the e-mail, what will Ms. Gray most likely send to the bank?

(A) Her credit card
(B) A statement for the bank to sign
(C) Money to credit to her account
(D) Her receipt

38. When is payment expected to be made to the bank?

(A) On 20 August
(B) On 25 August
(C) On 13 September
(D) On 10 September

39. What payment does Ms. Gray think there's an error with?

(A) Greengage Restaurant
(B) Porter Art
(C) Caspian Tour
(D) Misty Bakery

Double

P. 528

Questions 35-39 refer to the following e-mail and document.

E-Mail Message

To:	Client Service <csmanager@acertownbank.com>
From:	Tina Gray <tngray@online.net>
Date:	September 13
Subject:	Account Questions

To Whom It May Concern

❶ I am writing this e-mail because I don't know why an extra charge was put on my detailed statement. ❷ I think this is a mistake.

Unlike my detailed statement I received on August 30, ❸ I actually spent $40 on 12 August. ❹ You must investigate the cause of this error and credit $20 to my account. ❺ I would like you to send me a corrected one again.

I would like to resolve this problem immediately. ❻ If you need any other proof, I will send you the purchase receipt. The best way is to e-mail me at tngray@online.net, but if necessary, you may also leave me a message at 615-888-4121 and I will get back to you as quickly as possible.

Best regards,

Tina Gray

ACERTOWN Bank Credit Card Detailed Statement
30 August
Tina Gray
Account number: 875400
Card number: 4978-5321-7452-0808

Description	Date	Amount
Greengage Restaurant	08/11	$120.00
❼ Porter Art	08/12	$60.00
Caspian Tour	08/15	$270.00
Misty Bakery	08/20	$40.00
Wendy's Set	08/25	$60.00
Monthly Service Charge		$25.00
Total		$575.00

❽ Payment will be deducted from account number 875400 on 10 September.
The last payment was made on 10 August.

Eメール
☐ To Whom It May Concern ご担当者様宛　☐ detailed 詳細の　☐ statement 記載、明細書
☐ unlike ～のようではなく　☐ investigate ～を調査する　☐ cause 原因　☐ error 誤り
☐ credit $○○ to　○○ドルを～に入金する　☐ account 口座　☐ correct ～を訂正・修正する
☐ resolve ～を解決する　☐ immediately すぐに　☐ proof 証拠　☐ get back to ～に返答する
☐ as quickly as possible できるだけ急いで

書類
☐ deduct A from B AをBから控除する　☐ last payment 最終支払い

★★★★★

35. Why did Ms. Gray send her e-mail to the bank?

(A) She would like to pay the creditor $20.
(B) She wanted a total refund for a purchase.
(C) There was an inconsistency on her billing statement.
(D) She was undercharged on her billing statement.

Gray さんはなぜ銀行にEメールを送りましたか。

(A) 債権者に 20 ドルを支払いたかったため。
(B) 買い物について全額返金を求めたかったため。
(C) 請求明細書に矛盾があったため。
(D) 請求明細書に過少請求があったため。

Gray さんはなぜ銀行にEメールを送ったかが問われている。Gray さんは 1 文書目のEメールの❶・❷で「明細書へ過払い請求されている理由がわからず、間違いではないか」と主張している。よって、この間違いを "inconsistency（矛盾）" と言い換えた **(C)** が正解。(A) は、債権者に 20 ドル支払いたいのではなく、矛盾のある 20 ドルを返金してもらいたいため、不正解。今回の選択肢に使用されている語彙は若干難しめだが、TOEIC には頻出表現なので押さえておこう。

☐ creditor 債権者　☐ refund 払い戻し　☐ inconsistency 矛盾　☐ billing statement 請求明細書
☐ undercharge ～に過少請求する

★★★★☆

36. What does Ms. Gray ask the bank to do for her?

(A) Pay the difference to her and send a new statement
(B) Charge $40 on her account
(C) Cancel her credit card
(D) Loan $20 to her and send a revised statement

Gray さんは銀行に対し何をするように頼んでいますか。

(A) 差額を支払い、新しい明細を送る
(B) 口座に 40 ドルを入金する
(C) クレジットカードを解約する
(D) 20 ドルを貸し付け、訂正した明細を送る

Gray さんは銀行に対し何をするように頼んでいるかが問われている。Gray さんはEメールの❹で「今回の間違いの原因を調査し、私の口座に 20 ドルを入金してほしい」、❺で「訂正した明細書を再度送ってほしい」と述べている。よって、この 2 つを言い換えた **(A)** が正解。(D) は loan が「貸し付ける」という意味なので、文意に合わない。

☐ loan ～を貸し付ける　☐ revise ～を訂正・修正する

529

37. According to the e-mail, what will Ms. Gray most likely send to the bank?

- (A) Her credit card
- (B) A statement for the bank to sign
- (C) Money to credit to her account
- **(D)** Her receipt

Eメールによると、Gray さんは何を銀行に送ると考えられますか。

- (A) クレジットカード
- (B) 銀行に署名してもらうための明細
- (C) 口座に入金するお金
- **(D)** 領収書

> 🔍 Eメールから、Gray さんが銀行に送ると考えられるものが問われている。Gray さんはEメールの❺で「もし他に証拠が必要であれば、購入時のレシートを送る」と述べている。以上から、正解は **(D)**。

> ✎ □ sign ~に署名する

38. When is payment expected to be made to the bank?

- (A) On 20 August
- (B) On 25 August
- (C) On 13 September
- **(D)** On 10 September

銀行への支払いはいつ行われますか。

- (A) 8月20日
- (B) 8月25日
- (C) 9月13日
- **(D)** 9月10日

> 🔍 銀行への支払いはいつ行われるかが問われている。2文書目の書類の❽から、「9月10日に口座番号 875400 から引き落とす」と述べている。また、この書類の冒頭には、銀行のクレジットカードの明細書と書かれている。以上から、この9月10日が銀行への支払い期日だとわかる。よって正解は **(D)**。

 クロスリファレンス問題

39. What payment does Ms. Gray think there's an error with?

- (A) Greengage Restaurant
- **(B)** Porter Art
- (C) Caspian Tour
- (D) Misty Bakery

Gray さんが間違いがあると思っている支払いは何ですか。

- (A) Greengage Restaurant
- **(B)** Porter Art
- (C) Caspian Tour
- (D) Misty Bakery

> 🔍 Gray さんが間違いがあると思っている支払いは何かが問われている。まず Gray さんは、1文書目のEメールの❸で、「実際には8月12日に40ドルを使った」と述べ、❹で「この間違いの原因を調査し、私の口座に20ドルを入金するように」と続けている。次に2文書目の書類を読むと、❼に 8/12 付で費用が60ドルとなっている。つまり、この項目が実際には40ドルだったため、20ドルの差額を返金してほしいと主張していると考えられる。以上から、この品目に該当する **(B)** が正解となる。

受信者： 顧客サービス <csmanager@acertownbank.com>
送信者： Tina Gray <tngray@online.net>
日付： 9月13日
件名： 口座に関する質問

ご担当者様

なぜ明細書にもっと多くの料金が請求されているのかわかりませんでしたので連絡をしています。これは何かの間違いだと思います。

8月30日に受け取った明細書とは異なり、実際には8月12日に40ドルを使いました。この間違いの原因を調査し、私の口座に20ドルを入金してください。また、訂正したものを再度送ってください。

この問題をすぐに解決したいです。もし他に証拠が必要であれば、購入時のレシートをお送りします。一番良い方法は、tngray@online.net まで、私宛てにメールをいただくことですが、必要であれば、615-888-4121 にメッセージを残していただいても結構です。できるだけ早くお返事を差し上げます。

よろしくお願いいたします。

Tina Gray

ACERTOWN Bank クレジットカード明細書
8月30日
Tina Gray 様
口座番号：875400
カード番号：4978-5321-7452-0808

銘柄	日付	金額
Greengage Restaurant	08/11	120.00ドル
Porter Art	08/12	60.00ドル
Caspian Tour	08/15	270.00ドル
Misty Bakery	08/20	40.00ドル
Wendy's Set	08/25	60.00ドル
月額サービス料		25.00ドル
合計		575.00ドル

9月10日に口座番号 875400 から引き落とします。
前回の支払いは8月10日に行われました。

Questions 40-44 refer to the following report, e-mail, and article.

BRATTON PLAN

Bratton has been an essential part of used airplane sales since it was founded twenty years ago. Over the years, it has developed into a world-famous dealer.

We are sending a list of used private airplanes which meet your requirements. We will schedule you to see the planes in person, once you let us know which days and times you would be available.

1. Model: Casa-YU75
Sales Price: $25 million
Details: Contains an advanced air circulation system that improves airflow and leaves passengers feeling refreshed at the end of their journey.

2. Model: Zenice-CH600
Sales Price: $20 million
Details: Contains satellite phone, wireless network, and entertainment system. This plane has the logo of the previous owner's company on each wing. These will need to be removed.

3. Model: Gopro-BL888
Sales price: $16 million
Details: Features an advanced sound suppression system that reduces noise by 30 percent. Wide cabin with four separate seating areas and five bedrooms.

To: Carlos Suarez <sales@bratton.net>
From: Linda Tatum <president@sherwood.com>
Date: July 15
Subject: Private Airplane

Dear Mr. Suarez,

Thank you for taking the time to talk with me on the phone yesterday. As I mentioned, I have been searching for a new private airplane that I can use to attend various conferences and events internationally. I'll be happy to consider buying your merchandise, as far as my conditions are met and I receive full ownership. First of all, I would prefer something that is less than five years old and capable of long-flying trips. I'll be fine with any models if their prices are in the range of $15 million to $25 million. Of course, I would expect the interior of the airplane to have an attractive, contemporary design, and it should be able to comfortably accommodate at least 20 passengers.

I'd like to secure my new plane relatively quickly, but first I would like to find someone who will buy my current plane. If I can find a buyer in early August, I'd be willing to buy my new plane on August 20 in preparation for an awards show in Boston at the end of the month. I know that a used plane may require some modifications before I use it to visit a public event.

Regards,

Linda Tatum

Sherwood Entertainment President Purchases New Airplane
By Betty Rosenthal

New York (August 31)—Linda Tatum, president of the music and film production company Sherwood Entertainment, has bought a Zenice-CH600 private airplane, which she has named "Tatum One." She got on the plane for the first time yesterday when she flew into Boston for an awards ceremony.

The "Tatum One" boasts two Cheroki Hit III engines that make a total thrust power of 15,000 lbs. While these powerful engines produce more noise than those of some other planes, you can't hear it in the cabin at all due to the newly-equipped advanced sound-absorbing system. Even when the airplane is full of crew and passengers, it can travel impressive distances of up to 10,000 kilometers.

Ms. Tatum's new airplane may not seat as many people as her old one, but it comes with a wide array of modern amenities and technologies. But the cost of running the airplane will total approximately $1.5 million per year.

40. What is mentioned about Bratton?

(A) It will reduce its number of employees.
(B) It is an internationally well-known company.
(C) It has combined several of its departments.
(D) It will celebrate its 20th anniversary soon.

41. Who most likely is Mr. Suarez?

(A) A flying instructor
(B) An event planner
(C) An airline employee
(D) A sales representative

42. What is indicated about Ms. Tatum?

(A) She successfully sold her old airplane.
(B) She met with Mr. Suarez at her office.
(C) She would prefer to purchase a brand-new airplane.
(D) She spent more money than originally expected.

43. What can be inferred about "Tatum One"?

(A) Its previous logos were cleared away.
(B) It is a newly-built airplane.
(C) It was formerly owned by a famous actor.
(D) It was bought in Boston.

44. According to the article, how is the Zenice-CH600 different from Ms. Tatum's old one?

(A) It can fly for longer durations.
(B) It has a smaller capacity.
(C) It loads more powerful engines.
(D) It makes more sound in the cabin.

Triple

P. 534

Questions 40-44 refer to the following report, e-mail, and article.

BRATTON PLAN

Bratton has been an essential part of used airplane sales since it was founded twenty years ago. ❶ <u>Over the years, it has developed into a world-famous dealer.</u>

We are sending a list of used private airplanes which meet your requirements. We will schedule you to see the planes in person, once you let us know which days and times you would be available.

1. Model: Casa-YU75
Sales Price: $25 million
Details: Contains an advanced air circulation system that improves airflow and leaves passengers feeling refreshed at the end of their journey.

2. Model: ❷ Zenice-CH600
Sales Price: $20 million
Details: Contains satellite phone, wireless network, and entertainment system. ❸ <u>This plane has the logo of the previous owner's company on each wing. These will need to be removed.</u>

3. Model: Gopro-BL888
Sales price: $16 million
Details: Features an advanced sound suppression system that reduces noise by 30 percent. Wide cabin with four separate seating areas and five bedrooms.

To: Carlos Suarez <sales@bratton.net>
From: Linda Tatum <president@sherwood.com>
Date: July 15
Subject: Private Airplane

Dear Mr. Suarez,

Thank you for taking the time to talk with me on the phone yesterday. ❹ <u>As I mentioned, I have been searching for a new private airplane</u> that I can use to attend various conferences and events internationally. ❺ <u>I'll be happy to consider buying your merchandise, as far as my conditions are met and I receive full ownership.</u> First of all, I would prefer something that is less than five years old and capable of long-flying trips. I'll be fine with any models if their prices are in the range of $15 million to $25 million. Of course, I would expect the interior of the airplane to have an attractive, contemporary design, and it should be able to comfortably accommodate at least 20 passengers.

I'd like to secure my new plane relatively quickly, but first I would like to find someone who will buy my current plane. ❻ <u>If I can find a buyer in early August, I'd be willing to buy my new plane on August 20 in preparation for an awards show in Boston at the end of the month.</u> I know that a used plane may require some modifications before I use it to visit a public event.

Regards,

Linda Tatum

Sherwood Entertainment President Purchases New Airplane

By Betty Rosenthal

New York (August 31)— ❼ Linda Tatum, president of the music and film production company Sherwood Entertainment, has bought a Zenice-CH600 private airplane, which she has named "Tatum One." ❽ She got on the plane for the first time yesterday when she flew into Boston for an awards ceremony.

The "Tatum One" boasts two Cheroki Hit III engines that make a total thrust power of 15,000 lbs. While these powerful engines produce more noise than those of some other planes, you can't hear it in the cabin at all due to the newly-equipped advanced sound-absorbing system. Even when the airplane is full of crew and passengers, it can travel impressive distances of up to 10,000 kilometers.

❾ Ms. Tatum's new airplane may not seat as many people as her old one, but it comes with a wide array of modern amenities and technologies. But the cost of running the airplane will total approximately $1.5 million per year.

報告書
- [ ] essential 重要な [ ] used 中古の [ ] found ～を設立・創立する [ ] develop into ～へと成長する
- [ ] world-famous 世界的に有名な [ ] dealer 取引業者 [ ] private 自家用 [ ] meet requirement 要求を満たす
- [ ] in person 直接 [ ] detail 詳細 [ ] contain ～を含む・備える [ ] advanced 高度な
- [ ] air circulation 空気循環 [ ] airflow 空気の流れ [ ] refresh ～を元気づける・リフレッシュさせる
- [ ] satellite phone 衛星電話 [ ] wing 翼 [ ] feature ～という特徴がある [ ] suppression 抑制
- [ ] cabin 航空機内 [ ] separate 別になった

Eメール
- [ ] as I mentioned 私が言ったとおり [ ] search for ～を探す [ ] various さまざまな
- [ ] merchandise 商品 [ ] as far as SV S が V する限り [ ] ownership 所有権 [ ] less than ～以内
- [ ] capable of ～を可能とする [ ] be fine with ～があれば良い [ ] in the range of A to B A から B の範囲内で
- [ ] attractive 魅力的な [ ] contemporary 現代風の [ ] comfortably 快適に [ ] accommodate ～を収容する
- [ ] secure ～を確保する [ ] relatively 比較的 [ ] be willing to *do* 進んで～する
- [ ] in preparation for ～を準備する際に [ ] require ～を要求する [ ] modification 修正
- [ ] public event 公開イベント

記事
- [ ] awards ceremony 授賞式 [ ] boast ～を持つ・搭載する [ ] thrust power 推進力
- [ ] lbs. ポンド（重量単位 ※語源はラテン語の libra） [ ] newly-equipped 新しく備えつけられた
- [ ] impressive 驚くべき [ ] up to 上限～まで [ ] a wide array of 多様な [ ] amenity 設備 [ ] total 合計～となる
- [ ] approximately 約～

★★★☆☆

40. What is mentioned about Bratton?

(A) It will reduce its number of employees.
(B) It is an internationally well-known company.
(C) It has combined several of its departments.
(D) It will celebrate its 20th anniversary soon.

Bratton 社について何が言及されていますか。

(A) 従業員数を削減する。
(B) 国際的に有名な会社である。
(C) いくつかの部門を統合した。
(D) もうすぐ創立 20 周年を迎える。

🔍 Bratton 社について何が言及されているかを問う選択肢照合型の問題。1 文書目の報告書の❶に、「長い年月を経て世界でも有名な販売業者として成長」とある。これを "internationally well-known company" と表現した **(B)** が正解となる。(A) 従業員数の削減、(C) 部門統合、(D) 20 周年のお祝い、についてはそれぞれ言及がないので不正解。

✎ [ ] well-known よく知られた [ ] combine ～を統合する

41. Who most likely is Mr. Suarez?

(A) A flying instructor
(B) An event planner
(C) An airline employee
(D) A sales representative

Suarez さんは誰だと考えられますか。

(A) 飛行機操縦の指導員
(B) イベントの企画者
(C) 航空会社の従業員
(D) 営業担当者

🔍 Suarez さんがおそらくどんな人物であると考えられるかが問われている。Suarez さんは2文書目のEメールの受信者で、❹で「新しい飛行機を探している」、❺で「喜んで貴社の商品を検討する」という内容のメールを受け取っている。ここから、Suarez さんは、飛行機の販売担当（＝営業担当）だと考えられる。よって、正解は **(D)**。

✎ □ flying instructor 飛行操縦指導員

....

★★★★★ クロスリファレンス問題

42. What is indicated about Ms. Tatum?

(A) She successfully sold her old airplane.
(B) She met with Mr. Suarez at her office.
(C) She would prefer to purchase a brand-new airplane.
(D) She spent more money than originally expected.

Tatum さんについて何が示されていますか。

(A) 古い飛行機を売ることに成功した。
(B) Suarez さんと事務所で顔を合わせた。
(C) できれば新品の飛行機を購入したいと思っている。
(D) 当初予想していたよりも多くのお金を使った。

🔍 Tatum さんについて何が示されているかを問う選択肢照合型問題。Tatum さんは2文書目のEメールの送信者で、新しい飛行機の購入について触れた後、❻で「8月初旬に（所有している飛行機の）買い手が見つかれば、月末のイベントに備えて新しい飛行機を購入したい」と述べている。次に、3文書目の記事の❽に、「（Tatum さんが）新しい飛行機に乗ってイベント先のボストンへ向かった」とある。つまり、Tatum さんは無事に中古飛行機を売って、新しい飛行機を購入したことがわかる。以上から、正解は **(A)**。複数の文書を読んで、「買い手が見つかる」＝売れる、ということを読み換える少し難しい問題。

✎ □ brand-new 新しい　□ originally expected 当初予想していた

....

★★★★★ クロスリファレンス問題

43. What can be inferred about "Tatum One"?

(A) Its previous logos were cleared away.
(B) It is a newly-built airplane.
(C) It was formerly owned by a famous actor.
(D) It was bought in Boston.

"Tatum One" について何が推測できますか。

(A) 以前のロゴは取り除かれた。
(B) 新しく作られた飛行機である。
(C) 以前は有名な俳優によって所有されていた。
(D) ボストンで購入された。

🔍 "Tatum One" について何が推測されるかを問う選択肢照合型の問題。Tatum One は、3文書目の記事の❼で、Zenice-CH600 という型式の飛行機であることがわかる。1文書目の報告書の❷・❸で、この飛行機の紹介がなされており、「両翼に過去のオーナー会社のロゴがあり、これらを消す必要がある」と述べられている。つまり、Tatum One は、購入後に古いロゴを消したと推測される。よって、これを previous logos were cleared away と表した **(A)** が正解。

✎ □ clear away ～を除去する　□ newly-built 新しく建築された　□ formerly 過去に

★★★☆☆

44. According to the article, how is the Zenice-CH600 different from Ms. Tatum's old one?

(A) It can fly for longer durations.
(B) It has a smaller capacity.
(C) It loads more powerful engines.
(D) It makes more sound in the cabin.

記事によると、Zenice-CH600 は Tatum さんの前の飛行機と何が違いますか。

(A) より長時間の飛行が可能である。
(B) 定員が少ない。
(C) より強力なエンジンを搭載している。
(D) 客室の中の音が大きい。

記事から、Zenice-CH600 は Tatum さんの前の飛行機と何が違うかが問われている。3文書目の記事の❾で、「新しい飛行機は古いものより多く人を座らせられない」とあることから、収容人数能力が少なくなったことがわかる。これを a smaller capacity と表現した **(B)** が正解となる。

□ duration 持続時間　□ capacity 収容能力

問題 40 から 44 は次の報告書、Eメール、記事に関するものです。

BRATTON PLAN

Bratton は 20 年前に設立されて以来、中古飛行機販売業の重要な一端を担ってきました。長い年月を経て世界でも有名な販売業者として成長しました。

当社はお客様のご要望に応じた中古自家用飛行機のリストをお送りします。ご都合の良い日時をお知らせいただければ、実際に飛行機をご覧になれるように手配いたします。

1. 型式：Casa-YU75
販売価格：2500 万ドル
詳細：空気の流れを良くする高度な空気循環システムを備え、旅の終わりに乗客は快適な気分になる。

2. 型式：Zenice-CH600
販売価格：2000 万ドル
詳細：衛星電話、無線インターネット、エンターテインメントシステムを備える。この飛行機は両翼に前所有者の会社ロゴが付いているので、除去する必要がある。

3. 型式：Gopro-BL888
販売価格：1600 万ドル
詳細：高度な消音システムを搭載し騒音を 30 パーセント削減する。広い機内には 4 つに分けられた座席エリアと 5 つの寝室を備える。

受信者： Carlos Suarez <sales@bratton.net>
送信者： Linda Tatum <president@sherwood.com>
日付： 7月15日
件名： 自家用飛行機

Suarez 様

昨日はお電話でお話しさせていただきありがとうございました。お伝えしたとおり、私はさまざまな国際的な会議やイベントに出席する際に使用できる新しい自家用飛行機を探していました。私の条件が満たされ、完全な所有権を得られるのであれば、貴社の商品の購入を喜んで検討します。まず、機齢が5年以下で長距離の飛行が可能なものが望ましいです。価格が1500万ドルから2500万ドルの範囲であれば、型式に関わらず検討いたします。もちろん飛行機の内装は、魅力的で現代的なデザインが望ましく、また、最低でも20人の乗客が余裕をもって搭乗できる必要があります。

新しい飛行機を早めに手に入れたいですが、まずは現在所有している飛行機を購入してくれる方を探したいと思います。8月初旬に買い手が見つかれば、月末にボストンで行われる授賞式に備えて8月20日に新しい飛行機を購入したいと思っています。中古飛行機の場合、公共のイベントに行く前に、多少の改修が必要になることは承知しています。

よろしくお願いいたします。

Linda Tatum

Sherwood Entertainment の社長が新しい飛行機を購入
Betty Rosenthal

ニューヨーク（8月31日）— 音楽と映画の制作会社 Sherwood Entertainment の社長 Linda Tatum が Zenice-CH600 自家用飛行機を購入し、"Tatum One" と名付けた。昨日、授賞式のためにボストンに向かった際、初めてこの飛行機に搭乗した。

"Tatum One" には2つの Cheroki Hit III エンジンが搭載され、合計15000 ポンドの推力を生み出す。その強力なエンジンは他の飛行機に比べ多くの騒音を生み出すが、新しく装備された高度な吸音システムにより、客室では全く聞こえない。飛行機に乗務員と乗客が最大限搭乗している場合でも、最大1万キロメートルという驚くべき距離を飛行できる。

Tatum さんの新しい飛行機は以前の飛行機ほど多くの人が乗れないかもしれないが、さまざまな近代的な設備と技術が備わっている。しかし、この飛行機に掛かる費用は年間で合計約150万ドルになる。

GO ON
TO THE
NEXT PAGE!

August 16—The Braithwaite Mall in uptown Scottsdale will feature a gallery of photos by photographer Tom Zander in its lobby from the beginning of September to the end of November. Mall owner Lane Shelly has helped artists in the area for many years and the lobby has often been a great place to display various artworks.

"The lobby in the mall is a perfect place for people to gather, so I thought it would be a great place to display the works of talented artists from Scottsdale," said Mr. Shelly. He said everyone is welcome to come and appreciate the artworks. "We've also added some new restaurants to our dining area, where I think everyone should try to have a diverse cultural experience."

E-Mail Message

To:	Emory Robinson <emoryrbs@hmail.net>
From:	Lane Shelly <lshelly@braithwaitemall.org>
Date:	November 20
Subject:	Re>Your exhibition

Dear Mr. Robinson,

I'm so happy to be displaying your paintings in the Braithwaite Mall's lobby from December. I thought your works at the community center exhibit were fantastic and I think that even more people will be able to appreciate your works at our mall. Also, we will set up a souvenir shop in our mall where people could buy your merchandise like picture postcards.

I would like to know the dimensions of each piece in order to plan on arranging them in the lobby. If you let me know before the end of November, it would be a great help to us.

Sincerely,

Lane Shelly
Owner, Braithwaite Mall

Try it! Dishes at Great Wall
By Linda Arroyo

Great Wall, one of the new restaurants at Braithwaite Mall, is an interesting place that gives to you a different taste and cultural experience, very rare things in this area. I am not as experienced with Chinese cuisine that I can choose for myself, but the staff at Great Wall helped me decide what kind of food I should try.

I highly suggest Pork Chop Suey and Jalapeno Beef and Harritos as a drink. The restaurant is delightfully decorated and from its front window you can also see some of the paintings on display from famous local artists. Even if you've never had Chinese food before, don't be afraid. Try Chinese at Great Wall!

45. What is the report mainly about?

(A) A refurbished floor
(B) The works of a photographer
(C) A new artist
(D) The mall's description

46. What is true about Mr. Shelly?

(A) He has renovated the Braithwaite Mall.
(B) He supports the promotion of local artists.
(C) He is a photographer.
(D) He has experienced diverse cultures.

47. What would NOT be available to visitors who go to the Braithwaite Mall?

(A) An art exhibition
(B) A various of cuisine
(C) A community room
(D) A gift shop

48. What can be inferred about Mr. Robinson?

(A) He is a resident of Scottsdale.
(B) He has displayed his works from end of November.
(C) He is a friend of Ms. Arroyo's.
(D) He is a portrait painter.

49. What is suggested about Great Wall?

(A) It is a long-established restaurant.
(B) It has a view of the lobby from its window.
(C) It decorates a meal beautifully.
(D) It offers discounts to new customers.

Triple

 P. 542

Questions 45-49 refer to the following report, e-mail, and article.

August 16—The Braithwaite Mall in uptown Scottsdale will feature a gallery of photos by photographer Tom Zander in its lobby from the beginning of September to the end of November. ❶ Mall owner Lane Shelly has helped artists in the area for many years and ❷ the lobby has often been a great place to display various artworks.

"The lobby in the mall is a perfect place for people to gather, so ❸ I thought it would be a great place to display the works of talented artists from Scottsdale," said Mr. Shelly. He said everyone is welcome to come and appreciate the artworks. ❹ "We've also added some new restaurants to our dining area, where I think everyone should try to have a diverse cultural experience."

E-Mail Message

To:	Emory Robinson <emoryrbs@hmail.net>
From:	Lane Shelly <lshelly@braithwaitemall.org>
Date:	November 20
Subject:	Re>Your exhibition

❺ Dear Mr. Robinson,

❻ I'm so happy to be displaying your paintings in the Braithwaite Mall's lobby from December. I thought your works at the community center exhibit were fantastic and I think that even more people will be able to appreciate your works at our mall. Also, ❼ we will set up a souvenir shop in our mall where people could buy your merchandise like picture postcards.

I would like to know the dimensions of each piece in order to plan on arranging them in the lobby. If you let me know before the end of November, it would be a great help to us.

Sincerely,

Lane Shelly
Owner, Braithwaite Mall

Try it! Dishes at Great Wall
By Linda Arroyo

Great Wall, one of the new restaurants at Braithwaite Mall, is an interesting place that gives to you a different taste and cultural experience, very rare things in this area. I am not as experienced with Chinese cuisine that I can choose for myself, but the staff at Great Wall helped me decide what kind of food I should try.

I highly suggest Pork Chop Suey and Jalapeno Beef and Harritos as a drink. ❽ The restaurant is delightfully decorated and from its front window you can also see some of the paintings on display from famous local artists. Even if you've never had Chinese food before, don't be afraid. Try Chinese at Great Wall!

★★★☆☆

45. What is the report mainly about?

(A) A refurbished floor
(B) The works of a photographer
(C) A new artist
(D) The mall's description

報告書の主な内容は何ですか。

(A) 張り替えられた床
(B) 写真家の作品
(C) 新しい芸術家
(D) モールの紹介

報告書の主な内容について問われている。1文書目の報告書の冒頭で、「Braithwaite Mall のロビーでの写真展」について触れた後、❷「ロビーにさまざまな芸術作品を展示」、❸「スコッツデールの才能のある芸術家の作品の展示にぴったり」、❹「新しいレストランが加わった。多様な文化体験をしていただきたい」と、このモール内の説明をしていることがわかる。以上より、正解は **(D)**。

☐ refurbish 〜を改装する　☐ description 説明、描写

★★★☆☆

46. What is true about Mr. Shelly?

(A) He has renovated the Braithwaite Mall.
(B) He supports the promotion of local artists.
(C) He is a photographer.
(D) He has experienced diverse cultures.

Shelly 氏について正しいことは何ですか。

(A) Braithwaite Mall を改装した。
(B) 地元の芸術家の宣伝活動を手伝っている。
(C) 写真家である。
(D) 多様な文化を経験している。

モールオーナーの Shelly 氏について正しいことを問う選択肢照合型の問題。1文書目の報告書❶で「Shelly 氏が何年もその地域のアーティストを支援してきた」とある。このアーティストの支援のことを support the promotion of local artists と言い換えた **(B)** が正解。文書中で「宣伝活動」とまでは述べられていないが、「支援している」ということから、その範ちゅうまで行っていることが示唆されている。(A) の改装は、「新しいレストランもいくつか追加」とあるが、モール自体の改装は行っていないため、不正解。

☐ renovate 〜を修復・改装する　☐ promotion 宣伝活動

47. What would NOT be available to visitors who go to the Braithwaite Mall?

(A) An art exhibition
(B) A various of cuisine
(C) A community room
(D) A gift shop

Braithwaite Mall へ来た人が利用できないものは何ですか。

(A) 芸術の展覧会
(B) さまざまな料理
(C) 会議室
(D) 土産店

NOT 問題。Braithwaite Mall へ来た人が利用できないものが問われている。1 文書目の報告書から、❷のロビー展示が (A)、❹のレストラン追加による多様な文化体験が (B) に、2 文書目の E メールの❼での土産物設置が (D) に、それぞれ該当する。残った **(C)** が本文では述べられていないため、これが正解となる。複数文書の NOT 問題では、正解の根拠が文書をまたがっていることもあるので注意しよう。

□ community room 会議室

- -

48. What can be inferred about Mr. Robinson?

(A) He is a resident of Scottsdale.
(B) He has displayed his works from end of November.
(C) He is a friend of Ms. Arroyo's.
(D) He is a portrait painter.

Robinson さんについて何が推測できますか。

(A) スコッツデールの住民である。
(B) 11 月末から作品を展示した。
(C) Arroyo さんの友人である。
(D) 肖像画家である。

Robinson さんについて推測できることを問う選択肢照合型の問題。2 文書目の E メールの❺・❻で、モールオーナーの Shelly 氏が Robinson さんに対し、「ロビーに Robinson さんの絵画を展示すること」について述べている。これは、1 文書目の報告書の❸にあった、「スコッツデールの芸術家の作品を展示する」ということでもある。以上から、Robinson さんはスコッツデールに住んでいると考えられるため、正解は **(A)** となる。

□ portrait 肖像画

- -

49. What is suggested about Great Wall?

(A) It is a long-established restaurant.
(B) It has a view of the lobby from its window.
(C) It decorates a meal beautifully.
(D) It offers discounts to new customers.

Great Wall について何が示唆されていますか。

(A) 老舗のレストランである。
(B) 窓からロビーが見える。
(C) 料理を美しく盛り付ける。
(D) 新規顧客に割引を提供している。

Great Wall について示唆されていることを問う選択肢照合型の問題。3 文書目の記事に、新レストランである Great Wall についての記載があり、❽に「窓から地元の芸術家の展示絵画が見える」とある。モール内で絵画を展示している場所は、1 文書目の❸からロビーであることがわかるため、窓からはモールのロビーが見えると考えられる。以上から、正解は **(B)**。絵画の展示場所はどこなのかということと関連付ける必要があり、少し難しい問題だ。(A) は、このレストランは新規のため、(C) は、料理ではなくレストラン内を飾りつけているので、それぞれ不正解となる。

□ long-established 長期間経営している

8月16日―スコッツデールの住宅地区にある Braithwaite Mall では、9月の初めから11月の終わりまで、ロビーで写真家 Tom Zander さんの写真展を開催する。モールのオーナー、Lane Shelly 氏はこの地域の芸術家を長年支援してきており、ロビーはさまざまな芸術作品を展示するのに最適な場所となっている。

「モールのロビーは、人々が集まるのに最適な場所ですので、スコッツデールの才能のある芸術家の作品の展示にぴったりだと思いました。」と Shelly 氏は語った。いろいろな方に作品を鑑賞しに来てほしいとのことだ。「食事エリアには新しいレストランもいくつか加わりました。多様な文化体験を皆さまにしていただきたいと思っています。」

受信者： Emory Robinson <emoryrbs@hmail.net>
送信者： Lane Shelly <lshelly@braithwaitemall.org>
日付： 11月20日
件名： Re> 展示

Robinson 様

12月から Braithwaite Mall のロビーに Robinson さんの絵を展示できることをとてもうれしく思います。コミュニティーセンターで展示されていた Robinson さんの作品は素晴らしく、当モールではさらに多くの人たちに作品を鑑賞していただけると思います。また、当モールでは、絵葉書のような、あなたのグッズを購入できる土産店を設置します。

ロビーでの配置の仕方を考えますので、各作品の寸法を教えていただけますか。11月末までにお知らせいただければ、大変助かります。

よろしくお願いいたします。

Lane Shelly
Braithwaite Mall オーナー

Great Wall の料理は食べてみる価値あり！
Linda Arroyo 記者

Great Wall は Braithwaite Mall に新しくできたレストランの一つで、この地域では非常に珍しい、独特の味や文化体験を味わえる興味深い場所である。私は自分で選べるほど中華料理に詳しくないが、Great Wall の店員はどのような料理を選べばいいのか教えてくれた。

お勧めは Pork Chop Suey と Jalapeno Beef、飲み物は Harritos である。レストランは美しく装飾され、正面の窓からは地元の有名な芸術家による絵画の展示も見える。中華料理を食べたことがない人も、恐れることはない。Great Wall の中華料理をお試しあれ！

Freemont Movie Center
130 Oceanside Way, San Aldo
Phone: (650) 789-1154

CHECK OUT OUR ANNUAL SUMMER MOVIE SERIES.

We are going to present four movies by famous directors who will be invited as special guests. After the films, there will be time for the directors to address the audience and answer questions from the audience. Schedule is as follows.

Friday, July 23: The Movies of Ted Herrera
Friday, July 30: The Movies of Dina Trozelli
Friday, August 6: The Movies of Bao Wong
Friday, August 13: The Movies of Calista Potter

Tickets can only be bought on the day of the showing and will be sold on a first-come, first-served basis. Please remember that the box office will open at 9:00 A.M. in order to accommodate the expected high demand for tickets.

Visit www.freemontmc.org/summerseries for details of movies to show.

MEMO

To: All Film Guide Employees

From: Jack Monroe
Subject: Schedule
Date: 29 July

Dear All Film Guide Employees,

As you all have been informed, I will go out to the Freemont Movie Center tomorrow to have an interview with the special guest for *Film Guide*. I'd like some of you to come along and to help issue brief questionnaires to people exiting the movie center. I will reserve transportation through Compton Auto World in order for us to get there together nice and early and enjoy the movies. Please notify me by 5 P.M. today if you're interested in helping out.

Regards,

Jack Monroe
Senior Editor

ABOUT US	BRANCH LOCATIONS	SEARCH VEHICLES	**REVIEW**

Posted by Jack Monroe
On September 2

I had a pleasant experience with Compton Auto World and I am satisfied with your good service.

Firstly, the van was up-to-date, and spotless inside and out. Secondly, I thought it was very economical compared to the quotes I received from other businesses. Thirdly, the vehicle I rented had an incredible stereo sound. At the end of July this year, I took 7 people to an event in San Aldo, and they were all very impressed with the sound from the speakers.

I certainly wouldn't think twice about renting another Compton Auto World in the future.

50. According to the information, what will happen on Fridays?

(A) An awards ceremony will be hosted.
(B) Actors will deliver speeches to audience.
(C) Tickets will go on sale in the morning.
(D) Movie auditions will take place.

51. What does Mr. Monroe ask the employees of Film Guide to do?

(A) Survey event participants
(B) Review a movie
(C) Meet film directors
(D) Work in a box office

52. Who did Mr. Monroe interview at Freemont Movie Center?

(A) Ted Herrera
(B) Dina Trozelli
(C) Bao Wong
(D) Calista Potter

53. How many Film Guide employees responded to Mr. Monroe's request?

(A) 4
(B) 7
(C) 13
(D) 23

54. What is NOT mentioned in the online review?

(A) The competitiveness of the price
(B) The cleanliness of the vehicle
(C) The quality of the audio system
(D) The capacity of the vehicle

Triple

P. 548

Questions 50-54 refer to the following information, memo, and online review.

❶ Freemont Movie Center
130 Oceanside Way, San Aldo
Phone: (650) 789-1154

CHECK OUT OUR ANNUAL SUMMER MOVIE SERIES.

We are going to present four movies by famous directors who will be invited as special guests. After the films, there will be time for the directors to address the audience and answer questions from the audience. Schedule is as follows.

Friday, July 23: The Movies of Ted Herrera
❷ Friday, July 30: The Movies of Dina Trozelli
Friday, August 6: The Movies of Bao Wong
Friday, August 13: The Movies of Calista Potter

❸ Tickets can only be bought on the day of the showing and will be sold on a first-come, first-served basis. ❹ Please remember that the box office will open at 9:00 A.M. in order to accommodate the expected high demand for tickets.

Visit www.freemontmc.org/summerseries for details of movies to show.

MEMO

To: All Film Guide Employees

From: Jack Monroe
Subject: Schedule
❺ Date: 29 July

Dear All Film Guide Employees,

❻ As you all have been informed, I will go out to the Freemont Movie Center tomorrow to have an interview with the special guest for *Film Guide*. ❼ I'd like some of you to come along and to help issue brief questionnaires to people exiting the movie center. ❽ I will reserve transportation through Compton Auto World in order for us to get there together nice and early and enjoy the movies. ❾ Please notify me by 5 P.M. today if you're interested in helping out.

Regards,

Jack Monroe
Senior Editor

| ABOUT US | BRANCH LOCATIONS | SEARCH VEHICLES | **REVIEW** |

Posted by Jack Monroe
On September 2

I had a pleasant experience with Compton Auto World and I am satisfied with your good service.

Firstly, the van was up-to-date, and ❿ spotless inside and out. Secondly, I thought ⓫ it was very economical compared to the quotes I received from other businesses. Thirdly, ⓬ the vehicle I rented had an incredible stereo sound. ⓭ At the end of July this year, I took 7 people to an event in San Aldo, and they were all very impressed with the sound from the speakers.

I certainly wouldn't think twice about renting another Compton Auto World in the future.

案内
☐ there will be time for A to *do* A が〜する時間がある　☐ address 〜に向けて話す
☐ as follows 以下のとおり　☐ on a first-come, first-served basis 早い者勝ち　☐ in order to *do* 〜するために
☐ accommodate 〜を収容する　☐ expected 予想される　☐ high demand 高い需要　☐ detail 詳細

メモ
☐ be informed 知る　☐ come along 帯同する　☐ issue 〜を発行する　☐ brief 簡単な、簡潔な
☐ questionnaire アンケート　☐ in order for A to *do* A が〜するために　☐ notify 〜に知らせる　☐ help out 手伝う

オンラインレビュー
☐ pleasant 楽しい　☐ up-to-date 最新の　☐ spotless 汚れがない　☐ economical 経済的な
☐ compared to 〜と比較して　☐ quote 見積もり　☐ incredible 素晴らしい
☐ wouldn't think twice about *do*ing 2 度と〜しようと思わない　☐ in the future 今後

★★★★☆

50. According to the information, what will happen on Fridays?

(A) An awards ceremony will be hosted.
(B) Actors will deliver speeches to audience.
(C) Tickets will go on sale in the morning.
(D) Movie auditions will take place.

案内によると、金曜日に何が起こりますか。

(A) 授賞式が開催される。
(B) 俳優が観客に向けてスピーチをする。
(C) チケットが午前中に発売される。
(D) 映画のオーディションが行われる。

🔍 1 文書目の案内から、金曜日に何が起こるかが問われている。案内を見ると、すべての映画の上映日が金曜日であり、❸で「チケットは当日販売のみ」、❹で「多数のお客様のチケット購入が予測されることから、チケット売り場は午前 9 時に開く」と述べられている。以上から、「金曜日は午前中に映画のチケットが販売される」ことがわかる。よって、正解は **(C)**。

☐ host 〜を主催する　☐ deliver a speech スピーチをする　☐ take place 開催される

★★★☆☆

51. What does Mr. Monroe ask the employees of Film Guide to do?

(A) Survey event participants
(B) Review a movie
(C) Meet film directors
(D) Work in a box office

Monroe さんは Film Guide 社の従業員に対して何をするように頼んでいますか。

(A) イベント参加者を対象に調査を行う
(B) 映画を評価する
(C) 映画監督に会う
(D) チケット売り場で働く

Monroe さんが Film Guide 社の従業員に頼んでいることが問われている。2 文書目のメモの❼で、Monroe さんは、従業員宛てに「映画センターから出てきた人たちに簡単なアンケートを取ることを手伝ってほしい」と頼んでいる。ここから、「アンケート」→ survey、「映画センターから出てきた人」→ event participants、と言い換えた **(A)** が正解。(C) は、Monroe さんが特別ゲストつまり、映画監督にインタビューするとは言っているが、手伝うように言及しているのは「アンケートを取ること」のため不正解。

□ survey ～を調査・評価する

★★★★☆ クロスリファレンス問題

52. Who did Mr. Monroe interview at Freemont Movie Center?

(A) Ted Herrera
(B) Dina Trozelli
(C) Bao Wong
(D) Calista Potter

Monroe さんは Freemont Movie Center で誰にインタビューをしましたか。

(A) Ted Herrera
(B) Dina Trozelli
(C) Bao Wong
(D) Calista Potter

Monroe さんは Freemont Movie Center で誰にインタビューをしたかが問われている。まず、2 文書目のメモの❻で、Monroe さんは、「明日 Freemont Movie Center に行って特別ゲストにインタビューする」と述べている。❺から、このメモは 7 月 29 日に書かれたものであるため、インタビューは翌日の 7 月 30 日に行われることがわかる。次に、1 文書目の案内にある映画上映のリストを見ると、❶・❷から Freemont Movie Center で 7 月 30 日に行われる映画の監督が、Dina Trozelli さんであることがわかる。以上から、正解は **(B)**。書かれている情報と時系列をよく整理して解くようにしよう。

★★★★☆ クロスリファレンス問題

53. How many Film Guide employees responded to Mr. Monroe's request?

(A) 4
(B) 7
(C) 13
(D) 23

何人の Film Guide 社の従業員が Monroe さんの要望に応じましたか。

(A) 4
(B) 7
(C) 13
(D) 23

何人の Film Guide 社の従業員が Monroe さんの要望に応じたかが問われている。Monroe さんは、2 文書目のメモの❼でアンケートを取ることを手伝ってくれる従業員を募集し、❽・❾で「移動に使う車を予約するので、希望者は今日の 5 時までに知らせてほしい」と述べている。次に 3 文書目のオンラインレビューを見ると、冒頭の名前から Monroe さんが書いたレンタカーのレビューだとわかる。このレビューの⓬で「7 月末に San Aldo でのイベントに向かうため、7 名乗せた」と述べてられている。以上から、正解は **(B)**。ちなみに、⓭にある San Aldo という都市名は 1 文書目の案内の冒頭にも出てきており、解答のヒントになっている。3 つすべての文書を参照しておくと、より確信を持って正解を選べる。

54. What is NOT mentioned in the online review?

 (A) The competitiveness of the price
 (B) The cleanliness of the vehicle
 (C) The quality of the audio system
 (D) The capacity of the vehicle

オンラインレビューで言及されていないことは何ですか。

 (A) 競争力のある価格
 (B) 車両の清潔さ
 (C) 音楽再生機器の質
 (D) 車両の積載容量

NOT 問題。オンラインレビューで言及されていないことについて問われている。3 文書目のオンラインレビューを見ると、❿の「汚れがない」という記載が (B) に、⓫の「価格に関する記載」が (A) に、⓬の「音響に関する記載」が (C) に、それぞれ合致する。よって、残った記載のない **(D)** が正解。⓭に「7 名連れていった」とあるが、これは収容定員ではなく、実際に車に乗せた人数なので注意しよう。

□ competitiveness 競争優位性　□ cleanliness 清潔さ　□ capacity 収容・積載能力

問題 50 から 54 は次の案内、メモ、オンラインレビューに関するものです。

Freemont Movie Center
130 Oceanside Way, San Aldo 市
電話番号：(650) 789-1154

毎年恒例の夏の映画特集を開催します。

特別ゲストとして招待される有名な監督たちによる映画を 4 本上映します。映画の後には、監督が観客に挨拶し、観客からの質問に答える時間が設けられます。予定は以下のとおりです。

7 月 23 日（金）：Ted Herrera 監督の映画
7 月 30 日（金）：Dina Trozelli 監督の映画
8 月 6 日（金）：Bao Wong 監督の映画
8 月 13 日（金）：Calista Potter 監督の映画

チケットは各日とも上映当日のみ、先着順でご購入いただけます。多くのお客様がチケットを購入されることが予測されるため、チケット売り場は午前 9 時に開きますのでご注意ください。

上映する映画の詳細は www.freemontmc.org/summerseries をご覧ください。

メモ

宛先： Film Guide の全従業員
差出人：Jack Monroe
件名： 予定
日付： 7月29日

Film Guide 従業員の皆さま

お知らせしたとおり、私は明日、Film Guide の特別ゲストにインタビューを行うため、Freemont Movie Center に行きます。何人かの方に一緒に来ていただき、映画センターから出てきた人たちに簡単なアンケートを取ることを手伝っていただきたいと思います。Compton Auto World で移動に使う車を予約し、みんなで余裕をもって早めに到着し、映画を楽しみたいと思います。ご協力いただける方は、今日の午後5時までにお知らせください。

よろしくお願いいたします。

Jack Monroe
編集主任

---

http://www.comptonautoworld.net

当社について	支店の所在地	車両検索	評価

Jack Monroe 様の投稿
9月2日

Compton Auto World では不愉快なこともなく、良いサービスにとても満足しています。

まず、バンは最新のもので、内側にも外側にも汚れは一切ありませんでした。次に、他社の見積もりと比べて非常に経済的だと感じました。3つ目に、借りた車の音響システムは素晴らしいものでした。今年の7月の終わりに、San Aldo でのイベントに7人連れていきましたが、全員がスピーカーの音に非常に感動していました。

今後も迷わずに Compton Auto World で車を借りようと思います。

Test

8

Test 8

Questions 1-2 refer to the following Web page.

 1分30秒

◀ ▶ | www.vertecbakery.com | ▶

VERTEC BAKERY

The best supplier of all kinds of high quality bread for 50 years

To register for a Vertec Bakery online members account, click **here**.

There are many advantages of registering, such as:
▸ Updates on sales sent through e-mail
▸ Discount codes sent only to registered customers
▸ Faster order processing on our Web site

Entering your registration information is not difficult and takes only a few minutes. Just enter your contact information such as e-mail address and mobile phone number. Please keep in mind that we protect your information securely by using a state-of-art system.

1. What is NOT mentioned as a benefit of membership?

(A) Discounted delivery charges
(B) Notices about sales
(C) Special codes for discounted prices
(D) A quick ordering process

2. What is indicated about Vertec Bakery?

(A) It opened recently.
(B) It sends items around the world.
(C) It uses the latest confidential technology.
(D) It is family-owned company.

_P. 556_

Seoul Commercial Magazine—March 5
Business Journal Honors JK Financial

JK Financial was featured in Asian Commercial current news as one of the top five most influential companies in the financial consulting field in Asia. Founder and CEO Jina Kim served as president at North Pacific Bank in Beijing before starting her own agency eighteen years ago. Having been very successful at North Pacific Bank, she was eager to start a business venture in her hometown of Singapore. Today, the business has grown into an international corporation with branch offices in Seoul, Beijing, and Tokyo. Jina Kim reports that the company will open a fourth branch next February. As *Seoul Commercial Magazine* reported last month, the branch will be located in Bangkok, Thailand. Asian Commercial noted that JK Financial's emphasis on staff training has resulted in the rapid increase of customer support. No agency of a similar size to JK Financial has enjoyed so much support.

3. Why is the article written?

(A) To investigate why an investment banker has left her job
(B) To explain how a small corporation has expanded internationally
(C) To announce that a business has been discontinued
(D) To name the largest financial consulting firms in Asia

4. What can be inferred about JK Financial?

(A) Its headquarters is near that of North Pacific Bank.
(B) It received an award from *Seoul Commercial Magazine*.
(C) Its staff-training program has contributed to its success.
(D) Its founder started her career at North Pacific Bank.

P. 558

Questions 1-2 refer to the following Web page.

◀ ▶ | www.vertecbakery.com | ▶

VERTEC BAKERY

The best supplier of all kinds of high quality bread for 50 years

❶ To register for a Vertec Bakery online members account, click **here**.

❷ There are many advantages of registering, such as:
▸ ❸ Updates on sales sent through e-mail
▸ ❹ Discount codes sent only to registered customers
▸ ❺ Faster order processing on our Web site

Entering your registration information is not difficult and takes only a few minutes. Just enter your contact information such as e-mail address and mobile phone number. Please ❻ keep in mind that we protect your information securely by using a state-of-art system.

✏️ ☐ supplier 供給会社、サプライヤー ☐ all kinds of さまざまな ☐ high quality 高品質の
☐ register for ～に登録する ☐ account アカウント（インターネットサービスを利用する個人権利）
☐ advantage 利点 ☐ such as ～のような ☐ update 更新、最新情報 ☐ registered 登録済の
☐ order processing 注文処理 ☐ enter ～を入力する ☐ contact information 連絡先情報
☐ keep in mind that ～のことを留意する ☐ protect ～を保護する ☐ securely 安全に ☐ state-of-art 最新の

★★★☆☆ NOT 問題

1. What is NOT mentioned as a benefit of membership?

   (A) Discounted delivery charges
   (B) Notices about sales
   (C) Special codes for discounted prices
   (D) A quick ordering process

会員特典として言及されていないものは何ですか。

   (A) 配送料金の割引
   (B) セールに関するお知らせ
   (C) 割引料金のための特別コード
   (D) 注文時の迅速な処理

🔍 NOT 問題。会員特典として言及されていないものが問われている。❶でオンラインアカウントの登録を呼び掛け、❷〜❺で登録特典内容が記載されている。❸の「Eメールでのセール最新情報の提供」が (B) に、❹の「登録会員限定の割引コードの配信」が (C) に、❺の「注文時の迅速な処理」が (D) にそれぞれ当てはまる。残った **(A)** の配送料金の割引については述べられていないため、これが正解となる。

✏️ ☐ benefit 特典 ☐ membership メンバーシップ、会員権 ☐ delivery charge 配送料金 ☐ notice 通知

2. What is indicated about Vertec Bakery?

(A) It opened recently.
(B) It sends items around the world.
(C) It uses the latest confidential technology.
(D) It is family-owned company.

Vertec Bakery 社について何が示されていますか。

(A) 最近、開業した。
(B) 世界中に商品を発送する。
(C) 最新の機密技術を使用している。
(D) 家族経営の会社である。

Vertec Bakery 社について示されていることを問う選択肢照合型の問題。❻で「当社（Vertec Bakery 社）では最新の方法で顧客情報を厳重に保護している」と述べているため、これを言い換えた **(C)** が正解。"protect your information securely by using a state-of-art system" が uses the latest confidential technology と言い換えている。(A) は最近開業ではなく 50 年間経営しているため不正解。(B) 世界中への配送、(D) 家族経営、は記載がないため、いずれも不正解。

□ latest 最新の　□ confidential 秘密の　□ family-owned 家族経営の

問題 1 から 2 は次のウェブページに関するものです。

www.vertecbakery.com

VERTEC BAKERY 社
50 年間、あらゆる種類の高品質なパンを提供している最優良販売業者

Vertec Bakery 社のオンラインメンバーアカウントへの登録は、**こちら**をクリック

登録するとたくさんの特典があります。例えば：
▶ E メールでセールの最新情報を提供
▶ ご登録いただいたお客様限定の割引コードの配信
▶ 当ウェブサイトでのご注文時の迅速な処理

登録情報のご入力は簡単で、数分で終わります。E メールアドレスや携帯電話の番号などの連絡先情報を入力するだけです。当社では最新の方法を用いてお客様の情報を厳重に保護しておりますことをご承知おきください。

Questions 3-4 refer to the following article.

Seoul Commercial Magazine—March 5
Business Journal Honors JK Financial

❶ JK Financial was featured in Asian Commercial current news as one of the top five most influential companies in the financial consulting field in Asia. ❷ Founder and CEO Jina Kim served as president at North Pacific Bank in Beijing before starting her own agency eighteen years ago. ❸ Having been very successful at North Pacific Bank, she was eager to start a business venture in her hometown of Singapore. ❹ Today, the business has grown into an international corporation with branch offices in Seoul, Beijing, and Tokyo. Jina Kim reports that company will open a fourth branch next February. As *Seoul Commercial Magazine* reported last month, the branch will be located in Bangkok, Thailand. ❺ Asian Commercial noted that JK Financial's emphasis on staff training has resulted in the rapid increase of customer support. No agency of a similar size to JK Financial has enjoyed so much support.

□ feature ～を特集する   □ influential 影響のある   □ financial consulting field 金融コンサルティング分野
□ serve as ～として務める   □ agency 代理店   □ be eager to *do* ～することを熱望する
□ business venture ベンチャー企業、投機的事業   □ hometown 生まれ故郷   □ grow into ～へ成長する
□ branch office 支店   □ be located in ～に位置・所在している   □ note ～と述べる   □ emphasis on ～の強化
□ result in 結果として～になる   □ rapid 急速な   □ enjoy ～を享受する・(利益として) 得る

★★★☆☆

3. Why is the article written?

(A) To investigate why an investment banker has left her job
(B) To explain how a small corporation has expanded internationally
(C) To announce that a business has been discontinued
(D) To name the largest financial consulting firms in Asia

記事はなぜ書かれましたか。

(A) 投資銀行家がなぜ退職したかについて調査をするため
(B) 小さな企業がどのように国際的に発展したかについて説明するため
(C) 会社が廃業したことを周知させるため
(D) アジアで最大の金融コンサルティング会社の名を言うため

🔍 記事が書かれた理由が問われている。冒頭❶で「JK Financial 社が、アジアの金融コンサル分野で影響力のある企業として選ばれた」とあり、その後の❷～❹で「創業者の Kim さんは銀行に勤めた後に代理店を起業し、現在では国際的な企業へと成長した」と述べられている。この「小さな会社が国際的に発展した」という内容を言い換えた **(B)** が正解となる。

□ investigate ～を調査する   □ investment banker 投資銀行家   □ corporation 企業、会社   □ expand 拡張する
□ discontinue (会社等)を廃業する   □ name ～を指名・任命する

★★★☆☆

4. What can be inferred about JK Financial?

(A) Its headquarters is near that of North Pacific Bank.
(B) It received an award from *Seoul Commercial Magazine*.
(C) Its staff-training program has contributed to its success.
(D) Its founder started her career at North Pacific Bank.

JK Financial 社について何が示唆されていますか。

(A) 本社が North Pacific Bank の近くにある。
(B) *Seoul Commercial Magazine* から表彰された。
(C) 従業員研修プログラムが成功に貢献した。
(D) 創設者の経歴は North Pacific Bank から始まった。

JK Financial 社について示唆されていることを問う選択肢照合型の問題。❺で「JK Financial 社が従業員研修の強化により、顧客サポートが急増している」と述べている。ここから「顧客サポートが急増＝研修が顧客サポートの急増に役に立っている」ということが考えられる。よって、これを言い換えた (C) が正解。(A) 本社所在地、(B) 雑誌の表彰、については述べられていない。(D) は、創設者（Kim さん）が North Pacific Bank で頭取を務めたとはあるが、そこでキャリアをスタートさせたとは述べられていないため、不正解。

☐ headquarters 本社　☐ contribute to ～に貢献している　☐ founder 創設者

問題 3 から 4 は次の記事に関するものです。

Seoul Commercial Magazine — 3 月 5 日
ビジネス誌が JK Financial 社を称賛

JK Financial 社は、Asian Commercial の最近のニュースで、アジアの金融コンサルティング分野で最も影響力のある上位 5 位の企業として特集された。創業者兼 CEO である Jina Kim 氏は、自身の代理店を起こした 18 年前より以前に、北京の North Pacific Bank で頭取を務めた。North Pacific Bank で大成功を収めた彼女は、故郷のシンガポールで投機的事業を始めることに意欲的であった。現在、その事業は、ソウル、北京、東京に支店を持つ国際的な企業へと成長した。Jina Kim 氏は、その会社は来年 2 月に 4 つ目の支店を開設すると発表している。*Seoul Commercial Magazine* が先月報じたように、支店はタイのバンコクに開設される予定である。Asian Commercial は、JK Financial 社が従業員の研修に力を入れていることで、顧客サポートが急増していると述べている。JK Financial 社と同じ規模の代理店でこれほどの支持を得たところは他にない。

1分30秒

Jenna Oceanview
Perfect space for your functions

Thank you for your interest in Jenna Oceanview. Could you please complete the request form below? We'll call you with a plan and pricing that will satisfy the requirements of your special occasion.

Name: David Reinhardt
E-mail Address: dddrein@audiopro.com
Phone Number: 241-0967
Date(s) : 11 December

▶ Seating layout: Ceremony _√_   Private Dining __   Dinner with dance __
                Other _____

▶ Type of Event: Wedding __   Birthday __   Company function _√_
                Other _____

▶ Number of guests: 1~20 __   21~40 _√_   41~60 __   61+ __

▶ Equipment rental needed: Laptop __   Projector _√_   Internet connection __
                Other _____

▶ Accommodation for guests: Yes ____   No _√_

▶ How many guests require accommodation: _____

---

5. Why will Jenna Oceanview call the respondent on this form?

(A) To make a proposal based on the information provided
(B) To offer a discounted rate
(C) To recommend the event venue
(D) To send a newsletter

6. What is implied about Jenna Oceanview?

(A) It has multiple event spaces.
(B) It requires guests to bring all necessary equipment.
(C) It has been in business over a decade.
(D) It has a lodging facility.

P. 562

Questions 7-8 refer to the following online chat discussion.

 1分30秒

Sally McNichols 3:12 P.M.
Is recruiting drivers going well?

Timothy Slattery 3:14 P.M.
Terrible. It's going to take longer than I thought to get delivery drivers due to the new rules.

Sally McNichols 3:15 P.M.
What should we do about being short-staffed in the meantime?

Timothy Slattery 3:16 P.M.
I've already spoken to our customers about the situation, and they've all agreed to get supply deliveries twice a month instead of weekly.

Sally McNichols 3:17 P.M.
Didn't Hollander Service threaten to leave?

Timothy Slattery 3:18 P.M.
Yes, it actually did. However, it finally came around. What a relief.

Sally McNichols 3:19 P.M.
I'm happy to hear that.

7. According to the discussion, what is suggested about the problem?

(A) They do not have enough workers.
(B) They are facing too much competition.
(C) They've experienced a shortage of supplies.
(D) Their customers have made some complaints.

8. At 3:18 P.M., what does Mr. Slattery mean when he writes, "it finally came around"?

(A) He expected some supplies to be late.
(B) He was concerned that a rule wouldn't pass.
(C) He was worried that some visitors would not arrive.
(D) He was pleased a company reversed its decision.

P. 564

Questions 5-6 refer to the following form.

Jenna Oceanview
Perfect space for your functions

Thank you for your interest in Jenna Oceanview. Could you please complete the request form below? ❶ <u>We'll call you with a plan and pricing that will satisfy the requirements of your special occasion.</u>

Name: *David Reinhardt*
E-mail Address: *dddrein@audiopro.com*
Phone Number: *241-0967*
Date(s) : *11 December*

▶ Seating layout: Ceremony __√__   Private Dining ___   Dinner with dance ___
             Other _____
▶ Type of Event: Wedding ___   Birthday ___   Company function __√__
             Other _____
▶ Number of guests: 1~20 ___   21~40 __√__   41~60 ___   61+ ___
▶ Equipment rental needed: Laptop ___   Projector __√__   Internet connection ___
             Other _____
▶ ❷ Accommodation for guests: Yes _____   No __√__
▶ ❸ How many guests require accommodation: _____

☐ function イベント、催し ☐ interest in ～の関心 ☐ complete form 書式に記入する ☐ pricing 価格
☐ satisfy the requirement 要求を満たす ☐ special occasion 特別な状況 ☐ seating layout 座席配置
☐ ceremony お祝い事 ☐ company function 会社行事 ☐ laptop ノートパソコン ☐ projector プロジェクター
☐ Internet connection インターネット接続 ☐ accommodation 宿泊施設 ☐ require ～を必要とする

★★★☆☆

5. Why will Jenna Oceanview call the respondent on this form?

  (A) To make a proposal based on the information provided
  (B) To offer a discounted rate
  (C) To recommend the event venue
  (D) To send a newsletter

Jenna Oceanview 社はこの用紙の回答者になぜ電話をかけますか。

  (A) 提供された情報に基づいた提案をするため
  (B) 割引料金を提案するため
  (C) イベント会場を薦めるため
  (D) お知らせを送るため

🔍 Jenna Oceanview 社はこの用紙の回答者になぜ電話をかけるのかが問われている。❶に「お客様の特別な行事の要件を満たすプランと価格設定をご案内するために後日電話をする」とあるので、イベント開催を希望して書式に記入をした回答者（お客様）に、その情報を基にした提案をすることがわかる。よって、これを make a proposal と言い換えた **(A)** が正解となる。

☐ make a proposal 提案をする ☐ based on ～に基づく ☐ discounted rate 割引料金
☐ event venue イベント会場 ☐ newsletter お知らせ

6. What is implied about Jenna Oceanview?

(A) It has multiple event spaces.
(B) It requires guests to bring all necessary equipment.
(C) It has been in business over a decade.
(D) It has a lodging facility.

Jenna Oceanview 社について何が示唆されていますか。

(A) 多数のイベント会場を所持している。
(B) 出席者に必要な機材をすべて持参することを求めている。
(C) 10 年以上にわたって事業を行っている。
(D) 宿泊施設がある。

Jenna Oceanview 社について示唆されていることは何かを問う選択肢照合型の問題。❷で「宿泊の有無」、❸で「宿泊する場合の人数」を聞いていることから、この会社が宿泊施設を持っていると推測できる。よって、"accommodation" を lodging facility と言い換えた **(D)** が正解となる。(A) 多数の場所、(C) 事業年数は記載がなく、(B) 必要な機材はレンタルもできるため、いずれも不正解。

□ multiple 多数の　□ necessary equipment 必要な機器　□ over a decade 10 年にもわたり
□ lodging facility 宿泊施設

問題 5 から 6 は次の用紙に関するものです。

Jenna Oceanview 社
イベントに最適なスペース

Jenna Oceanview 社に関心をお寄せいただきありがとうございます。下記の申請書にご記入をお願いいたします。お客様の特別な行事の要件を満たすプランと価格設定をご案内するために後日お電話を差し上げます。

お名前：David Reinhardt
Eメールアドレス：dddrein@audiopro.com
お電話番号：241-0967
日程：12 月 11 日

▶ 座席配置：お祝い事 ✓　　会食 ＿＿＿　　お食事と舞踏会 ＿＿＿
　　　　　　 その他 ＿＿＿＿＿＿＿＿＿＿＿＿＿＿＿＿＿＿＿＿＿＿＿
▶ 催しの種類：結婚式 ＿＿＿　　誕生会 ＿＿＿　　会社のイベント ✓
　　　　　　 その他 ＿＿＿＿＿＿＿＿＿＿＿＿＿＿＿＿＿＿＿＿＿＿
▶ 出席人数：1 ～ 20 ＿＿＿　　21 ～ 40 ✓　　41 ～ 60 ＿＿＿　　61 以上 ＿＿＿
▶ 必要な機材のレンタル：ノートパソコン ＿＿＿　　プロジェクター ✓　　インターネット接続 ＿＿＿
　　　　　　 その他 ＿＿＿＿＿＿＿＿＿＿＿＿＿＿＿＿＿＿＿＿＿＿＿＿＿
▶ 出席者のための宿泊施設：要 ＿＿＿　　不要 ✓
▶ 宿泊を必要とする出席者の数：＿＿＿＿＿＿＿＿＿＿＿＿＿＿＿＿＿＿＿

Questions 7-8 refer to the following online chat discussion.

Sally McNichols 3:12 P.M.
❶ Is recruiting drivers going well?

Timothy Slattery 3:14 P.M.
❷ Terrible. It's going to take longer than I thought to get delivery drivers due to the new rules.

Sally McNichols 3:15 P.M.
❸ What should we do about being short-staffed in the meantime?

Timothy Slattery 3:16 P.M.
❹ I've already spoken to our customers about the situation, and they've all agreed to get supply deliveries twice a month instead of weekly.

Sally McNichols 3:17 P.M.
❺ Didn't Hollander Service threaten to leave?

Timothy Slattery 3:18 P.M.
❻ Yes, it actually did. However, ❼ it finally came around. ❽ What a relief.

Sally McNichols 3:19 P.M.
I'm happy to hear that.

☐ recruit ～を採用する ☐ go well 順調にいく ☐ terrible ひどい
☐ take longer than I thought 思ったより長くかかる ☐ due to ～により ☐ short-staffed 人員が不足している
☐ in the meantime その間に ☐ supply delivery 物品配送 ☐ instead of ～の代わりに
☐ threaten to *do* ～するとちらつかせてくる ☐ come around 意見を変えて同意する ☐ What a relief. ひと安心した。

★★★☆☆

7. According to the discussion, what is suggested about the problem?

(A) They do not have enough workers.
(B) They are facing too much competition.
(C) They've experienced a shortage of supplies.
(D) Their customers have made some complaints.

話し合いによると、問題について何が示唆されていますか。

(A) 労働者が不足している。
(B) 競争が激しすぎる。
(C) 物資が不足していた。
(D) 客から苦情が寄せられた。

🔍 問題について何が示唆されているかが問われている。McNichols さんと Slattery さんのやりとりの❶・❷で、新しい規則が原因で、運転手の採用が遅れていると述べられている。また、❸から、この採用は人員不足を解消するためだとわかる。以上より、人員不足を言い換えた **(A)** が正解となる。

☐ face ～に直面している ☐ competition 競争 ☐ shortage 不足 ☐ complaint 苦情

8. At 3:18 P.M., what does Mr. Slattery mean when he writes, "it finally came around"?

(A) He expected some supplies to be late.
(B) He was concerned that a rule wouldn't pass.
(C) He was worried that some visitors would not arrive.
(D) He was pleased a company reversed its decision.

午後 3 時 18 分に、Slattery さんは "it finally came around" という発言で、何を意味していますか。

(A) 供給が遅れる物資があると予想していた。
(B) 規則が承認されないことを懸念していた。
(C) 訪問者が到着しないのではないかと心配していた。
(D) 客が決定を覆したことを喜んだ。

意図問題。問われている❼の表現は、「(ある方向が) 最終的に違う方向になった」という意味。❽で「ほっとしている」とあるので、何がどう変わって「ほっとした」のかを読んでいく。その前の❹・❺・❻を読むと、「(人員不足の対応のため) 顧客に配送頻度を減らす調整をしたところ、Hollander Service 社が配送サービスの利用を停止すると言ってきた」と述べている。つまり、「サービスをもう利用しない」という意見だったが、最終的にはその意見を覆して提案に同意してくれたということになる。以上から、正解は **(D)** となる。❼の前に "However(しかしながら)" という接続副詞があり、この表現に注目すると、この前後で逆説の文脈になることがわかるので、この点も押さえておこう。

☐ be concerned that ～ということを心配する　☐ pass 承認される　☐ be pleased (that) 喜ぶ、うれしい
☐ reverse ～を覆す　☐ decision 決断

問題 7 から 8 は次のオンラインチャットの話し合いに関するものです。

Sally McNichols 午後 3 時 12 分
ドライバーの採用は順調ですか?

Timothy Slattery 午後 3 時 14 分
大変良くないです。新しい規則のせいで、配達ドライバーを採用するのに思っていたよりも時間がかかりそうです。

Sally McNichols 午後 3 時 15 分
その間、人員不足についてはどうしたらいいでしょうか?

Timothy Slattery 午後 3 時 16 分
すでにお客様には状況を説明しており、物品の配達は毎週ではなく月に 2 回ということで皆さんから同意を得ています。

Sally McNichols 午後 3 時 17 分
Hollander Service 社は利用を停止すると言ってこなかったのですか?

Timothy Slattery 午後 3 時 18 分
いいえ、たしかに言ってきました。しかし、最終的には同意していただきました。ほっとしました。

Sally McNichols 午後 3 時 19 分
それが聞けてよかったです。

Questions 9-11 refer to the following article.

 2分45秒

Baseball Series Finals
Return to Tucson

Tucson (March 5)—On August 1, the final series of the Golden League is going to start in Tucson. This is only the second time that the tournament has taken place here, the first time being a decade ago. The city's mayor Richard Baxter, who has worked diligently to regain this honor, is pleased to hear this good news.

"We are absolutely thrilled that the games will return," says Mr. Baxter. "Obviously, we are also rooting for our home team to be as victorious as the last time that the tournament was held here. They came in first place at that time." —[1]—.

The tournament is supposed to attract baseball fans in large numbers and will make up for the decline in tourism the city has experienced during the last decade. —[2]—.

The tournament couldn't come at a better time, as the late summer tends to be the slowest time of the year for tourism. Ticket holders should definitely reserve their hotel rooms far in advance since the overnight rates will just go up as the tournament dates approach. —[3]—.

This year the city will welcome the tournament by holding the games in Apollo Ball Park. The extensive remodeling work started at the ballpark just one month after the hosting decision was announced last year. The project is expected to be completed in two months. —[4]—.

In all, ten teams will play, with two teams playing in the final game of the tournament, which will occur on August 14.

9. When was the tournament last held in Tucson?

    (A) One year ago
    (B) Three years ago
    (C) Five years ago
    (D) Ten years ago

10. According to the article, what will happen in May?

    (A) Organizers will travel to Tucson.
    (B) An important tournament will take place.
    (C) Construction work will be finished.
    (D) A host city will be announced.

11. In which of the positions marked [1], [2], [3], and [4] does the following sentence best belong?

"In fact, the participants in the games will likely fill up the city's hotels"

    (A) [1]
    (B) [2]
    (C) [3]
    (D) [4]

P. 568

Questions 9-11 refer to the following article.

Baseball Series Finals
Return to Tucson

Tucson (❶ March 5)— ❷ On August 1, the final series of the Golden League is going to start in Tucson. This is only the second time that the tournament has taken place here, the first time being a decade ago. The city's mayor Richard Baxter, who has worked diligently to regain this honor, is pleased to hear this good news.

"We are absolutely thrilled that the games will return," says Mr. Baxter. "Obviously, we are also rooting for our home team to be as victorious as the last time that the tournament was held here. They came in first place at that time." —[1]—.

The tournament is supposed to attract baseball fans in large numbers and will make up for the decline in tourism the city has experienced during the last decade. —[2]—.

The tournament couldn't come at a better time, as the late summer tends to be the slowest time of the year for tourism. ❸ Ticket holders should definitely reserve their hotel rooms far in advance since the overnight rates will just go up as the tournament dates approach. —[3]—.

This year the city will welcome the tournament by holding the games in Apollo Ball Park. The extensive remodeling work started at the ballpark just one month after the hosting decision was announced last year. ❹ The project is expected to be completed in two months. —[4]—.

In all, ten teams will play, with two teams playing in the final game of the tournament, which will occur on August 14.

□ take place 開催される □ diligently 熱心に □ regain ～を取り戻す □ honor 名誉 □ absolutely 間違いなく
□ be thrilled that ～だとわくわくする □ obviously 明らかに □ root for ～を応援する □ victorious 勝利を得る
□ come in first place 優勝する、一等賞となる □ be supposed to *do* ～するはずである
□ in large numbers 多数の □ make up for ～を埋め合わせる □ decline in ～の減少 □ tourism 観光産業
□ decade 10年 □ couldn't come at a better time 絶好の時期である（直訳：これ以上良いタイミングで行われない）
□ ticket holder チケット保持者 □ definitely 必ず □ far in advance かなり余裕を持って
□ overnight rate 宿泊料金 □ go up （価格が）上がる □ extensive 大規模な □ remodeling work 改装工事
□ ballpark 球場 □ in all 全部で □ occur 行われる、起こる

★★☆☆☆

9. When was the tournament last held in Tucson?

(A) One year ago
(B) Three years ago
(C) Five years ago
(D) Ten years ago

トゥーソンで前回トーナメントが行われたのはいつですか。

(A) 1年前
(B) 3年前
(C) 5年前
(D) 10年前

トゥーソンで最後にトーナメントが開催されたのはいつかが問われている。❷に「この地でのトーナメント開催は今回が2回目で、1回目は10年前だ」とある。「この地」は、記事発信の場所であるトゥーソンだと直前の文からわかる。よって、前回は10年前に開催されたことがわかるので、正解は **(D)**。

★★★☆☆

10. According to the article, what will happen in May?

(A) Organizers will travel to Tucson.
(B) An important tournament will take place.
(C) Construction work will be finished.
(D) A host city will be announced.

記事によると、5月に何が起こりますか。

(A) 主催者がトゥーソンに行く。
(B) 重要なトーナメントが行われる。
(C) 建設工事が終了する。
(D) 開催都市が発表される。

✏️ ☐ host city 開催都市

....

★★★☆☆ 文挿入位置問題

11. In which of the positions marked [1], [2], [3], and [4] does the following sentence best belong?

"In fact, the participants in the games will likely fill up the city's hotels"

(A)　[1]
(B)　[2]
(C)　[3]
(D)　[4]

次の文は [1]、[2]、[3]、[4] のどの位置に最もよく当てはまりますか。

「実際、その試合の参加者が市のホテルを満室にしてしまう可能性が高い」

(A)　[1]
(B)　[2]
(C)　[3]
(D)　[4]

🔍 適切な文の位置を求める問題。問われている文は、「実際、その試合の参加者が市のホテルを満室にしてしまう可能性が高い」という意味になっている。ここから、試合に参加することや、宿泊に関する情報の後に該当すると考えられる。それを意識して本文を見ていくと、❸で「チケット保持者は、ホテルをかなり早めに予約をすべき」と書いているため、この直後に入れると、「早めにホテル予約を→満室になる可能性があるから」となり文意に合う。以上より、正解は **(C)** となる。

✏️ ☐ likely おそらく　☐ fill up ～を埋める

📝 問題 9 から 11 は次の記事に関するものです。

野球シリーズ決勝
トゥーソンに戻る

トゥーソン (3月5日) ― 8月1日、Golden League の決勝シリーズがトゥーソンで始まる。トーナメントがこの地で行われるのは今回がまだ2回目で、1回目は10年前のことである。この栄誉を取り戻そうと献身的に取り組んだ市長の Richard Baxter 氏は、この良いニュースを聞いて喜んでいる。

「私たちは試合が戻ってくることに心底わくわくしています。」と Baxter 氏は語る。「もちろん、前回ここでトーナメントが行われたときと同じように、ホームチームが勝つように応援しています。あの時、チームは優勝したのです。」―[1]―

トーナメントは多くの野球ファンを引きつけ、過去10年間に市が経験した観光客の減少を取り戻すこととなるだろう。―[2]―

夏の終わりは観光業が年間で最も低調な時期となる傾向があるため、トーナメントが行われるには絶好の時期である。トーナメントの日程が近づくにつれ、宿泊料金が上昇するため、チケットを持っている方は、ホテルをかなり早めに予約すべきだ。―[3]― 実際、その試合の参加者が市のホテルを満室にしてしまう可能性が高い。

今年、Apollo Ball Park で試合を開催することにより、市はトーナメントを歓迎する。球場の大規模な改装工事は、昨年開催決定が発表されてからわずか1カ月後に始まった。そのプロジェクトは2カ月後に完了する予定である。―[4]―

全部で10チームが試合を行い、2チームが8月14日にトーナメントの最終試合を行う。

Questions 12-14 refer to the following survey.

2分45秒

Wilson Online Mart Customer Survey

Would you mind taking a moment to fill in this survey form and mailing it back to us using the attached postpaid envelope? We greatly care about our delivery service to you. Thank you very much for sharing your opinions with us.

1. *Wilson Online Mart* is printed a week prior to the issue date. Does your copy arrive before the issue date?
___ Yes ___ No

2. On which day of the week does your copy of *Wilson Online Mart* usually arrive?
___ Monday ___ Tuesday ___ Wednesday ___ Thursday
___ Friday ___ Saturday ___ Sunday ___ irregular

3. Do you consider the arrival to be:
___ Satisfactory ___ Unsatisfactory

4. Has a copy of *Wilson Online Mart* ever failed to arrive in the last two months?
___ Yes ___ No

5. When it's time to renew your subscription to *Wilson Online Mart*, how likely would the following factors influence your renewal decision?
(Please rank from 1 to 5. 1=least important, 5=most important)

	1	2	3	4	5
Content of *Wilson Online Mart*					
Punctuality of delivery					
Customer service					
Subscription price					
Free gift					

12. What is the purpose of this survey?

    (A) To offer a discount to customers
    (B) To take a chance to win a prize
    (C) To get delivery information
    (D) To collect customer registration data

13. How is the form to be returned?

    (A) All customers are asked to fax the survey.
    (B) Any respondent will have to pay for the postage.
    (C) On Mondays, the form will be collected.
    (D) An envelope with a stamp is provided.

14. Which question is related to recent non-delivery of an issue of *Wilson Online Mart*?

    (A) Question 2
    (B) Question 3
    (C) Question 4
    (D) Question 5

P. 572

Questions 12-14 refer to the following survey.

Wilson Online Mart Customer Survey

Would you mind taking a moment to fill in this survey form and ❶ mailing it back to us using the attached postpaid envelope? ❷ We greatly care about our delivery service to you. Thank you very much for sharing your opinions with us.

1. *Wilson Online Mart* is printed a week prior to the issue date. Does your copy arrive before the issue date?
___ Yes ___ No

2. On which day of the week does your copy of *Wilson Online Mart* usually arrive?
___ Monday ___ Tuesday ___ Wednesday ___ Thursday
___ Friday ___ Saturday ___ Sunday ___ irregular

3. Do you consider the arrival to be:
___ Satisfactory ___ Unsatisfactory

❸ 4. Has a copy of *Wilson Online Mart* ever failed to arrive in the last two months?
___ Yes ___ No

5. When it's time to renew your subscription to *Wilson Online Mart*, how likely would the following factors influence your renewal decision?
(Please rank from 1 to 5. 1=least important, 5=most important)

	1	2	3	4	5
Content of *Wilson Online Mart*					
Punctuality of delivery					
Customer service					
Subscription price					
Free gift					

☐ take a moment to *do* 時間を取って~する　☐ fill in ~に記入する　☐ mail ~を郵送する　☐ attached 添付の
☐ postpaid 送料支払い済みの　☐ care about ~を重視している　☐ prior to ~に先立ち　☐ issue date 発行日
☐ unsatisfactory 不満である　☐ fail to *do* ~し損ねる　☐ renew ~を更新する　☐ subscription to ~の定期購読
☐ following 以下の　☐ factor 要因　☐ influence ~に影響する　☐ rank 評価する　☐ punctuality 時間厳取

12. What is the purpose of this survey?

    (A) To offer a discount to customers
    (B) To take a chance to win a prize
    (C) To get delivery information
    (D) To collect customer registration data

この調査の目的は何ですか。

    (A) 顧客に割引を提供すること
    (B) 賞品を当てるため、一か八かやってみること
    (C) 配送情報を得ること
    (D) 顧客の登録データを集めること

この調査の目的が問われている。文書の冒頭でアンケートに回答してほしい旨をお願いし、❷で「顧客への配送サービスを重視している」と述べている。ここから、配送サービスに関する顧客の意見・情報を得る目的だとわかる。以上より正解は **(C)**。

□ win ～を勝ち取る、～に当選する　□ registration data 登録データ

13. How is the form to be returned?

    (A) All customers are asked to fax the survey.
    (B) Any respondent will have to pay for the postage.
    (C) On Mondays, the form will be collected.
    (D) An envelope with a stamp is provided.

用紙はどのように返送されますか。

    (A) すべての顧客はファックスで調査票を送るように求められている。
    (B) 回答者全員が郵便料金を支払わなければならない。
    (C) 月曜日に用紙は回収される。
    (D) 切手の貼られた封筒が用意されている。

（調査）用紙がどのように返送されるかが問われている。❶で「添付の送料支払い済みの封筒で当社まで返送してほしい」とお願いしているので、切手もしくは支払い済印（=stamp）のある封筒が同封されていることがわかる。以上より、それを言い換えた **(D)** が正解。

□ respondent 回答者　□ postage 郵送料金　□ stamp 切手

14. Which question is related to recent non-delivery of an issue of *Wilson Online Mart*?

    (A) Question 2
    (B) Question 3
    (C) Question 4
    (D) Question 5

最近 *Wilson Online Mart* 誌が配送されなかったことについての質問はどれですか。

    (A) 2番
    (B) 3番
    (C) 4番
    (D) 5番

最近の Wilson Online 誌が配送されなかったことに関連する質問はどれかが問われている。❸の質問で、「過去2カ月間に、Wilson Online Mart 誌が届かなかったことがあるか?」と尋ねている。よって正解は **(C)**。❸の "fail to arrive" が設問文では non-delivery に言い換えられていることを押さえておこう。

□ related to ～に関連している　□ non-delivery 配送ができていない状態

Wilson Online Mart 誌顧客調査

このアンケート用紙にご記入の上、添付の送料支払い済みの封筒で当社までご返送いただけますでしょうか。当社では皆さまへの配送サービスをとても重視しています。ご意見をお聞かせいただきありがとうございます。

1. *Wilson Online Mart* 誌は発行日の 1 週間前に印刷されます。発行日までにお客様のお手元に届きますか？
____ はい ____ いいえ

2. *Wilson Online Mart* 誌は通常何曜日に届きますか？
____ 月曜日 ____ 火曜日 ____ 水曜日 ____ 木曜日
____ 金曜日 ____ 土曜日 ____ 日曜日 ____ 不定期

3. お届けについて：
____ 満足している ____ 不満である

4. 過去 2 カ月間に、*Wilson Online Mart* 誌が届かなかったことはありますか？
____ ある ____ ない

5. *Wilson Online Mart* 誌の購読を更新する際、次の要素が更新の判断にどの程度影響を与えますか？
（1 から 5 までで評価してください。1 ＝最も重要でない、5 ＝最も重要である）

	1	2	3	4	5
Wilson Online Mart 誌の内容					
お届け日の正確さ					
顧客サービス					
購読料					
贈呈品					

GO ON TO THE
NEXT PAGE!

Questions 15-17 refer to the following press release.

 2分45秒

Business: Amcor Group Inc., one of the leading fabricators in Canada, produces various kinds of hard plastic materials and most of them are converted into containers of different sizes. The company also makes plastic materials for home interior pieces, kitchen items, and waste bins as well as thin flexible plastics that are ideal for the production of disposable forks, spoons, and knives used by many restaurants. The company's main office is in Montreal, Quebec.

Sales: The company reported $508 million in annual sales last year, with customers in eleven northern hemisphere countries. The annual average increase in sales over the last decade has been nine percent.

History and Future: Established fifteen years ago as a division of Woodbridge Plasman Ltd., the company became independent seven years ago as Amcor Supply Company and was renamed Amcor Group Inc. one year ago. The company intends to build additional manufacturing plants within the next four years.

15. What kind of business is Amcor Group Inc.?

(A) A chain of kitchen appliance stores
(B) A producer of plastic materials
(C) A maker of restaurant furniture
(D) An interior decorating firm

16. What is indicated about Amcor Group Inc.?

(A) It is based in Montreal.
(B) Its sales have declined for the last four years.
(C) It makes fine cutlery.
(D) It carries products only domestically.

17. What is the relationship between Amcor Group Inc. and Woodbridge Plasman Ltd.?

(A) Amcor Group Inc. intends to merge with Woodbridge Plasman Ltd.
(B) Woodbridge Plasman Ltd. is a supplier for Amcor Group Inc.
(C) Woodbridge Plasman Ltd. is the name of Amcor Group Inc. overseas.
(D) Amcor Group Inc. was formerly part of Woodbridge Plasman Ltd.

P. 578

Questions 15-17 refer to the following press release.

Business: ❶ Amcor Group Inc., one of the leading fabricators in Canada, produces various kinds of hard plastic materials and most of them are converted into containers of different sizes. The company also makes plastic materials for home interior pieces, kitchen items, and waste bins as well as thin flexible plastics that are ideal for the production of disposable forks, spoons, and knives used by many restaurants. **❷** The company's main office is in Montreal, Quebec.

Sales: The company reported $508 million in annual sales last year, with customers in eleven northern hemisphere countries. The annual average increase in sales over the last decade has been nine percent.

History and Future: ❸ Established fifteen years ago as a division of Woodbridge Plasman Ltd., the company became independent seven years ago as Amcor Supply Company and was renamed Amcor Group Inc. one year ago. The company intends to build additional manufacturing plants within the next four years.

☐ leading 大手の ☐ fabricator 製造業者、製作者 ☐ various kinds of さまざまな
☐ hard plastic 硬質プラスチックの ☐ convert A to B A を B に加工する ☐ home interior 家庭用インテリア
☐ waste bin ゴミ箱 ☐ flexible 柔軟な ☐ ideal for 〜に適している ☐ disposable 使い捨ての
☐ northern hemisphere 北半球の ☐ over the last decade 最近 10 年にわたり ☐ independent 独立して
☐ rename A B　A の名前を B に変える ☐ intend to *do* 〜する予定である

★★★★★

15. What kind of business is Amcor Group Inc.?

(A) A chain of kitchen appliance stores
(B) A producer of plastic materials
(C) A maker of restaurant furniture
(D) An interior decorating firm

Amcor Group 社はどのような企業ですか。

(A) 台所用品店のチェーン
(B) プラスチック素材製造業者
(C) レストラン向け家具のメーカー
(D) 内装会社

Amcor Group 社はどのような企業かが問われている。冒頭❶で「Amcor Group 社は、さまざまな種類の硬質プラスチック素材を製造しており、…」とあるため、プラスチック素材製造会社であることがわかる。よって正解は **(B)**。会社名の後にその会社の概要について示すという典型的なパターンなので、すぐに正解にたどり着けるようにしよう。

☐ kitchen appliance 台所用品 ☐ interior decorating firm 内装会社

16. What is indicated about Amcor Group Inc.?

    (A) It is based in Montreal.
    (B) Its sales have declined for the last four years.
    (C) It makes fine cutlery.
    (D) It carries products only domestically.

Amcor Group 社について何が示唆されていますか。

    (A) モントリオールに本社がある。
    (B) 過去 4 年で売り上げが減少した。
    (C) 高級なカトラリーを製造している。
    (D) 国内でのみ製品を取り扱っている。

🔍 Amcor Group 社について示唆されていることを問う選択肢照合型の問題。❷で「同社の本社はケベック州モントリオールにある」とあるので、これを言い換えた **(A)** が正解。main office = be based in 場所、という言い換えは TOEIC では頻出であるため、この言い換えに反応できるようになっておこう。(C) は、ナイフ・フォークを製造するので、その点では "cutlery" を製造しているといえるが、"fine (高級な、上質の)" というタイプのものではなく、どのレストランでも使用する使い捨てのタイプの製造をしている。また (D) は海外にも顧客がいるため、いずれも不正解。

✎ ☐ cutlery (ナイフ・フォーク等の) 食卓食器、カトラリー　☐ carry ～を取り扱う　☐ domestically 国内で

---

17. What is the relationship between Amcor Group Inc. and Woodbridge Plasman Ltd.?

    (A) Amcor Group Inc. intends to merge with Woodbridge Plasman Ltd.
    (B) Woodbridge Plasman Ltd. is a supplier for Amcor Group Inc.
    (C) Woodbridge Plasman Ltd. is the name of Amcor Group Inc. overseas.
    (D) Amcor Group Inc. was formerly part of Woodbridge Plasman Ltd.

Amcor Group 社と Woodbridge Plasman 社はどんな関係ですか。

    (A) Amcor Group 社は Woodbridge Plasman 社と合併しようとしている。
    (B) Woodbridge Plasman 社は Amcor Group 社の供給会社である。
    (C) Woodbridge Plasman 社は Amcor Group 社の海外における名称である。
    (D) Amcor Group 社は、かつて Woodbridge Plasman 社の一部であった。

🔍 Amcor Group 社と Woodbridge Plasman 社の関係について問われている。最終段落の❸で、「同社 (Amcor Group 社) は Woodbridge Plasman 社の一部門として 15 年前に設立され、7 年前に Amcor Supply Company として独立した」とある。ここから、Amcor Group 社が以前は Woodbridge Plasman 社の一部だったことがわかる。よって、これを言い換えた **(D)** が正解。

✎ ☐ merge with ～と合併する　☐ overseas 海外で　☐ formerly 以前に

📝 問題 15 から 17 は次のプレスリリースに関するものです。

事業内容：カナダの大手製造業者の一つである Amcor Group 社は、さまざまな種類の硬質プラスチック素材を製造しており、ほとんどはさまざまな大きさの容器に加工されている。また、同社は家庭用インテリア、台所用品、ゴミ箱などに使われるプラスチック素材をはじめ、多くのレストランで使用される使い捨てのフォーク、スプーン、ナイフなどを製造するのに最適な薄くてしなやかなプラスチックも製造している。同社の本社はケベック州モントリオールにある。

売り上げ：同社は北半球の 11 カ国に顧客を持ち、昨年は年間で 5 億 8 百万ドルを売り上げたと報告している。この 10 年間の売り上げの年間増加率は平均で 9 パーセントである。

歴史とこれから：同社は Woodbridge Plasman 社の一部門として 15 年前に設立され、7 年前に Amcor Supply Company として独立し、1 年前に Amcor Group 社と社名を変更した。同社は今後 4 年で新たな製造工場を建設する予定である。

Questions 18-21 refer to the following online chat discussion.

4分00秒

Sophie Taylor [11:11 A.M.]	I'd like to raise an issue about the warehouse in Olathe. After the tornado last week, some serious cracks have been found on the wall of the building.
Danny Russel [11:12 A.M.]	We have to take care of that immediately. However, what about the merchandise we keep in there? How will we empty it out for building repairs?
Seth Harper [11:13 A.M.]	Our summer shipment shouldn't arrive for another week, should it? Let's delay that one. In the meantime we should move what we have in the Olathe warehouse to another one nearby.
Gwen Connel [11:14 A.M.]	In fact, the warehouse here in Belton is running low on inventory. Let's send their inventory here for now.
Sophie Taylor [11:15 A.M.]	Great. Seth, can you arrange for a few trucks to come here later today?
Danny Russel [11:16 A.M.]	Wait, let's send them to the Gardner branch instead. We can save a lot of time and money we would have to spend on the road.
Seth Harper [11:17 A.M.]	I think it would actually be a lot cheaper. I'll arrange for the drivers and the trucks. Sophie, get your loading crew ready. Danny, can your evening crew receive the shipment?
Danny Russel [11:18 A.M.]	That shouldn't be a big problem.

18. What problem does Ms. Taylor want to address?

(A) She needs to find a new building.
(B) A shipment has been postponed.
(C) Structural damage needs to be fixed.
(D) A warehouse is too low on inventory.

19. What most likely is Ms. Connel's position in the company?

(A) Chief financial officer
(B) Branch supply manager
(C) Transportation manager
(D) Customer service manager

20. What does Mr. Russel suggest about the branch in Belton?

(A) It has fewer workers than the Gardner branch.
(B) It is not wide enough for the merchandise.
(C) It is located farther away from Olath than the Gardner branch.
(D) It has much more inventory than the Gardner branch.

21. At 11:18 A.M., what does Mr. Russel mean when he writes, "That shouldn't be a big problem"?

(A) Goods will be transferred to a neighboring branch.
(B) A warehouse will be sold to another company.
(C) A shipment will be canceled.
(D) A clearance sale will be held.

P. 582

Questions 18-21 refer to the following online chat discussion.

Sophie Taylor [11:11 A.M.]	I'd like to raise an issue about the warehouse in Olathe. ❶ After the tornado last week, some serious cracks have been found on the wall of the building.
Danny Russel [11:12 A.M.]	We have to take care of that immediately. However, what about the merchandise we keep in there? How will we empty it out for building repairs?
Seth Harper [11:13 A.M.]	Our summer shipment shouldn't arrive for another week, should it? Let's delay that one. In the meantime we should move what we have in the Olathe warehouse to another one nearby.
Gwen Connel [11:14 A.M.]	❷ In fact, the warehouse here in Belton is running low on inventory. ❸ Let's send their inventory here for now.
Sophie Taylor [11:15 A.M.]	Great. Seth, can you arrange for a few trucks to come here later today?
Danny Russel [11:16 A.M.]	❹ Wait, let's send them to the Gardner branch instead. ❺ We can save a lot of time and money we would have to spend on the road.
Seth Harper [11:17 A.M.]	I think it would actually be a lot cheaper. I'll arrange for the drivers and the trucks. Sophie, get your loading crew ready. ❻ Danny, can your evening crew receive the shipment?
Danny Russel [11:18 A.M.]	❼ That shouldn't be a big problem.

□ raise 〜を提起する・取り上げる □ tornado（陸上で発生する）竜巻 □ crack ひび割れ
□ take care of 〜に対処する □ immediately すぐに □ empty out 〜の中にあるものを出して空にする
□ in the meantime その間に □ nearby 近くにある □ run low on 〜が欠乏している □ inventory 在庫
□ branch 支店 □ instead 代わりに □ on the road（比較的長距離の）輸送で □ loading crew 積み込み作業者

★★★☆☆

18. What problem does Ms. Taylor want to address?

(A) She needs to find a new building.
(B) A shipment has been postponed.
(C) Structural damage needs to be fixed.
(D) A warehouse is too low on inventory.

Taylor さんが取り組みたい問題は何ですか。

(A) 新しい建物を探す必要がある。
(B) 配送が延期された。
(C) 構造的な損傷を修繕する必要がある。
(D) 倉庫の在庫が少なすぎる。

Taylor さんが取り組みたい問題について問われている。チャットの冒頭で、Taylor さんが「問題を取り上げたい」と切り出し、❶で「先週の竜巻の後、建物の壁に深刻な亀裂が見つかった」と言っているため、建物の深刻な亀裂についての問題に取り組みたいことがわかる。よって、"serious cracks（深刻な亀裂）" を structural damage と表現している **(C)** が正解。(D) は、在庫不足の倉庫もあるが、それは Connel さんの❷の発言であり、Taylor さんが取り組みたい内容とは異なるので不正解。

□ address（問題）に対応する □ postpone 〜を延期する □ structural 構造的な □ fix 〜を修理する

★★★☆☆

19. What most likely is Ms. Connel's position in the company?

(A) Chief financial officer
(B) Branch supply manager
(C) Transportation manager
(D) Customer service manager

Connel さんの会社での役職は何であると考えられますか。

(A) 財務の最高責任者
(B) 支店の供給責任者
(C) 輸送の責任者
(D) 顧客サービスの責任者

Connel さんの会社での役職はおそらく何かが問われている。Connel さんは❷・❸で「こちらの支店の倉庫では、在庫が少なくなってきているので、在庫を送るように」と提案している。ここから Connel さんは、ある支店の倉庫で働いていて、在庫管理に関わる仕事を行っていることが考えられる。以上から、正解は **(B)**。❷の "here" が、働いている場所を指している。

★★★★★

20. What does Mr. Russel suggest about the branch in Belton?

(A) It has fewer workers than the Gardner branch.
(B) It is not wide enough for the merchandise.
(C) It is located farther away from Olathe than the Gardner branch.
(D) It has much more inventory than the Gardner branch.

Russel さんは Belton の支店について何を示唆していますか。

(A) Gardner 支店よりも働き手が少ない。
(B) 商品のための十分な広さがない。
(C) Gardner 支店よりも Olath からかなり遠くにある。
(D) Gardner 支店よりもかなり多くの在庫がある。

Russel さんが Belton の支店について示唆していることが問われている。Russel さんは、Connel さんが Belton 支店の倉庫に在庫を送る提案をしたことを受け、❹・❺で「それより Gardner 支店に送ったほうが、運送に費やす時間とお金を大幅に節約できる」と述べている。ここから、Belton 支店よりも、Gardner 支店の方が Olathe 倉庫からの運送時間とコストが安い、つまり「Belton 支店は Gardner 支店よりも遠い距離にある」ということがわかる。以上から正解はそれを言い換えた **(C)**。❺の "spend on the road" が「輸送にかかる」という意味となるため、ここをしっかり読み取って解く必要がある。

 ☐ merchandise 商品　☐ farther far（離れて、遠い）の比較級　☐ inventory 在庫

21. At 11:18 A.M., what does Mr. Russel mean when he writes, "That shouldn't be a big problem"?

(A) Goods will be transferred to a neighboring branch.
(B) A warehouse will be sold to another company.
(C) A shipment will be canceled.
(D) A clearance sale will be held.

午前 11 時 18 分に、Russel さんは "That shouldn't be a big problem" という発言で、何を意味していますか。

(A) 商品は近隣の支店に移される。
(B) 倉庫は別の会社に売却される。
(C) 配送は取り消しとなる。
(D) 在庫一掃セールが行われる。

🔍 意図問題。問われている❼は「それは大きな問題にならないはずだ」という意味。この "that（それ）" は、❻の、Harper さんが配送の件で Russel さんに「そちらの夜の作業員は荷物を受け取ることができるか？」という質問を指している。❻の質問は、❹・❺の「Belton 支店より近隣の Gardner 支店に配送する方が時間とお金を節約できる」という提案を受けたことによるものである。以上より、これを表した **(A)** が正解となる。

✏️ ☐ goods 商品　☐ transfer A to B A を B に輸送する　☐ neighboring 近隣の　☐ clearance sale 在庫一掃セール

📝 **問題 18 から 21 は次のオンラインチャットの話し合いに関するものです。**

Sophie Taylor［午前 11 時 11 分］	Olathe の倉庫についての問題を取り上げたいと思います。先週の竜巻の後、建物の壁に深刻な亀裂が見つかりました。
Danny Russel［午前 11 時 12 分］	早急に対応しないといけませんが、保管されている商品についてはどうしますか？　建物の修繕のためにどうやって倉庫を空にしたらいいでしょう？
Seth Harper［午前 11 時 13 分］	夏の荷物が届くまで、あと一週間ありますよね。それを遅らせましょう。その間に Olathe の倉庫にあるものを近隣の倉庫に移動させなければなりません。
Gwen Connel［午前 11 時 14 分］	実は、ここ Belton の倉庫では、在庫が少なくなってきています。あちらの在庫をこちらに送りましょう。
Sophie Taylor［午前 11 時 15 分］	いいですね。Seth さん、今日この後に数台のトラックにここへ来てもらうよう手配をしてもらえますか？
Danny Russel［午前 11 時 16 分］	待ってください、それよりも Gardner 支店に送りましょう。運送に費やす時間とお金を大幅に節約できます。
Seth Harper［午前 11 時 17 分］	そのほうが、かなり安くなりそうですね。運転手とトラックの手配をします。Sophie さん、積み込み作業員への指示をお願いします。Danny さん、そちらの夜の作業員は荷物を受け取ることができますか？
Danny Russel［午前 11 時 18 分］	大きな問題ではないと思います。

For years, a number of scientists have been attempting to find out a more effective way to make materials to repel water. But some plants and animals have already resolved the problem. For example, when the rain drops on the particular wings of Cultex butterflies, the water forms into beads that roll right off, carrying dirt away in the process.

A group of scientists in North America has made a decision to follow the rules of science by focusing on a type of white-winged Cultex butterfly. Using a blend of waterproofing elements and other chemicals, Savannah Martin and her colleagues managed to create a material called Mogone whose color changes from white to black.

This kind of new material will be used to make useful coatings for clothing and fabric, building materials, and other kinds of goods used outdoors. The coating would be also environmentally harmlessness due to the fact that there would be no need for harsh chemical to dye it black or detergents to clean it.

22. According to the article, what is true about Cultex butterflies?

    (A) They are found only in North America.
    (B) They have waterproof wings.
    (C) They make chemicals used for medicine.
    (D) They live for an unusually long time.

23. The word "follow" in paragraph 2, line 1, is closest in meaning to

    (A) accompany
    (B) pursue
    (C) issue
    (D) adopt

24. What is NOT the material created by Savannah Martin used for?

    (A) Construction materials
    (B) Fabrics
    (C) Beverages
    (D) Outer walls of a building

25. Why would the traditional coating method most likely be environmentally harmful?

    (A) It is combined with water.
    (B) It doesn't include detergents.
    (C) It works faster than other similar dyes.
    (D) It uses poisonous coloring matters.

P. 588

Questions 22-25 refer to the following article.

For years, a number of scientists have been attempting to find out a more effective way to make materials to repel water. But some plants and animals have already resolved the problem. ❶ For example, when the rain drops on the particular wings of Cultex butterflies, the water forms into beads that roll right off, carrying dirt away in the process.

❷ A group of scientists in North America has made a decision to follow the rules of science by focusing on a type of white-winged Cultex butterfly. Using a blend of waterproofing elements and other chemicals, Savannah Martin and her colleagues managed to create a material called Mogone whose color changes from white to black.

❸ This kind of new material will be used to make useful coatings for clothing and fabric, building materials, and other kinds of goods used outdoors. ❹ The coating would be also environmentally harmlessness due to the fact that there would be no need for harsh chemical to dye it black or detergents to clean it.

☐ for years 何年もの間 ☐ a number of 複数の ☐ attempt ～を試みる ☐ effective 効果的な
☐ repel ～をはじく ☐ resolve ～を解決する ☐ form into ～を形成する ☐ bead 水滴 ☐ roll off 転がり落ちる
☐ carry away ～を運び去る ☐ dirt 汚れ ☐ decision 決定 ☐ focus on ～に焦点を当てる
☐ waterproofing 防水の ☐ elements 要素 ☐ chemicals 化学物質 ☐ useful 有用な ☐ coating コーティング
☐ fabric 布地 ☐ environmentally 環境的に ☐ harmlessness 無害の ☐ harsh 色や香りが強すぎる
☐ dye 染料 ☐ detergent 洗剤

★★★☆☆

22. According to the article, what is true about Cultex butterflies?

(A) They are found only in North America.
(B) They have waterproof wings.
(C) They make chemicals used for medicine.
(D) They live for an unusually long time.

記事によると、Cultex チョウについて正しいことは何ですか。

(A) 北米のみに生息している。
(B) 防水の羽を持っている。
(C) 薬に使う化学物質を作り出す。
(D) 異常に長い期間生きる。

記事から Cultex チョウについて正しいことを問う選択肢照合型の問題。❶で「Cultex チョウの特殊な羽に雨が落ちるとしずくとなって流れ落ち…」とあるため、このチョウの羽は防水仕様であることがわかる。よって、これを "waterproof" と言い換えた **(B)** が正解。(A) は研究自体は北米で行われたが、生息地域については研究していないため、ここでは不正解。

☐ for medicine 医薬用の

★★★★☆ 同義語問題

23. The word "follow" in paragraph 2, line 1, is closest in meaning to

(A) accompany
(B) pursue
(C) issue
(D) adopt

第 2 段落・1 行目にある "follow" に最も意味が近いのは

(A) ～に同行する
(B) ～を遂行する
(C) ～を刊行する
(D) ～を取り入れる

同義語問題。問われている語が含まれた❷を見ていくと、目的語が「科学の法則」となっている。follow には「～に従う、のっとる」という意味があるため、「科学の法則にのっとって（取り入れて）…」とすると文意が通る。よって、この語と同じ意味は **(D)** となる。

★★☆☆☆ NOT 問題

24. What is NOT the material created by Savannah Martin used for?

(A) Construction materials
(B) Fabrics
(C) Beverages
(D) Outer walls of a building

Savannah Martin 氏が作成した素材が使用できないものは何ですか。

(A) 建築資材
(B) 生地
(C) 飲料
(D) 建物の外壁

NOT 問題。Savannah Martin 氏が作成した素材が使用できない用途について問われている。❸に Martin 氏の新素材の用途が述べられており、「衣類や布地、建築資材やアウトドアで使用されるさまざまな製品のコーティングを作る際に利用」とある。よって、飲食物については言及がないため、**(C)** が正解。

☐ outer wall 外壁

25. Why would the traditional coating method most likely be environmentally harmful?

伝統的なコーティング手法が環境に有害なのはなぜですか。

(A) It is combined with water.
(B) It doesn't include detergents.
(C) It works faster than other similar dyes.
(D) It uses poisonous coloring matters.

(A) 水と組み合わされているため。
(B) 洗剤を含まないため。
(C) 他の同様の染料より早く効くため。
(D) 有毒な色素が使用されているため。

伝統的なコーティング手法が環境に有害なのはなぜかが問われている。❹で、新しい素材によるコーティング手法について触れられており、「黒く染めるための刺激の強い化学薬品やそれを洗浄するための洗剤が不要であるため、環境的にも無害であろう」と述べている。つまり、これまでは無害ではない染料を使用していたと考えられる。以上より、正解は **(D)**。

□ combined A with B AとBを結びつける　□ poisonous 有毒な　□ coloring matter 色素

問題 22 から 25 は次の記事に関するものです。

何年もの間、多くの科学者たちが水をはじく物質を作るための、より効果的な方法を見つけようと試みてきた。しかし、植物や動物の中にはその問題をすでに解決しているものがいる。例えば、Cultex チョウの特殊な羽に雨が落ちると水はしずくとなってすぐ流れ落ち、その過程で汚れも運び去る。

北米の科学者たちのグループは、その科学の法則にのっとり、白い羽を持つ Cultex チョウの一種に焦点を当てることにした。Savannah Martin 氏とその同僚は、防水の要素と他の化学物質を調合したものを使い、色が白から黒に変化する Mogone と呼ばれる素材を作り出すことに成功した。

このような新しい素材は衣類や布地、建築資材やアウトドアで使用されるさまざま製品の有用なコーティングを作る際に利用されるだろう。また、このコーティングは、黒く染めるための刺激の強い化学薬品やそれを洗浄するための洗剤が不要であるため、環境的にも無害であろう。

August 10—After one month of delays because of funding shortfalls and staffing issues, construction on the Musienko Bridge will finally start on August 17. The plan contains broadening the bridge to accommodate a bike lane, adding additional safety lighting, and reinforcing the structure with support beams. Construction is expected to last approximately two months, during which time the bridge will be closed. A detour route over Red Van Bridge has been planned, and the city will be waiving Red Van Bridge's usual $7.00 toll per vehicle during this time.

—[1]—. The plan is expected to cost over $80 million, with funds coming from the state, county, and city. —[2]—. But almost all taxpayers think that the money would be better spent elsewhere. —[3]—. So, drivers dealing with these issues on a daily basis regard these as a higher priority. —[4]—.

Courtney Brielle, the supervisor of the Transportation Department, thinks the plan is very important. She said at a press conference yesterday, "This is not just about convenience. This is about ensuring the safety of everyone on the road." She also said that the department would hire more inspectors over the coming months to identify potentially dangerous sites in the roadway system.

26. When is the plan expected to end?

    (A) In July
    (B) In August
    (C) In September
    (D) In October

27. What change will take place on Red Van Bridge?

    (A) Its structure will be strengthened.
    (B) No rate will be changed under the construction.
    (C) A lane for bikes will be added.
    (D) It will be enlarged.

28. What did Ms. Brielle do on August 9?

    (A) She set up a plan.
    (B) She checked a bridge.
    (C) She hired more employees.
    (D) She spoke to journalists.

29. In which of the positions marked [1], [2], [3], and [4] does the following sentence best belong?

"For instance, most city streets are in disrepair, with faded lane lines."

    (A) [1]
    (B) [2]
    (C) [3]
    (D) [4]

P. 594

Questions 26-29 refer to the following article.

August 10—After one month of delays because of funding shortfalls and staffing issues, ❶ construction on the Musienko Bridge will finally start on August 17. The plan contains broadening the bridge to accommodate a bike lane, adding additional safety lighting, and reinforcing the structure with support beams. ❷ Construction is expected to last approximately two months, during which time the bridge will be closed. ❸ A detour route over Red Van Bridge has been planned, and the city will be waiving Red Van Bridge's usual $7.00 toll per vehicle during this time.

—[1]—. The plan is expected to cost over $80 million, with funds coming from the state, county, and city. —[2]—. ❹ But almost all taxpayers think that the money would be better spent elsewhere. —[3]—. ❺ So, drivers dealing with these issues on a daily basis regard these as a higher priority. —[4]—.

❻ Courtney Brielle, the supervisor of the Transportation Department, thinks the plan is very important. ❼ She said at a press conference yesterday, "This is not just about convenience. This is about ensuring the safety of everyone on the road." She also said that the department would hire more inspectors over the coming months to identify potentially dangerous sites in the roadway system.

- [ ] funding shortfall 資金不足　[ ] staffing issue 人員問題　[ ] contain ~を含む　[ ] broaden ~を拡張する
- [ ] accommodate ~を収容する　[ ] bike lane 自転車専用道路　[ ] lighting 照明　[ ] reinforce ~を補強・強化する
- [ ] support beam 支持梁（はり ※建物の荷重を支える部材）　[ ] approximately 約　[ ] during which time その間
- [ ] detour route 迂回路　[ ] waive ~を免除する　[ ] toll 通行料金　[ ] county 郡　[ ] taxpayer 納税者
- [ ] deal with ~に対処する　[ ] on a daily basis 日常的に　[ ] regard A as B A を B とみなす
- [ ] Transportation Department 運輸省　[ ] press conference 記者会見　[ ] inspector 調査官
- [ ] identify ~を特定する　[ ] potentially 潜在的に　[ ] roadway system 道路網

★★★☆☆

26. When is the plan expected to end?

    (A) In July
    (B) In August
    (C) In September
    (D) In October

計画はいつ終了する予定ですか。

    (A) 7 月
    (B) 8 月
    (C) 9 月
    (D) 10 月

（工事）計画がいつ終わる予定かが問われている。第 1 段落の❶で「8 月 17 日に着工」、❷で「工事は約 2 カ月かかると見込まれている」とあるため、8 月から 2 カ月後の 10 月に終了する予定だとわかる。よって、正解は **(D)**。いつの時点から 2 カ月か、という情報をしっかり整理して解こう。

★★★★☆

27. What change will take place on Red Van Bridge?

    (A) Its structure will be strengthened.
    (B) No rate will be changed under the construction.
    (C) A lane for bikes will be added.
    (D) It will be enlarged.

Red Van Bridge に対して、どのような変更が行われますか。

    (A) 構造が強化される。
    (B) 工事期間中は通行料が掛からない。
    (C) 自転車のための車線が追加される。
    (D) 拡張される。

Red Van Bridge の変更内容が問われている。❷・❸で「この橋は工事期間中の迂回ルートとして使われ、市は Red Van Bridge の通常の通行料を免除する」とある。ここから、工事期間中は通行料が掛からないことがわかるため、これを言い換えた **(B)** が正解。(C) は Musienko Bridge のことなので不正解。

□ strengthen ～を強化する　□ construction 工事　□ enlarge ～を拡張する

★★★☆☆

28. What did Ms. Brielle do on August 9?

    (A) She set up a plan.
    (B) She checked a bridge.
    (C) She hired more employees.
    (D) She spoke to journalists.

Brielle さんが 8 月 9 日に行ったことは何ですか。

    (A) 計画を立てた。
    (B) 橋を点検した。
    (C) より多くの従業員を雇った。
    (D) 記者に話をした。

Brielle さんが 8 月 9 日に行ったことが問われている。❻・❼で「Brielle さんは運輸省の責任者で、昨日記者会見を行った」という内容が述べられている。この記事は 8 月 10 日に書かれたものなので、Brielle さんが記者会見を開いたのは前日の 8 月 9 日だとわかる。よって、"press conference（記者会見）" を spoke to journalists と言い換えた **(D)** が正解となる。

□ set up（計画等）を立てる

29. In which of the positions marked [1], [2], [3], and [4] does the following sentence best belong?

"For instance, most city streets are in disrepair, with faded lane lines."

(A) [1]
(B) [2]
(C) [3]
(D) [4]

次の文は [1]、[2]、[3]、[4] のどの位置に最もよく当てはまりますか。

「例えば、市内のほとんどの道は線の色が薄くなっているなど、荒れた状態にある」

(A) [1]
(B) [2]
(C) [3]
(D) [4]

適切な文の位置を求める問題。問われている文は「例えば、市内のほとんどの道は線の色が薄くなっているなど、荒れた状態にある」という意味。この「例えば」から、例を挙げるきっかけとなった内容がこれよりも前に書かれていると考えられる。❹に、「しかし、ほぼすべての納税者は、お金を他のことに使った方がよいと考えている」とあり、❺で「したがって、日常的にこれらの問題に対処しているドライバーたちは、こちらが優先だと考えている」とある。つまり、予定している工事計画よりも、道の線の色の補修などが優先だということを示唆しており、❹の意見→具体例→その具体例の方が優先だ、という主張となり、文意に合う。よって、正解は **(C)** となる。

☐ for instance 例えば　☐ in disrepair 荒れた状態である　☐ faded 消えかかった　☐ lane line 道路上の線

📝 **問題 26 から 29 は次の記事に関するものです。**

8 月 10 日 ― 資金不足と人員配置の問題により 11 カ月遅れていた Musienko Bridge の工事が 8 月 17 日にようやく開始される。この計画には、拡張による自転車専用道路の設置、安全照明の追加、支持梁による構造の補強が盛り込まれている。工事は約 2 カ月かかると見込まれ、期間中、橋は閉鎖となる。Red Van Bridge を通る迂回ルートが計画されており、この間、市は Red Van Bridge の通常の通行料 1 車両あたり 7 ドルを免除する。

―[1]―計画には 8 千万ドル以上の費用が掛かると予想され、資金は州、郡、市が拠出する。―[2]―しかし、ほぼすべての納税者は、お金を他のことに使った方がよいと考えている。―[3]―例えば、市内のほとんどの道は線の色が薄くなっているなど、荒れた状態にある。したがって、日常的にこれらの問題に対処しているドライバーたちは、優先順位の高い問題はこちらのほうであると考えている。―[4]―

運輸省の責任者である Courtney Brielle さんは、計画がとても重要であると考えている。昨日の記者会見では「これは利便性だけに関わることではありません。これは道路上でのすべての人の安全を確保するということなのです。」と述べた。また、省は道路網において潜在的に危険な場所を特定するために、今後数カ月にわたり、より多くの検査員を雇うとも述べた。

GO ON TO THE NEXT PAGE!

EXCELLENT COOKGUIDE
P.O. Box 3124, Richmond, VA 31240

Customer Service
[616] 442-4124 (phone)
mustcare@excelcookingguide.org (e-mail)

Invoice: #00214587
Order Date: November 6
Shipping Date: November 7

Payments and Returns To: Excellent Cookguide
P.O. Box 3124, Richmond, VA 31240

Deliver To: Jack Doson
15478 Wilson St, 3124, Denton, TX 45785

Carrier: ACL Ground Residential
Other Information: #305-545-7854 (phone)

Dear Mr. Doson,
Thank you very much for placing an order with Excellent Cookguide. Please check the order sheet. You have a special discount as our author. If you have any queries, or would like to track the status of your order, do not hesitate to contact us by phone or e-mail. Please visit our Web site at www.excelcookguide.org for our newest products!

QUANTITY of ORDERING	SUBJECT	COST per book	Discount	Total PRICE
14	Garden Fresh Cook	$40.00	50.00%	$280.00
16	Garden Fresh Cook	$26.00	50.00%	$208.00
1	Great Pancakes	$38.00		$38.00

Sub Total	$526.00
Delivery	$14.05
Tax	$16.97
Amount Due	$557.02

To: Customer Service <mustcare@excelcookingguide.org>
From: Jack Doson <jackdoson_cook@tmail.com>
Date: November 8
Subject: Book condition

To Whom It May Concern,

On 6 November, I sent my purchase order to you through an e-mail for both 14 hardback and 16 paperback copies of my own book, *Garden Fresh Cook*, plus one paperback copy of *Great Pancakes* by Thomas Mark. I received them yesterday but I was very disappointed due to the fact that almost all of my books were in bad condition. I ordered new books, but those you sent to me were poorer than used copies I have seen. The book's jackets on the hardbacks were tattered and had a couple of scratches, and the edges were dented. Some of the paperbacks were greatly damaged. I had ordered my works to give as holiday presents, yet I can't give the books in poor condition. I would like to receive new and high quality copies quickly. Moreover, with concern to the book written by Mr. Mark, which is distributed by your firm, I think that I should be able to receive a 20% discount on it.

I ask you to contact me as soon as possible through e-mail or phone at [905] 857-8547. I expect to hear from you soon.

Jack Doson

---

30. Which of the following is NOT mentioned in the invoice?

(A) When the delivery will arrive
(B) Who delivers the books
(C) Where to be returned
(D) What the orderer should confirm

31. How many paperback books did Mr. Doson order?

(A) 14
(B) 16
(C) 17
(D) 31

32. Why did Mr. Doson order the books from Excellent Cookguide?

(A) To give them as gifts
(B) To cook a dish for the holidays
(C) To compensate for sales
(D) To learn how to make pancakes

33. According to the e-mail, what does Mr. Doson request in connection with *Great Pancakes*?

(A) New and good quality copies
(B) A full refund
(C) Gift wrapping for Mr. Mark
(D) An author's discount

34. What will most likely Excellent Cookguide do next?

(A) Complain to the transporter
(B) Deposit money into Mr. Doson's account
(C) Get in touch with Mr. Doson
(D) Ask Mr. Doson to order again

Double

P. 600

Questions 30-34 refer to the following invoice and e-mail.

EXCELLENT COOKGUIDE
P.O. Box 3124, Richmond, VA 31240

Customer Service
[616] 442-4124 (phone)
mustcare@excelcookingguide.org (e-mail)

Invoice: #00214587
Order Date: November 6
Shipping Date: November 7

❶ Payments and Returns To: Excellent Cookguide
P.O. Box 3124, Richmond, VA 31240

Deliver To: Jack Doson
15478 Wilson St, 3124, Denton, TX 45785

❷ Carrier: ACL Ground Residential
Other Information: #305-545-7854 (phone)

Dear Mr. Doson,
Thank you very much for placing an order with Excellent Cookguide. ❸ Please check the order sheet. You have a special discount as our author. If you have any queries, or would like to track the status of your order, do not hesitate to contact us by phone or e-mail. Please visit our Web site at www.excelcookguide.org for our newest products!

❹ QUANTITY of ORDERING		SUBJECT	COST per book	Discount	Total PRICE
14		Garden Fresh Cook	$40.00	50.00%	$280.00
16		Garden Fresh Cook	$26.00	50.00%	$208.00
1		Great Pancakes	$38.00		$38.00

Sub Total	$526.00
Delivery	$14.05
Tax	$16.97
Amount Due	$557.02

To: Customer Service <mustcare@excelcookingguide.org>
From: Jack Doson <jackdoson_cook@tmail.com>
Date: November 8
Subject: Book condition

To Whom It May Concern,

On 6 November, ❺ I sent my purchase order to you through an e-mail for both 14 hardback and 16 paperback copies of my own book, *Garden Fresh Cook*, plus one paperback copy of *Great Pancakes* by Thomas Mark. I received them yesterday but I was very disappointed due to the fact that almost all of my books were in bad condition. I ordered new books, but those you sent to me were poorer than used copies I have seen. The book's jackets on the hardbacks were tattered and had a couple of scratches, and the edges were dented. Some of the paperbacks were greatly damaged. ❻ I had ordered my works to give as holiday presents, yet I can't give the books in poor condition. I would like to receive new and high quality copies quickly. ❼ Moreover, with concern to the book written by Mr. Mark, which is distributed by your firm, I think that I should be able to receive a 20% discount on it.

❽ I ask you to contact me as soon as possible through e-mail or phone at [905] 857-8547. I expect to hear from you soon.

Jack Doson

請求書
☐ P.O. Box（= Post Office BOX）私書箱　☐ place an order 注文する　☐ query 問い合わせ
☐ track ～を追跡する　☐ status 状況　☐ sub total 小計　☐ amount due 支払合計

Ｅメール
☐ To Whom It May Concern ご担当者様宛　☐ hardback ハードカバー、堅表紙の
☐ paperback ペーパーバック、紙表紙の　☐ due to ～により　☐ the fact that SV S が V であるという事実
☐ in bad condition 悪い状態で　☐ scratch ひっかき傷　☐ edge 端部　☐ dented へこんでいる
☐ high quality 高品質の　☐ moreover さらに　☐ with concern to ～への懸念とともに
☐ distribute ～を発行する　☐ firm 会社

★★★☆☆ NOT 問題

30. Which of the following is NOT mentioned in the invoice?

(A) When the delivery will arrive
(B) Who delivers the books
(C) Where to be returned
(D) What the orderer should confirm

請求書に記載されていないことは次のうちどれですか。

(A) 配送物の到着日
(B) 本の配達業者
(C) 返品先
(D) 注文者が確認する事項

NOT 問題。請求書に記載されていないことは何かが問われている。❶の返品先が (C) に、❷の配達業者が (B) に、❸の注文者の確認事項が (D) にそれぞれ該当する。残った (A) が記載されていないため、これが正解。

☐ confirm ～を確認する

★★★★☆ クロスリファレンス問題

31. How many paperback books did Mr. Doson order?

(A) 14
(B) 16
(C) 17
(D) 31

Doson さんはペーパーバックの本を何冊注文しましたか。

(A) 14
(B) 16
(C) 17
(D) 31

Doson さんがペーパーバックの本を何冊注文したかが問われている。まず 1 文書目の請求書を読むと、❹から 14 冊、16 冊、1 冊と合計 31 冊を注文したことがわかる。次に 2 文書目のＥメールを読むと、❺に「Garden Fresh Cook のハードカバー 14 冊とペーパーバック 16 冊、Thomas Mark さんの書いた Great Pancakes のペーパーバック 1 冊の注文」とある。よって、ペーパーバック本は、16+1＝17 冊注文したことがわかるため、正解は **(C)** となる。このように、簡単な計算問題も時折出てくることがあるので、情報を整理して読み解くようにしよう。

★★☆☆☆

32. Why did Mr. Doson order the books from Excellent Cookguide?

(A) To give them as gifts
(B) To cook a dish for the holidays
(C) To compensate for sales
(D) To learn how to make pancakes

Doson さんはなぜ Excellent Cookguide に本を注文しましたか。

(A) 贈り物とするため
(B) 年末年始の料理を作るため
(C) 売り上げを補填するため
(D) パンケーキの作り方を知るため

Doson さんが Excellent Cookguide に本を注文した理由が問われている。2 文書目のＥメールの❻で、Doson さんは「私の著書は年末年始の贈り物として注文した」と述べている。よって、プレゼント用であることがわかるため、正解は "holiday presents" を gifts と言い換えた **(A)** となる。

☐ dish 料理　☐ compensate for ～を補償する

★★★☆☆

33. According to the e-mail, what does Mr. Doson request in connection with *Great Pancakes*?

(A) New and good quality copies
(B) A full refund
(C) Gift wrapping for Mr. Mark
(D) An author's discount

Ｅメールによると、Doson さんは *Great Pancakes* に関して何を求めていますか。

(A) 新品で質の良い本
(B) 全額返金
(C) Mark さんのためのギフト包装
(D) 著者割引

 Ｅメールから Doson さんが Great Pancakes に求めていることが問われている。Ｅメールで Doson さんは注文した本が傷んでいたことに触れ、❼では、「御社が発行している著作物については割引をしてもらえるはずだ」と主張している。以上から、正解は **(D)**。

 □ full refund 全額払い戻し　□ wrapping 包装

. . . .

★★★★☆

34. What will most likely Excellent Cookguide do next?

(A) Complain to the transporter
(B) Deposit money into Mr. Doson's account
(C) Get in touch with Mr. Doson
(D) Ask Mr. Doson to order again

Excellent Cookguide 社は次に何をすると考えられますか。

(A) 運送会社に抗議する
(B) Doson さんの口座にお金を入金する
(C) Doson さんに連絡をする
(D) Doson さんに再注文をお願いする

Excellent Cookguide 社は次に何をすると考えられるかが問われている。Doson さんはＥメールの締めくくりの❽で「Ｅメールか電話で、できるだけ早く連絡がほしい」と述べていることから、この後、Excellent Cookguide 社は Donson さんにＥメールか電話で連絡を取ることが考えられる。以上より、正解は "contact" を get in touch と表現した **(C)** が正解。

□ deposit 〜を入金する　□ get in touch 連絡を取る

EXCELLENT COOKGUIDE
私書箱 3124、リッチモンド、バージニア州 31240

カスタマーサービス
［616］442-4124（電話）
mustcare@excelcookingguide.org（E メール）

請求書：#00214587
注文日：11 月 6 日
発送日：11 月 7 日

支払い先・返品先：Excellent Cookguide
私書箱 3124、リッチモンド、バージニア州 31240

配送先：Jack Doson
15478 Wilson St 3124 デントン、テキサス州 45785

宅配業者：ACL Ground Residential
その他の情報：305-545-7854（電話）

Doson 様
Excellent Cookguide にご注文いただき誠にありがとうございます。注文票をご確認ください。著者の方には特別割引がございます。ご質問がある場合やご注文状況を確認したい場合は、お気軽にお電話または E メールにてお問い合わせください。当社の最新の商品については、ウェブサイト www.excelcookguide.org をご覧ください！

注文数	タイトル	1 冊の値段	割引率	合計額
14	Garden Fresh Cook	40.00 ドル	50.00 パーセント	280.00 ドル
16	Garden Fresh Cook	26.00 ドル	50.00 パーセント	208.00 ドル
1	Great Pancakes	38.00 ドル		38.00 ドル

小計	526.00 ドル
配送料	14.05 ドル
税金	16.97 ドル
合計額	557.02 ドル

受信者： カスタマーサービス〈mustcare@excelcookingguide.org〉
送信者： Jack Doson〈jackdoson_cook@tmail.com〉
日付： 11 月 8 日
件名： 本の状態

ご担当者様

11 月 6 日に私の著書 *Garden Fresh Cook* のハードカバー 14 冊とペーパーバック 16 冊、Thomas Mark さんの書いた *Great Pancakes* のペーパーバック 1 冊の注文票を E メールでお送りしました。昨日配達を受け取りましたが、拙著はほとんどすべての状態が悪かったため、とても残念でした。新品を注文しましたが、送られてきた本は私が見たことのある中古品よりも劣っていました。ハードカバーの本のカバーはボロボロでいくつかの傷があり、縁はへこんでいました。ペーパーバックの何冊かには、大きくて明らかな損傷がありました。私の著書は年末年始の贈り物として注文しましたが、このような状態の本を贈ることはできません。品質の良い新品の本をすぐに送っていただきたいです。また、御社が発行している Mark さんの本については、20 パーセントの割引をしていただけるはずです。

E メールかお電話［905］857-8547 にて、できるだけ早くご連絡ください。お返事をお待ちしております。

Jack Doson

Questions 35-39 refer to the following e-mails.

⏱ 5分00秒

To: Sam Webber <swebber@HM-Intl.com>
From: Michael Palma <palma@HM-Intl.com>
Date: March 4
Subject: Recommendations

Dear Sam,

I heard from your secretary that you will not come back until next month. However, I hope you see this e-mail and can help me.

I'm leaving on a business trip to the capital of Malaysia next week and am hoping you can offer me some general advice on doing business there. I know that much of your work takes you throughout Asia; therefore, any guidance you can offer will be a great help to me. Because this is the first trip I have taken as the sales manager, I'm especially eager for it to be a success.

Good luck with your business discussions. I trust they're going as well as you had hoped.

Take care, and see you soon.

Michael Palma

To: Michael Palma <palma@HM-Intl.com>
From: Sam Webber <swebber@HM-Intl.com>
Date: March 5
Subject: RE> Recommendations

Dear Michael,

It's my great pleasure to help you. I assume you are planning to do a little research on Malaysia before you go. When you arrive, you should try to visit a few places of cultural and historical interest. This will allow you to engage in some enjoyable discussions with your business partners.

Traffic could be a big problem in the capital city, Kuala Lumpur; you should consider this as it is important to arrive on time for appointments. Once your negotiations begin, be prepared to enter into them with a spirit of give-and-take. Perhaps figure out with your supervisor beforehand what kinds of compromises you should be willing to make.

The negotiations with our Swiss colleagues are going well so far, but we're right in the middle of this project, so I'm not counting on anything yet. We still have a lot of work to do before the deal is complete.

Have a great trip. See you at the next staff meeting at our headquarters in Los Angeles.

Sam Webber

35. Why does Mr. Palma write the first e-mail?

(A) To ask about business practices in Switzerland
(B) To discuss tourist attractions in Kuala Lumpur
(C) To ask a colleague about a business meeting in Asia
(D) To request advice about a business trip to Malaysia

36. What is true about Mr. Palma?

(A) He will move to another country in Asia next month.
(B) He has taken on a new position.
(C) He has visited Malaysia several times.
(D) He has just been introduced to Mr. Webber.

37. Which of the following is NOT Mr. Webber's suggestions?

(A) Visit some cultural and historical sites
(B) Be on time for business meetings
(C) Begin business discussions about sales figures
(D) Be flexible in business negotiations

38. In the second e-mail, the phrase "counting on" in paragraph 3, line 2, is closest in meaning to

(A) being certain of
(B) adding up
(C) traveling
(D) keeping records of

39. What will most likely happen in April?

(A) Mr. Palma will meet with Mr. Webber in Kuala Lumpur.
(B) Mr. Palma will leave on a business trip to Switzerland.
(C) Mr. Webber will accomplish a project with Swiss colleagues.
(D) Mr. Webber will help Mr. Palma at Kuala Lumpur.

Double

 P. 606

Questions 35-39 refer to the following e-mails.

Eメール（1）

To: Sam Webber <swebber@HM-Intl.com>
From: Michael Palma <palma@HM-Intl.com>
Date: ❶ March 4
Subject: ❷ Recommendations

Dear Sam,

❸ I heard from your secretary that you will not come back until next month. However, I hope you see this e-mail and can help me.

❹ I'm leaving on a business trip to the capital of Malaysia next week and am hoping you can offer me some general advice on doing business there. I know that much of your work takes you throughout Asia; therefore, any guidance you can offer will be a great help to me. ❺ Because this is the first trip I have taken as the sales manager, I'm especially eager for it to be a success.

Good luck with your business discussions. I trust they're going as well as you had hoped.

Take care, and see you soon.

Michael Palma

Eメール（2）

To: Michael Palma <palma@HM-Intl.com>
From: Sam Webber <swebber@HM-Intl.com>
Date: March 5
Subject: RE> Recommendations

Dear Michael,

It's my great pleasure to help you. I assume you are planning to do a little research on Malaysia before you go. ❻ When you arrive, you should try to visit a few places of cultural and historical interest. This will allow you to engage in some enjoyable discussions with your business partners.

❼ Traffic could be a big problem in the capital city, Kuala Lumpur; you should consider this as it is important to arrive on time for appointments. ❽ Once your negotiations begin, be prepared to enter into them with a spirit of give-and-take. Perhaps figure out with your supervisor beforehand what kinds of compromises you should be willing to make.

❾ The negotiations with our Swiss colleagues are going well so far, but we're right in the middle of this project, so I'm not counting on anything yet. ❿ We still have a lot of work to do before the deal is complete.

Have a great trip. See you at the next staff meeting at our headquarters in Los Angeles.

Sam Webber

E メール（1）
☐ capital 首都　☐ advice on ～に関する助言　☐ guidance 指針、助言　☐ eager 熱望している

E メール（2）
☐ assume ～と思っている　☐ cultural and historical interest 文化的・歴史的に興味深い場所、観光地
☐ engage in ～に従事・没頭する　☐ enjoyable 楽しめる　☐ negotiation 交渉事
☐ enter into ～と始める、～に参入する　☐ with a spirit of ～に精神で
☐ give-and-take ギブアンドテイク（互いに与え合う）　☐ figure out 考えだしておく　☐ beforehand 事前に
☐ compromise 妥協（点）　☐ be willing to do ～しようとする　☐ go well うまくいく
☐ so far これまでのところ　☐ in the middle of ～の最中である　☐ count on ～を予想・期待する
☐ deal 取引　☐ headquarters 本社

★★★★☆

35. Why does Mr. Palma write the first e-mail?

(A) To ask about business practices in Switzerland
(B) To discuss tourist attractions in Kuala Lumpur
(C) To ask a colleague about a business meeting in Asia
(D) To request advice about a business trip to Malaysia

Palma さんはなぜ 1 通目の E メールを書いていますか。

(A) スイスの商習慣について尋ねるため
(B) クアラルンプールの観光名所について話し合うため
(C) アジアでの商談について同僚に尋ねるため
(D) マレーシアへの出張に際し助言を求めるため

Palma さんはなぜ 1 通目の E メールを書いたのかが問われている。Palma さんは 1 文書目の E メール（1）の❷で「助言」という件名で E メールを書き、❹で「来週、マレーシアの首都に出張するので、ビジネスの一般的な助言がほしい」と依頼している。ここから **(D)** が正解だとわかる。(B) を選んだ人がいるかもしれないが、これは 2 文書目の E メール（2）で Webber さんが切り出したもので、E メール（1）には観光名所については言及がないため、不正解。

★★★☆☆

36. What is true about Mr. Palma?

(A) He will move to another country in Asia next month.
(B) He has taken on a new position.
(C) He has visited Malaysia several times.
(D) He has just been introduced to Mr. Webber.

Palma さんについて正しいことは何ですか。

(A) 来月、アジアの他の国に引っ越す。
(B) 新しい役職に就いたばかりである。
(C) マレーシアを何度か訪れたことがある。
(D) Webber さんに紹介されたばかりである。

Palma さんについて正しいことを問う選択肢照合型の問題。Palma さんは❺で「営業部長として初めての出張」と述べている。ここから、新たな役職に就いたということがわかるので、これを現在完了形で示した **(B)** が正解。

☐ position 役職　☐ take on ～の業務を行う、～の役職に就く

37. Which of the following is NOT Mr. Webber's suggestions?

(A) Visit some cultural and historical sites
(B) Be on time for business meetings
(C) Begin business discussions about sales figures
(D) Be flexible in business negotiations

Webber さんの提案ではないものは次のどれですか。

(A) 文化的・歴史的な場所を訪れる
(B) 商談には遅れない
(C) 売上高について商談を開始する
(D) 商談に柔軟に対応する

NOT 問題。Webber さんの提案でないものが問われている。2 文書目の Webber さんが書いた E メール（2）を見ると、❻の「文化的・歴史的に興味深い場所を訪れる」が (A) に、❼の「道路状況を考慮して約束の時間に間に合うように着く」が (B) に、❽の「交渉が始まれば、ギブアンドテイクの精神で臨む」が (D) に、それぞれ言い換えられている。よって、残った **(C)** が正解。売上高に関しては本文には記載がない。

🖊 ☐ sales figures 売上高　☐ be flexible 柔軟に対応する

★★★☆☆ 同義語問題

38. In the second e-mail, the phrase "counting on" in paragraph 3, line 2, is closest in meaning to

(A) being certain of
(B) adding up
(C) traveling
(D) keeping records of

2 通目の E メールの、第 3 段落・2 行目にある "counting on" に最も意味が近いのは

(A) ～について確かである
(B) ～を合計する
(C) 旅行をする
(D) ～を資料として保管する

同義語問題。問われている箇所は❾の後半部分で、"I'm not counting on anything yet（まだ何も予期していない）" という意味。つまり、「確かなことは何もない」ということがわかる。"count on" は「～をあてにする、頼りにする」という意味の他に、「～を予期する・期待する」という意味もある。今回は後者のニュアンスで使われている。よって、同じ意味となるのは **(A)**。

★★★★☆

39. What will most likely happen in April?

(A) Mr. Palma will meet with Mr. Webber in Kuala Lumpur.
(B) Mr. Palma will leave on a business trip to Switzerland.
(C) Mr. Webber will accomplish a project with Swiss colleagues.
(D) Mr. Webber will help Mr. Palma at Kuala Lumpur.

4 月に何が起こると考えられますか。

(A) Palma さんがクアラルンプールで Webber さんに会う。
(B) Palma さんがスイスに出張に行く。
(C) Webber さんがスイスの同僚たちとプロジェクトを成し遂げる。
(D) Webber さんがクアラルンプールで Palma さんを手伝う。

4 月に何が起こると考えられるかが問われている。まず、1 文書目の E メール（1）の❶・❸から、Webber さんは来月まで出張から戻らない、つまり、メールを出した 3 月の時点から来月（＝4 月）までは忙しい、ということがわかる。次に 2 文書目の E メール（2）の❾・❿を読むと、Webber さんは「スイスの同僚との交渉を行い、プロジェクトが真っ最中で、まだすべきことがたくさんある」と述べている。よって、4 月に出張から戻るまでにプロジェクトを完成させている、ということが予想されるので、これを未来形で表現した **(C)** が正解となる。

🖊 ☐ accomplish ～を達成する

E メール（1）

受信者：	Sam Webber <swebber@HM-Intl.com>
送信者：	Michael Palma <palma@HM-Intl.com>
日付：	3 月 4 日
件名：	助言

Sam さん

あなたの秘書から、あなたが来月になるまで戻ってこないとお聞きしました。しかし、この E メールを見て力を貸していただければ幸いです。

来週、マレーシアの首都に出張するのですが、そこでビジネスをするうえでの一般的な助言をいただけないでしょうか。Sam さんがお仕事でアジア中を回られていることについては知っていますので、提供していただけるどんな助言も私にとって大変役立ちます。今回は営業部長として初めての出張ですので、特に成功させたいと思っています。

Sam さんの商談がうまく行くことを願っています。Sam さんの期待どおりにうまく行きますよ。

よろしくお願いいたします。では、また。

Michael Palma

E メール（2）

受信者：	Michael Palma <palma@HM-Intl.com>
送信者：	Sam Webber <swebber@HM-Intl.com>
日付：	3 月 5 日
件名：	RE ＞助言

Michael さん

あなたのお役に立てて大変光栄です。出発の前にマレーシアのことを少し調べるつもりでいらっしゃるようですね。到着したら、文化的・歴史的に興味深い場所をいくつか訪れることをお勧めします。それでビジネスパートナーたちと楽しい議論ができるようになるでしょう。

首都のクアラルンプールでは交通渋滞が大きな問題となることがありますので、約束の時間に間に合うように、そのことを考慮すべきですね。交渉が始まったら、ギブアンドテイクの精神で臨むようにしてください。妥協できることについて事前に上司と話し合っておくほうがよいでしょう。

スイスの同僚との交渉は今のところ順調に進んでいますが、プロジェクトの真っ只中ですので、まだ何が起こるかわかりません。取り決めが完了するまでに、まだすべきことがたくさんあります。

良い旅を。次回のロサンゼルス本社でのスタッフ会議で会いましょう。

Sam Webber

Questions 40-44 refer to the following Web page and e-mails.

◯ 5分30秒

◀ ▶ | http://www.globalairlinershow.org/home | ▶

| HOME | ABOUT | PROGRAM | REGISTRATION |

GLOBAL AIRLINER SHOW
2020
In Las Vegas

It is certain that the show of the year will offer an educational and beneficial experience. Now in its eighth year, the Global Airliner Show (GAS) offers one of the largest displays of airliner technology internationally. Over 30 presenters have been added since last year, and we have an array of special events planned including:

▶ Presentation on the challenges of 21-century flying presented by famous pilot and best-selling writer Jeff Carroway
▶ The GAS Student Program, including workshops and small-group discussions
▶ Guided tour of the closest international airport
▶ Demonstration of digital airliner producing software by Trumarkia and other industry specialists

The Passenger Favorite Awards ceremony will be held again this year. Please look forward to seeing which company will win the glory.

Visit our **program page** for more details.

To: Keiran Vega
From: Liang Zhang
Subject: Update
Date: October 7

Dear Mr. Vega,

I had a great time at GAS.

I spent the whole afternoon in a workshop using digital airliner producing software. It was wonderful, and I think that the experience will make a very interesting future article.

Unfortunately, I didn't get a chance to hear Mr. Carroway yesterday. So, I spent the day touring the airport and talking to vendors. However, I did get an opportunity to interview students about the new software, and I also went to one of their small-group discussions.

The winner of this year's Passenger Favorite Awards is a very smart airliner maker from Toronto. His story would definitely engage our print audience, and it could possibly end up being a front page article. I am meeting with him later this evening to interview, and I will send you a draft of the article by tomorrow morning.

Truly,

Liang Zhang

To: Brian Hoffbauer
From: Liang Zhang
Subject: Photographs
Date: October 8

Dear Mr. Hoffbauer,

Thank you for taking the time to talk with me last night. I enjoyed it a great deal.

I e-mailed the article to my president, Keiran Vega. He liked it and made a special request. So I was hoping we could get together again for a few minutes to take some photos before you leave the show. I want to make sure that I have a few good pictures to go with the article.

Best Regards,

Liang Zhang

40. What is true about GAS?

(A) It is designed for new buyers to the industry.
(B) It has extended the duration of events.
(C) It has increased the number of its speakers.
(D) It takes place in a different state each year.

41. Who most likely is Mr. Zhang?

(A) A reporter
(B) An organizer of GAS
(C) A presenter
(D) An engineer

42. Which of the following didn't Mr. Zhang participate in?

(A) An airport tour
(B) A small-group discussion
(C) A software demonstration
(D) A presentation by a well-known author

43. What did Mr. Vega most likely ask Mr. Zhang to do?

(A) Send Mr. Zhang's article to GAS
(B) Take a picture of Mr. Hoffbauer
(C) Review Mr. Vega's e-mail
(D) Try digital airliner producing software

44. What can be inferred about Mr. Hoffbauer?

(A) He is a well-known photographer.
(B) He met Mr. Zhang in Toronto.
(C) He was a presenter at the award ceremony.
(D) He received a prize.

Triple

P. 612

Questions 40-44 refer to the following Web page and e-mails.

◀ ▶   http://www.globalairlinershow.org/home   ▶

| HOME | ABOUT | PROGRAM | REGISTRATION |

GLOBAL AIRLINER SHOW
2020
In Las Vegas

It is certain that the show of the year will offer an educational and beneficial experience. Now in its eighth year, the Global Airliner Show (GAS) offers one of the largest displays of airliner technology internationally. ❶ Over 30 presenters have been added since last year, and we have an array of special events planned including:

▶ ❷ Presentation on the challenges of 21-century flying presented by famous pilot and best-selling writer Jeff Carroway
▶ The GAS Student Program, including workshops and small-group discussions
▶ Guided tour of the closest international airport
▶ Demonstration of digital airliner producing software by Trumarkia and other industry specialists

The Passenger Favorite Awards ceremony will be held again this year. Please look forward to seeing which company will win the glory.

Visit our **program page** for more details.

Eメール（1）

To: Keiran Vega
From: Liang Zhang
Subject: Update
Date: October 7

Dear Mr. Vega,

I had a great time at GAS.

I spent the whole afternoon in a workshop using digital airliner producing software. It was wonderful, and I think that the experience will make a very interesting future article.

❸ Unfortunately, I didn't get a chance to hear Mr. Carroway yesterday. So, I spent the day touring the airport and talking to vendors. ❹ However, I did get an opportunity to interview students about the new software, and I also went to one of their small-group discussions.

The winner of this year's Passenger Favorite Awards is a very smart airliner maker from Toronto. ❺ His story would definitely engage our print audience, and it could possibly end up being a front page article. ❻ I am meeting with him later this evening to interview, and I will send you a draft of the article by tomorrow morning.

Truly,

Liang Zhang

Eメール（2）

To: Brian Hoffbauer
From: Liang Zhang
Subject: Photographs
Date: October 8

Dear Mr. Hoffbauer,

❼ Thank you for taking the time to talk with me last night. I enjoyed it a great deal.

I e-mailed the article to my president, Keiran Vega. ❽ He liked it and made a special request. ❾ So I was hoping we could get together again for a few minutes to take some photos before you leave the show. I want to make sure that I have a few good pictures to go with the article.

Best Regards,

Liang Zhang

ウェブページ
☐ certain 明らかである　☐ educational 教育的な　☐ beneficial 有益な　☐ airliner 旅客機
☐ an array of 多様な〜　☐ including 〜を含めて　☐ best-selling writer ベストセラー作家の　☐ workshop 研修
☐ small-group 小人数の　☐ guided ガイド付きの　☐ closest 最寄りの　☐ demonstration 実演
☐ ceremony 式典

Eメール（1）
☐ whole 全体、まるまる　☐ vendor 販売業者　☐ opportunity 機会　☐ definitely 間違いなく
☐ engage 〜を魅了する　☐ end up *do*ing 最終的に〜する　☐ draft ドラフト、草稿

Eメール（2）
☐ take the time to *do* 時間を取って〜する

★★★☆☆

40. What is true about GAS?

(A) It is designed for new buyers to the industry.
(B) It has extended the duration of events.
(C) It has increased the number of its speakers.
(D) It takes place in a different state each year.

GAS について正しいことは何ですか。

(A) 業界の新しいバイヤー向けに構想されている。
(B) イベントの期間を延長した。
(C) 発表者の数を増やした。
(D) 毎年違う州で行われている。

GAS について正しいことは何かを問う選択肢照合型の問題。1 文書目のウェブページの❶で、「昨年より30 人以上の発表者が追加された」とあることから、これを increase the number of its speakers と言い換えた **(C)** が正解。(A) 新バイヤー向けの構想、(B) イベント期間延長、(D) 毎年異なる州での開催、はそれぞれ述べられていないため不正解。

☐ extend 〜を延長する　☐ duration 期間　☐ take place 開催される

41. Who most likely is Mr. Zhang?

   (A) A reporter
   (B) An organizer of GAS
   (C) A presenter
   (D) An engineer

Zhang さんはどんな人物であると考えられますか。

   (A) 記者
   (B) GAS の主催者
   (C) 発表者
   (D) 技術者

🔍 Zhang さんはどんな人物なのかが問われている。Zhang さんは２文書目のＥメール（1）の発信者であり、❹で「学生たちへのインタビューの機会を得て、小グループでの討論にも参加した」と述べている。そして、その次の段落の❺で「記事化に関する話題」についても触れていることから、記者であることが考えられる。よって、正解は **(A)**。

✎ ☐ organizer 主催者

....

★★★★☆ クロスリファレンス問題

42. Which of the following didn't Mr. Zhang participate in?

   (A) An airport tour
   (B) A small-group discussion
   (C) A software demonstration
   (D) A presentation by a well-known author

Zhang さんが参加しなかったのは次のどれですか。

   (A) 空港のツアー
   (B) 小グループでの討論
   (C) ソフトウェアの実演会
   (D) 著名な作家による発表

🔍 Zhang さんが参加しなかったものについて問われている。Zhang さんは、２文書目のＥメール（1）の❸で「Carroway さんから話を聞けなかった」と述べている。１文書目のウェブページに書かれているイベントの❷で「有名なパイロットでベストセラー作家の Carroway さんによる発表」と述べられており、Zhang さんはこのイベントに参加できなかったと考えられる。よって、正解は **(D)**。なお、この設問は小文字の "not" 問題となっている。

✎ ☐ well-known 有名な

....

★★★★☆

43. What did Mr. Vega most likely ask Mr. Zhang to do?

   (A) Send Mr. Zhang's article to GAS
   (B) Take a picture of Mr. Hoffbauer
   (C) Review Mr. Vega's e-mail
   (D) Try digital airliner producing software

Vega さんは Zhang さんに何をするように頼んだと考えられますか。

   (A) Zhang さんの記事を GAS に送る
   (B) Hoffbauer さんの写真を撮る
   (C) Vega さんのＥメールを再確認する
   (D) デジタル旅客機製作ソフトを試す

🔍 Vega さんは Zhang さんに何を頼んだのかが問われている。３文書目のＥメール（2）の第２段落に Vega さんが登場する。Zhang さんは❽・❾で、「Vega さんから特別な指示を受けたため、Hoffbauer さんと会って写真を撮りたい」旨を述べている。ここから、Hoffbauer さんの写真を撮ることを頼んだと考えられるため、正解は **(B)**。

✎ ☐ review 〜を再確認する

44. What can be inferred about Mr. Hoffbauer?

    (A) He is a well-known photographer.
    (B) He met Mr. Zhang in Toronto.
    (C) He was a presenter at the award
        ceremony.
    (D) He received a prize.

Hoffbauer さんについて何が推測できますか。

    (A) 有名な写真家である。
    (B) トロントで Zhang さんに会った。
    (C) 授賞式で授与者を務めた。
    (D) 賞を受賞した。

Hoffbauer さんについて推測できることを問う選択肢照合型の問題。Zhang さんは2文書目のEメール（1）の❻で、「今日の夕方、受賞者に会ってインタビューをする」と述べている。次に、3文書目のEメール（2）の❼では、Zhang さんが Hoffbauer さんに対して「昨晩話す時間を取ってくれたお礼」を述べている。つまり、Hoffbauer さんは、賞を受賞した本人であることが推測できる。以上から、正解は **(D)**。Eメール（1）より、会う対象はどんな人かを考える必要があるが、このように代名詞が用いられた場合は、どういう人物かを常に意識して読み進めていこう。

□ prize 賞

問題 40 から 44 は次のウェブページと2通のEメールに関するものです。

http://www.globalairlinershow.org/home

メインページ	概要	プログラム	申し込み

Global Airliner Show
2020
ラスベガス

今年のショーでは、間違いなく教育的で有益な経験ができます。今回で8年目となった Global Airliner Show (GAS) では世界最大規模の旅客機技術に関する展示を行います。昨年から新たに30名以上の発表者が加わり、次のようなさまざまな特別イベントが予定されています：

▶ 有名なパイロットでベストセラー作家である Jeff Carroway さんによる 21 世紀の航空の課題に関する発表
▶ 講習会や小グループによる討論を含む、GAS 学生プログラム
▶ 最寄りの国際空港のガイドツアー
▶ Trumarkia などの業界の専門家によるデジタル旅客機製作ソフトウェアの実演

今年も Passenger Favorite Awards の授賞式が行われます。どの企業が栄冠を勝ち取るのか、ぜひご期待ください。

詳細については**プログラムページ**をご覧ください。

Eメール (1)

受信者:	Keiran Vega
送信者:	Liang Zhang
件名:	最新情報
日付:	10月7日

Vega さん

GAS では素晴らしい時間を過ごすことができました。

午後はずっと、デジタル旅客機製作ソフトを使った講習会に参加していました。素晴らしかったですし、この経験によってこれから興味深い記事が書けると思います。

残念ながら昨日は Carroway さんのお話を聞く機会を逃してしまいました。そのため、その日は空港の中を見学したり、お店の方たちとお話をしたりして過ごしました。しかし、新しいソフトウェアについて学生たちにインタビューをする機会は得られましたし、小グループでの討論にも参加しました。

今年の Passenger Favorite Awards を受賞したのは、トロントの非常に優秀な旅客機メーカーです。受賞者のお話は間違いなく当社の読者を魅了し、もしかすると一面の記事になるかもしれません。今日の夕方、彼に会ってインタビューをするので、明日の朝には記事の下書きをお送りします。

よろしくお願いいたします。

Liang Zhang

Eメール (2)

受信者:	Brian Hoffbauer
送信者:	Liang Zhang
件名:	写真
日付:	10月8日

Hoffbauer 様

昨晩はお話するお時間をいただきありがとうございます。非常に良い時間を過ごせました。

記事を社長の Keiran Vega にEメールで送ったところ、気に入ってもらえたようで、特別な指示を受けました。ショーの会場を発たれる前に、写真撮影のために数分ほどもう一度お会いいただけないでしょうか。記事に添える良い写真を何枚か撮らせていただければ幸いです。

よろしくお願いいたします。

Liang Zhang

Questions 45-49 refer to the following schedule and e-mails.

\multicolumn{5}{c}{The Harbortown Institute \\ Providing quality educational services since 1988}

\multicolumn{5}{c}{Summer Term Schedule (June 1—August 31)}
Code	Title	Date	Time	Instructor
CP605	Computer Programming	Tue/Thu	6:00P.M.–9:00P.M.	Margaret Medoza
PM472	Principles of Management	Wed/Fri	8:00P.M.–9:30P.M.	Phillip Danaher
IF513	Introduction to Finance	Mon/Thu	6:00P.M.–7:30P.M.	Karen Cataulin
PS726	Public Speaking	Tue/Wed	8:00P.M.–10:00P.M.	Ismael Augustine
ME934	Microeconomics	Thu/Fri	7:00P.M.–8:30P.M.	Jenna Gomez
IM589	International Marketing	Mon/Wed	6:30P.M.–8:00P.M.	Megan Toivanen

---

E-Mail Message

To:	Dionte Johnson <djdjdj@harbortown.net>
From:	Ryan Saunders <ryanlion@andovarsltd.com>
Date:	May 14
Subject:	Need your help

Dear Mr. Johnson,

I appreciate your kindness for having talks with me. The information that you offered was invaluable.

I am interested in taking a class at your institute this summer but am still unsure which one would be best. As I mentioned to you, I am now working at Andovar Supply Ltd. as a distributor. So I wanted to register for a management class. But my president has advised me that I won't be able to get promoted until I improve my presentation skills because I stutter a lot and get nervous when speaking in front of others. Do you have any classes that could help me overcome these problems because my main purpose is to move up the corporate ladder?

Moreover, I'm concerned whether or not all classes will definitely end on August 31. I am planning a business trip in September and don't want to make any reservations until I am sure that my travel plans won't interfere with my taking the classes.

Best regards,

Ryan Saunders

E-Mail Message

To: Steve Lin <stevelin@kinkmail.com>

From: Fred Razon <president@harbortown.net>

Date: May 15

Subject: New Classes

Dear Mr. Lin,

We are organizing classes that our institute will hold in this summer term. During the last week, so many applicants have enrolled in the educational service of the Harbortown Institute. So far, nearly all of our classes have at least 30 students registered for each of them. Owing to the fact that one of our instructors has cancelled, we are wondering if you could take the marketing class. If you are willing to accept this, please call me; my direct phone number is 723-1245.

Because we prefer to have a maximum of 20 students per class, we are thinking of dividing the classes into separate sections. It means that will double the amount of time each of you will teach. However, we think that this is a good opportunity, because enrollment at our institute had been declining for the last five years until this term. Please note that your pay will double because you will be teaching twice the hours.

I'd appreciate your getting in touch with me by no later than May 22.

Fred Razon
President, Harbortown Institute

45. According to the schedule, what is NOT true about the Harbortown Institute?

(A) It offers classes to students on the weekend.
(B) All of its classes begin in the evening.
(C) It has hired Mr. Danaher to teach a management course.
(D) All of its classes are twice a week.

46. What does Mr. Saunders request that Mr. Johnson do?

(A) Return his phone call
(B) Make a reservation for his business trip
(C) Suggest an effective class
(D) Send an application form to him

47. Which of the following will Mr. Saunders most likely enroll in?

(A) CP605
(B) PM472
(C) IF513
(D) PS726

48. Which instructor will be changed?

(A) Margaret Medoza
(B) Karen Cataulin
(C) Jenna Gomez
(D) Megan Toivanen

49. According to Mr. Razon, what does the Harbortown Institute suggest?

(A) Canceling the students' registration
(B) Closing the classrooms
(C) Splitting the classes
(D) Delaying the beginning of the classes

 P. 620

Triple

Questions 45-49 refer to the following schedule and e-mails.

The Harbortown Institute Providing quality educational services since 1988				
Summer Term Schedule (June 1—August 31)				
Code	Title ❶	Date ❷	Time	Instructor
CP605	Computer Programming	Tue/Thu	6:00P.M.–9:00P.M.	Margaret Medoza
PM472	❸ Principles of Management	Wed/Fri	8:00P.M.–9:30P.M.	❸ Phillip Danaher
IF513	Introduction to Finance	Mon/Thu	6:00P.M.–7:30P.M.	Karen Cataulin
❹ PS726	Public Speaking	Tue/Wed	8:00P.M.–10:00P.M.	Ismael Augustine
ME934	Microeconomics	Thu/Fri	7:00P.M.–8:30P.M.	Jenna Gomez
IM589	❺ International Marketing	Mon/Wed	6:30P.M.–8:00P.M.	❺ Megan Toivanen

Eメール（1）

	E-Mail Message
To:	Dionte Johnson <djdjdj@harbortown.net>
From:	Ryan Saunders <ryanlion@andovarsltd.com>
Date:	May 14
Subject:	Need your help

Dear Mr. Johnson,

I appreciate your kindness for having talks with me. The information that you offered was invaluable.

I am interested in taking a class at your institute this summer but am still unsure which one would be best. As I mentioned to you, I am now working at Andovar Supply Ltd. as a distributor. So I wanted to register for a management class. ❻ But my president has advised me that I won't be able to get promoted until I improve my presentation skills because I stutter a lot and get nervous when speaking in front of others. ❼ Do you have any classes that could help me overcome these problems because my main purpose is to move up the corporate ladder?

Moreover, I'm concerned whether or not all classes will definitely end on August 31. I am planning a business trip in September and don't want to make any reservations until I am sure that my travel plans won't interfere with my taking the classes.

Best regards,

Ryan Saunders

Eメール（2）

E-Mail Message

To:	Steve Lin <stevelin@kinkmail.com>
From:	Fred Razon <president@harbortown.net>
Date:	May 15
Subject:	New Classes

Dear Mr. Lin,

We are organizing classes that our institute will hold in this summer term. During the last week, so many applicants have enrolled in the educational service of the Harbortown Institute. So far, nearly all of our classes have at least 30 students registered for each of them. ❽ Owing to the fact that one of our instructors has cancelled, we are wondering if you could take the marketing class. If you are willing to accept this, please call me; my direct phone number is 723-1245.

❾ Because we prefer to have a maximum of 20 students per class, we are thinking of dividing the classes into separate sections. It means that will double the amount of time each of you will teach. However, we think that this is a good opportunity, because enrollment at our institute had been declining for the last five years until this term. Please note that your pay will double because you will be teaching twice the hours.

I'd appreciate your getting in touch with me by no later than May 22.

Fred Razon
President, Harbortown Institute

予定表
☐ institute（学校）機関　☐ educational service 教育サービス　☐ term 期間　☐ instructor 講師
☐ public speaking 演説　☐ microeconomics ミクロ経済

Eメール（1）
☐ kindness 親切心　☐ invaluable 貴重な　☐ as I mentioned to you 申し上げたとおり　☐ distributor 供給業者
☐ register for ～に登録する　☐ get promoted 昇進する　☐ stutter 言葉に詰まる　☐ nervous 緊張する
☐ overcome ～を克服する　☐ move up ～を登っていく　☐ corporate ladder 出世の階段　☐ moreover さらに
☐ concern whether or not ～か否かを心配している　☐ interfere with ～に支障となる

Eメール（2）
☐ organize ～を編成する　☐ applicant 申し込み志願者　☐ enroll in ～に登録する　☐ owing to ～が原因で
☐ wonder if ～かどうかと思う　☐ be willing to do ～しようとする気がある　☐ direct phone number 直通電話番号
☐ divide A into B A を B に分ける　☐ separate 分かれた　☐ section 区分　☐ double ～を 2 倍にする
☐ opportunity 機会　☐ enrollment 登録　☐ decline 減少する　☐ get in touch with ～と連絡を取る
☐ no later than おそくとも

45. According to the schedule, what is NOT true about the Harbortown Institute?

   (A) It offers classes to students on the weekend.
   (B) All of its classes begin in the evening.
   (C) It has hired Mr. Danaher to teach a management course.
   (D) All of its classes are twice a week.

予定表によると、Harbortown Institute について正しくないことは何ですか。

   (A) 週末に学生向けの授業がある。
   (B) すべての授業は夕方から始まる。
   (C) 経営のコースを教えてもらうために Danaher さんを雇った。
   (D) すべての授業は週 2 回である。

NOT 問題。予定表から、Harbortown Institute について正しくないことが問われている。1 文書目の予定表を見ていくと、❶のそれぞれの研修の日付欄が週 2 回であるため (D) と合致し、❷の開始時間が夕方からの開始であるため (B) と合致する。そして❸の経営に関するコースが Danaher 氏によって行われることがわかるので、(C) と合致する。よって、残った **(A)** が正解となる。**(A)** は❶から平日開催とわかるので、ここで不正解だとみることもできる。

---

46. What does Mr. Saunders request that Mr. Johnson do?

   (A) Return his phone call
   (B) Make a reservation for his business trip
   (C) Suggest an effective class
   (D) Send an application form to him

Saunders さんは Johnson さんに何をすることを要請していますか。

   (A) 折り返し電話する
   (B) 出張の予約をする
   (C) 効果的な授業を提案する
   (D) 申込書を送ってもらう

Saunders さんが Johnson さんに要請したことが問われている。Saunders さんは 2 文書目の E メール (1) の❼で、Johnson さんに宛てて、「自分の課題を克服するために役立つ授業はあるか」と尋ねている。つまり、役立つような効果的な授業があれば教えてほしいとお願いしていることがわかるので、これを言い換えた **(C)** が正解。

✎ ☐ effective 効果的な   ☐ application form 申込書

---

47. Which of the following will Mr. Saunders most likely enroll in?

   (A) CP605
   (B) PM472
   (C) IF513
   (D) PS726

Saunders さんが申し込むと考えられるのは次のどれですか。

   (A) CP605
   (B) PM472
   (C) IF513
   (D) PS726

Saunders さんが申し込む可能性の高いクラスが問われている。Saunders さんは、2 文書目の E メール (1) の❻で、「発表の技術を向上させない限り、昇進はできないと社長から言われた」と述べている。また❼で「問題を克服し、ステップアップしたい」とも述べていることから、発表の技術を向上するクラスを受講することが推測できる。以上から、1 文書目の予定表を見ると、❹に "Public Speaking（演説）" という発表に関すると思われるクラスがある。よって、正解は **(D)** となる。

48. Which instructor will be changed?

  (A) Margaret Medoza
  (B) Karen Cataulin
  (C) Jenna Gomez
  (D) Megan Toivanen

どの講師が変更されましたか。

  (A) Margaret Medoza
  (B) Karen Cataulin
  (C) Jenna Gomez
  (D) Megan Toivanen

変更となった講師は誰かが問われている。3 文書目の E メール (2) の❽で、校長の Razon さんが Lin さん宛てに「講師の一人がキャンセルになったので、マーケティングのクラスを受け持ってもらえないか」と尋ねている。ここから、マーケティングに関するクラスの講師が変更されるとわかるので、1 文書目の予定表から、そのクラスに相当する❺を受け持っている人物を探す。よって、**(D)** が正解となる。この問題も前の問題同様、E メールの内容→予定表を検索して正解を求める、というオーソドックスな解答プロセス。ここでしっかり解法をマスターしておこう。

★★★★☆

49. According to Mr. Razon, what does the Harbortown Institute suggest?

  (A) Canceling the students' registration
  (B) Closing the classrooms
  (C) Splitting the classes
  (D) Delaying the beginning of the classes

Razon さんによると、Harbortown Institute は何を提案していますか。

  (A) 学生の登録を取り消すこと
  (B) 教室を閉鎖すること
  (C) 授業を振り分けること
  (D) 授業の開始を遅らせること

所長の Razon さんの情報から、Harbortown Institute が提案していることは何かが問われている。3 文書目の E メール (2) を見ていくと、Razon さんは❾で「どのクラスも定員を最大 20 名にしたいため、クラスをいくつかに分けたい」と述べている。ここからそれを言い換えた **(C)** が正解となる。❾の "divide" が split に言い換えられていることも注目しよう。

□ registration 登録　□ classroom 教室　□ split 〜を分ける

The Harbortown Institute
1988 年から高品質の教育サービスを提供

夏学期予定表（6 月 1 日〜 8 月 31 日）

コード番号	タイトル	日程	時間	講師
CP605	コンピューター プログラミング	火曜日／木曜日	午後 6:00 から午後 9:00	Margart Medoza
PM472	経営理念	水曜日／金曜日	午後 8:00 から午後 9:30	Phillip Danaher
IF513	ファイナンス入門	月曜日／木曜日	午後 6:00 から午後 7:30	Karen Cataulin
PS726	演説	火曜日／水曜日	午後 8:00 から午後 10:00	Ismael Augustine
ME934	ミクロ経済学	木曜日／金曜日	午後 7:00 から午後 8:30	Jenna Gomez
IM589	国際マーケティング	月曜日／水曜日	午後 6:30 から午後 8:00	Megan Toivanen

E メール（1）

受信者：	Dionte Johnson <djdjdj@harbortown.net>
送信者：	Ryan Saunders <ryanlion@andovarsltd.com>
日付：	5 月 14 日
件名：	ご教示ください

Johnson 様

お話をするお時間をいただき誠にありがとうございます。いただいた情報は非常に貴重なものでした。

私はこの夏、研究所で授業を受けたいと思っていますが、どれが一番良いのかわかりません。お伝えしたとおり、現在、Andovar Supply Ltd. で物流担当者として働いていますので、経営の授業に申し込みをしたいと思いました。しかし、人前で話すと口ごもって緊張してしまうこともあり、発表の技術を向上させない限り、昇進はできないと社長から言われています。私の一番の目的は企業の中でステップアップすることですが、この問題を克服するのに役立つ授業はありますか？

また、すべての授業が 8 月 31 日に終了するのかどうかも心配です。9 月に出張を予定しており、それが授業を受けることの支障にならないと確認できるまでは、予約をしたくありません。

よろしくお願いいたします。

Ryan Saunders

Eメール（2）

受信者： Steve Lin <stevelin@kinmail.com>
送信者： Fred Razon <president@harbortown.net>
日付： 5月15日
件名： 新しい授業

Lin 様

この夏学期に当研究所で開催されるクラスを編成しています。先週、Harbortown Institute の教育サービスに非常に多くの申し込みがありました。現在のところ、ほぼすべての授業に少なくとも30名の学生が登録しています。講師の一人がキャンセルになったので、あなたにマーケティングのクラスを受け持ってもらえないかと思っています。もしよろしければ、私の直通電話（723-1245）までご連絡ください。

どのクラスも定員を最大20名にしたいため、クラスをいくつかに分けることを考えています。それはつまり、皆さんの講義時間が倍になるということです。しかしながら、今学期までの5年間、当学院の入学者数は減少し続けていたため、これは良い機会であると考えています。2倍の時間教えることになるので、給与も2倍になります。

遅くとも5月22日までにご連絡いただければ幸いです。

Fred Razon
Harbortown Institute 所長

Questions 50-54 refer to the following hotel review, Web page, and article. 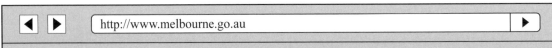 5分30秒

HOTEL REVIEW

	Very Bad	Bad	Average	Good	Very Good
Fixtures				✓	
Transportation	✓				
Cleanliness					✓
Meals					✓
Service				✓	

I had a very good time when I stayed here a week ago. My room was quite relaxing, and all my meals at the hotel restaurant were delightful. It was also very convenient for a commercial area nearby. The hotel provided me with excellent service as well.

However, I wish there had been transportation such as a shuttle service to the airport. Because it was my first visit, catching a taxi to the airport was difficult, and it wasn't cheap. Other than this problem, I enjoyed my stay on the whole.

Michelle Warren

◀ ▶ http://www.melbourne.go.au ▶

Melbourne City Center

Information about Hotels

Are you going to visit Melbourne? Then stay at one of the hotels of Melbourne City. Below are the most popular hotels in the downtown area.

Star Hotel & Resort
Amenities include complimentary wireless Internet service, double beds, 59-inch TVs, and an indoor swimming pool. This hotel is ready to offer everything to everyone. Perfect for Families!

Kingsgate Hotel
Try newly decorated guest rooms and enjoy quiet dining at the recently renovated eatery. You can visit nearby theatres, shopping malls, and other city attractions. And also, you can use the convention hall and free wireless Internet service.

Hotel Avani
Without a fee for transportation to the airport and a completely remodeled business centre, this is the best hotel for business travelers. It has various conference rooms and free wireless Internet service.

Travelodge Inn
This old-fashioned but convenient inn contains double beds, flat TVs, and free wireless Internet service in each room, like a modern hotel. It features charming decoration, appetizing free breakfasts, and nearby public transportation. This is a beautiful place to stay during your holiday in Melbourne.

Paxton Hotel Chain Acquires New Family

MELBOURNE (April 15)—The Paxton Hotel Chain has merged with the Blake Hotel Group. The Paxton Hotel Chain was a small company compared to the Star Hotel, which owns several properties in the local area. By acquiring the Blake Hotel Group, the Paxton Hotel Chain now owns 8 hotels and more than 1,200 guest rooms in Melbourne.

The Blake Hotel Group was widely known for its Blake Travel Centre, which was designed specifically for business travelers. Their three branches contain the deluxe Mancini Hotel, constructed in 1976, and the Emily Inn, an upscale hotel that was launched just last year.

"We welcome the Blake Hotel Group to be a part of the family," said the spokesperson of the Paxton Hotel Chain, Rayna Tang. "The Blake Hotel Group is getting a good reputation in Melbourne, and it will be a complete complement to Paxton's existing hotels."

Blake's loyal members are now able to earn points and use vouchers when they stay at Paxton Hotel Chain hotels.

50. What disappointed Ms. Warren about her stay?

(A) The lack of affordable transportation
(B) The low quality of the restaurant
(C) The high price of the room
(D) The unfriendly staff

51. What is a feature of the hotel where Ms. Warren stayed?

(A) It has an indoor swimming pool.
(B) The restaurant was renovated.
(C) Breakfast is free of charge.
(D) All rooms have double beds.

52. According to the Web page, what do the four hotels have in common?

(A) They were all built a long time ago.
(B) They all have swimming pools.
(C) They all offer discounts to business travelers.
(D) They all provide wireless Internet access free of charge.

53. In the article, the word "complement" in paragraph 3, line 3, is closest in meaning to?

(A) praise
(B) supplement
(C) fame
(D) no expense

54. Which of the following can be inferred to be a member of the Blake Hotel Group?

(A) Star Hotel
(B) Kingsgate Hotel
(C) Hotel Avani
(D) Travelodge Inn

Triple

P. 628

Questions 50-54 refer to the following hotel review, Web page, and article.

HOTEL REVIEW

	Very Bad	Bad	Average	Good	Very Good
Fixtures				✓	
Transportation	✓				
Cleanliness					✓
Meals					✓
Service				✓	

I had a very good time when I stayed here a week ago. My room was quite relaxing, and all my meals at the hotel restaurant were delightful. ❶ It was also very convenient for a commercial area nearby. The hotel provided me with excellent service as well.

❷ However, I wish there had been transportation such as a shuttle service to the airport. Because it was my first visit, catching a taxi to the airport was difficult, and it wasn't cheap. Other than this problem, I enjoyed my stay on the whole.

Michelle Warren

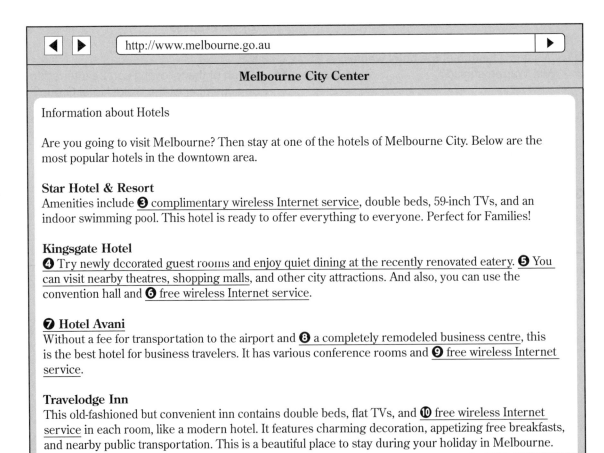

http://www.melbourne.go.au

Melbourne City Center

Information about Hotels

Are you going to visit Melbourne? Then stay at one of the hotels of Melbourne City. Below are the most popular hotels in the downtown area.

Star Hotel & Resort
Amenities include ❸ complimentary wireless Internet service, double beds, 59-inch TVs, and an indoor swimming pool. This hotel is ready to offer everything to everyone. Perfect for Families!

Kingsgate Hotel
❹ Try newly decorated guest rooms and enjoy quiet dining at the recently renovated eatery. ❺ You can visit nearby theatres, shopping malls, and other city attractions. And also, you can use the convention hall and ❻ free wireless Internet service.

❼ **Hotel Avani**
Without a fee for transportation to the airport and ❽ a completely remodeled business centre, this is the best hotel for business travelers. It has various conference rooms and ❾ free wireless Internet service.

Travelodge Inn
This old-fashioned but convenient inn contains double beds, flat TVs, and ❿ free wireless Internet service in each room, like a modern hotel. It features charming decoration, appetizing free breakfasts, and nearby public transportation. This is a beautiful place to stay during your holiday in Melbourne.

Paxton Hotel Chain Acquires New Family

MELBOURNE (April 15)—The Paxton Hotel Chain has merged with the Blake Hotel Group. The Paxton Hotel Chain was a small company compared to the Star Hotel, which owns several properties in the local area. By acquiring the Blake Hotel Group, the Paxton Hotel Chain now owns 8 hotels and more than 1,200 guest rooms in Melbourne.

⓫ The Blake Hotel Group was widely known for its Blake Travel Centre, which was designed specifically for business travelers. Their three branches contain the deluxe Mancini Hotel, constructed in 1976, and the Emily Inn, an upscale hotel that was launched just last year.

"We welcome the Blake Hotel Group to be a part of the family," said the spokesperson of the Paxton Hotel Chain, Rayna Tang. "The Blake Hotel Group is getting a good reputation in Melbourne, and **⓬** it will be a complete complement to Paxton's existing hotels."

Blake's loyal members are now able to earn points and use vouchers when they stay at Paxton Hotel Chain hotels.

ホテルレビュー
- ☐ fixture 設備　☐ cleanliness 清潔さ　☐ relaxing くつろげる　☐ delightful 素晴らしい　☐ convenient 便利な
- ☐ commercial area 商業区域　☐ as well 同様に　☐ such as ～のような　☐ shuttle service 往復輸送サービス
- ☐ on the whole 全体的に

ウェブページ
- ☐ below 下記に　☐ downtown 繁華街　☐ complimentary 無料の　☐ indoor 屋内の　☐ newly 新たに
- ☐ eatery 食堂施設、レストラン　☐ completely 完全に　☐ business traveler 出張者　☐ various さまざまな
- ☐ old-fashioned 古風の　☐ inn 宿泊施設　☐ contain ～を含む　☐ feature ～を特徴とする
- ☐ charming 魅力的な　☐ appetizing 食欲をそそるような　☐ public transportation 公共交通機関

記事
- ☐ merge with ～と合併する　☐ compared to ～と比較して　☐ acquire ～を買収する
- ☐ widely known 広く知られている　☐ branch 支店　☐ deluxe 豪華な　☐ construct ～を建設する
- ☐ upscale 高級な、高所得者向けの　☐ launch ～の営業を開始する　☐ spokesperson 広報担当者
- ☐ reputation 評判　☐ complement 補完　☐ earn ～を得る・稼ぐ　☐ voucher 金券・クーポン券

★★★★☆

50. What disappointed Ms. Warren about her stay?

(A) The lack of affordable transportation
(B) The low quality of the restaurant
(C) The high price of the room
(D) The unfriendly staff

Warren さんが滞在について失望したことは何ですか。

(A) 手ごろな移動手段がないこと
(B) レストランの質が低いこと
(C) 部屋の値段が高いこと
(D) 従業員が不親切なこと

Warren さんが滞在について失望したことが問われている。Warren さんは、1 文書目のホテルレビューの❷で「空港までのシャトルサービスがあればよかったのに」と述べている。ここから、費用の掛からない移動手段がなかったことが、がっかりしたことだと考えられるので、それを言い換えた **(A)** が正解。"wish＋過去完了（there had ＋ -ed)" で、「あの時あったらよかったのに（でもなかった）」という仮定法となり、この意味をくみ取る必要がある。

☐ disappoint ～をがっかりさせる　☐ lack of ～がないこと　☐ affordable （価格が）手ごろな　☐ unfriendly 不親切な

51. What is a feature of the hotel where Ms. Warren stayed?

(A) It has an indoor swimming pool.
(B) The restaurant was renovated.
(C) Breakfast is free of charge.
(D) All rooms have double beds.

Warren さんが宿泊したホテルの特徴は何ですか。

(A) 屋内にプールがある
(B) レストランをリニューアルした
(C) 朝食が無料である
(D) 全室ダブルベッドである

Warren さんが宿泊したホテルの特徴について問われている。まず、Warren さんは1文書目のホテルレビューの❶で「近所の商業施設が便利だった」と述べている。それを参考に2文書目のウェブページにある各ホテルの特徴をみると、❺に「劇場やショッピングモール」という記載があることから、Warren さんは Kingsgate Hotel に宿泊したことがわかる。❹に「最近リニューアルしたお食事処で静かなお食事をお楽しみください」とあることから、これを「レストランをリニューアルした」と言い換えた **(B)** が正解となる。

---

52. According to the Web page, what do the four hotels have in common?

(A) They were all built a long time ago.
(B) They all have swimming pools.
(C) They all offer discounts to business travelers.
(D) They all provide wireless Internet access free of charge.

ウェブページによると、4つのホテルに共通していることは何ですか。

(A) どれもかなり前に建設された。
(B) どれにもプールがある。
(C) どれも出張者に対し値引きをしている。
(D) どれも無料で無線インターネットを提供している。

ウェブページから、4つのホテルに共通していることが問われている。2文書目のウェブページで、それぞれのホテルの特徴を見ていくと、❸・❻・❾・❿で、いずれも「無線インターネット接続が無料」という情報がある。以上から、これを言い換えた **(D)** が正解。この問題は、「無料」を❸ "complimentary"、❻・❾・❿ "free" の他に、(D) の free of charge、のようにさまざまな形で表現している。これらが同じ意味であると早めに察知できれば正解しやすい。

☐ free of charge 無料で

---

53. In the article, the word "complement" in paragraph 3, line 3, is closest in meaning to?

(A) praise
(B) supplement
(C) fame
(D) no expense

記事の、第3段落・3行目にある "complement" に最も意味が近いのは

(A) 称賛
(B) 補足
(C) 名声
(D) 無償

同義語問題。問われている箇所は3文書目の記事の⓬で、「(Paxton の既存ホテルに完全に) 補完 (することになる)」と、「補完、補足するもの」という意味を持っている。これと同じ意味になるのは **(B)**。(A)「称賛」と (D)「無償」は "compliment" なら正解となるが、つづりが異なるのでここでは不正解。

54. Which of the following can be inferred to be a member of the Blake Hotel Group?

(A) Star Hotel
(B) Kingsgate Hotel
(C) Hotel Avani
(D) Travelodge Inn

Blake Hotel Group の一員だと推測できるのは次のどれですか。

(A) Star Hotel
(B) Kingsgate Hotel
(C) Hotel Avani
(D) Travelodge Inn

選択肢のどのホテルが Blake Hotel Group の一員だと推測できるかが問われている。3文書目の記事を見ていくと、❶に Black Hotel Group に関する記載があり、「特に出張者用にデザインされている」ということがわかる。次に2文書目のウェブページの各ホテルの特徴が記載された箇所をそれぞれ見ていくと、❼・❽から「"Hotel Avani" に、全面的に改装されたビジネスセンターがある」とわかる。また、❽以降で、ビジネスマン向けに会議室も有している、という記載もあることから、このグループのコンセプトに合致している。以上より、このグループの一員と推測できるのは **(C)**。このグループの一員である条件を記事で見つけ、それに合うホテルを2文書目のウェブページから検索するという解答プロセスとなっている。

問題 50 から 54 は次のホテルレビュー、ウェブページ、記事に関するものです。

ホテルの評価

	非常に悪い	悪い	平均的	良い	非常に良い
設備				✓	
交通の便	✓				
清潔さ					✓
食事					✓
サービス				✓	

1週間前にここに滞在したとき、私はとても良い時間を過ごしました。部屋ではかなりくつろぐことができましたし、ホテルのレストランの食事はどれも美味しかったです。また、近くには商業施設があり、とても便利でした。ホテルのサービスも素晴らしかったです。

しかし、空港シャトルサービスなどの移動手段があればよかったと思います。初めての訪問でしたので、空港に行くタクシーを捕まえるのは容易ではありませんでしたし、安くもありませんでした。この問題を除けば、全体的に滞在を楽しめました。

Michelle Warren

メルボルン市街地

ホテル情報

メルボルンを訪問する予定ですか？　では、メルボルン市のホテルに滞在するのはいかがでしょうか？　以下はダウンタウン地区で最も人気のあるホテルです。

Star Hotel & Resort
無料の無線インターネット接続、ダブルベッド、59 インチのテレビ、屋内プールをご利用いただけます。このホテルはすべての人にすべてを提供できます。ご家族にぴったりです！

Kingsgate Hotel
改装された客室に泊まって、最近リニューアルしたお食事処で静かなお食事をお楽しみください。近隣の劇場、ショッピングモール、その他の街の見どころへ行くことができます。また、会議場や無料の無線インターネット接続をご利用いただけます。

Hotel Avani
無料の空港送迎と全面的に改装されたビジネスセンターがあり、出張に最適なホテルです。さまざまな会議室があり、無料の無線インターネット接続ができます。

Travelodge Inn
この古風ながらも便利な宿屋には、近代的なホテルと同様に、各部屋にダブルベッド、薄型テレビ、無料の無線インターネット接続が完備されています。特筆すべき点はかわいらしい装飾、食欲をそそる無料の朝食、公共交通機関への容易なアクセスです。メルボルンで休暇を過ごすのにぴったりの場所です。

Paxton Hotel Chain に新しいメンバー

メルボルン（4 月 15 日）―Paxton Hotel Chain が Blake Hotel Group と合併した。Paxton Hotel Chain は、地域に複数の宿泊施設を所有する Star Hotel と比べると小さな会社だった。Blake Hotel Group を買収することにより、Paxton Hotel Chain は 8 つのホテルと 1,200 以上の客室をメルボルンで所有することになる。

Blake Hotel Group は、出張者向けに設計された Blake Travel Centre で広く知られている。その参加の 3 軒の中には、1976 年建設の豪華な Mancini Hotel、昨年開業した高級ホテル Emily Inn がある。

「Blake Hotel Group がファミリーの一員になることを歓迎します。」と Paxton Hotel Chain の広報担当 Rayna Tang は語る。「Blake Hotel Group はメルボルンで高い評価を得ており、Paxton の既存のホテルを完全に補完することになります。」

Blake の会員は、Paxton Hotel Chain のホテルに宿泊する際に、ポイントを取得したり、クーポンを利用したりすることが可能となった。

著者紹介

大里秀介　Shusuke Osato

TOEIC L&Rテスト990点、TOEIC S&Wテスト ライティング200点満点取得の経験を持つ現役サラリーマン。2006年から英語学習を開始して、2007年スコア730点を突破、社内選考でイギリス留学を経験する。2012年からカナダに駐在勤務し、北米間の大ビジネスプロジェクトをTOEICで磨いた英語力を駆使して成功に導く。著書に『3週間で攻略 TOEIC L&Rテスト900点！』(アルク)、『TOEIC テスト新形式完全攻略模試』(学研プラス)、『TOEIC L&Rテスト壁越えトレーニングPart 7』『TOEIC L&Rテスト 壁越え模試 リーディング』(旺文社)、『極めろ！ TOEIC L&R TEST 990点 リーディング特訓』(スリーエーネットワーク)などがある。

装幀・本文デザイン	斉藤 啓(ブッダプロダクションズ)
制作協力	ロゴポート、Testing Contents Service
編集協力	渡邉真理子
翻訳協力	河野伸治

解きまくれ！ リーディングドリル TOEIC® L&R TEST PART 7

2021年12月 1 日　初版第1刷発行
2024年10月 8 日　第 3 刷 発 行

著 者	大里秀介
発 行 者	藤嵜政子
発 行 所	株式会社　スリーエーネットワーク
	〒102-0083 東京都千代田区麹町3丁目4番 トラスティ麹町ビル2F
	電話:03-5275-2722 [営業]　03-5275-2726 [編集]
	https://www.3anet.co.jp/
印刷・製本	日経印刷株式会社

Answer Sheet

Answer Sheet

TEST 5 /54

TEST 6 /54

TEST 7 /54

TEST 8 /54

TEST 5

No.	ANSWER	No.	ANSWER
	A B C D		A B C D
1	A B C D	28	A B C D
2	A B C D	29	A B C D
3	A B C D	30	A B C D
4	A B C D	31	A B C D
5	A B C D	32	A B C D
6	A B C D	33	A B C D
7	A B C D	34	A B C D
8	A B C D	35	A B C D
9	A B C D	36	A B C D
10	A B C D	37	A B C D
11	A B C D	38	A B C D
12	A B C D	39	A B C D
13	A B C D	40	A B C D
14	A B C D	41	A B C D
15	A B C D	42	A B C D
16	A B C D	43	A B C D
17	A B C D	44	A B C D
18	A B C D	45	A B C D
19	A B C D	46	A B C D
20	A B C D	47	A B C D
21	A B C D	48	A B C D
22	A B C D	49	A B C D
23	A B C D	50	A B C D
24	A B C D	51	A B C D
25	A B C D	52	A B C D
26	A B C D	53	A B C D
27	A B C D	54	A B C D

TEST 6

No.	ANSWER	No.	ANSWER
	A B C D		A B C D
1	A B C D	28	A B C D
2	A B C D	29	A B C D
3	A B C D	30	A B C D
4	A B C D	31	A B C D
5	A B C D	32	A B C D
6	A B C D	33	A B C D
7	A B C D	34	A B C D
8	A B C D	35	A B C D
9	A B C D	36	A B C D
10	A B C D	37	A B C D
11	A B C D	38	A B C D
12	A B C D	39	A B C D
13	A B C D	40	A B C D
14	A B C D	41	A B C D
15	A B C D	42	A B C D
16	A B C D	43	A B C D
17	A B C D	44	A B C D
18	A B C D	45	A B C D
19	A B C D	46	A B C D
20	A B C D	47	A B C D
21	A B C D	48	A B C D
22	A B C D	49	A B C D
23	A B C D	50	A B C D
24	A B C D	51	A B C D
25	A B C D	52	A B C D
26	A B C D	53	A B C D
27	A B C D	54	A B C D

TEST 7

No.	ANSWER	No.	ANSWER
	A B C D		A B C D
1	A B C D	28	A B C D
2	A B C D	29	A B C D
3	A B C D	30	A B C D
4	A B C D	31	A B C D
5	A B C D	32	A B C D
6	A B C D	33	A B C D
7	A B C D	34	A B C D
8	A B C D	35	A B C D
9	A B C D	36	A B C D
10	A B C D	37	A B C D
11	A B C D	38	A B C D
12	A B C D	39	A B C D
13	A B C D	40	A B C D
14	A B C D	41	A B C D
15	A B C D	42	A B C D
16	A B C D	43	A B C D
17	A B C D	44	A B C D
18	A B C D	45	A B C D
19	A B C D	46	A B C D
20	A B C D	47	A B C D
21	A B C D	48	A B C D
22	A B C D	49	A B C D
23	A B C D	50	A B C D
24	A B C D	51	A B C D
25	A B C D	52	A B C D
26	A B C D	53	A B C D
27	A B C D	54	A B C D

TEST 8

No.	ANSWER	No.	ANSWER
	A B C D		A B C D
1	A B C D	28	A B C D
2	A B C D	29	A B C D
3	A B C D	30	A B C D
4	A B C D	31	A B C D
5	A B C D	32	A B C D
6	A B C D	33	A B C D
7	A B C D	34	A B C D
8	A B C D	35	A B C D
9	A B C D	36	A B C D
10	A B C D	37	A B C D
11	A B C D	38	A B C D
12	A B C D	39	A B C D
13	A B C D	40	A B C D
14	A B C D	41	A B C D
15	A B C D	42	A B C D
16	A B C D	43	A B C D
17	A B C D	44	A B C D
18	A B C D	45	A B C D
19	A B C D	46	A B C D
20	A B C D	47	A B C D
21	A B C D	48	A B C D
22	A B C D	49	A B C D
23	A B C D	50	A B C D
24	A B C D	51	A B C D
25	A B C D	52	A B C D
26	A B C D	53	A B C D
27	A B C D	54	A B C D

Answer Sheet

TEST 1   /54

TEST 2   /54

TEST 3   /54

TEST 4   /54

TEST 1

No.	ANSWER A B C D	No.	ANSWER A B C D
1	Ⓐ Ⓑ Ⓒ Ⓓ	28	Ⓐ Ⓑ Ⓒ Ⓓ
2	Ⓐ Ⓑ Ⓒ Ⓓ	29	Ⓐ Ⓑ Ⓒ Ⓓ
3	Ⓐ Ⓑ Ⓒ Ⓓ	30	Ⓐ Ⓑ Ⓒ Ⓓ
4	Ⓐ Ⓑ Ⓒ Ⓓ	31	Ⓐ Ⓑ Ⓒ Ⓓ
5	Ⓐ Ⓑ Ⓒ Ⓓ	32	Ⓐ Ⓑ Ⓒ Ⓓ
6	Ⓐ Ⓑ Ⓒ Ⓓ	33	Ⓐ Ⓑ Ⓒ Ⓓ
7	Ⓐ Ⓑ Ⓒ Ⓓ	34	Ⓐ Ⓑ Ⓒ Ⓓ
8	Ⓐ Ⓑ Ⓒ Ⓓ	35	Ⓐ Ⓑ Ⓒ Ⓓ
9	Ⓐ Ⓑ Ⓒ Ⓓ	36	Ⓐ Ⓑ Ⓒ Ⓓ
10	Ⓐ Ⓑ Ⓒ Ⓓ	37	Ⓐ Ⓑ Ⓒ Ⓓ
11	Ⓐ Ⓑ Ⓒ Ⓓ	38	Ⓐ Ⓑ Ⓒ Ⓓ
12	Ⓐ Ⓑ Ⓒ Ⓓ	39	Ⓐ Ⓑ Ⓒ Ⓓ
13	Ⓐ Ⓑ Ⓒ Ⓓ	40	Ⓐ Ⓑ Ⓒ Ⓓ
14	Ⓐ Ⓑ Ⓒ Ⓓ	41	Ⓐ Ⓑ Ⓒ Ⓓ
15	Ⓐ Ⓑ Ⓒ Ⓓ	42	Ⓐ Ⓑ Ⓒ Ⓓ
16	Ⓐ Ⓑ Ⓒ Ⓓ	43	Ⓐ Ⓑ Ⓒ Ⓓ
17	Ⓐ Ⓑ Ⓒ Ⓓ	44	Ⓐ Ⓑ Ⓒ Ⓓ
18	Ⓐ Ⓑ Ⓒ Ⓓ	45	Ⓐ Ⓑ Ⓒ Ⓓ
19	Ⓐ Ⓑ Ⓒ Ⓓ	46	Ⓐ Ⓑ Ⓒ Ⓓ
20	Ⓐ Ⓑ Ⓒ Ⓓ	47	Ⓐ Ⓑ Ⓒ Ⓓ
21	Ⓐ Ⓑ Ⓒ Ⓓ	48	Ⓐ Ⓑ Ⓒ Ⓓ
22	Ⓐ Ⓑ Ⓒ Ⓓ	49	Ⓐ Ⓑ Ⓒ Ⓓ
23	Ⓐ Ⓑ Ⓒ Ⓓ	50	Ⓐ Ⓑ Ⓒ Ⓓ
24	Ⓐ Ⓑ Ⓒ Ⓓ	51	Ⓐ Ⓑ Ⓒ Ⓓ
25	Ⓐ Ⓑ Ⓒ Ⓓ	52	Ⓐ Ⓑ Ⓒ Ⓓ
26	Ⓐ Ⓑ Ⓒ Ⓓ	53	Ⓐ Ⓑ Ⓒ Ⓓ
27	Ⓐ Ⓑ Ⓒ Ⓓ	54	Ⓐ Ⓑ Ⓒ Ⓓ

TEST 2

No.	ANSWER A B C D	No.	ANSWER A B C D
1	Ⓐ Ⓑ Ⓒ Ⓓ	28	Ⓐ Ⓑ Ⓒ Ⓓ
2	Ⓐ Ⓑ Ⓒ Ⓓ	29	Ⓐ Ⓑ Ⓒ Ⓓ
3	Ⓐ Ⓑ Ⓒ Ⓓ	30	Ⓐ Ⓑ Ⓒ Ⓓ
4	Ⓐ Ⓑ Ⓒ Ⓓ	31	Ⓐ Ⓑ Ⓒ Ⓓ
5	Ⓐ Ⓑ Ⓒ Ⓓ	32	Ⓐ Ⓑ Ⓒ Ⓓ
6	Ⓐ Ⓑ Ⓒ Ⓓ	33	Ⓐ Ⓑ Ⓒ Ⓓ
7	Ⓐ Ⓑ Ⓒ Ⓓ	34	Ⓐ Ⓑ Ⓒ Ⓓ
8	Ⓐ Ⓑ Ⓒ Ⓓ	35	Ⓐ Ⓑ Ⓒ Ⓓ
9	Ⓐ Ⓑ Ⓒ Ⓓ	36	Ⓐ Ⓑ Ⓒ Ⓓ
10	Ⓐ Ⓑ Ⓒ Ⓓ	37	Ⓐ Ⓑ Ⓒ Ⓓ
11	Ⓐ Ⓑ Ⓒ Ⓓ	38	Ⓐ Ⓑ Ⓒ Ⓓ
12	Ⓐ Ⓑ Ⓒ Ⓓ	39	Ⓐ Ⓑ Ⓒ Ⓓ
13	Ⓐ Ⓑ Ⓒ Ⓓ	40	Ⓐ Ⓑ Ⓒ Ⓓ
14	Ⓐ Ⓑ Ⓒ Ⓓ	41	Ⓐ Ⓑ Ⓒ Ⓓ
15	Ⓐ Ⓑ Ⓒ Ⓓ	42	Ⓐ Ⓑ Ⓒ Ⓓ
16	Ⓐ Ⓑ Ⓒ Ⓓ	43	Ⓐ Ⓑ Ⓒ Ⓓ
17	Ⓐ Ⓑ Ⓒ Ⓓ	44	Ⓐ Ⓑ Ⓒ Ⓓ
18	Ⓐ Ⓑ Ⓒ Ⓓ	45	Ⓐ Ⓑ Ⓒ Ⓓ
19	Ⓐ Ⓑ Ⓒ Ⓓ	46	Ⓐ Ⓑ Ⓒ Ⓓ
20	Ⓐ Ⓑ Ⓒ Ⓓ	47	Ⓐ Ⓑ Ⓒ Ⓓ
21	Ⓐ Ⓑ Ⓒ Ⓓ	48	Ⓐ Ⓑ Ⓒ Ⓓ
22	Ⓐ Ⓑ Ⓒ Ⓓ	49	Ⓐ Ⓑ Ⓒ Ⓓ
23	Ⓐ Ⓑ Ⓒ Ⓓ	50	Ⓐ Ⓑ Ⓒ Ⓓ
24	Ⓐ Ⓑ Ⓒ Ⓓ	51	Ⓐ Ⓑ Ⓒ Ⓓ
25	Ⓐ Ⓑ Ⓒ Ⓓ	52	Ⓐ Ⓑ Ⓒ Ⓓ
26	Ⓐ Ⓑ Ⓒ Ⓓ	53	Ⓐ Ⓑ Ⓒ Ⓓ
27	Ⓐ Ⓑ Ⓒ Ⓓ	54	Ⓐ Ⓑ Ⓒ Ⓓ

TEST 3

No.	ANSWER A B C D	No.	ANSWER A B C D
1	Ⓐ Ⓑ Ⓒ Ⓓ	28	Ⓐ Ⓑ Ⓒ Ⓓ
2	Ⓐ Ⓑ Ⓒ Ⓓ	29	Ⓐ Ⓑ Ⓒ Ⓓ
3	Ⓐ Ⓑ Ⓒ Ⓓ	30	Ⓐ Ⓑ Ⓒ Ⓓ
4	Ⓐ Ⓑ Ⓒ Ⓓ	31	Ⓐ Ⓑ Ⓒ Ⓓ
5	Ⓐ Ⓑ Ⓒ Ⓓ	32	Ⓐ Ⓑ Ⓒ Ⓓ
6	Ⓐ Ⓑ Ⓒ Ⓓ	33	Ⓐ Ⓑ Ⓒ Ⓓ
7	Ⓐ Ⓑ Ⓒ Ⓓ	34	Ⓐ Ⓑ Ⓒ Ⓓ
8	Ⓐ Ⓑ Ⓒ Ⓓ	35	Ⓐ Ⓑ Ⓒ Ⓓ
9	Ⓐ Ⓑ Ⓒ Ⓓ	36	Ⓐ Ⓑ Ⓒ Ⓓ
10	Ⓐ Ⓑ Ⓒ Ⓓ	37	Ⓐ Ⓑ Ⓒ Ⓓ
11	Ⓐ Ⓑ Ⓒ Ⓓ	38	Ⓐ Ⓑ Ⓒ Ⓓ
12	Ⓐ Ⓑ Ⓒ Ⓓ	39	Ⓐ Ⓑ Ⓒ Ⓓ
13	Ⓐ Ⓑ Ⓒ Ⓓ	40	Ⓐ Ⓑ Ⓒ Ⓓ
14	Ⓐ Ⓑ Ⓒ Ⓓ	41	Ⓐ Ⓑ Ⓒ Ⓓ
15	Ⓐ Ⓑ Ⓒ Ⓓ	42	Ⓐ Ⓑ Ⓒ Ⓓ
16	Ⓐ Ⓑ Ⓒ Ⓓ	43	Ⓐ Ⓑ Ⓒ Ⓓ
17	Ⓐ Ⓑ Ⓒ Ⓓ	44	Ⓐ Ⓑ Ⓒ Ⓓ
18	Ⓐ Ⓑ Ⓒ Ⓓ	45	Ⓐ Ⓑ Ⓒ Ⓓ
19	Ⓐ Ⓑ Ⓒ Ⓓ	46	Ⓐ Ⓑ Ⓒ Ⓓ
20	Ⓐ Ⓑ Ⓒ Ⓓ	47	Ⓐ Ⓑ Ⓒ Ⓓ
21	Ⓐ Ⓑ Ⓒ Ⓓ	48	Ⓐ Ⓑ Ⓒ Ⓓ
22	Ⓐ Ⓑ Ⓒ Ⓓ	49	Ⓐ Ⓑ Ⓒ Ⓓ
23	Ⓐ Ⓑ Ⓒ Ⓓ	50	Ⓐ Ⓑ Ⓒ Ⓓ
24	Ⓐ Ⓑ Ⓒ Ⓓ	51	Ⓐ Ⓑ Ⓒ Ⓓ
25	Ⓐ Ⓑ Ⓒ Ⓓ	52	Ⓐ Ⓑ Ⓒ Ⓓ
26	Ⓐ Ⓑ Ⓒ Ⓓ	53	Ⓐ Ⓑ Ⓒ Ⓓ
27	Ⓐ Ⓑ Ⓒ Ⓓ	54	Ⓐ Ⓑ Ⓒ Ⓓ

TEST 4

No.	ANSWER A B C D	No.	ANSWER A B C D
1	Ⓐ Ⓑ Ⓒ Ⓓ	28	Ⓐ Ⓑ Ⓒ Ⓓ
2	Ⓐ Ⓑ Ⓒ Ⓓ	29	Ⓐ Ⓑ Ⓒ Ⓓ
3	Ⓐ Ⓑ Ⓒ Ⓓ	30	Ⓐ Ⓑ Ⓒ Ⓓ
4	Ⓐ Ⓑ Ⓒ Ⓓ	31	Ⓐ Ⓑ Ⓒ Ⓓ
5	Ⓐ Ⓑ Ⓒ Ⓓ	32	Ⓐ Ⓑ Ⓒ Ⓓ
6	Ⓐ Ⓑ Ⓒ Ⓓ	33	Ⓐ Ⓑ Ⓒ Ⓓ
7	Ⓐ Ⓑ Ⓒ Ⓓ	34	Ⓐ Ⓑ Ⓒ Ⓓ
8	Ⓐ Ⓑ Ⓒ Ⓓ	35	Ⓐ Ⓑ Ⓒ Ⓓ
9	Ⓐ Ⓑ Ⓒ Ⓓ	36	Ⓐ Ⓑ Ⓒ Ⓓ
10	Ⓐ Ⓑ Ⓒ Ⓓ	37	Ⓐ Ⓑ Ⓒ Ⓓ
11	Ⓐ Ⓑ Ⓒ Ⓓ	38	Ⓐ Ⓑ Ⓒ Ⓓ
12	Ⓐ Ⓑ Ⓒ Ⓓ	39	Ⓐ Ⓑ Ⓒ Ⓓ
13	Ⓐ Ⓑ Ⓒ Ⓓ	40	Ⓐ Ⓑ Ⓒ Ⓓ
14	Ⓐ Ⓑ Ⓒ Ⓓ	41	Ⓐ Ⓑ Ⓒ Ⓓ
15	Ⓐ Ⓑ Ⓒ Ⓓ	42	Ⓐ Ⓑ Ⓒ Ⓓ
16	Ⓐ Ⓑ Ⓒ Ⓓ	43	Ⓐ Ⓑ Ⓒ Ⓓ
17	Ⓐ Ⓑ Ⓒ Ⓓ	44	Ⓐ Ⓑ Ⓒ Ⓓ
18	Ⓐ Ⓑ Ⓒ Ⓓ	45	Ⓐ Ⓑ Ⓒ Ⓓ
19	Ⓐ Ⓑ Ⓒ Ⓓ	46	Ⓐ Ⓑ Ⓒ Ⓓ
20	Ⓐ Ⓑ Ⓒ Ⓓ	47	Ⓐ Ⓑ Ⓒ Ⓓ
21	Ⓐ Ⓑ Ⓒ Ⓓ	48	Ⓐ Ⓑ Ⓒ Ⓓ
22	Ⓐ Ⓑ Ⓒ Ⓓ	49	Ⓐ Ⓑ Ⓒ Ⓓ
23	Ⓐ Ⓑ Ⓒ Ⓓ	50	Ⓐ Ⓑ Ⓒ Ⓓ
24	Ⓐ Ⓑ Ⓒ Ⓓ	51	Ⓐ Ⓑ Ⓒ Ⓓ
25	Ⓐ Ⓑ Ⓒ Ⓓ	52	Ⓐ Ⓑ Ⓒ Ⓓ
26	Ⓐ Ⓑ Ⓒ Ⓓ	53	Ⓐ Ⓑ Ⓒ Ⓓ
27	Ⓐ Ⓑ Ⓒ Ⓓ	54	Ⓐ Ⓑ Ⓒ Ⓓ

Answer Sheet

TEST 5	
	/54

TEST 6	
	/54

TEST 7	
	/54

TEST 8	
	/54

TEST 5

No.	ANSWER (A B C D)	No.	ANSWER (A B C D)
1	Ⓐ Ⓑ Ⓒ Ⓓ	28	Ⓐ Ⓑ Ⓒ Ⓓ
2	Ⓐ Ⓑ Ⓒ Ⓓ	29	Ⓐ Ⓑ Ⓒ Ⓓ
3	Ⓐ Ⓑ Ⓒ Ⓓ	30	Ⓐ Ⓑ Ⓒ Ⓓ
4	Ⓐ Ⓑ Ⓒ Ⓓ	31	Ⓐ Ⓑ Ⓒ Ⓓ
5	Ⓐ Ⓑ Ⓒ Ⓓ	32	Ⓐ Ⓑ Ⓒ Ⓓ
6	Ⓐ Ⓑ Ⓒ Ⓓ	33	Ⓐ Ⓑ Ⓒ Ⓓ
7	Ⓐ Ⓑ Ⓒ Ⓓ	34	Ⓐ Ⓑ Ⓒ Ⓓ
8	Ⓐ Ⓑ Ⓒ Ⓓ	35	Ⓐ Ⓑ Ⓒ Ⓓ
9	Ⓐ Ⓑ Ⓒ Ⓓ	36	Ⓐ Ⓑ Ⓒ Ⓓ
10	Ⓐ Ⓑ Ⓒ Ⓓ	37	Ⓐ Ⓑ Ⓒ Ⓓ
11	Ⓐ Ⓑ Ⓒ Ⓓ	38	Ⓐ Ⓑ Ⓒ Ⓓ
12	Ⓐ Ⓑ Ⓒ Ⓓ	39	Ⓐ Ⓑ Ⓒ Ⓓ
13	Ⓐ Ⓑ Ⓒ Ⓓ	40	Ⓐ Ⓑ Ⓒ Ⓓ
14	Ⓐ Ⓑ Ⓒ Ⓓ	41	Ⓐ Ⓑ Ⓒ Ⓓ
15	Ⓐ Ⓑ Ⓒ Ⓓ	42	Ⓐ Ⓑ Ⓒ Ⓓ
16	Ⓐ Ⓑ Ⓒ Ⓓ	43	Ⓐ Ⓑ Ⓒ Ⓓ
17	Ⓐ Ⓑ Ⓒ Ⓓ	44	Ⓐ Ⓑ Ⓒ Ⓓ
18	Ⓐ Ⓑ Ⓒ Ⓓ	45	Ⓐ Ⓑ Ⓒ Ⓓ
19	Ⓐ Ⓑ Ⓒ Ⓓ	46	Ⓐ Ⓑ Ⓒ Ⓓ
20	Ⓐ Ⓑ Ⓒ Ⓓ	47	Ⓐ Ⓑ Ⓒ Ⓓ
21	Ⓐ Ⓑ Ⓒ Ⓓ	48	Ⓐ Ⓑ Ⓒ Ⓓ
22	Ⓐ Ⓑ Ⓒ Ⓓ	49	Ⓐ Ⓑ Ⓒ Ⓓ
23	Ⓐ Ⓑ Ⓒ Ⓓ	50	Ⓐ Ⓑ Ⓒ Ⓓ
24	Ⓐ Ⓑ Ⓒ Ⓓ	51	Ⓐ Ⓑ Ⓒ Ⓓ
25	Ⓐ Ⓑ Ⓒ Ⓓ	52	Ⓐ Ⓑ Ⓒ Ⓓ
26	Ⓐ Ⓑ Ⓒ Ⓓ	53	Ⓐ Ⓑ Ⓒ Ⓓ
27	Ⓐ Ⓑ Ⓒ Ⓓ	54	Ⓐ Ⓑ Ⓒ Ⓓ

TEST 6

No.	ANSWER (A B C D)	No.	ANSWER (A B C D)
1	Ⓐ Ⓑ Ⓒ Ⓓ	28	Ⓐ Ⓑ Ⓒ Ⓓ
2	Ⓐ Ⓑ Ⓒ Ⓓ	29	Ⓐ Ⓑ Ⓒ Ⓓ
3	Ⓐ Ⓑ Ⓒ Ⓓ	30	Ⓐ Ⓑ Ⓒ Ⓓ
4	Ⓐ Ⓑ Ⓒ Ⓓ	31	Ⓐ Ⓑ Ⓒ Ⓓ
5	Ⓐ Ⓑ Ⓒ Ⓓ	32	Ⓐ Ⓑ Ⓒ Ⓓ
6	Ⓐ Ⓑ Ⓒ Ⓓ	33	Ⓐ Ⓑ Ⓒ Ⓓ
7	Ⓐ Ⓑ Ⓒ Ⓓ	34	Ⓐ Ⓑ Ⓒ Ⓓ
8	Ⓐ Ⓑ Ⓒ Ⓓ	35	Ⓐ Ⓑ Ⓒ Ⓓ
9	Ⓐ Ⓑ Ⓒ Ⓓ	36	Ⓐ Ⓑ Ⓒ Ⓓ
10	Ⓐ Ⓑ Ⓒ Ⓓ	37	Ⓐ Ⓑ Ⓒ Ⓓ
11	Ⓐ Ⓑ Ⓒ Ⓓ	38	Ⓐ Ⓑ Ⓒ Ⓓ
12	Ⓐ Ⓑ Ⓒ Ⓓ	39	Ⓐ Ⓑ Ⓒ Ⓓ
13	Ⓐ Ⓑ Ⓒ Ⓓ	40	Ⓐ Ⓑ Ⓒ Ⓓ
14	Ⓐ Ⓑ Ⓒ Ⓓ	41	Ⓐ Ⓑ Ⓒ Ⓓ
15	Ⓐ Ⓑ Ⓒ Ⓓ	42	Ⓐ Ⓑ Ⓒ Ⓓ
16	Ⓐ Ⓑ Ⓒ Ⓓ	43	Ⓐ Ⓑ Ⓒ Ⓓ
17	Ⓐ Ⓑ Ⓒ Ⓓ	44	Ⓐ Ⓑ Ⓒ Ⓓ
18	Ⓐ Ⓑ Ⓒ Ⓓ	45	Ⓐ Ⓑ Ⓒ Ⓓ
19	Ⓐ Ⓑ Ⓒ Ⓓ	46	Ⓐ Ⓑ Ⓒ Ⓓ
20	Ⓐ Ⓑ Ⓒ Ⓓ	47	Ⓐ Ⓑ Ⓒ Ⓓ
21	Ⓐ Ⓑ Ⓒ Ⓓ	48	Ⓐ Ⓑ Ⓒ Ⓓ
22	Ⓐ Ⓑ Ⓒ Ⓓ	49	Ⓐ Ⓑ Ⓒ Ⓓ
23	Ⓐ Ⓑ Ⓒ Ⓓ	50	Ⓐ Ⓑ Ⓒ Ⓓ
24	Ⓐ Ⓑ Ⓒ Ⓓ	51	Ⓐ Ⓑ Ⓒ Ⓓ
25	Ⓐ Ⓑ Ⓒ Ⓓ	52	Ⓐ Ⓑ Ⓒ Ⓓ
26	Ⓐ Ⓑ Ⓒ Ⓓ	53	Ⓐ Ⓑ Ⓒ Ⓓ
27	Ⓐ Ⓑ Ⓒ Ⓓ	54	Ⓐ Ⓑ Ⓒ Ⓓ

TEST 7

No.	ANSWER (A B C D)	No.	ANSWER (A B C D)
1	Ⓐ Ⓑ Ⓒ Ⓓ	28	Ⓐ Ⓑ Ⓒ Ⓓ
2	Ⓐ Ⓑ Ⓒ Ⓓ	29	Ⓐ Ⓑ Ⓒ Ⓓ
3	Ⓐ Ⓑ Ⓒ Ⓓ	30	Ⓐ Ⓑ Ⓒ Ⓓ
4	Ⓐ Ⓑ Ⓒ Ⓓ	31	Ⓐ Ⓑ Ⓒ Ⓓ
5	Ⓐ Ⓑ Ⓒ Ⓓ	32	Ⓐ Ⓑ Ⓒ Ⓓ
6	Ⓐ Ⓑ Ⓒ Ⓓ	33	Ⓐ Ⓑ Ⓒ Ⓓ
7	Ⓐ Ⓑ Ⓒ Ⓓ	34	Ⓐ Ⓑ Ⓒ Ⓓ
8	Ⓐ Ⓑ Ⓒ Ⓓ	35	Ⓐ Ⓑ Ⓒ Ⓓ
9	Ⓐ Ⓑ Ⓒ Ⓓ	36	Ⓐ Ⓑ Ⓒ Ⓓ
10	Ⓐ Ⓑ Ⓒ Ⓓ	37	Ⓐ Ⓑ Ⓒ Ⓓ
11	Ⓐ Ⓑ Ⓒ Ⓓ	38	Ⓐ Ⓑ Ⓒ Ⓓ
12	Ⓐ Ⓑ Ⓒ Ⓓ	39	Ⓐ Ⓑ Ⓒ Ⓓ
13	Ⓐ Ⓑ Ⓒ Ⓓ	40	Ⓐ Ⓑ Ⓒ Ⓓ
14	Ⓐ Ⓑ Ⓒ Ⓓ	41	Ⓐ Ⓑ Ⓒ Ⓓ
15	Ⓐ Ⓑ Ⓒ Ⓓ	42	Ⓐ Ⓑ Ⓒ Ⓓ
16	Ⓐ Ⓑ Ⓒ Ⓓ	43	Ⓐ Ⓑ Ⓒ Ⓓ
17	Ⓐ Ⓑ Ⓒ Ⓓ	44	Ⓐ Ⓑ Ⓒ Ⓓ
18	Ⓐ Ⓑ Ⓒ Ⓓ	45	Ⓐ Ⓑ Ⓒ Ⓓ
19	Ⓐ Ⓑ Ⓒ Ⓓ	46	Ⓐ Ⓑ Ⓒ Ⓓ
20	Ⓐ Ⓑ Ⓒ Ⓓ	47	Ⓐ Ⓑ Ⓒ Ⓓ
21	Ⓐ Ⓑ Ⓒ Ⓓ	48	Ⓐ Ⓑ Ⓒ Ⓓ
22	Ⓐ Ⓑ Ⓒ Ⓓ	49	Ⓐ Ⓑ Ⓒ Ⓓ
23	Ⓐ Ⓑ Ⓒ Ⓓ	50	Ⓐ Ⓑ Ⓒ Ⓓ
24	Ⓐ Ⓑ Ⓒ Ⓓ	51	Ⓐ Ⓑ Ⓒ Ⓓ
25	Ⓐ Ⓑ Ⓒ Ⓓ	52	Ⓐ Ⓑ Ⓒ Ⓓ
26	Ⓐ Ⓑ Ⓒ Ⓓ	53	Ⓐ Ⓑ Ⓒ Ⓓ
27	Ⓐ Ⓑ Ⓒ Ⓓ	54	Ⓐ Ⓑ Ⓒ Ⓓ

TEST 8

No.	ANSWER (A B C D)	No.	ANSWER (A B C D)
1	Ⓐ Ⓑ Ⓒ Ⓓ	28	Ⓐ Ⓑ Ⓒ Ⓓ
2	Ⓐ Ⓑ Ⓒ Ⓓ	29	Ⓐ Ⓑ Ⓒ Ⓓ
3	Ⓐ Ⓑ Ⓒ Ⓓ	30	Ⓐ Ⓑ Ⓒ Ⓓ
4	Ⓐ Ⓑ Ⓒ Ⓓ	31	Ⓐ Ⓑ Ⓒ Ⓓ
5	Ⓐ Ⓑ Ⓒ Ⓓ	32	Ⓐ Ⓑ Ⓒ Ⓓ
6	Ⓐ Ⓑ Ⓒ Ⓓ	33	Ⓐ Ⓑ Ⓒ Ⓓ
7	Ⓐ Ⓑ Ⓒ Ⓓ	34	Ⓐ Ⓑ Ⓒ Ⓓ
8	Ⓐ Ⓑ Ⓒ Ⓓ	35	Ⓐ Ⓑ Ⓒ Ⓓ
9	Ⓐ Ⓑ Ⓒ Ⓓ	36	Ⓐ Ⓑ Ⓒ Ⓓ
10	Ⓐ Ⓑ Ⓒ Ⓓ	37	Ⓐ Ⓑ Ⓒ Ⓓ
11	Ⓐ Ⓑ Ⓒ Ⓓ	38	Ⓐ Ⓑ Ⓒ Ⓓ
12	Ⓐ Ⓑ Ⓒ Ⓓ	39	Ⓐ Ⓑ Ⓒ Ⓓ
13	Ⓐ Ⓑ Ⓒ Ⓓ	40	Ⓐ Ⓑ Ⓒ Ⓓ
14	Ⓐ Ⓑ Ⓒ Ⓓ	41	Ⓐ Ⓑ Ⓒ Ⓓ
15	Ⓐ Ⓑ Ⓒ Ⓓ	42	Ⓐ Ⓑ Ⓒ Ⓓ
16	Ⓐ Ⓑ Ⓒ Ⓓ	43	Ⓐ Ⓑ Ⓒ Ⓓ
17	Ⓐ Ⓑ Ⓒ Ⓓ	44	Ⓐ Ⓑ Ⓒ Ⓓ
18	Ⓐ Ⓑ Ⓒ Ⓓ	45	Ⓐ Ⓑ Ⓒ Ⓓ
19	Ⓐ Ⓑ Ⓒ Ⓓ	46	Ⓐ Ⓑ Ⓒ Ⓓ
20	Ⓐ Ⓑ Ⓒ Ⓓ	47	Ⓐ Ⓑ Ⓒ Ⓓ
21	Ⓐ Ⓑ Ⓒ Ⓓ	48	Ⓐ Ⓑ Ⓒ Ⓓ
22	Ⓐ Ⓑ Ⓒ Ⓓ	49	Ⓐ Ⓑ Ⓒ Ⓓ
23	Ⓐ Ⓑ Ⓒ Ⓓ	50	Ⓐ Ⓑ Ⓒ Ⓓ
24	Ⓐ Ⓑ Ⓒ Ⓓ	51	Ⓐ Ⓑ Ⓒ Ⓓ
25	Ⓐ Ⓑ Ⓒ Ⓓ	52	Ⓐ Ⓑ Ⓒ Ⓓ
26	Ⓐ Ⓑ Ⓒ Ⓓ	53	Ⓐ Ⓑ Ⓒ Ⓓ
27	Ⓐ Ⓑ Ⓒ Ⓓ	54	Ⓐ Ⓑ Ⓒ Ⓓ

Answer Sheet

TEST 1   /54

TEST 2   /54

TEST 3   /54

TEST 4   /54

Answer Sheet

TEST 5   /54

TEST 6   /54

TEST 7   /54

TEST 8   /54